Global Perspectives on Social Media Influencers and Strategic Business Communication

Nicky Chang Bi
University of Nebraska at Omaha, USA

Ruonan Zhang
Rollins College, USA

IGI Global
PUBLISHER of TIMELY KNOWLEDGE

A volume in the Advances in Marketing, Customer Relationship Management, and E-Services (AMCRMES) Book Series

Published in the United States of America by
IGI Global
Business Science Reference (an imprint of IGI Global)
701 E. Chocolate Avenue
Hershey PA, USA 17033
Tel: 717-533-8845
Fax: 717-533-8661
E-mail: cust@igi-global.com
Web site: http://www.igi-global.com

Library of Congress Cataloging-in-Publication Data

Names: Bi, Nicky Chang, 1987- editor. | Zhang, Ruonan Zhang, 1991- editor.
Title: Global perspectives on social media influencers and strategic business communication / edited by Nicky Chang Bi, Ruonan Zhang.
Description: Hershey, PA : Business Science Reference, [2024] | Includes bibliographical references and index. | Summary: "This book provides a comprehensive overview of the contemporary research and practices of social media influencers. It also explores innovative methods to identify, assess, and reach out to influencers on a global scale"-- Provided by publisher.
Identifiers: LCCN 2024009404 (print) | LCCN 2024009405 (ebook) | ISBN 9798369309124 (hardcover) | ISBN 9798369309131 (ebook)
Subjects: LCSH: Social influence. | Social media.
Classification: LCC HM1176 .G563 2024 (print) | LCC HM1176 (ebook) | DDC 302/.13--dc23/eng/20240425
LC record available at https://lccn.loc.gov/2024009404
LC ebook record available at https://lccn.loc.gov/2024009405

This book is published in the IGI Global book series Advances in Marketing, Customer Relationship Management, and E-Services (AMCRMES) (ISSN: 2327-5502; eISSN: 2327-5529)

British Cataloguing in Publication Data
A Cataloguing in Publication record for this book is available from the British Library.

For electronic access to this publication, please contact: eresources@igi-global.com.

Advances in Marketing, Customer Relationship Management, and E-Services (AMCRMES) Book Series

Eldon Y. Li
National Chengchi University, Taiwan & California Polytechnic State University, USA

ISSN:2327-5502
EISSN:2327-5529

Mission

Business processes, services, and communications are important factors in the management of good customer relationship, which is the foundation of any well organized business. Technology continues to play a vital role in the organization and automation of business processes for marketing, sales, and customer service. These features aid in the attraction of new clients and maintaining existing relationships.

The Advances in Marketing, Customer Relationship Management, and E-Services (AMCRMES) Book Series

addresses success factors for customer relationship management, marketing, and electronic services and its performance outcomes. This collection of reference source covers aspects of consumer behavior and marketing business strategies aiming towards researchers, scholars, and practitioners in the fields of marketing management.

Coverage

- Online Community Management and Behavior
- CRM and customer trust
- Legal Considerations in E-Marketing
- Text Mining and Marketing
- Data mining and marketing
- CRM strategies
- Cases on CRM Implementation
- Database marketing
- Telemarketing
- Mobile CRM

IGI Global is currently accepting manuscripts for publication within this series. To submit a proposal for a volume in this series, please contact our Acquisition Editors at Acquisitions@igi-global.com or visit: http://www.igi-global.com/publish/.

The Advances in Marketing, Customer Relationship Management, and E-Services (AMCRMES) Book Series (ISSN 2327-5502) is published by IGI Global, 701 E. Chocolate Avenue, Hershey, PA 17033-1240, USA, www.igi-global.com. This series is composed of titles available for purchase individually; each title is edited to be contextually exclusive from any other title within the series. For pricing and ordering information please visit http://www.igi-global.com/book-series/advances-marketing-customer-relationship-management/37150. Postmaster: Send all address changes to above address.

Titles in this Series

For a list of additional titles in this series, please visit: http://www.igi-global.com/book-series/advances-marketing-customer-relationship-management/37150

Marketing and Big Data Analytics in Tourism and Events
Tareq Nael Hashem (Applied Science Private University, Jordan) Ahmad Albattat (Management and Science University, Malaysia) Marco Valeri (Niccolò Cusano University, Italy) and Anukrati Sharma (University of Kota, India)
Business Science Reference • copyright 2024 • 294pp • H/C (ISBN: 9798369333105) • US $295.00 (our price)

Impact of Teleworking and Remote Work on Business Productivity, Retention, Advancement, and Bottom Line
Harish Chandra Chandan (Independent Researcher, USA)
Business Science Reference • copyright 2024 • 311pp • H/C (ISBN: 9798369313145) • US $290.00 (our price)

AI-Driven Marketing Research and Data Analytics
Reason Masengu (Middle East College, Oman) Option Takunda Chiwaridzo (University of Science and Technology Beijing, Beijing, China) Mercy Dube (Midlands State University, Zimbabwe) and Benson Ruzive (Modern College of Business and Science, Oman)
Business Science Reference • copyright 2024 • 490pp • H/C (ISBN: 9798369321652) • US $290.00 (our price)

Marketing Innovation Strategies and Consumer Behavior
Belem Barbosa (University of Porto, Portugal)
Business Science Reference • copyright 2024 • 469pp • H/C (ISBN: 9798369341957) • US $325.00 (our price)

Corporate Governance and CSR Strategies for Sustainability
Maja Pucelj (Faculty of Organisation Studies, University of Novo Mesto, Slovenia) and Rado Bohinc (Scientific Research Centre Koper, Slovenia)
Information Science Reference • copyright 2024 • 368pp • H/C (ISBN: 9798369358634) • US $290.00 (our price)

Balancing Automation and Human Interaction in Modern Marketing
Arjun J. Nair (St. Lawrence College, Canada) Sridhar Manohar (Chitkara Business School, Chitkara University, India) Amit Mittal (Chitkara Business School, Chitkara University, India) and Wasim Ahmed (University of Hull, UK)
Business Science Reference • copyright 2024 • 326pp • H/C (ISBN: 9798369322765) • US $290.00 (our price)

Building Strong Brands and Engaging Customers With Sound
Minna-Maarit Jaskari (School of Marketing and Communication, University of Vaasa, Finland)
Business Science Reference • copyright 2024 • 267pp • H/C (ISBN: 9798369307786) • US $265.00 (our price)

Globalized Consumer Insights in the Digital Era

IGI Global
PUBLISHER of TIMELY KNOWLEDGE

701 East Chocolate Avenue, Hershey, PA 17033, USA
Tel: 717-533-8845 x100 • Fax: 717-533-8661
E-Mail: cust@igi-global.com • www.igi-global.com

Table of Contents

Section 3

Influencers in Industries

Section 4

Influencers and Engagement

Detailed Table of Contents

Influencer marketing on YouTube has become an increasingly popular method for building engagement with consumers. This study examines how perceived homophily and interactivity with social media influencers impact the effectiveness of food-related YouTube influencer marketing and consumer engagement with social media. An online survey (N = 404) found that perceived homophily and interactivity both positively relate to intentions to engage with social media. In addition, perceived expertise and physical attractiveness of the social media influencer mediated the relationship between both perceived homophily and interactivity and social media engagement. Study results provide evidence-based implications for influencer marketing strategies and insight into consumer engagement with food-related YouTube content.

There are more than 64 million social media influencer accounts as of June 2023, evidence influencers are not a passing trend (trendHERO, 2023). Influencers have shifted the way information is disseminated, how public opinion is swayed, and how brands are promoted. However, pet influencers are an under-researched type of influencer. These influencers create content that shares their pets' personalities and adventures with others. The pet is the star of the social media account – not the owner. Millions of social media users follow the pet influencers such as Grumpy Cat, Smudge – Table Cat, and Doug the Pug (Feedspot, 2023).Pets with large followings such as Venus the Cat or JiffPom can earn thousands to millions of dollars for their promotional efforts (Myers et al., 2022). A survey of more than 400 followers of pet influencers found they deem pet influecers credible and likeable. They also find the brands being promoted credible and have high purchase intent. The more time one spends on social media influences perceptions of pet influencers.

This critical literature review explores sustainable fashion consumption (repurposing) influenced by Edu-influencers on Instagram, addressing the limitations of traditional behavioral change theories on social media. It evaluates various perspectives on consumer behavior, sustainable consumption, and social media, highlighting the shortcomings of current behavioral change theories. The review aims to establish the groundwork for forthcoming theoretical and empirical advancements by critically analyzing and synthesizing recent studies associated with the three distinctive bodies of literature. Additionally, it aims to lay the groundwork for future research endeavors within these domains. The findings could inform consumer education, policy recommendations, and communication strategies for sustainable fashion consumption, laying the groundwork for future research and behavioral interventions.

Section 4

Influencers and Engagement

Influencers are a powerful tool in the worlds of communication and marketing. The relationships that influencers build with audiences can affect consumer behaviors as can the brand that they create. Both the audience's perception of a relationship with the influencer as well as the audience's desire to be like the influencer can impact consumer purchasing behaviors. The purpose of this study is to explore how wishful identification and parasocial relationships serve as mediating factors in influencer impact on audience consumer behavior outcomes. This purpose is addressed via a quantitative survey (n = 948) in collaboration with a YouTube influencer disseminated to her audience. Results show that viewers' reported income, interactions with influencers, and parasocial relationships all have a positive impact on predicting participants' purchase behavior of influencer-recommended products. The findings contribute to an in-depth understanding of how wishful identification serves as a mediating variable between parasocial relationships and consumer purchasing behaviors in audiences.

Social media has emerged as a powerful platform that revolutionized the way the fashion industry operates. Fashion influencers have significantly impacted global consumer trends and brand perceptions with their large followings and engaging content. This chapter investigated the ways in which fashion influencers leverage social media platforms to shape consumer behavior, promote sustainable fashion practices, and bridge cultural boundaries to create a more inclusive fashion community across borders. This chapter has contributed to a better understanding of fashion beyond borders, social media influencers' role in transforming the fashion landscape, and their potential to influence positive change in the industry by conducting a comprehensive literature review. This chapter explores social media influencers' multifaceted roles in redefining fashion globally.

This chapter explores the mediation role of influencer trust in gender and expertise congruency effects on consumers' attitudes and purchase intentions, focusing on a cross-national comparison between

Preface

Social media influencers have become a popular source of information around the world and thus affect consumer decisions on a global scale. They have been increasingly important for brands and organizations that aim to reach a larger but more precisely targeted audience, especially digital natives (Schaffer, 2020). As editors, it is with great pleasure that we present *Global Perspectives on Social Media Influencers and Strategic Business Communication*.

The research of social media influencers has grown rapidly in recent years. Social media influencers are a group of individuals who produce high-quality content that assists their audiences in learning new skills and recruiting fresh information on a particular topic (Kessel, 2019). Social media influencers can make an impact on their audiences' purchasing decisions through information dissemination, product try-ons, brand endorsement, and sponsored or user-generated reviews of products and services. Social media influencers not only have the ability to make a significant difference in their followers' brand loyalty and purchase intention but also help shape cultural norms and build communities around shared interests (Bi & Zhang, 2022). For instance, live streaming and off-site interactions are effective ways that influencers can adopt to build relationships with their audience and drive sales (e.g. Chen & Yang, 2023; Lange, 2019). This calls for attention from brands that intend to reach out to influencers. Businesses and organizations should make ethical decisions in choosing influencers. It is important for them to carefully assess social media influencers and avoid working with those who have a history of engaging the audience through unethical methods.

Throughout the pages of this book, readers will find a rich tapestry of topics, ranging from the impacts of influencers on audience attitudes and purchase intentions to the ethical considerations inherent in influencer collaborations. Exploring motivations, characteristics, and emerging trends within the influencer contexts, our contributors offer insights into the complex interplay between content creators, brands, and consumers.

Furthermore, we recognize the significance for businesses and organizations to navigate this terrain with ethical consideration, ensuring that influencer partnerships align with the organizational core values and principles. As such, discussions surrounding the ethics and potential negative consequences of influencer marketing are given due consideration, offering readers a balanced perspective on this evolving phenomenon.

Topics on social media influencers were explored through a variety of research methods. Some scholars have used quantitative methods to explore the factors impacting the product adoption process. For example, survey studies examined predictions of the credibility of influencers (Lee & Kim, 2020), influencers' popularity (e.g. Pittman & Abell, 2021), homophily (Bu, 2022), emotional attachment (e.g. Ladhari et al., 2020), parasocial interaction and relationship with influencers (e.g. Wei et al, 2022), wishful identification (Schouten et al., 2021), and others on customers' attitudes towards product endorsement, product attitudes, and purchase behaviors. Qualitative methods such as ethnography and in-depth interviews were also used to explore social media influencers' production processes and audiences' interactions with influencers (e.g. Lange, 2019; Lou, 2022). In addition to the current literature, this book includes chapters using a wide breadth of methodology including case studies, discourse analysis, surveys, experiments, systematic reviews, in-depth interviews, and big data analysis to comprehensively examine the role of influencers in strategic business communication.

Chapter 1, "Shaping Style: The Rise of Fashion and Beauty Social Media Influencers" by Faren Karimkhan, differentiated social media influencers from traditional celebrities. The chapter navigates through the significance of perceived similarity, identification, and authenticity in shaping fashion and beauty influencers' success. Moreover, it provides an insightful exploration of the trends within the fashion and cosmetic industries, since these two influential sectors exhibit numerous similarities.

Chapter 2, Surjit Singha's "Exploring Motivations of Social Media Influencers in Content Production," offers a comprehensive examination of the underlying motivations driving content creation among social media influencers. Through meticulous analysis, the chapter uncovers various incentives such as personal enthusiasm, monetary rewards, and the pursuit of recognition, providing insight into how these motivations influence the authenticity and caliber of influencer-generated content. With valuable insights from case studies, this chapter serves as a roadmap for businesses seeking collaborations with influencers.

Chapter 3, "Influencers' Perception of Personal Branding on Social Media in Vietnam" by Tuong-Minh Ly-Le and Truc Hoang, provides a comprehensive understanding of influencers' perspectives on personal branding in Vietnam's social media landscape. Through in-depth interviews, the chapter explored influencers' strategies shaped by social trends, audience expectations, and the pursuit of authenticity. This chapter also offers practical implications for personal branding strategies and helps us understand influencer practices in the Vietnamese context.

Chapter 4, David Stephens' chapter, "The Wendy's Retweet Challenge: Neoliberalism, Social Media, and the Creation of an Influencer," evaluates Wendy's viral Retweet Challenge campaign. By the analysis of Wendy's strategic utilization of neoliberal tactics including gamification, individualism, and positivity, the chapter highlights the campaign's effectiveness in positioning the brand and fostering consumer engagement. Through insightful analysis, it presents Wendy's as a dynamic player in the evolving landscape of influencer marketing.

Chapter 5, Tricia Farwell's chapter, "Influencers Using Instagram to Promote Change in the Knitting Community," looks at the power of micro-influencers within the crafting community on Instagram. Through Kelman's framework, the study explores how these influencers advocate for change and how social media creates a safe space for marginalized voices. This research highlights the role of micro-influencers in creating narratives and fostering a community on Instagram.

Chapter 6, "Exploring Communication Practices of Influencers on Commerce Focused Social Media: Whatnot" by Victoria McDermott, Amy May, and Olivia Truban, examines the Whatnot sellers' strategic communication. Through qualitative analysis, the chapter reveals sellers' techniques in engaging users and fostering community during product promotions. Contrary to traditional e-commerce, this study introduces the notion of "strategic communication performance" in the act of selling, providing insights into communicative strategies for business owners in the social commerce landscape.

Chapter 7, David Painter, Tanja Vierrether, and Camilla Guimaraes' chapter, "Skin Deep: Body Positivity Influencer Campaigns," employs the Expectancy Violation Theory to investigate the impact of body positivity influencer's attire and portrayal of skin on consumer responses to branded Instagram posts. Through experiments, the chapter highlights the important role of authenticity and emotional responses in influencing purchase intentions. This research offers practical guidance for brands and influencers seeking to adopt body positivity as a promotional strategy.

Chapter 8, Linda Dam's chapter, "Food-Related YouTube Influencer Marketing: The Impact of Homophily and Interactivity on Social Media Engagement," explores the effectiveness of food-related YouTube influencer marketing in driving social media engagement. Through an online survey, the chapter discovers the positive impacts of perceived homophily and interactivity on consumer engagement. Furthermore, it examines the mediating role of influencer expertise and physical attractiveness in enhancing social media engagement, offering practical implications for influencer businesses.

Chapter 9, Michel Haigh and Shelley Wigley's chapter, "Doug the Pug, Eggnog, and Boo: The Impact of Pet Influencers on Stakeholders' Purchase Intentions and Attitudes Toward the Brand," investigates the impact of pet influencers on consumer purchase intentions and brand attitudes. Through the analysis of survey data, the chapter underscores the credibility and likability of pet influencers, highlighting their potential to drive purchase intent among social media users. This research reveals the burgeoning phenomenon of pet influencer marketing and its impact on consumer behavior.

Chapter 10, Lujain Hassoubah, Daniella Ryding, and Gianpaolo Vignali's chapter, "Revolutionizing Edu-Influencers as Minorities Nudging Sustainable Fashion Consumption on Instagram," critically examines sustainable fashion consumption influenced by edu-influencers on Instagram. Through a comprehensive literature review, the chapter identifies the limitations of current behavioral change theories and proposes frameworks for future studies on sustainable fashion. This research also lays the groundwork for future behavioral interventions aimed at fostering sustainable fashion consumption through social media platforms.

Chapter 11, Trinidee Mercado and Ruonan Zhang's chapter, "Investigating the Impact of Influencer Wishful Identification and Parasocial Relationships on Purchasing Behavior: Insights From Influencer Fan Data," examines the mediating factors in influencing audience purchase behavior in response to influencer recommendations by surveying an influencer's fans. Through quantitative survey analysis, the chapter reveals the significant impacts of wishful identification and parasocial relationships on the audience's actual purchasing behaviors of the recommended products. These findings provide valuable insights for marketers aiming to enhance the effectiveness of influencer collaborations.

Chapter 12, Poornima Nair and Sunita Kumar's chapter, "Beyond the Borders: Fashion Influencers Shaping Global Trends," explores the transformative role of fashion influencers in transcending cultural boundaries and shaping global consumer trends. Through a comprehensive literature review, the chapter elucidates influencers' impact on consumer behavior, brand perceptions, and sustainable fashion practices. This research highlights the pivotal role of fashion influencers in fostering inclusivity and driving positive change in the global fashion industry.

Chapter 13, Yang Yang's chapter, "Does Influencer Trust Matter? Influencer Trust, Gender Congruency, and Expertise Congruency: A Cross-National Comparison Between Douyin and TikTok Users in China and the USA," looks at the mediation role of influencer trust in influencing consumer attitudes and purchase intentions. Through a cross-national comparison between Douyin and TikTok users, the chapter examines the impact of influencers' gender and expertise congruency on consumer behavior. This research offers valuable insights for marketers seeking to enhance the credibility and effectiveness of influencer collaborations in diverse cultural contexts.

Chapter 14, Rajni Bala, Vinod Kumar, and Ritu Sharma's chapter, "Navigating Consumer Engagement: Unveiling the Influence of Social Media Influencers," investigates social media influencers' pivotal role in promoting consumer engagement in the digital era. Through a comprehensive analysis, the chapter examines influencers' impact on consumer engagement and brand perceptions. This research also provides conceptualizations of consumer engagement, dimensions of consumer engagement, and engagement models. It highlights the advantages of social media influencers for Indian consumers.

Chapter 15, Albérico Rosário and Anna Boechat's chapter, "Systematic Literature Review Bibliometrics on Ethics Practiced by Influencers," offers a systematic review of literature on ethics practiced by influencers. Through rigorous analysis, the chapter evaluates influencers' ethical behaviors and calls for transparent and authentic content. This research provides valuable insights for scholars and practitioners seeking to understand the ethical dimensions of influencer marketing in the digital age.

Chapter 16, Ranjit Singha, Surjit Singha, V. Muthu Ruben, Melita Stephen Natal, Amenla Longkumer, and Alphonsa Diana Haokip's chapter, "The Ethics of Collaborating With Social Media Influencers: Influencers and Psychological Well-Being," highlights the importance of prioritizing influencers' psychological well-being in influencer marketing collaborations. Through a comprehensive examination, the chapter highlights the ethical considerations inherent in influencer partnerships and proposes strategies for fostering a supportive and sustainable influencer ecosystem. This research offers insights for marketers aiming to establish ethical and mutually beneficial collaborations with influencers.

Chapter 17, Isuru Hewapathirana's chapter, "Leveraging Artificial Intelligence for Ethical Social Media Influencer Communication," explores the ethical concerns of influencer communication in the age of artificial intelligence (AI). Through empirical investigation using Reddit data and case study analysis, the chapter evaluates AI's impact on influencer communication practices and offers guidance for ethical decision-making in influencer marketing. This research contributes to a deeper understanding of AI's role in influencer communication and provides practical recommendations for industry professionals and policymakers.

The book is a valuable resource for business owners, strategic communicators, marketers, scholars, content creators, and anyone interested in learning more about social media influencers and influencer marketing. It would be a great textbook for students of any level who are interested in understanding the related concepts and methodology adopted to inquire about social media influencer topics. The book offers individuals who want to become content creators a toolbox for fostering audience engagement by considering the ethical practices in production while leading public opinion on a particular topic. The book also provides business owners a comprehensive understanding of the influencers' motivations for content production, influencer-customer interaction and intimacy, and ethical considerations in collaboration, which provides them with a clear roadmap of what to expect in executing influencer communication and management.

In conclusion, this book provides a comprehensive overview of the contemporary research and practices of social media influencers from a global perspective. It covers a wide range of topics, including social media influencers in different industries and sectors, their impact on audiences, their motives and characteristics, and their use in business management, public relations, advertising, and strategic communication. It explores innovative methods to identify, assess, and reach out to influencers in a global context. Overall, the book represents a salutary addition to the current academic studies of social media influencers and strategic communication.

Nicky Chang Bi
University of Nebraska at Omaha, USA

Ruonan Zhang
Rollins College, USA

REFERENCES

Bi, N. C., & Zhang, R. (2022). Electronic Word-of-Mouth and social media. In J. H. Lipschultz, K. Freberg, & R. Luttrell (Eds.), *The Emerald Handbook of Computer-Mediated Communication and Social Media* (pp. 37–50). Emerald Group Publishing.

Bu, Y., Parkinson, J., & Thaichon, P. (2022). Influencer marketing: Homophily, customer value co-creation behaviour and purchase intention. *Journal of Retailing and Consumer Services*, *66*, 102904. doi:10.1016/j.jretconser.2021.102904

Chen, N., & Yang, Y. (2023). The role of influencers in live streaming e-commerce: Influencer trust, attachment, and consumer purchase intention. *Journal of Theoretical and Applied Electronic Commerce Research*, *18*(3), 1601–1618. doi:10.3390/jtaer18030081

Kessel, P. V. (2019, December 4). 10 facts about Americans and YouTube. *Pew Research Center*. Retrieved from https://www.pewresearch.org/fact-tank/2019/12/04/10-facts-about-americans-and-youtube/

Ladhari, R., Massa, E., & Skandrani, H. (2020). YouTube vloggers' popularity and influence: The roles of homophily, emotional attachment, and expertise. *Journal of Retailing and Consumer Services*, *54*, 102027. doi:10.1016/j.jretconser.2019.102027

Lange, P. (2019). *Thanks for watching: an anthropological study of video sharing on YouTube*. University Press of Colorado.

Lee, S., & Kim, E. (2020). Influencer marketing on Instagram: How sponsorship disclosure, influencer credibility, and brand credibility impact the effectiveness of Instagram promotional post. *Journal of Global Fashion Marketing*, *11*(3), 232-249.

Lou, C. (2022). Social media influencers and followers: Theorization of a trans-parasocial relation and explication of its implications for influencer advertising. *Journal of Advertising*, *51*(1), 4–21. doi:10.1080/00913367.2021.1880345

Pittman, M., & Abell, A. (2021). More trust in fewer followers: Diverging effects of popularity metrics and green orientation social media influencers. *Journal of Interactive Marketing*, *56*(1), 70–82. doi:10.1016/j.intmar.2021.05.002

Schaffer, N. (2020). *The Age of Influence: The Power of Influencers to Elevate Your Brand*. HarperCollins Leadership.

Schouten, A. P., Janssen, L., & Verspaget, M. (2021). Celebrity vs. Influencer endorsements in advertising: the role of identification, credibility, and Product-Endorser fit. In *Leveraged marketing communications* (pp. 208–231). Routledge. doi:10.4324/9781003155249-12

Wei, X., Chen, H., Ramirez, A., Jeon, Y., & Sun, Y. (2022). Influencers as endorsers and followers as consumers: Exploring the role of parasocial relationship, congruence, and followers' identifications on consumer–brand engagement. *Journal of Interactive Advertising*, *22*(3), 269–288. doi:10.1080/15252019.2022.2116963

Section 1
Motivations and Influencers

Chapter 1

Shaping Style:
The Rise of Fashion and Beauty Social Media Influencers

Faren Karimkhan
https://orcid.org/0000-0002-8793-8207
Syracuse University, USA

ABSTRACT

In this chapter, the authors explore the distinctions between social media influencers and traditional celebrities in fashion and beauty. Next, they discuss the significance of perceived similarity, identification between social media influencers and their audience, and authenticity for fashion and beauty influencers' success. Finally, they examine the evolving landscape, current trends, and the anticipated trajectory of the fashion and cosmetic industries. Generally, the fashion and cosmetic industries share many characteristics and accept influence from one another. Therefore, it would be beneficial to examine these two industries together.

In February 2000, Jennifer Lopez gained significant attention at the 42nd Grammy Awards ceremony when she wore a striking green Versace dress, an iconic moment that remains vivid in a generation's collective memory. The dress captured immediate global attention, and people around the world eagerly searched online to catch a glimpse of it, to the point that it turned into one of the most searched queries of its time. This unprecedented demand for images led to the development of Google Images.

Before this moment, Google Search results were primarily text and web links. However, the overwhelming desire to visually experience the now-famous dress marked a pivotal moment in internet history. Much has transformed since the year 2000, yet the enduring power of a single image—a dress—continues to captivate our attention even in the present day.

DOI: 10.4018/979-8-3693-0912-4.ch001

INTRODUCTION

The landscape of the Internet has been transformed by the influence of social media, reshaping the way we consume information. Today, platforms like X have become our go-to sources for news, while Instagram and Pinterest have emerged as hotspots for fashion inspiration. However, many of those inspirations no longer come from traditional celebrities like Jennifer Lopez; instead, they stem from ordinary social media individuals who have captivated our attention with their content and style.

Accessibility and availability of the Internet and the popularity of social media have given birth to a new breed of celebrities known as social media influencers (Appel et al., 2019). Social media influencers (SMIs) are particularly dominant sources of inspiration for consumers in the realm of fashion and beauty (Chu & Seock, 2020; Driver, 2018). In the past, most fashion and cosmetic brands relied on celebrity collaborations to bring attention and visibility to their brand and establish consumer trust. However, in the past decade, we have observed a significant pivot towards SMIs (Jin et al. 2019; Linqia, 2019).

While the efficacy of celebrity endorsements remains undeniable, the surge in social media influencer endorsements cannot be overlooked. Brands, both high-end luxury and every day, are increasingly turning to influencers to bridge the gap between themselves and consumers, amplifying brand awareness and promoting trust. Although brands have had success with celebrity endorsements, there are still drawbacks to this technique. Celebrity endorsement can be both costly and risky due to the potential for attracting negative publicity (Wei & Lu, 2013).

Existing research results do not give a definite verdict on whether celebrity or social media influencer endorsement is more effective, but recent studies have found evidence for the effectiveness of social media influencers over traditional celebrities. For example, results of a recent empirical study suggested that sponsored content shared by SMIs increases purchase intentions more than those of traditional celebrities (Pöyry et al., 2021) However, the effectiveness of social media influencer endorsement and the popularity of this technique in the fashion and beauty industries is undeniable (e.g., Jin et al., 2021; Sokolova & Kefi, 2020). SMIs have reshaped the dynamics of brand promotion and consumer engagement. The shift towards SMIs reflects a new era where authenticity, relatability, and direct audience connection take precedence in the evolving landscape of digital influence.

Instagram, specifically, has become dominant in the fashion industry as one of the most influential sources for fashion insights (Chu & Seock, 2020). As a visual-based platform, Instagram aligns well with the fashion industry's reliance on visual appeals (Djafarova & Rushworth, 2017). Instagram, YouTube, and recently, TikTok have become the perfect place for social media fashion and beauty influencers to create and share their content and build a fan base.

In this chapter, we will explore the distinctions between SMIs and traditional celebrities in fashion and beauty. Next, we will discuss the significance of perceived similarity, identification between SMIs and their audience, and authenticity for fashion and beauty influencers' success. Finally, we will examine the evolving landscape, current trends, and the anticipated trajectory of the fashion and cosmetic industries. Generally, the fashion and cosmetic industries share many characteristics and accept influence from one another (Driver, 2018; Yan & Bissell, 2014). Therefore, it would be beneficial to examine these two industries together.

What Sets Social Media Influencers Apart from Traditional Celebrities?

Ordinary users on social media evolve into SMIs as they draw a substantial audience by producing content that attracts significant attention (Khamis et al., 2017; Tan, 2017). As they continue to grow their careers, SMIs may gain an audience population that is comparable to celebrities. For instance, Chiara Ferragni is a social media fashion influencer, who has gained over 29 million followers on Instagram and even has started her own clothing brand. So, if SMIs can reach an audience size that is comparable to or even sometimes bigger than those of celebrities, are they essentially the same? Although it may look that way at first glance, SMIs are inherently different from traditional celebrities.

Ordinary Status

The key distinguishing factor between SMIs and traditional celebrities lies in their ordinary status. SMIs are recognized as trusted trendsetters within their specific niches (Gräve, 2017; De Veirman et al., 2017). They participate in brand endorsements by seamlessly integrating brand messages into their content in exchange for rewards, such as free products, brand trips, tickets to shows and events, etc., that are typically determined by their outreach metrics (such as follower count, monthly views, engagement, etc.) (Audrezet et al., 2020; Luvaas, 2017). This contrasts with collaborations and endorsements by traditional celebrities, where the audience is clearly aware of the financial incentives for the celebrities involved (Gräve, 2017), which take away from their authenticity and affect consumers' trust. While followers tend to perceive branded content from SMIs as peer endorsements; therefore, they show lower resistance to their promotional messages (Pöyry et al., 2019).

Path to Fame

Celebrities and SMIs are very different in their paths to prominence. Traditional celebrities attain fame through careers in entertainment, professional sports, and similar industries, whereas influencers rely solely on social media to cultivate their audience and establish a career (Brooks et al., 2021; Carrillat & Ilicic, 2019; Harnish & Bridges, 2016). For instance, celebrities are often in the spotlight, starring in movies, showing off their looks on red carpets, and appearing on talk shows—opportunities that influencers generally lack. SMIs instead rely on social media to grow their audience base. For this reason, the relationship dynamics between celebrities and their audiences are inherently different from those of influencers.

Friendship-Like Relationship

To remain relevant and expand their reach, influencers must sustain a constant and direct connection with their audiences on social media as their primary platform. They must consistently share content on social media, participate in Q&A sessions, produce daily life vlogs, and offer glimpses into their personal moments to stay connected and relevant. Influencers are often seen as more relatable and approachable, similar to having a "long-distance friend" (Djafarova & Rushworth, 2017). They frequently address their followers directly in their posts, reply to their comments, and answer their questions which creates a sense of closeness with their audience (Chung et al., 2023; Erz & Christensen, 2018). Consequently, the type of relationship that influencers establish with their audience is more authentic (Scott, 2015,

p. 295), and real (Senft, 2008). This phenomenon cultivates a dynamic similar to a friendship between SMIs and their followers (Djafarova & Rushworth, 2017; Mudambi & Schuff, 2010; Schouten et al., 2019). This unique connection contributes significantly to their influence over followers and consumers (Jun & Yi, 2020; Ki et al., 2020).

It is important to acknowledge that SMIs have the potential to gain significant follower counts and develop into the status of micro-celebrities. However, it's essential to recognize that a notable discrepancy typically exists in audience size between SMIs and traditional celebrities.

Lesson From Dior: From High-Profile Celebrity Endorsement to Influencers' Campaign

Celebrity endorsements are practically inseparable from high-end and luxury fashion and cosmetic brands. Brands, like Dior, often utilize celebrity endorsements to align themselves with the prestige and allure of famous figures. In 2004, Charlize Theron established a groundbreaking record by securing an 11-year contract as a brand ambassador for the luxury fashion and cosmetics brand Dior, with a staggering value of 55 million USD (Nelson, 2023). Engaging in celebrity endorsement is a common practice for luxury fashion houses and is true to Dior's DNA. However, this deal, in particular, was attention-grabbing in the industry and was placed in the category of most high-profile celebrity endorsement deals with celebrities.

While it's less common for luxury fashion houses to venture into social media influencer campaigns, in 2017 Dior engaged in a social media campaign known as #DiorLoveChain. the #DiorLoveChain. The campaign was, in fact, a charitable initiative in which Dior pledged to donate $1 to organizations established to end poverty among children and provide schooling for girls in Kenya each time the #DiorLoveChain hashtag was shared on social media.

High-profile celebrities including Charlize Theron, Natalie Portman, and Jennifer Lawrence (Weil, 2017), as well as several influencers with followers of fewer than 500,000 were selected to participate in this campaign and answer the question of "What would you do for love?" in an Instagram post and use the #DiorLoveChain hashtag. The campaign distinguished itself through its innovative fusion of celebrity partnerships and influencer-style engagement. This inclusive strategy elevated the campaign's reach and authenticity, bridging the gap between celebrity endorsements and influencer marketing in a unique and impactful way. By leveraging high-profile celebrities in a manner similar to influencers, Dior effectively capitalized on the prestige and status of celebrities while simultaneously utilizing the authenticity and engagement potential of SMIs. This approach allowed Dior to maintain the allure of celebrity endorsement while also connecting with their target audience through social media platforms, thereby enhancing the campaign's authenticity and impact. Although this campaign surely cost Dior less than the 55 million USD contract, it brought significant visibility and engagement to the brand. The campaign was widely successful and marked the beginning of luxury fashion designer brands engaging in social media influencer endorsements.

This example shows that more and more brands are beginning to recognize the value of SMIs and are actively seeking to integrate influencers into their advertising strategies. The key takeaway from this example is that leveraging social media influencer endorsements can serve as a complementary approach to primary brand advertisements. This method proves to be highly effective in harnessing the influence of social media personalities while remaining authentic to the brand's core values, avoiding any sense of forced or misplaced promotion.

Figure 1. The image shows a post from Beatrice Gutu's Instagram, (@beatrice.gutu) one of the SMIs selected by Dior to participate in the #DiorLoveChain campaign

What Makes Fashion and Beauty Influencers Unique?

The era of SMIs has created a participation culture as opposed to exposure. Social media fashion influencers have the power to create trends and make certain fashion items a "must-have." This power shift from traditional celebrities to ordinary individuals in an industry that has spent far too many years selling the ideal beauty is noteworthy.

Today, thousands of influencers exist in every niche and on different platforms. Fashion and cosmetics stand out as particularly popular and densely populated with influencers (Chu & Seock, 2020;

Driver, 2018). It is typical for consumers today to watch their favorite influencers get ready, do their makeup, etc., to find inspiration for their personal aesthetic. Many consumers turn to influencers for product recommendations and are heavily influenced by the trends they promote. This is a revolutionary shift for the cosmetics and fashion industries, where the traditional glossy pages of magazines featuring professional photoshoots with supermodels are seemingly giving way to the influence of ordinary individuals sharing their personal style online. In contemporary times, the accessibility of digital platforms has democratized the fashion and beauty industry by enabling virtually anyone to become an influencer (Karlovitz, 2020). This phenomenon has empowered previously marginalized voices and images to gain visibility within the industry (Suk, 2021), thereby fostering greater inclusivity and diversity in fashion and beauty narratives. Research results show that SMIs can play a significant role in contributing to the culture of body positivity (Cohen et al., 2019; Cohen, Fardouly, et al., 2019). Cosmetic and fashion influencers are unique in the sense that they offer an alternative source of expression and inspiration, away from the old-school beauty standard —rich, thin, tall, heterosexual, and white—which many consumers seem to find refreshing and relevant (Rocamora, 2011). Fashion related content created by influencers is believed to be more real than mainstream magazines because they promote street fashion used by real and everyday people (Rocamora, 2012).

Fashion and beauty influencers are unique in the sense that they have contributed to the transformation of the industry from an exclusive space accessible only to the privileged minority into an inclusive platform where everyone can freely express themselves and explore their unique style, regardless of their body size or sociodemographic status (Trequattrini et al., 2019). This shift has caught the attention of brands across the spectrum, from high-end and luxury to everyday, and has encouraged brands to embrace the "realness movement" as a response to the new industry climate (Anderson, 2023). From this perspective, influencers effectively bridge the gap between brands and consumers by bringing visibility to consumers' authentic desires and preferences and reshaping the landscape to align more closely with what people genuinely want.

Social media fashion and cosmetics influencers today play a prominent role in the industry and sit in the front row of fashion shows. As noted earlier, influencers are trendsetters. Therefore, brands have turned to influencers to adapt themselves to the current and gauge consumer preference. Marketers in the fashion industry are increasingly turning to influencers to influence both current and potential consumers' purchasing decisions, reaching wider audiences at a lower cost (Britt et al., 2020). The effectiveness of this strategy lies in influencers presenting brands' products in alignment with their personal tastes and styles (Audrezet et al., 2020). This approach is perceived more as inspiration or peer endorsement rather than a traditional advertisement, making it a more effective strategy.

Fashion and beauty influencers are also unique in the way they foster a personal connection with their followers within the intimate realm of clothing and cosmetics (Hudders et al., 2020). This connection serves as a critical mechanism, allowing influencers to create an impact on their audiences. Beyond the utilitarian aspect of clothing, fashion and cosmetic products are often used to fulfill deeper, personal, and intricate needs linked to self-expression and identity (Evans, 1989). Individuals frequently utilize fashion and makeup as powerful tools to articulate their self-concept, attain image congruence, and signify group membership (Carroll & Ahuvia, 2006; Lundblad & Davies, 2016).

The role of these products in shaping personal identity highlights the importance of the interpersonal connection between influencers and their audience (Khamis & Munt, 2010). This connection, founded on shared values and aesthetic preferences, not only influences consumer choices but also forms a symbiotic relationship where followers find inspiration, guidance, and a sense of belonging in the influencer's curated world. As a result, influencers become not just fashion guides but also pathways for self-discovery and empowerment, solidifying their impact in the ever-evolving world of fashion influence (Kim, 2023; Limatius, 2020).

Is It Still All About the "Ideal Beauty" Standards?

Historically, the fashion and cosmetic industries have been centered around pursuing a glamorous and visually appealing aesthetic. Brands have consistently promised consumers a sense of perfection through their products and an elevated sense of allure and visual enchantment. The traditional narrative of these industries has often portrayed an idealized image of glamour, which is also often unrealistic and unattainable. Physical attractiveness has always been crucial for brands related to physical appearances, such as fashion and cosmetic brands (Kamins, 1990). For example, in celebrity endorsement, the physical attractiveness of the endorser has been a crucial factor in the fashion and cosmetics industries. The persistent use of the "ideal thin" concept in fashion advertising and the presentation of models with flawless skin and facial features- often extensively altered and retouched- in cosmetics advertising has been the industry norm for a long time.

Research results have continuously shown that exposure to thin models, especially in fashion advertising, can lead to negative consequences and severe symptoms such as body dissatisfaction, eating disorders, self-esteem issues, and depression (e.g., Fardouly & Vartanian, 2015; Kim & Lennon, 2007). Despite the overwhelming amount of evidence, the majority of retail brands have been reluctant to change their approach because "thinness sells" (Dittmar & Howard, 2004). However, in recent years, audiences have become more aware of digital alteration and the fact that many images shown in advertising are, in fact, unrealistic and unhealthy.

There has been an undeniable change in consumers' tastes regarding fashion and cosmetics. As a result, few brands have started to take a different approach, such as incorporating average or plus-size models in their advertising campaigns (Clayton et al., 2017; Convertino et al., 2019). For instance, intimate apparel brand Aerie has gained attention by advocating for body positivity and showcasing diverse models in their campaigns—a departure from the standardized "ideal thin" image often promoted by brands like Victoria's Secret. In 2014, Aerie launched their #AerieReal campaigns and featured unretouched photos of models with various body sizes and skin colors to celebrate natural beauty. They asked other women on social media to participate. The campaign has been a massive financial success for the brand and brought them significant positive attention (Kohan, 2022).

The rise of influencer culture significantly influences the transformative shift we observe in the industry. Unlike celebrities, a majority of influencers defy the conventional ideals of beauty standards. Instead, they present diverse body sizes, ethnicities, skin colors, and personal tastes. This diversity in the influencer landscape contributes substantially to creating a more inclusive and varied space within the fashion and cosmetics industry. In contrast to the traditionally narrow portrayals of beauty, influencers bring forth a multitude of perspectives, fostering a more authentic and relatable representation for their audiences. This shift is indicative of a broader movement towards embracing and celebrating diverse forms of beauty within the realms of fashion and cosmetics (Talbot, 2019). Social media has enabled individuals to express their unique fashion tastes and preferences on a personal level, as opposed to conforming to overarching global narratives (Camiciottoli, 2015). Regardless of race, ethnicity, gender, age, or body type, individuals can utilize social media platforms to articulate their identity, culture, and personal fashion choices, allowing for the sharing of diverse styles, tastes, and opinions (Belk, 2013).

Remi Bader, known on social media as Remi Jo, is a plus-size fashion influencer and content creator. She has gained 2.3 million followers on TikTok and 686 thousand followers on Instagram. She also made it to the Forbes 30 under 30 list among social media creators and personalities (Adebonojo, 2023). Remi Bader has launched her own collaborative collection with fashion brand Revolve and has partnered with major brands such as L'Oréal.

Bader's looks and aesthetic appear to be very popular among her audience, but she does not stop there. Remi Bader has been a vocal advocate against size discrimination within the fashion industry and has criticized brands for size discrepancies. Standing apart from the standardized norms of fashion and cosmetics brands, she represents a growing cohort of influencers challenging conventional norms. Prior to the advent of SMIs, curvy models were rarely featured in mainstream fashion magazines. However, in contemporary times, the widespread popularity of influencers from previously marginalized groups has compelled brands to acknowledge and address their needs. Influencers like Bader play a significant role in this shift towards a more inclusive culture within the fashion and cosmetic industries.

Another example is Grece Ghanem, a 56-year-old fashion influencer who has gained significant attention on social media for her unique sense of fashion and style that is ageless. Ghanem, with 1.5 million followers on Instagram and 394 thousand followers on TikTok, has brought attention to another group of consumers whom the fashion and beauty industries have often marginalized due to their age.

Conventional beauty standards that fashion and cosmetic brands embrace often overlook individuals beyond their 20s and 30s. Anti-aging skincare products and conservative clothing items are typically marketed toward consumers in their 40s and 50s. However, in recent times, influencers such as Ghanem have played a significant role in challenging age discrimination that has become ingrained in the industry. These influencers question the traditional narrative by showcasing ageless style and beauty and contribute to a broader cultural shift that embraces and celebrates beauty across all age groups. Their influence and popularity highlight the need for the industry to recognize and cater to the diverse beauty needs of consumers at every stage of life.

Today, there is still predominant discrimination and exclusion because of body size, race, age, etc., in the fashion industry and its media, despite the consumers' demanding a more inclusive and diverse market (Lewis, 2019). Although the industry has not entirely moved past the exclusive and discriminatory culture, there has been slow and steady progress made in representation. The landscape of the fashion and beauty industries is much more inclusive today and welcoming of all aspects of diversity, and influencers, in many respects, have played a role in fostering this positive change. Influencers have created a significant shift in these industries where "authenticity" and "realness" are celebrated over "perfection."

The Winning Formula for Fashion and Cosmetic Influencers: Similarity, Wishful Identification, and Authenticity

A fair question to ask at this point is: What makes social media fashion and beauty influencers effective and impactful? What qualities lead to their credibility and ability to influence their consumers and what they decide to purchase? Persuasion and advertising theories have tried to answer this question. Source credibility theory (Ohanian, 1990) is a commonly applied theory to answer this question. According to this theory, trustworthiness, expertise in the field, and attractiveness constitute the three components that enhance the credibility and, consequently, the effectiveness of the source, including influencers. While this theory adeptly explains the effectiveness of celebrity endorsers and captures the impact of SMIs in

Figure 2. The image is selected from Remi Bader's Instagram (@remibader)

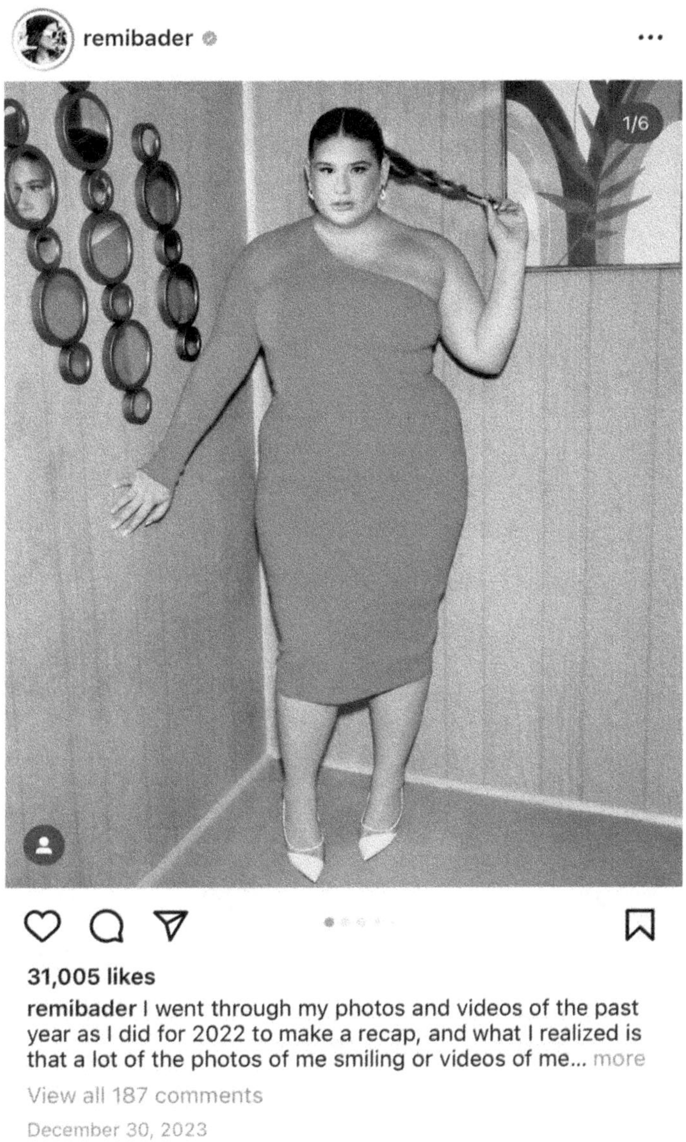

areas that align with celebrities, it does not capture the distinctive aspects and qualities that also play a role in the effectiveness of influencers.

In academic research, various factors have been examined to understand their contribution to the effectiveness of influencers, including source-product congruency, authenticity, relatability, similarity, para-social relationship, identification, physical and social attractiveness, etc (e.g., Chu & Kamal, 2008; Ki & Kim, 2019; Kim & Kim, 2021; Martensen et al., 2018; Sokolova & Kefi, 2020; Taillon et al., 2020; Tolbert & Drogos, 2019; Van Esch et al., 2018). While all these factors play a role in the overall success of an influencer, in the fashion and cosmetics domain, the key to success can be distilled into

Figure 3. The image is selected from Grece Ghanem's Instagram (@greceghanem)

three main elements: perceived similarity, identification, and authenticity. These factors emerge as the primary contributors that solidify influencers as successful sources of information and inspiration. It is important to note that this does not diminish the significance of other mentioned qualities; instead, the discussion here emphasizes the specific importance of these qualities in fashion and cosmetics, which can sometimes be overlooked.

Perceived Similarity

SMIs thrive on the perception of similarity between themselves and their audiences (Yuan & Lou, 2020). SMIs enhance the feeling of similarity by posting content about their personal life to make their profiles appear ordinary, humanized, approachable, and authentic (Djafarova & Rushworth, 2017; Schouten et al., 2019). The possibility of direct interaction between influencers and their audiences, though, for example, comments, etc., strengthens the feeling that the influencer is similar to oneself (Schmidt, 2007). Similarities in demographics, background, interests, attitudes, social status, and lifestyles can create a sense of similarity between influencers and their followers (McPherson et al., 2001; Phillips et al., 2006) which can enhance SMIs' effectiveness. For instance, findings from an empirical study examining beauty influencers revealed a significant relationship between attitude homophily and perceived credibility and para-social interaction between the influencer and the audiences, which in turn, led to higher purchase intention (Sokolova & Kefi, 2020). Another study found that perceived similarity with SMIs positively impacts consumers' purchase intention and loyalty to the influencer (Kim & Kim, 2021). Other research findings indicate that consumers tend to be receptive to information when they perceive the source as similar to themselves (Yaniv et al., 2011). Research results also suggest that influencers who are perceived as similar by their audience can influence consumers' purchase decisions (e.g., Shang et al., 2017), which is also one of the mechanisms that contribute to the effectiveness of influencers.

Perceived similarity is even more critical in the fashion and cosmetic industries (Kozar & Damhorst, 2008). Fashion and makeup choices are closely tied to one's physical appearance, which is also influenced by demographics such as ethnicity. Therefore, similarities in demographic characteristics may enhance the feeling of similarity between influencers and their audiences. People choose to follow particular fashion and beauty influencers because they appreciate their style, and they find their content relatable. For instance, petit women might be more interested and willing to take fashion advice and inspiration from petit influencers because they are familiar with that body type. Similarly, someone with a darker skin tone may be more interested in following makeup tutorials from an influencer with a similar complexion, as they trust that the suggested products and techniques would complement their features (Childs, 2022). These shared characteristics and similarities establish a close connection between influencers and their audience, a particularly crucial aspect in fashion and beauty, where physical attributes take center stage.

Beyond physical characteristics, shared values and sociodemographic traits also play a significant role in creating a perception of similarity between influencers and their audience. Consumers often select specific clothing items and brands not only for their aesthetic appeal but also to convey social meaning and attain social acceptance (Pham, 2011). For instance, an individual earning $300,000 annually seeking to establish social class and status through fashion might find an influencer with similar values and preferences more relatable than someone in a lower-income group who values minimalism. In this way, influencers become not just style guides but relatable figures who resonate with their audience's diverse social and economic backgrounds.

Wishful Identification

Identification is "a persuasion process that occurs when an individual adopts the behavior or attitudes of another individual or group based on a self-defining relationship" (Kelman, 1961, p. 63). Bandura's (2001) social cognitive theory further characterizes identification as a psychological matching process wherein individuals change their emotional responses or behaviors to align with those of another person. In the case of influencers, wishful identification, or the desire to be more "like them," is particularly important as it can influence the consumers' purchase decisions (Ki & Kim, 2019). When individuals adopt behaviors to become more similar to influencers, it extends to influencing their purchase intentions. Identification occurs when one is attracted to an endorser and strongly desires to become like them (Erdogan, 1999). From this perspective, if the audience admires an influencer to the extent that they aspire to be more like them, it is likely they will also follow the influencer's purchase decisions as a means to achieve that resemblance.

Identification and similarity are often interconnected (Schouten et al., 2019). Previous research indicates that audiences are more inclined to experience wishful identification with influencers rather than celebrities, primarily due to a higher perceived similarity (Gong & Li, 2017; Gräve, 2017; Jain & Roy, 2016; Jin & Phua, 2014). Wishful identification is more likely when audiences perceive the source as similar and share commonalities (Hoffner & Buchanan, 2005). This dynamic appears prevalent in the relationship between fashion and beauty influencers and their followers.

Wishful identification remains crucial in the realm of fashion and cosmetics. The frequent and easily modifiable decision-making nature in the fashion and cosmetics domain prompts consumers to engage in purchases influenced by wishful identification more regularly. Products within the fashion and cosmetic industry are characterized as low involvement and low risk. For instance, when a consumer makes a purchase influenced by wishful identification, seeking to align their style and appearance with their favorite influencer, the financial investment is typically limited, such as spending $100 on a pair of jeans or $20 on lipstick. The potential outcomes, even in less favorable scenarios, involve minimal risk – perhaps the consumer may not end up wearing the jeans or find the lipstick suits them. These consequences are comparatively low risk, highlighting the relatively low stakes associated with decisions in the fashion and cosmetics realm influenced by wishful identification.

Authenticity

Authenticity is another aspect of the success formula for influencers. The concept of authenticity revolves around notions of truth, genuineness, and reality (Beverland & Farrelly, 2010). According to the self-determination theory, authenticity entails individuals engaging in behaviors driven by intrinsic motivation—driven by one's inherent desires and passions (Deci & Ryan, 2000). Conversely, inauthenticity entails participating in extrinsically motivated behaviors, which are propelled by external incentives or pressures, such as the anticipation of rewards (Ryan & Deci, 2000), similar to financial compensations in the case of SMIs.

From this perspective, authenticity can be understood as how genuine the influencers are perceived by their followers, which also depends on their motives. As previously mentioned, audiences are aware of the financial motivations when celebrities engage in brand endorsement, which contrasts with their perceived authenticity. Although financial compensation in influencer brand endorsement is becoming more common, influencers still approach it differently. They strive to persuade their audience that the endorsed products align with their personal preferences and that their recommendations remain authentic (Hund & McGuigan, 2019). Even when creating sponsored content, influencers frequently emphasize the independence of their reviews and recommendations. They also feature the product in non-sponsored content, reinforcing the authenticity of their recommendations to the audience. This approach aims to build trust by assuring viewers that the influencer's endorsement is genuine and not solely motivated by a paid partnership. The combination of sponsored and non-sponsored content provides a more authentic and transparent representation of the product, strengthening the bond between influencers and the audience. A recent study found that influencers perceived authenticity positively impacts consumers' attitudes toward the sponsored product, purchase intention, and loyalty to the influencer (Kim & Kim, 2021).

Authenticity is even more critical for fashion and beauty influencers. Audiences expect influencers to be more "real" and "authentic" compared to traditional celebrities and models, which fosters a relationship that is in many ways similar to a friendship between influencers and their followers (Mudambi & Schuff, 2010; Djafarova & Rushworth, 2017; Schouten et al., 2019). Authenticity in fashion and beauty influencers is a dynamic interplay of transparency, genuine self-expression, and trustworthy recommendations. Those who successfully embody these qualities are more likely to build lasting connections with their audience and wield significant influence in the ever-evolving landscape of fashion and beauty. Several research studies focused on beauty, fashion, and lifestyle influencers have concluded that the authenticity of SMIs is an essential element that contributes to their effectiveness (Duffy, 2013; Gannon & Prothero, 2016; García-Rapp, 2017; Marwick, 2013).

Influencers employ various strategies to enhance perceptions of authenticity, including sharing unfiltered selfies (Gannon & Prothero, 2016), engaging in intimate dialogue (Suhr, 2014), fostering direct interactions with their audience (Marwick, 2013), and creating original content (Duffy & Wissinger, 2017). Followers often seek inspiration from influencers who stay true to their unique aesthetics and preferences rather than conforming to trends solely for commercial purposes. In the era dominated by photo editing and filters, influencers who embrace their natural selves and advocate for body positivity contribute to an authentic narrative. This commitment to authenticity not only challenges conventional notions of beauty but also resonates deeply with followers seeking relatable and genuine representation in the world of fashion and beauty influencers.

Case Study

A Success Story: ASOS and Social Media Influencers

This case study seeks to provide insights into the factors that facilitated the success of ASOS's collaboration with social media influencers. According to Yin (2009, p. 18), a case study is an empirical investigation that examines a phenomenon within its natural context. The design of this case study follows a descriptive single-case study approach (Priya, 2021), aiming to portray the phenomenon within its real-world setting. Various data sources have been utilized, including industry population statistics, academic literature, observations, and narrative analysis (Baxter & Jack, 2015).

ASOS, a prominent online retailer specializing in clothing and cosmetics, has emerged as a frontrunner in the digital marketplace, mainly targeting a youthful consumer base. Today, ASOS carries over 850 brands and has its own clothing and accessories label. ASOS is known as an international brand and ships to 196 countries. ASOS also offers fast shipping, and its next-day shipping (available in the UK, US, and other countries) is very popular among consumers.

The brand's effective use of social media influencer marketing has played a key role in positioning it at the forefront of the industry. This case is significant as it highlights the essential elements that lead to the success of a social media influencer campaign and emphasizes the pivotal role influencers can play as a brand's backbone. Influencers have contributed significantly to enhancing ASOS's visibility and connecting more deeply with consumers (McCormick & Livett, 2012). The collaboration between ASOS and influencers stands out as not only one of the earliest but also among the most achieving examples in the realm of social media influencer partnerships within the fashion industry.

ASOS, previously known as "As Seen On the Screen" (ASOS), is a British fashion and cosmetic retailer launched in 2000 as a celebrity-linked clothing website. As Seen On the Screen initially focused on providing consumers with imitations and replicas of clothing items celebrities wear. In 2003, ASOS rebranded itself and evolved its strategy, which was a pivot point in the brand's success. Recognizing shifts in consumer preferences, ASOS departed from its celebrity-centric approach and aimed to deliver a seamless shopping experience, offering affordable clothing items with tasteful and trendy designs to younger consumers (Robert, 2018). A significant part of ASOS's success today is due to its well-planned and executed social media influencer campaigns that are rooted in the DNA of the new ASOS. In this case study, we will review the core elements that led to ASOS success with SMIs:

Social Media Influencers at the Forefront

ASOS has achieved significant success with influencers by placing them at the core of their brand rather than using influencers as a supplementary element to other advertising efforts. This unique approach has led consumers to view influencers as brand ambassadors rather than mere advertising outlets. ASOS's strategy regarding influencers has resonated with the audience, making the integration of influencers into ASOS's identity feel natural and aligned with the brand's core.

ASOS carefully curates a group of influencers, referred to as "insiders," who showcase various fashion styles and body shapes to contribute to ASOS's social media. By frequently featuring ASOS clothing, accessories, and beauty products in their daily content, ASOS insiders not only enhance the brand's visibility but also contribute to the perception of authenticity.

ASOS rarely posts content created by the brand itself. Instead, the majority of their content has been created and re-posted by ASOS) by a diverse array of influencers representing various niches, body sizes, ethnicities, styles, and more. This strategy reinforces the perception of influencers as authentic advocates for the brand. It not only showcases a variety of perspectives but also strengthens the organic and genuine connection between ASOS, its influencers, and the broader consumer base.

Community Building

ASOS launched the #AsSeenOnMe campaign in 2004, encouraging consumers to share photos and videos showcasing themselves wearing ASOS products and use the hashtag across different social media platforms. As of January 2024, the hashtag remains active and has been shared over 1.4 million times, highlighting the lasting success and impact of the campaign.

This campaign is very beneficial for ASOS as it generated substantial engagement and visibility without incurring costs. The user-generated content, which is viewed as trustworthy and authentic by consumers, became a valuable asset for ASOS, and the popularity of the hashtag served as a vote of confidence for the brand from consumers.

ASOS also recognized that for the campaign to be sustainable, they must offer something of value in exchange. ASOS reciprocated by featuring user-generated content on its official Instagram page with 14.8 million followers (as of January 2024) and on the product pages on its website. This strategy was very well-received, especially by micro-influencers who were trying to establish their careers on social media and needed the visibility that ASOS offered. This reciprocal approach not only empowered individual creators by featuring their content but also created value for the broader community. Users participating in the #AsSeenOnMe campaign had the opportunity to enhance their own social media presence but also contributed value to the entire community, allowing consumers to receive recommendations from fellow advocates within the ASOS community.

This strategy established a reciprocal relationship between the brand and consumers, establishing a powerful community of ASOS fans. The #AsSeenOnMe campaign effectively positioned these fans at the forefront of ASOS's most influential media outlets – their official website and Instagram page. This community-centric approach has proven to be a compelling force in strengthening the brand-consumer relationship for ASOS.

No Platform Is Too Small; No Platform Is Too Big

Another element of ASOS's success story is platform diversity. ASOS has not only leveraged various social media platforms but also has the ability to pivot, for example, from Facebook to Instagram and TikTok, as a response to the dynamic shifts in the market and evolving consumer culture. By maintaining a strong presence across multiple platforms, ASOS achieves a broader reach and stays attuned to the preferences and trends that resonate with diverse audiences.

Recognizing the distinct user demographics and purposes of each platform, ASOS has adapted its influencer content to suit the preferences and behavior of users on each platform. For instance, on YouTube, influencers often share longer videos, such as lifestyle content or weekly product reviews. This platform caters to users who seek in-depth and comprehensive content. In contrast, on Instagram, the same influencers may utilize the Stories feature to engage with the audience more casually and frequently. Understanding the unique characteristics of each social media platform allows ASOS to effectively connect with diverse audiences, optimizing content for the specific expectations and preferences of users on Instagram, YouTube, TikTok, Snapchat, etc.

As mentioned earlier, ASOS relies heavily on influencers for their Instagram content, but they also extend their influencer collaborations across multiple platforms. ASOS frequently re-posts and collaborates with influencers on its TikTok account, which has 2 million followers and a remarkable 20 million daily engagements. The TikTok content often includes short videos offering glimpses into quick "get ready with me" or other styling-related content, aligning with the platform's focus on short and engaging videos.

On YouTube, ASOS features series that serve as a "guide" into various styles and aesthetics, each featuring different influencers known for their distinct fashion preferences. This strategy on YouTube provides audiences with a more in-depth exploration of diverse styles, which also aligns with the purpose of the platform. By tailoring its influencer content to suit the characteristics of each platform, ASOS effectively maximizes its reach and engagement across all major social media platforms.

Body Positivity and Inclusivity

Influencers have played a pivotal role in aiding ASOS to embrace and highlight body positivity and inclusivity. In addition to the brand's progressive steps, such as eliminating gender-specific sections for clothing and accessories on its website and substituting "beauty" with "face+body," ASOS's collaborations with influencers have enabled the brand to better practice and showcase its inclusivity.

ASOS takes a distinctive approach by delving into influencer content instead of relying solely on traditional models. This strategy allows them to showcase a diverse range of styles, body sizes, and unique approaches to fashion and style. Influencers, being real individuals, proudly display features like stretch marks, freckles, cellulite, and other perceived "imperfections" without digitally altering their content. This bold move is not only a significant step in the right direction but also a direct response to consumers' increasing demand for realness and authenticity in the fashion industry. By embracing and celebrating the authentic beauty of influencers, ASOS has effectively bridged the gap between the brand and consumers and has established a closer and more relatable connection.

Beyond The Glamour: The Critiques and Challenges of Influencer Culture

Authenticity Under Threat

While we have discussed the positive contributions of social media fashion and beauty influencers, it is also essential to acknowledge the downsides. One prevalent critique aimed at influencers in general (not specifically fashion and beauty influencers) is that the oversaturation of the space has compromised influencers' authenticity. Today, in every given niche, there are thousands of influencers driven to expand their follower count and land brand deals.

Fashion and cosmetics are among the most crowded and saturated niches across all social media platforms. As influencers navigate the crowded and competitive landscape, some find themselves compelled to compromise authenticity for the sake of career advancement. A common scenario involves influencers accepting endorsement deals from brands they may not genuinely appreciate. The pressure to seize every opportunity to enhance their career leads individuals to endorse products or services that do not align with their true preferences or values. This compromises the integrity of their content and raises questions about the sincerity of their recommendations.

There is a delicate balance between genuine content creation and the pursuit of professional growth. This paradox prompts a larger conversation about the sustainability and ethics of influencer culture, urging both influencers and their audience to critically evaluate the motivations behind the content they create and consume.

Encouraging Overconsumption

As mentioned earlier, in order to stay connected and relevant, influencers need to engage with their audiences and post new content constantly. For fashion and beauty influencers, this dynamic often translates into constantly showcasing new products on their social media platforms. However, constantly promoting various products may contribute to an overconsumption culture among the audience.

Video topics like "Brand hauls," "Unboxing," "Get ready with me using all new beauty products," or "Come shopping with me" are very common among fashion and beauty influencers. While it is understandable that influencers, as part of their job, need to shop for the latest trends consistently, the frequency and enthusiasm with which they showcase new, and often entirely unnecessary products can have negative consequences. The constant exposure to such content may influence consumers to emulate these behaviors, leading them to overspend on products they probably do not need.

Social media fashion influencers have significantly contributed to the surge in the popularity of fast-fashion brands such as the Chinese giant Shein and H&M. Known for their frequent release of new collections every few weeks, as opposed to the traditional seasonal approach, these brands specialize in offering clothing items designed for short-term use, available at very low price point. This continuous cycle aligns with the influencers' need for regular content as they eagerly unbox, showcase, and style the latest collections every few weeks. While this practice enhances their visibility on the platform, it encourages a culture of fast-fashion consumption and overconsumption among audiences. The emphasis on rapid turnover and low prices perpetuates the idea that clothing is disposable, encouraging consumers to engage in frequent, impulsive purchases that may not align with sustainable and mindful consumer practices.

The influencer's role as a trendsetter, coupled with the nature of their content creation, has the potential to contribute to a culture of excessive consumerism. Fashion and beauty influencers constantly create and embrace new trends, which gives them new content ideas but also creates a need for new items to be purchased. This perpetual cycle introduces a stream of "must-have" items that remain trendy for only a few weeks. The desire to keep up with the latest and trendiest items endorsed by influencers may drive consumers to make purchasing decisions influenced more by social media trends than practical necessity. This phenomenon reflects the broader impact of influencer content on consumer behavior and raises questions about the responsibility influencers bear in shaping consumer culture and consumption patterns.

What Does the Future Hold?

Despite the critiques discussed above, the positive impacts of fashion and beauty influencers outweigh the negatives. This is not intended to diminish the fair and significant criticisms discussed earlier; rather, it emphasizes that by fostering awareness and responsibility among brands, influencers, and audiences, influencers can indeed be a sustainable and powerful force for positive change in the fashion and cosmetic industries.

The prevailing trend in the market strongly indicates that influencers are here to stay. As discussed earlier in the chapter, even esteemed designer houses, such as Dior, are starting to acknowledge the power of influencers and embrace this new world of fashion and beauty. There has been consistent growth in influencer marketing, and the trajectory is rising.

The consistent growth in influencer marketing highlights its enduring trajectory and a continuous and upward trend. This trend signifies a fundamental shift in how brands approach marketing and engage with their audiences. Influencers have become integral players in shaping consumer preferences and driving brand visibility. As the influencer landscape continues to evolve, it is evident that influencers will remain a potent and influential force in fashion and beauty.

Another notable trend in the fashion and cosmetic industry is the shift towards collaborating with micro-influencers rather than mega-influencers (Hosie, 2019). Micro-influencers, with a smaller follower count, are generally perceived as more authentic and relatable, which makes it easier for audiences to trust their content and recommendations (Britt et al., 2020; Ehlers, 2021). This shift towards micro-influencers provides brands with a distinct advantage over traditional celebrities or mega-influencers. The emphasis on micro-influencers reflects a strategic move within the industry to establish more genuine connections between influencers and their audiences, ultimately benefiting the brands involved.

CONCLUSION

In conclusion, social media fashion and beauty influencers have created a dynamic landscape marked by distinctions from traditional celebrities. The uniqueness of influencers lies not only in their diverse backgrounds and styles but also in their transformative role in steering the industry towards a more inclusive culture by challenging conventional beauty standards.

Social media influencers in the fashion and beauty industries have played a pivotal role in democratizing a space historically dominated by traditional and often unattainable beauty standards. These standards have perpetuated a sense of exclusion and marginalization among individuals who do not conform to them. Today, attributes such as age, race, skin color, body size, and personal fashion and makeup preferences are no longer constrained by universal norms. Instead, individuality is celebrated and embraced, thanks to the diverse representation and inclusive messages promoted by social media influencers.

Factors such as similarity, wishful identification, and authenticity are pivotal in establishing genuine connections between influencers and their audiences. While criticisms about authenticity and the promotion of overconsumption have been raised, the discussion highlights the industry's ongoing evolution. The future trends indicate a shift towards micro-influencers and a continued dependence on influencers as powerful agents shaping the fashion and beauty narrative. SMIs play a central role in reshaping the industry, advancing it towards authenticity, inclusivity, and dynamic transformations in the realms of beauty and fashion. Social media influencers play a pivotal role in holding brands accountable for their exclusionary practices and contribute substantially to amplifying consumer opinions. with the sustained presence of social media influencers, the landscape of the fashion and beauty industry is positioned to evolve into a more diverse and inclusive space.

REFERENCES

Adebonojo, R. (2023). *Remi Bader*. Forbes. https://www.forbes.com/profile/remi-bader/?sh=17ab80cf7de2

Anderson, M. (2023, September 13). *How brands are embracing the "realness movement."* Forbes. https://www.forbes.com/sites/forbescommunicationscouncil/2023/09/13/how-brands-are-embracing-the-realness-movement/

Appel, G., Grewal, L., Hadi, R., & Stephen, A. T. (2020). The future of social media in marketing. *Journal of the Academy of Marketing Science*, *48*(1), 79–95. doi:10.1007/s11747-019-00695-1 PMID:32431463

Audrezet, A., de Kerviler, G., & Guidry Moulard, J. (2020). Authenticity under threat: When social media influencers need to go beyond self-presentation. *Journal of Business Research*, *117*, 557–569. doi:10.1016/j.jbusres.2018.07.008

Bandura, A. (2001). Social cognitive theory: An agentic perspective. *Annual Review of Psychology*, *52*(1), 1–26. doi:10.1146/annurev.psych.52.1.1 PMID:11148297

Baxter, P., & Jack, S. (2015). Qualitative case study methodology: Study design and implementation for novice researchers. *The Qualitative Report*. Advance online publication. doi:10.46743/2160-3715/2008.1573

Belk, R. W. (2013). Extended self in a digital world: Table 1. *The Journal of Consumer Research*, *40*(3), 477–500. doi:10.1086/671052

Beverland, M. B., & Farrelly, F. J. (2010). The quest for authenticity in consumption: Consumers' purposive choice of authentic cues to shape experienced outcomes. *The Journal of Consumer Research*, *36*(5), 838–856. doi:10.1086/615047

Britt, R. K., Hayes, J. L., Britt, B. C., & Park, H. (2020). Too big to sell? A computational analysis of network and content characteristics among mega and micro beauty and fashion social media influencers. *Journal of Interactive Advertising*, *20*(2), 111–118. doi:10.1080/15252019.2020.1763873

Brooks, G., Drenten, J., & Piskorski, M. J. (2021). Influencer celebrification: How social media influencers acquire celebrity capital. *Journal of Advertising*, *50*(5), 528–547. doi:10.1080/00913367.2021.1977737

Camiciottoli, C. B. (2015). All those Elvis-Meets-Golf-Player looks: A corpus-assisted analysis of creative compounds in fashion blogging. *Discourse, Context & Media*, *12*, 77–86. doi:10.1016/j.dcm.2015.10.002

Carrillat, F. A., & Ilicic, J. (2019). The celebrity capital life cycle: A framework for future research directions on celebrity endorsement. *Journal of Advertising*, *48*(1), 61–71. doi:10.1080/00913367.2019.1579689

Carroll, B. A., & Ahuvia, A. C. (2006). Some antecedents and outcomes of brand love. *Marketing Letters*, *17*(2), 79–89. doi:10.1007/s11002-006-4219-2

Childs, K. M. (2022). "the shade of it all": How Black women use Instagram and YouTube to contest colorism in the beauty industry. *Social Media + Society*, *8*(2). doi:10.1177/20563051221107634

Chu, S.-C., & Kamal, S. (2008). The effect of perceived blogger credibility and argument quality on message elaboration and brand attitudes: An exploratory study. *Journal of Interactive Advertising*, *8*(2), 26–37. doi:10.1080/15252019.2008.10722140

Chu, S.-C., & Seock, Y.-K. (2020). The power of social media in fashion advertising. *Journal of Interactive Advertising*, *20*(2), 93–94. doi:10.1080/15252019.2020.1802955

Chung, J., Ding, Y., & Kalra, A. (2023). I really know you: How influencers can increase audience engagement by referencing their close social ties. *The Journal of Consumer Research*, *50*(4), 683–703. doi:10.1093/jcr/ucad019

Clayton, R. B., Ridgway, J. L., & Hendrickse, J. (2017). Is plus size equal? The positive impact of average and plus-sized media fashion models on women's cognitive resource allocation, social comparisons, and body satisfaction. *Communication Monographs*, *84*(3), 406–422. doi:10.1080/03637751.2017.1332770

Cohen, R., Fardouly, J., Newton-John, T., & Slater, A. (2019). #BoPo on Instagram: An experimental investigation of the effects of viewing body positive content on young women's mood and body image. *New Media & Society*, *21*(7), 1546–1564. doi:10.1177/1461444819826530

Cohen, R., Irwin, L., Newton-John, T., & Slater, A. (2019). #bodypositivity: A content analysis of body positive accounts on Instagram. *Body Image*, *29*, 47–57. doi:10.1016/j.bodyim.2019.02.007 PMID:30831334

Convertino, A. D., Rodgers, R. F., Franko, D. L., & Jodoin, A. (2019). An evaluation of the *Aerie Real* campaign: Potential for promoting positive body image? *Journal of Health Psychology*, *24*(6), 726–737. doi:10.1177/1359105316680022 PMID:27888254

De Veirman, M., Cauberghe, V., & Hudders, L. (2017). Marketing through Instagram influencers: The impact of number of followers and product divergence on brand attitude. *International Journal of Advertising*, *36*(5), 798–828. doi:10.1080/02650487.2017.1348035

Deci, E. L., & Ryan, R. M. (2000). The "what" and "why" of goal pursuits: Human needs and the self-determination of behavior. *Psychological Inquiry*, *11*(4), 227–268. doi:10.1207/S15327965PLI1104_01

Dittmar, H., & Howard, S. (2004). Professional hazards? The impact of models' body size on advertising effectiveness and women's body-focused anxiety in professions that do and do not emphasize the cultural ideal of thinness. *British Journal of Social Psychology*, *43*(4), 477–497. doi:10.1348/0144666042565407 PMID:15601505

Djafarova, E., & Rushworth, C. (2017). Exploring the credibility of online celebrities' Instagram profiles in influencing the purchase decisions of young female users. *Computers in Human Behavior*, *68*, 1–7. doi:10.1016/j.chb.2016.11.009

Driver, R. (2018). *Instagram reigns supreme for fashion and beauty influencers.* Fashionnetwork.com. https://us.fashionnetwork.com/news/instagram-reigns-supreme-for-fashion-and-beauty-influencers,942744.html

Duffy, B. E. (2013). *Remake, remodel: Women's magazines in the digital age.* University of Illinois Press. doi:10.5406/illinois/9780252037962.001.0001

Duffy, B. E., & Wissinger, E. (2017). Mythologies of Creative Work in the Social Media Age: Fun, Free, and "Just Being Me.". *International Journal of Communication*, 11.

Ehlers, K. (2021, June 2). *Micro-influencers: When smaller is better.* Forbes. https://www.forbes.com/sites/forbesagencycouncil/2021/06/02/micro-influencers-when-smaller-is-better/?sh=2795a40b539b

Erdogan, B. Z. (1999). Celebrity endorsement: A literature review. *Journal of Marketing Management*, *15*(4), 291–314. doi:10.1362/026725799784870379

Erz, A., & Heeris Christensen, A.-B. (2018). Transforming consumers into brands: Tracing transformation processes of the practice of blogging. *Journal of Interactive Marketing*, *43*, 69–82. doi:10.1016/j.intmar.2017.12.002

Evans, M. (1989). Consumer behaviour towards fashion. *European Journal of Marketing*, *23*(7), 7–16. doi:10.1108/EUM0000000000575

Fardouly, J., & Vartanian, L. R. (2015). Negative comparisons about one's appearance mediate the relationship between Facebook usage and body image concerns. *Body Image*, *12*, 82–88. doi:10.1016/j.bodyim.2014.10.004 PMID:25462886

Gannon, V., & Prothero, A. (2016). Beauty blogger selfies as authenticating practices. *European Journal of Marketing*, *50*(9/10), 1858–1878. doi:10.1108/EJM-07-2015-0510

García-Rapp, F. (2017). 'Come join and let's BOND': Authenticity and legitimacy building on YouTube's beauty community. *Journal of Media Practice*, *18*(2–3), 120–137. doi:10.1080/14682753.2017.1374693

Gong, W., & Li, X. (2017). Engaging fans on microblog: The synthetic influence of parasocial interaction and source characteristics on celebrity endorsement. *Psychology and Marketing*, *34*(7), 720–732. doi:10.1002/mar.21018

Gräve, J.-F. (2017). Exploring the perception of influencers vs. Traditional celebrities: Are social media stars a new type of endorser? *Proceedings of the 8th International Conference on Social Media & Society - #SMSociety17.*

Harnish, R. J., & Bridges, K. R. (2016). Mall haul videos: Self-presentational motives and the role of self-monitoring. *Psychology and Marketing*, *33*(2), 113–124. doi:10.1002/mar.20858

Hoffner, C., & Buchanan, M. (2005). Young adults' wishful identification with television characters: The role of perceived similarity and character attributes. *Media Psychology*, *7*(4), 325–351. doi:10.1207/S1532785XMEP0704_2

Hosie, R. (2019, April 9). Why brands are turning away from big Instagram influencers to work with people who have small followings instead. *Business Insider*. https://www.businessinsider.com/brands-turning-to-micro-influencers-instead-of-instagram-stars-2019-4

Hudders, L., De Jans, S., & De Veirman, M. (2020). The commercialization of social media stars: A literature review and conceptual framework on the strategic use of social media influencers. *International Journal of Advertising*, *40*(3), 327–375. doi:10.1080/02650487.2020.1836925

Hund, E., & McGuigan, L. (2019). A shoppable life: Performance, selfhood, and influence in the social media storefront. *Communication, Culture & Critique*, *12*(1), 18–35. doi:10.1093/ccc/tcz004

Jain, V., & Roy, S. (2016). Understanding meaning transfer in celebrity endorsements: A qualitative exploration. *Qualitative Market Research*, *19*(3), 266–286. doi:10.1108/QMR-03-2015-0020

Jin, S.-A. A., & Phua, J. (2014). Following celebrities' tweets about brands: The impact of twitter-based electronic word-of-mouth on consumers' source credibility perception, buying intention, and social identification with celebrities. *Journal of Advertising*, *43*(2), 181–195. doi:10.1080/00913367.2013.827606

Jin, S. V., Muqaddam, A., & Ryu, E. (2019). Instafamous and social media influencer marketing. *Marketing Intelligence & Planning*, *37*(5), 567–579. doi:10.1108/MIP-09-2018-0375

Jin, S. V., Ryu, E., & Muqaddam, A. (2021). I trust what she's #endorsing on Instagram: Moderating effects of parasocial interaction and social presence in fashion influencer marketing. *Journal of Fashion Marketing and Management*, *25*(4), 665–681. doi:10.1108/JFMM-04-2020-0059

Jun, S., & Yi, J. (2020). What makes followers loyal? The role of influencer interactivity in building influencer brand equity. *Journal of Product and Brand Management*, *29*(6), 803–814. doi:10.1108/JPBM-02-2019-2280

Kamins, M. A. (1990). An investigation into the "match-up" hypothesis in celebrity advertising: When beauty may be only skin deep. *Journal of Advertising*, *19*(1), 4–13. doi:10.1080/00913367.1990.10673175

Karlovitz, T. J. (2020). The democratization of technology – and its limitation. In *Managing Customer Experiences in an Omnichannel World: Melody of Online and Offline Environments in the Customer Journey* (pp. 13–25). Emerald Publishing Limited. doi:10.1108/978-1-80043-388-520201004

Kelman, H. C. (1961). Processes of Opinion Change. *Public Opinion Quarterly*, *25*(1), 57. doi:10.1086/266996

Khamis, S., Ang, L., & Welling, R. (2017). Self-branding, 'micro-celebrity' and the rise of Social Media Influencers. *Celebrity Studies*, *8*(2), 191–208. doi:10.1080/19392397.2016.1218292

Khamis, S., & Munt, A. (2010). The three Cs of fashion media today: convergence, creativity and control. *SCAN Journal of Media Arts Culture, 7*(3).

Ki, C.-W., Cuevas, L. M., Chong, S. M., & Lim, H. (2020). Influencer marketing: Social media influencers as human brands attaching to followers and yielding positive marketing results by fulfilling needs. *Journal of Retailing and Consumer Services*, *55*(102133), 102133. doi:10.1016/j.jretconser.2020.102133

Ki, C.-W., & Kim, Y.-K. (2019). The mechanism by which social media influencers persuade consumers: The role of consumers' desire to mimic. *Psychology and Marketing*, *36*(10), 905–922. doi:10.1002/mar.21244

Kim, D. (2023). Racialized beauty, visibility, and empowerment: Asian American women influencers on YouTube. *Information Communication and Society*, *26*(6), 1159–1176. doi:10.1080/1369118X.2021.1994626

Kim, D. Y., & Kim, H.-Y. (2021). Trust me, trust me not: A nuanced view of influencer marketing on social media. *Journal of Business Research*, *134*, 223–232. doi:10.1016/j.jbusres.2021.05.024

Kim, J.-H., & Lennon, S. J. (2007). Mass media and self-esteem, body image, and eating disorder tendencies. *Clothing & Textiles Research Journal*, *25*(1), 3–23. doi:10.1177/0887302X06296873

Kohan, S. E. (2020, June 28). *AEO's Aerie brand, built on body positivity and inclusion, is slowly edging out sexy supermodel juggernaut Victoria's Secret*. Forbes. https://www.forbes.com/sites/shelleykohan/2020/06/28/aeos-aerie-brand-built-on-body-positivity-and-inclusion-is-slowly-edging-out-sexy-supermodel-juggernaut-victorias-secret/?sh=2d3d4d3d42ba

Kozar, J. M., & Lynn Damhorst, M. (2008). Older women's responses to current fashion models. *Journal of Fashion Marketing and Management*, *12*(3), 338–350. doi:10.1108/13612020810889290

Lewis, R. (2019). Modest body politics: The commercial and ideological intersect of fat, black, and Muslim in the modest fashion market and media. *Fashion Theory*, *23*(2), 243–273. doi:10.1080/1362704X.2019.1567063

Limatius, H. (2020). *Communities of empowerment: Exploring the discourse practices of plus-size fashion bloggers* [Tampere University]. https://urn.fi/URN:ISBN:978-952-03-1489-7

Linqia. (2019). *The State of Influencer Marketing 2019*. https://linqia.com/wp-content/uploads/2019/04/Linqia-State-of-Influencer-Marketing-2019-Report.pdf

Lundblad, L., & Davies, I. A. (2016). The values and motivations behind sustainable fashion consumption. *Journal of Consumer Behaviour*, *15*(2), 149–162. doi:10.1002/cb.1559

Luvaas, B. (2017). What does a fashion influencer look like? Portraits of the Instafamous. *Fashion, Style & Popular Culture*, *4*(3), 341–363. doi:10.1386/fspc.4.3.341_7

Martensen, A., Brockenhuus-Schack, S., & Zahid, A. L. (2018). How citizen influencers persuade their followers. *Journal of Fashion Marketing and Management*, *22*(3), 335–353. doi:10.1108/JFMM-09-2017-0095

Marwick, A. E. (2013). They're really profound women, they're entrepreneurs. Conceptions of Authenticity in Fashion Blogging.

McCormick, H., & Livett, C. (2012). Analysing the influence of the presentation of fashion garments on young consumers' online behaviour. *Journal of Fashion Marketing and Management*, *16*(1), 21–41. doi:10.1108/13612021211203014

McPherson, M., Smith-Lovin, L., & Cook, J. M. (2001). Birds of a feather: Homophily in social networks. *Annual Review of Sociology*, *27*(1), 415–444. doi:10.1146/annurev.soc.27.1.415

Mudambi & Schuff. (2010). Research note: What makes a helpful online review? A study of customer reviews on Amazon.com. *MIS Quarterly: Management Information Systems, 34*(1), 185. doi:10.2307/20721420

Munnukka, J., Uusitalo, O., & Toivonen, H. (2016). Credibility of a peer endorser and advertising effectiveness. *Journal of Consumer Marketing*, *33*(3), 182–192. doi:10.1108/JCM-11-2014-1221

Nelson, A. (2023, May 18). *Charlize Theron's net worth, "Monster" Bank Account—Charlize Theron's Net Worth Is Almost as Big as Her Acting Range!* Parade. https://parade.com/celebrities/charlize-theron-net-worth

Ohanian, R. (1990). Construction and validation of a scale to measure celebrity endorsers' perceived expertise, trustworthiness, and attractiveness. *Journal of Advertising*, *19*(3), 39–52. doi:10.1080/00913367.1990.10673191

Pham, M.-H. T. (2011). Blog ambition: Fashion, feelings, and the political economy of the digital raced body. *Camera Obscura*, *26*(1), 1–37. doi:10.1215/02705346-2010-013

Phillips, K. W., Northcraft, G. B., & Neale, M. A. (2006). Surface-level diversity and decision-making in groups: When does deep-level similarity help? *Group Processes & Intergroup Relations*, *9*(4), 467–482. doi:10.1177/1368430206067557

Pöyry, E., Pelkonen, M., Naumanen, E., & Laaksonen, S.-M. (2019). A call for authenticity: Audience responses to social media influencer endorsements in strategic communication. *International Journal of Strategic Communication*, *13*(4), 336–351. doi:10.1080/1553118X.2019.1609965

Pöyry, E., Pelkonen, M., Naumanen, E., & Laaksonen, S.-M. (2021). A Call for Authenticity: Audience Responses to Social Media Influencer Endorsements in Strategic Communication. In N. S. Borchers (Ed.), *Social Media Influencers in Strategic Communication*. Routledge. doi:10.4324/9781003181286-6

Priya, A. (2021). Case study methodology of qualitative research: Key attributes and navigating the conundrums in its application. *Sociological Bulletin*, *70*(1), 94–110. doi:10.1177/0038022920970318

Robert, Y. (2018, October 23). *How ASOs is making E-commerce all-inclusive*. Forbes. https://www.forbes.com/sites/yolarobert1/2018/10/23/now-trending-how-asos-is-making-e-commerce-all-inclusive/?sh=521a65b9297d

Rocamora, A. (2011). Personal fashion blogs: Screens and mirrors in digital self-portraits. *Fashion Theory*, *15*(4), 407–424. doi:10.2752/175174111X13115179149794

Rocamora, A. (2012). Hypertextuality and remediation in the fashion media: The case of fashion blogs. *Journalism Practice*, *6*(1), 92–106. doi:10.1080/17512786.2011.622914

Ryan, R. M., & Deci, E. L. (2000). Self-determination theory and the facilitation of intrinsic motivation, social development, and well-being. *The American Psychologist*, *55*(1), 68–78. doi:10.1037/0003-066X.55.1.68 PMID:11392867

Schmidt, J. (2007). Blogging practices: An analytical framework. *Journal of Computer-Mediated Communication*, *12*(4), 1409–1427. doi:10.1111/j.1083-6101.2007.00379.x

Schouten, A. P., Janssen, L., & Verspaget, M. (2019). Celebrity vs. Influencer endorsements in advertising: The role of identification, credibility, and Product-Endorser fit. *International Journal of Advertising*, *39*(2), 258–281. doi:10.1080/02650487.2019.1634898

Scott, D. M. (2015). *The new rules of marketing and PR: How to use social media, online video, mobile applications, blogs, news releases, and viral marketing to reach buyers directly* (D. M. Scott, Ed.; 5th ed.). John Wiley & Sons. doi:10.1002/9781119172499.ch02

Senft, T. M. (2008). *Camgirls: Celebrity and community in the age of social networks*. Peter Lang Publishing.

Shang, S. S. C., Wu, Y.-L., & Sie, Y.-J. (2017). Generating consumer resonance for purchase intention on social network sites. *Computers in Human Behavior*, *69*, 18–28. doi:10.1016/j.chb.2016.12.014

Sokolova, K., & Kefi, H. (2020). Instagram and YouTube bloggers promote it, why should I buy? How credibility and parasocial interaction influence purchase intentions. *Journal of Retailing and Consumer Services*, *53*(101742), 101742. doi:10.1016/j.jretconser.2019.01.011

Suhr, H. C. (2014). *Online Evaluation of Creativity and the Arts*. Routledge. doi:10.4324/9781315795836

Suk, H. (2021). The characteristics of democratization of fashion and fashionocracy in the global fashion industry. *The Research Journal of the Costume Culture*, *29*(4), 488–504. doi:10.29049/rjcc.2021.29.4.488

Taillon, B. J., Mueller, S. M., Kowalczyk, C. M., & Jones, D. N. (2020). Understanding the relationships between social media influencers and their followers: The moderating role of closeness. *Journal of Product and Brand Management*, *29*(6), 767–782. doi:10.1108/JPBM-03-2019-2292

Talbot, K. (2019, June 2). *Diversity in influencer marketing: Why representation matters*. Forbes. https://www.forbes.com/sites/katetalbot/2019/06/02/diversity-in-influencer-marketing-why-representation-matters/?sh=9f5aad47a3e6

Tan, D. (2017). *The Commercial Appropriation of Fame*. Cambridge University Press. doi:10.1017/9781316488744

Tolbert, A. N., & Drogos, K. L. (2019). Tweens' Wishful Identification and Parasocial Relationships With YouTubers. *Frontiers in Psychology*, *10*, 2781. Advance online publication. doi:10.3389/fpsyg.2019.02781 PMID:31920829

Trequattrini, R., Manfredi, S., Lardo, A., & Cuozzo, B. (2019). Social media as a new opportunity for female entrepreneurs: An analysis of the fashion industry. In *Advances in Gender and Cultural Research in Business and Economics* (pp. 287–298). Springer International Publishing. doi:10.1007/978-3-030-00335-7_19

van Esch, P., Arli, D., Castner, J., Talukdar, N., & Northey, G. (2018). Consumer attitudes towards bloggers and paid blog advertisements: What's new? *Marketing Intelligence & Planning*, *36*(7), 778–793. doi:10.1108/MIP-01-2018-0027

Wei, P.-S., & Lu, H.-P. (2013). An examination of the celebrity endorsements and online customer reviews influence female consumers' shopping behavior. *Computers in Human Behavior*, *29*(1), 193–201. doi:10.1016/j.chb.2012.08.005

Weil, J. (2017, August 28). Dior launches digital 'Love Chain' initiative. *The Los Angeles Times*. https://www.latimes.com/fashion/la-ig-wwd-dior-love-chain-20170828-story.html

Yan, Y., & Bissell, K. (2014). The globalization of beauty: How is ideal beauty influenced by globally published fashion and beauty magazines? *Journal of Intercultural Communication Research*, *43*(3), 194–214. doi:10.1080/17475759.2014.917432

Yaniv, I., Choshen-Hillel, S., & Milyavsky, M. (2011). Receiving advice on matters of taste: Similarity, majority influence, and taste discrimination. *Organizational Behavior and Human Decision Processes*, *115*(1), 111–120. doi:10.1016/j.obhdp.2010.11.006

Yin, R. K. (2009). *Case study research: Design and methods*. SAGE Publications.

Yuan, S., & Lou, C. (2020). How social media influencers foster relationships with followers: The roles of source credibility and fairness in parasocial relationship and product interest. *Journal of Interactive Advertising*, *20*(2), 133–147. doi:10.1080/15252019.2020.1769514

Chapter 2
Exploring Motivations of Social Media Influencers in Content Production

Surjit Singha
https://orcid.org/0000-0002-5730-8677
Kristu Jayanti College, India

ABSTRACT

This chapter examines the underlying motivations that propel the creation of content by social media influencers. Social media influencers have emerged as individuals of considerable power, capable of moulding consumer sentiments, affecting brand interactions, and exerting influence. A comprehensive comprehension of the motivations of influencers is imperative for businesses and marketers aiming to establish fruitful collaborations with them. It analyzes the various motivations that drive influencers to generate content. These motivations encompass personal enthusiasm, monetary rewards, the aspiration for recognition, and the quest for originality. This study examines how these incentives affect the authenticity and calibre of influencer-generated content and analyzes the ramifications for strategic business communication. Through case studies and discussions, this chapter illuminates the intricacies of influencer motivations and provides valuable perspectives for organizations seeking to establish fruitful collaborations with influencers.

INTRODUCTION

The digital realm has recently experienced a significant paradigm shift due to the emergence and proliferation of social media influencers. These individuals exhibit an extraordinary capacity to engage and accumulate substantial online communities. The rise of these entities has significantly influenced modern consumer behavior, moulding the preferences and selections of an international audience. It explores the inception and development of social media influencers, analyzing the transition from conventional celebrity endorsements to the widespread availability of influence on digital platforms. The democratization process has granted agency to individuals from various origins, offering them a genuine

DOI: 10.4018/979-8-3693-0912-4.ch002

and relatable substitute for well-known public figures. Significant turning points in this progression, characterized by the introduction of platforms such as TikTok, YouTube, and Instagram, act as catalysts for the ascent of influencers.

Further probing into the influencer ecosystem, this chapter examines the diverse industries and sectors in which influencers have had a substantial impact, establishing themselves as authorities in their respective fields and cultivating devoted communities around their content. The discourse further explores influencers' significant effect on consumer behavior, elaborating on how they mould perceptions and decisions via persuasive narratives, relatable materials, and genuine engagements. Lajnef (2023) analyzes the psychological mechanisms by which influencers establish and maintain their position as key opinion leaders, impacting lifestyle choices, purchasing decisions, and brand perceptions. This chapter highlights influencers' cultural impact and worldwide reach, focusing on their ability to transcend geographical boundaries and foster a globally interconnected digital culture. It establishes the foundation for a more thoughtful investigation into the motivations of influencers and the strategic ramifications that ensue for organizations that employ influencer-led communication.

Acknowledging the significant influence of social media influencers is critical in strategic business communication; therefore, establishing a nuanced comprehension of their motivations becomes fundamental for fostering fruitful collaborations. It provides an in-depth analysis of the motivations that propel social media influencers to create content, focusing on the strategic implications for companies aiming to capitalize on this influential force. Gaining insight into the motivations of influencers is comparable to deciphering the structure of compelling content. It lets organizations know the genuine motivating influencers who interact with their followers. By translating these incentives, organizations can harmonize their communications and principles with those of influencers, cultivating authentic collaborations that deeply resonate with the intended demographic.

Furthermore, the motivations of influencers play a crucial role in formulating strategic communication approaches. Enterprises can customize their collaborations, campaigns, and outreach according to the enthusiasm, concerns, and principles that motivate influencers to produce captivating content. Su et al. (2021) argue that this unity bolsters the message's authenticity and fosters a deeper rapport with the audience by seamlessly incorporating the content into the influencer's narrative.

Strategic business communication is predicated on the formation of mutually advantageous relationships. Organizations can customize their interactions to align with the ambitions and objectives of influencers by understanding the motivations that drive them. It discusses how businesses can balance their goals and build real stories. This way, they can build partnerships beyond simple transactions and help everyone grow in the long run. Furthermore, gaining insight into influencer motivations gives organizations a strategic guide for discerning appropriate influencers to represent their brand. Organizations can foster a more authentic and fruitful partnership by establishing associations with influencers whose motivations harmonize with the brand's. By selecting a strategic alignment, the brand not only bolsters its credibility but also aids in constructing a unified narrative that effectively connects with the intended demographic (Zitzmann et al., 2024; Bellina et al., 2020). It emphasizes the importance of investigating the underlying motivations that propel influencers on social media. Recognizing this as a fundamental element of strategic business communication empowers organizations to construct genuine narratives, forge significant partnerships, and nurture connections beyond mere transactions. Ultimately, this knowledge aids in the triumph of influencer-driven campaigns amidst the perpetually changing digital environment.

The background portion of the study establishes the study's context by providing a historical overview or contextual information that supports the purpose of the investigation. The background section of the chapter on strategic business communication and global perspectives on social media influencers examines the rapid advancement of digital communication, the increasing reliance on social media platforms, and influencers' transformative role in contemporary marketing strategies. The theoretical framework serves as a cornerstone for the research, employing relevant theories or models to clarify and analyze the phenomena under investigation. By integrating communication theories, marketing models, and sociological perspectives, the theoretical framework of the chapter provides a lens through which to examine the motivations of social media influencers and their effect on business communication. The conceptual framework delineates the fundamental concepts, variables, and interconnections investigated in the research, expanding upon the theoretical underpinnings. It is a navigational guide for comprehending the diverse components and their interrelationships. The conceptual framework of the chapter encompasses pivotal notions, including consumer behavior, influencer motivations, and strategic communication strategies. Its purpose would be to depict the intricate interplay between these components within the ever-changing digital environment.

The study's intention communicates the research's purpose or overarching objective. The chapter aims to investigate, scrutinize, and comprehend the incentives that drive social media influencers and the ramifications that this may have for global strategic business communication. It may require examining how influencer motivations impact content development and the strategic ways companies can collaborate with influencers to improve their communication tactics. The study's scope specifies its limitations and boundaries. The scope manages the audience's expectations by defining the research's inclusions and exclusions. The scope of the chapter delineates the industries, geographic regions, and social media platforms that fall under the investigation's jurisdiction. Additionally, it includes potential limitations or temporal restrictions on the categories of influencers considered. The background, conceptual framework, theoretical framework, aim, and scope collectively establish a comprehensive chapter structure that directs the investigation into the global realm of strategic business communication and social media influencers.

MOTIVATIONS OF SOCIAL MEDIA INFLUENCERS

Gaining insight into the underlying incentives that propel social media influencers is paramount to deciphering the intricacies of their content generation methodologies and forging efficacious alliances in strategic business communication (Kim & Kim, 2022; Taillon et al., 2020). A considerable number of influencers on social media initiate their content creation endeavors with an authentic enthusiasm for particular subjects or sectors. Personal interests and pastimes can be powerful motivators, facilitating a genuine connection between influencers and their audience (Zniva et al., 2023; Lee & Eastin, 2021).

Financial incentives and monetization tactics are important as driving factors for social media influencers rather than being motivated solely by enthusiasm. With the constant evolution of digital platforms, influencers are progressively investigating ways to generate income from their online presence sustainably (Everett et al., 2021; Peleg-Oren, 2002). The desire for prominence and sway is a powerful incentive for numerous social media influencers. The influencers endeavor to establish personal identities, acquire extensive acclaim, and amass substantial audiences. The ramifications of this motivation are explored by probing into the ever-changing connection between influencers who pursue fame and their audiences and the strategic factors that organizations should consider when attempting to establish partnerships with influencers motivated by this aspiration (Malik et al., 2020). Influencers are primarily motivated by the pursuit of authenticity and the opportunity for creative expression. Influencers utilize digital platforms as innovative channels to showcase their distinct viewpoints and personal styles. It explores the dynamic relationship between authenticity and creativity, specifically focusing on how influencers develop a unique aesthetic and voice to strengthen their audience bonds and augment the effectiveness of their messaging (Lee & Eastin, 2021), recognizing the intricate terrain of motivations that influencers frequently traverse and the complexities and ramifications that arise from the need to reconcile numerous driving forces. Influencers often face the challenge of reconciling their pursuit of renown with their passion, financial obligations, and other competing priorities. Furthermore, it considers the strategic ramifications for organizations seeking to partner with influencers adeptly manoeuvring through various motivational terrains. By comprehending these incentives, organizations can cultivate more genuine and productive partnerships with influencers in strategic business communication.

INFLUENCER MOTIVATIONS AND CONTENT QUALITY

A comprehensive comprehension of the complex correlation between influencer motivations and content quality is critical when evaluating the efficacy of communication strategies led by influencers (Chang & Wu, 2023; Zhang & Choi, 2022). Motivations drive influencers in their creative pursuits. Influencers generate content with inherent creativity and innovation, influenced by various motivational factors such as personal passion, financial incentives, and the pursuit of fame. It clarifies how particular motivations contribute to creating distinctive, captivating narratives that captivate the audience and distinguish influencers amidst a saturated digital environment through the analysis of case studies and examples (Lajnef, 2023). Motivations have a critical impact on brand perception and audience engagement dynamics. The implications of various influencer motivations on the degree of audience engagement. This study investigates the establishment of psychological bonds between influencers and their followers and the potential ramifications for enterprises seeking to exploit these bonds (Ao et al., 2023; Hugh et al., 2022).

Transparency and authenticity are of the utmost importance in influencer-led communication. The motivations of influencers either support or contradict the integrity and openness of their content. It investigates the strategies influencers utilize to balance financial motivations and maintain an authentic voice, thereby examining the potential tension that may arise (Zniva et al., 2023; Lee & Eastin, 2021). Comprehending the dynamic relationship between the motivations of influencers and the quality of their content is crucial for organizations seeking to optimize the effects of their partnerships. By understanding how they affect the creative process, audience engagement, and brand perception, organizations can customize their approaches to correspond with these motivations.

Furthermore, bolstering the overall efficacy of influencer-led communication endeavors and fostering audience confidence are outcomes of influencer partnerships that prioritize transparency and authenticity (Zhang & Choi, 2022; Su et al., 2021). Gaining insight into the underlying incentives that propel social media influencers is paramount in deciphering the intricacies of their content generation methodologies and alliances in strategic business communication (Kim & Kim, 2022; Taillon et al., 2020).

A considerable number of influencers on social media initiate their content creation endeavors with an authentic enthusiasm for particular subjects or sectors. Personal interests and pastimes can be powerful motivators, facilitating a genuine connection between influencers and their audience (Zniva et al., 2023; Lee & Eastin, 2021). Financial incentives and monetization tactics are important driving factors for social media influencers rather than being motivated by passion. With the constant evolution of digital platforms, influencers are progressively investigating ways to sustainably generate income from their online presence (Everett et al., 2021; Peleg-Oren, 2002). The desire for notoriety, prominence, and sway is a powerful incentive for numerous social media influencers. The influencers endeavor to establish personal identities, acquire extensive acclaim, and amass substantial audiences. The consequences of this motive include the constantly evolving relationship between influencers seeking recognition and their audiences and the strategic elements that businesses should consider when trying to form relationships with influencers driven by this goal (Malik et al., 2020).

The pursuit of authenticity and the opportunity for creative expression primarily motivate influencers. Influencers utilize digital platforms as innovative channels to showcase their distinct viewpoints and personal styles. The dynamic relationship between authenticity and creativity focuses on how influencers develop a unique aesthetic and voice to strengthen their audience bonds and augment the effectiveness of their messaging (Lee & Eastin, 2021). They recognize the intricate terrain of motivations that influencers frequently traverse and the complexities and ramifications that arise from the need to reconcile numerous driving forces. Influencers often face the challenge of reconciling their pursuit of fame with their passion, financial obligations, and other competing priorities. Furthermore, it considers the strategic ramifications for organizations seeking to partner with influencers adeptly manoeuvring through various motivational terrains. By comprehending these incentives, organizations can cultivate more genuine and productive partnerships with influencers in strategic business communication.

INFLUENCER-BRAND PARTNERSHIPS

In influencer-led strategic business communication, establishing successful collaborations between brands and influencers requires a meticulous synchronization of objectives (Joshi et al., 2023; Borchers, 2019). A successful influencer-brand partnership is predicated on identifying and aligning common values and goals. A cohesive marketing story that matches the motives and objectives of the influencer is essential. This study explores methods for discerning influencers whose principles correspond with those of the brand, guaranteeing the genuineness of communication and establishing an authentic rapport with the target audience (Oprea, 2023; Hugh et al., 2022).

Efficient collaboration is critical during the content creation process to convert common values into persuasive messaging. Synergistic content production leverages the distinct strengths of corporations and influencers. This study examines the potential of integrating influencer ingenuity with brand communication to generate genuine, captivating content that effectively connects with the intended demographic (Hugh et al., 2022; Berné-Manero & Marzo-Navarro, 2020). Although specific campaigns may have a significant impact, establishing enduring partnerships between influencers and brands provides enduring advantages. Understanding and promoting the mutual motivations underlying these connections is essential. It examines tactics for demonstrating consistency, loyalty, and trust in partnerships between influencers and brands. By recognizing the dynamic characteristics of influencer incentives and adjusting their approaches accordingly, organizations can establish long-lasting partnerships that transcend temporary advertising initiatives. To effectively navigate the intricacies of influencer-led communication, businesses can cultivate enduring relationships founded on mutual motivations, identify shared values, and implement collaborative content-creation strategies. Strategic alignment optimizes the efficacy of specific campaigns and fosters the enduring expansion and triumph of influencer-brand partnerships within the dynamic realm of strategic business communication. The chapter provides several cases of showcasing influencer-brand partnerships.

CASE STUDY 1

Within the ever-changing realm of the fashion sector, social media influencers possess considerable sway over consumers' purchasing decisions and preferences. This case study examines the trajectory of CS, a 28-year-old fashion devotee whose captivating fashion content has amassed more than one million followers on social media platforms, including Instagram and YouTube. CS's content predominantly comprises trend forecasts, fashion hauls, and ensemble designs, exemplifying her lifelong enthusiasm for the industry she has nurtured since her youth. Motivated by an authentic passion for fashion, CS's material strikes a chord with her audience, facilitating robust bonds predicated on mutual interests. Social media platforms function as a medium through which CS can manifest her unique identity and exhibit her artistic prowess, allowing her to investigate a wide range of aesthetics and produce visually captivating material.

Social media platforms cultivate a collective atmosphere that CS values, providing a forum for fashion enthusiasts to share thoughts, seek guidance, and build relationships. Driven by audience engagement and feedback, CS endeavours to provide fashion content that is both of superior quality and relatable. CS's interest has developed into a successful professional trajectory characterized by collaborations with renowned fashion labels and active engagement in industry gatherings. These opportunities yield monetary benefits and augment CS's standing, reputation, and knowledge of burgeoning trends in the fashion industry.

The varied motivations of CS highlight the substantial influence that social media has on contemporary influencers, providing businesses that are traversing the influencer market with valuable insights. Through comprehending and capitalizing on these incentives, organizations can augment their strategic communication endeavors within the digital domain. To ascertain influencers, the organization implemented an all-encompassing research methodology. The organization conducted thorough analyses on various social media platforms, such as YouTube and Instagram, to identify individuals with substantial followings and active participation rates in the fashion niche. Using analytics tools, they evaluated metrics such as subscriber demographics, content engagement, and posting frequency.

Furthermore, the organization employed sentiment analysis to ascertain how audience sentiment agreed with potential influencers. Analyzing remarks likes, and shares on influencer posts provided valuable insights into the audience's receptivity and the influencer's overall reputation. Network analysis shows a significant relationship between influencers and their audiences, including key opinion leaders and potential collaboration impacts. By initiating direct outreach and communication with influencers, it became possible to directly assess their authenticity, passion for fashion, and congruence with the brand's values. To ensure that the selection process was strict and based on data-driven decisions aligned with brand goals, the organization used a research method that combined qualitative and quantitative methods and direct communication with influential people.

CASE STUDY 2

SM has amassed a sizable fan base on social media sites like YouTube and Instagram. Her journey started when SM realized she was passionate about exercise and a healthy life. Her desire to live a healthy lifestyle inspired her to share her fitness journey, exercise regimens, and dietary advice with her audience. SM's genuine love of fitness and assisting others in leading healthier lives is what drives her to create content. Her belief in the transformational power of exercise and nutrition inspires and motivates her to encourage her followers to prioritize their health and well-being. She establishes a personal connection with the audience by openly sharing her experiences, obstacles, and triumphs. SM builds a relationship of trust and sincerity with her audience by sharing the honest and genuine parts of her path toward health. SM's audience has attained high levels of engagement and loyalty due to her genuine approach to content development. Her fans value her openness and honesty, and they frequently mention in their comments how her posts have motivated them to take up better routines. Because of her genuine ability to connect with her audience, SM has secured brand relationships with companies that offer fitness-related goods and services, further confirming her standing as a reliable influencer in the field.

SM's incentive motivation stems from her genuine enthusiasm for physical activity and maintaining a healthy lifestyle. Her inclination to effortlessly maintain a healthy lifestyle is reflected in her material, as she divulges personal experiences and offers pragmatic guidance. Her genuine story resonates with her audience, instilling a sense of motivation among her followers, inspired by her journey and its positive impact on her life. SM's content showcases her fitness regimens and emphasizes the profound impact of physical activity and proper nutrition. She forges a relatable bond with her audience by transparently divulging her difficulties and achievements. The relationship between SM's inspirational material and followers' adoption of healthy behaviors is crucial in driving incentive motivation.

SM's capacity to establish genuine connections with her audience has made her a reliable influencer in the fitness industry. Brands recognize the importance of this association and actively pursue collaborations with SM to capitalize on her influence. The success of these collaborations stems from SM's authentic dedication to health, which strongly resonates with her audience's interests and objectives. Influencers and brands establish effective collaborations by adopting similar principles and synchronizing communication strategies. Brands that provide fitness-related products and services are a natural fit inside SM's content ecosystem due to their alignment with her sincere promotion of health and well-being. This alignment boosts the credibility of sponsored content, guaranteeing that promotions feel seamlessly integrated rather than coerced.

SM fosters a network of committed and devoted fans through her inspirational material. Brands recognize the importance of this active audience and partner with social media influencers to target potential customers. They use their influence to motivate action and foster brand loyalty among their followers. The reciprocal advantages between incentive motivation and influencer-brand partnerships create a synergy. SM's sincere enthusiasm inspires her audience to participate and make a difference actively, while brands reap the benefits of this engaged audience through true partnerships. These collaborations are sustainable because they are based on trust and common ideals, promoting long-term relationships that benefit both parties.

The path of SM serves as a prime example of how the combination of incentive motivation and genuine enthusiasm can propel successful partnerships between influencers and brands. SM has become a trusted influencer in the fitness niche by focusing on authenticity, creating value, and engaging with the community. This has helped her establish brand partnerships that increase her impact and influence. This case study highlights the significance of authenticity and alignment in influencer marketing, demonstrating how genuine enthusiasm can inspire action and foster meaningful collaborations with businesses.

CASE STUDY 3

AK has amassed a sizable fan base on social media sites like TikTok and Instagram. AK offered his audience fashion advice and insights from his wardrobe as a hobby. This was the beginning of his career in the fashion industry. AK's love of fashion and self-expression was his original driving force behind creating material. He liked to play around with various looks and fashions, and he tried to encourage others to embrace their sense of style. However, as his fan base increased, AK started looking at the business potential of being an influencer.

AK's content strategy creates a harmonious whole by combining sponsored material and corporate relationships with his flair. AK carefully incorporates sponsored posts and business partnerships into his content mix while staying true to his love of fashion and self-expression. He ensures that these collaborations reflect his ideals and style to be authentic with his audience. AK has built a devoted and enthusiastic following because of his ability to balance his love of design with his business potential. His followers value his sincere passion for fashion and his deft integration of sponsored content into his feed without sacrificing authenticity. As a result, AK has become a sought-after influencer for fashion companies trying to successfully connect with their audience while preserving their reputation in the industry.

CASE STUDY 4

EH is a prominent figure in the travel blogging world due to her passion for exploration and influential position as a travel influencer. EH started her journey when she decided to post updates about her travels on social media and her blog. EH's passion for exploring new places and cultures drives her to create content. Her motivation stems from her desire to inspire others to appreciate the natural beauty of various places. Traveling can transform people, and EH wants to share this belief with her audience through her experiences.

Immersion experiences and authentic narratives are the cornerstones of EH's content approach. She uses appealing imagery and compelling storytelling to transport her audience to breathtaking landscapes, energetic cities, and off-the-beaten-path locations while capturing each place's spirit. EH places a high value on authenticity in her material and avoids highly controlled or manufactured moments to maintain a real connection with her audience. EH's audience has found resonance in her genuine approach to travel writing, which stokes wanderlust and motivates people to go out on their trips. Her fans frequently ask for her advice while making trip arrangements because they like her frank and relatable content. Because of her popularity, EH has worked with travel agencies and tourism boards, allowing her to continue travelling and share her experiences with the public.

EH's incentive motivation stems from her authentic enthusiasm for travel and exploring. The core of her content creation lies in her genuine desire to explore novel destinations and immerse herself in diverse cultures. EH's belief in the profound impact of travel and her goal to inspire her audience to value the magnificence of diverse locations drive her to communicate her experiences. EH's content strategy focuses on creating immersive experiences and delivering authentic narratives. EH effectively transports the audience to many geographies and cultural settings by presenting fascinating images and relatable anecdotes. This genuineness strikes a chord with her supporters, igniting a strong desire to travel and inspiring them to embark on their journeys.

EH's focus on genuineness cultivates a robust sense of trust and relatability with her audience. Her admirers want her advice and suggestions for itinerary preparation because they value her authentic viewpoint and personal encounters. Establishing trust in this relationship amplifies EH's impact and inspires her audience to take action based on her trip suggestions. EH's success as a travel influencer has led to collaborations with travel firms and tourism organizations. These relationships are mutually beneficial: EH can access exclusive travel opportunities and resources to investigate further and communicate her experiences, while companies use her influence to connect with a highly engaged audience seeking genuine travel inspiration.

EH's approach to sponsored content demonstrates her dedication to maintaining honesty. She preserves her voice and narrative approach while working with businesses, guaranteeing that promotional content smoothly blends with her overarching story. The authenticity of EH's audience enhances the effectiveness of influencer-brand partnerships, as they perceive sponsored recommendations as dependable and trustworthy. EH's strong motivation and genuine content have an enduring impact on her audience and brand partners. EH cultivates a network of committed followers who actively seek her advice and recommendations by regularly providing value and inspiration. The active and interested audience contributes to the significance of EH's collaborations with travel brands, building enduring connections founded on shared principles and reciprocal advantages.

EH's journey as a travel influencer exemplifies how incentives-driven motivation and genuine content creation foster successful partnerships between influencers and brands in the travel industry. EH's unwavering commitment to her passion for exploration and her genuine approach to storytelling motivate her audience to embark on their journeys. It garners valuable partnerships with travel firms looking to capitalize on its popularity and trustworthiness. This case study highlights the significance of passion, authenticity, and engagement in developing influential influencer marketing tactics in specialized industries such as travel blogging.

DISCUSSION

Influencer marketing inextricably links to content creation incentives. Many factors significantly influence the qualities and outcomes of content provided by influencers. An essential incentive for influencers is usually sincere passion and interest in particular topics or niche markets. Their audience feels engaged and connected to them because of the genuineness with which they present their content. Monetary incentives also have a significant influence on content creation. Their monetization techniques, such as sponsored content and brand collaborations, influence the frequency and type of material influencers produce. Occasionally, the convergence of financial incentives and passion can compromise the integrity of the material, creating a fragile equilibrium. Three powerful motivators that drive influencers are fame, recognition, and the desire to have an impact. As businesses work to build their brand and preserve a positive public image, this incentive may affect their content. Within this context, finding a balance between being true to oneself and meeting the audience's expectations is crucial.

The pursuit of authenticity and artistic expression are fundamental motivations for many influencers. The digital landscape enables a more customized and creative approach to content creation. Influencers improve the diversity and richness of information by using their unique voices, aesthetics, and points of view to set themselves apart in a crowded digital space. Navigating these motives, however, may be difficult, and influencers often need help to balance several goals simultaneously. Challenges may arise when the desire for actual self-expression clashes with monetary rewards or when the aspiration for fame compromises the content's authenticity. Understanding these nuances is essential for companies looking to work with influencers because it provides them with knowledge about the incentives behind producing content that will serve as a brand ambassador. Analyzing influencers' motivations can help us understand the mechanisms influencing content creation. Understanding the nuances of these incentives is essential for companies looking to form genuine, fruitful alliances in the ever-changing field of influencer-driven strategic business communication. A purposeful and intentional approach is required to effectively align influencer motivations with the goals of strategic corporate communication. The following approaches establish a structure for organizations to cultivate partnerships that are not solely genuine but also aid in attaining more extensive communication goals, such as performing extensive research to identify influencers whose motivations are highly congruent with the brand's values and communication objectives. It necessitates looking at the themes, messaging, and engagement levels of influencers, as well as the demographics of their fan base. Selecting influencers whose passions coincide with the brand ensures a more genuine partnership. Give priority to influencers whose goals and principles coincide with the brand's. Collaborations motivated by shared objectives and interests produce more creative work. Communicate the brand's mission and values throughout the influencer selection process to ensure the influencers align with the overall marketing plan. Ensure you have open, honest lines of communication with influencers immediately. Encourage candid conversations with all stakeholders on the campaign's objectives, expectations, and rewards. This type of communication ensures that influencers agree with the brand's communication goals by fostering mutual understanding and supporting conflict resolution.

Reach agreements and conditions that align with the goals of the influencers and the company. We may need to modify collaboration agreements, establish clear standards, and determine expectations for content development. The company ensures a more effective and harmonious collaboration by aligning terms with influencers' incentives. Give influencers the artistic freedom to integrate the brand's message into their material legitimately. Encourage influencers to share their stories and personal encounters with the brand. This approach ensures that the content looks real and resonates with the influencer's audience, which boosts the effectiveness of the whole communication plan. Conscious of the long-term value of connections with influencers beyond particular initiatives. Promote long-term collaborations and engagements that go above and beyond what contracts require. Supporting influencers in their personal and professional endeavours can create a win-win relationship that increases customer loyalty to the brand and strengthens the legitimacy of the connection. Regularly evaluate the influencer relationships' contribution to the brand's communication goals. Utilize analytics and performance data to evaluate campaign effectiveness and adjust strategy as needed. By utilizing this iterative process, organizations can put improvements and changes into practice, guaranteeing that future collaborations are even more closely aligned with the brand's objectives. By implementing these methods, organizations can successfully navigate the complexities of aligning influencers' motivations with their strategic communication goals. As a result, the brand forges long-lasting alliances and triumphant campaigns that bolster its image and story in the dynamic field of influencer-driven strategic business communication. Co-creating content with influencers can enhance authenticity and relevance. Brands can enlist influencers to help develop and create content, utilizing their knowledge and insights to produce material that appeals to the target audience and supports the goals and messaging of the brand. This cooperative strategy guarantees that the content reflects the influencers' authentic voice and style while giving them a sense of ownership. In today's globalized world, brands must consider diversity and cultural sensitivity when interacting with influencers. Influencers from different areas and backgrounds can help brands show their inclusivity and reach a larger audience. Additionally, to prevent any potential reaction or misinterpretation, marketers should ensure that their marketing and content are sensitive to cultural differences and relevant.

Influencer marketing should go beyond product or service promotion; brands should support influencers in connecting with their audience on a genuine level. This could be leaving comments, engaging in dialogue, or offering personal tales or experiences connected to the company. Genuine interaction creates a stronger bond between influencers and their fans, boosting brand loyalty and the effect of the brand's messaging. Educating and training influencers on brand standards, values, and goods and services can guarantee coherence in their content production endeavors. To assist influencers with comprehending the brand's messaging, target audience, and communication goals, brands can provide workshops, webinars, or written instructions. Influencers can provide material that appeals to their audience more effectively and profoundly by putting money into education. Ethical issues are becoming more and more crucial as influencer marketing grows, ethical issues become more critical. Brands should keep influencer marketing best practices and moral norms in mind. These include disclosing sponsored material, being transparent in collaborations, and abstaining from dishonest or misleading tactics. Brands can improve the efficacy of their influencer marketing initiatives by cultivating trust among consumers and influencers and maintaining ethical standards.

Social media and influencer marketing are dynamic fields constantly changing due to the frequent emergence of new platforms, trends, and technologies. To stay ahead of the curve, brands should remain flexible and agile, eager to try new tactics. This could entail experimenting with different formats, platforms, or content types to find what appeals to their target audience the most. By adding these extra tactics and factors to their influencer marketing campaigns, brands can improve the congruence between influencer incentives and strategic business goals. In the end, influencer marketing efforts that are more genuine, interesting, and effective can benefit from a deliberate and comprehensive approach and help organizations achieve tangible outcomes. Influencer marketing is dynamic; thus, a comprehensive strategy that matches strategic corporate goals with influencer motivations is required. Brands can effectively navigate the complexities of influencer-driven communication by embracing diversity and ethical standards, cultivating genuine connections, and comprehending and utilizing influencer incentives. Influencer marketing initiatives that successfully connect with audiences and produce tangible outcomes for businesses integrate cooperative content development, cultural sensitivity, genuine engagement, influencer education, and flexibility. Ultimately, a deliberate and thorough approach to influencer marketing produces real, compelling, and effective campaigns that help achieve measurable business results.

CONCLUSION

A deep comprehension of influencers' motivations is necessary to lay the groundwork for successful influencer marketing efforts. Analyzing the many motivations behind influencer content creation is critical, as relatability and authenticity are essential in today's digital world. These motivations are solid catalysts, including financial incentives and the need to approve unique interests and passions. By understanding and appropriately using these incentives, organizations can successfully navigate the constantly shifting influencer environment and achieve their marketing objectives. Influencer rewards must be consistent with communication goals and brand values. Influencers who genuinely resonate with a brand's values and messaging generate content that fortifies the relationship between the company and its target market. Ultimately, this genuine connection shapes customer behaviour and brand perceptions, which build brand affinity and loyalty.

Building on this understanding, the recommended steps provide a comprehensive guide for businesses looking to develop genuine partnerships between influencers and brands. Organizations can form partnerships that yield authentic and influential content by emphasizing long-term relationships versus one-time efforts, promoting open communication, and providing influencers with creative latitude. Additionally, by tracking and refining tactics according to performance metrics, firms may effectively maximize their marketing efforts and adapt to the shifting landscape of influencers.

Ultimately, businesses may establish profound connections with their intended audiences by aligning influencer motivations and cultivating common values. In the constantly changing realm of strategic corporate communication, this tactic lays the groundwork for influencer marketing campaigns that enhance business results and support the development of a compelling brand narrative. As the landscape of influencer marketing evolves, companies must understand and capitalize on influencer incentives to establish authentic and meaningful brand partnerships.

REFERENCES

Ao, L., Bansal, R., Pruthi, N., & Khaskheli, M. B. (2023). Impact of social media influencers on customer engagement and purchase Intention: A Meta-Analysis. *Sustainability (Basel)*, *15*(3), 2744. doi:10.3390/su15032744

Berné-Manero, C., & Marzo-Navarro, M. (2020). Exploring how influencer and relationship marketing serve corporate sustainability. *Sustainability (Basel)*, *12*(11), 4392. doi:10.3390/su12114392

Borchers, N. S. (2019). Social media influencers in strategic communication. *International Journal of Strategic Communication*, *13*(4), 255–260. doi:10.1080/1553118X.2019.1634075

Chang, S., & Wu, J. (2023). A content-based metric for social media influencer marketing. *Industrial Management & Data Systems*, *124*(1), 344–360. doi:10.1108/IMDS-05-2022-0303

Everett, Y., Martin, C. G., & Zalewski, M. (2021). A Systematic Review Focusing on Psychotherapeutic Interventions that Impact Parental Psychopathology, Child Psychopathology and Parenting Behavior. *Clinical Child and Family Psychology Review*, *24*(3), 579–598. doi:10.1007/s10567-021-00355-3 PMID:34254219

Hugh, D. C., Dolan, R., Harrigan, P., & Gray, H. (2022). Influencer marketing effectiveness: The mechanisms that matter. *European Journal of Marketing*, *56*(12), 3485–3515. doi:10.1108/EJM-09-2020-0703

Joshi, Y., Lim, W. M., Jagani, K., & Kumar, S. (2023). Social media influencer marketing: Foundations, trends, and ways forward. *Electronic Commerce Research*. Advance online publication. doi:10.1007/s10660-023-09719-z

Kim, D. Y., & Kim, H. (2022). Social media influencers as human brands: An interactive marketing perspective. *Journal of Research in Interactive Marketing*, *17*(1), 94–109. doi:10.1108/JRIM-08-2021-0200

Lajnef, K. (2023). The effect of social media influencers on teenagers Behavior: An empirical study using cognitive map technique. *Current Psychology (New Brunswick, N.J.)*, *42*(22), 19364–19377. doi:10.1007/s12144-023-04273-1 PMID:36742063

Lee, J. A., & Eastin, M. S. (2021). Perceived authenticity of social media influencers: Scale development and validation. *Journal of Research in Interactive Marketing*, *15*(4), 822–841. doi:10.1108/JRIM-12-2020-0253

Malik, M. J., Ahmad, M., Kamran, M. R., Aliza, K., & Elahi, M. Z. (2020). Student use of social media, academic performance, and creativity: The mediating role of intrinsic motivation. *Interactive Technology and Smart Education*, *17*(4), 403–415. doi:10.1108/ITSE-01-2020-0005

Oprea, C. (2023). Influencer branding in brand management. In Innovatives Markenmanagement (pp. 51–60). doi:10.1007/978-3-658-41364-4_6

Peleg-Oren, N. (2002). Group intervention for children of drug-addicted parents—Using expressive techniques. *Clinical Social Work Journal*, *30*(4), 403–418. doi:10.1023/A:1020768011128

Su, B., Wu, L., Chang, Y., & Hong, R. (2021). Influencers on social media as references: Understanding the importance of parasocial relationships. *Sustainability (Basel)*, *13*(19), 10919. doi:10.3390/su131910919

Taillon, B. J., Mueller, S., Kowalczyk, C. M., & Jones, D. N. (2020). Understanding the relationships between social media influencers and their followers: The moderating role of closeness. *Journal of Product and Brand Management*, *29*(6), 767–782. doi:10.1108/JPBM-03-2019-2292

Zhang, X., & Choi, J. (2022). The importance of social influencer-generated content for user cognition and emotional attachment: An information relevance perspective. *Sustainability (Basel)*, *14*(11), 6676. doi:10.3390/su14116676

Zitzmann, J., Rombold-George, L., Rosenbach, C., & Renneberg, B. (2024). Emotion regulation, parenting, and psychopathology: A systematic review. *Clinical Child and Family Psychology Review*, *27*(1), 1–22. doi:10.1007/s10567-023-00452-5 PMID:37704867

Zniva, R., Weitzl, W., & Lindmoser, C. (2023). Be constantly different! How to manage influencer authenticity. *Electronic Commerce Research*, *23*(3), 1485–1514. doi:10.1007/s10660-022-09653-6

ADDITIONAL READING

Bi, C. N., & Zhang, R. (Eds.). (2024). Global perspectives on social media influencers and strategic business communication. IGI Global. https://doi.org/ doi:10.4018/979-8-3693-0912-4

Rosário, A. T., & Da Silva, J. M. (2023). Social media influencers in fashion: Challenges and opportunities. In T. Tarnanidis, E. Papachristou, M. Karypidis, & V. Ismyrlis (Eds.), *Social Media and Online Consumer Decision Making in the Fashion Industry* (pp. 243–266). IGI Global. doi:10.4018/978-1-6684-8753-2.ch014

Singha, S. (2024). Social media's influence on consumer decision-making: A roadmap for success. In F. Sahin & C. Soylemez (Eds.), *Globalized Consumer Insights in the Digital Era* (pp. 85–109). IGI Global. doi:10.4018/979-8-3693-3811-7.ch004

KEY TERMS AND DEFINITIONS

Authenticity: It is not a cosmetic characteristic but rather a fundamental aspect that resides in the very essence of a person. It captures the core of authenticity, portraying one's natural nature without any pretence or facade. When an influencer genuinely exemplifies authenticity, their content connects deeply with sincerity and honesty, accurately expressing their true identity. This attribute is not merely a trendy term; it establishes the basis of a robust bond between an influencer and their audience. Influencers cultivate a connection based on trust and dependability by engaging in genuine communication. They cultivate an authentic connection with their supporters by remaining steadfast in their convictions, principles, and personal encounters.

Consumer Behaviour: Understanding consumer behaviour is a complex area of study that necessitates a sophisticated comprehension of how human psychology, social interactions, cultural forces, and environmental elements interact. By utilizing knowledge gained from studying consumer behaviour, firms and marketers may create focused strategies, improve customer experiences, and cultivate enduring relationships with their intended audience. In today's dynamic environment, generating corporate success and maintaining competitiveness requires anticipating and adapting to developing consumer behaviour.

Content Production: Content production is a complex process that encompasses creating and developing diverse digital assets specifically designed for distribution on internet platforms. This versatile discipline comprises diverse media, such as videos, photographs, text, audio, and interactive features, with the primary objective of captivating and connecting with a particular target demographic. Essentially, creating content starts with generating ideas and carefully organizing them. Material creators engage in creativity, research, and strategizing to ensure that their material aligns with their target audience's interests, needs, and preferences. This stage frequently entails conducting market studies, researching competitors, and segmenting the audience to guarantee that the generated content is both pertinent and captivating.

Influencer Marketing: A marketing strategy involves collaborating with social media influencers to promote products or services, leveraging their credibility and reach to connect with a larger audience.

Motivations: In this context, the driving forces or reasons behind an individual's actions refer to the influencers' reasons for engaging in content creation and online influence.

Social Media Influencers: Social media influencers significantly impact the moulding of digital culture, consumer behavior, and brand views in today's interconnected world. Influencers have become essential collaborators for businesses aiming to establish genuine and impactful connections with consumers, as they possess the power to captivate audiences, generate engagement, and sway purchasing decisions. Authenticity, openness, and relevance will continue to be crucial in the evolving influencer ecosystem for building trust and establishing genuine connections with audiences.

Strategic Business Communication: Businesses should make purposeful and planned communication efforts, utilizing various channels, to achieve specific objectives and enhance their overall brand image.

Chapter 3
Influencers' Perception of Personal Branding on Social Media in Vietnam

Tuong-Minh Ly-Le
https://orcid.org/0000-0001-8203-7357
University of Management and Technology Ho Chi Minh City, Vietnam

Truc Ngoc Hoang
Van Lang University, Vietnam

ABSTRACT

This research aims to explore influencers' perceptions of personal branding on social media in Vietnam and examine the factors that shape their understanding and practices. The study employs in-depth interview method. Thirteen influencers were interviewed to gather their perspectives and insights on personal branding. Research findings indicate that influencers in Vietnam perceive social trends as influential in shaping their personal branding strategies. They prioritize staying updated and adapting their content and image to match the expectations and needs of their target audience. Additionally, influencers recognize the significance of showcasing their expertise and maintaining authenticity in building their personal brand. The findings provide practical guidance for influencers and practitioners in building effective personal brands on social media. They highlight the need for influencers to stay updated with social trends, leverage expertise, express authenticity, utilize technology, and consider public reception. This research contributes to the specific context of Vietnam, shedding light on the perception of personal branding among influencers in this cultural setting. The findings provide a deeper understanding of the influencers' practices and offer practical implications that can inform personal branding strategies on social media in Vietnam.

INTRODUCTION

In today's technologically advanced society, social media has become an integral part of our daily lives, significantly transforming the way we communicate and interact with others. With the rise of social

DOI: 10.4018/979-8-3693-0912-4.ch003

media, the concept of personal branding has gained prominence as a crucial element in the competitive market economy. Vietnam has witnessed a significant presence on social media platforms. As of January 2023, there were over 70 million active social media users in Vietnam, accounting for 71% of the national population using social media (Kemp, 2023). Moreover, consumer behavior has undergone a notable shift, with over 90% of customers in Vietnam placing trust in influencers rather than traditional advertising methods (Tuan Ha, 2020). This shift highlights the power of influencer marketing and the role of influencers as opinion leaders within society.

The social media revolution has brought forth the most influential force in the form of word-of-mouth marketing through influencers. According to Kerpen et al. (2019), the personal pages of influencers play a pivotal role in establishing public trust by sharing personal experiences, evaluations, and recommendations. The inherent trust built through these platforms has made influencer marketing a simple and highly effective form of promotion.

The emergence of influential groups on social media has given rise to a new wave of opportunities and challenges for active influencers. To thrive in this competitive landscape, influencers must not only focus on content creation but also adopt a long-term strategic approach to building their personal brand. This process necessitates continuous learning, knowledge deepening, and skill development to formulate effective personal brand strategies (Kerpen et al., 2019).

Given the significance of personal branding on social media, it is crucial to explore influencers' awareness and perception of personal branding in Vietnam. By understanding the role and importance of personal brands, influencers can leverage this knowledge to effectively build and develop their personal brand strategies on Vietnamese social networking platforms. Additionally, the findings of this research can benefit businesses and communicators who seek to identify suitable influencers for their brands and establish meaningful connections with target audiences through influencer marketing.

This study aims to investigate influencers' perceptions of personal branding on social media in Vietnam and shed light on the importance of personal branding for influencers. This study seeks to understand the factors that contribute to the formation of a personal brand for an influencer, and how influencers can build a strong personal brand on social media. Accordingly, the research aims to bridge the gap between theoretical knowledge and practical application, enabling influencers to effectively build and enhance their personal brands on social media platforms.

LITERATURE REVIEW

Personal Branding

In the modern era of marketing and communication, the concept of personal branding has gained significant attention as individuals strive to distinguish themselves in a crowded and competitive landscape.

The term "brand" is widely discussed in the marketing literature. Fournier (1998) defined a brand as the perception, feelings, and beliefs held by customers and partners about all elements of an organization. Within the domain of personal branding, scholars like Pawar (2016) have defined it as the perception or feeling maintained by others about an individual's outstanding qualities and the impact they have on relationships. Llopis (2013) expanded on this definition by stating that personal branding encompasses the total experience of an individual or public figure in relation to the image they represent as a leader or expert. This perception reflects how the public evaluates them socially.

Personal branding is a multifaceted concept that is discussed in various fields, as noted by Charon (1992), who emphasized two main aspects of personal branding: identity and image. Identity refers to how individuals are perceived and valued, acting as representatives of the organizations or groups they are associated with. It encompasses the elements and characteristics that people use to identify and remember a particular individual. On the other hand, image refers to how society perceives an individual. It can be reflected through visual materials associated with a brand or organization and represents the public's perception and valuation of that individual.

The significance of personal branding has been increasingly acknowledged, especially with the rise of social media platforms. Philbrick and Cleveland (2015) emphasized the role of personal branding in enabling individuals to establish themselves in their careers by effectively communicating their unique qualities. Similarly, Pawar et al. (2022) highlighted the role of online personal branding in conveying individuals' outstanding qualities in the digital sphere, aiding them in achieving their career aspirations and differentiating themselves from others.

Social media platforms, such as Facebook, play a pivotal role in personal branding journeys. According to Kerpen et al. (2019), social media platforms serve as virtual cocktail parties, facilitating effortless interactions and connections among individuals. This interconnectedness not only allows individuals to interact, share, and connect, fostering new relationships, but also expands the reach of personal brands, benefiting businesses and influencers alike. In the context of influencers, social media provide favorable environments for them to develop and strengthen their personal brands, leveraging digital tools to become influential figures and share their values with their audience effectively.

In summary, personal branding is a vital aspect of modern marketing and communication. It involves the perception, feelings, and beliefs held by others about an individual's outstanding qualities and the impact they have on relationships. Personal branding encompasses the identity and image of an individual, with identity representing how individuals are perceived and valued and image reflecting society's perception. Personal branding plays a significant role in individuals' careers, enabling them to stand out and achieve their goals. Social media, with their widespread reach and connectivity, provide influencers with platforms to build and enhance their personal brands, connecting with audiences and sharing their values effectively. Understanding the definition and conceptualization of personal branding is essential for influencers seeking to navigate the competitive landscape of social media in Vietnam and establish meaningful connections with their target audience.

Personal Branding and Influencers

Personal branding has become increasingly crucial for professionals across various domains, particularly in the context of social media platforms. Several studies underscore the importance of effective communication and audience engagement in personal branding activities. Brems et al. (2016) and Jacobson (2020) emphasized the need for individuals to convey their personality and skills while engaging with their audience, stressing that continuous engagement was key to establishing a successful personal brand.

Authenticity and positive content are identified as fundamental elements of effective personal branding. Vitelar (2019) highlighted the significance of honesty, technological savvy, and hard work for Generation Z individuals leveraging personal branding on social media. Similarly, Devos et al. (2022) explored how Instagram influencers emphasize appearance, expertise, and socio-cultural factors to bolster their personal brand success. These studies collectively underline the importance of authenticity, positivity, and diligence in building personal brands on social media platforms.

Social dynamics and stakeholder relationships are another critical aspect of personal branding. Dumont and Ots (2020) emphasized that personal branding was an interactive process involving social motivation and relationships with family, friends, coworkers, and online communities. These relationships played a significant role in shaping and promoting personal brands. Self-awareness and self-knowledge were also crucial factors in personal branding, according to the same study. These findings highlight the importance of building and nurturing relationships as well as developing self-awareness for successful personal branding.

Measuring the strength of a personal brand is another aspect explored in the literature. Faliagka et al. (2018) proposed a methodology for quantifying personal brand influence based on web activity. They suggest evaluating relevance to the recruiting company's brand, investment in personal brand building, leadership skills, and technological proficiency as indicators of personal brand strength. This framework offers a systematic approach to assessing personal brand impact and effectiveness.

The influence of social media on personal branding, particularly for celebrities, is a notable focus of research. Wróblewski and Grzesiak (2020) highlighted the role of openness, transparency, engaging dialogue, compelling content, and diverse communication methods in shaping celebrity personal brands on social media platforms. These platforms offer celebrities opportunities to interact with fans, enhance their brand equity, and shape their personal brands effectively.

To sum up, personal branding on social media platforms is a multi-faceted process that requires effective communication, continuous engagement, authenticity, positive content, social dynamics, self-awareness, and relationship-building. Understanding these themes and implementing them strategically can contribute to successful personal branding across various professional domains.

The Scope of This Research

While previous research has explored various factors contributing to personal branding, there remains a gap in understanding how Vietnamese influencers perceive and navigate personal branding on social media platforms.

With the unique social media landscape, a significant presence of active users, and a distinct consumer behavior trend, it is important to delve deeper into the Vietnamese influencers' awareness and perception of personal branding to tailor strategies that resonate with the local audience and cultural nuances. Understanding influencers' perceptions will not only enhance the current comprehension of personal branding dynamics but also contribute to refining strategies for building and strengthening personal brands on social media platforms in Vietnam.

In this research, the authors examined the social trends, influencers' expertise, influencers' personalities, influencers' attitudes toward personal branding, technological advancements, and public perception.

First, the social trends, particularly the widespread usage of the internet and social media platforms, significantly influence personal branding on social media. Vietnam has experienced a substantial increase in internet and social media users, indicating the growing importance of these platforms in people's lives (Kemp, 2023). The rise in social media usage for various purposes, such as connecting with others, staying updated, expressing opinions, and sharing daily activities, has contributed to the increasing need for personal branding.

Besides, expertise plays a crucial role in establishing trust and credibility among individuals in society (Pormpitakpan, 2004). Within the context of personal branding on social media, expertise is a fundamental factor in building a strong personal brand (Brems et al., 2016). It is important for influencers to effectively communicate their professional skills on social media platforms.

The personality of influencers plays a significant role in attracting and engaging the public. Personal branding on social media requires influencers to maintain their personal identity, live according to their personalities, selectively interact with others, and share positive messages (Jacobson, 2020). Influencers' attitudes towards personal branding, including self-awareness and self-knowledge, are crucial factors in building a compelling personal brand (Dumont & Ots, 2020). Understanding their self-worth, talents, and skills and how they want others to perceive them is essential.

Another factor is technological advancements, which have provided influencers with convenient tools and features that enhance the personal branding process on social media platforms. These tools include user-friendly interfaces, analytics, content creation and scheduling platforms, and social media management applications. Integrating technology into personal branding processes improves efficiency and effectiveness, allowing influencers to reach a wider audience and optimize their online presence.

Finally, public reception is influenced by effective interaction between the influencer and the audience, coupled with personalized communication, which enhances the reception of information. Additionally, leveraging technological utilities contributes to capturing communication trends in the digital age.

All the above factors are used to analyze and discuss the two research questions of this study:

RQ1. What factors contribute to the formation of a personal brand for an influencer?

RQ2. How can influencers build a strong personal brand on social media?

RESEARCH DESIGN

This research employed a qualitative research design with in-depth interviews to gain rich and detailed insights into the experiences and opinions of the participants. The inclusion criteria are influencers on social media platforms. such as Facebook, Instagram, or TikTok, with a minimum of 10,000 followers. The research used a purposive, convenient sampling technique to choose the participants.

Data saturation was determined after conducting 13 interviews with qualified participants, where a high degree of consistency in theme responses was observed. The participants are influencers with 12,000 - 300,000 followers on popular social media channels in Vietnam, belonging to a group of small and medium influencers. The participants use different platforms, with varying ranges of followers and content.

All potential participants were emailed about the data-gathering procedure and the research problem of the study. If a person decided to participate, the researcher read them the Interview consent information so that they could understand the purpose of the research, as well as their role and rights as a participant in more detail. Information about how to withdraw was also included. Only if the participant agreed to give consent, the interview would continue. The participants were asked one question at a time and could choose to stop the interview at any time or have their answers withdrawn. The withdrawn participants would have had their data destroyed and would not be used in the research. Participation in this research is entirely voluntary, and the participants could withdraw their consent at any point up to the completion of the interview. No participant chose to withdraw.

The participants' profiles are as below.

Table 1. Interview participants' profiles

Participant	*Platform(s) Used*	*Follower Count (Thousands)*
01	Instagram	12.6
02	Facebook	13.5
03	Facebook TikTok	20 2.6
04	Instagram	34.7
05	TikTok	40.7
06	Facebook TikTok	58 51.9
07	Facebook TikTok	8.1 53
08	Instagram TikTok	15.8 70.6
09	TikTok	86.1
10	TikTok	111.5
11	Facebook	199.4
12	Facebook TikTok	65 259.1
13	TikTok	312.9

FINDINGS

Influencers' Perception of Personal Branding is Influenced by Social Trends and Audience Understanding

Seven out of the 13 influencers who participated in this study demonstrated a keen awareness of the impact of societal trends on their content creation and personal brand. They acknowledged the significance of staying updated with current trends and aligning their content to resonate with their target audience. For these influencers, social trends played a crucial role in shaping their personal branding strategies.

"I pay attention to current trends and popular topics among my target audience. It helps me create relevant and relatable content that resonates with them." (Participant 6)

Two other participants expressed disinterest in building a personal brand:

"I only share content I like and that can benefit my followers. Besides, my current job keeps me too busy [to follow trends]." (Participant 10)

When prompted about their levels of interest in personal branding, two participants were aware of personal branding but had not actively pursued it…

"I've only recently started to pay attention to [building a personal brand], and I don't really understand how to do it. Maybe I will do it in the near future." (Participant 1)

Nine influencers expressed a genuine interest in personal branding and actively sought to build their personal brands on social media.

"Building a personal brand is essential. Continuously refining your image is crucial. When companies reach out to me [for endorsement or marketing activities], they first check my social media profile to understand my style and preferences. What I post on my profile becomes a strength and an opening for brands to connect with me." (Participant 11)

These nine influencers also had strategic plans for developing their personal brands on social media. These plans involved transitioning their content and approach to align with their evolving goals.

"I used to focus mainly on reviews, but now I plan to become someone who provides value to my viewers, being approachable and authentic. At different stages, I have various directions and plans." (Participant 6)

"I always plan ahead. Before starting any project, I undergo training, even for my very first video." (Participant 8)

Moreover, these participants actively set goals for their personal branding journey on social media, demonstrating a commitment to personal growth and strategic development:

"I'm currently aiming to transition into a professional key opinion leader (KOL). I plan to stay updated on the societal trends to know which products to endorse and how to introduce them to users." (Participant 8)

"I am focusing on completing the projects I'm involved in. Based on the results, I will prove myself and have the opportunity to work with larger clients." (Participant 7)

On the other hand, three influencers shared that they did not have any specific goals related to personal branding.

"I haven't looked into this yet, but I think my followers share similar interests with me, so they naturally follow my channel." (Participant 5)

It is worth noting that all participants discussed the importance of understanding their followers. They believed that knowing their audience's preferences and insights was vital to creating content that resonated with them and forming meaningful connections.

"When I understand my [social media] followers, I can tailor my content and choose products from brands that suit my audience. For example, if my audience consists mainly of young people, I must focus on providing content that resonates with them." (Participant 11)

These findings show diverse attitudes and strategies of influencers in Vietnam regarding personal branding on social media. While some are highly strategic and goal-oriented, others are more relaxed and content-driven. Nonetheless, the common thread among these influencers is their recognition of the significance of societal trends and audience understanding in shaping their personal branding efforts.

Expertise Factor Plays a Significant Role in Developing Influencers' Personal Brands

Among the 13 influencers interviewed, six acknowledged the importance of leveraging their expertise and knowledge in the development of their personal brands on social media. These influencers believed that their specialized knowledge allowed them to create content that resonated with their target audiences. They used their expertise as a strategic advantage to attract and engage their followers.

Participant 8, who had a career in fashion production and sales, shared their view:

"I am building my personal brand based on my knowledge of fashion. For more than a year, I have focused on sharing fashion knowledge with educational content on TikTok. I think that developing this type of content resonates with my followers, thus bringing more value to them and more [business] opportunities for me."

The other seven participants focused on their personal interests and strengths when creating content. Despite not being specialists in particular fields, these influencers recognized their unique abilities and interests and used them as the foundation for their content. They created content that resonated with their personal preferences, effectively aligning their content with their own passions.

"I simply share the content that I find funny and relevant with my friends... I share according to what I like and what is related to my work." (Participant 5)

"I started creating content during the pandemic to attract more attention and engage in conversations. When I saw content from other [well-known] influencers, I was inspired, and my goal was to become an influencer myself and reach 1,000 followers. Later on, as I became more known, I started refining and taking it more seriously. My expertise is in finance, but I only focus on content that is relatable to my audience, rather than delving into the technical aspects." (Participant 12)

"I enjoy playing games and sharing my gaming clips on TikTok. It started as a hobby and has now become my job. I build my personal brand based on my genuine personality and interests, but I also approach it with a structured and professional mindset." (Participant 13)

In brief, there are varying approaches that influencers in Vietnam could take when developing their personal brands. While some rely on their expertise in specific fields to create content, others use their personal interests and strengths as the foundation for their content, demonstrating the diversity of strategies employed by influencers in the country.

The Personality Factor Emerges as a Crucial Element in Building a Personal Brand on Social Media

In the realm of personal branding on social media, the role of an influencer's personality is evident, and five out of the 13 influencers interviewed expressed their perspectives on this matter. These influencers held diverse views regarding the establishment of a framework or model for themselves on social media.

Participant 4 conveyed their discomfort with the idea of setting a framework for their personal brand:

"I feel like setting a framework on social media makes me feel uncomfortable like I'm living pretending to be someone else, not me." This sentiment highlights the influencer's preference for authenticity and resistance to conforming to predefined models.

On the contrary, other influencers expressed their desire to be perceived within the framework they have deliberately constructed for themselves. They aimed to shape a particular public image based on specific traits and values.

"I have built myself in front of the public as a well-mannered image, has musical expertise, and actively spreads love through social activities." (Participant 3)

"I tend to show different [self-images] on different social media platforms. On TikTok, I present a friendly and informative image; while on Facebook, I build a professional image that could increase my credibility and draw business cooperation." (Participant 7)

Further in the process of personal branding, the participants acknowledged that influencers must also navigate negative feedback and comments. All 13 influencers agreed that responding to such feedback required a flexible approach to maintain a balance between fostering public affection and safeguarding personal reputation.

"I am ready to respond to negative comments or information, depending on the situation. If it's just gossip, I don't care. However, if the information affects my personal reputation, I will speak up to protect myself." (Participant 8)

"Depending on the situation, I may choose different strategies. I could remain silent and continue to build a positive image. If I make a mistake, I might speak up to show a sense of responsibility. In extreme cases, I might respond but always in a civilized manner." (Participant 9)

The findings here underscore the significant role of influencers' personalities in the construction of their personal brands on social media. While some influencers prefer to remain authentic and resist conforming to established frameworks, others actively shape their public image according to their chosen values and expertise. Moreover, all influencers acknowledged the importance of a tailored approach in handling negative feedback and comments, striving to maintain public affection while protecting their personal reputation.

The Attitude Factor Influences Influencers' Perception of Personal Branding on Social Media

The influencers interviewed held varying levels of interest and commitment to personal branding on social media. While most participants considered it a priority, two of them were indifferent or had not yet fully embraced the concept.

"I don't care about personal branding on social media because I don't aspire to be famous." (Participant 5)

"I simply enjoy sharing content that I like and that can help my followers. At the moment, my job keeps me occupied, and I don't have enough time to focus on social media." (Participant 10)

Nine out of the 13 influencers had specific plans and goals related to personal branding on social media. They approached personal branding strategically to achieve their objectives.

"I used to focus on reviews primarily, but recently, I plan to transition into a role where I provide value to my audience, be more relatable, and informative. At each stage, I have different directions and plans." (Participant 6)

In summary, the participants vary in their level of interest and commitment to personal branding. Those who are actively engaged in personal branding have concrete plans and goals and emphasize the importance of understanding their audience to tailor their content effectively.

Technological Advancements Play a Crucial Role in Shaping Influencers' Personal Branding Strategies

All the influencers who participated in the interviews recognized the pivotal role that technological advancements play in shaping their personal branding strategies. They acknowledged the importance of staying updated with the latest trends, tools, and features in social media platforms and actively utilized technology to enhance their personal brand.

"I constantly explore and experiment with new features and trends on platforms like Instagram and YouTube. It helps me stay relevant and engage my audience in innovative ways." (Participant 10)

Additionally, all influencers admitted to using various apps and software for photo and video editing to support their content creation. For instance:

"I had to attend design courses for a few months when I started. Content creation is no longer just a supplementary skill; it's a necessity." (Participant 12)

"To create the image I want to present to the public, using these tools is an investment that showcases my attention to detail." (Participant 1)

"Knowing how to use these applications is crucial. Even without assistance, I can edit images to meet the requirements of brands and ensure everything is ready before posting on social media." (Participant 3)

The participants held various opinions on using AI-based tools for content support, including AI-driven writing and information retrieval tools. These opinions ranged from complete agreement to non-use, with some influencers expressing their intention to explore AI tools.

Two influencers actively used AI-based tools to assist in generating content ideas and information retrieval:

"I make the most of the utilities that support everything, from information retrieval to outlining ideas. If you know how to leverage them, they can save a lot of time." (Participant 6)

"I also consult, but I have to be selective and distill the main ideas. For example, when writing an essay, I read sample essays not to copy but to understand the structure and how to create a story for myself. I don't just copy and paste; that wouldn't be beneficial for my creative ideas." (Participant 11)

Five participants expressed an intention to explore AI tools in the future:

"Given my current content, which mainly focuses on images, I haven't needed AI support for content creation yet. However, I might consider it for future projects." (Participant 1)

"I don't object to people using AI tools. However, my current content is event-based and emotional, so I haven't needed it yet. I will explore it as it has many advantages." (Participant 12)

Six other influencers expressed skepticism and reluctance regarding the use of AI-based content generation tools:

"Regarding AI, like chatbots, I haven't used them. My content is meant to provide value to my viewers, and I want it to truly be my idea, not someone else's, including AI." (Participant 8)

"I don't hold AI-generated content in high regard. For me, personal branding involves showcasing one's individuality and unique traits. Using AI could diminish the creativity and personal touch." (Participant 7)

These influencers perceived AI-generated content as potentially diminishing their creative input and the uniqueness of their personal brands. They placed a higher value on content that reflects their distinct characteristics and creativity.

To review, all influencers acknowledged the importance of staying updated with the latest social media trends and tools. They actively used technology, including apps for photo and video editing, to enhance their content creation. Opinions on AI-based content support varied among influencers, with some actively using these tools, some planning to explore them, and others expressing concerns about potential impacts on personal creativity and uniqueness.

Public Perception Plays a Significant Role in Influencers' Perception of Personal Branding

Ten out of the 13 influencers recognized the significant role that managing their public image and reputation plays in shaping their personal branding strategies. They acknowledged the importance of how they are perceived by their audience and the general public. Maintaining authenticity, transparency, and credibility were key principles for them to build trust and loyalty among their followers.

"I am mindful of how I am perceived by my audience and the general public. I strive to maintain authenticity, transparency, and credibility to build trust and loyalty." (Participant 1)

Moreover, participant 12 emphasized the need for consistency and careful messaging through their content. They were conscious of shaping their personal brand to align with their desired public perception.

"I ensure that my content aligns with my values and beliefs. I want my audience to perceive me as someone who is genuine and trustworthy."

Eleven out of the 13 influencers affirmed that their content is well-received by the public. They expressed positive sentiments about the resonance of their content with their audience and the broader public.

"Since I made the decision to change my content and rebrand myself, I've been fortunate to receive a lot of support. Many people expressed joy and congratulations for my decision to change during this time." (Participant 6)

However, two influencers mentioned that they often encountered mixed reactions from their followers:

"From the content I share on TikTok, I knew it would be controversial due to the easily misunderstood headlines. Those who don't like it will use it to critique me." (Participant 7)

"Previously, I mainly created positive content, but now, I also create content based on real events and emotional stories. As a result, it's not all rosy anymore, and there are many who empathize and accept it, but there are also many who don't like me this way." (Participant 12)

Seven of the influencers disclosed that they had faced backlash or strong negative reactions from the public due to content that was perceived as inappropriate or controversial. These influencers actively addressed such issues and learned from them.

All influencers expressed a willingness to adapt and adjust their content strategy if it did not resonate with the public:

"Initially, my focus is on regularly sharing content. From this content, I can gauge what my audience likes and dislikes and make adjustments accordingly." (Participant 9)

"When you have a certain number of fans, you need to review content before posting it on social media. For me, it's about listening and changing in a positive direction, showing adaptability and self-improvement." (Participant 2)

It can be seen that public perception significantly impacts influencers' personal branding. The influencers actively manage their public image, emphasizing authenticity, transparency, and credibility. While most influencers reported a positive reception of their content, some experienced mixed reactions. Seven influencers learned from instances of negative public reactions, indicating their readiness to adapt their content to better align with their desired public perception and maintain a positive personal brand.

DISCUSSION

Factors Contributing to the Formation of a Personal Brand for an Influencer

The findings reveal that social trends play a pivotal role in shaping influencers' personal branding strategies. The participating influencers demonstrated a keen awareness of the importance of staying updated with current trends and aligning their content to resonate with their target audience. This finding aligns with previous research highlighting the dynamic nature of social media and the need for influencers to adapt to changing trends (Kaplan & Haenlein, 2010). It underscores the significance of market orientation (Llopis, 2013), where influencers actively tailor their content to meet the evolving demands and preferences of their audience.

Furthermore, understanding the audience emerged as a key factor. The participants acknowledged the need to know their audience's preferences and insights to create content that resonated with them. This emphasis on audience understanding is consistent with prior studies emphasizing the importance of audience engagement (Brems et al., 2016) and authenticity (Vitelar, 2019) in personal branding. It reinforces the idea that a strong personal brand is built on a foundation of genuine connection with the audience.

The study also found that influencers could leverage their expertise and specialized knowledge to create content that resonated with their target audiences. This aligns with the concept of content expertise and credibility (Pornpitakpan, 2004) and emphasizes the importance of influencers' professional skills in establishing trust and credibility with their followers.

On the other hand, several influencers focused on personal interests and strengths when creating content. They recognized their unique abilities and interests and used them as the foundation for their content. This approach resonates with the idea of personal authenticity and self-expression in personal branding (Jacobson, 2020). It suggests that influencers can build strong personal brands by staying true to their passions and strengths, provided they effectively communicate their genuine interests.

Finally, the research findings underscore the significance of influencers' personalities in shaping their personal brands. While some influencers preferred authenticity and resisted conforming to predefined models, others actively shaped their public image based on specific traits and values. This finding resonates with previous research highlighting the role of authenticity (Devos et al., 2022) and personal identity (Charon, 1992) in personal branding. It suggests that influencers have the flexibility to choose between projecting their true selves or strategically crafting a persona based on their desired public image.

Building a Strong Personal Brand on Social Media

The study reveals that influencers who were committed to building a strong personal brand on social media often had strategic plans and clear goals. They recognized the importance of setting objectives and continuously refining their image. This aligns with the idea of personal branding as an ongoing process (Philbrick & Cleveland, 2015) and emphasizes the role of goal orientation (Faliagka et al., 2018) in building a robust personal brand. It highlights the need for influencers to establish a roadmap for their personal branding journey to ensure consistency and relevance.

The research findings also emphasize the importance of influencers' adaptability and responsiveness to audience feedback and changing perceptions. Influencers acknowledged that public perception significantly impacted their personal branding efforts. Those who encountered mixed reactions or negative feedback demonstrated a willingness to adapt and adjust their content strategy to better align with their desired public image. This adaptive approach aligns with the concept of responsiveness in personal branding (Dumont & Ots, 2020) and reflects the influencer's ability to maintain public affection while safeguarding their personal reputation.

Lastly, the study highlights the pivotal role of technological advancements in shaping influencers' personal branding strategies. Influencers actively used technology for content creation, including photo and video editing apps. This aligns with the idea of leveraging digital technology to enhance personal branding efforts (Pawar et al., 2022) and emphasizes the importance of staying updated with the latest trends and tools. It suggests that influencers should view technology as an essential tool for optimizing their online presence.

However, opinions on AI-based content support tools varied among influencers. While some embraced these tools for content generation and information retrieval, others expressed concerns about their potential impact on creativity and personal touch. This divergence of views highlights the need for influencers to carefully evaluate the use of AI tools and consider how they align with their personal branding goals.

Theoretical Contributions

This research fills the gap in the current literature by giving Vietnamese influencers' insights into how they perceive and apply personal branding tactics. Through analyzing the ways the influencers think, behave, and manage their brands, the research expands the knowledge of personal branding practices in a certain cultural context and socio-economic context.

This research also adds to the scholarship of personal branding. By delving into the area of social trends, expertise, personality, attitude, technological developments, and public perception, this research stresses the complexity of personal branding processes on social media, incorporating different viewpoints and experiences of the influencers that are dealing with the digital environment of Vietnamese people.

The findings also highlight the role of culture in personal branding. Influencers in Vietnam, like those in other countries, are influenced by societal trends, norms, and values. Understanding and aligning with the cultural context is essential for effective personal branding.

Practical Implications

For influencers and practitioners, these findings provide practical guidance in building effective personal brands on social media in Vietnam. Staying updated with social trends, showcasing expertise, maintaining authenticity, leveraging technology, and considering public reception are key strategies for success. By incorporating these factors into their personal branding strategies, influencers can enhance their impact and engagement with their target audience.

In terms of contributions to the field of personal branding and influencers, this research offers a nuanced understanding of the specific context of Vietnam. By focusing on influencers in Vietnam and considering the socio-cultural factors that influence their personal branding strategies, this study fills a gap in the existing literature. The findings contribute to the ongoing discourse on personal branding and influencers by providing context-specific insights and practical implications for influencers and practitioners operating in the Vietnamese market.

For businesses and marketers, this study offers practical insights into identifying suitable influencers for their brand campaigns and developing effective influencer marketing campaigns. By understanding the influencers' perceptions of personal branding and their strategies for developing their personal brands, businesses can choose the most suitable influencers that resonate with the organization's values and their target audience. Besides, the findings can be used to shape their marketing strategies and messaging to better align with the influencers' personal branding efforts, thus maximizing the impact of influencer engagement.

Overall, the findings of this study could reach different stakeholders that engage in influencer marketing. Such insights can be used to build strong personal brands as well as to strategize a profitable partnership with influencers and to capitalize on emerging trends and technologies in the Vietnamese market.

CONCLUSION

This research examined the influencers' perception of personal branding on social media in Vietnam and explored the factors that shape their understanding and practices. The findings have important implications for influencers and practitioners in the field of personal branding, as well as contributing to the existing body of knowledge in this area.

Despite the valuable insights provided by this research, it is important to acknowledge its limitations. The research focused solely on influencers' perspectives, and it would be beneficial to investigate the audience's perception and reception of influencers' personal branding. Understanding how the audience engages with influencers' content and how it influences their personal branding process can provide a more comprehensive view of the phenomenon.

It is anticipated that a future where influencers not only shape trends but also adapt to them. Building a personal brand that stands the test of time demands a blend of innovation and timeless values. The influencers of tomorrow will be those who skilfully balance the art and science of personal branding, fostering meaningful relationships in the digital age while embracing the technological tools that empower their creativity and reach.

REFERENCES

Brems, C., Temmerman, M., Graham, T., & Broersma, M. (2016). Personal branding on Twitter. *Digital Journalism (Abingdon, England)*, *5*(4), 443–459. doi:10.1080/21670811.2016.1176534

Charon, J. (1992). *Sociology: A conceptual approach*. Allyn & Bacon.

Devos, S., Eggermont, S., & Vandenbosch, L. (2022). Instagram influencers as superwomen: Influencers' lifestyle presentations observed through framing analysis. *Media and Communication*, *10*(1), 173–184. doi:10.17645/mac.v10i1.4717

Dumont, G., & Ots, M. (2020). Social dynamics and stakeholder relationships in personal branding. *Journal of Business Research*, *106*, 118–128. doi:10.1016/j.jbusres.2019.09.013

Faliagka, E., Ramantas, K., Rigou, M., & Sirmakessis, S. (2018). Measuring personal branding in social media: Towards an influence indication score. In I. Garrigós & M. Wimmer (Eds.), *Current trends in web engineering*. Springer. doi:10.1007/978-3-319-74433-9_23

Fournier, S. (1998). Consumers and their brands: Developing relationship theory in consumer research. *The Journal of Consumer Research*, *24*(4), 343–373. doi:10.1086/209515

Ha, T. (2020). *Báo cáo về thị trường KOLs, influencer Việt Nam* [Report on Vietnam KOLs and influencer market]. https://issuu.com/tuanha/docs/state_of_influencer_marketing_in_vietnam_2020_7sat

Jacobson, J. (2020). You are a brand: Social media managers' personal branding and "the future audience". *Journal of Product and Brand Management*, *29*(6), 715–727. doi:10.1108/JPBM-03-2019-2299

Kemp, S. (2023, February 13). *Digital 2023: Vietnam*. DataReportal. https://datareportal.com/reports/digital-2023-vietnam

Kerpen, D., Greenbaum, M., & Berk, R. (2019). *Likeable social media*. McGraw Hill.

Llopis, G. (2013, April 8). Personal branding is a leadership requirement, not a self-promotion campaign. *Forbes*. https://www.forbes.com/sites/glennllopis/2013/04/08/personal-branding-is-a-leadership-requirement-not-a-self-promotion-campaign/?sh=50b73bd8226f

Pawar, A. (2016). The power of personal branding. *International Journal of Engineering and Management Research*, *6*(2), 840–847.

Pawar, A., Kusmiati, M., & Sundari, S. (2022). The building of online personal branding. *Journal of Business and Management Inaba*, *1*(1), 1–15. doi:10.56956/jbmi.v1i1.6

Philbrick, J. L., & Cleveland, A. D. (2015). Personal branding: Building your pathway to professional success. *Medical Reference Services Quarterly*, *34*(2), 181–189. doi:10.1080/02763869.2015.1019324 PMID:25927510

Pornpitakpan, C. (2004). The persuasive effect of circadian arousal, endorser expertise, and argument strength in advertising. *Journal of Global Marketing*, *17*(2-3), 141–172. doi:10.1300/J042v17n02_07

Vitelar, A. (2019). Like me: Generation Z and the use of social media for personal branding. *Management Dynamics in the Knowledge Economy*, *7*(2), 257–268. Advance online publication. doi:10.25019/mdke/7.2.07

Wróblewski, Ł., & Grzesiak, M. (2020). The impact of social media on the brand capital of famous people. *Sustainability (Basel)*, *12*(16), 6414. doi:10.3390/su12166414

Section 2

Practices of Influencers

Chapter 4
The Wendy's Retweet Challenge:
Neoliberalism, Social Media, and the Creation of an Influencer

David F. Stephens
University of Memphis, USA

ABSTRACT

The purpose of this chapter is to evaluate the strategies the Wendy's food brand implements during their viral Retweet Challenge in which they wager a year's worth of chicken nuggets in exchange for teenager Carter Wilkerson to achieve 18 million retweets. This chapter argues for the effectiveness of this campaign due to Wendy's utilizing neoliberal strategies of gamification, individualism, and positivity, positioning the brand as antagonist to Wilkerson's efforts, and thus, encouraging the support from other Twitter users, only to revert back to a supportive role once the challenge commences. This, while possessing some possible drawbacks, Wendy's is framed not as corporate oppressor but as a supporter of not only Wilkerson's goal but of the creative exchange that often characterizes the relationship between producers and consumers via new media.

1. INTRODUCTION

April 5, 2017, marked a day in Twitter history as one user, Carter Wilkerson, playfully asked Wendy's how many retweets he needed to receive a year's supply of chicken nuggets.

The terms of the challenge were relatively simple for the average American Twitter user. He had to amass 18 million retweets to reach his goal. The numbers one must achieve to reach virality are always contingent on several factors (Van Dijck 2013; Kaplan & Haenlein 2011; Jenkins, Green & Ford 2013), but if Wilkerson achieves even a 1/10 of the goal, then it will have been a viral sensation for Wendy's. This cooperation between producer and consumer is an extension of Henry Jenkins's theory of digital participatory culture (2006). To this end, Wendy's has engaged in various social media performances

DOI: 10.4018/979-8-3693-0912-4.ch004

to cultivate their savvy, relatable, and ironic online persona mainly through their witty retorts to other fast-food companies and users. With over 3 million retweets, the tweet would ultimately become one of Twitter's most viral tweets, becoming the fourth most popular retweeted post on the platform, and the second most retweeted tweet of all time overall. But how does Wendy's elevate Wilkerson to the position of influencer, such that he can persuade others to join his noble cause?

Fuchs's (2013) argues, "[c]apitalism produces potentials and germforms of communism and at the same time intensifies exploitation of labour in order to create ever more profit during one hour of labour," a statement which alludes to the potentially unifying impetus of the RT challenge for users while acknowledging the unequal benefits Wendy's stands to gain in contrast to Wilkerson and others who participate. Wendy's advances their economic goals by investing in Carter the image of the underdog waging a war against oppressive corporate institutions, happily playing the antagonist, only to, in the final instance, voice their support for Wilkerson, the challenge, and the communal possibility present therein. In other words, Wendy's and Wilkerson re-enact the historical power struggle between consumers and producers.

Precarity as an affective mode is central to this discussion because it represents the uncertainty that motivates parties within the challenge and also within a larger socio-economic context. Within the context of the challenge, precarity is expressed by users who question the parameters of the challenge, but also by Wendy's who must regulate any discontent they detect in the comments, for fear of undermining the challenge or Wilkerson himself. In the macro context, this precarity represents the way social media has disturbed the traditional relationship between consumer and producer. As with the introduction of any new technology, how and for whom it will be used are questions that are constantly being negotiated. In this case, precarity is produced from the question of whether social media will be dominated by corporate accounts or rooted in the agency and free expression of everyday users.

Thus, this paper discusses the process by which Wendy's frames Wilkerson as an influencer, even if momentarily, by adopting an antagonistic position throughout the challenge. Such a framing, as my evidence suggests, makes Wilkerson a relatable figure whom others are encouraged to support. Drawing on the discourse between users, and Wendy's themselves, as well as other sources, I argue the structure of the challenge mirrors themes within neoliberal thought including a) efficiency and fairness, b) the valorization of the individual, and c) the obsession with positivity. This framework is critical to understanding the construction of Wilkerson as an influencer since neoliberalism represents a strain of thought that encourages those to believe that, like Wilkerson, they could be plucked from obscurity by a popular brand and allowed to accumulate social, cultural, and economic capital. Ultimately, this chapter is interested in the often spontaneous conditions that frame everyday users as influencers.

Similar to other studies on brand cultures, this article explores the digital strategies of popular brands, highlighting the way social media offers new terrain for both consumers and producers. However, this article focuses on a specific aspect of neoliberal techno-capitalist power and how it is interwoven into the relationship between individuals, platforms, and brands—affect. Additionally, this article is also interested in the way that, despite the age of the challenge, it has become institutionalized within the platform's history and user memory.

Review of Literature

The purpose of this literature review is to work through the affective modes present within the economic and cultural logic of neoliberalism to understand the tactics Wendy's utilizes to encourage participation in the challenge, as well as how users resist these strategies. I begin with the concept of precarity because it frames the motivations of both consumers and producers within the challenge itself, but also in the larger dialectical struggle over social media as a site of grassroots social formation or a platform structured by corporate dominance. In a broad sense, precarity has to do with the feeling of uncertainty or unpredictability of economic and cultural outcomes (Berlant, 2012). Han (2018) discusses the role of precarity in our contemporary moment, especially as a result of changing labor conditions, but also as a defining feature of social existence. The shifts in capitalism motivated by the information/network economy have increased the experience of precarity for workers as new forms of labor come into being such as the gig economy (Morgan & Nelligan, 2018). Gill and Pratt (2013) discuss precarity specifically in cultural and creative work, prioritizing the role of immaterial and affective labor as central commodities.

Conversely, social media has provided an avenue for consumers to question and resist corporate dominance (Fuchs, 2014), thus producing a sense of uncertainty regarding the efficacy of corporate power. The social media manager is a position created by businesses to manage precarity by performing a friendly and relatable identity for a brand. Sarah T. Robert's (2019) analyzes the role of screeners and moderators who help companies and brands craft their online presence. According to Banet-Weiser (2012), corporate use of social media is "a way of recouping a loosening of control over messaging" (p. 45). As opposed to traditional media, where consumer feedback options were limited, the opportunity for online users to resist corporate narratives has complicated the discursive dynamic between consumers and brands.

This dynamic is precarious precisely because of the platforms on which it is produced. The tendency towards monetization and commodification of the positive affects (Jarrett, 2015) on which digital communities are based is one of the primary tensions this project is concerned with because it structures the ideas of equity and fairness that impact the rollout of the challenge itself. However, the larger implication regards the dialectic between consumers and producers on social media as they struggle to define either a grassroots or hyper-commercial ethos (by which I mean the character or general characteristics of groups or platforms) for the social media site. In other words, Wendy's, in its efforts to commercialize social media, draws from neoliberal tactics such as individualism, and positivity to increase its virality. These strategies have the effect of transferring the precarity or anxiety onto consumers, as they struggle to overcome the challenge Wendy's poses, and ultimately represent the power these corporate accounts have to shape the experience of social media. Conversely in consumers' attempt to exercise their agency within the platform, users question these strategies through their discourse on community and displays of skepticism which resist the organized efforts of corporate influence.

The cultural influence of neoliberalism manifests through several strategies including gamification, individualism, and positivity. Regarding the first strategy, Woodcock and Johnson (2017) define gamification in one instance as "the imposition of systems of regulation, surveillance, and standardization upon aspects of everyday life, through forms of interaction and feedback drawn from games (ludus) but severed from their original playful (paidia) contexts" (p. 543). The ability to play, whether in the form of memes, videos, viral tweets, or other cultural products is part of what creates value on social media platforms. Social media, then, is a site through which cultural and creative work has been conducted, resulting in the formation of affective communities bonded through the production of immaterial labor (Jarrett, 2015). It is the spontaneity between users that is often co-opted in ways similar to play but that serve a commercial purpose. In this case, Wendy's takes the playful ethos of social media and disciplines it by directing it towards a particular goal. It takes naturally occurring phenomena like online sharing and transforms them into a methodical, calculated business decision. This strategy represents the elisions between work and play. Fuchs (2013) writes "[u]sers are productive consumers who produce commodities and profit – their user labour is exploited. But this exploitation does not feel like toil, it is rather more like play and takes place during leisure time outside of wage labour – it is unpaid labour and play labour" (p. 16). As this division collapses, user-generated content becomes an unpaid commodity for companies to exploit: "'web 2.0' reflects a new web-based marketing approach that strategically employs user-generated content in the production and targeting of commercial messages." (Manzarolle 2010, p. 462). Gamification also presents itself as a focus on efficiency where "neoliberalism expects public life generally… to understand its principal elements and activities either as inputs or products" (Lissavoy, 2013: p. 423). However, the focus on efficiency allows users to resist, through their expressions of doubt, whether their labor will be fairly compensated given the near impossibility of Wilkerson amassing 18 million retweets.

Second, neoliberalism has ushered in a new era of individualism motivated by the promise of increased social and economic mobility through the free market. Wrenn and Waller (2017) write, "[n]eoliberalism as an ideology valorizes autonomy as a state of being and as an ethics of self-interest and personal responsibility exclusively" (p. 499). The neoliberal emphasis on the individual is also magnified by media technologies through programs like *American Idol* and *You've Got Talent* that "repeatedly address ordinary subjects who can 'make it to the top of their particular profession" (Litter, 2017: p. 59). Crystal Abidin's (2018) work on microcelebrities and Brooke Erin Duffy's research on aspirational labor (2015, 2017) have laid the groundwork for thinking about how social media technologies, in particular, are sustained through the affective and aspirational forms of labor conducted through them by individuals seeking to profit from the promises of the neoliberal marketplace.

The dynamics I have outlined have placed a renewed focus on emotion and affect as a facet of neoliberal life. As Davies (2015) explains, "the future of successful capitalism depends on our ability to combat stress, misery, and illness, and put relaxation, happiness and wellness in their place. Techniques, measures, and technologies are now available to achieve this, and they are permeating the workplace, the high street, the home and the human body" (p. 10). The insistence on happiness or positivity presents itself in several interactions including comments from Wendy's urging participants to have faith in the process, as well as a small controversy over Wilkerson's decision to tag an anti-feminist Twitter page. Sara Ahmed's (2010; 2021) critical works on affect and gender reveal how feminist politics interrupts the utopic desires of the patriarchy. Similarly, Kanai and Gill (2020) point to the "feel-good" mode of affect present within consumer culture, specifically "woke capitalism." This particular dynamic is important as it provides fruitful ground for challenging the trust and faith that Wendy's asks of consumers through the challenge, while also highlighting the often-exploitative nature of neoliberal capitalism which encourages financial accumulation in opposition to social justice.

What follows is a deconstruction of this challenge through the lens of two neoliberal strategies: gamification, individualism, and positivity where I will discuss how these strategies work to marshall support for his causes.

Method and Methodology

Methodologically, this research was performed as a case study into the various discourses produced from this challenge. In order to capture the contours of the challenge, tweets were collected that represent interactions between users and between Wendy's and users, respectively; discourses produced by users over time; and discourse produced by users during a time of techno-mediated crises. The first phase involved collecting tweets during the initial days of the challenge from users between users, and from

Wendy's themselves and the various correspondences they have with users as they were actively being produced. Most tweets collected for this study fall between April 5th and April 17th of 2017 with some falling 1-2 years after. Many of the user tweets featured in this essay received at least 75+ likes with many reaching over 1000, which indicates a general agreement with the sentiments expressed. The few that did not were selected because they highlighted an important dynamic within the challenge. 250 Comments were chosen based on how they fit into the analytical categories of gamification/efficiency, individuality, and positivity. Additionally, the section on "Managing Affect" draws on Wendys' tweets, and their conversations with other users. These tweets were selected based on their representing an affective stance by the brand, primarily optimism.

Individual tweets were analyzed using hand-coded textual analysis to produce what culminated into an "affective discourse analysis." In *Affect and Emotion: A New Understanding*, Wetherell argues for the unification of affect and discourse, stating, "investigating the range and entire patterning of affective assemblages operating in important scenes in everyday life along with their social consequences and entailments" (52). Additionally, several works highlight the utility of affect and discourse (Wetherell, 2013; Duncan 2017; Glepka, 2019). This essay contributes to these works by arguing that the discourse produced from these tweets and interactions bespeaks a larger affective mode produced by the precarity of neoliberal economics and culture. Thus, I read comments from users and even Wendy's themselves as representing the negotiations of traditional brand power with that of increased user agency made available through social media. Together, these multiple forms of data tell a complex story of how brands use new media to elicit participation in ways that are unpredictable and expand beyond the intended outcome. Despite the success of the challenge, the creative resistance of users, as well as how Wendy's adapts to this resistance, symbolizes the ongoing dialectic between consumers and producers on social media—a dialectic that is bound up with the perception and fate of the platform itself.

Finally, there are certainly limitations to conducting a study such as this which traverses years of data. For instance, while using the Twitter Academic API feature, which allows scholars and researchers to explore the ever-expanding archive of Tweets, was disrupted by Elon Musk's purchase of the platform, thus limiting the period and site of data collection. Additionally, collecting the tweets via the comment section limits the available data as only so much of the tweet's comments and retweets are viewable outside of API access. To make up for some of these limitations, I chose tweets that contained 100+ likes which arguably represents a common sentiment possessed by other users.

2. GAMIFICATION AND EFFICIENCY

I begin by addressing the competition as an aspect of neoliberal gamification. This strategy is perhaps the most appropriate for encouraging users to articulate support for Wilkerson and his mission. By framing the challenge in terms of a competition, Wendy's leverages its identity as a powerful food brand against an average consumer with an empathetic goal, thus making Wilkerson more appealing as an influencer. This occurs specifically through users calling out aspects of the gamified challenge they feel are unfair or exploitative providing an impetus for the emotional investment of users in the outcome of the challenge. Rather than acquiescing to the rules, users participate in the challenge in a way that uplifts Wilkerson and deems him worthy of influencing the masses. For example, users reflect on their precarious labor, and connect this precarity with time itself—whether the time they have invested is wasted or not.

Efficiency in this context is about whether users feel the value they generate will be rewarded. In this case, that means whether their efforts are making it more possible for Wilkerson to reach his goal. User sentiments indicate they are unsure whether their actions are being considered equitably but because of their precarious position as prosumers, they are unable to secure that certainty. However, the gamification of this challenge also presents an opportunity for consumer resistance via the constant calculations they make. Rather than acquiescing to the rules, they participate in the challenge in a way that expresses their agency. Take, for instance,

the above tweets. These calculations serve as ways to structure their affective investments. By adhering to a rationalist logic, users can determine whether to place their hopes into a positive outcome or to retreat into cynicism. The skepticism is expressed by users who think Wendy's may be undermining the challenge, thus encouraging them to argue on Wilkerson's behalf.

These tweets signify just one of the ways that users are regulating the concepts of possibility and fairness. The user in Figure 1 indicates that she was curious as to whether 18 million was a number that could be reached until she googled the number of worldwide Twitter users which far outweighs the

Figure 1. User Comment 1 (Twitter, 2017)

Figure 2. User Comment 2 (Twitter, 2017)

amount Wilkerson needed. She hedges her bets and must secure a certain level of confidence before she can be optimistic. Figure 2 depicts another kind of calculation that runs throughout the comment section, in which a user takes the number of retweets at the time they posted as a way of making a statement on the possibility of pushing past that limit. The user in this figure calculates the number of current retweets at 3.6 million, which is $1/5^{th}$ of the goal and amounts to a certain percentage of the year's supply of chicken nuggets. These calculations serve to constantly evaluate the fairness of the challenge. These considerations feature heavily in tweets that are explicitly skeptical or dismissive of Wilkerson's chances. These users tread lightly before they fully invest in the possibility of Wilkerson reaching his goal. For them, they need some level of certainty, and that comes in the form of calculations and odds. Such a strategy is effective for its re-appropriation of quantitative logics that Wendy's imposes on Wilkerson.

In some ways, users agree that there is some level of exploitation occurring in this process. However, tensions arise from whether Wendy's will base Wilkerson's success on his ability to reach the proposed number of retweets in the most literal manner, or if they will acknowledge the labor performed by both Wilkerson and other users by conceding some kind of prize, whether in the form of the full year's supply or some fraction of it based on a certain number of retweets. In other words, gamification, as a neoliberal strategy, risks being perceived as celebrating unequal access to knowledge and resources. By focusing on the "required" number of retweets, much to the chagrin of Wendy's as will be explained later, users can highlight the exploitation that neoliberalism relies on, specifically in the realm of digital capitalism—how the actions of everyday users are co-opted for corporate gains. In this way, Wendy's possible exploitation works to raise Wilkerson to the level of influencer as he embodies the common struggle of man against an oppressive corporate entity.

The idea of fairness is a major theme that traverses these comments. They are expressed through comments such as one asking Wendy's which specific tweet to retweet such that Wilkerson would get the maximum impact of his petition. Many users see themselves as regulating how this game is conducted, fashioning themselves as referees who ultimately determine the equity of the challenge. And in many respects, they are correct. The company has multiple investments in the rollout of this marketing scheme, not the least of which is making it appear fair and transparent.

Figure 3. User Comment 3 (Twitter, 2017)

Their long-term strategy is an increase in profits, thus, the binary opposition they arrange between themselves and Wilkerson can only be utilized to an extent, lest they risk permanently damaging their reputation. For example, one of the first tweets Wendy's sends out is in response to a user who was enlisting others to help Wilkerson because he only had 5k retweets. Without

prompt, Wendy's responds saying they will use another tweet of Wilkerson's as the metric since it has more retweets. That they voluntarily choose the other tweet is a recognition that they prioritize how users view the rollout of the game.

Evidence of how invested people were in this challenge are comments from people watching or "checking back" to see the results:

Figure 4. User Comment 4 (Twitter, 2017)

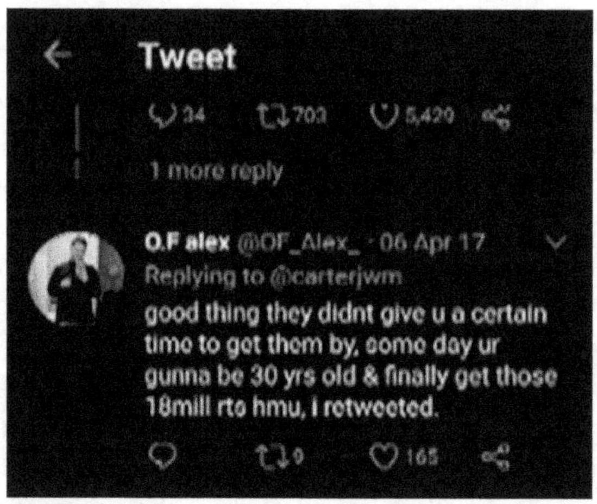

Figure 5. User Comment 5 (Twitter, 2017)

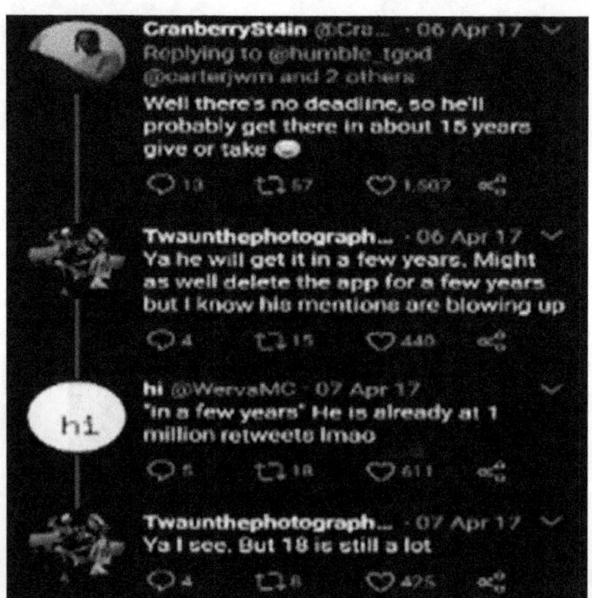

@Lindsay_Henry: "I need an update on this guy. DID HE GET FREE NUGGS FROM WENDY'S OR WHAT?"

@slypig89: "I've been watching religiously…I haven't been this emotionally invested since the UW Madison Snapchat saga"

These comments suggest that Wendy's marketing strategy is effective in generating interest in this challenge beyond immediate engagements such as retweets, likes, and comments. This is primarily accomplished through the neoliberal focus on gamification and an emphasis on rules, which then frames Wilkerson as a relatable consumer striving for a simple goal. Such a strategy relies on a well-worn narrative of corporate exploitation. By aligning themselves with Wilkerson, users display an investment of personal time and energy in both their promotion of Wilkerson and their lingering desire to see him win. The simple desire for chicken nuggets influences others to join his simple cause.

This waiting is itself, a type of precarity because it involves the deferment of pleasure or excitement until such time that Wilkerson reaches his goal. This waiting is extended by the fact that, as far as most users might have assumed, Wendy's was not going to decrease the required number of retweets, meaning if users were hoping he would reach 18 million, they did so knowing it would take a significant amount of time. Yes, there is room for faith, but it is the very battle between faith and pessimism (or even ignorance) that produces the feeling of precarity. Checking back works to confirm whether their original emotional investments have paid off.

While the upshot of the challenge sets aside some trepidation of users, Wendy's initial strategy of gamification is an implicit reminder of traditional dynamics between consumers and producers whereby producers maintain control via their social, economic, and media power. The gamified aspects of this challenge, rather than inducing a sense of relatability, may position Wendy's as relishing in Wilkerson's impossible goal. However, both Wendy's and Wilkerson ultimately reap the benefits of this temporarily imposed binary opposition between consumer and producer. By "playing" as antagonistic to Wilkerson, Wendy's crafts an average Twitter user into the image of the micro-celebrity influencer.

Against the unlikely goal, Wilkerson becomes an underdog for whom others will cheer on. The oscillation between Wilkerson as an individual, and the necessity of grassroots involvement underscores the precarious social formations that compose this challenge.

Neoliberalism and Individualism

This section focuses on how Wendy's strategy of neoliberal individualism works to craft Wilkerson into a micro-influencer. To reiterate, Wendy's raises Wilkerson to the status of influencer by utilizing neoliberal strategies that temporarily frame them as antagonistic to Wilkerson's goal, thus encouraging other users in his effort to overcome to challenge set before him.

One way this occurs is by reorienting the ethics and value of online participation from one rooted in the capitalist manipulation of the attention economy to one that celebrates communal online activity. The attention economy in this case being a condition where "the attention of each user is being translated into new forms of knowledge that is then utilized by corporations and advertising agencies to make a profile" (Celis, 2016, pg. 1). However, while Wendy's and other companies might prefer users who passively participate in advertising and marketing campaigns, by paying attention, albeit more intensely than Wendy's desires, users can push back against the individual capitalist ethics of the challenge.

To begin, if we think about this challenge as a microcosm for social mobility under neoliberal times, then the individual is responsible for exercising their presumed agency to reach a certain class or economic status. Furthermore, "the individual is taught that to have a responsibility for the care of others diminishes one's own identity, constraining the possibilities of the responsible individual. (Wrenn & Waller, 2017: p. 501). The individual, then, is the foci of affective investments in neoliberal economics meaning the individual stands as confirmation of the fidelity of the system. The individual encapsulates all that is possible and achievable within the socio-economic system.

Wendy's capitalizes on the strategy of exceptionalism by selecting Wilkerson as worthy of an opportunity for elevated social status and celebration. In many ways, Wilkerson can be considered the quintessential neoliberal entrepreneurial influencer. He is tasked with finding 18 million people who would freely help him towards his goal. On one hand, Wilkerson shows his entrepreneurial spirit by even asking in the first place, and then again when he readily accepts the challenge. The labor he performs in the comment section by interacting with other users and tagging celebrities puts his efforts on display. Thus Wilkerson engages in the work of influencing by utilizing the affordances of the platform to mobilize other users towards his goal.

His entrepreneurial spirit also transforms him into a micro-celebrity of sorts. As Angela Cirucci (2020: p. 42) argues, the structure and affordances of social media provide users the opportunity to achieve micro-celebrity status. Cirucci is interested in how "[t]he guiding structures and values that support microcelebrity practices are also guiding 'regular,' everyday users through a process of unintentional celebrification" (2020: p. 42). Throughout this challenge, Wilkerson gains a following that is supportive of his efforts. As his tweet spreads, so does he and his story and the various narratives attached to him. The structure of social media makes it such that he can gain notoriety within a few hours based on hashtags and trending topics. His exceptionalism is underscored more by the fact that he was unknown, and yet was able to find a way to mobilize his human capital to encourage people to follow him.

While Wendy's relies on the neoliberal impulse towards individual capital accumulation in the challenge, the investments that other users have in Carter resist this dominant frame. The conversation above

Figure 6. User Comments 6 (Twitter, 2017)

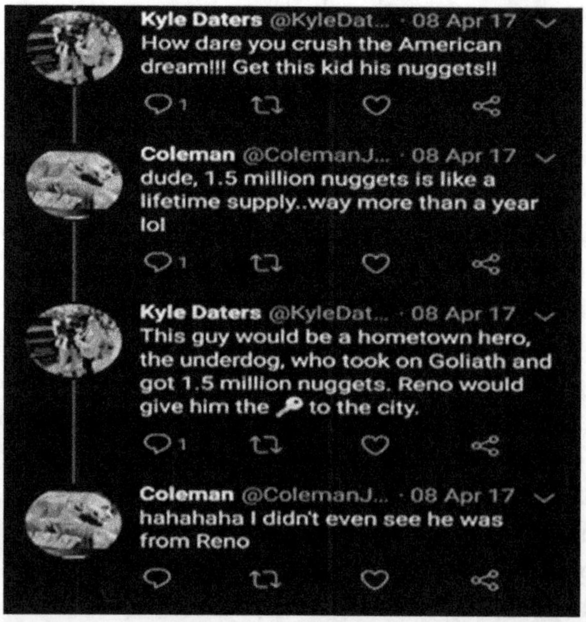

demonstrates the optimistic investments some users have in the outcome of the challenge. Wilkerson's success, according to the user, is more valuable for its symbolism--"The Hometown Hero" overcoming the Goliathan forces of a commercial entity to come out on top. The user mentions that Reno would probably give him the key to the city. Even when the other user expresses doubt about the possibility of it happening, the opposing user is not

speaking in realistic terms. Their affective investments are more abstract than the specifics of the challenge itself. This discourse is about recentering the power and influence of the communal rather than massive corporate or governmental institutions. When they say that Reno could even give Wilkerson the key to the city, it represents a reoriented value system where local and community recognition is more important than online fame. Thus, Carter's diminutive status as a Twitter user influences others to support him for the fulfillment of personal and communal narratives of triumph.

Interestingly, enough, Twitter utilizes this hyperbolic language on their trending topics page shown above: Even calling him a "man" ironically elevates his task to that of a Herculean status. Furthermore, such rhetoric frames Wilkerson and his mission as universally relatable. Additionally, Wilkerson's diminutive status as a high schooler with glasses, curly hair, and visible acne frames him as relatable, and thus worthy of positive affective investments. Wilkerson does garner some level of fame, as his local news station posted a story of Wilkerson being interviewed shortly after the beginning of this challenge[1]. So, the invocations of the hometown hero are not unfounded.

Wilkerson's mission characterizes his identity as an everyman. is used to induce support for his cause, despite the impossibility of shared benefit. Users who share the tweet may have an emotional orientation towards the challenge or the parties involved. According to Ho (2010), this affection is rooted in altruism, a quality that is integral to the success of the challenge. Even though retweeting is a basic function of Twitter, the act of sharing a post on which you are not the recipient of the prize requires a level of altruism or selflessness, a trait that runs counter to the neoliberal focus on the individual. Thus,

Figure 7. Carter featured on Twitter trending story

Figure 8. User Comments 7 (Twitter, 2017)

Wilkerson influences people through the combination of his own efforts, but also the way he is framed as an everyman whom everyday users desire to support.

Though the challenge could potentially highlight the efforts of Wilkerson himself, and while he is the topic of several articles and interviews it is the efforts of users, Wilkerson, and Wendy's that help to frame Wilkerson as an influencer worthy of support and ultimately provide an impetus for the labor that users engage in to aid him towards his goal.

This communal ethos is also a strategy for how users resist the next neoliberal strategy—the fixation on positivity.

3. NEOLIBERAL POSITIVITY

The final neoliberal strategy leveraged by Wendy's in this campaign is the tension between positivity and cynicism. By requiring such a high retweet value, Wilkerson begins this challenge as the underdog who must maintain positivity and faith in the face of a monumental task that inspires doubt in the most confident of people. However, this doubt springs users into action as they seek to defy the parameters of the challenge. Thus, despite being an individual, users have elected him as a worthy representative of their vicarious desires.

However, in the final instance, the reliance on neoliberal positivity is interrupted by the introduction of negative affects or emotions which, while detracting from Wilkerson's goal, represents the risks associated with investing in regular, unvetted individuals, the hopes and desires of an influential figure.

To begin, this positivity is an extension of the emphasis on the individual and the personal responsibility logic where people are encouraged to believe they contain within themselves the power to change their material or mental circumstances. This focus on happiness is, as Catherine Kingfisher (2013) notes, "[d]riven in part by the newly emergent sub-disciplines of positive psychology and happiness economics, and highlighted in local, national, and international fora, these new engagements with happiness signal a paradigm shift in orientations to governance – to work on society and work on the self" (p. 67). This happiness has pervaded virtually every aspect of our culture from self-help books on positive thinking to its manifestations in the form of wellness and fitness cultures.

The following conversations represent, in some way or another, a tension between hope and doubt, optimism and pessimism. The focus on positivity derives from a neoliberal discourse that says possibility rests in the mental capacity of the individual to believe or have faith. When they bear out, they have the potential to create affective utopias. However, as I will articulate drawing from the anti-feminist comments present under Wilkerson's post, these utopias are often about whose voices they exclude. Differences in opinion regarding faith, logic, and possibility create a precarious atmosphere where these competing affects structure the discourse between users and themselves as well as their communication with Wendy's.

Some users expressed doubt about the chances of the tweet reaching the requisite amount, claiming that it would be nearly impossible to beat the likes of Ellen whose selfie received almost 3.5 million retweets. One user, Jon Acuff, a NYT best-selling author expressed some doubt about reaching the goal. Another user responded, saying, "Records were made to be broken."

It is useful to juxtapose Wilkerson's tweet vs The Oscars Selfie as they represent different modes of virality. Ellen and her group selfie crashed the internet earning thousands of retweets a minute at one point. The selfie, taken at the Oscars and adorned with likable figures like Bradley Cooper and Meryl Streep, quickly became the most retweeted tweet at the time in part for its quirky and relatable authenticity, embodied through Ellen, despite its sophisticated setting. This image of an elegant and luxurious Hollywood condensed within a picture and distributed freely and quickly across the internet is representative of a celebrity-fueled culture where recognition of stars and figures provides a stimulus for sociality. Furthermore, these celebrities have an infrastructure of fame and influence that allows for their media to go viral. So, while the feat is impressive, it is still within the realm of what is "possible" and thus not representative of any sort of unique combination of effort and quality.

As compared to the Oscars Selfie, Carter Wilkerson represents the everyman--instead of ornate dreams of making it big in his career, Wilkerson's mission is relatable.

And beyond support, the words of encouragement posted by users highlight their investment in Wilkerson's regardless of whether they share in the prize. Wilkerson's eventual success can be interpreted as a moment whereby grassroots efforts by users resulted in the overturning of a particular model of social media stardom. Still, Acuff persists adding that he would give the user who tagged him 100 dollars if Wilkerson reached his goal. Even his financial offer is littered with doubt as he doesn't expect that he'll have to cough up the money. However, one comment under the tweet captures the tension between the folksy optimism of users and the perceived dominance of celebrity culture. One user added "Not everyone likes

those celebrities. Everyone likes when random dudes on the internet get free nuggets for a year." The user's position is that Wilkerson can reach his goal because he and his desires are more relatable to the average person than a selfie with people whose combined net worth amounts to billions of dollars. Thus the very doubt that is instituted by the formal structure of the challenge actually induces support for Wilkerson.

Finally, before I turn to the section on Wendy's strategy of affective management, another interesting phenomenon that plays out in the comment section includes people debating the logic of feminism.

Figure 9. User exchange (Twitter, 2017)

Figure 10. User Comments 8 (Twitter, 2017)

It is easy to miss the origins of this issue, but it began when Wilkerson, fueled by his entrepreneurial spirit, tagged @MeninistTweets under his tweet. The phrase "meninist" is a subversion of feminism and refers to people who advocate on behalf of me in the face of hegemonically constructed feminism and who generally mock its beliefs. It mostly has a pejorative association which explains why people reacted so negatively to him tagging a page like that. As a result, a debate ensued about social justice under a post about chicken nuggets.

I make this observation to discuss how the introduction of controversial topics interferes with the intended affective structure of this dialogue, ultimately hurting Wilkerson's chances of reaching his goal and calling into question his influencer status. Some have invested in this challenge as a kind of utopic space where people of disparate political and social interests can come together in support of a single mission. As a result, some users are bewildered to discover such an intense conversation occurring under this tweet. Some noted the contrasts between the light-hearted efforts of Wilkerson striving for chicken nuggets and the serious political discussion about feminism. The invocation of feminism or anti-feminism, in this case, is a reminder of the polemical debates that structure cultural discourses. The deterministic undertone of "we brought politics into this" is indicative of a particular emotional

Figure 11. User Comment 9 (Twitter, 2017)

Figure 12. User Exchange (Twitter, 2017)

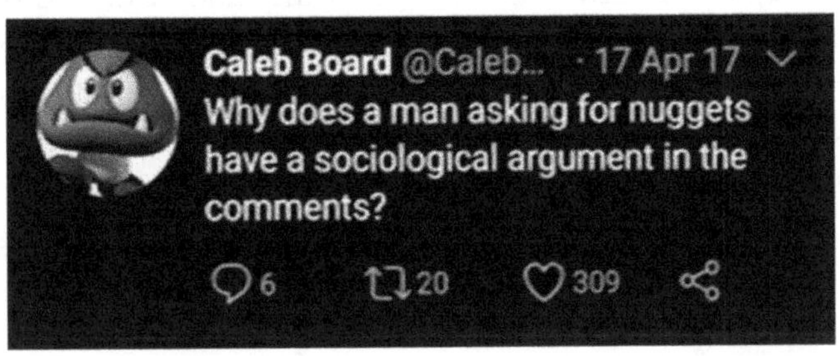

orientation--that even in such a positive and affirming space, the politics of difference always exists as a specter representing the potential for conflict.

Sarah Ahmed's *Willful Subjects* (2014) has much to offer regarding "woman" as an interrupter to joy. She says, "Feminist killjoys: those who refuse to laugh at the right points; those who are unwilling to be seated at the table of happiness…Feminist killjoys: willful women, unwilling to get along, unwilling to preserve an idea of happiness" (p. 2). Here, Ahmed highlights the way feminists are often viewed as unwilling to ignore injustice for the sake of others' happiness.

In this case, users could have chosen to ignore the fact that Wilkerson tagged @Meninist, or could have chosen not to acknowledge it, and by doing so, refrain from introducing a negative affective charge within the discourse. There is an impulse to designate this space as politics-free, but in speaking of the specific consequences of this purposeful ignorance, Ahmed warns,

> *…feminist critiques of the figure of "the happy housewife;" Black critiques of the myth of "the happy slave"; queer critiques of the sentimentalisation of heterosexuality as "domestic bliss…Around these specific critiques are long histories of scholarship and activism…teaching us how happiness is used to redescribe social norms as social goods. (Merha, 2017).*

Based upon Ahmed's observation, a contrast can be drawn between the feel-good sentiments produced in the RT challenge, and the seemingly objectively positive prospect of equality for women. However, for some, the conditions that produce this positivity depend on the absence of certain identities, and it is when those who are made absent by these gaps appear that the affective politics of positivity are disrupted.

What is the larger meaning of the observations I have brought to bear? Lauren Berlant's *Cruel Optimism* (2012) is a useful framework for discussing the tensions that exist between these particular users. What produces this precarity is the idea and awareness of difference. This difference in either identity or viewpoint creates uncertainty regarding allegiance and loyalty. Berlant describes cruel optimism in these very terms:

But, again, optimism is cruel when the object/scene that ignites a sense of possibility actually makes it impossible to attain the expansive transformation for which a person or a people risks striving; and, doubly, it is cruel insofar as the very pleasures of being inside a relation have become sustaining regardless of the content of the relation, such that a person or a world finds itself bound to a situation of profound threat that is, at the same time, profoundly confirming. (p. 2)

Wilkerson's challenge requires a certain amount of loyalty and efforts to disrupt his potential may be viewed as an affront to users and their efforts, and more importantly, the affective investments they have placed into Wilkerson and the challenge itself. Managing this loyalty is difficult when the challenge ostensibly requires 18 million retweets. As the comments are a necessary component of spreading this challenge, it also requires the mingling of people with different opinions. Put simply, the factors that make it necessary for Wilkerson to win, are the very factors that provide a challenge to his success. Thus while doubt provides a rationale for supporting Wilkerson and celebrating his ability to overcome, expressly negative sentiments such as sexist or misogynistic discourses can disrupt efforts to organically craft an individual into the figure of an influencer.

While this utopic space faces many challenges including the affects of doubt and pessimism, and the invocation of anti-feminist politics, it is the job of Wendy's to manage the overall affect of the comments and the challenge itself. What solidifies Wilkerson's status as an influencer, as I discuss in this final section, is Wendys' ability to occupy the role of corporate oppressor, urging other users to support Wilkerson in the first place, only to reverse their position in their comments as they reassure users that Wilkerson's success is possible. This results in an environment where Wilkerson's influence is bolstered by his backing by Wendy's.

4. MANAGING AFFECT

This final section highlights the ways that Wendy's solidifies Wilkerson's role as an influencer through the efforts of the Wendy's social media manager who encourages users to support the micro-influencer. This is in contrast to the efforts discussed in previous sections, however. By framing Wilkerson's success as a real possibility, Wendy's creates in Wilkerson an influencer who can achieve both his personal goal, and that of the Wendy's corporation.

Increasingly this emotional work is becoming a task that must be mediated through the digital world. In Affective Labor, Michael Hardt (1999) argues that immaterial labor has become a feature of capitalist exploitation. Emotional or affective labor is categorized as immaterial "even if it is corporeal and affective, in the sense that its products are intangible: a feeling of ease, well-being, satisfaction, excitement, passion-even a sense of connected-ness or community" (p. 96). During the execution of this challenge, which occurs over days and weeks, Wendy's must consistently monitor the sentiments of user comments. Though affective labor is associated with the service industry and in-person interactions, increasingly "that contact can be either actual or virtual. In the production of affects in the entertainment industry, for example, the human contact, the presence of others, is principally virtual, but not for that reason any less real" (p. 96) As an ongoing affair, the Wendy's SMM must be sensitive to negative emotions that may impact the spirit of the challenge or the brand itself. Many of the comments from the Wendy's account represent their attempts to maintain an atmosphere of levity, despite user cynicism.

In some ways, the exorbitant proposition backfires as the high number becomes the foci of the challenge for some users rather than the positive affective experience Wendy's is attempting to generate. They spend a significant amount of time trying to manage the doubt that users express. Despite knowing that Wilkerson reaching 18 million retweets is extremely unlikely, they must perform "sincerity" to give the impression that Wilkerson has a chance. There are numerous instances of Wendy's responding to users who are expressing doubt. They write comments like "that's the spirit there" or "it can definitely happen." These comments are a periodic reminder that the bet is real, but also position Wendy's as almost altruistic in their attempts to aid Wilkerson. Wendy's has a stake in the number of retweets as that translates into free advertising for them. But they are also assuming an affective position that aligns with Wilkerson himself. It allows Wendy's to appear accessible and down to earth like most of its consumers. If, for instance, Wendy's responded with a more cynical tone, it might have encouraged others to retweet Wilkerson more to prove them wrong, but it might have produced a negative affect of resentment towards Wendy's for proposing such an impossible challenge. Take as an example, the following conversations:

1. @BenBriggs34: "@Wendy's I bet @McDonalds would give him the nugget for the effort. Quit slacking. (2017) @Wendy's: "Just be patient, have faith, and let a beautiful thing happen" (2017)
2. @calekiekhaefer2: @Wendy's lower this for this man (2017) @ Wendy's: "He's doing well. Don't doubt the hustle" (2017)

Another user even compliments the way Wendy's is managing expectations. On that same thread user @Seth_Kaplan writes, "Wendy's is playing this perfectly" (2017). After posing such a challenge, it might have seemed cold and almost cruel to abandon Wilkerson in his efforts to meet the goal. In some ways, this constant encouragement is a manifestation of knowledge they already possess. If it is true that Wilkerson was going to receive the nuggets all along, and that they knew that, then their behavior in the comment section makes sense. Knowing that Wilkerson probably will not reach his goal, they must perform sincerity so that they are not depicted as unfair. Their unwillingness to budge on the number is not about being inflexible, but rather they know this number will serve as a motivation to further their goals as well as Wilkerson's. It's as if they placed the number that high such that it would be impossible to reach because the point of the tweet was not to reach the goal, but all the free advertising, creative communication, and interaction that it generated. In other words, there are no opposing sides, just a continuum of positive relationality. It also ultimately makes them look good if, despite Wilkerson failing to reach his goal, they are encouraging others to participate the entire time.

Further proof of this continuum of relationality is how the brand aligns itself with Wilkerson through the phrasing of "our boy."

@Wendy's: "It just keeps climbing. Our boy is gonna make it all the way"

This language creates a personal connection that shows the brand is not antagonistic to Wilkerson. When one user implies Wendy's is nervous about the tweet reaching even 1 million retweets, they coolly respond, "It's over 2 million," thus dispelling the notion that they are anything other than in full support of Wilkerson's mission. Another user responded to Wendy's and found the "our boy" phrasing humorous. @allygroom wrote, "" our boy' lol I love it. Like give him a commercial at this point...maybe one where its just him being surrounded by nuggets." This language of adoption brings Wilkerson, Wendy's, and their consumer base together into a closer affective relationship by implying the universality of the desire to see Wilkerson win.

Perhaps the best maneuver employed in this entire spectacle is the company's promise to donate $100,000 to Dave Thomas Foundation for Adoption if Wilkerson beats the Oscars Selfie. By making this offer, the overall goal of Wendy's in proposing this challenge is the accumulation of as much goodwill and social capital as possible. While offering Wilkerson the chance of a lifetime is one aspect of that goal, a donation of such magnitude sends a positive message about the brand—that they value real/offline issues as they do play. It also makes them somewhat more trustworthy as, even though some users are skeptical about whether Wendy's will hold up their end of the bargain, it's more believable that they would do so behind the weight of such an altruistic claim.

Ultimately, what makes this such a successful campaign is that Wendy's has mastered the art of "playing it cool" and appearing nonplussed despite criticisms that the number was too high. Their ability to manage affects such as anxiety and precarity contributes to the overwhelmingly positive view of the challenge. This kind of challenge risks being reduced to numbers and calculations, however. Users are aware of how they are exploited on social media. This does not mean that they are unwilling to engage in friendly challenges Given the right circumstances and the right person, users will divert their time and attention towards a spectacle like this. Furthermore, by creating a fun, easy-going atmosphere, Wendy's possibly endears itself to other consumers who see them as social.

On May 9th, 2017, when the popular tweet had reached around 3 million retweets, Wendy's announced that Wilkerson would receive his year's supply of chicken nuggets, while simultaneously fulfilling their promise to donate $100,000 to the Dave Thomas Foundation for Adoption. This outcome is evidence that, despite the company's status as a corporate giant, they can use social media to incur social capital through positive relationality with its audience. While offering Wilkerson the chance of a lifetime is one aspect of that goal, a donation of such magnitude sends a positive message about the brand—that they value real/offline issues as they do play. It also makes them somewhat more trustworthy as, even though some users are skeptical about whether Wendy's will hold up their end of the bargain, it's more believable that they would do so behind the weight of such an altruistic claim.

As a result of challenges like this, Wendy's is one of the most followed food brands on Twitter and has provided a blue-print for other companies as well. What makes Wendy's so successful in this realm is how interactions between the social media managers and Twitter users maintain a humorous, often-biting, but rarely unkind tone. In this way, they encourage a dialogue between users, one where user creativity and contributions matter within the discourse.

CONCLUSION

The Wendy's retweet challenge stands as an example of not simply how corporate entities leverage influencers to attract and motivate audiences, but how companies themselves work to actually create influencers and micro-celebrities for express purposes. By staging the challenge as the historical confrontation between producers and consumers of culture, Wendy's incentivizes users to support Wilkerson in his quest to achieve his simple goal, if only to see him live up to the challenge and topple a corporate giant, even if just metaphorically. However, by reversing their position, Wendy's ensures that, as an influencer, Wilkerson is rewarded his prize, but more importantly, that the labor of those involved in his success is celebrated as well.

Interestingly, almost two years later, Wendy's engages in a similar challenge when independent artist Chance the Rapper tweeted his desire to see the brand's spicy chicken nugget back on the menu. Announcing that if their tweet reached 2 million likes, they would acquiesce to the rapper's demands. While this spectacle did not have the reach of the original challenge, the tweet still received 1.8 million likes as of the time of this writing. And while the rapper's star status might seem at odds with their use of Wilkerson years prior, what connects these contrasting figures is the image of relatability, of desiring simple pleasures in life, and being able to leverage this relatability to contribute to the sense of parity between consumers and producers. Far from designating this challenge as a true site of equality, such challenges do offer momentary opportunities of connection mediated by users like Wilkerson, who, rather than expend the time and energy necessary to create a brand that Wilkerson can later leverage, can serve as temporary microcelebrity and hero for the masses.

REFERENCES

Ahmed, S. (2010). *The Promise of Happiness*. Duke University Press.

Ahmed, S. (2021). *Complaint!* Duke University Press.

@allygroom. (2019, April 11). "Our boy" lol i love it. like give him a commercial at this point... maybe one where its just him being surrounded by nuggets. Twitter. https://twitter.com/allygroom/status/851805748719964160

@BenBriggs34. (2017). @Wendys I bet @McDonalds would give him the nuggets for the effort. Quit slacking. Twitter. https://twitter.com/BenBriggs34/status/850091859808595968?s=19

Berlant, L. (2012). *Cruel Optimism*. Duke University Press.

Bueno, C. C. (2017). *The attention economy: Labour, time and power in cognitive capitalism*. Rowman & Littlefield International.

@calekiekhaefer2. (2017, Apr. 6). @Wendys lower this for this man. Twitter. https://twitter.com/calekiekhaefer2/status/850024284487548928?s=19

Campopiano, J. (2014). Memory, temporality, & manifestations of our tech-nostalgia. *Preservation. Digital Technology & Culture*, *43*(3), 75–85. doi:10.1515/pdtc-2014-0004

Cirucci, A. (2020). Facebook and Unintentional Celebrification. In C. Abidin & M. L. Brown (Eds.), *Microcelebrity Around the Globe: Approaches to cultures of internet fame* (pp. 33–47). Emerald Publishing Group.

@cwilso… (2017, Apri. 6). Records were made to be broken,haha! Twitter.

Duffy, B. (2015). The Romance of work: Gender and aspirational labour in the digital culture industries. *International Journal of Cultural Studies*, *19*(4), 441–457. doi:10.1177/1367877915572186

Duffy, B. E. (2017). *Not Getting Paid to Do What You Love: Gender, Social Media, and Aspirational Work*. Yale University Press. doi:10.12987/yale/9780300218176.001.0001

Fuchs, C. (2013). Digital prosumption labour on social media in the context of the capitalist regime of time. *Time & Society*, *23*(1), 97–123. doi:10.1177/0961463X13502117

Fuchs, C. (2014). Social Media and the Public Sphere. *tripleC: Communication, Capitalism & Critique. Open Access Journal for a Global Sustainable Information Society*, *12*(1), 57–101. https://doi.org/https://triple-c.at/index.php/tripleC/article/view/552

Gill, R., & Pratt, A. (2008). In The Social Factory?: Immaterial Labour, Precariousness and Cultural Work. *Theory, Culture & Society*, *25*(7-8), 1–30. doi:10.1177/0263276408097794

Hardt, M. (1999). Affective Labor. *Boundary, 26*(2), 89-100.

Ho, J. Y. C., & Dempsey, M. (2010). Viral marketing: Motivations to forward online content. *Journal of Business Research*, *63*(9-10), 1000–1006. doi:10.1016/j.jbusres.2008.08.010

Jarrett, K. (2017). *Feminism, Labour and Digital Media: The Digital Housewife*. Routledge, Taylor & Francis Group.

Jenkins, H., Green, J., & Ford, S. (2018). *Spreadable media: Creating value and meaning in a networked culture*. New York University Press.

Kanai, A., & Gill, R. (2020). Woke? affect, neoliberalism, marginalised identities and consumer culture. *New Formations*, *102*(102), 10–27. doi:10.3898/NewF:102.01.2020

Kaplan, A. M., & Haenlein, M. (2011). Two hearts in three-quarter time: How to waltz the Social Media/viral marketing dance. *Business Horizons*, *54*(3), 253–263. doi:10.1016/j.bushor.2011.01.006

Kingfisher, C. (2013). Happiness: Notes on History, Culture and Governance. *Health, Culture and Society (Pittsburgh, Pa.)*, *5*(1), 67–82. doi:10.5195/HCS.2013.145

Lissavoy, N. W. (2013). Pedagogy of the Impossible: Neoliberalism and the Ideology of Accountability. *Policy Futures in Education*, *11*(4), 423–435. doi:10.2304/pfie.2013.11.4.423

Littler, J. (2018). *Against Meritocracy: Culture, Power and Myths of Mobility*. Routledge.

Manzerolle, V. (2010). Mobilizing the audience commodity: Digital labour in a wireless world. *Ephemera*, *10*(4), 455–469.

Morgan, G., & Nelligan, P. (2018). *The creativity hoax: Precarious work in the Gig Economy*. Anthem Press. doi:10.2307/j.ctt1z27hwj

Niemeyer, K., & Siebert, O. (2023). Nostalgia, media, and technologies of the future. *Current Opinion in Psychology*, *50*, 101561. doi:10.1016/j.copsyc.2023.101561 PMID:36889050

Scharff, C. (2016). The Psychic Life of Neoliberalism: Mapping the Contours of Entrepreneurial Subjectivity. *Theory, Culture & Society*, *33*(6), 107–122. doi:10.1177/0263276415590164

@Seth_Kaplan. (2017, Apr. 6). Wendy's is playing this perfectly. Twitter. https://twitter.com/Seth_Kaplan/status/850149089928990721?s=19

Van Dijck, J., & Poell, T. (2013). Understanding social media logic. *Media and Communication*, *1*(1), 2–14. doi:10.17645/mac.v1i1.70

@Wendys. (2017a, Apr. 8). Attempt? It's still climbing. He's going to crush that record. Twitter. https://twitter.com/Wendys/status/850821313920991234?s=19

@Wendys. (2017b), Apr. 6). He's doing well. Don't doubt the hustle. Twitter. https://twitter.com/Wendys/status/850024538305961984?s=19

@wendys. (2017c, Apr. 7). It can definitely happen. Twitter. https://twitter.com/Wendys/status/850443001428144129?s=19

@Wendys. (2017d, Apr. 9). It's over 2 million. Twitter. https://twitter.com/Wendys/status/851195851972202498?s=19

@Wendys. (2017e, Apr. 6). Just be patient, have faith, and let a beautiful thing happen. Twitter. https://twitter.com/Wendys/status/850092618881130496?s=19

@Wendys. (2017f, Apr. 7). That's the spirit right there. Twitter. https://twitter.com/Wendys/status/850418239729545216?s=19

Woodcock, J., & Johnson, M. R. (2018). Gamification: What it is, and how to fight it. *The Sociological Review*, *66*(3), 542–558. doi:10.1177/0038026117728620

Wrenn, M. V., & Waller, W. (2017). Care and the Neoliberal Individual. *Journal of Economic Issues*, *51*(2), 495–502. doi:10.1080/00213624.2017.1321438

ENDNOTE

1 https://mynews4.com/news/local/nuggets-watch-reno-teen-honored-on-nevada-senate-floor

Chapter 5
Influencers Using Instagram to Promote Change in the Knitting Community

Tricia M. Farwell
https://orcid.org/0000-0003-2209-9411
Middle Tennessee State University, USA

ABSTRACT

This chapter examines the online discussions and resulting changes in an online crafting community on Instagram. Using Kelman's framework of attitude change, this study of qualitative textual analysis looked at how micro-influencers in the fiber crafting community identified a problem and advocated for changes within the community. The use of the social media platform allowed for marginalized voices to share their lived experiences in their own words, unfiltered by mainstream media. The resulting discussion caused a shift in the community to create a safe space for marginalized voices to express their lived experiences and gain support from allies. The findings in this study show how micro-influencers created a narrative on Instagram and provided motivation for others to internalize change.

INTRODUCTION

On January 7, 2019, a blog post by a prominent businesswoman unintentionally sparked a conversation about white privilege that disrupted perceptions in the fiber crafting community and businesses serving them. The post was the catalyst that opened eyes and began a discussion on how the community, both online and offline, treated its Black and Indigenous People of Color (BIPOC) members. The words in the blog were "not wrong, per se, just that the tone felt like [she] thought India only existed to be all those things for" her (Saxena, 2019). The post was criticized for perpetuating white privilege and a colonizing agenda. The conversations that followed on social media and the impact of those conversations on business practices are the focus of this chapter.

It is well established that online discussions can be used as a way of presenting information to shape discourse and influence the public through the selection of words and phrases. Often, influencers and

DOI: 10.4018/979-8-3693-0912-4.ch005

businesses use social media as a way to directly communicate with their audience without others interpreting or changing the message. This direct, real-time communication, added to the fact that the person presenting the information may be seen as a trustworthy member of the online community with whom they are communicating, may make for a larger impact than messages from those outside the community. The more trust an audience places in a source, the more likely the audience members will respond to the messages used in the conversation (Druckman, 2001).

Social media platforms have made it increasingly easier for less-heard voices to have an outlet to share their views and build a following in which their opinions are not only shared by them, but amplified by others. Thus, minority voices can be heard without being translated and they can become community influencers promoting their message in their own words. This kind of message is privileged among online communities as 92 percent of people surveyed said they trusted influencers over traditional advertising (Linquia, 2019). It is clear that community members trust community insiders for messages of products, services and viewpoints online.

Instagram had long been a platform embraced by the fiber-crafting community as a place that allowed businesses to show their products (yarn, fiber, and related items) and for crafters to show their skills. For many small businesses selling fiber products, Instagram is the primary way to gain awareness of their products and services through self-promotion and user promotion. The company, Fringe Supply Co, was no exception. Bags sold through Fringe Supply Co. owned by Karen Templer, a maker in the fiber crafting community, were seen as the "Birkin of knitting bags" (Saxena, 2019). However, Templer's blog post, "2019: My year of color," triggered a community discussion that went in a direction that Templer neither intended nor anticipated. For Templer, the post focused on her excitement about her plans for the new year, which included a trip to India. She shared her story of growth, but also that international travel was still "so daunting" (Templer, "My Year," 2019). Templer added "This year's resolution: Wear color. Be color. Live in color" (2019). She brought the color and travel threads together by informing readers that a trip to India was one of her 2019 goals. She mentioned that she passed up a trip to India when she was younger because "[t]o a suburban midwestern [sic] teenager with a severe anxiety disorder, that was like being offered a seat on a flight to mars[sic]" (Templer, "My Year," 2019). Due to Templer's words and the popularity of Fringe Supply Co.'s products, members of the community saw and commented on the blog post. However, not all the comments were positive. Although Templer did issue an apology for her blog post and explained how she was going to make changes to herself and her business, Fringe Supply Company closed its doors in August 2020.

Although many of the initial responses to the post made by the owner of the business reflected that some members thought the fiber crafting community was already inclusive, as the influencer-led discussion progressed, a different view of the community emerged. Over the months that followed, BIPOC makers and businesses used their online platforms to create a narrative that demanded others hear them. These conversations, started on social media, have led to widespread changes in the knitting community including representation in mainstream magazines such as *Vogue Knitting* and movements supporting size inclusivity in patterns and representation. Although it is difficult to determine the number of knitters worldwide, Ravelry, a web community founded in 2007, developed specifically surrounding fiber crafting has approximately 9 million users with 5-6 million page views per day (Ravelry About, 2020).

This study explores how micro-influencers used Instagram and a post by a prominent businesswoman to create a narrative through curated content and shared experiences as a means for discussion and motivation towards diversity, equity, and inclusion within the niche community of fiber crafting. Using Kelman's framework, this chapter shows how an online discussion started with influencers who accepted the role they had in influencing a community (compliance). The community responded by identifying the influencers as having the influence, being the voice of the topic and leaders in the change. Eventually, a portion of the community internalized the change as evidenced by their continued discussion and expansion of inclusivity in the community.

While researchers have explored the effect of other social media tools on student movements (Bosch, 2017; Bosch & Mutsvario, 2017; Yan, Pegoraro, & Watanabe, 2018), no studies could be found regarding the use of Instagram specifically and solely in social movements. Using the fiber crafting discussion as a case study, this study explores how micro-influencers used Instagram to promote discussion, connectivity, and change. The outcome of this crafting-connected online discussion opened doors for BIPOC and other marginalized voices to share their experiences, their pain, and their desire to see the community be as inclusive as some had thought it already was.

LITERATURE REVIEW

Social Media Platforms and Influencers

Businesses are often told that a best practice for their social media presence is to create a community for their users. *Forbes*, for example, lists 16 suggestions for leaders to use online interaction to create an "inspiring" community. Included in those suggestions are tips such as responding to comments and sharing audience content that is engaging, provide content that is in line with the brand story, showcase active participants and create a space where people feel safe to share their views (Forbes, 2021).

Often, these community includes influencers who are considered leaders or celebrities in the community for their style, viewpoint, and shared content. These influencers often are engaged to promote and sing the praises of the business and products. Influencers are not business employees, they are social media users whose online postings and conversations have an impact on audience members and businesses (Freberg et al., 2011). For the fiber community as a whole, these online communities created both by businesses and influencers are essential ways to communicate about new products and services as most of the businesses online are small, independent organizations without the resources to create a national advertising campaign. Therefore, these business owners turn to social media such as Instagram to promote their products through original postings, test makes (where community members apply, are selected, and make an item using a pattern and/or fiber by the company, post their progress online, and tag and provide feedback to the business, but the community member keeps the finished product), sample makes (where the business provides all the materials necessary to make an item and the selected community member makes the item, posts on social media, and sends the completed project back to the business to be used for promotion) and other activities to draw users into a conversation.

Although social media users are third-party endorsers of products, services, and businesses, they too are aware of the need to be strategic in their communications to keep followers engaged. Those deemed successful in engaging followers could potentially rise to the level of social media influencers who have an active platform to express their views. While macro-influencers are easily identified, micro-influencers (those with follower counts ranging from 10,000-100,000) may have a larger impact on their communities in that they have closer relationships with their followers than their macro-influencer counterparts (Hart, 2017; Pierucci, 2018). The appeal of social media influencers for businesses and users is that their followers see the influencer as a trusted resource for information and advice (Liu et al. 2012; Freberg et al., 2011). Although society may be more aware of the fact that influencers receive free products and/ or compensation for their online support of organizations, research shows that micro-influencers still carry a significant amount of credibility with their followers and therefore are trusted voices which can impact action such as purchase decisions (Crnjak-Karanović, 2023).

Due to the ease of access, social media platforms have made it increasingly easier for less-heard voices to have an outlet to share their views and build a following in which their opinions are not only shared by them, but also amplified by others. Thus, minority voices can be heard without being translated and they can become community influencers promoting their message in their own words. This kind of message is privileged among online communities as 92 percent of people surveyed said they trusted influencers over traditional advertising (Linquia, 2019). In 2021, Nielsen reported that 71 percent of people surveyed "completely or somewhat" trusted opinions about brands and product placements by influencers (Getting, 2022). It is clear that community members trust community insiders for messages of products, services, and viewpoints online.

Digital Activism and Online Participation

Increasingly, activists are turning to social media and other digital platforms as a communication method. Bennett and Segerberg (2012) found distinguishing features in frames between movements that were "collective action" supported by advocacy organizations and "connective action" those that were not associated with advocacy organizations (p. 739). These self-organized movements, which are characterized by connective action, have content creators who focus their communication on "personal action frames" (Bennett & Segerberg, 2012, p. 756). These frames are then shared over social networks which allow others to encounter messages on a more personal level through their community connections.

Advocacy groups, both formal and informal, have used social media to advance their causes. The power and consequences of social media have also been studied in connection to political protest. Freelon et al. (2018) argued that social media not only serves as a communication tool for protests, but also can be measured in terms of power through participation numbers, unified messages, and commitment. When looking at Twitter conversations surrounding Black Lives Matter, Freelon et al. (2018) showed social media can be a dominant outlet for movements to communicate with others and used effectively to draw media attention to a topic.

Smith et al. (2019) argued that the connection between participation in activism and social media's influence was more complex than previous studies had shown. Although others have characterized activism on social media as "slacktivism" due to the minimal effort needed to participate (Bastos et al., 2015), Smith et al. (2019) found that social media activism could both help and hurt protests. Although the researchers found it difficult to pinpoint the true effectiveness of social media activism, they did find that those who used social media in their efforts may have felt more empowered in having their voices heard without filters.

Using social media as a platform to initiate change is also seen in the retail industry. Fashion discussions online, specifically plus-sized fashion, have been a significant site of change spurred by plus-sized bloggers using their platform to promote body and size inclusiveness (Scaraboto & Fischer, 2013). Online tools such as blogs, social media platforms, and sites such as change.org, allow those speaking for change to motivate others to join their cause and amplify their voices. These tools allow creators to show the level of support for their viewpoints, vocally question current practices, and, perhaps, even change organizational policies and behaviors (Minocher, 2019). While it could be argued that simply signing a change.org petition is a form of slacktivism, Minocher found that the platform's focus on results promoted engagement beyond the signature.

Sometimes, however, using social media to amplify voices may distract from the cause. In looking at the online beauty community, Lawson (2021) found that the drama happening around conversations overshadowed the change the community was trying to enact. Specifically, Lawson found that using call-out measures and not connecting the incidents to larger social issues left the online beauty community focusing on the drama instead of communicating the need for lasting change (2021).

Case Background

Bags sold through Fringe Supply Co. owned by Karen Templer, a maker in the fiber crafting community, were seen as the "Birkin of knitting bags" (Saxena, 2019). However, Templer's blog post, "2019: My year of color," triggered a community discussion that went in a direction that Templer neither intended nor anticipated. For Templer, the post focused on her excitement about her plans for the new year, which included a trip to India. She shared her story of growth, but also that international travel was still "so daunting" (Templer, "My Year," 2019). Templer added, "This year's resolution: Wear color. Be color. Live in color" (2019). She brought the color and travel threads together by informing readers that a trip to India was one of her 2019 goals. She mentioned that she passed up a trip to India when she was younger because "[t]o a suburban midwestern [sic] teenager with a severe anxiety disorder, that was like being offered a seat on a flight to mars[sic]" (Templer, "My Year," 2019).

Due to Templer's words and the popularity of Fringe Supply Co.'s products, members of the community saw and commented on the blog post. However, not all the comments were positive. One of the first BIPOC to criticize and share the criticism was Korina Yoo, @thecolormustard on Instagram. Yoo annotated the blog post and shared it through her Instagram story. Soon, her story was shared by others. As the stories were shared across the platform, other BIPOC added their thoughts and experiences to the posts. The discussion changed from a post about personal change for the new year to showcasing tone-deaf wording and how the blog post exemplified white privilege of colonizers over the colonized. As the discussion continued, Maria Tusken of Tusken Knits posted a YouTube video regarding her thoughts on white privilege in the knitting community. Tusken's video, now deleted, was a stand in support of white fiber crafters who might have felt "attacked" in the discussion. The only post left of Tusken's interaction with the online discussion is a somewhat rambling, video explaining why she is leaving Instagram. In this video, she accuses BIPOC makers of "trolling" and "bullying" (Tusken, 2019).

On January 12, 2019 Templer posted an apology to her blog. In it she addressed the criticism by saying that she "spent the week listening hard, learning, . . . And thinking about all the things I can do . . . To be more inclusive and supportive of people of color" (Templer, "Words," 2019). She included a recap of what people found offensive in the original post and thanked @thecolormustard for clearly annotating the post. Templer closed by repeating her apology and stating she was working to educate herself beginning by reading *The Origin of Others* by Toni Morrison.

Social Influence and Problem Solving

Long before social media became so pervasive, Kelman (1958) and others explored the nature of change brought about by communication efforts. Specifically, Kelman stated, "it is not enough to know that there has been some measurable change in attitude; . . . we would also want to know what kind of change it is" (51). Kelman's research led to a framework to be applied to forms of social influence which impact a person's decision making. Specifically, the framework identified compliance, identification and internalization as key factors to message acceptance. Compliance is "when an individual accepts influence . . . to achieve favorable reaction from" the community (53). Identification is "when an individual accepts influence . . . to establish or maintain" their identity within a specific community (53). Internalization is "when an individual accepts influence . . . because the content . . . is intrinsically rewarding . . . [and] it is congruent with his value system" (53). In identifying this framework, Kelman provided a basis to evaluate the depth and motivations of message acceptance that also applies to social media messaging. This framework provides keys to how and when an individual will react to messaging on social media relating to issues that have been presented on the platform.

METHODOLOGY

To study the conversation surrounding white privilege in the online knitting community, the researcher conducted a qualitative textual analysis of select story highlights from micro-influencers within the fiber crafting community on Instagram. Textual analysis can be used by researchers to discover how people "make sense of the world" (McKee, 2003). Through textual analysis, researchers can explore how people construct their world and their identities. Instagram story highlights were collected from accounts that were active in the online knitting community in continuing and amplifying the conversation on the issues BIPOC members faced, and who had follower counts of at least 8000. This follower count placed all the accounts studied in the range of micro-influencers. Micro-influencers are seen as strong voices in a niche market and are considered to be a true voice in the community who are still approachable by community members. These micro-influencers were identified by being shared through other users' Instagram stories and being referenced in blog posts, including posts by Karen Templer responding to and engaging with the discussion. Although the online discussion started in early January, 2019, data collection and analysis spanned several months to allow for the discussion to develop or fade out via the online platform.

Instagram proved the ideal platform for the micro-influencers to engage the fiber crafting community in the discussion in that it allowed users to easily create content using words and images, allowing users to tag, save, and categorize content using hashtags and stories, and providing ease of sharing of content by the creator and other users. It should be noted that the online conversation did not appear to develop as part of any sponsored organization or advocacy group, but as a natural grassroots conversation in reaction to Templer's blog post. As the online discussion progressed, the highlights from 6 key micro-influencers were selected for textual analysis: @thecolormustard (Korina Yoo) with more than 18,000 followers, @ su.krita (Sukrita Mahon) with more than 16,500 followers, @ocean_bythesea (Ocean Rose) with more than 25,000 followers, @transitory (Candace Last name unknown) with more than 8,500 followers, @ tina.say.knits (Tina Tse) with more than 20,000 followers, and @astitchtowear (Grace Anna Farrow) with more than 11,500 followers. Additionally, these accounts were often referenced and thanked for leading the discussion about racism in the knitting community by others in the fiber crafting community. Four of the six micro-influencers (Grace Anna Farrow, Sukrita Mahon, Korina Yoo, and Ocean Rose) subsequently created a blog called *Unfinished Objec*t (unfinishedobject.com) in which they intended to continue their work as makers, writers and disruptors (https://www.unfinishedobject.com/about). A 2023 review of the *Unfinished Object* website shows little action since 2019.

Each of the identified micro-influencers had created easily identifiable highlight reels on Instagram with tags such as "KT stuff," "Racist Knitters," and "Diversity." The researcher captured the Instagram story highlights using Blueberry FlashBack Express Recorder, a free program that allows users to capture video and audio directly from their computer screen. Video capture occurred from April 17 to May 17, 2019. The researcher selected story highlights for recording and analysis because of their longevity. Instagram stories disappear within 24-hours and, therefore, were no longer accessible, however, highlights are available until the user deletes the highlight. Each of the micro-influencers saved several of their stories as story highlights. Altogether, there were approximately two hours of story highlight footage to analyze. Often community members referred to and shared these saved highlights as part of the ongoing discussion.

The researcher reviewed each collected highlight multiple times. The purpose of this was not to provide a usage count of certain words or phrases, but to allow for a nuanced interpretation of the discussion through a "long preliminary soak" (Hall, 1975, p. 15) in the captured highlights. This was followed by taking extensive notes which allowed for content topics to be grouped and for themes, patterns, and experiences with keywords and phrases noted. Repeated content was not removed from the analysis as the story highlights are carefully curated by the micro-influencer and repetition most likely signified the importance of the content and reinforced the message the micro-influencer was communicating. Although many of the items in the story highlights were clickable, click-through content was not analyzed due to the fact the researcher and micro-influencer could not guarantee viewers clicked through to read the full post.

RESULTS

The conversation surrounding Karen Templer's blog post and the impact on those in the fiber crafting community started as an educational effort by influencers, but grew to have a long-lasting and expansive impact on the members and businesses that serve the fiber crafting community. While each micro-influencer created and curated information about the discussion, the highlights often contained shared content from other users that was useful, well-written, supportive of their stance, or needing support. Due to this extensive sharing, there was no one unifying look to the posts and in some cases, it was difficult to tell original versus shared content. The posts had a variety of visual approaches ranging from text on a solid color background, images with very little or no words, and a combination of text and words. All capitalization and punctuation from quotes have been maintained from the original post. However, spelling has been corrected when it was an obvious typing error and the layout has not been maintained.

Education and Lived Experiences

At the start of the online conversation, many of the initial posts by the identified influencers focused on bringing attention to the hurt brought on by Karen Templer's blog post and deconstructing the language to reveal what the words in the post spoke to members of the BIPOC community. In starting the conversation, the influencers were in the compliance stage of social change. Their influence served to both inform the community of what was happening and get reactions from community members. Through the content posted, the messaging was to educate both the business owner and the community regarding the content and the impact of the messages. These types of posts ranged from detailed analysis such as "so, you're talking about how scary and 'foreign' the world outside america is . . . and then to appease that fear, you cite increasing globalization and westernization . . . so really, aren't you actually saying that you've decided to take this bucket list trip because you've realized that this world will bend over backwards to accommodate the likes of you?" (@thecolormustard, 2019). Another analysis post said, "caution: romanticization, exocitization, fetishization. diminishing someone's cultural background to a stupid fashion fad? equating a trip to india to a flight to mars? that's quite a literal take on alienation if I've ever seen one. i thought you had a lifelong obsession with india? But only for the pink and not for the food? why do you regret it? Because it's 'woke' now?" (@thecolormustard, 2019). Through these posts, @thecolormustard asked people to see beyond their personal point-of-view and think about the larger implications and how seeing these words, while perhaps not meant to hurt, had marginalized people and reduced their lives to a limited view through a reductionist lens.

As more people joined in the discussion, the theme of education expanded beyond the analysis of the original blog post, thus showing that the community was joining in with the communication. However, although they were joining in, the original influencers were still seen as identifying with and being the face of the conversation. Some of the posts were pointed out in trying to show how different races would receive different reactions in comments and in life. One post questioned, "how is it that a white woman can add 'going to india' to her 2019 resolutions and receive praise for following her heart, but when we come here to make a living, we're met with degradation and violence?" (@thecolormustard, 2019). Other posts asked people to examine their reactions to the educational topics. In directly addressing designers in the community, @su.krita said, "Speaking of designers talking about this: If you are saying shit like 'I know Karen meant no harm' you are part of the problem and I see you. If you don't cite poc voices and instead niceify the issue, you are part of the problem and I. See. You." These posts which asked members of the knitting community to look at their own values regarding their reactions to the conversation continued to bring the conversation to a personal level. With this request, community members were asked to internalize the conversation and the results as part of their value systems. The problem was no longer something that happened to someone else, it was something that the community needed to address.

To further illuminate the long-standing nature of the issue, Yoo noted that the discussion of racism in the knitting community did not start in 2019, "but to say that white women noticed it when it happened to Karen Templer is more accurate. . .. That's shitty, but if that's what it takes to get the conversation started, I have trouble spending a lot of time feeling bad about it" (Saxena, 2019). Templer's post was the tipping point for BIPOC in the community and served as a starting point to share lived experiences. As Lim points out, it is not unusual for movements to have a trigger point. Movements are often a mix of long-term factors, short-term issues, and a triggering event (Lim, 2018). The stories that BIPOC was able to share online reflected widespread experiences they were forced to confront for years. Templer's blog post only served as a provoking incident for the much-needed discussion and the Instagram platform provided a space for multiple BIPOC voices to express their views.

As part of educating the community, @su.krita opened a safe space where members of the BIPOC community were able to direct message their lived experiences connected to the fiber community to the account holder for her to re-post anonymously. The lived experiences when shopping in yarn stores included:

- Being ignored, not being asked if help was needed, or being locked out of conversations
- Being followed when others aren't

- Being told "you're not that dark," being asked "what are you," or being asked if knitting was "common among black people"
- Being told where the "cheaper yarns" are, being questioned if they could afford yarn or having to prove worth by donating/buying expensive yarn
- Missing representation in yarn shops or not being asked to teach classes
- Having to keep hands in sight while shopping for fear of being accused of stealing
- Having to use white or white passing models to showcase designs.

However, just learning from these experiences was not enough. The influencers directly addressed the community as a whole throughout their posts to draw readers into the conversation and to personalize it. As @tina.say.knits wrote, "You saying my lived, and living, experiences are something else other than what it is, is dismissing my experiences completely. Everyone is intersectional. Sure, you might have experienced something similar but it isn't what the story is about. So please, do not come into anyone['s] spaces to tell them their experience is anything other than what they have experienced. If you can't relate because you aren't Asian American or Asian minority living in a predominantly white country, then you can take it in and understand that these stories exist and to be compassionate about our stories. It can't always be about you when it's clearly a lived experience someone else had" (@tina.say.knits, 2019).

As part of the educational experience, members of the BIPOC community shared how to process lived experiences if they were not experiences that were familiar to the audience. One post said, ". . . I share my lived experiences to inspire, to spark, to educate, to be some kind of light to those who can relate, to those who are still living it. If you can not relate to the situation, do not compare it to something else. Do not take the context on my lived experience and turn it into something more palatable to your understanding. Do not tell me my lived, and living, experience is that of a 'generational' one rather than a 'cultural' one. If you can't understand in the context, I have shared my experience, then the story isn't for you. The story is then for you to be compassionate rather than relate to" (@tina.say.knits, 2019). Another post shared, ". . . Word choice is important. Educate yourself on the words you should use. And if someone corrects you, DO NOT TAKE OFFENSE. Open your heart and realize you just hurt another human being and be bigger than yourself and apologize" (@transitory, 2019).

Another component of the education and lived experiences discussion was asking the audience what were seemingly simple questions such as how many people of color were they following or how many hashtags supporting people of color were they following. For example, @ocean_bythesea said, "I've changed my mind. Im [sic] not going to talk about this whole issue of racism in the knitting community. Im [sic] actually triggered. Ok maybe I will talk about it. I live this every. Single. day. All of these micro-aggressions add up. Pile up. leaving us near bundled on the floor. I'll post a few questions and then collect my thoughts. I would really appreciate it if you can answer one, a few or all. If you can't, ask yourself why. Start there." These questions had a request for accountability which asked the audience to explore why they were or were not following accounts and hashtags supporting the BIPOC community.

Additionally, the educational and lived experiences theme took on another feature of sharing that having these conversations about racism and lived experiences was difficult for everyone involved, no matter their race. This brought some in the community to see the problem from the viewpoint of the group and not of an individual. Despite the pain, those leading the conversation felt it was necessary to share and continue the discussion. One post said, "These conversations are not easy to have. It takes a lot of energy and patience to effectively get the right message across, to make a progressive impact and not encourage negative and unconstructive dialogue. But silence isn't the answer. Being uncomfortable is not an excuse for not having the conversation. We live in a time where we can make effective change and we should be" (@tina.say.knits, 2019) The account @transitory said, "The whole point of this conversation is that knitters who are POC, don't get to simply 'escape' being a POC. This is our lived experience. Dismissing that is incredibly privileged and ignorant. Check. Your. Privilege." Additionally, "As it has been said before: it is a privilege to learn about racism. Rather than having to experience it your entire life" (@transitory, 2019).

As more members of the community engaged with the content, they became active problem solvers, but not necessarily self-supported problem solvers. Instead of seeking information from a variety of sources, they turned to the influencers for answers. Thus, it became necessary to remind people that members of the BIPOC community were not on the platform to answer everyone's questions and that people could make the effort to educate themselves (@thecolormustard, 2019). Others took this as an opportunity to reveal the emotional stress that one places on BIPOC in expecting them to serve as the educational resource. A post shared by @transitory said that "this is an emotionally labor intensive and draining conversation" for those who identify as BIPOC (2019). Thus, the message to educate was multi-layered in that not only did the influencers request that followers be educated on the topic, but also that they should educate themselves and not expect someone else to do all the work. A post in @ ocean_bythesea's highlights summarized, "This wasn't our job to do, but the fear of not being represented is greater" (2019). Perhaps the most difficult expression of the weight of educating other crafters was expressed in a highlight from @tina.say.knits as she shared that "I also found myself, a few months in, at a point where I felt that the pain I was sharing, mine and others, was being consumed as twisted entertainment, trauma porn. There was pressure to write posts with long captions every day to continue the conversation, whilst white companies and makers got away with saying noting or posting a vague 'I support diversity' message" (2019).

In leading the conversation, the influencers showed that the views they expressed were more than surface-level problems of a single person. These views were expressed to gain a reaction from the community and served as a platform for the influencers to express an identity surrounding inclusiveness. Their sharing led others in the community to become active problem solvers and internalize the messaging of being more sensitive towards and thoughtful about the impact their language and viewpoints have on others. Due to this internalization of content, after the education messaging had taken root, the community embraced messaging that led to allyship and helped correct the identified problem.

Being an Ally

These posts showed the wide range of actions and factors that go into allyship and helped community members decide how best to become an ally and engage in the conversation in a meaningful way. The allyship posts were the community's ways of expressing identification and internalization of the change promoted by the influencers. As with the educational posts, the content of this part of the conversation evolved from easy entry points such as sharing of posts by members of the BIPOC community, sharing posts on how to be an ally, sharing educational materials such as a link to Layla F. Saad's book (which was a free download at the time), *Me and White Supremacy*, to a deeper commitment of supporting BIPOC makers through buying their products or supporting them with a Ko-Fi donation, and curating lists of BIPOC makers who could be supported by others. Thus, the messages of how followers could support BIPOC makers could be enacted at several levels depending on the reader's status, finances, and engagement levels. The micro-influencers estimated that during the time they were actively sharing the link to *Me and White Supremacy*, users downloaded the book approximately 5,000 times.

While the notion of sharing posts seems to be a simple action with a minimal level of engagement from the followers, influencers positioned this request as a meaningful show of support but also something that needed to be done with care. As @thecolormustard said, "and to any other white person following me, if you: don't have any POC friends who you actually LOVE and can take the back seat and listen to without feeling the need to soothe your with guilt our [sic] defend your white fragility . . . check yourself before you share your 'opinions.' because if you don't, you're doing harm" (@thecolormustard, 2019). The micro-influencers also pointed out that by not speaking up or sharing posts, people who claimed they were supporting members of the BIPOC community were actually doing harm. For instance, @ su.krita said "Your silence on this issue is very loud to me. If you are a white knitter friend, and have seen this, and not spoken to me, nor shared anything publicly, please now that I see this. It is not okay." For those using the explanation that they were trying to think about what to say or how to say it, it was pointed out how that was not an acceptable response for long. As @su.krita said, "Ok, deep breaths. It's been a week and some people are still 'processing' what it means that racism is a reality in the knitting community. This little bit of hesitation on your part speaks V O L U M E S to me and every other poc. It tells us you don't care! You never cared! And that your spaces are NOT safe for everyone, no matter how cute/grammable you think they are."

With the calls to share the messages about the identified problem in the knitting community and to amplify BIPOC voices being heard and enacted, a concern arose for thoughtful sharing, not just mindless reposting. Thus, the influencers were asking for more than a person's showing they identify with the community through sharing someone's content to actually internalizing the content as they became active problem solvers. Sharing opened the door for people to see the posts, but internalizing the content promoted change and protection of the BIPOC voices. Eventually, calls for thoughtfulness and protection were included in allyship as people amplifying voices needed to consider consequences. As @thecolormustard said, "a gentle reminder to those amplifying our voices: please also consider what kind of traffic you're bringing to us. We need your vocal support at our doorsteps too. starting is one thing, follow-through is another." The call for protection and thoughtfulness extended beyond the online platform as @astitchtowear wrote, "How many times do you see nonblack people risk their bodies for black people? How often can we expect protection? How much of how we learned to move through this world is with the expectation that we won't receive it?" In other words, the influencers were having their messaging being shared by and among supporters in the community, but with the pervasiveness of social media, the messaging also went beyond the supporters and the intended community.

Community Change

Ultimately, the conversation asked that people "make an accountable effort to learn, improve and change" (@astitchtowear, 2019) in order to better themselves and the community. The goal, however, was a wider understanding and safer, more inclusive place that was more representative of the fiber community. In other words, the influencers asked that the community internalize the change. The depth and range of the conversation was noted by Layla F. Saad, "What's most striking to me however is just how "big" this discussion has been in that community. Because it tells me that it has probably been a very white-cantered space for a v long time. I'm happy to see many people from that community coming to my work. AND, I would remind all of those doing so (and anyone doing my workbook), that this is not a thought experiment or personal development experience. This is real work. Hard work. Necessary work." Her post was shared by several members of the community. The micro-influencers reminded members of the fiber community "How about using all the energy you are putting into your next knit along into some effort to better the community for all of us . . . Just to be completely clear. I am suggesting putting in the work to dismantle white supremacy within knitting instead of actually knitting." (@astitchtowear, 2019). The request, simply put, was to not just endorse the conversation with a like or share, but to truly internalize the discussions and outcomes for solving the identified problem.

The importance of the conversation was highlighted through comments such as "it's week four, fiber friends. much longer for many of us, actually. again, are you still with us? And by that, I mean: do you understand why we can't hug it out?" (@thecolor mustard, 2019). By keeping the conversation going and not allowing others to divert the messaging to other topics, the call for change in the community stayed at the forefront. People acknowledged that, "When someone within our community does harm we want to believe that it was unintentional because we don't want to damage the shared bond of community. . . It follows that we want to believe that if they just became aware of the harm that they would find a way to correct it and do better." (@astitchtowear, 2019). However, people were still asked to consider larger implications, "what's it mean? this is not a world apart. you want to implement positive, inclusive change in our community? we're here. where else are you looking? whose paths are you tracing and following are you putting up boundaries or are you putting up wall? your non-engagement is engagement and it is what's undermining this conversation" (@thecolormustard, 2019). Being passive was not a response that the influencers would accept. Instead, they promoted active engagement with the situation in order to solve the problem.

The consistent theme that arose in promoting community change was that all the members of the knitting (and fiber) community needed to work together to make the change. It was not easier for some or harder for others. At many points in the discussion, the micro-influencers acknowledged that this would not be an easy conversation for the community. They made the difficulty of the conversation inclusive in that it was "an uncomfortable position for all of us" (@astitchtowear, 2019). A post included in @ocean_bythesea's highlight story encouraged people to "Please speak up in whatever capacity you can. WE will meet you where YOU are" (2019). In thinking about community change, people were reminded that, "There has been quite a few messages since my last story . . . People saying they are too scared to speak up, for fear of losing followers, and fear of saying the wrong thing. Do you really want people following you who don't care about humanity/ community? & The "wrong" thing can be worked on. I'm Terrified that this might just be a trend, please speak up in whatever capacity you can. WE will meet you where you are" (@ocean_bythesea, 2019). Also, that, "The amount of messages pouring in tells me that as a wider community we should be speaking about this more. There is so much love, kindness, encouragement . . . there are also many things that are being swept under the rug. I think it's time to air the issues out." (@ocean_bythesea, 2019)

DISCUSSION

Using Kelman's framework, this study looked at how micro-influencers in the fiber crafting community identified a problem and advocated for change within the community and across businesses that serve the community. Kelman's framework shows how both the influencers and the community embraced the change. By bringing the issue before the community, the influencers took on the role of compliance in that their content was established to get a reaction to bring about change. The community responded by both identifying the influencers as change agents and by helping them maintain that identity through message amplification. Eventually, the discussion was so meaningful that the community internalized and propagated the change beyond the initial conversation to include other forms of inclusiveness. The micro-influencers used Templer's initial post as an entry point to identify a community-wide problem for discussion and change. This reference point gave the micro-influencers and community members a shared starting point for discussion that was expanded upon as the conversation continued. By deconstructing Templer's blog post, the micro-influencers were able to create a narrative that was accessible through the shared Instagram content and visiting the blog itself. Once this initial narrative was established, the micro-influencers were able to curate and contextualize content and lived experiences for the community. These actions made it possible for community members to move beyond compliance where people join in conversations just for the glory of identifying with the problem and, ultimately, internalizing change brought about. This change also led to businesses internalizing the change through modifying their business practices.

Through curating content to promote self-education and highlighting lived experiences, the micro-influencers were able to draw Instagram users into the conversation at a variety of levels. Story highlights became a message for social change based on lived experience, and the educational tools allowed others to join in the conversation, increase awareness, and promote change. Although the conversation was not sponsored by any outside organization, the micro-influencers identified a community-wide problem that had been present, but not openly discussed. Having the conversation on social media, specifically Instagram, made it more difficult for some people to dismiss the presence of racism as the saved story highlights served as a constant reminder of what BIPOC makers experienced.

The curated content, however, was not uncontested and did not always work as intended. After the identification of the problem, the micro-influencers assumed that others in the community would teach themselves about the problems instead of feeding on the BIPOC experiences. While this happened in some cases, it did not happen for all. This reaction could be a result of a passive audience or it could be a sign that followers are more reliant on influencer viewpoints when dealing with controversial issues that are not part of their lived experience. Although fiber crafting influencers encouraged finding ways to meet their audience where their audience was comfortable, they may not have realized how much emotional effort that would take with a passive audience. Knowing that this was a difficult conversation for all, the influencers provided a variety of ways for community members to participate ranging from financial support to amplifying voices. This provided a way for community members to engage in the conversation at points they felt reflected their commitment, financial resources, and knowledge level on the topic.

Although the micro-influencers actively created the narrative surrounding the problem of racism in the knitting community, they soon realized that they were opening their social media spaces to negative and hostile comments. When this happened, the requests began for those who were amplifying their voices to also be aware of who they were sending to these accounts. In June 2019, several of the influencers noted in this study took steps to change their Instagram names so they would be less of a target, and some have since changed back to the handles mentioned in this study. Additionally, some accounts were targeted by people with opposing views for doxxing and removal from sites claiming the accounts were in violation of the platform's terms of service.

Having this conversation on Instagram allowed members of the crafting community who were already present on the platform to have easy access to curated content in a format that was easily shared. This allowed for initial points of entry to be accomplished with ease. This could have allowed those who were sharing content to feel comfortable with that action and then motivated them to create their own content in aid of asking for specific changes and joining in the fight against racism in the knitting community. Through sharing and creating content, they were able to develop an additional group identity within the crafting community. Thus, the members of the online community used social media as an information engine; as a way to connect with others, as a way to maintain the conversation, and, ultimately, as a form of empowerment once prominent makers and magazines spoke up in support of what they were reading and pledged to make changes.

Additionally, the visibility of the conversation had an impact on the businesses which serve the fiber crafting community. Many yarn dyers and magazines devoted space in their Instagram stories and feeds to amplify the conversation. The change for the businesses was more than compliance, but reflected an internalization of the change in that they included greater representation and ended contracts with those who did not agree with the community stance. This change in representation went beyond racial representation to be more inclusive of body types and other forms of inclusivity.

This study is not without its limitations. One of the primary limitations is that the study did not explore posted online responses to the Instagram story highlights. Also, due to the online nature of the conversation, the researcher was not able to evaluate direct messages. Given the responses in some of the highlights, it became clear that people were reaching out to the influencers in private messages with both requests and hate speech. The private nature of these messages made them inaccessible to outsiders. Additionally, the researcher is a white woman who is outside of the BIPOC lived experiences. While she did her best to acknowledge and check any privilege, having a BIPOC person analyze the data may have explored a different perspective.

This community is also a source for future research. Although a tightly focused online community, these initial conversations have stemmed more discussions regarding race, being inclusive, and representation. Given the prominence of this discussion, future research could investigate the amount of change and the lasting impacts, if any, of the changes.

Through this online discussion, the influencers identified a problem and drove change through providing alternate experiences and interpretations. They acknowledged that this was a difficult, yet necessary, discussion to have in order to truly embrace diversity. In bringing the discussion surrounding racism to the forefront in an open platform such as Instagram, they also opened the doors for other socially relevant conversations regarding being inclusive. This allowed community members to go beyond compliance regarding the discussion to truly internalize change to actively address the problem This community discussion is just one example of how influencers are using their power to communicate to, engage with, and motivate their followers to transform their community.

REFERENCES

@astitchtowear. (2019). *Instagram photos and videos*. Retrieved May 17, 2019, from https://www.instagram.com/astitchtowear/

Bastos, M. T., Mercea, D., & Charpentier, A. (2015). Tents, tweets, and events: The interplay between ongoing protests and social media. *Journal of Communication*, *65*(2), 320–350. doi:10.1111/jcom.12145

Bennett, W. L., & Segerberg, A. (2012). The logic of connective action: Digital media and the personalization of contentious politics. *Information Communication and Society*, *15*(5), 739–768. doi:10.1080/1369118X.2012.670661

Black, S. (2017). Knit + Resist: Placing the Pussyhat project in the context of craft activism. *Gender, Place and Culture*, *24*(5), 696–710. doi:10.1080/0966369X.2017.1335292

Bosch, T. (2017). Twitter activism and youth in South Africa. The case of #RhoeesMustFall. *Information Communication and Society*, *20*(2), 221–232. doi:10.1080/1369118X.2016.1162829

Bosch, T., & Mutsvairo, B. (2017). Pictures, Protests and politics: Mapping Twitter images during South Africa's fees must fall campaign. *African Journalism Studies*, *38*(2), 71–89. doi:10.1080/23743670.2017.1368869

Crnjak-Karanović, B., Milaković, I. K., & Elez, J. (2023). Which decision-making stages matter more? Influencer's perceived credibility, sponsorship and moderating role of trust. *Young Consumers*, *24*(6), 649–668. doi:10.1108/YC-08-2022-1590

Dawkins, N. (2011). Do-it-yourself: The precarious work and postfeminist politics of handmaking (in) Detroit. *Utopian Studies*, *22*(2), 261–284. doi:10.5325/utopianstudies.22.2.0261

Druckman, J. N. (2001). The Implications of Framing Effects for Citizen Competence. *Political Behavior*, *23*(3), 225–256. doi:10.1023/A:1015006907312

Forbes. (2021, March 25). 16 Inspiring ways to build a community on social media. *Forbes*. https://www.forbes.com/sites/forbescommunicationscouncil/2021/03/25/16-inspiring-ways-to-build-a-community-on-social-media/?sh=46770f7f30b9

Freberg, K., Graham, K., McGaughey, K., & Freberg, L. A. (2011). Who are the social media influencers? A study of public perceptions of personality. *Public Relations Review*, *37*(1), 90–92. doi:10.1016/j.pubrev.2010.11.001

Freelon, D., McIlwain, C., & Clark, M. (2018). Quantifying the power and consequences of social media protest. *New Media & Society*, *20*(3), 990–1011. doi:10.1177/1461444816676646

Getting closer: Influencers help brands build more personal consumer connections. (May 2022). Nielsen. https://www.nielsen.com/insights/2022/getting-closer-influencers-help-brands-build-more-personal-consumer-connections/

Hackney, F. (2013). Quiet Activism and the New Amateur. *Design and Culture*, *5*(2), 169–193. doi:10.2752/175470813X13638640370733

Hallahan, K. (1999). Seven Models of Framing: Implications for Public Relations. *Journal of Public Relations Research, 11*(3), 205–242. doi:10.1207/s1532754xjprr1103_02

Hart, B. (2017, October 30). *Why 2018 Will Be the Year of the Micro-Influencer, According to a Millennial Expert.* Retrieved May 23, 2019, from Inc.com website: https://www.inc.com/brian-hart/this-game-changing-strategy-will-help-your-business-reach-millennials-heres-how-to-use-it.html

Jefferies, J. (2016). Crocheted Strategies: Women Crafting their Own Communities. *Textile (Oxford), 14*(1), 14–35. doi:10.1080/14759756.2016.1142788

Kelman, H. C. (1958). Compliance, identification, and internalization three processes of attitude change. *The Journal of Conflict Resolution, 2*(1), 51–60. doi:10.1177/002200275800200106

Lawson, C. E. (2020). Skin deep: Callout strategies, influencers, and racism in the online beauty community. *New Media & Society, 23*(3), 596–612. Advance online publication. doi:10.1177/1461444820904697

Lim, M. (2018). Roots, Routes, and Routers: Communications and Media of Contemporary Social Movements. *Journalism & Communication Monographs, 20*(2), 92–136. doi:10.1177/1522637918770419

Linquia. (2019). *2020 Influencer Marketing Playbook.* Retrieved November 27, 2019, from https://linqia.com/insights/the-2020-influencer-marketing-playbook/

Liu, B., Yan, J., Briones, R., & Kuch, B. (2012). Managing turbulence in the blogosphere: Evaluating the blog-mediated crisis communication model with the American Red Cross. *Journal of Public Relations Research, 24*(4), 353–370. doi:10.1080/1062726X.2012.689901

Luckman, S. (2013). The Aura of the Analogue in a Digital Age: Women's Crafts, Creative Markets and Home-Based Labour After Etsy. *Cultural Studies Review, 19*(1), 249–270. doi:10.5130/csr.v19i1.2585

McKee, A. (2003). *Textual Analysis: A Beginner's Guide.* Sage Publications. doi:10.4135/9780857020017

Minocher, X. (2019). Online consumer activism: Challenging companies with Change. org. *New Media & Society, 21*(3), 620–638. doi:10.1177/1461444818803373

@ocean_bythesea. (2019). *Instagram photos and videos.* Retrieved May 17, 2019, from https://www.instagram.com/ocean_bythesea/

Orton-Johnson, K. (2012). Knit, purl and upload: New technologies, digital mediations and the experience of leisure. *Leisure Studies, 33*(3), 305–321. doi:10.1080/02614367.2012.723730

Pentney, B. A. (2018). Feminism, Activism, and Knitting: Are the Fibre Arts a Viable Mode for Feminist Political Action? *Thirdspace: A Journal of Feminist Theory & Culture, 8*(1), 14.

Pierucci, S. (2018, January 17). *Why MICRO-INFLUENCER Marketing is still 'The Game' in 2019.* Retrieved May 23, 2019, from Medium website: https://medium.com/swlh/why-micro-influencer-marketing-is-the-game-in-2018-fdeda0993c36

Saxena, J. (2019). *Racism in the knitting community is finally being talked about.* Retrieved Feb 27, 2019, from *Vox* website: https://www.vox.com/the-goods/2019/2/25/18234950/knitting-racism-instagram-stories

Scaraboto, D., & Fischer, E. (2013). Frustrated fashionistas: An institutional theory perspective on consumer quests for greater choice in mainstream markets. *The Journal of Consumer Research*, *39*(6), 1234–1257. doi:10.1086/668298

Smith, B. G., Krishna, A., & Al-Sinan, R. (2019). Beyond Slactivism: Examining the entanglement between social media engagement, empowerment, and participation in activism. *International Journal of Strategic Communication*, *13*(3), 182–196. doi:10.1080/1553118X.2019.1621870

Springgay, S. (2010). Knitting as an Aesthetic of Civic Engagement: Re-conceptualizing Feminist Pedagogy through Touch. *Feminist Teacher*, *20*(2), 111–123. doi:10.1353/ftr.2010.0009

@su.krita. (2019). *Instagram photos and videos*. Retrieved May 17, 2019, from https://www.instagram.com/su.krita/

Templer, K. (2019, January 7). *2019: My year of color*. Retrieved July 3, 2019, from Fringe Association website: https://fringeassociation.com/2019/01/07/2019-my-year-of-color/

Templer, K. (2019, January 12). *Words Matter*. Retrieved April 22, 2019, from Fringe Association: Knit and Let Knit website: fringeassociation.com/2019/01/12/words-matter.

Tewksbury, D., & Scheufele, D. A. (2009). News framing theory and research. In J. Bryant & M. B. Oliver (Eds.), Media Effects: Advances in theory and research (3rd ed., pp. 17–33). New York: Routledge.

@thecolormustard. (2019). *Instagram photos and videos*. Retrieved May 17, 2019 from https://www.instagram.com/thecolormustard/

@tina.say.knits. (2019). *Instagram photos and videos*. Retrieved May 17, 2019, from https://www.instagram.com/tina.say.knit/

@transitory. (2019). *Instagram photos and videos*. Retrieved May 17, 2019, from https://www.instagram.com/transitory/

Tusken, M. (2019, January 23). *Knitting, Instagram, and some new bases for the shop!* YouTube [Video]. Retrieved May 17, 2019, from YouTube website: https://www.youtube.com/watch?v=Dv1TxdkwdIY

Winslow, L. (2018). Frame Analysis. In The Sage Encyclopdia of Communication Research Methods (pp. 584-586). doi:10.4135/9781483381411

Yan, G., Pegoraro, A., & Watanabe, N. (2018). Student-athletes' organization of activism at the University of Missouri: Resource mobilization on Twitter. *Journal of Sport Management*, *32*(1), 24–37. doi:10.1123/jsm.2017-0031

Zweiman, J., & Suh, K. (n.d.). *Our Story*. Retrieved May 29, 2019, from PUSSYHAT PROJECT™ website: https://www.pussyhatproject.com/our-story

KEY TERMS AND DEFINITIONS

Craftivism: This term is used to explain activism in the craft world or using crafts. Knitting is a craft and the accounts discussed in this chapter used their social media presence as a form of activism in the community.

Influencers: Influencers are defined as a person with a platform, typically online, who holds some sort of influence over a specific audience or community. The accounts studied in this chapter fit that definition.

Micro-Influencers: Micro-influencers are defined as those with an online following of 10,000-100,000. All of the influencers studied in this chapter fall into that category except for one who had approximately 8,000 followers.

Social Media Activism: Social media activism is a form of online support of a cause using hashtags or other means to encourage change in society or a community. The accounts in this chapter all encouraged community members and businesses to change in a way that is intended to foster inclusivity.

Chapter 6
Exploring Communication Practices of Influencers on Commerce-Focused Social Media:
Whatnot

Victoria McDermott
https://orcid.org/0000-0001-9837-5545
University of Alaska, Fairbanks, USA

Amy May
University of Alaska, Fairbanks, USA

Olivia Truban
https://orcid.org/0000-0002-4138-4907
University of Maryland, USA

ABSTRACT

Social commerce sites continue to rise in popularity due in large part to their ability to integrate content creation and selling. Platforms like Whatnot provide new avenues for public relations scholarship to explore the communication strategies and techniques used by influencers to engage with users to cultivate community during product promotions. Through the qualitative analysis of 10 livestream auctions across five categories, this study adds to the literature the concept of the strategic communication performance of selling, e.g., the ways in which influencers engage in strategic communication to put on a performance of selling products. Counter to the traditional digital culture recommendations that tout authenticity, this study presents the idea of explicit performance of selling that occurs among influencers which seeks to leverage social capital through transparency/vulnerability, the use of established norms, and the increase of engagement through the dispersion of power among users.

DOI: 10.4018/979-8-3693-0912-4.ch006

INTRODUCTION

The rapid growth and influence of digital media have led to a rise in social media influencers (SMIs) as a new form of content curators and disseminators (Freberg, 2022). While scholarship has traditionally explored major social media platforms such as Instagram, Facebook, and TikTok, lesser-known platforms, such as Whatnot, provide important niche spaces for SMIs to reach potential audiences to "buy, sell and go live" (Whatnot, 2023a). As a commerce platform, Whatnot provides a different experience than traditional social media or content creation applications (i.e., apps), as the purpose of the app for influencers is to sell and for users is to buy.

This chapter explores the relationship between SMIs and strategic communication tactics that seek to foster rapport associated with product sales specifically on the platform Whatnot. Informed by the theoretical constructs of strategic communication (Heide et al., 2018), social capital (Kennan & Hazelton, 2006), and engagement (Dhanesh, 2017), we sought to understand how influencers on Whatnot utilize communication to cultivate community through the promotion of products during auctions.

From the analysis of 10 livestreams with 10 different influencers across five categories, we identified three overarching themes that sought to answer the proposed research question: the use of the platform functions, establishment and maintenance of platform norms, and communication strategies. Platform functions refer to the capabilities allowed by the Whatnot platform, such as thumbnails, music, and the chat feature to enhance livestream experience. Establishment and maintenance of norms refers to the use of specific terminology, actions, and expectations created on the platform that are known by insiders within the community. Lastly, communication strategies refer to the use of tactics, such as transparency, dialogue, and user agency, to build a sense of community between influencers and users as well as amongst users.

From these findings, we argue the new concept of *the strategic communication performance of selling,* i.e., how influencers engage in strategic communication to put on a performance of selling products. Based on previous scholarship of livestreaming and SMIs, as well as the theories of social capital and engagement, we identified four elements used by SMIs to foster engagement that comprise *the strategic communication performance of selling*: performing-performing vs. performing-not performing, transparency/vulnerability, established norms, and perception of dispersion of power. We close the chapter with an overview of limitations and areas for future research.

LITERATURE REVIEW

The following review of literature begins with an overview of the perspective of strategic communication, outlining two important concepts that assist in the creation of strategic communication: social capital and engagement. Next, we explore the current literature on social media influencers (SMIs) and livestreaming. We close the literature review with an overview of the development of S-commerce (e.g., social commerce) and an explanation of the Whatnot application (app).

Strategic Communication

Strategic communication broadly encompasses a variety of theories and paradigmatic approaches that seek to study "how organizations use communication purposefully to fulfill their overall missions" (Heide et al., 2018, p. 452). In their 2018 article, Zerfass et al. (2018) proposed that strategic communication "encompasses all communication that is substantial for the survival and sustained success of an entity" (p. 487). Thus, used throughout a multitude of communication subdisciplines, including advertising and public relations, marketing communication, and organizational communication (Grunig, 2006; Heide et al., 2018; Zerfass et al., 2018), strategic communication, in essence, is communicating with purpose (Hallahan et al., 2007).

Specifically related to public relations scholarship, strategic communication has been used to help inform how relationships between organizations and publics are cultivated (Cheng, 2018). Depending on paradigmatic assumptions, the strategic function of communication in public relations is viewed as either a process or product for fostering meaningful relationships that can translate to organizations achieving their business goals (Hallahan et al., 2007; Kitchen & Moss, 1995). Thus, intentional communication can be used to help build relationships between organizations and key publics. Because strategic communication seeks to be purposeful, scholarship and practice of strategic communication are focused on deploying messages geared towards optimizing organizational effectiveness and enhancing organizational legitimacy (i.e., Zerfass et al., 2018). It is important to note that landscape, context, and medium all play a role in the form strategic communication may take (Freberg, 2022).

Two concepts that have been used to further explicate the concept of strategic communication are social capital and engagement. Both require the use and contribute to the development of purposeful communication used by organizations to connect with key publics.

Social Capital

Social capital is a concept that has been used across disciplines to explain the relationships that form the foundations of power structures in a society (Kennan & Hazelton, 2006). Bourdieu (1986) defines social capital as "the aggregate of the actual or potential resources which are linked to possession of a durable network of more or less institutionalized relationships of mutual acquaintance or recognition" (p. 243). In other words, social capital is an intangible resource based on societal structures that lends power and legitimacy to an individual or organization based on access to resources (e.g., knowledge, expertise, relationships, and respect).

Importantly, social capital is built and used through communication as it is grounded in social relationships. Through communication, people produce and define the resources, as well as decide who has access to them (Kennan & Hazelton, 2006). As such, social capital is built through the perception of reputation among others. Social capital is an important consideration in strategic communication, as social capital can be used to build relationships to achieve desired outcomes (Kennan & Hazelton, 2006). For example, those with social capital can partner with organizations to endorse actions or products to lend legitimacy and social acceptance (Dodd, 2015). Through purposeful and intentional communication, one can build their own social capital.

Engagement

Engagement is a multifaceted concept that has been used to loosely refer to the interaction between an organization and publics. Within public relations scholarship, some research has conceptualized engagement at a surface level using the metrics of clicks, likes, views, and shares to make sense of interactions with publics (Agostino, 2013; Men et al., 2018). This perspective of engagement positions engagement as short, abrupt, unidirectional communication loops from organizations to publics.

This chapter uses the definition of engagement proposed by Dhanesh (2017; Dhanesh et al., 2022), who challenged organizational communication to go beyond simply message dissemination to consider engagement as collaboration. From a digital perspective, Dhanesh (2017, p. 931) defines engagement as:

an affective, cognitive, and behavioral state wherein publics and organizations who share mutual interests in salient topics interact along continua that range from passive to active and from control to collaboration, and is aimed at goal attainment, adjustment, and adaptation for both publics and organizations.

From this perspective, engagement is seen as a way for both publics and organizations to engage in the communication process to foster the creation of quality relationships.

Engagement is an important concept to consider when thinking about strategic communication. For example, engagement with publics can help to determine what messages do and do not work to reach organizational outcomes and meet the needs of publics. Messages with intended outcomes of persuasion or action that are not taken can show the limitations or errors of communication messages. Finally, engagement with an organization's messages can help identify new needs, keep an organization at the forefront of public consciousness, and increase satisfaction with an organization (Men & Tsai, 2013; Wang et al., 2018).

Ultimately, the relationship between social capital and engagement is important to consider in relation to strategic communication. Social capital helps to lend power and legitimacy to an organization's reputation. Related to engagement, considering the architecture of the social media landscape (Kent & Taylor, 2021), effective engagement can inform avenues for elevated organizational presence online. In tandem, organizations with high levels of social capital can increase the communication they have with publics, strengthening their overall relationship and meeting organizational goals. Today, one way that many brands and organizations seek to increase their social capital and engagement is through the use of social media influencers, i.e., those who may be perceived as having legitimacy and connection to specific publics in digital spaces. These influencers often utilize strategic communication to cultivate their own brand and aesthetic to build a following based on their perceived expertise and connection to followers.

Social Media Influencers

An influencer is someone who has an online presence and is viewed as an authority on a specific topic, practice, or position (Freberg, 2022). There are various types of influencers that are identified based on a spectrum of status and following, including mega-influencers, micro-influencers, and nano-influencers (Freberg, 2022). In function, influencers operate similarly to organizations in that influencers must establish relationships with publics and stakeholders of interest in order to progress their reputation and brand. One of the ways influencers achieve this goal is through partnering with other organizations, also known as influencer marketing (i.e., selling, Freberg, 2022).

Influencer marketing has become increasingly popular in the past decade, where organizations partner with influencers to help promote a product or service (Freberg, 2022). Examples of partnerships include influencers providing reviews of products, talking about an organization's brand, or launching a product with an organization they collaborated on (Freberg, 2022). With the influencer marketing industry netting over $14 billion dollars since 2016 (West, 2023), it is important that strategic communication scholarship considers the unique role influencers play in endorsing products and services online. Specifically, how influencers utilize various strategic communication tactics based on community standards (e.g., guidelines set forth by the online platform being used, Kent & Taylor, 2021) to promote products. One benefit of influencer marketing is that influencers possess the ability to convey more interpersonal messages with key audiences online, which allows them to spark engagement and provide unique value in a way that organizations traditionally may not be able to.

SMI Livestreaming

One way SMIs have sought to build relationships with followers is through the use of livestreaming. Livestreaming is when a video is sent over the Internet in real time without being recorded first (CloudFlare, n.d.). It has been likened to live television in which creators react, in real time, to situations or comments without reciting memorized content. While the concept of livestreaming has existed since the 1990s, it was not well-known until the first YouTube livestream in 2008. Livestreaming rose in popularity starting in 2016 and today, most social media platforms have some sort of livestreaming capabilities (Shodipe-Dosunmu, 2023). Today, livestreaming merges real-time video content with chat interaction creating a new digital space for content creation and consumption (Luo et al., 2023).

Previously, scholars have explored what factors impact users watching and buying intentions during livestreams (Hou et al., 2019; Liu et al., 2023; Sun et al., 2019) and livestreaming from an influencers' perspective (Wongkitrungrueng et al., 2020). For users, research has found that elements like visibility (i.e., ease of access and quality of the live stream, Sun et al., 2019), perceived enjoyment and serendipity (Liu et al., 2023), and use of humor appeals (Hou et al., 2019) all play a role in users' intentions to continue watching livestreams and effects if they chose to buy something. Wongkitrungrueng et al. (2020) identified four main categories of transaction-based approach (e.g., influencers focus on providing details about products and rarely talk about other things beyond products, price/promotion and payment/delivery details), persuasion-based approach (e.g., when influencers seek to entice, entertain customers, and differentiate themselves from other influencers who sell the same products), content-based approach (e.g., influencers share content that may or may not be related to a product), and relationships-based approach (e.g., influencers consider their customers as friends whom they care about and seek to build relationships with viewers) for characterizing how influencers approached the livestream selling process on Facebook. Ultimately, a systematic review of existing research on livestreaming found that much of the current scholarship on livestreaming has sought to categorize motivations for selling and watching, identify key characteristics of the shopping/relationship experience, and take a quantitative approach to data analysis (e.g., structural equation modeling and regression analysis). Furthermore, the researchers argued that future scholarship should seek to focus on communication skills and engagement techniques employed by influencers (Luo et al., 2023).

Social Commerce (S-Commerce)

One way that SMIs use livestreams is to engage in social commerce (S-commerce), e.g., the selling of products in real-time through digital platforms (Ventre et al., 2021). S-commerce has a rich history that dates back to Yahoo!, who coined the term "me commerce" with the launch of their Shoposphere (Arrington, 2005). Facebook Marketplace and Amazon Wishlists soon followed; however, the popularity of

S-commerce exploded during the COVID-19 pandemic as housebound consumers, desiring to connect with others, sought out more interactive and community-based shopping experiences (Arula, 2021).

For existing social media platforms, such as Instagram and TikTok, S-commerce is achieved through the integration of an online marketplace. For commerce-driven sites like Amazon, social elements are added to their platforms to connect, engage, and drive sales (Deloitte Analysis, 2023). For online shoppers, S-commerce is driven by relationship development and perceived trust between the SMI selling the product, the individual user, and the overall community members who engage in social interaction before, during, and after the sale (Ventre et al., 2021). By 2025, analysts predict S-commerce will account for roughly 30% of online purchases, contributing over two (2) trillion dollars to the U.S. economy (Deloitte Analysis, 2023).

Whatnot

While existing social media platforms sites are integrating commerce elements, new applications are launching with a sole focus on S-commerce as described above. One of the most popular new S-commerce sites is Whatnot. Whatnot specifically "aim(s) to enable anyone to turn their passion into a business & bring people together through commerce" (Whatnot, 2023b, para. 1). Whatnot launched in December 2019 as a United States (U.S.) based company quickly captured the attention of viewers looking for a dynamic and interactive commerce platform. Billed as a "shopping unicorn," (Shah, 2021) for its ability to capture the attention of consumers in a crowded marketplace, Whatnot founders boast their platform is now "most value independent livestream shopping in the U.S." (Gagne & Maini, 2022, para. 2). The current valuation is roughly four billion in 2023 (Crunchbase, 2023).

Touted as a site for connection and commerce, the main function of Whatnot is to connect buyers and influencers. Whatnot is unique in that there is a limited marketplace of traditional classified ads. Instead the platform thrives on live auctions, combining livestream selling with the thrill of real-time bidding (Balestra, 2022). Moreover, during auctions, users can chat amongst each other and the influencer(s), building community as users encourage their fellow Whatnoters[1] to "bid up," get "steals and deals," and share topics of interest.

Exploring commerce-centric platforms is important for strategic communication because it helps explicate the relationship between marketing and public relations (Kitchen & Moss, 1995), specifically how relational considerations inform successful business models online. Filling a dearth of research on S-commerce SMIs, this chapter used a multimodal qualitative content analysis (Sommer, 2020) to understand how SMIs on Whatnot use strategic communication to connect with audiences to sell their products. Specifically, our analysis of these auctions provides further insight into how moving visual elements of digital communication inform relational connections online between influencers and buyers.

RQ: How do influencers on Whatnot utilize communication to cultivate community through the promotion of products during auctions?

METHODS

The following methods section begins with an overview of how the influencers analyzed in this study were chosen and data was collected. We close with an overview of the data analysis process.

Selection of Influencers

Whatnot currently has 35 categories of product offerings, which are further broken down into subcategories (Whatnot, 2023c). For example, *Bags and Accessories* represent one category with the following subcategories: *Luxury Bags & Accessories, Midrange & Fashion Bags,* and *Other Accessories* (Whatnot, 2023d). On the app, thumbnails are used to highlight active livestreams and tease upcoming shows. Typically, there are over 1,000 livestreams at any given time in each category. Because of the wide range of categories and subcategories, as well as the variation of those currently livestreaming, determining the most popular influencers in each category is challenging.

To ease data collection and ensure a manageable data set, five categories were selected based on published demographic data by *ContraryResearch*, the only site offering information of Whatnot users (Gagne & Maini, 2022). Gagne and Maini (2022) characterize Whatnot users as follows:

...young (typically Gen Z), have plenty of disposable income, and are enthusiastic collectors of items like Pokémon cards, designer toys, and NFL/NBA trading cards. Whatnot's most prominent group of shoppers are American men between 25 and 34. They tend to be tech early adopters and spend a lot of time online (Market & Customer, para. 2).

Based on this information, the researchers selected the following categories: *Trading Card Games, Sports Cards,* and *Toys & Hobbies*. To expand the dataset, the researchers also included *Bags & Accessories* and *Sneakers & Streetwear* because these two categories had the highest number of livestreams at the time of data collection. Once the categories were selected, *Shop All* was used to ensure all subcategories had an equal chance of being included in the data. Under *Shop All*, the two shows with the highest number of viewers in each category were selected for analysis. The livestreams were chosen based on number of viewers, as number of viewers gives an indication of audience engagement; moreover, more users provided an opportunity to further assess not only engagement with the influencer but other Whatnoters. In the end, the following influencers were selected (see Table 1):

Data Collection

The researchers watched two live auctions from the livestreams with the most viewers over two weeks of data collection (n=10) from December 4th 2023 to December 18th 2023. By watching livestreams from a variety of influencers on the platform, the researchers were able to gather thick descriptive information about the communication tactics SMIs used to effectively engage with buyers on Whatnot (Tracy, 2019).

Table 1. Whatnot influencers

Category	Influencer #1	Influencer #2
Trading Card Games	@krakenhits	@pokemonwizard
Sports Cards	@cardboard47	@nflhumor
Toys & Hobbies	@evend	@7bucksapop
Bags & Accessories	@fashionica	@thedonsluxurygoods
Sneakers & Streetwear	@blazendary	@keevadokicks

Given average Whatnoters watch approximately one hour of livestreams per day (Shah, 2021), the researchers used this timeframe for data collection in each livestream as a guide. During the livestreams, the researchers took copious notes, documenting not only the verbal communication but also non-verbal aspects of delivery. In addition, the researchers took notes on the level of engagement by the influencer with the viewers and the level of engagement between Whatnoters via the chat. Finally, the researchers took note of discussions that de-centered selling and provided space for community building. At the end of data collection, the researchers viewed 10 hours of livestreaming, resulting in approximately 100 pages of handwritten notes.

Data Analysis

After completing data collection, the researchers used content analysis to analyze the data and answer the research question (Neuendorf, 2017; Patton, 2014). Phase one involved reading through the data to get a feel for how strategic communication is used by influencers during livestreams; in addition, the researchers took note of the strategic communication used by Whatnoters to connect and engage to build community. The goal of this phase was to gain familiarity with the dataset and start to formulate loose categories. To engage in deeper coding and develop more defined categories, each researcher analyzed the data individually during phase two to map out a loose coding strategy to ensure consistency (Patton, 2014). After testing a subset of the data, the researchers came together to discuss preliminary findings and finalize a codebook to guide further analysis and generate themes. During the final phase, researchers discussed their findings and generated a final list of themes, including representative quotes to answer the research questions (Neuendorf, 2017).

FINDINGS

Three overarching themes were identified from the analyzed data that seek to answer the research question. Further subthemes use exemplars from the data to illustrate the findings.

RQ: How do influencers on Whatnot utilize communication to cultivate community through the promotion of products during auctions?

Use of the Platform Functions

The first overarching theme to emerge related to influencers' communication to cultivate community was the use of platform functions to enhance the livestream experience. For example, through the use of thumbnails, influencers were able to tease future livestreams and get users excited to engage in the auction process, thus proactively sparking purchasing intentions of users. Influencers also used the chat function to connect with users and build community through conversation, which further promoted user buy-in of goods. Finally, music often played a critical role in setting the "vibe," establishing the pacing, and often indicates whether or not the show will be explicit.

Thumbnails

Thumbnails are small images or video clips that represent the influencer and/or the content of the livestream. A well-designed thumbnail serves to attract viewers and increase user purchase intentions via persuasive aesthetic resonance. As noted by one influencer, "ahhhh ya'll like that sexy thumbnail. I had more saves for this show than any other one." The thumbnail featured a scantily clad woman with breasts bulging out of a bra. The influencer sells cards, which seems like a disconnect; however, considering key demographics of Whatnot users (i.e., predominantly young men), the image may have been strategically selected to entice viewers and enhance buyer appeal. Some influencers prefer to feature themselves in all of their thumbnails for upcoming shows (i.e., emphasizing influencer branding) while others focus on products, giveys (e.g., free giveaways), sponsorships, or teasers (e.g., a major announcement or themed show). A well-designed thumbnail helps influencers stand out in categories where livestreams number in the thousands at any given time.

Thumbnails take many shapes and forms, but they contain shared elements. In the top left-hand corner, the day and time of the show are displayed if scheduled in the future. The top right-hand corner contains bookmarks (i.e., the number of times the show has been saved by viewers) or the number of live audience members. The bulk of the thumbnail contains a video or image of the influencer or products. On the left side of the screen, the influencer *@fashionica* chose to present herself along with a high-end luxury bag (Birkin) to attract viewers. *@7dollarsapop*, on the other hand, chose to display an image featuring the show's theme. The image is bright and colorful, aesthetically drawing in potential viewers looking to pay *@7bucksapop* for Marvel and DC Funko Pops that are rare and hard to find, described by the influencer as "grails."

Chat Function

The chat function is an integral part of the Whatnot platform. The chat is often used by the influencers and users to build community and promote transparency during the selling process. The chat allows users to share text and emoticons; however, images or videos are not allowed. The chat also includes moderators or "mods," trusted users or fellow influencers who help keep the discussion focused. These moderators help establish the community parameters of the chat and determine what are deemed appropriate contributions based on platform guidelines. Moderators also have the ability to block users who are deemed problematic (i.e., those who breach the community standards or moderator guidelines set forth by the platform).

Music

Music is often featured by many influencers to set the mood and vibe of the show. All influencers in the data set chose to use music during the data collection period, often stopping to sing lyrics. Chat participants frequently commented on the music, confirming "I loooooovvvvv this song" or "damn, I haven't heard this one in years." One chat participant even asked the influencer if they could share their playlist on Spotify, to which the influencer responded with "hell yeah." Music often served to compliment the pacing of the show. From Jazz and elevator music with lower beats per minute (BPM) to Electronic Dance Music (EDM), influencers were strategic in their music selections. EDM, for example, music was often featured in shows that auctioned items back-to-back on sudden death, i.e., auctions that do not restart the clock when a higher bid is made. Notably, in influencers strategically pairing music with their livestreams, they also provide an opportunity for users to listen to and/or be encouraged to purchase select songs, demonstrating how additional promotions of secondary products (i.e., music) correspondingly can occur during shows.

Establishment and Maintenance of Platform Norms

The second overarching theme identified from the data was the creation and use of platform-specific norms. This includes the creation and use of lingo and selling activities unique to the platform of Whatnot that sought to build engagement and excitement among users who had insider knowledge of how the platform works. Through the establishment and maintenance of norms, a sense of community was built regardless of category which, in turn, can enhance user buy-in for Whatnot influencers

Giveys and Giveys Goblins

Giveaways (often referred to as giveys or "for the free") are a staple of Whatnot livestreams and represent a strategic form of communication. They are "pinned" by influencers at the start of the show while they welcome in users and preview the items for auction or buy it now. Giveys are also offered at multiple points during the livestream to maintain audiences or build audiences when viewership wanes, thus pairing influencer social capital with user social capital (i.e., winning a givey). Some influencers offer back-to-back giveys during the entire duration of the show. While giveys may be drawn at any time, the default is a five-minute countdown where Whatnoters must be present and following the influencer in order to win. Giveys are paid for by the influencers and are eligible for rating by the winner.

Some influencers proudly show their givey and assign a monetary value while others pin "random giveys to be determined by the host" or "my gift to you," deemphasizing the "what" and focusing on the "free." The giveys often represent the theme of the show or further represent the influencers and their brand (i.e., influencer branding). For example, *@krakenhits* usually offers a mystery pack of cards, meaning cards unopened, sealed in the pack "for the free" to entice hesitant influencers who are risk-avoidant. The goal is to show "good cards" are available, so "bid bid bid chat." *@Thedonsluxurygoods* often gives away branded coasters and shirts to build community and further the reputation of "the dons" as the "best place for luxury goods on Whatnot at the best prices."

Giveys were also used by all influencers in the sample to celebrate raids. Raids happen when a fellow influencer ends their show and sends their viewers to another livestream. Raids can range from a few viewers to hundreds of Whatnoters who may or may not be familiar with the influencer selected to receive the raid. Raids may even cross categories. Whatnoters may also sponsor a givey for a set price ranging from 10 dollars to hundreds of dollars. Whatnoters, especially fellow influencers, use sponsored giveaways as strategic communication to gain followers and get publicity as the raided influencer exclaims "RAID" and "follow X host a follow right now." They are also influencers on Whatnot. They also use the sponsored influencer's Whatnot screen name in the description of the giveaway, making it easy for Whatnoters to view their profile, follow, and bookmark other shows. This strategic allocation of attention from one influencer to another on the app can be viewed as platform capital, which we define as the perceived social capital and value of a influencer/user in a platform context. In allocating platform capital, those with existing social capital and platform endorsement are vouching for another influencer on the platform, thus driving captured interest on the platform.

While giveys are described by influencers as "necessary for getting y'all in here" and "don't go anywhere - let me pin another givey," there is also negative framing of "givey goblins," Whatnoters who come "for the free" and then immediately leave after the winner is drawn are known as givey goblins. When the winner is drawn, some influencers stop and encourage the chat to "say goodbye to the givey goblins. Bbbbbyyyyyyyeeeeeee." Influencers will also celebrate a givey winner who is a known buyer or fellow influencer, further driving platform capital. However, some influencers spend time trying to "figure out who that was who won" or dismissing them as a "givey goblin."

Givey goblins can also be aggressive in the chat, showing up and demanding the influencer run a giveaway. All of the influencers maintained a respectful tone in the livestreams analyzed by saying things like "Thanks for asking. I will be running more giveys later in the show. All the more reason to stay around and shop." While influencers maintained a positive tone, fellow Whatnoters often in the chat called out the users and accused them of being "rude" or "disrespectful" to the livestream influencer. To counter givey goblins and "celebrate the chat who has been here for the whole show and letting me know what they want to see," some influencers will pin a givey for only a few seconds, screaming at the chat "get in there" before doing a final countdown to inform the chat they will pull the winner in "five, four, three and half, two, aaaaaannnnnddddddddd one."

A special givey influencers may use as a strategic communication tool is the buyers-only givey. These giveys have a higher cost associated with them when compared to your typical giveaway and often include items such as luxury goods, highly collective cards or toys, and iPads or Apple Watches. A big buyer givey is perceived as a tool to "get you to buy something" and "stay here until we pull the buyer givey at the end of the show." In order to be eligible for a buyers-only givey, there must be a purchase made during the livestream. In other words, financial investment helps to inform platform capital. However, it is important to note due to federal lottery laws (as described by one influencer), givey goblins can bypass the buyer part and fill out a form which makes them eligible regardless of if they purchased something or not. Many influencers will pull a buyers-only givey almost immediately to ensure givey goblins do not win and "take away the big prize from a real buyer."

Giveys also create space for community building in the chat between Whatnoters. When a winner is drawn, there is often a slew of "congratulations," "so deserved a win" or "so jelly. I wanted that." The winner will often share with the chat "OMG I can't believe I won" and "I never win giveys." If the winner does not engage with the chat, they may face a backlash from fellow Whatnoters. Whatnot rules specifically require winners to be present to win, and "when a user enters a giveaway but leaves the livestream, they will be automatically removed from the list of entries for that giveaway" (Whatnot, 2023f, *FAQs*, para. 7). Moreover, the rules state that an influencer may not ask if the winner is present (Whatnot, 2023f); however, the chat is free to challenge if the winner is present. They will often claim "they aren't even here," or "I hate givey goblins. It's not fair" They will prod the influencer to run another givey, which may result in additional back and forth in the chat.

Dolla Holla

During a livestream, influencers may choose to auction items at a starting bid, or they may choose to set a price for an item in the *buy it now* feature. The *buy it now* feature allows buyers to make offers up to 80% off depending on the influencer's specifications. However, Whatnot is increasingly known for their "dolla hollas." Dolla hollas are auctions that start at $1 dollar. For bidders, there is excitement over the possibility of obtaining a luxury item or collectible for a very low price, thus driving financial interest and investment in influencer livestreams. In the chat, they ask for $1 dollar to start consistently across categories. For influencers, there is a risk that an item will go for less than what they paid; however, to be competitive, influencers must meet the demand for dolla hollas or their buyers will move on to the next livestream. Therefore, it is important for influencers to not only capture initial attention from users, but convert such attention into both financial and social return-on-investment (i.e., financial and social gain). When a Whatnoter joins a chat, their name is displayed. During the data collection period, it was common to see Whatnoters rejoining multiple times, suggesting they were showing hopping, i.e., moving in and out of livestreams and back and forth between competing influencers.

Influencers across categories reacted very differently to dolla hollas. Some influencers, such as @ *blazendary*, start their auctions at $1 dollar. These influencers tend to have a larger number of followers and viewership in any given show, thus the bidding often reaches a number that allows them to make a profit. However, some influencers are very dramatic before, during, and after the dolla holla. For example, they often spend a great deal of time talking about the condition of the item, the going price for similar items on other sites (showing screenshots of what a similar item sold for online), and the price they paid for the item.

During the dolla holla auction, influencers may scream and jump while exclaiming "don't do this to me" or "I paid way more than this chat" or accusing the chat of robbery and threatening to call the police (in a joking manner based on tone). A select few started to get frustrated and angry (facial expressions, body language) with the chat, creating tension during the livestream. Chat participants will often question "why did you start it at a dolla then. We didn't make you" or "next time start the auction at a price you feel comfortable with. You don't have to do dollar starts." In one case, an influencer decided to end their show early because the "loss was too great" and "chat keeps doing this to me." There was no ending givey or raid, which are commonplace for most influencers about to end their show. Instead, there was just an abrupt ending to the show.

Blessing the Chat. Some influencers choose to use dolla hollas as a way to "bless the chat." The influencer frames this as "I know that I am taking a loss, but I want to give back. I want to bless the chat." Influencers will often speak about how appreciative they are for the chat, shares, sells, and "chat members who show up for every show." In one instance, an influencer wanted to bless the chat because they met their sales goals, thus meeting their financial obligations helped foster community appreciation. One influencer blessed the chat in a religious way, lifting arms up, wrapping a scarf around their head, and repeatedly saying "I am blessing you chat" over and over again during the auction. The influencer continued to bless the chat with multiple dolla hollas. Chat members often respond enthusiastically to being blessed, often expressing "thank you thank you thank you" if they win the auction. Even for chat members who do not win, there is an expression of gratitude, further demonstrating effective community cultivation on the platform through this tactic.

Communication-Based Strategies

The last theme identified from the dataset was the use of communication strategies deployed by influencers, such as transparency, starting conversations not related to the item to build rapport, and user agency. These communication strategies sought to build a sense of community and trust with app users, as well as enhance both the platform's and influencers' social capital.

Transparency

S-commerce is built on relationship building and perceived trust between buyers and influencers. Whatnot has an all sales final and no returns policy unless an item is lost in shipping, inaccurately described, or counterfeit (Whatnot, 2023g). For community members who perceive an item was inaccurately described, both influencers and buyers have a level of protection by viewing the "video receipt." Whatnot offers video receipts or a video featuring the description of the item and bidding process before, during, and after the sale. The goal for influencers is to prevent a negative rating (i.e., loss of social capital), which can impact their sales or get them in trouble with Whatnot, jeopardizing their position and legitimacy as a streamer on the platform. To ensure transparency, influencers spend a significant amount of time discussing callouts and ensuring no sleight of hand, which is considered a deceptive practice.

Callouts. For pre-loved items and vintage items, accurately describing callouts or imperfections in the item for sale or auction is critical for building and maintaining trust. For the influencers in the *Toys & Hobbies, Bags & Accessories,* and *Sneakers & Streetwear* categories, this is standard practice. Some influencers choose to take detailed pictures featuring the callouts for items in the *buy it now* or for *items up for auction.* They often add a generic disclaimer such as "all items are pre-loved or vintage. Expect small imperfections and minor defects. If you are looking for perfect items, I am not the seller for you."

Additionally, a rating is added to quantify conditions. The most common rating systems include letter grades (A+ to F) and a number between 1-to-10. The closer to A and 10 an item is rated, the better the overall condition. Other influencers choose to list as "toy #1" or "sneakers sz 10" without detailed pictures. For these influencers, the livestream allows them to walk through each callout for their viewers. If this step is skipped or rushed, community members will commonly ask "callouts?," "show again," or question if a callout was missed by asking "is that a stain?" or "any smell?" Prior to pinning the item for auction or sale, influencers frequently ask the chat if there are any questions about the item and "did everyone see the callouts."

No Sleight of Hand. For influencers in the *Trading Card Games, Sports Cards*, and *Toys & Hobbies* categories, the items tended to be new, i.e., in the package, or graded by professional grading agencies for cards and collectibles. The major concern for these influencers is to avoid being charged with "sleight of hand," an accusation that indicates the winning item was substituted for a less valuable or less rare item prior to shipping. To avoid the sleight of hand charge, influencers in this category often use a different setup. While many influencers choose to position their cameras in front of them, showing their entire physical presence and selection of goods in the background, influencers in card and toy categories often choose to position the camera at an angle where the only part of their body that is visible is their hands. Their hands are often centered in the camera lens with cards and toys for auctions in front of them.

When a pack of cards is won, they have the choice to "rip or ship." Rip means that the pack of cards are opened, requiring the influencer to show the cards to the livestream one by one. The names of the characters featured on the cards are often called out with added commentary about their rareness or collectability. For card winners, this ensures they know exactly which cards they won and how many. Any variation from this will often result in negative reviews and negative comments in the chat about how they "were ripped off last time" which, in turn, can decrease their platform capital as an influencer.

Ship, on the other hand, means the winner wants to be surprised. The pack of cards is sent unopened and in the original packaging.

Off Topic

In addition to selling and greeting chat members as they join the live, some influencers focus more on community building than selling. During the data collection period, influencers discussed reality TV, polled the chat on their favorite Disney characters, and shared their holiday plans. The chat was invited to share their thoughts, opinions, and ideas. The influencer responded to the majority of the chat, laughing, pointing out disagreements in the chat, and continuing the discussion by introducing a new topic to discuss. For many influencers, this appears to happen organically; however, some influencers schedule shows that are focused on community building. Some of the shows scheduled by the influencers include *Christmas Cookies, Meditation, Prayer Requests,* and even sitting on the beach listening to the waves. The most common topic for these scheduled shows is the *Seller Question & Answer*. During these shows, the chat (i.e., active users) is encouraged to ask the influencer questions about anything related to selling, livestreaming, how to ship items, and common issues with buyers.

The most common question posed by chat related to selling is sourcing. Fellow influencers in the chat looking to expand into different categories or buyers interested in becoming influencers, often ask "how do you source your items to sell." All of the influencers during the data collection period declined to reveal their sources, i.e., vendors they use to stock their Whatnot stores. Influencers did explain why they declined to provide this information. Many influencers shared the length of time it takes to build relationships with credible sources, or they chose to share how they got started, e.g., selling from their personal collections, going to auctions, or traveling to foreign countries to find rare items. One influencer was more direct and told the chat members to Google it or "check out YouTube." A few influencers hinted that fellow Whatnoters were their suppliers, but refused to identify them directly, instead encouraging the chat "if you think about it - they are one of the big influencers in this category - you can figure it out."

Another common question related to dealing with negative buyer feedback. This was a touchy subject for some influencers, seizing the opportunity to rant about buyers with unrealistic expectations. This was especially true for Whatnot streamers who sell preloved or vintage items. They disclosed strategies to reduce the risk for negative feedback by adding disclaimers to the auction items and repeating over and over "this is a preloved item. I tried to explain the condition to the best of my ability." Two influencers also noted they most often receive negative feedback from other influencers and from chat members who do not like the givey. Influencers expressed frustration and confusion regarding other influencers leaving negative feedback. The chat often weighed in and "called bullshit." Other influencers often shared similar stories in the chat, further building community through shared experience.

Disruptors and Defenders

Whatnot influencers often choose to have moderators or "mods" in their chat to help make sure they do not miss item requests, to reinforce policies, or answer simple questions presented by chat. One of the most common questions asked during the data collection period include "are these items authentic." In the luxury and sneaker categories, for example, influencers and mods often stressed the use of Entrupy, a handheld device that scans each item in various locations to compare the item to millions of stock photos of both counterfeit and real luxury items (Entrupy, 2023). One critical function of mods, depending on the influencer's setting, is the ability to temporarily or permanently block or silence/mute Whatnoters who are perceived to be disruptive based on the established community parameters.

Whatnot chat members may engage in a multitude of behaviors that are deemed by influencers as disruptive. The most common observed during the data collection period included the following: (1) disgruntled buyers who want a public platform to confront the influencer; (2) fellow Whatnot influencers who take offense to an influencer who sells items outside of their assigned category; (3) Whatnoters who challenge the influencer's business model; and (4) Whatnoters who accuse influencers of crashing the value of the market in a particular category. For example, one chat member was banned because they took offense to a card influencer auctioning toys during a show scheduled in the card category. One chat member was banned after they accused an influencer who starts luxury items as dolla hollas for crashing the luxury market. They were unable to make money because "influencers like them underprice and undervalue their items."

While "mods" play a more formal role in advocating for influencers, the chat was also observed defending their favorite influencers. When buyers share negative feedback, they may reply with "this is not the appropriate time or place. The seller is very responsive if you just message them." When chat members accuse influencers of crashing the market with dolla hollas, they may challenge the buyer by saying "no one makes you sell on this platform. No one makes you start your items at a dollar" or "maybe this isn't the platform for you." Chat participants often join forces and may present comment after comment in an attempt to silence the disrupter. Influencers may choose to directly engage in a disrupter; however, the influencers observed during the data collection period chose to let other community members be "the bad guy. I am just grateful for all my customers. Whatnot is about community."

DISCUSSION

Strategic communication is an important consideration for SMIs, especially those seeking to engage in S-commerce, an emerging form of creation, connection, and selling. As argued by Sundermann and Raabe (2019), more scholarship is needed from a strategic communication perspective to better understand the communication practices and strategies of SMIs. Through the analysis of 10 livestreams on the platform Whatnot, this chapter sought to respond to this call for additional scholarship to better understand the strategic communication tactics of SMIs through the theoretical constructs of social capital and engagement.

Often SMIs in public relations scholarship are considered third-party entities hired by an organization to leverage their legitimacy to sell a product. Whatnot is a unique platform in which SMIs may not be connected with a specific brand and instead, seek to leverage their own social capital and ability to cultivate engagement to sell specific items. Furthermore, livestreaming is a unique space different from static social media posts in that it requires SMIs to engage in unique utterances to foster audience engagement. As a result, we identified *the strategic communication performance of selling,* as the ways in which influencers engage in strategic communication to put on a performance of selling products. We define *the strategic communication performance of selling* through the combination of four communication elements: performing-performing vs. performing-not performing, transparency/vulnerability, established norms, and perception of dispersion of power. We further explicate these elements below.

Performance of Performing

Oftentimes on social media, authenticity is touted as the most important communication technique used by SMIs. Authenticity, defined as "presenting a consistent, positive, and 'true' self across online and offline context which necessitated sharing both positive and negative content on social media" (Haimson et al., 2021, p. 2). Associated with authenticity is the idea of performing-not-performing (Dubrofsky & Ryalls, 2014; McDermott & Caslin, in press), i.e., creating the illusion that a performance is natural behavior. Dubrofsky and Ryalls (2014) note performing not-performing is defined as when people perform their seemingly true selves unconsciously in front of a camera and audience to achieve the presentation of an authentic self.

Contrary to these assumptions, the findings in this study identified that the influencers in this study engaged in the performance of performing. Specifically, the influencers in this study were overt in their performance of selling and thus, actively acknowledged that they were selling products and wanted to receive more money. Instead of attempting to perform not-performing to foster a sense of authenticity, influencers explicitly engaged in a performance of performing to sell their products. For example, during Dolla Holla's and giveys, influencers were not shy in calling out low bids and acknowledging how a low bid would impact their profits. Influencers encouraged users to bid more and take action in the chat to receive giveys.

As a result, the overt performance of performing played a role in the engagement of the users in the auction overall and expectations of influencers' behavior on the app. Whatnot influencers overtly performing selling products is important to note considering recent calls for platforms to have stricter standards regarding SMIs promoting products (i.e., being strategically vague about a social media post being an ad or not; e.g., Freberg, 2022). Thus, the relationship between SMIs' ability to sell products on S-commerce and engage with respective users about their platform capital helps demonstrate the parallels between strategic communication and marketing practices.

Transparency and Vulnerability

Even though users are aware of the selling performance, influencers still have to engage in transparent and vulnerable communication. Previous research has found that SMIs are more influential than other celebrities because consumers feel more intensely connected to the daily lives of SMIs due to the accessibility of the information they share about their experiences (Angraini, 2023). Thus, SMIs occupy as unique space as both a person and an organization. Because of this positionality, SMIs must be strategic in the communication they employ. From the data we identified that influencers must engage in the use of transparency and vulnerability with users to maintain engagement and, correspondingly, continue successful sales practices.

Related to transparency, SMIs must accurately describe the product they are selling to build trust with users, as well as share factually correct information about the product or history of the industry to avoid negative impacts to their organizational reputation. Repeating phrases such as "this is a preloved item," sharing anything wrong with the item, giving context to the product, and explaining its rareness were some of the communication strategies influencers used to try to build and maintain transparency with users. Influencers were also able to build and maintain transparency with users by responding respectfully to disrupters and partnering with users if there was an issue with a product. These community relations help further inform trust related to user purchasing intentions, as influencers who were open and transparent regarding the auction products could help maintain positive community feedback loops, enhancing platform capital.

Additionally, to build community, SMIs engaged in vulnerable communication. Vulnerability was cultivated by sharing aspects of themselves as a person, e.g., expressing gratitude, discussing the TV shows they are watching, and sharing holiday plans. This strategic disclosure of information created a sense of vulnerability as influencers shared details about themselves that were not directly related to selling, emphasizing their personhood. Some influencers even schedule specific shows that were not related to selling such as providing an inside look into the influencers' lives or answering questions about the livestreaming profession. Importantly, these conversations helped to move an influencer from surface level engagement (e.g., metrics of likes and clicks) to a collaborative engagement (Dhanesh, 2017) that helped to create positive, memorable experiences for users. In turn, this positive engagement with SMIs can effect buyer intentions and auction loyalty as social capital helps inform financial investment (Freberg, 2022; Kennan & Hazelton, 2006; Kitchen & Moss, 1995).

Established Norms

Importantly, to build social capital (Kennan & Hazelton, 2006), as well as showcase insider knowledge, SMIs engaged in the established norms of the platform. From using platform specifics such as thumbnails to tease upcoming events to the use of language such as "blessing the chat," the adherence to already established communication norms was integral for influencers to build and maintain their social capital on the app. Using platform specific norms also helped to increase user engagement as influencers encouraged users to communicate with each other in the chat to share congratulations and engage in bidding wars. Things like giveys, "blessing the chat," and raids, unique to Whatnot as a platform, contributed to the cultivation of an insider knowledge network to make users feel like a part of a tight-knit closed community. These norms were also used to entice users to join auctions, help increase engagement when there was a lull in the auction, and maintain overall user engagement during a livestream. Notably, such investment and knowledge of an online community helps establish brand loyalty and platform validation, further informing the effectiveness of Whatnot's influencer commerce actions (Freberg, 2022).

Dispersion of Power

Lastly, the dispersion of power was an important element for enhancing engagement with users and played an important role in the overall strategic performance of selling. Notably, power was not held by either influencers or users at any given time but was perceived as a give-and-take through discourse among influencers and users. While influencers hosted the livestream, had accessibility to the products, and were the only ones able to use verbal communication, they shared power with the users.

One example of the dispersion of power is through the chat function. Through the chat, users were able to converse directly with the influencer, connect with others, and share their thoughts and opinions. For example, through the chat, as the auction occurred, users were able to call out influencers to express their happiness or dismay. Users had the opportunity to share their voice and perspective through the use of the chat directly with the influencer and those in the auctions. The chat function also allowed influencers to ask users to answer questions, participate in polls, and share information as influencers engaged in conversations related or unrelated to selling.

Second, users were able to use the platform specific norms of callouts to hold influencers accountable. Callouts refer to influencers showing all the imperfections of a product or showcasing that a product was unopened before bidding to ensure it was a high-quality product. This required accountability from influencers as lying about a product can result in bad ratings and getting booted from the platform.

Third, influencers shared power by asking users to help monitor the chat, giving users agency in who was allowed to continue to participate in the community of the auction. Users were allowed to remove others who might be disruptive or have ill-intentions (e.g., givey goblin), helping to set and maintain the tone of the livestream. These cited examples of the platform's shared allocation of power provides unique insight into the structural dimension of Whatnot's platform capital (Kennan & Hazelton, 2006), as the communities formed by the influencers and chat engagement co-construct the value and direction of Whatnot's avenues for S-commerce. This connection helps to emphasize the relationship between public relations and marketing (Kitchen & Moss, 1995), specifically how social capital helps to inform financial influence and power.

LIMITATIONS AND FUTURE RESEARCH

This research had some limitations. First, the data collected represented only 10 influencers on a platform that has tens of thousands of influencers. Moreover, the researchers only viewed one hour for each influencer, limiting the amount of data collected. Additional inquiry into other influencers, as well as longer viewing sessions could yield more tactics and characteristics of communication among influencers and users. Second, only one S-commerce platform was used for analysis. Additional research across S-commerce sites, as well as non-western platforms and platforms outside of the U.S. could provide insights into different norms and expectations of selling. It is important to note, however, that Whatnot continues to open in new markets, including the United Kingdom and India.

CONCLUSION

Overall, S-commerce sites provide new avenues for scholarship to understand the communication strategies and techniques used to cultivate community during product promotions. The findings from this study add to the literature the concept of *the strategic communication performance of selling,* e.g., the ways in which influencers engage in strategic communication to put on a performance of selling products. Because of the unique scenario of explicit selling performance in a digital culture that touts authenticity, understanding the elements that can be used in conjunction to foster community on a commerce-based app helps to further our understanding of the role of strategic communication in public relations and financial decision-making.

REFERENCES

Agostino, D. (2013). Using social media to engage citizens: A study of Italian municipalities. *Public Relations Review*, *39*(3), 232–234. doi:10.1016/j.pubrev.2013.02.009

Angraini, N. (2023). Social media marketing influencer: Literature review on promotional strategies using the influence of social media celebrities. *International Journal of Economic Research and Financial Accounting*, *1*(4). Advance online publication. doi:10.55227/ijerfa.v1i4.42

Arrington, M. (2005, November 14). Yahoo Shoposphere just launched. *TechCrunch.* https://techcrunch.com/2005/11/14/yahoo-shoposphere-launches-tonight/

Arula, K. (2021, December 1). *The evolution of social commerce: What, when, how and why?* Insights for Professionals. https://www.insightsforprofessionals.com/marketing/ecommerce/evolution-of-social-commerce

Balestra, D. (2022, December 19). *WhatNot app: Pros & cons of auction apps like WhatNot.* Vendoo. https://blog.vendoo.co/live-selling-the-pros-cons-of-selling-on-whatnot-app

Bourdieu, P. (1986). The forms of capital. In J. G. Richardson (Ed.), *Handbook of theory and research for the sociology of education* (pp. 241–258). Greenwood.

Cheng, Y. (2018). Looking back, moving forward: A review and reflection of the organization–public relationship (OPR) research. *Public Relations Review*, *44*(1), 120–130. doi:10.1016/j.pubrev.2017.10.003

CloudFlare. (n.d.). *What is live streaming? How live streaming works.* https://www.cloudflare.com/learning/video/what-is-live-streaming/

Crunchbase. (2023). *Whatnot financials.* https://www.crunchbase.com/organization/Whatnot

Deloitte Analysis. (2023, February). *The rise of social commerce: A growth opportunity for brands.* https://www2.deloitte.com/content/dam/Deloitte/nl/Documents/deloitte-nl-consumer-the-rise-of-social-commerce.pdf

Dhanesh, G., Duthler, G., & Li, K. (2022). Social media engagement with organization-generated content: Role of visuals in enhancing public engagement with organizations on Facebook and Instagram. *Public Relations Review*, *48*(2), 102174. Advance online publication. doi:10.1016/j.pubrev.2022.102174

Dhanesh, G. S. (2017). Putting engagement in its PRoper place: State of the field, definition and model of engagement in public relations. *Public Relations Review*, *43*(5), 925–933. doi:10.1016/j.pubrev.2017.04.001

Dodd, M. D. (2016). Intangible resource management: Social capital theory development for public relations. *Journal of Communication Management (London)*, *20*(4), 289–311. doi:10.1108/JCOM-12-2015-0095

Dubrofsky, R. E., & Ryalls, E. D. (2014). The Hunger Games: Performing not-performing to authenticate femininity and whiteness. *Critical Studies in Media Communication*, *31*(5), 395–409. doi:10.1080/15295036.2013.874038

Entrupy. (2023). *Luxury retailers.* https://www.entrupy.com/luxury-reinfluencers/

Freberg, K. (2022). *Social media for strategic communication: Creative strategies and research-based applications*. Sage Publications.

Gagne, N., & Maini, S. (2022, October 29). *Whatnot.* Contrary Research. https://research.contrary.com/reports/Whatnot

Grunig, J. E. (2006). Furnishing the edifice: Ongoing research on public relations as a strategic management function. *Journal of Public Relations Research*, *18*(2), 151–176. doi:10.1207/s1532754xjprr1802_5

Haimson, O. L., Liu, T., Zhang, B. Z., & Corvite, S. (2021). The online authenticity paradox: What being" authentic" on social media means, and barriers to achieving it. *Proceedings of the ACM on Human-Computer Interaction*, *5*(2), 1–18. doi:10.1145/3479567

Hallahan, K., Holtzhausen, D., Van Ruler, B., Vercic, D., & Sriramesh, K. (2007). Defining strategic communication. *International Journal of Strategic Communication*, *1*(1), 3–35. doi:10.1080/15531180701285244

Heide, M., von Platen, S., Simonsson, C., & Falkheimer, J. (2018). Expanding the scope of strategic communication: Towards a holistic understanding of organizational complexity. *International Journal of Strategic Communication*, *12*(4), 452–468. doi:10.1080/1553118X.2018.1456434

Hou, F., Guan, Z., Li, B., & Chong, A. Y. L. (2020). Factors influencing people's continuous watching intention and consumption intention in live streaming: Evidence from China. *Internet Research*, *30*(1), 141–163. doi:10.1108/INTR-04-2018-0177

Kennan, W. R., & Hazelton, V. (2006). Internal public relations, social capital, and the role of effective organizational communication. In C. H. Botan & V. Hazelton (Eds.), *Public relations theory II* (pp. 311–341). Lawrence Erlbaum.

Kent, M. L., & Taylor, M. (2021). Fostering dialogic engagement: Toward an architecture of social media for social change. *Social Media + Society*, *7*(1), 205630512098446. Advance online publication. doi:10.1177/2056305120984462

Kitchen, P. J., & Moss, D. (1995). Marketing and public relations: The relationship revisited. *Journal of Marketing Communications*, *1*(2), 105–106. doi:10.1080/13527269500000012

Liu, Z., Li, J., Wang, X., & Guo, Y. (2023). How search and evaluation cues influence consumers' continuous watching and purchase intentions: An investigation of live-stream shopping from an information foraging perspective. *Journal of Business Research*, *168*, 114233. Advance online publication. doi:10.1016/j.jbusres.2023.114233

Luo, X., Lim, W. M., Cheah, J. H., Lim, X. J., & Dwivedi, Y. K. (2023). Live streaming commerce: A review and research agenda. *Journal of Computer Information Systems*, 1–24. doi:10.1080/08874417.2023.2290574

McDermott, V., & Caslin, T. (in press). Day 206 of being a girl: How LGBTQ+ GenZ are communicatively performing and disrupting traditional expectations of gender on TikTok. In R. R. Reynolds (Ed.), *Mediating Sex, Gender, and Sexuality in the Gen Z Era*. New York University Press.

Men, L. R., & Tsai, W. H. S. (2013). Beyond liking or following: Understanding public engagement on social networking sites in China. *Public Relations Review*, *39*(1), 13–22. doi:10.1016/j.pubrev.2012.09.013

Men, L. R., Tsai, W. S., Chen, Z. F., & Ji, Y. G. (2018). Social presence and digital dialogic communication: Engagement lessons from top social CEOs. *Journal of Public Relations Research*, *30*(3), 83–99. doi:10.1080/1062726X.2018.1498341

Neuendorf, K. A. (2017). The content analysis guidebook. *Sage (Atlanta, Ga.)*.

Patton, M. Q. (2014). Qualitative research & evaluation methods: Integrating theory and practice. *Sage (Atlanta, Ga.)*.

Shah, S. (2021, September 17). *'A monstrous market': Whatnot co-founder Grant Lafontaine on what's next for the livestream shopping unicorn*. ModernRetail. https://www.modernretail.co/retailers/a-monstrous-market-Whatnot-co-founder-grant-lafontaine-on-whats-next-for-the-livestream-shopping-unicorn/

Shodipe-Dosunmu, A. (2023, June 9). *The history and evolution of live streaming*. Make Use Of. https://www.makeuseof.com/history-of-live-streaming/

Sommer, V. (2020). Multimodal analysis in qualitative research: Extending grounded theory through the lens of social semiotics. *Qualitative Inquiry*, *27*(8-9), 1102–1113. Advance online publication. doi:10.1177/1077800420978746

Sun, Y., Shao, X., Li, X., Guo, Y., & Nie, K. (2019). How live streaming influences purchase intentions in social commerce: An IT affordance perspective. *Electronic Commerce Research and Applications*, *37*, 100886. Advance online publication. doi:10.1016/j.elerap.2019.100886

Sundermann, G., & Raabe, T. (2019). Strategic communication through social media influencers: Current state of research and desiderata. *International Journal of Strategic Communication*, *13*(4), 278–300. doi:10.1080/1553118X.2019.1618306

Tracy, S. J. (2019). *Qualitative research methods: Collecting evidence, crafting analysis, communicating impact*. John Wiley & Sons.

Ventre, I., Mollá-Descals, A., & Frasquet, M. (2021). Drivers of social commerce usage: A multi-group analysis comparing Facebook and Instagram. *Ekonomska Istrazivanja*, *34*(1), 570–589. doi:10.1080/1331677X.2020.1799233

Wang, Y., & Yang, Y. (2020). Dialogic communication on social media: How organizations use twitter to build dialogic relationships with their publics. *Computers in Human Behavior*, *104*, 106183. Advance online publication. doi:10.1016/j.chb.2019.106183

West, C. (2023, October 26). *22 influencer marketing statistics to guide your brand's strategy in 2023.* Sprout Social. https://sproutsocial.com/insights/influencer-marketing-statistics/

Whatnot. (2023a). https://www.Whatnot.com/

Whatnot. (2023b). *About us.* https://www.Whatnot.com/about-us

Whatnot. (2023c). *Browse by category.* https://www.Whatnot.com/explore

Whatnot. (2023d). *Bags & accessories.* https://www.Whatnot.com/category/bags_jewelry_accessories

Whatnot. (2023e). *Understanding how rankings work on Whatnot.* https://help.Whatnot.com/hc/en-us/articles/12190921464461-Understanding-how-ranking-works-on-Whatnot

Whatnot. (2023f, December 22). *Giveaways overview.* https://help.Whatnot.com/hc/en-us/articles/11329417780365-Giveaways-Overview

Whatnot. (2023g, December 22). *Whatnot return policy.* https://help.Whatnot.com/hc/en-us/articles/360061194552-Whatnot-Return-Policy

Wongkitrungrueng, A., Dehouche, N., & Assarut, N. (2020). Live streaming commerce from the sellers' perspective: Implications for online relationship marketing. *Journal of Marketing Management*, *36*(5-6), 488–518. doi:10.1080/0267257X.2020.1748895

Zerfass, A., Verčič, D., Nothhaft, H., & Werder, K. P. (2018). Strategic communication: Defining the field and its contribution to research and practice. *International Journal of Strategic Communication*, *12*(4), 487–505. doi:10.1080/1553118X.2018.1493485

KEY TERMS AND DEFINITIONS

Engagement: A way for both publics and organization to interact through the communication process to foster the creation of quality relationships.

Livestream(ing): Real-time video content with chat interaction.

Social Capital: An intangible resource based on a societies' social structures that lends power and legitimacy to an individual or organization based on access to resources (e.g., knowledge, expertise, relationships, and respect).

Social Commerce: Combines the social interaction functions of traditional social media platforms with the convenience of the online retail experience, creating an immersive experience for consumers.

Social Media Influencers (SMIs): Someone who has an online presence and is viewed as an authority on a specific topic, practice, or position.

Strategic Communication: Communicating with purpose.

Whatnot: A commerce app that combines live stream selling with the thrill of real-time bidding connecting buyers and influencers.

Whatnoters: Whatnoters is a term coined by the authors to define the community of buyers and influencers on the Whatnot platform. Any user of the Whatnot platform is considered a Whatnoter for research purposes.

ENDNOTE

1 Whatnoters is a term coined by the authors to define the community of buyers and influencers on the Whatnot platform. Any user of the platform is considered a Whatnoter for research purposes.

Section 3
Influencers in Industries

Chapter 7
Skin Deep:
Body Positivity Influencer Campaigns

David Lynn Painter
https://orcid.org/0000-0001-5808-6319
Rollins College, USA

Tanja Vierrether
https://orcid.org/0000-0003-3066-1523
Rollins College, USA

Camilla L. Guimaraes
Rollins College, USA

ABSTRACT

This investigation used expectancy violation theory (EVT) to explain how a body positivity influencer's clothing styles (modest or revealing) and skin tones (filtered or unfiltered) affected viewers' responses to branded Instagram posts violating (i.e., unfiltered and revealing) or confirming (i.e., filtered and modest) appearance norms. Specifically, viewers' attractiveness and authenticity ratings as well as their emotional responses were measured to verify that their appearance norm internalization triggered EVT's effects. Finally, this study explored how viewers' attractiveness, authenticity, and emotional response ratings mediated the effect of the influencer's appearance on their purchase intentions. The results indicate viewers punished norm violations in their attractiveness ratings but rewarded them in their authenticity and emotional response ratings. Finally, viewers' emotional responses and authenticity ratings more powerfully shaped their purchase intentions than their attractiveness ratings. These results suggest body positivity influencer marketing may mutually benefit both sponsors and consumers while countering toxic appearance norms on social media and society at large.

INTRODUCTION

Research indicates Instagram has joined other visual media (e.g., television, magazines, and movies) in cultivating unrealistic appearance norms for women that negatively affect their self-image, body satis-

DOI: 10.4018/979-8-3693-0912-4.ch007

faction, and overall well-being (Brown and Tiggemann, 2020; Tiggemann and Anderberg, 2020). This literature also suggests the use of filters and photo-editing software significantly contributes to these negative outcomes (Kleemans et al., 2018; McComb et al., 2021). These issues are particularly salient because about 90% of women who use Instagram indicate they edit or filter photos before posting them (Gill, 2023).

At the same time as filtering became the norm on Instagram, the body positivity movement also became popular on social media. This movement addresses society's unrealistic and unattainable beauty standards through posts showing more genuine and representative images of women to cultivate an appreciation for body diversity and self-love (Lazuka et al., 2020; Stevens and Griffiths, 2020). Over time, social media influencers and brands have also used body positivity messages to promote their products and services. However, we are only beginning to understand how viewers respond to these sponsored posts. For example, Brathwaite and DeAndrea (2022) used the persuasion knowledge model to explain why promotional body positivity Instagram posts were less effective than non-promotional posts at promoting body inclusivity, acceptance, and appreciation. Moreover, Vendemia and colleagues (2021) used objectification and warranting theories to explain why body positivity Instagram posts labeled as edited or sexualized (i.e., "posed suggestively with most of body unclothed") were less effective than posts labeled as unedited and not sexualized (i.e., "posed non-suggestively and fully clothed") at promoting body positivity (p. 139).

While interesting and informative, most of this research analyzed the body positivity movement using psychological theories and wellness outcomes (e.g., Brown and Tiggemann, 2020; Cohen et al., 2019; McComb et al., 2021). Alternately, some studies used marketing communications theories and outcomes to analyze the effects of sponsored Instagram posts (e.g., Brathwaite and DeAndrea, 2022; Shoenberger et al., 2020). To date, however, this literature is limited to comparisons of thin-ideal to plus-size models, sponsored to unsponsored content, or uses textual cues to indicate edits were made to change the model's body. Thus, many questions remain about the influence of body positivity posts on viewers' responses to sponsoring brands. To address these gaps in the literature, Vendemia and colleagues (2021) called for experiments that manipulated images of the same body positivity model or influencer to explore how the post's appearance characteristics and the viewers' psychological traits influenced their responses. Moreover, Brathwaite and DeAndrea (2022) called for research that included market-driven outcome variables in their analyses.

To answer these calls, this study used a communication theory to explain how a body positivity influencer's clothing styles and skin filters affected viewers' responses to branded or sponsored Instagram posts. Specifically, expectancy violation theory (EVT) provided a framework for organizing existing knowledge while also exploring the effects of branded boy positivity Instagram influencer posts on women viewers' perceptions, attitudes, and behavioral intentions. To do so, participants' perceived attractiveness and authenticity ratings as well as their emotional responses to the posts were used as dependent variables to measure the strength, direction, and boundaries of EVT's effects. In particular, the influencer's clothing style (modest or fully clothed versus revealing or mostly bare) and skin tones (filtered or unfiltered) were manipulated to compare the effects of posts violating (i.e., unfiltered and revealing) rather than confirming (i.e., filtered and modest) appearance norms. Next, the extent to which the viewers' internalization of society's appearance norms triggered EVT's effects was measured. Finally, this study explored how attractiveness, authenticity, and emotional response ratings mediated the effect of the influencer's appearance condition on viewers' purchase intentions.

LITERATURE REVIEW

Body Positivity

Body positivity refers to the social movement challenging restrictive, unrealistic, and unattainable appearance norms and urging people of all body types, skin tones, abilities, gender, and racial identities to accept their bodies, celebrate self-love through body appreciation, and resist all forms of body shame (Avalos et al., 2005; Leboeuf, 2019). Body positivity is closely linked to the fat acceptance movement that originated in the 1960s to fight discrimination against overweight people and draw attention to the culture of fat-shaming and weight stigma. Indeed, the knowledge generated through the fat acceptance movement and scholarship are the foundation of body positivity activism and research. For instance, we know that overweight women are sexualized and objectified less frequently than thin women because they are dehumanized, held to stricter standards of modesty, and face negative social pressures when dressed revealing (Holland and Haslam, 2013: Sokolova et al., 2022). However, body positivity is broader than fat acceptance, encompassing people of all body shapes and sizes because body image issues and eating disorders are not limited to overweight people. These differences notwithstanding, both movements challenge the dominant thin, White, cisgendered, and able-bodied appearance norms to shift the focus from the body's appearance to its health and functionality (Sastre, 2014).

While the media's propagation of unrealistic appearance norms and the negative outcomes they cause women have been established for decades (Frederick et al., 2017; Grabe et al., 2008), recent research indicates social media also exert powerfully negative responses from women (Fioravanti et al., 2022). To address concerns over these toxic practices and outcomes, Tessa Holliday (formerly Munster) founded the social media dimension of the body positivity movement when she created the @effyourbeautystandards on Instagram in 2013 (Cwynar-Horta, 2016). This Instagram account called on women of every shape, size, and background to post images celebrating their bodies to counter unrealistic appearance norms, including prohibitions against plus-sized women wearing revealing clothing (Caldeira and De Ridder, 2017).

Although the body positivity movement's goals are laudable and the most popular social media accounts adhere to the movement's mission, it is not without critics. For example, one content analysis indicated nearly 80% of all body positivity Instagram posts "at least somewhat embodied culturally based beauty ideals including smooth skin" (Lazuka et al., 2020, p. 87). Further, while seeing body positive posts may reduce body dissatisfaction compared to thin-ideal posts, they also may increase women's body objectification due to their focus on appearance (Cohen et al., 2019). Finally, one of the most salient criticisms of body positivity is its use in promotional campaigns (Braithwaite and DeAndrea, 2022; Cwynar-Horta, 2016).

Commodification

Many brands have adopted the body positivity movement's values, images, and messages in their promotional campaigns. Specifically, Dove's *Real Beauty* campaign is one of the most prominent examples. Dove's campaign showed women who were "wrinkled, freckled, pregnant, had stretch marks, or might be seen as fat" (Johnston and Taylor, 2008, p. 942). The Dove campaign was so successful that other brands began using the movement for promotional purposes (Cwynar-Horta, 2016).

Perhaps most prominently, many fashion brands and influencers use body positivity messages in their campaigns. For example, *Aerie Real* uses unedited images of models with diverse body types to promote its products, and research indicates they elicit more positive emotional responses than traditional ads (Rodgers et al., 2019). Thus, commodification has increased body diversity in many promotional campaigns, which may positively influence women's body satisfaction compared to traditional campaigns that have the opposite effect (Clayton et al., 2017). And while branded body positive posts may be perceived as less authentic than non-promotional posts, they may nonetheless positively influence viewers' body image, satisfaction, and wellness (Brown and Tiggemann, 2020; Stevens and Griffiths, 2020).

Clothing and Filter Norms

These positive outcomes notwithstanding, some critics contend commodification undermines the movement's efficacy because people may perceive body positivity as just another superficial marketing strategy. This argument is based on research indicating there was an inverse relationship between viewers' recognition of body positivity posts' promotional purposes and their belief that they endorsed inclusive beauty standards (Brathwaite and DeAndrea, 2022). Similarly, Vendemia and colleagues (2021) found that "the perceived sexualization and modification of body positive images substantively influence how viewers evaluate and respond to body positive images on Instagram" (p. 144). Specifically, images showing women dressed revealingly and posed suggestively triggered viewers to sexually objectify themselves, to perceive the posts as self-serving, and to endorse traditional appearance standards (Vendemia et al., 2021). However, this line of research has not yet compared branded body positivity Instagram influencer posts to each other, leaving many questions unanswered. For example, how do viewers' responses vary depending on whether the influencer is dressed modestly or revealingly, and her skin tones are unfiltered or filtered?

To answer these questions, the current study examines the effects of revealing dress, not sexualization, because many body positivity posts, including sponsored content for swimwear and lingerie, do not show women in sexually suggestive poses. This distinction is important because the poses (e.g., seductive gaze, arching back, tilting head toward camera), not revealing clothing (most of the body bare), characterize sexualization and trigger objectification (Biefeld and Brown, 2021; Bernard et al., 2019). Additionally, prior research used text to indicate photo-editing software was used to change the size and shape of the women in the body positivity posts (Shoenberger et al., 2020). However, the current study relies on visual cues to compare responses to the same body positivity influencer with filtered and smooth skin or with unfiltered skin, acne, and stretch marks. The purpose of this exploration is not only to demonstrate that posts showing the body positivity influencer with unfiltered skin in revealing clothing violate appearance norms, but also to use EVT as the framework for measuring how those violations shaped viewers' responses.

Expectancy Violation Theory

To explain how clothing styles and skin filtering may influence viewers' responses to branded body positivity influencer Instagram posts, appearance norm internalization is conceptualized as the mechanism triggering viewers' more powerful responses to the posts violating normative expectations (i.e., unfiltered and dressed revealingly). These powerful responses may be explained by EVT, which was originally developed to explain the effects of nonverbal (i.e., proxemics) violations during interpersonal interactions (Burgoon, 1978). More recently, EVT is becoming increasingly popular as an analytic framework explaining responses to norm-violating practices in online advertising, digital public relations, and social media marketing (e.g., Boerman et al., 2017; Park et al., 2021; Yim, 2019).

Put simply, prior research suggests both offline and online norm-violating behaviors elicit higher levels of arousal and more powerful responses than norm-confirming behaviors. The effects' direction, however, "are a function of the rewardingness of the initiator, the direction of deviations from expectations, and the magnitude of deviation" (Burgoon, 2015, p. 3). That is: the direction of the effects (positive or negative) is shaped by an assessment of individual (e.g., attractiveness and charisma) and contextual (e.g., relationship and status) factors, as well as the extent to which the behavior confirms or violates norms (Nicholls and Rice, 2017). For example, people may respond more positively to norm violating behaviors from social media influencers than from "regular" users due to their distinct status (Vendemia and DeAndrea, 2018). Further, users respond more positively to transparently rather than covertly sponsored posts (Dhanesh and Duthler, 2019). Thus, it is important to compare branded body positivity posts to each other when assessing how images that violate (i.e., unfiltered and revealing) rather than confirm (i.e., filtered and modest) other appearance norms influence viewers' responses. And while all posts showing a plus-sized model may violate the thin-ideal appearance norm, EVT explains that additional violations (e.g., unfiltered skin and revealing dress) may elicit even more powerful responses. The direction of those effects in terms of viewers' attractiveness, authenticity, and emotional response ratings, however, has not yet been determined.

Attractiveness

Physical attractiveness has been broadly defined as the extent to which a person's image elicits favorable responses from others within a particular culture (Morrow, 1990). While seemingly subjective, attractiveness ratings are remarkably reliable (e.g., Sprecher and Hatfield, 2022), and closely associated with advertisement and influencer effectiveness (e.g., AlFarraj et al., 2020; Brumbaugh, 1993). Broadly, this research indicates "what is beautiful is good" (Eagly et al., 1991, p. 109) because attractiveness has been linked to a wide range of positive responses (Caballero et al., 1989; Eisend and Langner, 2010; Taillon et al., 2020). However, we were unable to locate prior research that used attractiveness as a dependent rather than a control variable when testing viewers' responses to body positivity posts. Therefore, attractiveness in this study is conceptualized as an aesthetic judgment based on cultural appearance norms so that we can compare ratings across conditions and explore relationships with purchase intentions.

Authenticity

Next, authenticity is defined as the extent to which a brand is perceived as genuine, unique, honest, and committed to enduring values (Campagna et al., 2023). Although long recognized as influential, authenticity has become an increasingly popular variable as social media transformed relationships between brands and publics over the last 15 years (Kowalczyk et al., 2016; Vrontis et al., 2021). This line of research indicates authenticity is critical to influencer credibility and positively related to brand trust, attitudes, and purchase intentions (Portal et al., 2019; Wang and Weng, 2024; Yang et al., 2021).

Of particular interest in this study, Shoenberger and colleagues (2020) found that plus-sized models whose body shapes and sizes were labeled as unedited in *Aeire Real* Instagram posts elicited higher authenticity ratings than posts labeled as edited posts showing thin-ideal models. However, other researchers found revealing clothing and photo-editing may negatively influence authenticity ratings (Rodgers et al., 2019; Vendemia et al., 2020). Moreover, perceptions of authenticity, or the viewers' belief that the brand is genuinely committed to body positivity values, may determine whether sponsored and promotional body positivity messages bolster or undermine the movement's efficacy (Vendemia et al., 2020).

Emotional Responses

Viewers' emotional responses are conceptually defined as "a predisposition to respond in a favourable or unfavourable manner to a particular advertising stimulus during a particular exposure" (MacKenzie & Lutz, 1989, p. 49). This attitudinal variable is frequently used in studies of advertisements and promotional social media content (e.g., Campbell and Farrell, 2020; Lee and Hong, 2016: Olney et al., 1991) because of its ability to predict ad recall, persuasiveness, purchase intentions (Burton et al., 2019; Mehta, 2000). Moreover, this literature provides compelling bases for expecting the influencer's appearance characteristics may elicit distinct responses based on the extent to which they confirm or violate normative expectations. However, we were unable to predict the direction of EVT's effects because prior findings are mixed (Bullock and Hubner, 2020; Yim, 2019). Thus, this study's first research question asks:

RQ1: How do the influencer's appearance characteristics influence viewers' responses to the branded body positivity influencer posts?

Appearance Norm Internalization

Beyond the influencers' appearance characteristics, the viewers' appearance norm internalization is also expected to influence their responses to the branded body positivity posts. This expectation is based on EVT's proposition that norm-violating behaviors elicit more powerful responses than norm-confirming behaviors. Thus, the extent to which viewers have internalized these norms may influence how they perceive and interpret behaviors in relation to those standards. Operationally, the Sociocultural Attitudes Towards Appearance Questionnaire (SATAQ) has been widely used to measure participants' appearance norm internalization (Schaefer et al., 2016).

While much of the this research used participants' SATAQ scores as a dependent variable because it approaches body positivity from a psychological angle with body image and other wellness outcomes (Huang et al., 2020), some studies more focused on marketing communications outcomes have used SATAQ scores as an independent variables because they may shape viewers' responses to body positive social media content. For example, Tiggemann and colleagues (2020) found that women with high levels of appearance norm internalization (i.e., high SATAQ scores) were more aware of and influenced by body positive social media posts than women with low levels of internalization (i.e., low SATAQ scores). Therefore, the second research question asks:

RQ2: How do viewers' appearance norm internalization influence their responses to the branded body positivity influencer posts?

Interaction Effects

In addition to the main effects of appearance characteristics and norm internalization, we also wanted to determine how these variables may interact to influence viewers' responses. The expectation that these variables may interact is based on EVT's prediction that viewers with high levels of appearance norm internalization will respond more powerfully to the norm-violating posts than viewers with lower levels of appearance norm internalization. Thus, viewers' responses to the branded body positivity influencer posts may depend not only on the influencer's appearance characteristics in each condition, but also on the extent to which they have internalized appearance norms. In this way, viewers' appearance norm internalization may function as the theoretical mechanism triggering their responses to the posts. That is: the greater their norm internalization, the more powerfully viewers may respond to the norm-violating (e.g., revealing and unfiltered) versus norm-confirming (e.g., modest and filtered) posts.

In addition to verifying its theoretical role in precipitating EVT's effects, the interaction between appearance condition and norm internalization may also provide insight into the distinctive effects that different types of body positivity messages exert on different types of viewers. In the context of this study, these interactions may identify how women with differing levels of norm internalization respond to different types of norm-confirming and norm-violating body positivity posts. This insight could provide body positivity influencers and brands with guidance in developing posts that not only improve their marketing communication strategies, but also elicit positive emotional responses from viewers with differing levels of appearance norm internalization. In particular, the expectation is that women with higher levels of appearance norm internalization will not only respond more powerfully to the posts overall in terms of main effects, but also that they will report particularly strong responses to the norm-violating posts compared to both norm-confirming posts and to women with lower levels of norm internalization. To test this expectation, the third research question asks:

RQ3: How does norm internalization interact with condition to influence viewers' responses to the branded body positivity influencer posts?

Mediation Effects: Purchase Intentions

The main reason for selecting attractiveness, authenticity, and emotions to measure viewer responses in our first three research questions was their relationships with purchase intentions. Indeed, research indicates that these variables are important measures of brand perceptions and attitudes that may mediate relationships between the sponsors' messages and the viewers' purchase intentions (Burton, 2019; Kim et al., 2020; Yang et al., 2021). Moreover, brands are probably most interested in the ways sponsored influencer posts shape consumer behavior and affect their revenue. Thus, we hypothesize that responses to the branded body positivity posts will mediate the relationship between the influencer's appearance condition and the viewers' purchase intentions.

H1: The effect of the influencer's appearance condition on viewers' purchase intentions will be mediated by (a) attractiveness, (b) authenticity, and (c) emotional response.

METHOD

Pretest: Stimuli Images

To answer the research questions, an image search and a pretest were conducted to locate and validate that they were perceived as representing each condition's defining characteristic (i.e., modest-filtered; modest-unfiltered; revealing-filtered; revealing unfiltered). This search yielded four images of Denise Bidot, a plus-size fashion model whose publicly available images were appropriate for the conditions. Thus, all four images showed the same model in varying states of skin conditions (filtered versus unfiltered) and dress (modest versus revealing). The images were then used to create mock-up Instagram posts with the fictional brand name, Bon Form, in the upper-right corner, and shown in the profile picture. Each mock-up post was liked by "Sue and 120 others" and used the hashtag "#BoPo," but no other captions (see Appendix).

Next, a pretest was conducted to ensure participants perceived the model's appearance as intended for each condition. Participants in this pretest were 104 women undergraduate students at a small liberal arts college in the southeastern U.S. Using a five-point Likert scale, these participants rated the modest-filtered image (M =1.82, SD = 1.05) significantly less revealing than the revealing-filtered image (M =4.18, SD = 1.07), $t(101) = -12.93$, $p < .01$. Similarly, the modest-unfiltered image (M =3.53, SD = 1.36) showed significantly rougher skin tones and textures than the modest-filtered image (M =1.62, SD = 0.81), t 101) = -11.89, $p < .01$. Next, the revealing-unfiltered image (M =4.29, SD = 0.90) was rated significantly more revealing than the modest-unfiltered image (M =1.65, SD = 0.73), $t(101) = 18.84$, $p < .01$. And finally, the revealing- unfiltered image (M =4.26, SD = 0.95) showed significantly rougher skin tones and textures than the revealing-filtered image (M =1.79, SD = 1.03), $t(101) = 18.32$, $p < .01$.

Design and Participants

This project's treatment conditions (modest-filtered; modest-unfiltered; revealing-unfiltered, revealing-filtered) and participants' internalization levels (low or high) created a four-by-two posttest-only factorial design. As required for Institutional Review Board approval, participants were first presented with an informed consent form explaining that "the purpose of this study is to better understand people's attitudes toward branded body positivity marketing campaigns. Additionally, you will be asked a series of questions about how you formed your body image, your feelings about your own body, and your opinions of a body positivity model in a branded Instagram post."

Next, 820 women participants were recruited from Prolific Academic to complete the questionnaire on Qualtrics between October 17-21, 2023. However, 36 participants failed the attention check item asking them to identify *Bon Form* as the name of the clothing brand sponsoring the post. The remaining 784 participants' ages ranged from 18- to 44-years-old with a median age of 30, closely mirroring the ages of most Instagram users (Dixon, 2023). The participants' racial identities were also largely representative of the population: 14% Black; 21% Hispanic or Latina; 6% Asian; 1% Native American; 5% Multiracial; and 53% White.

Procedure

First, the participants answered five items (α = .85) adapted from the Sociocultural Attitudes Towards Appearance Questionnaire (SATAQ) to measure their appearance norm internalization. Then, participants were randomly assigned to one of the four conditions and asked to view the sponsored body positivity Instagram post from *Bon Form*, a new women's clothing company. After viewing the post, participants answered a single item asking them to rate the extent to which they agreed that the influencer in the post was physically attractive on a five-point Likert scale. Next, to measure authenticity, participants were asked to answer six items (α = .91) on a five-point Likert scale: (1) This brand's model represents real people; (2) This brand connects people with their real selves; (3) This is an authentic brand; (4) This brand reflects important values people care about; (5) This brand is honest; and (6) This brand cares about its customers. Next, participants' emotional responses to the post were measured using three items (α = .81) on a five-point Likert scale: (1) This post got my attention; (2) I liked this post; and (3) This post made me feel good. Finally, purchase intentions were measured using a single item on a five-point Likert scale asking participants to indicate the extent to which they agreed with this statement: "Based on this post, I would buy something from this brand."

RESULTS

First, to answer the research questions, a median-split technique was used to create an internalization level variable with high and low values. Then, a multivariate analysis of variance (MANOVA) test was conducted to determine how the influencer's appearance (four conditions) and the participants' internalization level (high or low) influenced attractiveness, authenticity, and purchase intention ratings. Significant differences were found for condition, Wilks's $\Lambda = .67$, $F(3, 742) = 26.29$, $p < .01$, $\eta^2 = .12$, and internalization, Wilks's $\Lambda = .88$, $F(3, 742) = 33.45$, $p < .01$, $\eta^2 = .12$). Additionally, the interaction between these two independent variables was also significant, Wilks's $\Lambda = .83$, $F(3, 742) = 12.76$, $p < .01$, $\eta^2 = .05$. See Table One for means and standard deviations of all dependent variables across conditions and internalization levels.

Main Effects

Condition. First, the MANOVA results indicate the differences in attractiveness ratings across conditions were significant, (F (3, 746) = 23.50, $p < .01$, $\eta^2 = .09$). Specifically, post-hoc Bonferroni results indicate participants rated the revealing-unfiltered post significantly less attractive than the modest-unfiltered post, which was rated significantly less attractive than the revealing-filtered and modest-filtered posts, which were not significantly different from each other, p > .05 (see Table One's third row).

Norm Internalization. The second research question asked how appearance norm internalization influenced their responses. First, the MANOVA results (see rows one and two in Table One) indicate there were significant differences in attractiveness ratings (F (3, 746) = 26.23, $p < .01$, $\eta^2 = .08$) because participants with high internalization rated the posts more attractive than participants with low internalization. Second, authenticity ratings (F (3, 746) = 26.23, $p < .01$, $\eta^2 = .13$) were also significantly different

Table 1. Attractiveness, Authenticity, and emotional responses by condition and internalization

	Total (n = 748)	Modest Filtered (n = 177)	Modest Unfiltered (n = 207)	Revealing Filtered (n = 180)	Revealing Unfiltered (n = 184)
Attractiveness					
High Internalization (n = 418)	4.20* (88)	4.71^{a*} (.45)	4.37^{b*} (.48)	4.36^{b} (.89)	3.50^{c*} (.91)
Low Internalization (n = 330)	3.89* (.91)	3.86^{a*} (.95)	3.58^{a*} (1.02)	4.33^{b} (.67)	3.90^{a*} (.69)
Total (n = 748)	4.04 (.91)	4.17^{a} (.91)	3.96^{b} (.91)	4.35^{a} (.79)	3.71^{c} (.89)
Authenticity					
High Internalization (n = 418)	3.70* (.79)	3.10^{a*} (.669)	3.67^{b*} (.89)	3.76^{b*} (.83)	4.08^{c*} (.34)
Low Internalization (n = 330)	3.14* (.68)	2.83^{a*} (.60)	3.09^{b*} (.53)	3.35^{c*} (.64)	3.37^{c*} (.79)
Total (n = 748)	3.40 (.78)	2.93^{a} (.63)	3.37^{b} (.78)	3.72^{c} (.71)	3.58^{c} (.77)
Emotional Responses					
High Internalization (n = 418)	3.37* (.86)	2.81^{a} (.80)	3.52^{b*} (.87)	3.55^{b*} (1.02)	3.42^{b*} (.45)
Low Internalization (n = 330)	2.92* (.66)	2.61^{a} (.58)	2.83^{a*} (.81)	3.11^{b*} (.57)	3.24^{b*} (.42)
Total (n = 748)	3.13 (.80)	2.68^{a} (.67)	3.16^{b} (.91)	3.35^{b} (.87)	3.33^{b} (.44)

*Differences between high and low internalization scores significant, $p < .05$

$^{a, b, c}$Scores with different superscripts are significantly different from each other, $p < .05$

due to high internalization participants rated the posts more authentic than low internalization participants (see rows four and five in Table One). Third, the significant differences in emotional responses, (F (3, 746) = 48.92, $p < .01$, $\eta^2 = .06$) were due to high internalization participants reporting more positive emotional responses than low internalization participants (see rows seven and eight in Table One).

Interaction Effects

Attractiveness. The third research question asked how the influencer's appearance interacted with the viewers' norm internalization to influence their responses. First, the MANOVA results reveal the interaction effect on attractiveness was significant, (F (3, 746) = 24.14, $p < .01$, $\eta^2 = .09$). Specifically, as shown in Table One's top rows, high internalization participants' attractiveness ratings were significantly greater than low internalization participants' ratings in both modest (filtered and unfiltered) conditions. However, low internalization participants' attractiveness ratings were greater than high internalization participants in the revealing-unfiltered condition.

Authenticity. Next, the MANOVA results reveal the interaction effect on authenticity was also significant, (F (3, 746) = 3.62, $p = .01$, $\eta^2 = .02$). First, authenticity ratings among high internalization participants were significantly higher than low internalization participants across conditions. However, high internalization participants rated the revealing-unfiltered condition the most authentic while low internalization participants rated the revealing-filtered and revealing-unfiltered conditions significantly more authentic than the modest-unfiltered or the modest-filtered condition (see middle rows own in the top section of Table One).

Emotional Responses. Finally, the MANOVA results reveal the interaction on attitudes toward the posts was also significant, ($F\,(3, 746) = 5.04, p < .01, \eta^2 = .04$). As shown in the bottom section of Table One, low internalization participants' attitudes toward the revealing-filtered and revealing-unfiltered posts were not significantly different, but they were significantly higher than the modest-filtered and modest-unfiltered posts. For the high internalization participants, however, attitudes toward the modest-unfiltered, revealing-filtered or unfiltered posts were not significantly different, but they were significantly higher than their attitudes toward the modest-filtered post.

Mediation Analyses

Research question four asked how attractiveness, authenticity, and emotional response mediated the relationship between the influencer's appearance and the viewer's purchase intentions. To answer this question, three analyses were conducted using Model 4 of Hayes' Process Macro for SPSS (2022) with experimental conditions as the independent variable, purchase intention as the dependent variable, and authenticity, attractiveness, and attitudes as mediating variables. The modest-filtered (MF) condition was selected as the reference group because it most closely aligns with viewers' expectations. Thus, the models in Figures 1-3 show the relative direct, indirect, and total effects of the norm violation conditions: modest-unfiltered (MU), revealing-filtered (RF), and revealing-unfiltered (RU) on purchase intention as mediated by viewers' response ratings. The reported path coefficients are unstandardized. Paths *a* (connecting conditions and mediators) represent the mean differences in attractiveness, authenticity, and emotional responses caused by each condition.

Table 2. Indirect effects of condition on purchase intentions mediated by attractiveness, authenticity, and emotional response ratings

	Effect	SE	LLCI	ULCI
Attractiveness				
MU-MF	-.06	.03	-.11	-.01
RF-MF	-.12	.03	-.18	-.07
RU-MF	.05	.02	.00	.09
Authenticity				
MU-MF	.31	.05	.21	.41
RF-MF	.55	.06	.44	.67
RU-MF	.45	.05	.35	.55
Emotional Responses				
MU-MF	.39	.07	.26	.52
RF-MF	.53	.05	.43	.63
RU-MF	.55	.06	.42	.67

Notes: 95% confidence interval and 5000 bootstraps

Attractiveness. Figure One shows that for participants within the same condition, those rating the post higher in attractiveness also indicated higher purchase intentions, ($b = 0.26$, $t(743) = 7.34$, $p < 0.01$). The top rows of Table Two list the effects, standard errors, and confidence interval limits for each group. The indirect effects indicate that compared to participants in the MF condition, those in the RF condition reported the lowest, and those in the MU condition reported the next lowest purchase intentions due to the expectancy violation effects on their attractiveness ratings. Although the indirect effect for those in the RU condition was not significant, the effect of the independent variable on the dependent variable "can be said to be mediated by M if at least one of the [three] relative indirect effects is different from zero" (Hayes 2021, p. 206). Therefore, these results provide moderately strong support for H1a.

Authenticity. Figure Two shows that authenticity was a stronger predictor of purchase intentions than attractiveness, ($b = 0.69$, $t(743) = 18.7$, $p < 0.01$). The indirect effects of the expectancy violation effects on authenticity ratings indicate that those in the MU condition reported higher purchase intentions than those in the RU condition, who were higher than those in the RF condition, who were higher than those in the MF condition. The middle rows of Table Two list the effects, standard errors, and confidence interval limits for each group. All three indirect effects are statistically significant, therefore supporting H1b.

Emotional Responses. Figure Three shows that emotional response was a stronger predictor of purchase intentions than attractiveness and authenticity, ($b = 0.82$, $t(743) = 25.9$, $p < 0.01$). The indirect effects indicate that those in the MU condition were higher than those in the RF condition, who were higher than those in the RU condition, who were higher than those in the MF condition in their likelihood of buying the product because of the expectancy violation effect on their emotional response ratings. The bottom rows of Table Two list the effects, standard errors, and confidence interval limits for each group comparison. All three indirect effects are statistically significant, therefore supporting H1c.

Figure 1. Model of attractiveness (Attr.) mediating the effect of condition (C) represented by three grouping variables (MU-MF, RF-MF, RU-MF) on purchase intention (PI)
Notes: **** p<0.01; ** p<0.05; dashed paths in grey represent non-significant relationships.*

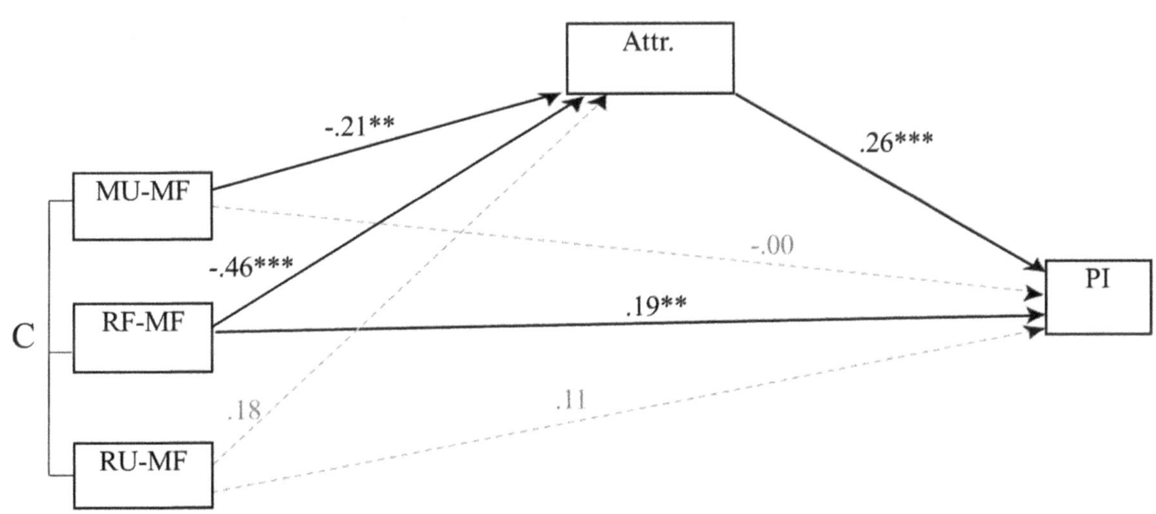

Figure 2. Model of authenticity (Auth.) mediating the effect of condition (C) represented by three grouping variables (MU-MF, RF-MF, RU-MF) on purchase intention (PI)
Notes: *All paths are significant with $p < 0.01$*

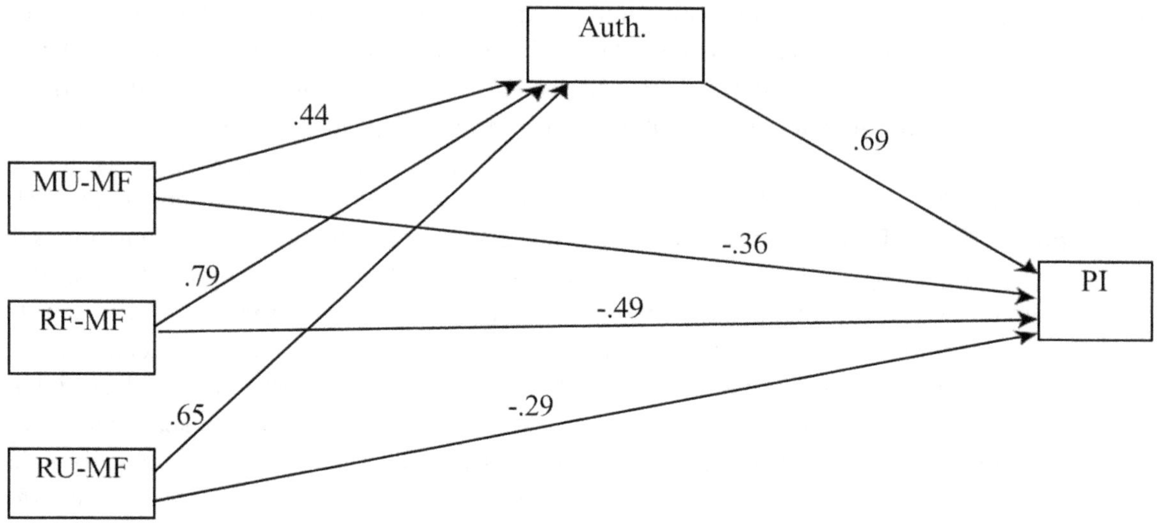

Figure 3. Model of emotional response (ER) mediating the effect of condition (C) represented by three grouping variables (MF-MU, MF-RF, MF-RU) on purchase intention (PI)
Notes: *All paths are significant with $p < 0.01$*

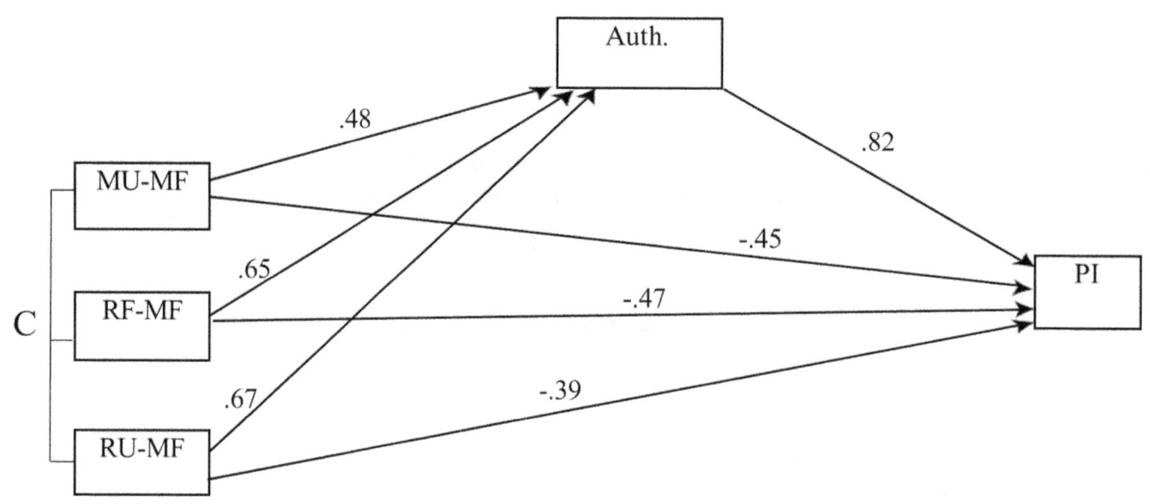

DISCUSSION

Altogether, these findings offer compelling implications for scholars analyzing body positivity's commodification and brands using the movement as part of their marketing strategy. First, the main effects indicate participants punished clothing and filter norm violations in their attractiveness ratings because the revealing-unfiltered post was rated the lowest but the modest-filtered post confirming both norms was rated the highest. Further, filters were more important than clothing because both filtered posts were rated more attractive than both unfiltered posts regardless of whether the influencer was dressed modestly or revealingly. Second, participants rewarded clothing norm violations in their authenticity ratings because both revealing posts were rated higher than the modest-unfiltered post violating the filter norm, which was more authentic than the modest-filtered post confirming both norms. Third, participants' emotional response ratings rewarded clothing and filter norm violations because the three posts violating either norm elicited stronger responses than the norm-confirming post.

Next, the interaction results support our expectation that norm internalization would function as the theoretical mechanism triggering EVT's effects because high internalization participants' more powerful responses drove the main effects. In particular, high internalization participants rated the revealing-unfiltered post violating both norms the least attractive but most authentic. Next, they rated the modest-filtered post confirming both norms the most attractive but least authentic. Moreover, high internalization participants' reported stronger positive emotional responses to the posts violating at least one norm than low internalization participants.

Theoretical Implications

More broadly, this study is one of the first to answer calls to use EVT as a framework for organizing and explaining existing knowledge about body positivity messages and their effects on viewers (Vendemia and Robinson, 2022). The results not only support EVT, but also explain the strength, direction, and limits of its effects. For example, high internalization participants rated the norm-confirming (modest-filtered) post distinctly differently from any of the three norm-violating posts across all dependent variables. On the other hand, low internalization participants largely discriminated only between modest and revealing, but not filtered or unfiltered posts. Next, attractiveness ratings were inverted, mirror images of authenticity and emotional response ratings, which aligns with research suggesting people may make cognitive appraisals of same-sex others' attractiveness disconnected from their affective responses (Kenrick et al., 1993; Martin & Gentry, 1997). That is: women participants' ratings of another woman's attractiveness may be unrelated to their attitudes or behavioral intentions.

The results also support our expectation that norm internalization would function as the theoretical mechanism triggering EVT's effects because high internalization participants were more attuned to the influencer's appearance and the extent to which the post deviated from normative expectations than low internalization participants. These results also suggest the positive emotional responses elicited from norm-violating posts may be concentrated among those who most need them. Indeed, women with high internalization levels may be the most concerned about the ways their bodies violate the norms, and the most negatively affected by unrealistic and unobtainable media images (e.g., Halliwell, 2013; Tiggemann et al., 2017).

Practical Implications

The average weight of U.S. women between 20- and 74-years-old increased from about 140 pounds in the 1960s (Ogden et al., 2004) to about 171 pounds by 2016 (Fryar et al., 2018). Additionally, the average U.S. woman at least 20-years-old wears a "size 16–18, which corresponds to a Women's Plus size 20W" (Christel et al., 2016, p. 132). Thus, it is not surprising that women are embracing the body positivity movement countering society's thin-ideal appearance norms while promoting body satisfaction, appreciation, and self-love. Of particular interest in this study, body positivity's popularity on social media has grown exponentially since it began a little more than a decade ago, with many influencers associated with the movement. The body positivity movement's popularity has also inspired brands to adopt its messages and images in promotional campaigns designed to engage their target audience on social and visual media such as Instagram.

Overall, participants' responses to the branded body positivity Instagram posts suggest the movement's commodification may positively influence viewers' perceptions of and attitudes toward sponsoring brands, and these responses powerfully mediate relationships among the messages and the viewers' purchase intentions. In particular, this study's results suggest that branded body positivity influencer posts are most effective when they are not superficial or skin deep commodifications of the movement. Rather, the most effective posts not only violate the thin-ideal beauty standard, but also norms against plus-sized women showing skin, especially if it is unfiltered. Put simply: the posts violating the clothing and filter norms were the most authentic and elicited the strongest positive emotions, variables that are more powerful than attractiveness in shaping viewers' purchase intentions.

These findings contradict traditional advertising practices of using aspirational images of "flawless and thin models to encourage more typical-sized women with stretchmarks to purchase products to aspire to the 'perfection' advertised to her" (Shoenberger et al., 2020, p. 200). Indeed, authenticity and emotional responses are important not only for brands attempting to build relationships with their publics on social media, but also are critical components of effective influencer marketing (Kim et al., 2020; Lee and Hong, 2016; Wang and Weng, 2024). Further, these norm-violating posts may both strengthen branded body positivity marketing campaigns and benefit viewers who are more frequently exposed to images confirming the toxic and restrictive appearance norms propagated on social media.

Limitations and Future Research

As with all other research projects, the current study includes some limitations that must be noted. First, we used images of the same plus-sized influencer and model in all four treatment conditions to maximize external validity. However, some participants may have been familiar with Denise Bidot, which may have influenced their responses. Moreover, this influencer and model is widely considered very attractive even though her body does not conform to the thin-ideal appearance norm because she weighs 200 pounds. Thus, every condition violated society's thin-ideal beauty standard to some extent, the featured influencer and model is probably considered attractive in every condition, and she may have been known to some participants. To address these limitations, future researchers may want to use unknown models with varying body shapes and attractiveness ratings to investigate viewers' responses to branded body positivity Instagram posts.

Second, we used a 4 (treatment condition) by 2 (high or low internalization) between-subjects, posttest-only factorial design that did not include a control group. However, we intentionally used this design because we wanted to compare viewers' responses to four different images of the same model. That said, future research using control groups and comparing the influence of branded body positivity Instagram posts on viewers' body images or other elements of their psychological, physical, and/or emotional well-being may provide insights into these campaigns beyond the current investigation.

REFERENCES

AlFarraj, O., Alalwan, A. A., Obeidat, Z. M., Baabdullah, A., Aldmour, R., & Al-Haddad, S. (2021). Examining the impact of influencers' credibility dimensions: Attractiveness, trustworthiness and expertise on the purchase intention in the aesthetic dermatology industry. *Review of International Business and Strategy*, *31*(3), 355–374. doi:10.1108/RIBS-07-2020-0089

Avalos, L., Tylka, T. L., & Wood-Barcalow, N. (2005). The Body Appreciation Scale: Development and psychometric evaluation. *Body Image*, *2*(3), 285–297. doi:10.1016/j.bodyim.2005.06.002 PMID:18089195

Bernard, P., Hanoteau, F., Gervais, S., Servais, L., Bertolone, I., Deltenre, P., & Colin, C. (2019). Revealing clothing does not make the object: ERP evidences that cognitive objectification is driven by posture suggestiveness, not by revealing clothing. *Personality and Social Psychology Bulletin*, *45*(1), 16–36. doi:10.1177/0146167218775690 PMID:29877123

Biefeld, S. D., & Brown, C. S. (2022). Fat, sexy, and human? Perceptions of plus-size sexualized women and dehumanization. *Body Image*, *42*, 84–97. doi:10.1016/j.bodyim.2022.05.002 PMID:35671637

Boerman, S. C., Kruikemeier, S., & Zuiderveen Borgesius, F. J. (2017). Online behavioral advertising: A literature review and research agenda. *Journal of Advertising*, *46*(3), 363–376. doi:10.1080/00913367.2017.1339368

Brathwaite, K. N., & DeAndrea, D. C. (2022). BoPopriation: How self-promotion and corporate commodification can undermine the body positivity (BoPo) movement on Instagram. *Communication Monographs*, *89*(1), 25–46. doi:10.1080/03637751.2021.1925939

Brown, Z., & Tiggemann, M. (2020). A picture is worth a thousand words: The effect of viewing celebrity Instagram images with disclaimer and body positive captions on women's body image. *Body Image*, *33*, 190–198. doi:10.1016/j.bodyim.2020.03.003 PMID:32289571

Brumbaugh, A. M. (1993). Physical attractiveness and personality in advertising: More than just a pretty face? In L. McAlister & M. L. Rothschild (Eds.), *Advances in consumer research* (Vol. 20, pp. 159–164). Association for Consumer Research.

Bullock, O. M., & Hubner, A. Y. (2020). Candidates' use of informal communication on social media reduces credibility and support: Examining the consequences of expectancy violations. *Communication Research Reports*, *37*(3), 87–98. doi:10.1080/08824096.2020.1767047

Burgoon, J. K. (1978). A communication model of personal space violations: Explication and an initial test. *Human Communication Research*, *4*(2), 129–142. doi:10.1111/j.1468-2958.1978.tb00603.x

Burgoon, J. K. (2015). Expectancy Violations Theory. In C. R. Berger, M. E. Roloff, S. R. Wilson, J. P. Dillard, J. Caughlin, & D. Solomon (Eds.), *The International Encyclopedia of Interpersonal Communication* (Vol. 26, pp. 1–9). John Wiley & Sons, Inc.

Burton, J. L., Gollins, J., McNeely, L. E., & Walls, D. M. (2019). Revisiting the relationship between ad frequency and purchase intentions: How affect and cognition mediate outcomes at different levels of advertising frequency. *Journal of Advertising Research*, *59*(1), 27–39. doi:10.2501/JAR-2018-031

Caballero, M. J. (1989). Using physical attractiveness as an advertising tool: An empirical test of the attraction phenomenon. *Journal of Advertising Research*, *29*(4), 16.

Caldeira, S. P., & De Ridder, S. (2017). Representing diverse femininities on Instagram: A case study of the body-positive@ effyourbeautystandards Instagram account. *Catalan Journal of Communication & Cultural Studies*, *9*(2), 321–337. doi:10.1386/cjcs.9.2.321_1

Campagna, C. L., Donthu, N., & Yoo, B. (2023). Brand authenticity: Literature review, comprehensive definition, and an amalgamated scale. *Journal of Marketing Theory and Practice*, *31*(2), 129–145. doi:10.1080/10696679.2021.2018937

Campbell, C., & Farrell, J. R. (2020). More than meets the eye: The functional components underlying influencer marketing. *Business Horizons*, *63*(4), 469–479. doi:10.1016/j.bushor.2020.03.003

Christel, D. A., & Dunn, S. C. (2017). Average American women's clothing size: Comparing national health and nutritional examination surveys (1988–2010) to ASTM international misses & women's plus size clothing. *International Journal of Fashion Design, Technology and Education*, *10*(2), 129–136. doi:10.1080/17543266.2016.1214291

Clayton, R. B., Ridgway, J. L., & Hendrickse, J. (2017). Is plus size equal? The positive impact of average and plus-sized media fashion models on women's cognitive resource allocation, social comparisons, and body satisfaction. *Communication Monographs*, *84*(3), 406–422. doi:10.1080/03637751.2017.1332770

Cohen, R., Fardouly, J., Newton-John, T., & Slater, A. (2019). #BoPo on Instagram: An experimental investigation of the effects of viewing body positive content on young women's mood and body image. *New Media & Society*, *21*(7), 1546–1564. doi:10.1177/1461444819826530

Cwynar-Horta, J. (2016). The commodification of the body positive movement on Instagram. *Stream: Culture/Politics/Technology, 8*(2), 36-56.

Dhanesh, G. S., & Duthler, G. (2019). Relationship management through social media influencers: Effects of followers' awareness of paid endorsement. *Public Relations Review*, *45*(3), 101765. doi:10.1016/j.pubrev.2019.03.002

Dixon, S. J. (2023, August 25). *Instagram: distribution of global audiences 2023, by age group.* Statista. https://www.statista.com/statistics/325587/instagram-global-age-group/

Eagly, A. H., Ashmore, R. D., Makhijani, M. G., & Longo, L. C. (1991). What is beautiful is good, but...: A meta-analytic review of research on the physical attractiveness stereotype. *Psychological Bulletin*, *110*(1), 109–128. doi:10.1037/0033-2909.110.1.109

Eisend, M., & Langner, T. (2010). Immediate and delayed advertising effects of celebrity endorsers' attractiveness and expertise. *International Journal of Advertising*, *29*(4), 527–546. doi:10.2501/S0265048710201336

Fioravanti, G., Bocci Benucci, S., Ceragioli, G., & Casale, S. (2022). How the exposure to beauty ideals on social networking sites influences body image: A systematic review of experimental studies. *Adolescent Research Review*, *7*(3), 419–458. doi:10.1007/s40894-022-00179-4

Frederick, D. A., Daniels, E. A., Bates, M. E., & Tylka, T. L. (2017). Exposure to thin-ideal media affect most, but not all, women: Results from the Perceived Effects of Media Exposure Scale and open-ended responses. *Body Image*, *23*, 188–205. doi:10.1016/j.bodyim.2017.10.006 PMID:29132044

Fryar, C. D., Kruszon-Moran, D., Gu, Q., & Ogden, C. L. (2018, December 20). *Mean body weight, waist circumference, and body mass index among adults: United States, 1999-2000 through 2015-2016.* Centers for Disease Control and Prevention. https://www.cdc.gov/nchs/data/nhsr/nhsr122-508.pdf

Gill, R. (2023). *Perfect: Feeling judged on social media.* Polity Press.

Grabe, S., Ward, L. M., & Hyde, J. S. (2008). The role of the media in body image concerns among women: A meta-analysis of experimental and correlational studies. *Psychological Bulletin*, *134*(3), 460–476. doi:10.1037/0033-2909.134.3.460 PMID:18444705

Halliwell, E. (2013). The impact of thin idealized media images on body satisfaction: Does body appreciation protect women from negative effects? *Body Image*, *10*(4), 509–514. doi:10.1016/j.bodyim.2013.07.004 PMID:23972728

Hayes, A. F. (2022). *Introduction to mediation, moderation, and conditional process analysis: A regression-based approach* (3rd ed.). The Guilford Press.

Holland, E., & Haslam, N. (2013). Worth the weight: The objectification of overweight versus thin targets. *Psychology of Women Quarterly*, *37*(4), 462–468. doi:10.1177/0361684312474800

Huang, Q., Peng, W., & Ahn, S. (2021). When media become the mirror: A meta-analysis on media and body image. *Media Psychology*, *24*(4), 437–489. doi:10.1080/15213269.2020.1737545

Johnston, J., & Taylor, J. (2008). Feminist consumerism and fat activists: A comparative study of grassroots activism and the Dove Real Beauty campaign. *Signs (Chicago, Ill.)*, *33*(4), 941–966. doi:10.1086/528849

Kenrick, D. T., Montello, D. R., Gutierres, S. E., & Trost, M. R. (1993). Effects of physical attractiveness on affect and perceptual judgments: When social comparison overrides social reinforcement. *Personality and Social Psychology Bulletin*, *19*(2), 195–199. doi:10.1177/0146167293192008

Kim, J. H., Song, H., & Youn, H. (2020). The chain of effects from authenticity cues to purchase intention: The role of emotions and restaurant image. *International Journal of Hospitality Management*, *85*, 102354. doi:10.1016/j.ijhm.2019.102354

Kleemans, M., Daalmans, S., Carbaat, I., & Anschütz, D. (2018). Picture perfect: The direct effect of manipulated Instagram photos on body image in adolescent girls. *Media Psychology*, *21*(1), 93–110. do i:10.1080/15213269.2016.1257392

Kowalczyk, C. M., & Pounders, K. R. (2016). Transforming celebrities through social media: The role of authenticity and emotional attachment. *Journal of Product and Brand Management*, *25*(4), 345–356. doi:10.1108/JPBM-09-2015-0969

Lazuka, R. F., Wick, M. R., Keel, P. K., & Harriger, J. A. (2020). Are we there yet? Progress in depicting diverse images of beauty in Instagram's body positivity movement. *Body Image*, *34*, 85–93. doi:10.1016/j.bodyim.2020.05.001 PMID:32534269

Lee, J., & Hong, I. B. (2016). Predicting positive user responses to social media advertising: The roles of emotional appeal, informativeness, and creativity. *International Journal of Information Management, 36*(3), 360–373. doi:10.1016/j.ijinfomgt.2016.01.001

Lubitz, R. (2016, June 22). *Model Denise Bidot wants you to know that there is no wrong way to be a woman.* Yahoo News. https://news.yahoo.com/news/model-denise-bidot-wants-know-140226584.html?guccounter=1&guce_referrer=aHR0cHM6Ly93d3cuZ29vZ2xl

MacKenzie, S. B., & Lutz, R. J. (1989). An empirical examination of the structural antecedents of attitude toward the ad in an advertising pretesting context. *Journal of Marketing, 53*(2), 48–65. doi:10.1177/002224298905300204

Martin, M. C., & Gentry, J. W. (1997). Stuck in the model trap: The effects of beautiful models in ads on female pre-adolescents and adolescents. *Journal of Advertising, 26*(2), 19–34. doi:10.1080/00913367.1997.10673520

McComb, S. E., Gobin, K. C., & Mills, J. S. (2021). The effects of self-disclaimer Instagram captions on young women's mood and body image: The moderating effect of participants' own photo manipulation practices. *Body Image, 38*, 251–261. doi:10.1016/j.bodyim.2021.04.011 PMID:33964566

Mehta, A. (2000). Advertising attitudes and advertising effectiveness. *Journal of Advertising Research, 40*(3), 67–72. doi:10.2501/JAR-40-3-67-72

Morrow, P. C. (1990). Physical attractiveness and selection decision making. *Journal of Management, 16*(1), 45–60. doi:10.1177/014920639001600104

Nicholls, S. B., & Rice, R. E. (2017). A dual-identity model of responses to deviance in online groups: Integrating social identity theory and expectancy violations theory. *Communication Theory, 27*(3), 243–268. doi:10.1111/comt.12113

Ogden, C., Fryar, C. D., Carroll, M. D., & Flegal, K. M. (2004, October 27). Mean body weight, height, and body mass index, United States 1960+2002. *Centers for Disease Control and Prevention.* https://www.cdc.gov/nchs/data/ad/ad347.pdf

Olney, T. J., Holbrook, M. B., & Batra, R. (1991). Consumer responses to advertising: The effects of ad content, emotions, and attitude toward the ad on viewing time. *The Journal of Consumer Research, 17*(4), 440–453. doi:10.1086/208569

Park, S. Y., Cho, M., & Kim, S. (2021). The effect of CSR expectancy violation: Value from expectancy violation theory and confirmation bias. *Journal of Marketing Communications, 27*(4), 365–388. doi:10.1080/13527266.2019.1671478

Portal, S., Abratt, R., & Bendixen, M. (2019). The role of brand authenticity in developing brand trust. *Journal of Strategic Marketing, 27*(8), 714–729. doi:10.1080/0965254X.2018.1466828

Rodgers, R. F., Kruger, L., Lowy, A. S., Long, S., & Richard, C. (2019). Getting Real about body image: A qualitative investigation of the usefulness of the Aerie Real campaign. *Body Image, 30*, 127–134. doi:10.1016/j.bodyim.2019.06.002 PMID:31260946

Sastre, A. (2014). Towards a radical body positive: Reading the online "body positive movement". *Feminist Media Studies*, *14*(6), 929–943. doi:10.1080/14680777.2014.883420

Schaefer, L. M., Burke, N. L., Thompson, J. K., Dedrick, R. F., Heinberg, L. J., Calogero, R. M., & Anderson, D. A. (2016). Development and validation of the sociocultural attitudes towards appearance questionnaire-4 (SATAQ-4). *Psychological Assessment*, *27*(1), 54–67. doi:10.1037/a0037917 PMID:25285718

Shoenberger, H., Kim, E. A., & Johnson, E. K. (2020). #BeingReal about Instagram ad models: the effects of perceived authenticity: How image modification of female body size alters advertising attitude and buying intention. *Journal of Advertising Research*, *60*(2), 197–207. doi:10.2501/JAR-2019-035

Sokolova, K., Kefi, H., & Dutot, V. (2022). Beyond the shallows of physical attractiveness: Perfection and objectifying gaze on Instagram. *International Journal of Information Management*, *67*, 102546. doi:10.1016/j.ijinfomgt.2022.102546

Sprecher, S., & Hatfield, E. (2022). Ratings of the physical attractiveness of an interaction partner after a getting-acquainted interaction. *Personal Relationships*, *29*(2), 366–385. doi:10.1111/pere.12422

Stein, J.-P., Krause, E., & Ohler, P. (2021). Every (Insta)gram counts? Applying cultivation theory to explore the effects of Instagram on young users' body image. *Psychology of Popular Media Culture*, *10*(1), 87–97. doi:10.1037/ppm0000268

Stevens, A., & Griffiths, S. (2020). Body Positivity (# BoPo) in everyday life: An ecological momentary assessment study showing potential benefits to individuals' body image and emotional wellbeing. *Body Image*, *35*, 181–191. doi:10.1016/j.bodyim.2020.09.003 PMID:33068893

Taillon, B. J., Mueller, S. M., Kowalczyk, C. M., & Jones, D. N. (2020). Understanding the relationships between social media influencers and their followers: The moderating role of closeness. *Journal of Product and Brand Management*, *29*(6), 767–782. doi:10.1108/JPBM-03-2019-2292

Tiggemann, M., & Anderberg, I. (2020). Social media is not real: The effect of 'Instagram vs reality' images on women's social comparison and body image. *New Media & Society*, *22*(12), 2183–2199. doi:10.1177/1461444819888720

Tiggemann, M., Anderberg, I., & Brown, Z. (2020). #Loveyourbody: The effect of body positive Instagram captions on women's body image. *Body Image*, *33*, 129–136. doi:10.1016/j.bodyim.2020.02.015 PMID:32151992

Tiggemann, M., Brown, Z., Zaccardo, M., & Thomas, N. (2017). "Warning: This image has been digitally altered": The effect of disclaimer labels added to fashion magazine shoots on women's body dissatisfaction. *Body Image*, *21*, 107–113. doi:10.1016/j.bodyim.2017.04.001 PMID:28456058

Vaidhyanathan, S. (2021, September 18). Leaks just exposed how toxic Facebook and Instagram are to teen girls and, well, everyone. *The Guardian*. https://www.theguardian.com/commentisfree/2021/sep/18/facebook-instagram-zuckerberg-teenagers

Vendemia, M. A., DeAndrea, D. C., & Brathwaite, K. N. (2021). Objectifying the body positive movement: The effects of sexualizing and digitally modifying body-positive images on Instagram. *Body Image*, *38*, 137–147. doi:10.1016/j.bodyim.2021.03.017 PMID:33887562

Vendemia, M. A., & Robinson, M. J. (2022). Promoting body positivity through stories: How protagonist body size and esteem influence readers' self-concepts. *Body Image*, *42*, 315–326. doi:10.1016/j.bodyim.2022.07.005 PMID:35908298

Vrontis, D., Makrides, A., Christofi, M., & Thrassou, A. (2021). Social media influencer marketing: A systematic review, integrative framework and future research agenda. *International Journal of Consumer Studies*, *45*(4), 617–644. doi:10.1111/ijcs.12647

Wang, E. S. T., & Weng, Y. J. (2024). Influence of social media influencer authenticity on their followers' perceptions of credibility and their positive word-of-mouth. *Asia Pacific Journal of Marketing and Logistics*, *36*(2), 356–373. doi:10.1108/APJML-02-2023-0115

Yang, J., Teran, C., Battocchio, A. F., Bertellotti, E., & Wrzesinski, S. (2021). Building brand authenticity on social media: The impact of Instagram ad model genuineness and trustworthiness on perceived brand authenticity and consumer responses. *Journal of Interactive Advertising*, *21*(1), 34–48. doi:10.1080/15252019.2020.1860168

Yim, M. C. (2019). CEOs' political tweets and perceived authenticity: Can expectancy violation be a pleasant surprise? *Public Relations Review*, *45*(3), 101785. doi:10.1016/j.pubrev.2019.05.006

APPENDIX: STIMULI

Figure 4. Modest-filtered post

Figure 5. Modest-unfiltered post

Figure 6. Revealing-filtered post

Figure 7. Revealing-unfiltered post

Chapter 8
Food-Related YouTube Influencer Marketing:
The Impact of Homophily and Interactivity on Social Media Engagement

Linda Dam
University of Nevada, Las Vegas, USA

ABSTRACT

Influencer marketing on YouTube has become an increasingly popular method for building engagement with consumers. This study examines how perceived homophily and interactivity with social media influencers impact the effectiveness of food-related YouTube influencer marketing and consumer engagement with social media. An online survey (N = 404) found that perceived homophily and interactivity both positively relate to intentions to engage with social media. In addition, perceived expertise and physical attractiveness of the social media influencer mediated the relationship between both perceived homophily and interactivity and social media engagement. Study results provide evidence-based implications for influencer marketing strategies and insight into consumer engagement with food-related YouTube content.

INTRODUCTION

Influencer marketing has become a popular and lucrative marketing strategy (Statista, 2023). In 2023, the global influencer market was evaluated at 21.1 billion U.S. dollars and is expected to reach $52 billion U.S. by 2028 (Statista, 2023). In 2018, 4.7 million brand sponsored social media influencer posts were published (Statista, 2019). Moreover, Gen Z consumers (i.e., born between 1997-2012) reported that social media plays an important role in their purchasing decisions and provides a platform to learn, research, and be inspired by different brands (Gutierrez, 2022). Specifically, YouTube influencer marketing is an increasingly popular and effective method for building brand awareness with consumers (Delbaere et al., 2020; Xiao et al., 2018).

DOI: 10.4018/979-8-3693-0912-4.ch008

Research has found that the perceived credibility of content created by YouTube social media influencers, and the blending of content and advertisements contributes to the popularity and growth of influencer marketing on the YouTube platform (Fidelman, 2017; Saima & Khan, 2021; Xiao et al., 2018). Approximately 91% of content on YouTube consists of content created by influencers (Statista, 2023) and among U.S. teens, YouTube social media influencers have been found to be more popular than celebrities (Haryacha, 2014). Furthermore, the affordances on social media platforms such as the ability to like, comment, and share content increases interactivity between viewers and the social media influencers, which could lead to increased source credibility, consumer evaluation, and social media engagement (e.g., Lin et al., 2021; Munnukka et al., 2019; Sokolava & Kefi, 2020).

Additionally, the ability for influencers to interact on social media could lead to parasocial interactions or perceived homophily (Balabanis & Chatzopoulou, 2019; Burchill, 2024; Kurtin et al., 2018). For example, affordances such as commenting or liking a post on social media platforms allow consumers to interact with influencers, which may create the illusion of a potential one-sided interpersonal relationship (Kurtin et al., 2018; Lin et al., 2021; Reinikainen et al., 2020). In addition, the amount of followers that social media influencers have is positively related to perceived similarity to the average person, or perceived homophily (Foxwell, 2020). For instance, micro-influencers – those with approximately 1,000 to 10,000 followers – have the most successful engagement rates due to their authenticity and perceived relatability with their audience (Burchill, 2024). Thus, relatability and authenticity with the social media influencers may create a sense of perceived homophily with the influencer, which may enhance consumer evaluation. While many studies on the effectiveness of social media influencers have centered on parasocial interactions, this study seeks to explore the role of perceived homophily on influencer effectiveness.

In the food and beverage industry, the use of influencer marketing has become increasingly popular (Brown, 2021; Holmberg et al., 2016; Jin, 2018; Spence et al., 2016). Approximately 46% of online consumers report using social media to learn about different foods (Hartman Group, 2012) and among U.S. Millennials, 82% seek out YouTube for food-related tips (Delgado et al., 2014). In 2020, U.S. and Canadian food and beverage companies that utilized YouTube campaigns generated approximately 120.57 million views (Statista, 2023). Research has found that food marketing can lead to purchase intentions (Dam et al., 2024) and the overconsumption of food products (Lee & Wan, 2023). Therefore, it is important to explore the role of social media influencers in promoting food products on social media and the impact on consumer evaluation. Utilizing the similarity-attraction and source credibility theoretical frameworks, the current study explores the effectiveness of YouTube influencer marketing and consumer engagement with social media in the context of food-related YouTube content. Specifically, this study aims to expand knowledge on the effectiveness of food-related social media influencers, while also exploring consumer evaluation when exposed to food-related YouTube content.

LITERATURE REVIEW

Social Media Influencers, Homophily, and Interactivity

Influencer marketing utilizes social media influencers to enhance consumer evaluation (Hudders et al., 2021). Social media influencers are conceptualized as "individuals who have accrued a sizable and engaged following on one or more social media platforms, and who possess the power to shape attitudes, opinions, and behaviors of their audience through their online content" (Freberg et al., 2011, p. 90). Research has identified a positive relationship between number of followers and credibility of the source on Twitter and Instagram (De Veirman et al., 2017; Janssen et al., 2022; Jin & Phua, 2014). For instance, social media influencers are grouped into several categories based on the number of followers: mega-influencers are those who have more than 1 million followers (i.e. celebrities, athletes), macro-influencers are those who have reached a following of more than 40,000 individuals and who are lesser known celebrities or successful online experts within a field, and micro-influencers are those with more than 1000 followers and who are everyday people specialized on niche topics (Geyser, 2022). Janssen et al. (2022) found that macro influencers were more likeable than micro influencers, suggesting that consumers may utilize the quantity of followers as a metric for credibility. In contrast, Foxwell (2020) reported that micro-influencers were found to be more relatable to the average person.

Research has suggested that social media influencers may be more influential than celebrities due to the relatability to their audiences (Jin et al., 2019; Schouten, 2020). Similarity-attraction theory (Byrne, 1971) purports that relation formation are more likely among individuals who share attributes that are similar. For instance, perceived homophily can be defined as the "degree to which people who interact are similar in beliefs, education, social status and the like" (Eyal & Rubin, 2003, p. 80). The theory posits that these perceived similarities can positively influence source credibility and attitudinal and behavioral outcomes. Research has found that perceived homophily with a social media influencer positively related to the effectiveness of the influencer (Balabanis & Chatzopoulou, 2019; Lee & Watkins, 2016; Shoenberger & Kim, 2023). For example, in a study on YouTube vloggers', Lee and Watkins (2016) reported that greater perceived homophily positively predicted parasocial interaction, which in turn, predicted luxury brand perceptions such as brand value, brand-user-imagery fit, and brand luxury. Similarly, Balabanis and Chatzopoulou (2019) noted that participants who indicated greater perceived homophily with a beauty blogger predicted positive consumer evaluation. Perceived homophily has also been found to positively predicted the perceived authenticity of the influencer, which predicted purchase intentions (Shoenberger & Kim, 2023). In a qualitative study on gratifications sought from food-related social media influencers, Alhothali and Aljefree (2023) reported that individuals who perceived influencers as more authentic were more likely to engage with their content.

Research has also shown that social media influencers who interact with their audience can positively impact consumer evaluation (Hayes & Carr, 2015; Ott et al., 2016; Xiao et al., 2018). Interactivity can be conceptualized as the activeness of social media influencers to engage in communication with their audience (Xiao et al., 2018). Specifically, social media influencers can effectively strengthen interactivity with consumers (Hayes & Carr, 2017; Majid et al., 2019). For example, in an online experiment, Hayes and Carr (2017) reported that the socialness with a blogger (i.e., comments and conversations between the social media blogger and viewer) predicted the perceived expertise of the blogger, which predicted brand attitudes and purchasing intentions. Similarly, Ott et al. (2016) noted that message interactivity on a company's Facebook page had a positive indirect effect on consumer evaluation through perceived informativeness of the message.

While interactivity addresses the interaction between social media influencers and their audiences, social media engagement refers to the audience interactions with the social media platforms such as commenting, clicks, reactions, and sharing (Blowers, 2012; Roccapriore & Pollock, 2023). For example, higher-level social media engagement consists of replying or commenting on an influencer post whereas lower-level social media engagement consists of passively following the influencer (Roccapriore & Pollock, 2023). In a study on brand engagement, Delbaere et al. (2021) found that influencers positively impacts consumers' engagement with brands on social media. Thus, based on previous literature on perceived homophily and interactivity, the following hypotheses are proposed:

H1: Homophily with a YouTube social media influencer will positively relate to social media engagement.

H2: Interactivity from a YouTube social media influencer will positively relate to social media engagement.

Source Credibility and Social Media Influencer

One of the factors influencing the success of a social media influencer is the perceived credibility of the influencer (Mannukka et al., 2019; Reinikainen et al., 2020; Sokolova & Kefi, 2020). Source credibility influences not only message acceptance (Ohanian, 1990), but also impacts consumers' attitudes towards the brands endorsed by the influencers (Reinikainen, et al., 2020; Weismueller et al., 2020). Perceived source credibility is defined as "judgments made by a perceiver (e.g., message recipient) concerning the believability of a communicator" (O'Keefe, 1990, p. 131). In general, sources that are perceived as being trustworthy and have expertise influence consumers' attitudes, behaviors, and purchase intentions (Ohanian, 1990; Solokova & Kefi, 2020; Wang & Scheinbaum, 2018). Similarly, research showed that perceived expertise is positively related to attitudes toward the ad and purchase intentions (i.e. digital camera) (Hayes & Carr, 2015; Ohanian, 1991).

Research examining the effectiveness of social media influencers has found that source credibility has a positive effect on consumer attitudes and behavior (Wang & Scheinbaum, 2018; Uribe et al., 2016). In the context of social media, source credibility is conceptualized as "the degree to which content producers are perceived as trustworthy, knowledgeable and credible" (Zha et al., 2018, p. 300). Message effectiveness increases when the source celebrity is perceived as being trustworthy and having expertise in the field (Keel & Nataraajan, 2012). Additionally, research has shown that influencers' perceived credibility influences viewers' choice of content (Johnson & Kaye, 2013; Solokova & Kefi, 2020). In a study examining a popular influencer video blogger on the topic of maternity and childcare, Monge- Benito et al. (2020) demonstrated that perceived expertise of the influencer was positively related to purchase intentions among YouTube viewers. Therefore, the following hypotheses are proposed regarding the mediating effects of perceived expertise and trustworthiness:

H3: Perceived expertise with a YouTube social media influencer will mediate the relationship between perceived homophily and social media engagement.

H4: Perceived trustworthiness with a YouTube social media influencer will mediate the relationship between perceived homophily and social media engagement.

Expertise and trustworthiness can also be enhanced by interactivity with a social media influencer (Jun & Yi, 2020). Jun and Yi (2020) found that social media influencer interactivity positively predicted perceived authenticity, which in turn, predicted trust in the brand. Similarly, Ooi et al. (2023) reported that interactivity with a social media influencer positively predicted attitudes towards the influencer, highlighting the importance of engaging with one's audience. In doing so, social media influencers can strengthen audience perceptions of their credibility. Therefore, the following is hypothesized regarding the mediating effects of expertise and trustworthiness:

H5: Perceived expertise with a social media YouTube influencer will mediate the relationship between interactivity and social media engagement.

H6: Perceived trustworthiness with a social media YouTube influencer will mediate the relationship between interactivity and social media engagement.

Additionally, credibility dimensions often utilized in exploring advertising effectiveness include source likeability and physical attractiveness. While source attractiveness can encompass various dimensions of attractiveness such as likeability, similarity, and physical attractiveness, prior studies have also measured source attractiveness as separate dimensions (Lou & Yuan, 2019; Taillon et al., 2020; Wiedmann & Von Mettenheim, 2021). Past research on advertising effectiveness has found the likeability of the source is a positive predictor for consumer evaluation (Belch & Belch, 2013; Infanger & Sczensny, 2015; Yilmaz et al., 2011). For instance, Belch and Belch (2013) reported that celebrities are often utilized in magazine advertisements because of their likeability. Similarly, Infanger and Sczensny (2015) found that endorser likeability positively predicted attitudes toward the advertisements. In a study on print advertisements, Yilmaz et al. (2011) demonstrated that source likeability positively related to attitudes towards the brand, the ad, and purchase intentions. In terms of social media influencers, perceived likeability toward Instagram influencers was related to higher engagement with followers (Myers, 2021). In a study on social media influencers in the fitness and nutrition industry, Roccapriore and Pollock (2023) found that warmth characteristics from social media influencers was positively related to positive social media engagement interactions. Similarly, perceived likeability of virtual influencers positively mediated the relationship between the effect of diverse virtual influencers and consumer evaluation (Ferraro et al., 2023). Taillon et al. (2020) analyzed the separate roles of physical attractiveness and likeability of the social media influencer and found that perceived likeability positively predicted attitude toward the influencer and word-of mouth while physical attractiveness positively predicted purchase intentions but negatively predicted attitudes toward the influencer.

Thus, physical attractiveness of the source can also impact the effectiveness of the message (Choi & Lee, 2019; Na et al., 2005; Taillon et al., 2020). Specifically, greater perceived physical attractiveness of the source predicts positive consumer evaluation (Na et al., 2005). Physical attractiveness can be defined as "the degree to which a stimulus person's facial features are pleasing to observe" (Ohanian, 1990). For example, Choi and Lee (2019) reported that greater physical attractiveness of a fashion vlogger was positively related to intentions to share content. In a meta-analysis of social media influencer effectiveness, Han et al. (2024) reported that in Western countries, greater effect sizes for influencer attractiveness on purchase intentions. Among food influencers, Luong and Ho (2023) reported that the physical attractiveness of food vloggers positively predicted attitudes toward the content. Therefore, the following hypotheses are proposed regarding likeability and physical attractiveness and social media engagement:

H7: Perceived likeability with a YouTube social media influencer will mediate the relationship between perceived homophily and social media engagement.

H8: Physical attractiveness of a YouTube social media influencer will mediate the relationship between perceived homophily and social media engagement.

H9: Perceived likeability with a YouTube social media influencer will mediate the relationship between interactivity and social media engagement.

H10: Physical attractiveness of a YouTube social media influencer will mediate the relationship between interactivity and social media engagement.

Consumers' Attitudes and Social Media Engagement

Marketing models predict that attitudes toward messages mediate the effect of exposure to a message and attitudes toward the object or behavior in the message (Brown & Stayman, 1992; MacKenzie, Lutz, & Belch, 1986; Spears & Singh, 2004). Attitudes toward the message or ad have been defined as "a psychological tendency that is expressed by evaluating a particular entity with some degree of favor or disfavor" (Eagly & Chaiken, 1993, p. 1). For example, studies indicated that individuals' attitudes toward restaurant ads influenced their decision to visit a restaurant (Xu & Yeong, 2018). Among digital influencers in the fashion and beauty industry, consumer attitudes was positively related to purchase intentions (Torres et al., 2019). Moreover, looking at the fashion industry in Malaysia, Chin et al. (2019) found that positive attitudes toward a brand do influence consumers' purchase intentions. Similarly, Lee et al. (2016) explored attitudes toward ads and brands in the South Korean golf industry and indicated that attitudes toward a golf brand influenced consumers' intentions to buy the product.

While past research has found a significant relationship between attitudes toward ads and consumers' behavioral intentions to consume or purchase a product (Ha et al., 2014; Lee et al., 2016), few studies have examined the impact of attitudes toward the social media influencer and YouTube video on intentions to engage in social media. Drawing on previous research on consumers' attitudes, the present study proposes that attitudes toward the social media influencer and attitudes toward the video will also positively impact intentions to engage with the social media content: Thus, the following hypotheses are proposed:

H7: Attitudes toward the YouTube video will be positively related to social media engagement.

H8: Attitudes toward the YouTube social media influencer will be positively related to social media engagement.

METHODS

Upon university Institutional Review Board (IRB) approval, participants completed an online survey hosted on Qualtrics during November, 2019. Amazon's Mechanical Turk platform (MTurk) was utilized to recruit participants. Participants were informed on the consent form that they can skip questions or cease participation at any time. Of the 404 completed surveys, 41.8% were male participants and 57.9% were female participants with an average reported age of 31.65 (SD = 9.38). The survey consisted of 60.1% Caucasian, 14.6% Black, 14.4% Asian, 5.2% Hispanic, 2.7% two or more races, 2.0% American Indian/Alaskan Native, .5% Native Hawaiian/Pacific Islander, and .5% Other. The educational profile of participants consisted of 44.6% indicating a Bachelor's degree, 19.6% with some college (no degree), 15.3% with a Masters degree, 9.7% with a High School degree or equivalent (GED), 7.9% with an Associates degree, 1.5% with a Professional degree (i.e., MD, JD, DDS, DVM), 1.2% with less than a high school diploma, and .2% with a doctorate degree (i.e., Ph.D., EdD).

Participants reported spending M = 9.13 hrs (SD = 7.19) watching YouTube on weekdays and M = 8.14 hrs (SD = 7.19) watching YouTube on the weekends. From 1 (never) to 7 (always), participants reported watching the following on YouTube: product review videos M = 4.37 (SD = 1.61), How-to guides and tutorial videos M = 4.50 (SD = 1.47), Vlogs (e.g., unscripted dialogue that looks into the video maker's mind) videos M = 4.42 (SD = 1.66), gaming videos M = 3.98 (SD = 1.81), comedy and sketch videos M = 4.31 (SD = 1.67), shopping sprees/haul videos M = 3.78 (SD = 1.61), tag or challenge videos M = 3.66 (SD = 1.90), favorite/best of videos M = 4.21 (SD = 1.76), educational (e.g.,

Ted Talks, National Geographics) videos $M = 4.27$ ($SD = 1.56$), unboxing (e.g., seeing for the first time the contents of the package) videos $M = 3.93$ ($SD = 1.81$), funny animal videos $M = 4.03$ ($SD = 1.66$), and celebrity gossip videos $M = 3.56$ ($SD = 1.89$). Only participants who indicated they have viewed food-related YouTube videos were included for this survey. Participants reported watching $M = 5.29$ hrs ($SD = 5.91$) food-related YouTube videos during a typical weekend and $M = 5.29$ hrs ($SD = 5.91$) food-related YouTube videos during a typical weekday.

Measures

Expertise. Influencer sources' expertise was measured with a 5-item scale adapted from Ohanian (1990). Respondents' answers were measured on a 7-point semantic-differential scale (e.g. "You feel the YouTube influencer is…" (1) Not an expert to (7) An expert). Sample items include: "inexperienced/experienced," "unknowledgeable/knowledgeable," "unqualified/qualified," and "unskilled/skilled." A composite variable was created by averaging items ($\alpha = .92$, $M = 5.12$, $SD = 1.31$).

Trustworthiness. Influencer sources' trustworthiness was measured with a 5-item scale adapted from Ohanian (1990). Respondents' answers were measured on a 7-point semantic-differential scale (e.g. "You feel the YouTube influencer is…" (1) untrustworthy to (7) trustworthy). Sample items include: "dishonest/honest," "unreliable/reliable," "insincere/sincere," and "undependable/dependable." A composite variable was created by averaging items ($\alpha = .93$, $M = 5.26$, $SD = 1.28$).

Likeability. Influencer trustworthiness was measured with a 4-item scale adapted from Reysen (2005). Respondents' answers were measured on a 7-point semantic-differential scale (e.g. "You feel the YouTube influencer is…" (1) Unfriendly to (7) friendly). Sample items include: "unfriendly/friendly," "unlikeable/likeable," "Not warm/warm," and "not approachable/approachable." A composite variable was created by averaging items ($\alpha = .93$, $M = 5.26$, $SD = 1.28$).

Physical Attractiveness. 7, 9, 10 The physical attractiveness of the YouTube influencer was measured with a 3-item scale adapted from Ohanian (1990) with responses on a 7-point Likert-type scale ("strongly disagree = 1" to "strongly agree = 7"). Items include: "I think he (she) is quite handsome (pretty)," "He (she) is very sexy looking," and "I find him (her) very physically attractive." A composite variable was created by averaging items ($\alpha = .84$, $M = 4.71$, $SD = 1.33$).

Interactivity. Interactivity with the YouTube influencer was measured with an adapted scale from Xiao et al. (2018), with responses on a 7-point Likert-type scale ("strongly disagree = 1" to "strongly agree = 7"). The 4-items scale included: "It is easy to contact this YouTube influencer," "This YouTube influencer is willing to interact with me," "This YouTube influencer is influenced by me," "This influencer interacts with me frequently," "A composite variable was created by averaging items ($\alpha = .90$, $M = 4.30$, $SD = 1.53$).

Homophily. Homophily with the YouTube influencer was measured on a 7-point Likert-type scale (e.g., You feel that your favorite YouTube influencer …(1) "Doesn't think like me" (7) "thinks like me") adapted from McCroskey et al. (1975). Sample items include the following: "Doesn't think like me/Thinks like me," "Doesn't behave like me/behaves like me," "Different from me/Similar to me," and "Unlike me/like me." A composite variable was created by averaging items ($\alpha = .95$, $M = 4.59$, $SD = 1.66$).

Video Attitudes. Video attitudes was measured on a 7-point Likert-type scale (e.g., The YouTube video is…(1) "not fun" (7) "fun"). The scale had five items and included: "Not fun/fun", "dull/exciting," "not delightful/delightful," "not thrilling/thrilling," and "not enjoyable/enjoyable." A composite variable was created by averaging items ($\alpha = .95$, $M = 5.29$, $SD = 1.36$).

Attitudes toward the YouTube influencer. Attitudes toward the YouTube influencer was measured on a 7-point Likert-type scale (e.g., I feel that my favorite YouTube influencer is…(1) "Not an expert" (7) "expert"). The scale had four items and included: "Unrelatable/relatable," "reserved/outgoing," "Unsociable/sociable," and "Insincere/sincere." A composite variable was created by averaging items ($\alpha = .87$, $M = 5.49$, $SD = 1.22$).

Social Media Engagement. Engagement with YouTube Videos was measured with the following: "How often do you engage in each of the following activities while viewing YouTube Videos…(1) "never" (5) "often")." The scale had six items and included: "Watching videos," "sharing videos," "leaving your comments on the shared videos," "clicking "like" or "dislike" if you like the video," "having food," and "making or preparing food." A composite variable was created by averaging items ($\alpha = .86$, $M = 2.79$, $SD = 1.00$).

RESULTS

To assess the interrelations among variables, Pearson correlations were conducted to examine the interrelations among variables. Social media engagement was positively correlated with homophily ($r = .54$, $p < .001$), interactivity ($r = .55$, $p < .001$), expertise ($r = .46$, $p < .001$), trustworthiness ($r = .37$, $p < .001$), likeability ($r = .29$, $p < .001$), physical attractiveness ($r = .47$, $p < .01$), video attitudes ($r = .47$, $p < .001$), and attitudes toward the influencer ($r = .36$, $p < .001$). Correlation results and VIF indicators < 5 suggest there was no multicollinearity.

To test H1, H2, and H11-12 on whether homophily and interactivity, along with dimensions of credibility, would impact social media engagement, a hierarchal regressions were conducted. (See Table 1). Sex, race, age, and education were entered as control variables in Block 1. Block 2 contained homophily and interactivity with the influencer. Block 3 contained credibility dimensions such as perceived expertise, likeability, trustworthiness, and physical attractiveness of the social media influencer. Block 4 contained attitudes toward the video and attitudes toward the influencer.

The regression model was significant, $F(12, 391) = 27.459$, $p < .001$, $R^2 = .44$. Overall, the final model explained 44% of the variance in social media engagement with 32% of the variance in interactivity and homophily, 5% of the variance in credibility dimensions, and 2% of the variance in attitudes. Homophily ($\beta = .16$, $p < .01$), interactivity ($\beta = .28$, $p < .001$), expertise ($\beta = .17$, $p < .01$), physical attraction ($\beta = .14$, $p < .01$), and video attitudes ($\beta = .24$, $p < .001$) positively predicted social media engagement. Thus, H1, H2, and H11 were supported and H12 was not supported.

Mediation Analyses

To test H3-H10, which investigate the mediating roles of source credibility on one's engagement with social media, parallel multiple-mediator models using the PROCESS macro model 4 for SPSS written by Hayes (2022), were conducted. (See Figures 1 and 2). The analysis used 5000 bootstrapped resamples and a 95% bias corrected confidence interview (CI). In both mediation models, homophily was entered as the predictor (X), perceived expertise (M), perceived likeability (M), perceived trustworthiness (M), and physical attractiveness (M) were entered as mediators, and social media engagement was entered as the outcome (Y). Sex, race, education, and age were entered as covariates.

Table 1. Multiple regression predicting social media engagement

	B	*SE*	β	*p*
Block 1				
White Race	-.02	.02	-.03	.380
Gender	.12	.08	.06	.108
Education	.06	.03	.09	.032
Age	.00	.06	.03	.388
R^2 = .05				
Block 2				
Perceived Homophily	.09	.03	.16	.005
Interactivity	.18	.03	.28	.001
ΔR^2 = .32				
Block 3				
Expertise	.13	.05	.17	.003
Trust	-.02	.06	-.03	.679
Likeability	-.06	.06	-.08	.300
Physical Attractive	.10	.04	.14	.004
ΔR^2 = .05				
Block 4				
Influencer attitude	-.03	.05	-.04	.517
Video attitude	.17	.04	.24	.001
ΔR^2 = .02				
Total R^2 = .44				

Mediation analyses confirmed that perceived homophily predicted perceived expertise (β = .43, SE = .03, t(398) = 12.50, p < .001), perceived trustworthiness (β = .44, SE = .03, t(398) = 13.40, p < .001), perceived likeability (β = .36, SE = .04, t(398) = 10.26, p < .001), and physical attractiveness (β = .40, SE = .03, t(398) = 11.60, p < .001). Perceived homophily (β = .19 SE = .03, t(394) = 5.78, p < .001), perceived expertise (β = .18, SE = .05, t(394) = 3.98, p < .001), and physical attractiveness (β = .16, SE = .04, t(394) = 4.42, p < .001) predicted social media engagement. Additionally, the effect of perceived homophily on social media engagement was significantly mediated by perceived expertise (β = .08, SE = .03, 95% CI = [.03, .13]) and physical attractiveness (β = .06, SE = .02, 95% CI = [.03, .10]). Thus, H3 and H6 are supported.

Mediation analyses confirmed that interactivity predicted perceived expertise (β = .31, SE = .04, t(398) = 7.39, p < .001), perceived trustworthiness (β = .33, SE = .04, t(398) = 8.09, p < .001), perceived likeability (β = .37, SE = .04, t(398) = 4.80, p < .001), and physical attractiveness (β = .40, SE = .03, t(398) = 9.09, p < .001). Interactivity (β = .24, SE = .03, t(394) = 7.77, p < .001), perceived expertise (β = .20, SE = .04, t(394) = 4.47, p < .001), and physical attractiveness (β = .15, SE = .03, t(394) = 4.34, p < .001) predicted social media engagement. Additionally, the effect of interactivity on social media engagement was significantly mediated by perceived expertise (β = .06, SE = .02, 95% CI = [.03, .10]) and physical attractiveness (β = .05, SE = .02, 95% CI = [.03, .09]). Thus, H7 and H10 are supported.

Figure 1. Mediation analyses for homophily, expertise, likeability, trust, physical attraction, and social media engagement

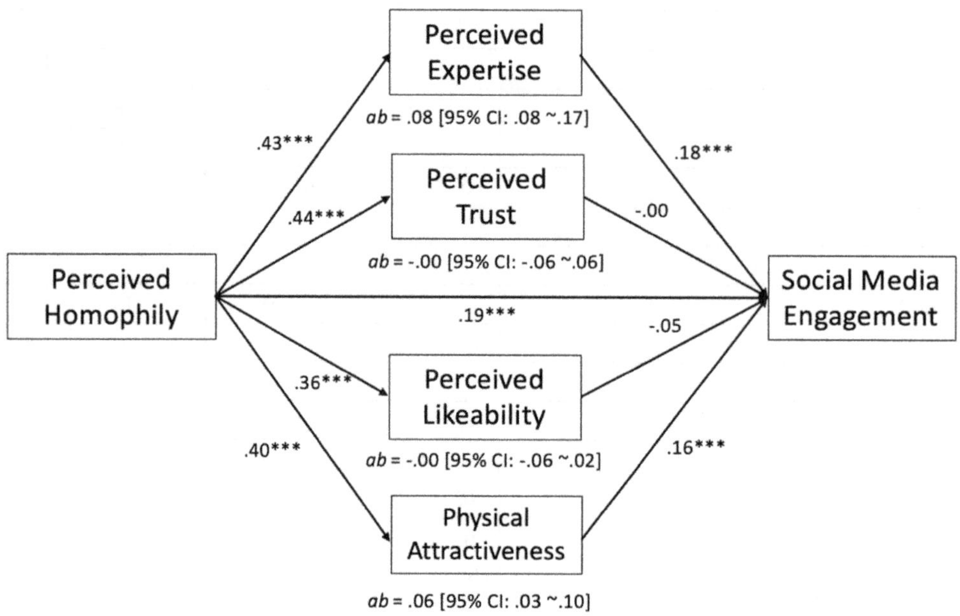

Figure 2. Mediation analyses for interactivity, expertise, likeability, trust, physical attraction, and social media engagement

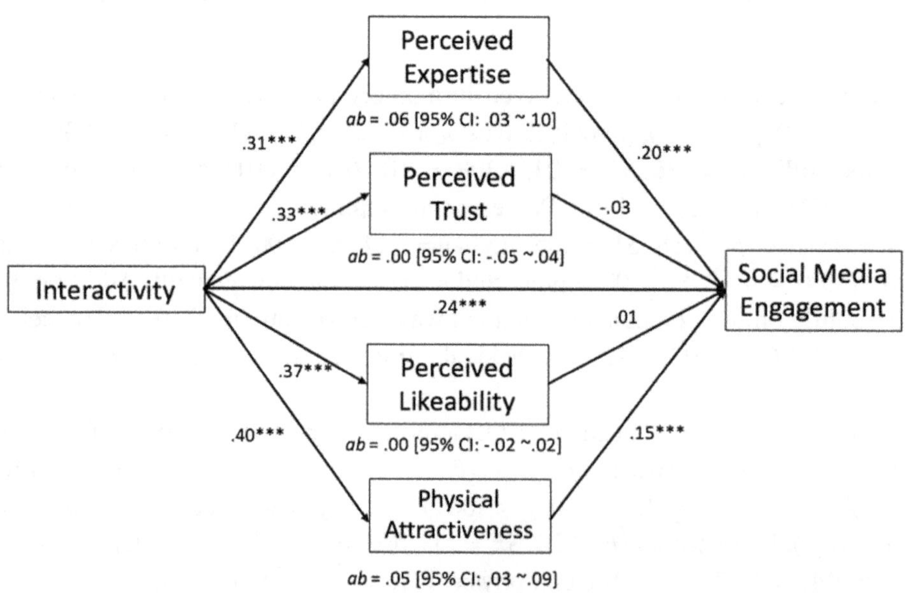

DISCUSSION

Research has found that social media has become an increasingly popular method for food-related displays (Holmberg et al., 2016; Jin, 2018). This study explores the effects of perceived homophily and interactivity with food-related YouTube social media influencers on various dimensions of perceived credibility and the impact on consumer evaluation and social media engagement. Specifically, the study explores the mediating roles of social media influencer source credibility dimensions such as expertise, trustworthiness, likability, and physical attractiveness on intentions to engage with social media. The present research contributes to social media influencer literature by examining consumer processes in developing consumer relationships through food-related social media influencers.

Overall, findings revealed significant relationships among perceived homophily with a food-related YouTube social media influencer, perceived expertise and physical attractiveness, and attitudes toward the YouTube video on consumer social media engagement. Specifically, results demonstrated that greater levels of perceived homophily with a YouTube social media influencer positively related to perceived expertise and physical attractiveness of the influencer, which was related to positive consumer evaluation of food-related YouTube content. Findings provide empirical support for social media influencer marketing research (e.g, Jin et al., 2019; Reinikainen et al., 2020; Sokolova & Kefi, 2020), which demonstrated significant relationships between perceived homophily with social media influencers and perceived source credibility. These findings provide managerial implications for food and beverage companies who may utilize social media influencers as part of their marketing plan. Specifically, food and beverage companies should aim to obtain influencers who are perceived to be more similar and relatable to their target audience such as micro-influencers rather than macro-influencers (Foxwell, 2020). For example, micro-influencers, those with approximately 1,000 to 10,000 followers, are perceived to be more relatable to the average person, which has been found to generate more social engagement from consumers (Foxwell, 2020).

Findings also provide practical implications for individuals seeking a profession as a food-related social media influencer and provide tactics on how to better engage with consumers. For instance, for food-focused social media content, influencers should aim to draw similarities to their target audiences in order to enhance their own credibility. This suggests that if consumers perceive social media influencers as similar to themselves, they are more likely to perceive the influencer as more credible and physically attractive, which may lead to more engagement with social media. Findings also provide theoretical implications for similarity-attraction theory (Byrne, 1971) and source credibility framework in the context of food marketing. Byrne's (1971) similarity-attraction theory posits that individuals are more likely to build relationships with others who share similar characteristics. Thus, an influencer who is positioned to be relatable to their audience are able to establish greater expertise, which may increase positive attitudes toward the influencers' content and increase social media engagement. For instance, influencers can aim to endorse food products that appeal to local preferences and are easily attainable.

Because social media offers the ability for influencers to connect with consumers, the role of interactivity was also examined. Findings revealed that greater interactivity between social media influencers and consumers increased perceived source credibility and consumer evaluation. Specifically, higher interactivity was related to perceived expertise, physical attractiveness, and social media engagement. These results align with past research findings (Hayes & Carr, 2015; Ott et al., 2016; Xiao et al., 2018), which indicated the positive effect of interactivity in strengthening consumer attitudes and behaviors. For influencers, higher levels of interactivity can be achieved by engaging with the audience through tactics such as requesting food recommendations or soliciting feedback on food products. Additionally, posting questions or creating opportunities to converse with the audience can further increase the influencer's perceived credibility, which in turn, positively impacts social media engagement.

Study findings also revealed that perceived expertise and physical attractiveness of the social media influencer mediated the relationship between perceived homophily (and interactivity) on social media engagement. This suggests that for food-related social media marketing, influencers must aim to being knowledgeable in order to enhance their expertise. In regards to physical attractiveness, findings provide insight into the importance that physical attractiveness may play on the advertising effectiveness of a social media influencer. These findings align with past research, which also found the physical attractiveness of food vloggers to positively predict consumer behavior (Luong & Ho, 2023). For example, the physical attractiveness of restaurant servers can impact the taste perceptions of customers (Lin et al., 2018). Thus, food brand managers who seek to utilize social media influencers must also take into consideration the role that physical attractiveness can have on credibility and consumer evaluation.

Surprisingly, perceived likeability and trustworthiness did not emerge as significant predictors of social media engagement. Findings align with Luong and Ho (2023), who also did not find trustworthiness to emerge as a significant predictor for consumer evaluation on food vloggers. A plausible explanation could be that consumers are more aware of the possibility of sponsorship compensation that influencers may receive for their posts, which may create distrust in the influencer. For example, in a study on YouTube influencers, Stubb et al. (2019) reported that lack of fully disclosing sponsorship compensation could negatively impact consumer responses. Specifically, simply disclosing sponsorship compensations versus emphasizing sponsorship compensations resulted in less credibility and consumer evaluation towards the influencer (Stubb et al., 2019). Thus, the role of sponsorship could plausibly explain the insignificance of trustworthiness and likeability towards the influencer on one's intentions to engage with social media.

Findings provide practical insight into the importance of social media influencers connecting with their audiences through the social media platform. For instance, social media influencers can engage with viewers by providing an opportunity to viewers to connect with them. Study results provide practical implications for managers who seek to utilize YouTube influencer marketing to strengthen their consumer base in the food industry. Results suggest that by providing greater interactivity with consumers, consumers are more likely to engage further with the social media platform.

Future research on food-related social media influencers should aim to explore the effectiveness of different social media platforms. For example, TikTok is widely use by social media influencers to display food reviews. Future studies can explore whether greater perceived homophily and interactivity can be obtained through other social media platforms.

REFERENCES

Absolom, S., & Roberts, A. (2011). Connecting with others: The meaning of social eating as an everyday occupation for young people. *Journal of Occupational Science*, *18*(4), 339–346. doi:10.1080/14427591.2011.586324

Alhothali, G. T., & Aljefree, N. M. (2023). Young adults' sought gratifications from, and perceptions of food advertising by, social media influencers: A qualitative approach. *Journal of Health, Population and Nutrition*, *42*(1), 1–12. doi:10.1186/s41043-023-00449-4 PMID:37752524

Alvaro, E. M., Crano, W. D., Siegel, J. T., Hohman, Z., Johnson, I., & Nakawaki, B. (2013). Adolescents' attitudes toward antimarijuana ads, usage intentions, and actual marijuana usage. *Psychology of Addictive Behaviors, 27*(4), 1027–1035. doi:10.1037/a0031960 PMID:23528197

Atika, A., Kusumawati, A., & Iqbal, M. (2018). The effect of electronic word of mouth, message source credibility, information quality on brand image and purchase intention. *Jurnal Ekonomi dan Keuangan, 20*, 94-108. doi:10.24034/j25485024.y2016.v20.i1.94

Balabanis, G., & Chatzopoulou, E. (2019). Under the influence of a blogger: The role of information-seeking goals and issue involvement. *Psychology and Marketing, 36*(4), 342–353. doi:10.1002/mar.21182

Ballantine, P., & Martin, B. (2005). Forming parasocial relationships in online communities. *Advances in Consumer Research. Association for Consumer Research (U. S.), 32*, 197–201.

Belch, G. E., & Belch, M. A. (2013). A content analysis of the use of celebrity endorsers in magazine advertising. *International Journal of Advertising, 32*, 369–389. doi:10.2501/IJA-32-3-369-389

Bellissimo, N., Pencharz, P. B., Thomas, S. G., & Anderson, G. H. (2007). Effect of television viewing at mealtime on food intake after a glucose preload in boys. *Pediatric Research, 61*(6), 745–749. doi:10.1203/pdr.0b013e3180536591 PMID:17426650

Blowers, H. (2012). Measuring social media and the greater digital landscape. *Computers in Libraries, 32*, 27–29.

Browne, M. W., & Cudeck, R. (1992). Alternative ways of assessing model fit. *Sociological Methods & Research, 21*(2), 230–258. doi:10.1177/0049124192021002005

Burchill, A. (2024, January). *Influencer marketing statistics to know in 2024.* Dash. Retrieved from: https://www.dash.app/blog/influencer-marketing-statistics#:~:text=65%25%20of%20influencers%20on%20Instagram,to%20work%20with%20content%20creators

Chen, Y.-L., Chang, C.-L., & Sung, A.-Q. (2021). Predicting eWOM's influence on purchase intention based on helpfulness, credibility, information quality and professionalism. *Sustainability (Basel), 13*(13), 7486. doi:10.3390/su13137486

Cheung, C. M. K., Lee, M. K. O., & Rabjohn, N. (2008). The impact of electronic word-of-mouth: The adoption of online opinions in online customer communities. *Internet Research, 18*(3), 229–247. doi:10.1108/10662240810883290

Choi, W., & Lee, Y. (2019). Effects of fashion vlogger attributes on product attitude and content sharing. *Fashion and Textiles, 6*(1), 1–18. doi:10.1186/s40691-018-0161-1

Chung, S., & Cho, H. (2017). Fostering parasocial relationships with celebrities on social media: Implications for celebrity endorsement. *Psychology and Marketing, 34*(4), 481–495. doi:10.1002/mar.21001

Clendenen, V. I., Herman, C. P., & Policy, J. (1994). Social facilitation of eating among friends and strangers. *Appetite, 23*(1), 1–13. doi:10.1006/appe.1994.1030 PMID:7826053

Coates, A. E., Hardman, C. A., Halford, J. C. G., Christiansen, P., & Boyland, E. J. (2019). Food and beverage cues featured in youtube videos of social media influencers popular with children: An exploratory study. *Frontiers in Psychology, 10*, 21–42. doi:10.3389/fpsyg.2019.02142 PMID:31616344

Dam, L., Basaran, A., & Burroughs, B. (2024). (Over)Eating with our eyes: An examination of Mukbang influencer marketing and consumer engagement with food brands. *Journal of Promotion Management, 30*(2), 227–251. doi:10.1080/10496491.2023.2253244

De Veirman, M. D., Cauberghe, V., & Hudders, L. (2017). Marketing through Instagram influencers: The impact of number of followers and product divergence on brand attitude. *International Journal of Advertising, 36*(5), 798–828. doi:10.1080/02650487.2017.1348035

Delbaere, M., Michael, B., & Phillips, B. J. (2021). Social media influencers: A route to brand engagement for their followers. *Psychology and Marketing, 38*(1), 101–112. doi:10.1002/mar.21419

Ferraro, C., Sands, S., Zubcevic-Basic, N., & Campbell, C. (2024). Diversity in the digital age: How consumers respond to diverse virtual influencers. *International Journal of Advertising*, 1–23. Advance online publication. doi:10.1080/02650487.2023.2300927

Foxwell, B. (2020). A Guide to Social Media Influencers: Mega, Macro, Micro, and Nano. *Iconosquare.* https://blog.iconosquare.com/guide-to-social-media-influencers/

Griffin, R. J., Neuwirth, K., Giese, J., & Dunwoody, S. (2002). Linking the heuristic-systematic model and depth of processing. *Communication Research, 29*(6), 705–732. doi:10.1177/009365002237833

Hayes, R. A., & Carr, C. T. (2015). Does being social matter? Effects of enabled commenting on credibility and brand attitudes in Social Media. *Journal of Promotion Management, 21*(3), 371–390. doi:10.1080/10496491.2015.1039178

Horton, D., & Wohl, R. (1956). Mass communication and para-social interaction: Observations on intimacy at a distance. *Psychiatry, 19*(3), 215–229. doi:10.1080/00332747.1956.11023049 PMID:13359569

Hughes, C., Swaminathan, V., & Brooks, G. (2019). Driving brand engagement through online social media influencers: An empirical investigation of sponsored blogging campaigns. *Journal of Marketing, 83*(5), 78–96. doi:10.1177/0022242919854374

Infanger, M., & Sczesny, S. (2015). Communion-over-agency effects on advertising effectiveness. *International Journal of Advertising, 34*(2), 285–306. doi:10.1080/02650487.2014.993794

Janseen, L., Schouten, A. P., & Croes, E. A. J. (2022). Influencer fit and number of followers affect advertising outcomes and influencer evaluations via credibility and identification. *International Journal of Advertising, 41*(1), 101–127. doi:10.1080/02650487.2021.1994205

Jin, S. V., Muqaddam, A., & Ryu, E. (2019). Instafamous and social media influencer marketing. *Marketing Intelligence & Planning, 37*(5), 567–579. doi:10.1108/MIP-09-2018-0375

Jun, S., & Yi, J. (2020). What makes followers loyal? The role of influencer interactivity in building influencer brand equity. *Journal of Product and Brand Management, 29*(6), 803–814. doi:10.1108/JPBM-02-2019-2280

Kenny, D. A. (1979). *Correlation and causality*. Wiley-Interscience.

Khan, S., & Khan, M. A. (2021). Effect of social media influencer marketing on consumers' purchase intention and the mediating role of credibility. *Journal of Promotion Management*, *27*(4), 503–523. doi:10.1080/10496491.2020.1851847

Ki, C., & Kim, Y. (2019). The mechanism by which social media influencers persuade consumers: The role of consumers' desire to mimic. *Psychology and Marketing*, *36*(10), 905–922. doi:10.1002/mar.21244

Kline, R. B. (2005). *Principles and practice of structural equation modeling*. Guilford publications.

Kurtin, K. S., O'Brien, N., Roy, D., & Dam, L. (2018). The development of parasocial relationship on YouTube. *The Journal of Social Media in Society*, *7*, 233–252.

Labrecque, I. I. (2014). Fostering consumer-brand relationships in social media environments: The role of parasocial interaction. *Journal of Interactive Marketing*, *28*(2), 134–148. doi:10.1016/j.intmar.2013.12.003

Lee, D., & Wan, C. (2023). The impact of Mukbang live streaming commerce on consumers' overconsumption behavior. *Journal of Interactive Marketing*, *58*(2-3), 198–221. doi:10.1177/10949968231156104

Lee, J. E., & Watkins, B. (2016). YouTube vloggers' influence on consumer luxury brand perceptions and intentions. *Journal of Business Research*, *69*(12), 5753–5760. doi:10.1016/j.jbusres.2016.04.171

Lin, C. A., Crowe, J., Pierre, L., & Lee, Y. (2021). Effects of parasocial interaction with an *Instafamous* influence on brand attitudes and purchase intentions. *Journal of Social Media in Society*, *10*, 55–78.

Lin, L., Hoegg, J., & Aquino, K. (2018). When beauty backfires: The effects of server attractiveness on consumer taste perceptions. *Journal of Retailing*, *94*(3), 296–311. doi:10.1016/j.jretai.2018.04.003

Lou, C., & Yuan, S. (2019). Influencer marketing: How message value and credibility affect consumer trust of branded content on social media. *Journal of Interactive Advertising*, *19*(1), 58–73. doi:10.1080/15252019.2018.1533501

Luong, T.-B., & Ho, C.-H. (2023). The influence of food vloggers on social media users: A study from Vietnam. *Heliyon*, *9*(7), e18259. doi:10.1016/j.heliyon.2023.e18259 PMID:37501978

MacKenzie, S. B., Lutz, R. J., & Belch, G. E. (1986). The role attitude toward the ad as a mediator of advertising effectiveness: A test of competing explanations. *JMR, Journal of Marketing Research*, *23*(2), 130–143. doi:10.1177/002224378602300205

McCroskey, J. C. (1966). Scales for the measurement of ethos. *Speech Monographs*, *33*(1), 65–72. doi:10.1080/03637756609375482

Monge-Benito, S., Elorriaga-Illera, A., & Olabarri-Fernandez, E. (2020). YouTube celebrity endorsement: Audience evaluation of source attributes and response to sponsored content. A case study of influencer Verdeliss. *Communicatio Socialis*, *33*, 149–166.

Munnukka, J., Maity, D., Reinikainen, H., & Luoma-aho, V. (2019). "Thanks for watching". The effectiveness of YouTube vloendorsements. *Computers in Human Behavior*, *93*, 226–234. doi:10.1016/j.chb.2018.12.014

Myers, S. (2021). Instagram source effects: The impact of familiarity and likeability of influencer outcomes. *Journal of Marketing Development and Competitiveness*, *15*, 50–55.

Neely, E., Walton, M., & Stephens, C. (2014). Young people's food practices and social relationships. A thematic synthesis. *Appetite*, *82*, 50–60. doi:10.1016/j.appet.2014.07.005 PMID:25017130

Ogden, J., Coop, N., Cousins, C., Crump, R., Field, L., Hughes, S., & Woodger, N. (2013). Distraction, the desire to eat and food intake. Towards an expanded model of mindless eating. *Appetite*, *62*, 119–126. doi:10.1016/j.appet.2012.11.023 PMID:23219989

Ohanian, R. (1990). Construction and validation of a scale to measure celebrity endorsers' perceived expertise, trustworthiness, and attractiveness. *Journal of Advertising*, *19*(3), 39–52. doi:10.1080/00913367.1990.10673191

Ohanian, R. (1991). The impact of celebrity spokespersons' perceived image on consumers' intentions to purchase. *Journal of Advertising*, *31*, 46–54.

Ott, H. K., Vafeiadis, M., Kumble, S., & Waddell, T. F. (2016). Effects of message interactivity on product attitudes and purchase intentions. *Journal of Promotion Management*, *22*(1), 89–106. doi:10.1080/10496491.2015.1107011

Roccapriore, A. Y., & Pollock, T. G. (2023). I don't need a degree, I've got abs: Influencer warmth and competence, communication mode, and stakeholder engagement on social media. *Academy of Management Journal*, *66*(3), 979–1006. doi:10.5465/amj.2020.1546

Sanderon, J. (2009). "You are all loved so much" Exploring relational maintenance within the context of parasocial relationships. *Journal of Media Psychology*, *21*(4), 171–182. doi:10.1027/1864-1105.21.4.171

Schouten, A. P., Janssen, L., & Verspaget, M. (2020). Celebrity vs. influencer endorsement in advertising: The role of identification, credibility, and product-endorser fit. *International Journal of Advertising*, *39*(2), 258–281. doi:10.1080/02650487.2019.1634898

Shan, Y., Chen, K., & Lin, J. (2020). When social media influencers endorse brands: The effects of self-influencer congruence, parasocial identification, and perceived endorser motive. *International Journal of Advertising*, *39*(5), 590–610. doi:10.1080/02650487.2019.1678322

Shareef, M. A., Mukerji, B., Dwivedi, Y. K., Rana, N. P., & Islam, R. (2019). Social media marketing: Comparative effect of advertisement sources. *Journal of Retailing and Consumer Services*, *46*, 58–69. doi:10.1016/j.jretconser.2017.11.001

Sokolava, K., & Kefi, H. (2020). Instagram and YouTube bloggers promote it, why should I buy? How credibility and parasocial interaction influence purchase intentions. *Journal of Retailing and Consumer Services*, *53*, 1–9. doi:10.1016/j.jretconser.2019.01.011

Spears, N., & Singh, S. N. (2004). Measuring attitude toward the brand and purchase intentions. *Journal of Current Issues and Research in Advertising*, *26*(2), 53–66. doi:10.1080/10641734.2004.10505164

Statista. (2023a). *Influencer marketing worldwide – statistics & facts.* Retrieved from: https://www.statista.com/topics/2496/influence-marketing/#topicOverview

Statista. (2023b). *YouTube food & drink industry sponsored video views in the U.S. & Canada 2020.* Retrieved from: https://www.statista.com/statistics/1269589/youtube-food-drink-industry-sponsored-video-views/#statisticContainer

Stubb, C., Nystrom, A. G., & Colliander, J. (2019). Influencer marketing: The impact of disclosing sponsorship compensation justification on sponsored content effectiveness. *Journal of Communication Management (London), 23*(2), 109–122. doi:10.1108/JCOM-11-2018-0119

Taillon, B. J., Mueller, S. M., Kowalczyk, C. M., & Jones, D. N. (2020). Understanding the relationships between social media influencers and their followers: The moderating role of closeness. *Journal of Product and Brand Management, 29*(6), 767–782. doi:10.1108/JPBM-03-2019-2292

Thorson, K. S., & Rodgers, S. (2006). Relationships between blogs as eWOM and interactivity, perceived interactivity, and parasocial interactions. *Journal of Interactive Advertising, 6*(2), 34–44. doi:10.1080/15252019.2006.10722117

Torres, P., Augusto, M., & Matos, M. (2019). Antecedents and outcomes of digital influencer endorsement: An exploratory study. *Psychology and Marketing, 36*(12), 1267–1276. doi:10.1002/mar.21274

Turner, P. G., & Lefevre, C. E. (2017). Instagram use is linked to increase symptoms of orthorexia nervosa. *Eating and Weight Disorders, 22*(2), 227–284. doi:10.1007/s40519-017-0364-2 PMID:28251592

Uribe, R., Buzeta, C., & Velasquez, M. (2016). Sidedness, commercial intent, and expertise in blog advertising. *Journal of Business Research, 69*(10), 4403–4410. doi:10.1016/j.jbusres.2016.04.102

Wang, S. W., & Scheibaum, A. C. (2018). Enhancing brand credibility via celebrity endorsement: Trustworthiness trumps attractiveness and expertise. *Journal of Advertising Research, 58*(1), 16–32. doi:10.2501/JAR-2017-042

Wiedmann, K. P., & von Mettenheim, W. (2021). Attractiveness, trustworthiness, and expertise-social media influencers' winning formula? *Journal of Product and Brand Management, 30*(5), 707–725. doi:10.1108/JPBM-06-2019-2442

Xiao, M., Wang, R., & Chan-Olmstead, S. (2018). Factors affecting YouTube influencer marketing credibility: A heuristic-systematic model. *Journal of Media Business Studies, 15*(3), 188–213. doi:10.1080/16522354.2018.1501146

Yilmaz, C., Telci, E. E., Bodur, M., & Iscioglu, T. E. (2011). Source characteristics and advertising effectiveness: The roles of message processing motivation and product category knowledge. *International Journal of Advertising, 30*(5), 889–915. doi:10.2501/IJA-30-5-889-914

Chapter 9
Doug the Pug, Eggnog, and Boo:
The Impact of Pet Influencers on Stakeholders' Purchase Intentions and Attitudes Toward the Brand

Michel M Haigh
Texas State University, USA

Shelley Wigley
University of Texas, Arlington, USA

ABSTRACT

There are more than 64 million social media influencer accounts as of June 2023, evidence influencers are not a passing trend (trendHERO, 2023). Influencers have shifted the way information is disseminated, how public opinion is swayed, and how brands are promoted. However, pet influencers are an under-researched type of influencer. These influencers create content that shares their pets' personalities and adventures with others. The pet is the star of the social media account – not the owner. Millions of social media users follow the pet influencers such as Grumpy Cat, Smudge – Table Cat, and Doug the Pug (Feedspot, 2023).Pets with large followings such as Venus the Cat or JiffPom can earn thousands to millions of dollars for their promotional efforts (Myers et al., 2022). A survey of more than 400 followers of pet influencers found they deem pet infleucers credible and likeable. They also find the brands being promoted credible and have high purchase intent. The more time one spends on social media influences perceptions of pet influencers.

INTRODUCTION

There are more than 64 million social media influencer accounts as of June 2023, evidence influencers are not a passing trend (trendHERO, 2023). In fact, influencer marketing has increased at least 50 percent

DOI: 10.4018/979-8-3693-0912-4.ch009

every year since 2016 (Geyser, 2021). Influencers have shifted the way information is disseminated, how public opinion is swayed, and how brands are promoted. Influencers can have anywhere from 1,000 to more than a million followers; and they can specialize in various topics including fashion, food, and lifestyle. Research has examined influencers from a variety of perspectives (see for example: Belanche et al., 2021; Jamil et al., 2023; Jin et al., 2019; Martinez-Lopez, et al., 2020; Trivedi & Sama, 2019; Saima & Khan, 2021). However, pet influencers are an under-researched type of influencer. These influencers create content that shares their pets' personalities and adventures with others. The pet is the star of the social media account – not the owner. Millions of social media users follow pet influencers such as Grumpy Cat, Smudge—Table Cat, and Doug the Pug (Feedspot, 2023).

There are very few studies examining the relationship between pet influencers and their followers. This chapter provides an overview of the influencer literature, the current pet influencer literature, and then examines if pet influencers are deemed credible sources of information and if pet influencers influence the credibility of the brand. The study presented is one of the first studies evaluating stakeholders' perceptions of pet influencers using a survey rather than a content analysis.

Social Media Influencers

Individuals must meet certain criteria to be an influencer. Social media influencers are individuals who meet the following conditions: (1) they must be experts in a specific area (2) they must have a considerable following on one or more social media platforms, and (3) they must produce content that is valuable and engaging to both their audience and brand partners (Lou & Yuan, 2019).

There are different types of influencers. Celebrity influencers have more than 1 million followers; macro influencers have 100,000 to 1 million followers; micro influencers have 10,000 to 100,000 followers; and nano influencers have between 1,000 and 10,000 followers (Andrii, 2023).

In the summer of 2023, most influencers fell in the nano category (91.07%, 58.2 million). Around 8 percent were considered micro influencers (5.1 million), .83 percent were macro influencers (.5 million), and less than .05 percent were celebrities (34,300). The top three countries with the most influencers are Brazil (5.4 million), the United States (4.7 million), and India (2.3 million) (Andrii, 2023).

Social media influencers are different from traditional celebrities such as actors, athletes, and models. These influencers have been described as microcelebrities or instafamous (Poyry et al., 2019). While some celebrities may in fact use social media to influence others, the current study examines influencers who were unknown before establishing a following on social media. These influencers are regular people who may be health and fitness fanatics, fashionistas, or parents. They are not, however, famous, or professionally trained (Zhang et al., 2023). To qualify as an influencer, these everyday individuals must have a well-established social media following and established authenticity and credibility in their area of expertise (Cheng et al., 2020). Research has found that bloggers, YouTubers, and other influencers may be even more powerful than traditional celebrities because they are more relatable (Djafarova & Rushworth, 2017). The foundation for understanding influencers has been laid, so now the impact influencers have will be examined.

The Power of an Influencer

Influencers do not exist merely to entertain their followers. In fact, influencers have two goals: enhancing product knowledge and increasing purchase intention (Kay et al., 2020). Brands partner with influencers who post promotional content for the brand from their own social media accounts. The best influencer marketing is created to seamlessly blend with other influencer created content, often referred to as native advertising. The brand content looks the same as the influencer's organic content and is sometimes differentiated with hashtags like #ad or #sponsored that are embedded in the post. Influencers are compensated by brands through sales commissions via affiliate marketing programs, direct payments, or in-kind products (Geyser, 2021). Influencers, sometimes referred to as brand ambassadors, leverage their established relationships with followers to increase purchase likelihood (Jiménez-Castillo & Sánchez-Fernández, 2019). Influencers are powerful; they not only attract followers, but they can expand their initial reach through followers' likes and shares. This means an influencer's audience can expand exponentially to followers of followers and so on (Kay et al., 2020).

Influencers have changed how companies spend their advertising dollars. The influencer market was $16.4 billion in the U.S. during 2022. Instagram continues to be the major social platform used for influencer content because the brand website can be linked in the post or through the addition of a shopping tab (Dencheva, 2023). This matters because consumers use social platforms to help with their buying decisions (De Veirman & Hudders, 2020). It is expected this trend will continue as teens turn into adults and look for recommendations on products and services (Forbes, 2019; Lou & Yuan, 2019).

Not all social media influencers are people. In fact, some are pets whose owners manage their online profiles (Myers et al., 2022). People enjoy following other people's pets on social media. This is likely because most U.S. households own at least one pet and nearly one-third of that number indicates they follow pet influencers on social media (Roberts, 2021). Now that the power of the influencer has been discussed, the power of the pet influencer will be examined more closely from the beginning of the first pet influencer, to the relationships people form with this unique type of influencer.

PET INFLUENCERS

Brands have taken advantage of pet influencers not only in the pet care market but even brands like Budweiser, Google, Subaru, and The Body Shop have deals with pet influencers and their humans (Myers et al., 2022). The pet care market alone is expected to top $200 billion globally by 2025 (Niemietz, 2020). Pets with large followings such as Venus the Cat or JiffPom can earn thousands to millions of dollars for their promotional efforts (Myers et al., 2022). Pet influencers are such big business for brands that talent agencies have been created exclusively to focus on the pet influencer niche (Myers et al., 2022).

Although pet influencers can garner money and fame from their online posts, research reveals one of the primary reasons for owners to maintain these pet social media accounts is to bring joy and happiness to a corner of the Internet that is often mired in toxicity and negative content (Hartama, 2021; Maddox, 2020).

Pet Influencer Beginnings

One might consider Boo the original pet influencer. Boo was a Pomeranian who had a Facebook page starting in 2009. Boo's page said "My Name is Boo. I am a dog. Life is good." His popularity grew in 2010 after the singer Kesha sent a tweet with a link to the page. He was known as the World's Cutest Dog. Boo and his brother Buddy had 5 million Facebook fans when his first book was published. Six books were published about Boo, including a cut-out book, and several stuffed animals were manufactured by the toy company Gund. In July 2012, Virgin America named Boo its Official Pet Liaison; he also modeled sunglasses for The Monocle and promoted Dogswell Jerky Treats. In October of 2013, Boo was interviewed by Anderson Cooper. In the end, he had more than 17 million followers, and Facebook created Boo Stickers for users in posts, comments, and in messenger.

Boo used his status to raise money for Operation Smile; Freedom House; Lucile Packard Children's Hospital's pet therapy program; Charity: Water; and San Francisco Animal Care for his birthdays. Boo passed away in 2018 (boothedog.net, 2023). Boo had a large fan following without Instagram, TikTok, or the other social media platforms that came later. Now in the year 2023, there is a list of the Top 100 Pet Influencers (Feedspot, 2023). Pet influencers are usually dogs or cats, but a variety of animals have social media pages. Doug the Pug made the list of top pet influencers with 3.7 million followers on Instagram. He's also won two People's Choice Awards. Hosico Cat has 1.9 million followers, Smudge—Table Cat has 1.7 million followers, Mr. White (a cat) has 2.2 million followers, Grumpy Cat has 2.7 million followers, and Hamlet (a pig) has 322,000 followers.

Despite their large followings and significant impact on the advertising and marketing industries, research on pet influencers and their followers is scarce. Influencers create relationships with their followers, and this type of relationship is often considered a parasocial relationship.

Influencers and Relationships

The appeal of social media influencers among followers is the parasocial relationships formed. Parasocial relationships have been shown to increase purchase intent as well as product interest (Lou & Kim, 2019; Yuan & Lou, 2020). The term parasocial interaction explains the illusionary bonds that develop between consumers of media and media personalities (Horton & Wohl, 1956).

Traditional parasocial research focused on the personae, or performers, who appeared on the primary modes of programming at the time—radio and TV. These media personalities, or personae, offer regular appearances that are dependable and routine for media consumers. Over time, this association leads to shared past experiences between the media consumer and media personality that can result in a one-sided relationship. Research challenges the idea of a one-sided relationship—now saying it is bidirectional—meaning the relationship between the influencer and their followers is more interactive and reciprocal than a traditional parasocial relationship (Lou & Kim, 2019).

Following an influencer allows the follower "to get to know" the media persona—in this case, the influencer. "Behind the scenes" looks and insider information offered by the influencer can translate into an intimate bond between influencers and their followers.

Followers can also interact with the influencer through comments, likes, and shares; develop feelings of intimacy by checking the influencer's content on a regular basis; and develop attitudes toward the influencer (Boerman, 2020). When this interaction occurs repeatedly and on a regular basis, the contact can resemble a real relationship, at least to the media consumer, and develop into a parasoical relationship. The followers feel a bond with the influencer and believe they know the influencer better than others do (Haigh & Wigley, 2015).

Social media platforms are perfect for fostering parasocial relationships because followers are exposed to details of an influencer's daily life. Followers can even set notifications so that they never miss an influencer's post or them "going live" to interact with followers. These actions further perpetuate the illusion of intimacy and closeness between influencers and their followers (Chen, 2018; Munnukka et al., 2019).

Influencers are unique compared to traditional media personalities because their entire job is based on sponsorships and endorsement deals - meaning they are making money off the relationship. Their goal is to get the followers to like, comment, share, and purchase the products they are sharing in their posts. This makes the parasocial relationship with an influencer unique compared to a traditional media personality. The relationships stakeholders have with the influencer often determines how credible an influencer is–so credibility is examined next.

Influencer Credibility

Parasocial relationships do not happen between influencers and their followers without elements such as trust and source credibility. Followers must believe and have faith in what the influencers tell them. Yuan and Lou (2020) argue source credibility is a precursor for parasocial relationships to form. Three factors drive an individual's perceptions of source credibility: expertise, trustworthiness, and attractiveness (Ohanian, 1990).

Expertise is the extent to which a communicator is believed to have competence, qualifications, or skills and be a valid source of information; trustworthiness refers to the communicator's perceived honesty, believability, and integrity (Erdogan, 1999; Ohanian, 1990); and attractiveness, which includes liking or familiarity with a communicator (McGuire, 1985). While Ohanian's model is widely used and acknowledged, other dimensions of source credibility have been explored including similarity between the communicator and media consumers (Morimoto & La Ferle, 2008).

Influencer honesty, openness, and transparency led to greater trust and satisfaction in influencers from their followers (Dhanesh & Duthler, 2019). Similarity and attractiveness led to a stronger parasocial relationship with an influencer. The parasocial relationship is mediated by perceived similarity and product interest. Followers will form stronger parasocial relationships with influencers they find attractive and comparable to themselves. The relationship then leads to greater product interest. Munnukka et al. (2016) found that a higher degree of similarity led to more positive attitudes toward the advertised brand. Credibility and trust are important factors in influencers' ability to impact consumer purchase decisions (Zhang & Wei, 2021).

An influencer's authenticity impacts credibility, and that authenticity lends credibility to both the message and the messenger. These influencers are seen as credible because they are authentic and true to themselves, which makes them trustworthy (Poyry et al., 2019). In their examination of authenticity among influencers, Poyry et al. (2019) defined the concept as comprising elements such as sincerity, genuineness, and truthfulness. In fact, research reveals that brands should work with influencers that fit the brand and are known among the target audience (Jin et al., 2019; Shan et al., 2020).

It may come as a surprise to some that influencers reportedly have more influence than either traditional celebrities or advertisements. Talavera (2015) found influencer-generated content was considered more authentic and organic than brand-generated ads. Other researchers also suggest that influencers impact consumer preferences more than traditional advertising or traditional celebrities because they possess higher authenticity and credibility (Djafarova & Rushworth, 2017; Giles, 2017).

Martinez-Lopez et al. (2020) recommend that brands work with non-celebrities who are experts in their field because those types of influencers have the greatest attitudinal and behavioral responses. Lou and Yuan (2019) found influencers' trustworthiness, attractiveness, and similarity to their followers positively impacted followers' trust in influencers' branded posts, which thereby influenced brand awareness and purchase intentions.

Research Questions

Pet influencers give humanlike features to their pets through their social media accounts. These accounts tend to act like a brand community because members have a deep connection to the other members of the community and a sense of belonging. There is a deep connection between the members and the influencer, and the community has rituals and traditions (Muniz & O'guinn, 2001).

Influencer honesty, openness, and transparency lead to greater trust and satisfaction in influencers (Dhanesh & Duthler, 2019). Influencer–follower relationships are also stronger when the follower finds them comparable to themselves. Similarity and attractiveness lead to stronger relationships with an influencer (Yuan & Lou, 2020). However, expertise and trustworthiness did not predict stronger relationships (Yuan & Lou, 2020). All these things – honesty, openness, transparency, similarity, trust, attractiveness – are measured as a form of credibility. Most research examines perceptions of influencers' credibility, but pet influencers are a unique type of influencer. In most cases, the pet is the star of the show, not the human. Do followers think pet influencers are credible considering they are showcasing the pet and not themselves the way most influencers do? The following research questions are asked:

RQ1: How do followers perceive the credibility of the pet influencer (trust, expert, similarity, attractiveness)?

RQ2: How do followers perceive the likeability of the influencer?

It's understood that followers form stronger relationships with influencers they find attractive and comparable to themselves, and the relationship leads to more interest in the product the influencer is promoting (Yuan & Lou, 2020). The higher degree of similarity can lead to more positive attitudes toward the advertised brand (Munnukka et al., 2016), and credibility and trust are important factors in influencers' ability to impact consumer purchase decisions (Zhang & Wei, 2021). When conducting a content analysis of pet influencer posts, Myers et al. (2022) found that the engagement rate for a pet influencer post was negatively impacted by disclosing it was an ad or paid partnership. There was also less engagement when the pet influencer post included the brand logo in the promotional post. This finding was similar when looking at regular influencers (De Cicco et al., 2020). Pet influencers are unique. The followers are unique. People find them credible and look to them for advice. Even though the content analysis findings (Myers et al., 2022) indicate a lack of engagement, it is worth pursuing if followers are turned off from the product featured by the pet influencer. It is also worth examining how it impacts the brand credibility when partnering with a pet influencer and the followers' purchase intent. If pet influencers are deemed credible, pet parents may transfer that credibility and positive attitude to the brand and purchase it. The following research question is asked:

RQ3: What are pet influencer followers' perceptions of (a) brand credibility, (b) brand attitude, and (c) brand purchase intent for the brands featured in sponsored content from pet influencers?

Pet influencers are unique because they promote products relevant and useful to pets and pet owners (Hartama, 2021). Lou and Yuan (2019) argue social media influencer content is similar to online advertising. The content could be informative or entertaining (Ducoffe, 1996). Advertising informativeness is the ability of the ad to provide information so consumers are more likely to purchase a product. When an ad is entertaining, it is there to entertain the consumer and rely on the affective value of an ad instead of the cognitive elements of an ad (Ducoffe, 1996). Dao et al. (2014) found social media advertising informativeness, entertainment, and credibility determined how they perceive the value of the ad and influenced their purchase intent. Lou and Yuan (2019) found informative value of a post and the entertainment value of a post did not affect brand awareness. The informative value of a branded-post influenced purchase intent. Their study examined regular influencer posts. It would be interesting to see if followers of pet influencers deem a post informative or entertaining or both.

RQ4: How do followers perceive the pet influencer posts—entertaining or informative?

There is little research examining the differences in perceptions between men and women when it comes to influencers. This study examines if there are differences. The following research question is asked:

RQ5: Are there gender differences in perceptions of credibility when it comes to following pet influencers?

Finally, the amount of time an individual spends on social media, social media intensity, should influence how credible they deem social media influencers as well as the products they endorse. When examining past research on social media influencers (e.g., Boerman, 2019; Dhanesh & Duthler, 2019; Munnukka et al., 2016; Zhang et al., 2023) researchers have not measured social media intensity to predict the credibility of influencers or brand variables. Very few researchers included a measure of social media intensity in the method section of their studies. The current study measured social media intensity thinking the amount of time participants spend on social media would impact how credible they deem an influencer as well as the brand the influencer is promoting. The pattern would follow the same idea found in social media and psychology research indicating the amount of time one spends on social media impacts their well-being (Cramer, Song, & Drent, 2016). The following research question is asked:

RQ6: How does Instagram intensity (use) influence followers' perceptions of credibility of an influencer and the brand featured in a sponsored post?

METHOD

Procedures

Participants were recruited from an M-Turk panel. They were paid $1 to complete the survey. They were required to live in the United States and be 18 years of age.

First participants implied consent. Before answering survey questions, a sample of two sponsored posts from pet influencers were provided as exemplars. Participants were then told to think of those types of posts while taking the survey. They were then asked to provide the name of a pet influencer they followed. If participants did not provide a pet influencer, they were dismissed from the study. Participants then started answering a variety of questions that asked about credibility, brand perceptions, social media use, and demographics.

Participants

The final sample included 244 males (59.8%) and 164 females (40.0% female) with an average age of 29.39 ($SD = 6.50$, $N = 408$), ranging from 18 to 78. Thirteen percent of participants (12.2%) had a high school diploma. Most participants had earned college credit (67.4% bachelor's degree, 2.0% associate's degree, 1.7% had some college classes, 1.2% had a Ph.D., and 14.2% had a professional degree). Over 90% of participants were Caucasian (96.3%), .7% identified as African American, and .7% identified as Asian/Pacific Islander. Two percent (2.0%) identified as American Indian, and .2% selected "other" as ethnicity.

Social Media Demographics

One question asked how many Facebook friends the individual had (Ellison et al., 2007). Eight percent (8.1%) had 100 friends or more on Facebook, 30.4% had 200 Facebook friends or more, 29.9% had 300 Facebook friends or more, 14.2% had 400 or more Facebook friends, 10.0% had 500 or more Facebook friends, and 7.4% had 600 or more Facebook friends. The question was repeated for Instagram. Nine percent (9.6%) had 100 friends or more on Instagram, 25.5% had 200 Instagram friends or more, 32.1% had 300 Instagram friends or more, 14.7% had 400 or more Instagram friends, 9.8% had 500 or more Instagram friends, and 8.3% had 600 or more Instagram friends.

Measures

Instagram Intensity

The Facebook Intensity measure was updated for Instagram for the purpose of this study. Participants were asked to indicate how often they do the following activities on Instagram posts tied to pet influencers. Questions were placed on a 5-point scale where 1 indicated never and 5 indicated always. Statements included: Make posts, like/react to others' posts, comment on others' posts, and share others' posts ($\alpha = .90$; $M = 5.79$, $SD = 1.00$) (Ellison et al., 2007).

Instagram Intensity with Pet Influencers. Participants were asked, "in the past week, on average, approximately how many minutes per day do you spend on Instagram posts tied to pet influencers?" Seven percent (7.1%) of participants spent less than 30 minutes a day engaging with posts tied to pet influencers; 43.4% spent 31 to 60 minutes a day engaging with posts tied to pet influencers; 24.3% spent 61 to 90 minutes a day engaging with posts tied to pet influencers, and 25.2% spent more than 90 minutes a day engaging with posts tied to pet influencers.

Another question asked how many times a week they liked or commented on Instagram posts tied to pet influencers. Around 10.5% indicated they would like or comment 0 to 5 times a week, 31.6% liked/commented 6 to 10 times a week, 34.8% indicated they would like/comment 11 to 15 times a week, 13.7% indicated they like/comment on influencers' posts 16 to 20 times a week, and 9.3% indicated they like/comment on influencers' posts 20 or more times a week.

Purchase Intent

Purchase intent was measured by combining two scales from Gill et al. (1988) and Urbany et al. (1997). The questions asked if participants would purchase the brand's products/services. Adjective pairs included: unlikely/likely; nonexistent/existent; improbable/probable; impossible/possible; uncertain/certain; definitely would not/definitely would ($\alpha = .89$, $M = 5.90$, $SD = 1.00$). Items were placed on 7-point semantic-differential scales.

Brand Attitude

Attitude toward the brand comprised four items on a 7-point semantic-differential scale (Rodgers, 2003; Shiv, Edell, & Payne, 1997). Adjective pairs were bad/good, negative/positive, unacceptable/acceptable, and unfavorable/favorable ($\alpha = .87$, $M = 5.98$, $SD = 1.00$).

Brand Credibility

Brand credibility was measured using three items: honest/dishonest, trustworthy/not trustworthy, and ethical/unethical on a 7-point semantic-differential scale ($\alpha = .82$, $M = 5.97$, $SD = 1.00$) (Kirmani, 1997).

Credibility of the Source

Credibility was measured using a scale from Munnukka et al. (2016). Participants indicated their agreement with a series of statements. Each statement was placed on a 7-point scale starting with, "Concerning the influencer you mentioned..." There was a note that the questions should be applied to the pet owner – not the pet. The scale had multiple dimensions. The first dimension measured was ***expert*** ($\alpha = .81$, $M = 5.83$, $SD = .94$) with four statements: I feel the endorser knows a lot about the product, I feel the endorser is competent to make assertions about the product, I consider the endorser an expert on the product, and I consider the endorser sufficiently experienced to make assertations about the product. The next dimension, ***trust*** ($\alpha = .83$, $M = 5.87$, $SD = 1.00$), consisted of four statements: I feel the endorser was honest, I consider the endorser trustworthy, I feel the endorser was truthful, and I consider the endorser earnest. The dimension ***similarity***, ($\alpha = .80$, $M = 5.80$, $SD = 1.00$), consisted of three statements including: The endorser and I have a lot in common, the endorser and I are a lot alike, and I can easily identify with the endorser. The final dimension was ***attractiveness*** ($\alpha = .85$, $M = 5.80$, $SD = 1.00$). It consisted of four statements including: I consider the endorser very attractive; I consider the endorser very stylish; I think the endorser is good looking, and I think the endorser is sexy.

Likeability of the Influencer

Likeability of the influencer was measured by three, 7-point semantic-differential scales ($\alpha = .84$, $M = 5.95$, $SD = 1.01$). The question told participants to think of the pet owner–not the pet. Scale points included: cold/warm, unlikeable/likeable, and unfriendly/friendly (Dimofte et al., 2003).

Informativeness/Entertainment Value of Post

Influencer-generated content's informativeness and entertainment value were measured by asking participants' responses to a statement: "Concerning the pet influencer whom I follow, I personally think their social media posts/updates are …" Responses were anchored by five, 7-point semantic-differential scales (Lou & Yuan, 2019; Voss et al., 2003). The informativeness dimension included the following scales ineffective/effective; unhelpful/helpful; not functional/functional; unnecessary/necessary; and impractical/practical ($\alpha = .91$, $M = 5.88$, $SD = 1.01$). For the entertainment dimension, the following scales were included: not fun/fun; dull/exciting; not delightful/delightful; not thrilling/thrilling; and unenjoyable/enjoyable ($\alpha = .89$, $M = 5.92$, $SD = 1.00$).

RESULTS

The purpose of this study was to examine the credibility of pet influencers. It also intended to examine whether pet influencers impacted brand attitude, credibility, and purchase intent.

Research Question 1 asked how followers perceive the credibility of pet influencers (trust, expert, similarity, attractiveness). Descriptive statistics were examined for the dimensions of credibility. Pet influencers were deemed ***trustworthy*** ($M = 5.87$, $SD = 1.00$). For the dimension of ***expert***, the pet influencers ($M = 5.83$, $SD = .94$) were deemed expert sources. Pet influencers were deemed ***similar*** ($M = 5.80$, $SD = 1.00$) to the followers, and they were also deemed ***attractive*** ($M = 5.80$, $SD = 1.00$). On the 7-point scale, anything above 4.0 would indicate positive perceptions and anything below would indicate negative perceptions. Therefore, pet influencers were deemed credible sources.

Research Question 2 asked if followers would deem the pet influencer as likeable. Descriptive statistics indicate followers deemed pet influencers very likeable ($M = 5.95$, $SD = 1.01$). The mean score is approaching 6.0, indicating followers deem influencers very likeable.

Research Question 3 asked about pet influencer followers' perceptions of (a) brand credibility, (b) brand attitudes, and (c) purchase intent for the brands featured in sponsored content from pet influencers. Descriptive statistics indicate followers have very positive perceptions of the brands featured in the sponsored content ($M = 5.97$, $SD = 1.00_{\text{credibilty}}$; $M = 5.98$, $SD = 1.00_{\text{attitude}}$; $M = 5.90$, $SD = 1.00_{\text{purchase intent}}$). They deem the brands very credible, have very positive brand attitudes, and are likely to purchase the products featured in the sponsored posts.

Research Question 4 asked if followers would perceive the pet influencer posts as more entertaining or informative. Descriptive statistics indicate followers find the posts more entertaining ($M = 5.92$, $SD = 1.00$) than informative ($M = 5.88$, $SD = 1.01$). The means are not statistically significant, but the entertainment mean is slightly higher than the informative mean.

Research Question 5 asked if there were gender differences in perceptions of source credibility and brand attitudes when examining followers. An analysis of variance (ANOVA) test was run with the independent variables **gender identity** and the dependent variables four dimensions measuring source credibility (trust, expert, similarity, and attractiveness), likeability, and brand variables (brand attitude, brand credibility, and purchase intent). The omnibus test result is provided before looking at the pattern of means for each of the independent variables.

There were statistically significant results for the dependent variables: *likeability* $F(2, 407) = 11.91$, $p < .05$, $\eta^2 = .06$; and *brand attitude* $F(2, 407) = 7.29$, $p < .05$, $\eta^2 = .04$. Females ($M = 6.11$, $SD = .77$) indicated higher scores on likeability than men ($M = 5.89$, $SD = 1.10$). Females also had more positive perceptions of the brand ($M = 6.06$, $SD = .81$) than men ($M = 5.95$, $SD = 1.04$).

There were no statistically significant differences for the dependent variables *trust* $F(2, 407) = .16$, $p > .05$, $\eta^2 = .00$, *expert* $F(2, 407) = .01$, $p > .05$, $\eta^2 = .00$, *similarity* $F(2, 407) = .11$, $p > .05$, $\eta^2 = .00$, *attractiveness* $F(2, 407) = .69$, $p > .05$, $\eta^2 = .00$; *purchase intent* $F(2, 407) = .43$, $p > .05$, $\eta^2 = .00$; and *brand credibility* $F(2, 407) = .92$, $p > .05$, $\eta^2 = .00$.

Table 1 includes the means and standard deviations for the independent variable gender and the dependent variables.

Research Question 6 asked if Instagram intensity influenced perceptions of credibility and brand variables. Instagram intensity was recoded into three categories based on mean scores. The categories were low intensity, medium intensity, and high intensity. The recoded variable was used as the independent variable in an ANOVA. Because the groups were not the same size, Welch's Anova was computed. The Welch's degrees of freedom are reported in the results. There were statistically significant results for all dependent variables: *trust* $F(2, 21.53) = 26.52$, $p < .00$; *expert* $F(2, 21.23) = 25.60$, $p < .00$; *similarity* $F(2, 21.14) = 25.39$, $p < .00$; *attractiveness* $F(2, 21.65) = 35.31$, $p < .00$; *likeability* $F(2, 22.71) = 21.89$,

Table 1. Gender differences for dependent variables

Variables	Male	Female
	(n=244)	(n=163)
Source Credibility		
Trust	5.86 (1.02)	5.89 (.70)
Expert	5.83 (1.00)	5.84 (.70)
Similarity	5.81 (1.04)	5.79 (.82)
Attractiveness	5.83 (1.04)	5.75 (.85)
Likeability	5.89 (1.10)	6.11 (.77)*
Brand Variables		
Purchase Intent	5.88 (1.03)	5.94 (.76)
Brand Attitude	5.95 (1.04)	6.06 (.81)**
Brand Credibility	5.9. (1.07)	6.07 (.82)

Notes: Means and standard deviations (shown in parentheses) for gender and the dependent variables. Source credibility was measured by three dimensions. Statements were placed on 7-point Likert scales (Munnukka et al., 2016). Likeability was measured by a 7-point semantic-differential scales (Dimofte et al., 2003). Purchase intent was measured by 7-point semantic-differential scales from Gill et al. (1988) and Urbany et al. (1997). Brand attitude was measured by a 7-point semantic differential scale (Rodgers, 2003; Shiv, Edell, & Payne, 1997). Brand credibility was measured by 7-point semantic-differential scales (Kirmani, 1997).

$^{**}p < .001$

$p < .00$; *purchase intent* $F(2, 21.50) = 27.48, p < .00$; *brand attitude* $F(2, 22.65) = 23.26, p < .00$; and *brand credibility* $F(2, 22.67) = 26.33, p < .00$.

When examining the pattern of means, Instagram intensity did make a difference in perceptions of the credibility of the pet influencer as well as the brand. Those who spent more time on Instagram had more positive perceptions of the influencer as well as the brand. When looking at source credibility dimensions, there were statistically significant differences for trust ($M = 3.87, SD = 1.60_{low}; M = 4.75, SD = 1.14_{medium}; M = 6.03, SD = .70_{high}$). The less time one spends on Instagram, the less trust they had for a pet influencer. The less time one spent on Instagram, the less they judged the pet influencer as an expert ($M = 3.87, SD = 1.59_{low}; M = 4.75, SD = 1.07_{medium}; M = 6.00, SD = .69_{high}$). The more time one spent on Instagram, the more likely they thought the pet influencer was similar ($M = 3.60, SD = 1.79l_{ow}; M = 4.54, SD = 1.25_{medium}; M = 5.99, SD = .70_{high}$), attractive ($M = 3.50, SD = 1.62_{low}; M = 4.50, SD = 1.09_{medium}; M = 5.99, SD = .73_{high}$), and likeable ($M = 4.00, SD = 1.75_{low}; M = 4.72, SD = 1.38_{medium}; M = 6.14, SD = .78_{high}$).

The more time one spent on Instagram, the more likely they were to purchase a product the pet influencer was promoting ($M = 3.48, SD = 1.77l_{ow}; M = 4.81, SD = 1.13_{medium}; M = 6.07, SD = .68_{high}$). The less time one spent on Instagram, the less positive their perceptions of the brand a pet influencer was promoting ($M = 3.71, SD = 1.82_{low}; M = 4.90, SD = 1.26_{medium}; M = 6.16, SD = .72_{high}$). They also found the brand less credible ($M = 3.93, SD = 1.90_{low}; M = 4.65, SD = 1.22_{medium}; M = 6.17, SD = .80_{high}$). Therefore, when examining the pattern of means, Instagram intensity/use played a large role in deeming pet influencers as credible as well as the brands they were promoting. Table 2 includes the means and standard deviations.

Table 2. Social media intensity (use) differences for dependent variables

Variable	Low (n=13)	Medium (n=24)	High (n=364)
Source Credibility			
Trust	3.87 (1.60)	4.75 (1.14)	6.03 (.70)**
Expert	3.87 (1.59)	4.75 (1.07)	6.00 (.69)**
Similarity	3.60 (1.79)	4.54 (1.25)	5.99 (.70)**
Attractiveness	3.50 (1.62)	4.50 (1.09)	5.99 (.73)**
Likeability	4.00 (1.75)	4.72 (1.38)	6.14 (.78)**
Brand Variables			
Purchase Intent	3.48 (1.77)	4.81 (1.13)	6.07 (.68)**
Brand Attitude	3.71 (1.82)	4.90 (1.26)	6.16 (.72)**
Brand Credibility	3.9. (1.90)	4.65 (1.22)	6.17 (.80)**

Notes: Means and standard deviations (shown in parentheses) for gender and the dependent variables. Source credibility was measured by three dimensions. Statements were placed on 7-point Likert scales (Munnukka et al., 2016). Likeability was measured by a 7-point semantic- differential scales (Dimofte et al., 2003). Purchase intent was measured by 7-point semantic-differential scales from Gill et al. (1988) and Urbany et al. (1997). Brand attitude was measured by a 7-point semantic-differential scale (Rodgers, 2003; Shiv, Edell, & Payne, 1997). Brand credibility was measured by 7-point semantic-differential scales (Kirmani, 1997). A Welch Test was used because of the differences between group size. The differences were statistically significant when using the Welch Test.

**$p < .001$

DISCUSSION

Pet influencers are a unique type of social media influencer. They are often narrating the page on behalf of their pet (Zhang et al., 2023). Most pet influencer research focuses on the owners of the accounts (e.g., Berzleja & Kertész; Hartama, 2021; Maddox, 2020; Shamayleh & Arsel, 2020) and not on the followers' perceptions. The current study extends the current literature by looking at followers of pet influencers (Zhang et al., 2023).

Research Question 1 asked how followers perceive the credibility of pet influencers. Past pet influencer research did not examine the credibility of the influencer from the follower perspective (e.g., Zhang et al., 2023; Berzleja & Kertész, 2019; Myers et al., 2022; Maddox, 2020). The current study engages with pet influencer followers to determine perceptions of credibility. Pet influencers were deemed very credible sources on all dimensions of source credibility including being seen as an expert, trustworthy, similar, and attractive. This research confirms past findings for other types of influencers on social media (e.g., Dhanesh & Duthler, 2019; Yuan & Lou, 2020). Belanche et al. (2021) found when influencers are seen as a credible source, followers have positive attitudes toward them. Publishing sponsored posts or non-sponsored posts from the pet's point of view did not impact the credibility of the account.

Research Question 2 asked if the pet influencer would be likeable. Findings indicate pet influencers are very likable. This finding supports past research that found influencers should be authentic (Djafarova & Rushworth, 2017; Giles, 2017; Jin et al., 2019; Shan et al., 2020). It supports the conclusion from Martinez-Lopez et al. (2020) and Lou and Yuan (2019) that brands should work with non-celebrities who are "experts." Pet influencers were deemed likeable because they were authentic, non-celebrities, living regular lives. Participants found the influencer likable through the content they posted about their pets. The positive feelings followers have toward the pets transfer to the pet owners who are managing the account.

Research Question 3 asked if followers would have positive perceptions of the brand being promoted by the pet influencer. Findings indicate followers had positive attitudes about the brand being promoted by the influencer. Participants found the brand very credible, and they were very likely to purchase products the pet influencer promoted. These findings are similar to findings for other types of influencers (Alrwashdeh et al., 2022). Alrwashdeh et al. (2022) found the quality of information and likability of the influencer impacted the likelihood of purchasing a product. The current findings also support Belanche et al. (2021). It is important that influencers promote products that are congruent with being a pet influencer. This means pet influencers need to continue to promote pet products or they risk losing the credibility they have built up among their followers. Positive attitudes toward an influencer predict if a follower will purchase a product (Belanche et al., 2021), so it is not surprising that the participants in the current study indicated they were very likely to purchase the products the pet influencer was promoting because they deemed the pet influencer credible and likeable. It is important to note those positive associations the followers had for the pet influencers transferred to the brand as well.

One reason participants had positive perceptions of the brand may be because they find pet influencers similar to themselves (Munnukka et al., 2016). Because participants in this study considered the pet influencers to be credible sources, it makes sense they will purchase the products the pet influencers promote (Zhang & Wei, 2021). This study did not include specific branded posts by pet influencers, which is why it contradicts the content analysis findings from Myers et al. (2022) and De Cicco et al. (2020). Rather, the current study asked about the likelihood of purchasing the products pet influencers promoted. In the end, participants in this study found the brand credible, their attitudes toward the brand were positive, and they were very likely to purchase the product featured. But it should be noted, that if a pet influencer was promoting a brand not congruent with being a pet influencer, the findings may have been different.

Research Question 4 asked if followers would perceive the pet influencer posts as more entertaining or informative. Findings indicate they find the posts more entertaining than informative. When pet influencers were interviewed, they noted they extend humanlike features to their pets by the storytelling shared in posts (Shamayleh & Arsel, 2020). Maddox (2020, p. 3) states pet influencers use their accounts to create a "fur baby" which then makes the influencer look like a "loving pet parent." They are posting to create joy on social media (Maddox, 2020). The current study's findings support past research showing people find posts entertaining and less informative. Granted, because participants indicated they are more likely to purchase a product from a sponsored post, one could assume branded posts are also informative. The current study did not differentiate between branded or non-branded posts.

Research Question 5 asked if there were gender differences in perceptions of source credibility and brand attitudes when examining followers. Past research had not examined gender differences when examining pet influencers (e.g., Zhang et al., 2023). It was worth examining gender differences regarding pet influencers because Chae (2018) found females envy social media influencers. When examining the pattern of means, all means were very positive regarding credibility of the source, likability, and brand variables. However, two statistically significant findings occurred between the genders—the perceptions of likeability and attitudes toward the brand. Females rated the pet influencer they followed as slightly more likable than male participants. They also indicated more positive attitudes toward the brands their pet influencer promoted than men.

Research Question 6 asked if the more time one spends on Instagram predicts their perceptions of pet influencers and the brands they promote. The answer is yes. The more time one spends on Instagram, the more credible their perceptions of the pet influencer as well as the brand the pet influencer promotes. These findings support previous research (Stojanovic et al., 2018). Stojanovic et al. (2018) did not look at influencers like the current study did, but the same pattern was found - the more time one spent on social media, the more aware they were of the brand and the quality of the brand. As Myers et al. (2022) note, pet influencers provide intimate self-disclosures about their personal lives. It makes sense then that the more a follower sees these types of posts, the more positive their perceptions of the pet influencer and the brands are compared to those who spend less time on social media and are exposed to fewer posts by the pet influencer.

Limitations, Future Directions, and Practical Implications

Every study has some limitations. One limitation of this study is the number of males versus females or those who are non-binary. The M-Turk hit was available to anyone over the age of 18 living in the U.S. It was surprising that more men than others would take part in a study about pet influencers. Everyone had to list a pet influencer they followed, otherwise they were dismissed from the study. Even this question did not disqualify more men from taking part.

Followers' personal traits could impact their perceptions of the influencer. The study did not ask any questions about the followers' perceptions of animals in general or even if they had a pet at home. These types of variables as well as their motivations for following a pet influencer could play a role in credibility and brand research.

Future research should include an experiment of sponsored content and non-sponsored content to compare the findings to experimental results found for non-pet influencers. More research should also be conducted on pet influencer posts that promote pet products compared to those who feature other types of products. Are pet influencers seen as less credible when promoting brands that aren't pet-related? The type of post should be examined. There may be differences in perceived credibility when an influencer posts photos of themselves rather than the pet. It is not clear if stakeholders expect posts only about the pets, pets with their humans, or posts of just the humans.

In addition, one of the overarching questions this study did not address is the ethical nature of humans deploying their pets for consumerism. The influencer is the pet. Some may consider the human owner to be exploiting the pet to make money. The pet is much the same as a child, so what are the ethical considerations to examine moving forward? This is important to think about since the number of pet influencers continues to grow as well as the number of followers.

CONCLUSION

Brands have taken advantage of building relationships with pet influencers (Myers et al., 2022). The pet care market alone is expected to top $200 billion globally by 2025 (Niemietz, 2020). Understanding the followers of pet influencers is important as the pet market continues to grow. There is still more to learn about why people follow pet influencers, their perceptions of the brands partnering with pet influencers, and how pet influencers are unique compared to other types of social media influencers since their accounts are really stories about their pets.

REFERENCES

Alrwashdeh, M., Ali, H., Helalat, A., & Alkhodar, D. (2022). The mediating role of brand credibility between social media influencers and patronage intentions. *International Journal of Data and Network Science*, *6*(2), 305–314. doi:10.5267/j.ijdns.2022.1.007

Andrii. (2023). *How many influencers are there in 2023*. trendHERO. Available at: https://trendhero.io/blog/how-many-influencers-are-there/

Belanche, D., Casalo, L. V., Flavian, M., & Ibanez-Sanchez, S. (2021). Understanding influencer marketing: The role of congruence between influencers, products and consumers. *Journal of Business Research*, *132*, 186–195. doi:10.1016/j.jbusres.2021.03.067

Berzleja, Z., & Kertész, F. (2019). *The furry side of Instagram: A study about dog influencers on Instagram*. Unpublished thesis. Malmö Universitet.

Boerman, S. C. (2020). The effects of the standardized Instagram disclosure for micro-and meso-influencers. *Computers in Human Behavior*, *103*, 199–207. doi:10.1016/j.chb.2019.09.015

Chae, J. (2018). Explaining females' envy toward social media influencers. *Media Psychology*, *21*(2), 246–262. doi:10.1080/15213269.2017.1328312

Chen, H. (2018). College-aged young consumers' perceptions of social media marketing: The story of Instagram. *Journal of Current Issues and Research in Advertising*, *39*(1), 22–36. doi:10.1080/10641734.2017.1372321

Cheng, Y., Wei, W., & Zhang, L. (2020). Seeing destinations through vlogs: Implications for leveraging customer engagement behavior to increase travel intention. *International Journal of Contemporary Hospitality Management*, *32*(10), 3227–3248. doi:10.1108/IJCHM-04-2020-0319

Clow, K., James, K., Kranenburg, K., & Berry, C. (2006). The relationship of the visual element of an advertisement to service quality expectations and source credibility. *Journal of Services Marketing*, *20*(6), 404–411. doi:10.1108/08876040610691293

Cramer, E. M., Song, H., & Drent, A. M. (2016). Social comparison on Facebook: Motivation, affective consequences, self-esteem, and Facebook fatigue. *Computers in Human Behavior*, *64*, 739–746. doi:10.1016/j.chb.2016.07.049

Dao, W. (2014). Social media advertising value: The case of transitional economies in Southeast Asia. *International Journal of Advertising*, *33*(2), 271–294. doi:10.2501/IJA-33-2-271-294

De Cicco, R., Silva, S. C., & Alparone, F. R. (2020). Millennials' attitude toward chatbots: an experimental study in a social relationship perspective. *International Journal of Retail & Distribution Management*, *48*(11), 1213–1233. doi:10.1108/IJRDM-12-2019-0406

De Veirman, M., & Hudders, L. (2020). Disclosing sponsored Instagram posts: The role of material connection with the brand and message-sidedness when disclosing covert advertising. *International Journal of Advertising*, *39*(1), 94–130. doi:10.1080/02650487.2019.1575108

Dencheva, V. (2023). *Influencer marketing –worldwide—statistics & facts*. Statista. Available at: https://www.statista.com/topics/2496/influence-marketing/#topicOverview

Deshpandé, R., & Stayman, D. (1994). A tale of two cities: Distinctiveness theory and advertising effectiveness. *JMR, Journal of Marketing Research*, *31*(1), 57–64. doi:10.1177/002224379403100105

Dhanesh, G. S., & Duthler, G. (2019). Relationship management through social media influencers: Effects of followers' awareness of paid endorsement. *Public Relations Review*, *45*(3), 101765. doi:10.1016/j.pubrev.2019.03.002

Dimofte, C. V., Forehand, M. R., & Deshpande, R. (2003). Ad schema incongruity as elicitor of ethnic self-awareness and differential advertising response. *Journal of Advertising*, *32*(4), 7–17. doi:10.1080/00913367.2003.10639142

Djafarova, E., & Rushworth, C. (2017). Exploring the credibility of online celebrities' Instagram profiles in influencing the purchase decisions of young female users. *Computers in Human Behavior*, *68*, 1–7. doi:10.1016/j.chb.2016.11.009

Ducoffe, R. H. (1996). Advertising value and advertising on the web. *Journal of Advertising Research*, *36*(5), 21–35. https://link.gale.com/apps/doc/A76914157/AONE?u=anon~4e336c6a&sid=googleScholar&xid=c32e5dbb

Ellison, N. B., Steinfield, C., & Lampe, C. (2007). The benefits of Facebook "friends:" Social capital and college students' use of online social network sites. *Journal of Computer-Mediated Communication*, *12*(4), 1143–1168. doi:10.1111/j.1083-6101.2007.00367.x

Erdogan, B. Z. (1999). Celebrity endorsement: A literature review. *Journal of Marketing Management*, *15*(4), 291–314. doi:10.1362/026725799784870379

Feedspot. (2023). *Top 100 pet influencers*. Available at: https://influencers.feedspot.com/pet_instagram_influencers/

Forbes. (2019, April 2). *Taking a stand on authenticity in influencer marketing*. Forbes Media LLC. Retrieved from https://www.forbes.com/sites/forbesagencycouncil/2019/03/29/taking-a-stand-on-authenticity-in-influencer-marketing/#3abc5a6c7270

Geyser, W. (2021). *The state of influencer marketing 2021*. Benchmark report. Influencer Marketing (Influencer Marketing Hub). https://influencermarketinghub.com/influ encer-marketing-benchmark-report-2021/

Giles, D. C. (2017). How do fan and celebrity identities become established on Twitter? A study of 'social media natives' and their followers. *Celebrity Studies*, *8*(3), 445–460. doi:10.1080/19392397.2017.1305911

Gill, J. D., Grossbart, S., & Laczniak, R. N. (1988). Influence of involvement, commitment and familiarity on brand beliefs and attitudes of viewers exposed to alternative claim strategies. *Journal of Advertising*, *17*(2), 33–43. doi:10.1080/00913367.1988.10673111

Haigh, M. M., & Wigley, S. (2015). Butter, Facebook, and Paula Deen: Examining fans' use of social media in crisis. In A. Slade, A. Narro, & D. Given-Carroll (Eds.), *Television, Social Media, and Fan Culture* (pp. 261–275). Lexington Books.

Hartama, E. (2021). *Possibilities of influencer marketing through pet Instagram accounts: A fast lane to a pet owner's pocket?* Lut University. https://lutpub.lut.fi/handle/10024/163069

Horton, D., & Richard Wohl, R. (1956). Mass communication and para-social interaction: Observations on intimacy at a distance. *Psychiatry, 19*(3), 215–229. doi:10.1080/00332747.1956.11023049 PMID:13359569

Hovland, C. I., & Weiss, W. (1951). The influence of source credibility on communication effectiveness. *Public Opinion Quarterly, 15*(4), 635–650. doi:10.1086/266350

Influencity. (2023). *The largest influencer study in the U.S. in 2023. The state of influencer marketing in the United States in 2023*. Available at: https://influencity.com/resources/studies/the-largest-influencer-study-of-the-united-states-2023/

Jamil, R., Qayyum, U., ul Hassan, S., & Khan, T. (2023). Impact of social media influencers on consumers' well-being and purchase intention: a TikTok perspective. *European Journal of Management and Business Economics*. doi:10.1108/EJMBE-08-2022-0270

Jiménez-Castillo, D., & Sánchez-Fernández, R. (2019). The role of digital influencers in brand recommendation: Examining their impact on engagement, expected value and purchase intention. *International Journal of Information Management, 49*, 366–376. doi:10.1016/j.ijinfomgt.2019.07.009

Jin, S. V., Muqaddam, A., & Ryu, E. (2019). Instafamous and social media influencer marketing. *Marketing Intelligence & Planning, 37*(5), 567–579. doi:10.1108/MIP-09-2018-0375

Kay, S., Mulcahy, R., & Parkinson, J. (2020). When less is more: The impact of macro and micro social media influencers' disclosure. *Journal of Marketing Management, 36*(3–4), 248–278. doi:10.1080/0267257X.2020.1718740

Keel, A., & Nataraajan, R. (2012). Celebrity endorsements and beyond: New avenues for celebrity branding. *Psychology and Marketing, 29*(9), 690–703. doi:10.1002/mar.20555

Kirmani, A. (1997). Advertising repetition as a signal of quality: If it's advertised so much, something must be wrong. *Journal of Advertising, 26*(3), 77–86. doi:10.1080/00913367.1997.10673530

Lou, C., & Kim, H. K. (2019). Fancying the new rich and famous? Explicating the roles of influencer content, credibility, and parental mediation in adolescents' parasocial relationship, materialism, and purchase intentions. *Frontiers in Psychology, 10*, 2567. doi:10.3389/fpsyg.2019.02567 PMID:31803110

Lou, C., & Yuan, S. (2019). Influencer marketing: How message value and credibility affect consumer trust of branded content on social media. *Journal of Interactive Advertising, 19*(1), 58–73. doi:10.1080/15252019.2018.1533501

Maddox, J. (2020). The secret life of pet Instagram accounts: Joy, resistance, and commodification in the Internet's cute economy. *New Media & Society, 23*(11), 3332–3348. doi:10.1177/1461444820956345

Martínez-López, F. J., Anaya-Sánchez, R., Fernández Giordano, M., & Lopez-Lopez, D. (2020). Behind influencer marketing: Key marketing decisions and their effects on followers' responses. *Journal of Marketing Management*, *36*(7–8), 579–607. doi:10.1080/0267257X.2020.1738525

McGuire, W. J. (1985). Attitudes and Attitude Change. In Handbook of Social Psychology (vol. 2, pp. 233–346). Random House.

Morimoto, M., & La Ferle, C. (2008). Examining the influence of culture on perceived source credibility of Asian Americans and the mediating role of similarity. *Journal of Current Issues and Research in Advertising*, *30*(1), 49–60. doi:10.1080/10641734.2008.10505237

Muniz, A. M. Jr, & O'guinn, T. C. (2001). Brand community. *The Journal of Consumer Research*, *27*(4), 412–432. doi:10.1086/319618

Munnukka, J., Maity, D., Reinikainen, H., & Luoma-aho, V. (2019). "Thanks for watching." The effectiveness of YouTube vlogendorsements. *Computers in Human Behavior, 93*, 226–234. 10.1016/j.chb.2018.12.014

Munnukka, J., Uusiltalo, O., & Toivonen, H. (2016). Credibility of a peer endorser and advertising effectiveness. *Journal of Consumer Marketing*, *33*(3), 182–192. doi:10.1108/JCM-11-2014-1221

Myers, S., Sen, S., Syrdal, H., & Woodroof, P. (2022). The impact of persuasion knowledge cues on social media engagement: A look at pet influencer marketing. *Journal of Marketing Theory and Practice*, 1–18. doi:10.1080/10696679.2022.2093224

Niemietz, B. (2020, January 5). They bark, we buy: Pet influencers having big impact on what humans spend. *New York Dailey News*. https://www.nydailynews.com/2020/01/05/they-bark-we-buy-pet-influencers-having-big-impact-on-what-humans-spend/

Ohanian, R. (1990). Construction and validation of a scale to measure celebrity endorsers' perceived expertise, trustworthiness, and attractiveness. *Journal of Advertising*, *19*(3), 39–52. doi:10.1080/00913367.1990.10673191

Pöyry, E., Pelkonen, M., Naumanen, E., & Laaksonen, S. M. (2019). A call for authenticity: Audience responses to social media influencer endorsements in strategic communication. *International Journal of Strategic Communication*, *13*(4), 335–351. doi:10.1080/1553118X.2019.1609965

Roberts, R. (2021, March 10). *Pet industry trends, growth & statistics in 2021 and beyond: Unleashing your ecommerce pet marketing strategies*. Common Thread. https://commonthreadco.com/blogs/coachs-corner/pet-industry-trendsgrowth-ecommerce-marketing

Rodgers, S. (2003). The effects of sponsor relevance on consumer reactions to internet sponsorships. *Journal of Advertising*, *32*(4), 67–76. doi:10.1080/00913367.2003.10639141

Saima, & Khan, M. (2021). Effect of social media influencer marketing on consumers' purchase intention and the mediating role of credibility. *Journal of Promotion Management, 27*(4), 503–523. doi:10.1080/10496491.2020.1851847

Shan, Y., Chen, K. J., & Lin, J. S. (2020). When social media influencers endorse brands: The effects of self-influencer congruence, parasocial identification, and perceived endorser motive. *International Journal of Advertising*, *39*(5), 590–610. doi:10.1080/02650487.2019.1678322

Shiv, B., Edell, J. A., & Payne, J. W. (1997). Factors affecting the impact of negatively and positively framed ad messages. *The Journal of Consumer Research*, *24*(3), 285–294. doi:10.1086/209510

Stojanovic, I., Andreu, L., & Curras-Perez, R. (2018). Effects of the intensity of use of social media on brand equity: An empirical study in a tourist destination. *European Journal of Management and Business Economics*, *27*(1), 83–100. doi:10.1108/EJMBE-11-2017-0049

Talavera, M. (2015, July 14). 10 reasons why influencer marketing is the next big thing. *Adweek*. https://www.adweek.com/digital/10-reasons-why-influencer-marketing-is-the-next-big-thing/

Trivedi, J., & Sama, R. (2019). The effect of influencer marketing on consumers' brand admiration and online purchase intentions: An emerging market perspective. *Journal of Internet Commerce*, *19*(1), 103–124. doi:10.1080/15332861.2019.1700741

Urbany, J. E., Bearden, W. O., Kaicker, A., & Borrero, M. S. (1997). Transaction utility effects when quality is uncertain. *Journal of the Academy of Marketing Science*, *25*(1), 45–55. doi:10.1007/BF02894508

Yuan, S., & Lou, C. (2020). How social media influencers foster relationships with followers: The roles of source credibility and fairness in parasocial relationship and product interest. *Journal of Interactive Advertising*, *20*(2), 133–147. doi:10.1080/15252019.2020.1769514

Zhang, L., & Wei, W. (2021). Influencer Marketing: A comparison of traditional celebrity, social media influencer, and AI influencer. *Boston Hospitality Review*. https://www.bu.edu/bhr/2021/10/04/influencer-marketing-a-comparison-of-traditional-celebrity-social-media-influencer-and-ai-influencer

Zhang, L., Wei, W., Rathjens, B., & Zheng, Y. (2023). Pet influencers on social media: The joint effect of message appeal and narrator. *International Journal of Hospitality Management*, *110*, 103453. doi:10.1016/j.ijhm.2023.103453

Chapter 10
Revolutionizing Edu-Influencers as Minorities Nudging Sustainable Fashion Consumption on Instagram

Lujain Nabeel Hassoubah
The University of Manchester, UK

Daniella Ryding
The University of Manchester, UK

Gianpaolo Vignali
https://orcid.org/0000-0002-4408-1282
Manchester Metropolitan University, UK

ABSTRACT

This critical literature review explores sustainable fashion consumption (repurposing) influenced by Edu-influencers on Instagram, addressing the limitations of traditional behavioral change theories on social media. It evaluates various perspectives on consumer behavior, sustainable consumption, and social media, highlighting the shortcomings of current behavioral change theories. The review aims to establish the groundwork for forthcoming theoretical and empirical advancements by critically analyzing and synthesizing recent studies associated with the three distinctive bodies of literature. Additionally, it aims to lay the groundwork for future research endeavors within these domains. The findings could inform consumer education, policy recommendations, and communication strategies for sustainable fashion consumption, laying the groundwork for future research and behavioral interventions.

INTRODUCTION

The textile industry is experiencing a significant increase in production and global consumption (Özdil et al., 2023; Shirvanimoghaddam et al., 2020). By 2027, the market volume is projected to reach $1.45

DOI: 10.4018/979-8-3693-0912-4.ch010

trillion, with an annual growth rate of 9.99%. (Statista, 2023). Also, this growth is accompanied by environmental concerns, ranking the industry second-largest contributor to environmental issues after the oil industry. As a result, there is a growing focus on sustainable fashion consumption (SFC), but there is a significant gap in research on this crucial aspect highlighting a substantial need for further investigation (Garcia-Torres et al., 2022; Hasbullah et al., 2022; UN, 2022).

Predominantly, the growing global emphasis on promoting SFC, particularly during the disposal phase, has gained considerable attention in recent years (UN, 2022; Mukendi et al., 2020). In this study, SFC in the disposal stage is defined as the responsible discarding of unwanted fashion items (Testa et al., 2021). Gao (2023) and Sambargi and Tripathi (2023) highlight the significant impact of this critical phase in fashion consumption on the environment, society, and economy, with Millennials and Gen-Z being a key demographic in this context (Kim et al., 2022; Gonçalves and Silva, 2021).

The disposal phase in fashion consumption significantly impacts the achievement of multiple SDGs (Sambargi and Tripathi, 2023). This is due to fostering sustainable consumption practices, responsible resource management, environmental protection, minimizing hazardous materials in textiles, and economic growth that benefits present and future generations (UN fashion alliance, 2023; Dominguez and Bhatti, 2022; UN, 2022; Kidd et al., 2020).

Moreover, the fashion disposal stage involves second-hand clothing (Geegamage et al., 2021), recycling (Desa et al., 2023) and repurposing (Krismawan et al., 2021). Primarily, this study highlights the benefits of repurposing on social media, focusing on shifting consumer behavior toward SFC and the role of social media influencers (SMI) in promoting repurposing. It is crucial because it positively generates environmental and social benefits (Eike et al., 2020), and economic benefits (Sambargi and Tripathi, 2023; Testa et al., 2021; Hassan et al., 2022). Predominantly, repurposing is one of the most effective sustainable fashion strategies that is defined in this study as reusing old items into new products from a consumption standpoint (Eike et al., 2020).

However, despite the relevance of SFC in achieving the United Nations' SDGs, there is a notable scarcity of research focusing specifically on the clothing disposition stage (Mason et al., 2022). This absence of concentrated study is seen as a drawback in understanding and improving sustainable fashion practices leading to criticism of the field being fragmented (Hassan et al., 2022). Besides, while research on upcycling (Lepesant, 2022), repair (Li, 2023), and second-hand clothing (Geegamage et al., 2021; Borusiak et al., 2020), the literature review represents a lack of investigation into repurposing unwanted fashion items, highlighting a knowledge gap.

Furthermore, the United Nations emphasizes the need for contemporary approaches to shift the current unsustainable consumption behavior in fashion presenting four main global calls (UNfashionalliance, 2023; UN, 2020). First, leveraging SMIs as a bottom-up approach to shift behavior. Second, develop a behavioral framework that makes SMIs the default option to drive sustainable consumption behavior. Third, called nations to respond to SDGs. Finally, called academia to collaborate to shift consumption behavior toward sustainable consumption. Furthermore, it acknowledges academia's role in exploring ways to increase sustainable consumption practices, focusing on the negative environmental, societal, and economic impacts of fashion consumption (UNfashionalliance, 2023; UN, 2020).

Parallel to this, there has been a noticeable surge in discussions regarding the influence of sustainable fashion through social media platforms (Marcella-Hood, 2023; UN, 2020). Particularly, through SMIs and their tailored content strategies aimed at shaping consumer behavior (Hudders et al., 2021). This has sparked discussions about the emerging influencers' phenomenon, Educational-influencers (Edu-Influencer) due to their impact on teacher practices, prompting calls for further exploration and contextualization of this phenomenon within behavioral change literature (Arantes and Buchanan, 2022). Arantes and Buchanan (2022) suggest that future studies on Edu-influencers should be comprehensive, examining their content across various domains and using empirical data from followers. The focus of this study delves into the notion of influencers being likened to minorities, aligning with Moscovici's Minority Influence Theory. Minority Influence Theory suggests that a smaller group within a larger population can influence the majority to accept their views or behaviors (Mosccovici, 1980) particularly, in remote areas like online settings (Yilmaz and Youngreen, 2016). In this context, Edu-influencers are perceived as minorities within the realm of influence due to their limited number, yet significant impact on the behaviors of Millennials and Generation-z. This perception stems from their distinct behavioral and thinking styles, as well as their adaptability. Moreover, their strong sense of identification with their followers' community further reinforces their role as minorities' influential figures. Specifically, the study examines Edu-influencers, leveraging Instagram to prompt their followers to adopt minority viewpoints, such as embracing repurposing behaviors. Primarily, the study highlights how Edu-influencers as minorities nudge repurposing behavior, leverage consistency, thinking style, flexibility, and identification to nudge behavioral change among their followers on Instagram.

Recent behavioral change studies highlight the importance of understanding millennials and Generation-Z demographics, as 75% are more likely to adopt sustainable behaviors after watching sustainability content (Unilever, 2023; Mohr et al., 2022; Roozen et al., 2021). Edu-influencers are emphasized for their role in shaping online behavior and contributing to socio-economic transformation in developing nations like Saudi Arabia (Curcio et al., 2023; Theunissen, 2023; Gillespie, 2019; Hickman, 2019). Instagram is a significant social media platform, with Edu-influencers inducing visual and verbal nudges, offering an opportunity to influence sustainable consumption online Curcio et al., 2023; Theunissen, 2023; Madani, 2022; Gil-Quintana and Vida de León, 2021).

This research synthesis sheds light on gaps and limitations within three literature, behavioral changes, sustainable fashion, and social media. Mainly, it critically represents the deficiencies and gaps within behavioral change literature. Specifically, it lacks a diverse range of theoretical perspectives, restricting the scope of findings. Additionally, there is a notable absence of a comprehensive framework for the development of online behavioral interventions. Thus, the study highlights the need for a comprehensive diversification of existing behavioral theories to develop a behavioral intervention that meets both the literature gaps and the United Nations Sustainable Development Goals (SDGs). It addresses the shortcomings of traditional top-down interventions such as government campaigns to achieve the global SDGs (UN, 2022; Gonzales-Arcos et al., 2021). This paper stands out by proposing a conceptual framework for investigating behavioral change in social media through two novel theories, setting itself apart from others in the field. First, Nudge Theory, which is used to guide the selection criteria for visual and verbal posts driving repurposing in Edu-influencers' Instagram content through drawing directly from their followers. Second, to explore Minority Influence Theory through the lens of the selected visual and verbal nudges to reinforce the investigation of behavioral change in social media.

The Present Work

The current chapter aims to bridge a theoretical gap within the realm of consumer behavior, particularly in the field of behavioral change. It serves as a foundational platform for future studies in this area. Traditional theories of consumer behavior have shortcomings, leading to a lack of new and diverse findings (Duckworth and Gross, 2020; Gilal et al., 2019). This is because the United Nations has called for future research on sustainable consumption to influence consumer behaviors globally, as significant changes in adverse consumer behaviors have not been realized (UN, 2023). Thus, underscoring the necessity for the adoption of new theories in this field and filling a gap in existing literature, emphasizing the need for comprehensive theoretical frameworks to impact behaviors (Paul, and Gray, 2011). Additionally, it emphasizes the role of modern digital technologies that could provide valuable insights into overlooked behavior-change interventions, advancing theories and enhancing understanding of various aspects of altering behavior (Zhang et al., 2021).

This is because, in conjunction with the recent emphasis on the importance of diversifying behavioral change theories, behavioral economics has emerged as a thriving new subfield to improve consumer behavior (Abhyankar, 2022). This raises the question of whether - and if so, how– insights from behavioral economy (Thaler and Sunstein, 2008) and social influence (Moscovici, 1976) could potentially impact SFC (Nogueira et al., 2023). Thus, the implications of this new field for consumer behavior and achieving the United Nations SDGs have been emphasized by Parashar (2022) and Unilever (2023). Finally, the identified limitations and research gaps serve as catalysts for the present study, which aims to construct a conceptual framework and delineate future research directions, envisioning a transformative impact on SDGs and consumer behavior.

This chapter makes four contributions: first, the critical review identified gaps and limitations, and synthesized recent literature on three distinct fields: consumer behavior, sustainable fashion, and social media. Second, based on the synthesized gaps, it suggested an integrated conceptual framework drawing on two theories: Minority Influence Theory (Moscovici and Lage, 1976) and Nudge Theory (Thaler and Sunstein, 2008) to promote SFC behavior online (see, Figure 5). It reveals the importance of the integration between behavioral economy and social psychology theories into consumer behavior studies to understand the intricate relationship between cognitive biases and social influences on the impact of online complex behavior. Third, the conceptual framework paves the way for academics to empirically investigate how Edu-influencers influence SFC, focusing on repurposing through Nudge Theory and Minority Influence Theory. Fourth, it provides practical implications enabling practitioners such as, marketers, policymakers, and educators to develop effective interventions through Edu-influencers who have the potential to shift consumer behavior as minorities nudging behavioral shift.

METHOD

The critical literature review followed six main steps to be conducted:

1. **Defining Research Objectives and Scope**

The research was conducted according to the objectives outlined in the introduction and its scope was as presented in Figure 1.

2. **Identification of keywords and search strategy**

Figure 1. The scope and the concepts of the study within three literature

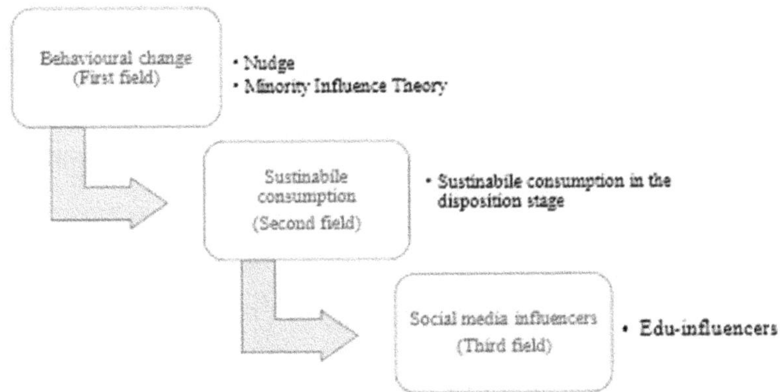

In this step, the researcher used all the keywords include terms like "sustainable fashion consumption," "disposition stage of sustinabile fashion," " behavioral intervention," "social influence," "social media Nudging," "Nudging AND sustinabile fashion," "Minority influence," " Minority Influence AND social media," "Edu-influencers AND behavioral change."

The keywords are derived from previous research and have been adapted to form the core focus of this paper (e.g., Unilever, 2023; Pozharliev et al., 2022; Roozen et al., 2021; Chwialkowska, 2019).

3. Selection of database and search engines

Select reputable academic databases (e.g., Scopus, Web of Science, PubMed, Google Scholar, and University of Manchester database) and search engines that cover interdisciplinary research in consumer behavior, environmental science, and behavioral economics.

4. Inclusion and exclusion criteria

The research conducted in this study involved the synthesis of contemporary studies pertaining to a specific concept across three selected literature domains. Those concepts are illustrated in Figure 1. In addition, older seminal studies were purposefully integrated into the review process to establish the foundational groundwork for defining and contextualizing each theory. These foundational studies traced the historical evolution, conceptual development, and fundamental principles of the theories examined, providing a robust framework for contemporary interpretations and applications. The paper includes research that specifically examines minority influence and nudging consumer behavior or sustainability context or in social media context. On the other hand, it excludes studies that utilized Minority influence and Nudge Theory in other fields such as psychology or behavioral economy.

5. Systematic Search and Screening Process

The systematic search process involves conducting searches using identified keywords, reviewing results, and excluding non-relevant studies to retrieve full-text articles for further assessment.

6. Critical Appraisal and Data Extraction

Extracts relevant information such as research methods, key findings, theoretical frameworks, and implications that answer the research aim and objectives.

This chapter focuses on theory development, presenting a conceptual framework following the steps identified by Hulland (2020) as presented in Figure 2, presenting theoretical syntheses, and introducing a novel integrative framework (Jaakkola, 2020).

THEMES AND CONCEPTUAL FRAMEWORK DEVELOPMENT

Sustainable Fashion Consumption (SFC)

The concept of SFC has evolved from a focus on sustainable production practices to acknowledging the role of consumers in driving positive change in the fashion industry (Hasbullah et al., 2022; Iran, 2018). This shift emphasizes the importance of consumer behavior, choices, and influence on achieving sustainability goals (Dabas and Whang, 2022). This is because it represents the consumption aspects of 'consumer behavior' in sustainable fashion (Brandão and da Costa, 2021). The concept now integrates production and consumption aspects, with two distinct study paths (Mukendi et al, 2020; Iran, 2018) as illustrated in Figure 3. Previous studies have primarily examined the supply chain aspect from a garment standpoint (Garcia-Torres et al., 2022; Tam and Lung, 2022), but scholars argue that consumption has a vital impact on sustainable fashion (Hasbullah et al., 2022; Mukendi et al, 2020). As presented by Busalim

Figure 2. Constructing a conceptual paper: Guided by Hulland's (2020) steps

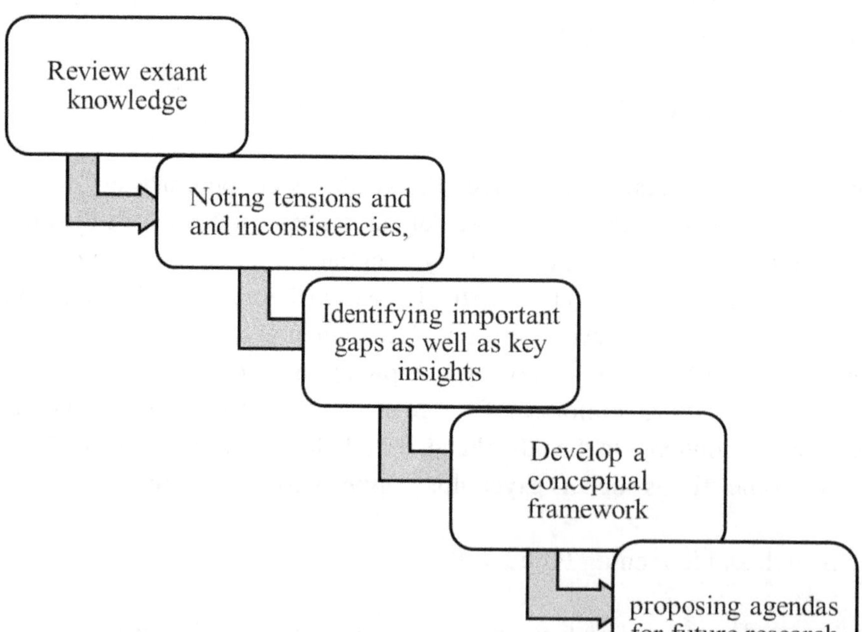

et al. (2022) and Vesterinen and Syrjälä (2022) the scope of sustainable fashion now encompasses not only the production and supply side but also the consumer perspective and behaviors. However, there is a lack of research on SFC, suggesting future research to particularly investigate how to shift consumers' behaviors toward the consumption of sustainable fashion through an effective communication strategy (Dabas and Whang, 2022).

Moreover, SFC involves three stages: Busy, Use, and Dispose (Stål and Jansson, 2017). The disposition stage involves the post-purchase activities that include reusability, reconditioning, recycling, and repurposing (Hassan et al, 2022; Bianchi, and Gonzalez, 2021). Testa et al. (2021) explained that consumers play a significant role in promoting sustainable fashion in different ways, especially during the disposition stage. For example, second-hand clothing (Geegamage et al., 2021), recycling (Koch and Domina, 1999) and repurposing (Krismawan et al., 2021).

Besides, SFC in the disposition stage is particularly relevant to multiple SDGs. For example, SDGs 12, 13, 11, and 6. This is because it ensures sustainable consumption (SDGs 12), reduces the negative impact of fashion consumption on the climate (SDGs 13), manages waste such as repurposing of fashion items and reduces hazardous material (SDGs 11), reduces fashion consumption, water pollution in textiles (SDGs 6) (UNfashionalliance, 2023; Dominguez and Bhatti, 2022; UN, 2022). Thus, the disposition stage contributes to achieving SDGs (Kidd et al., 2020).

Repurposing Within The Disposition Stage

Repurposing fashion helps consumers identify and reuse valuable items, as they are often purchased for outdated styles rather than the lack of functionality, thereby bridging the gap between buying and discarding (Eike et al., 2020). Bianchi and Gonzalez (2021) argued that it reduces demand for new clothing production, conserves natural resources, and minimizes pollution. In addition, it promotes circularity, waste reduction, and sustainable production processes, leading to social benefits (Rotimi et al., 2021; Saksena, 2020). Finally, Repurposing clothes during the disposable phase can significantly extend their

Figure 3. Sustainable fashion source: Adapted from Iran (2018)

Note: Reprinted from sustainable fashion: from production to alternative consumption by S. Iran, 2018, SpringerLink. Copyright 2018 Springer International Publishing AG, part of Springer Nature.

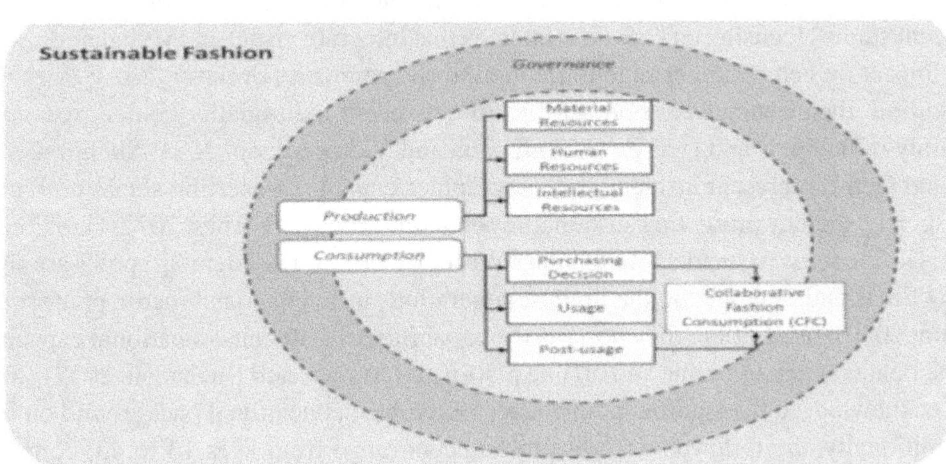

lifespan, reduce environmental impacts, and tap into the untapped economic potential of efficient waste use (Zhang and Hale, 2022). Also, it leads to reducing textile waste in landfills which enhances social and economic conditions in the industry, highlighting the untapped economic potential of efficient waste management (Sambargi and Tripathi, 2023; Testa et al., 2021). Thus, the disposition stage particularly repurposing aims to balance environmental, social, and economic factors (Hassan et al., 2022; Bianchi and Gonzalez, 2021; Gonçalves and Silva, 2021). Furthermore, developing countries offer a venue for repurposing fashion as a sustainable practice (Lewis, et al., 2017) due to its social, environmental, and economic benefits (Hassan et al., 2022). This practice challenges the sustainability agenda by balancing environmental protection and economic development and reducing the negative impact of environmental impacts. It also challenges fashion consumption and contributes to environmental protection (Gao, 2023; Krismawan et al., 2021).

Revolution of Edu-influencers: Catalysts of Behavioral Change

Edu-influencers are a growing trend in consumer behavior, with scholars examining their unique attributes from various perspectives (Arantes and Buchanan, 2022; Gil-Quintana and Vida de León, 2021).

Predominantly, those influencers have a great presence in different SM platforms including TikTok (Fiallos, and Figueroa, 2023), Twitter (Carpenter et al., 2022; Marcelo and Marcelo, 2021), and Instagram which serves as the primary platform for these types of influencers (Gil-Quintana and Vida de León, 2021), Moreover, prior research suggests that Edu-influencers exhibit both shared traits and distinct characteristics to other categories of SMIs previously situated within behavioral studies (e.g., Fiallos, and Figueroa, 2023; Marcelo and Marcelo, 2021). Additionally, the unique traits exhibited by these influencers have prompted scholars to advocate for the initiation of contextualizing them within behavioral studies (e.g., Carpenter et al., 2022; Shelton et al., 2020). Thus, it offers potential avenues for future research within the behavioral change context (Arantes and Buchanan, 2022; Gil-Quintana and Vida de León, 2021).

Primarily, some of their distinctive features identified from the review includes their significant contribution to the socio-economic transformation of developing nations like Saudi Arabia through Instagram (Curcio et al., 2023; Hickman, 2019; Theunissen, 2023). Moreover, the study highlights their use of visual and verbal nudges on Instagram which is considered a key strategy used by Edu-influencers to engage with followers (Gil-Quintana and Vida de León, 2021; Shelton et al., 2020). This is due to the growing interest in recent studies focusing on content strategies that integrate visual and verbal nudges to promote SFC and its impact on behavioral change in the online environment (Unilever, 2023; Pozharliev et al., 2022). In addition, their distinctive approach lies in delivering high-quality content to a high-quality audience mainly millennials and Gen-Z (Gil-Quintana and Vida de León, 2021; Shelkton et al., 2020). Millennials and Gen Z represent influential demographics capable of exerting social pressure on other members of society, thereby promoting sustainable behavioral change (Forbes, 2022; Dabija et al., 2019). Moreover, this influence is particularly heightened through SMIs, as both demographics are significantly influenced by SMIs and rank among the highest generations utilizing social media platforms (Mohr et al., 2022; Shin, 2020). In addition, they possess the capability to foster an educational capacity to influence teachers' behavior across online and offline platforms (Arantes and Buchanan, 2022). Also, Curcio et al. (2023) acknowledged the significant influence of a robust educational background on influencing behavior. Additionally, the followers of those influencers range from ages 13 to 45, comprising both

Millennials and Gen Z, with Millennials forming the larger portion at 67% (Gil-Quintana and Vida de León, 2021). Hence, this makes them appropriate target segments for the current study.

Edu-Influencers: Minorities Nudging in Instagram

Correspondingly, Edu-influencers' Instagram content leverages information influence through posting visual and verbal cues (Gil-Quintana et al., 2021), providing a potential venue to test these cues' impact on followers' behavior. Particularly, this research highlights their capabilities to significantly influence millennials' and Gen-Z's behavior (Gil-Quintana and Vida de León, 2021). This is because Gil-Quintana and Vida de León (2021) indicated that millennials and Gen-Z represent the highest number of Edu-influencers' followers in SM platforms, making them a prime target segment for the research.

The influence wielded by these individuals on platforms like Instagram has been documented, primarily in their capacity as educators impacting classroom behavior. However, their unique traits, including a strong educational background (Curcio et al., 2023), high-quality content (Carpenter et al., 2022), and a significant following among millennials and Gen-Z (Gil-Quintana and Vida de León's, 2021) and their educational capacity extends to shaping the behavior of teachers through both online and offline platforms, positioning them as minorities within the Instagram sphere (Arantes and Buchanan, 2022). Also, it offers an opportunity to explore their potential impact on fostering sustainable behavior among millennials and Gen Z (Curcio et al., 2023). Parallel to this, there is a clear call to contextualize them within both behavioral change and sustainability literature to utilize those unique features (Curcio et al., 2023) that intersect with Minority Influence Theory as per this study investigation. Precisely, previous research findings indicate that Millennials and Gen-Z individuals are affected by sustainable fashion portrayed on social media, alongside other elements like brand reputation, trust, and intentions to purchase (Palomo-Domínguez et al., 2023; Bouvier, and Cho, 2022). These demographics, who constitute a significant portion of the consumer market, are likely to drive future consumption patterns, making them key targets for analysis and study (Mohr et al., 2022).

Uncovering the Boundaries: Addressing Gaps of Behavioral Change Theories 'Diversifying for Expansion'

The review of conventional behavioral theories highlights their shortcomings and calls for their expansion in the digital age (e.g., Akhtar et al., 2023; Zhang et al., 2021; Sniehotta, et al., 2014). Correspondingly, the latest studies shed light on behavioral economics that challenges traditional theories and highlight their limitations (Pérez, 2022) specifically within the realm of social media and sustainable consumption (Lotti et al., 2023; Roozen et al., 2021). Strong theory-practice alignment is needed in online behavioral change studies, and a shift in focus from initiation to maintenance is needed as argued by Pera (2023) and Rothman (2000). Besides, other scholars discussed the need to diversify behavioral change theories as crucial for successful interventions and impacting sustainable fashion consumption (e.g., Akhtar et al., 2023; Zhang et al., 2021; Sniehotta, et al., 2014).

Recent studies have used various theories to contextualize SMIs in behavioral change literature such as the theory of Planned Behavior (TPB) (Chopra et al., 2021), the Congruity Theory of Attitude Change (Sun et al., 2021), and the theory of Reasoned Action (Hoo et al., 2022). However, these theories have limitations in understanding complex behaviors (Duckworth and Grosa, 2020) like SFC in social media. Some scholars argue that these theories overlook the process of translating intentions into behavioral changes, use intention as a proxy, and rely on rational decision-making in behavioral change (Sun et al., 2021; Ajzen, 1991). In addition, the research on fashion repurposing as a sustainable fashion consumption method is limited by a lack of theoretical frameworks, primarily focusing on social cognition or reflective processes (e.g., TPB) (Zhang and Halem 2022). Zhang and Hale (2022) have also discussed that within fashion repurposing studies, those theories are too individualistic-centric, structural, and environmental factors can significantly influence material consumption, outweighing individual factors as mentioned. This limits their utility, as many behaviors are governed by routines and habits Zhang and Hale (2022), which brings the Nudge Theory and Minority Influence Theory to discussions.

In addition, traditional behavior change theories lack theoretical integration and a comprehensive framework, hindering their application in behavior change-driven strategies, particularly online. Since 2014, there has been a lack of diversification in these theories (Zhang et al., 2021; Montanaro et al., 2018; Paul, and Gray, 2011), limiting the scope of findings. Moreover, Schlüter et al. (2022) call for the adoption of multiple theories to address the complexity of sustainable behavior. Since 2014, there has been a lack of diversification in behavioral change theories, limiting the scope of findings, as previous studies have mentioned various documentation of these drawbacks (e.g., Akhtar et al., 2023; Sniehotta, et al., 2014). The scientific community is advocating for the retirement of the traditional theories of behaviors such as, TPB due to criticism and concerns about the last time the behavioral field gained new knowledge from traditional theories (Sniehotta et al., 2014). Recent literature on social media and behavioral change often overlooks social and environmental factors, focusing on individualistic decision-making and intention rather than actual behavior (Akhtar et al., 2023; Leclercq-Machado, 2021; Hollebeek et al., 2019; Ajzen, 1991). Future studies should address the gap in the literature by other factors driving behavioral change and expanding conventional theories to diversify findings and interventions (Zhang et al., 2021). Zhang et al. (2021) identified a gap in traditional behavioral change theories, particularly in the impact of digital technology on interventions. Thus, the integration of theory-driven behavioral change interventions with social media is crucial as it offers valuable insights into overlooked interventions, advancing theories, and enhancing behavior alteration understanding (Zhang et al., 2021).

As a first step to doing so, scholarly literature from 2014 such as Sniehotta et al. (2014) to 2023 like Akhtar et al. (2023) and Zhang et al. (2021) consistently supports and strengthens the proposition of broadening or diversifying behavioral theories beyond TPB and TRA with clear contexts and empirical evidence. To do so, previous research emphasizes the importance of understanding the theoretical foundations of combining behavioral change theories with behavioral interventions to enhance their effectiveness and synergy (Prestwich et al., 2014). This is because often, those interventions are designed without reference to theory, neglecting the importance of theory-based interventions to change behavior (Zhang et al., 2021; Dombrowski et al., 2012). As a result, the UN has urged academic collaboration to support the SDGs (UN, 2022). This involves investigating societal shifts towards sustainable consumption, driving substantial changes in behavior (UN, 2022). Simultaneously, recent studies have started to investigate various theories from different fields like behavioral economy and social psychology in consumer behavior (Pozharliev et al., 2022; Chwialkowska, 2019). However, these studies revealed a lack of utilization of those theories within the context of sustainable fashion and social media, indicating a need for further investigation to fully comprehend their potential impact on these areas.

The Conceptual Framework: Its Theorizing Lenses

Nudge Theory as a Vehicle to Analyze Instagram Content Through Minority Influence Theory

Nudge Theory suggests that a subtle change in the presentation of choice or information can influence and change behavior without forbidding or mandating certain actions (Thaler and Sunstein, 2008, p. 6). Nudging is a strategy that utilizes cognitive or heuristic biases and choice architecture representing both internal and external elements to influence behavior (Thaler and Sunstein, 2009).

First, **individual/internal** factors impact behavior. Nudging is a cognitive shortcut method that encourages behavior by addressing instinct or impulsivity rather than rational thinking (Banerjee et al., 2023), challenging conventional theories in behavioral change (Martin and Morich, 2011). Daniel Kahneman's two types of cognitive systems shape human thinking: System-1 (automatic thinking) and System-2 (reflective thinking). Banerjee et al. (2023) and Tzikas and Koulierakis (2023) identified Nudging as part of System-1 thinking, which is influenced by automatic thinking. The debates surrounding the impact of System-1 and System-2 thinking on human behavior and decision-making are crucial. Previous research indicates that System-1 thinking influences consumer decisions which involves sustainable consumption behaviors (Chen et al., 2023; Blackford, 2021; Roozen et al., 2021).

Second, **environmental/external** factors (Choice Architecture). It refers to the design of the environment where the behavior takes place, in this context, Instagram aims to influence choices while maintaining freedom (Thaler and Sunstein, 2009). Ensaff (2021) explained that designing the environment and presenting options using nudges can alter behavior, particularly in promoting sustainable fashion through visual and verbal information (Pozharliev et al., 2022). Choice architecture involves using visual and verbal nudges to guide individuals towards specific behaviors. (Lee et al., 2020). The use of SM nudging automatically influences behavior (Hallsworth, and Kirkman, 2020), challenging the assumption of human rational behavior (Banerjee et al., 2023). Thus, it has the potential to challenge other behavioral theories. Furthermore, despite limited research, recent studies have demonstrated that Nudge can effectively promote sustainable behavior, leading to the positive impact on behavior (Lotti et al., 2023; Tening, and Harder, 2023) (see, Table 1 and Table A1 in Appendix A).

Visual and Verbal Nudges within Social Media Context. Visual and verbal nudges on social media platforms like Instagram target behaviors without forbidding choices through SMIs, images, videos, and comments (Pozharliev et al., 2022; Roozen et al., 2021). Primarily, it draws attention (Rettie and Brewer, 2000; Schoormans and Robben, 1997) and drives behavioral change specifically when generated through SMIs' content (Unilever, 2023). Visual nudges are images, graphics, or videos that encourage SFC through visual cues (Gies College of Business, 2023sk). Second, verbal nudges are messages that encourage behavioral shifts through written language (Roozen et al., 2021). Fundamentally, visual, and verbal nudges include the type of information presented (verbal nudge) and the presentation of the information through visualization (visual nudge) (Roozen et al., 2021). For example, use an image of an SMI wearing eco-friendly clothing that nudges consumers toward SFC (Gies College of Business, 2023). Pozharliev et al. (2022) research was one of the limited studies that tested visual and verbal nudging in SM platforms. It indicates that the interaction between verbal and visual cues in influencer advertising and posts significantly impacts behavior, but no studies have explored how those nudges impact SFC within the disposition stage in SM.

Table 1. The latest studies explored visual and verbal nudges online

Reference	Findings and Nudge type	Limitations	Method
Roozen et al. (2021)	Verbal nudge influence consumers choice towards SFC online. Providing additional environmental information on fashion items increases consumer willingness to pay more, and verbal nudges in a positive environment drive SFC behaviour. (Online-Website)	Limited to website, calling to exploring the nudges in social media.	Quantitative (Online Survey)
Girgis (2022)	Information nudge through Visual and Verbal Nudge drives sustainable fashion behaviour, "sustainable clothing shopping" (Online- website).	Limited to websites.	Qualitative (semi- structure focus group)
Pozharliev et al. (2022)	The study utilized eye-tracking and EEG measurements. It indicates in a positive response to the advertising message. The study found that the product description and the social influencer's photo significantly attract more attention than the influencer's number of followers. Both visual and verbal nudges influence behaviour, but verbal cues have stronger impact on behaviour (SMI in Instagram)	Limited to analyse SMI ads posts to one product. SMI (micro) use of both visual and verbal cues (nudge) draws more attention from followers within Instagram. Called to expand the implication in other aspects in SM and to invetsigate real content and expand the investigation to other visual and verbal cues within their contemt to impact behaviour.	Quantitative (Laboratory study)
Lotti et al. (2023)	It concluded that combining both information with visual nudges significantly improves sustainable consumption behaviour within the disposition stage, recycling clothes. (Offline)	Limited to offline context and did not draw a conclusion of how nudge work as an intervention giving the nature of eye tracking experiment.	Quasi-experimental setting
Chen et al (2023)	This study did not focus on nudge, rather it draws a conclusion about the theory. It concluded that visual cues combined with social norm are powerful when communicated though SM, it focused on SMI in Twitter endorse CSR initiatives.	Limited to CSR initiatives in twitter and type of SMI (Non-CSR SMI) It called for exploring visual and verbal cues in relation to sustainability in SM.	Quantitative (online survey)
Unilever (2023)	Visual and Verbal nudges by SMI through text videos and photos change behaviours and drive sustainable consumption. (SMI). It called future action to be taken within SMI and nudges.	----	Experiment

Furthermore, as represented in Table 1, various online studies have been conducted to investigate the use of visual and verbal nudges to encourage behavioral shifts (Chen et al., 2023; Unilever, 2023). Figures 4 represent some examples of visual and verbal nudges that encourage sustainable consumption (Lotti et al., 2023; Roozen et al., 2021). Primarily, the reviewed literature identifies two types of studies focusing on visual and verbal nudges to influence online behavior (See Table 1). First, some studies conducted online on fashion retailers' websites examined the use of visual and verbal cues to drive sustainable fashion behavior (Lotti et al., 2023; Girgis, 2022; Roozen et al., 2021). Those studies reported positive results regarding nudging; nevertheless, they excluded SMI applications and urged further exploration of these nudges across diverse online contexts, such as social media.

Secondly, other studies have examined the influence of social media visual and verbal nudges on driving behavioral change but have not focused on SFC (Chen et al., 2023; Pozharliev et al., 2022; Rossi et al., 2022). Overall, insufficient attention has been given to exploring SMIs implications of various types of nudges, as highlighted by Chen et al. (2023) and Pozharliev et al. (2022). Particularly, to the best of the researcher's knowledge, no study tested visual and verbal nudges to impact sustainable fashion consumption in SM. In addition, Table 1 highlights a significant gap in research on the impact of visual and verbal cues within influencers' content, highlighting the need for further investigation.

Leveraging influencers' content to shape behavior: Visual and Verbal Content/Nudge Theory. Mainly, SMIs strategically leverage content strategies as a key marketing tactic (Hudders et al., 2020). In addition, Instagram influencers utilize visual consistency to establish robust connections with their followers, subsequently enhancing their brand engagement (Argyris et al., 2020). Similarly, Edu-influencers leverage both visual and verbal nudges within their Instagram content strategy which captures millennials and Gen-z attention (Gil-Quintana and Vida de León, 2021). These nudges, including visual and

Figure 4. Visual nudge and verbal nudges in website to drive sustainable fashion consumption in website
Note: Adapted from "Do Verbal and Visual Nudges Influence Consumers' Choice for Sustainable Fashion?" by I. Roozen, M. Raedts, M. and Meijburg, L, 2021, Journal of Global Fashion Marketing, 12(4) (https://doi.org/10.1080/20932685.2021.1930096). Copyright 2015 by Taylor & Francis.

written content, are instrumental in driving behavioral change within the online sphere (Unilever, 2023; Pozharliev et al., 2022). Furthermore, Pozharliev et al. (2022) study yielded intriguing findings about Instagram influencers' content indicating that both visual and verbal cues serve as a primary catalyst in capturing followers' attention.

It's worth noting that research is advancing on the impact of influencer content on consumer behavior, on the other hand, key areas are being underexplored for further investigations (Apasrawirote and Yawised, 2022; Hudders et al., 2020). Correspondingly, a recent systematic literature review by Hudders et al. (2021) emphasized the lack of research on the content strategies of SMIs and their potential to influence behavior. Hence, the review suggests conducting future studies focusing on influencers' content to further enrich the existing literature in this field (Hudders et al., 2021). On the other hand, Vrontis et al. (2021) latest systematic literature review on SMIs revealed that although several theories have been employed to investigate SMIs in consumer behavior, these theories possess limitations due to their traditional essence and restricted scope of influence. These limitations hinder the diversification of the findings. For example, the theory of reasoned action, social exchange theory, source-credibility theory, two-step flow of communication, persuasion knowledge model, social comparison theory, and attribution theory (Hudders et al., 2021). It is worth noting that many studies within SMIs lack coherent theoretical underpinning (Vrontis et al., 2021).

Minority Influence Theory

Minority Influence Theory suggests that a smaller group within a larger population can influence the majority to accept their views or behaviors (Mosccovici, 1980), particularly, in remote areas like online settings (Yilmaz and Youngreen, 2016). Minority Influence Theory is a social influence concept that focuses on the ability of a minority, like Edu-Influencers, to influence the majority's behaviors through information, driven primarily by environmental and external factors (Chwialkowska, 2019; Moscovici, 1976).

Previous research has primarily focused on face-to-face settings, indicating a lack of online studies (Brijnath et al., 2022; Kardosh et al., 2022). First, research on minority influence has grown alongside the cognitive orientation in social psychology (e.g., Erb and Bohner, 2001). Primarily, those studies have focused on information processing and persuasion within the field of social psychology granting valuable insights into the nature and outcomes of minority influence, outlining the conditions under which a minority exerts influence (e.g., Brijnath et al., 2022; Stroebe, et al., 2010). Nevertheless, they fall short of providing a comprehensive understanding of minority influence driving social change (Kardosh et al., 2020; Martin, and Hewstone, 2008; Erb and Bohner, 2001).

A further set of investigations of the theory has been explored in the consumer behavior field, mainly in offline contexts (e.g., Kardosh et al., 2020; Martin, and Hewstone, 2008; Erb and Bohner, 2001). However, the literature revealed that limited theoretical studies on SMIs as minorities and their role in peer communication, on the other hand, the recent focus is on SMIs as credible minorities (e.g., Wu et al., 2022). Mainly, Wu et al.'s (2022) study explored the relationship between credibility and identifications within the identity of the minority and the decision-making process of human vs. AI minority. In contrast, Yilmaz and Youngreen (2016) study investigated the behavioral style, anonymity, and status of minorities in computer-mediated communication through a literature review but called to study Minority Influence Theory in an online context to expand the literature.

Nonetheless, one of the latest reviews of the theory is Prislin (2022) study that provided a future research agenda to fill the theoretical gap. His review concluded that research on minority influence, which aimed to understand social change, grew until the 1990s, but it has mainly focused on cognitive processes and attitudinal change in response to minority advocacy or presence. Also, it is concentrated on the role of minorities in decision-making and group tasks. Besides, it has been followed by a decrease and stabilization in the 2000s and 2010s as presented in Prislin (2022) review. Despite a remarkable scientific output, research on minority influence has failed to address its original question about social change and social influence (Prislin, 2022). Correspondingly, Peris' review aligns with current research evaluations of past literature on the implications of the theory.

Extensively, the call raised by Yilmaz and Youngreen (2016) to investigate Minority Influence Theory in social media is underpinned by critical reasons, drawing from its theoretical origins, particularly Moscovici's work in 1976. First, Wood et al. (1994) discovered that studies conducted in face-to-face settings revealed fewer instances of minority influence than those conducted in written or audiotaped contexts, hence demonstrating the contrast between different settings. Despite a few exceptions (e.g., Bazarova et al., 2012) the majority of minority influence research was conducted in face-to-face group settings or environments devoid of contact among group members (Prislin, 2022). Platforms for computer-mediated communication (CMC) provide less immediate and more private interactive venues for group discussions. CMC's distinct properties, such as asynchronous communication and anonymity, create boundary conditions critical for understanding minority-majority influence dynamics (Yilmaz and Youngreen, 2016). As a result, the purpose of Yilmaz and Youngreen (2016) literature review is to show how CMC groups can provide a study environment that meets the objectives of Minority Influence Theory while not compromising its essential principles. On the contrary, urging empirical studies to prioritize investigations within the online context presents a valuable opportunity for in-depth exploration, particularly within the realm of social media (Yilmaz and Youngreen, 2016). Additionally, Yilmaz and Youngreen (2016) and Chwialkowska's (2019) study reveal that social media minorities have a greater impact on behavior in private/social media settings, as clarified by Moscovici in 1976. Also, minorities' influence on social media is attributed to their unique, authentic, and engaging content that resonates with their niche audience and the wider online community seeking diverse perspectives and authenticity (Wu et al., 2022; Chwialkowska, 2019). furthermore, Chwialkowska's (2019) study examined how a minority group, sustainable influencers, in Facebook advocacy for sustainable lifestyles influences environmentally conscious behaviors among a larger online community, focusing on how their shared information influences these behaviors. The study analyzed over 8,000 Facebook posts of sustainable influencers via Netnography followed by semi-structured interviews with their followers. Furthermore, the study explored Minority Influence Theory through the lens of information influence, examining four constructs: behavioral style, thinking style, flexibility, and identifications as presented in Table 2. In addition, the study integrated Minority Influence Theory with Social Learning Theory to advance the investigations into normative influence that impacts behavior. To elaborate, Minority influence in online contexts can establish and surpass social learning theories, leading to both information influence and normative influence (Politi et al., 2017; Moscovici, Faucheux, 1972). This influence goes beyond the typical mechanisms of social learning theories, which focus on learning through observation and imitation. Minority influence can challenge existing norms and opinions, making the minority group's perspectives or actions the norm, guiding the behavior of the larger community as explained by Chwialkowska's (2019). This process demonstrates how the influence of a minority group in an online setting can surpass conventional explanations, leading to the establishment of new norms or attitudes within the broader online community (Moscovici, Faucheux, 1972). Chwialkowska (2019) explained that sustainability influencers initiate information influence, stimulating initial modelling behaviors that are spread through peer communication within their profile. Also, it concluded by highlighting that Minority influence is more significant in remote and written interactions than in immediate, public, face-to-face interactions.

Table 2. Conceptualized definitions of minority influence theory's constructs

Reference	Findings and Nudge type	Limitations	Method
Roozen et al. (2021)	Verbal nudge influence consumers choice towards SFC online. Providing additional environmental information on fashion items increases consumer willingness to pay more, and verbal nudges in a positive environment drive SFC behaviour. (Online-Website)	Limited to website, calling to exploring the nudges in social media.	Quantitative (Online Survey)
Girgis (2022)	Information nudge through Visual and Verbal Nudge drives sustainable fashion behaviour, "sustainable clothing shopping" (Online- website).	Limited to websites.	Qualitative (semi- structure focus group)
Pozharliev et al. (2022)	The study utilized eye-tracking and EEG measurements. It indicates in a positive response to the advertising message. The study found that the product description and the social influencer's photo significantly attract more attention than the influencer's number of followers. Both visual and verbal nudges influence behaviour, but verbal cues have stronger impact on behaviour (SMI in Instagram)	Limited to analyse SMI ads posts to one product. SMI (micro) use of both visual and verbal cues (nudge) draws more attention from followers within Instagram. Called to expand the implication in other aspects in SM and to investigate real content and expand the investigation to other visual and verbal cues within their content to impact behaviour.	Quantitative (Laboratory study)
Lotti et al. (2023)	It concluded that combining both information with visual nudges significantly improves sustainable consumption behaviour within the disposition stage, recycling clothes. (Offline)	Limited to offline context and did not draw a conclusion of how nudge work as an intervention giving the nature of eye tracking experiment.	Quasi-experimental setting
Chen et al (2023)	This study did not focus on nudge, rather it draws a conclusion about the theory. It concluded that visual cues combined with social norm are powerful when communicated though SM, it focused on SMI in Twitter endorse CSR initiatives.	Limited to CSR initiatives in twitter and type of SMI (Non-CSR SMI) It called for exploring visual and verbal cues in relation to sustainability in SM.	Quantitative (online survey)
Unilever (2023)	Visual and Verbal nudges by SMI through text videos and photos change behaviours and drive sustainable consumption. (SMI). It called future action to be taken within SMI and nudges.	----	Experiment

Adopted from Moscovici (1976) and Moscovici, Faucheux (1972) identified two types of influence through Minority Influence: informational and normative influence. Informational influence occurs when a minority presents new and persuasive arguments or information that challenges the majority's existing norms or perspectives. Therefore, the influence of minority information can prompt the majority to reconsider their stance, leading to normative influence and potentially a revaluation of their stance as explained by Martín et al. (2015) and Moscovici, (1980). On the other hand, normative influence is based on social norms and conformity (Kende et al., 2023). The concept arises when the behavior or opinions of a minority are seen as favorable or suitable by the larger majority (Hardecker et al., 2023). Primarily, this type of influence doesn't necessarily involve new information but stems from a desire to conform to the perceived norms set by the minority group (Moscovici, 1976). Both types of influence can interact and complement each other through a consistent minority (Hardecker et al., 2023).

Minority Influence Theory: Millennials and Gen-Z Context. Millennials, born between 1980 and 2000 (Kim and Park, 2020), and Gen Z born between 1997 and 2013 also known as post-millennials, share many traits and bring new behaviors in comparison to previous generations. Future research on social media and sustainability should involve these generations due to their high engagement in these topics (Kovanci, and Karakoc, 2022). On another note, social media platforms are a platform that represents a legitimate venue to explore and induce minority influence (Wu et al., 2022; Cummings et al., 2019; Yilmaz, and Youngreen, 2016), particularly, through information influence presented by minorities such as Edu-influencers in social media context (Chwialkowska, 2019). These influencers' content reinforces behaviors, particularly among millennials and Gen-Z (Gil-Quintana and Vida de León, 2021). However, the examination of existing literature unveiled this area that requires deeper exploration, specifically within the realms of sustainability, social media, and behavioral change. More research is essential to comprehend this overlooked domain.

Millennials and Gen-Z can reinforce both types of influence in different ways. First, informational influence is influenced by their receptiveness to new information and diverse viewpoints (Kovanci and Karakoc, 2022), particularly in the realm of SMI and sustainable consumption. Both generations have exhibited increased awareness of conscious consumption, especially within the fashion industry, displaying a notable inclination towards SFC (Lee et al., 2022). Additionally, SMIs wield significant influence on these topics within these demographics; (Barbe and Neuburger, 2021; Curtis et al., 2019). Millennials and Gen-z have high digital engagement, reliance on peer validation, and endorsements within their networks, and influence family and friends' consumption behavior (Forbes, 2022; Dabija et al., 2019).

In addition, SMIs who significantly impact Millennials and Gen-z's sustainable consumption behavior (Djafarova and Foots, 2022), are frequently viewed as minorities in the realm of sustainability topics (Chwialkowska, 2019). Also, the latest studies about Edu-influencers revealed that those segments represent the highest percentage of their followers, making them a crucial focus for influencing millennials and Gen-Z behavior (Gil-Quintana and Vida de León, 2021). Gen-z's reliance on social media has significantly influenced their values and guided their individual preferences (Kovanci and Karakoc, 2022). They are exposed to ideas related to the collaborative economy, environmentally friendly purchases, and sustainability, which have become ingrained in their social norms (Dahlquist and Garver, 2022; Artese, 2020; Shin, 2020). Normative influence, where individuals conform to societal expectations to gain approval, plays a significant role in shaping Gen-Z's attitudes towards these concepts (Dahlquist and Garver, 2022; Artese, 2020). As a result, Gen-z is more likely to adopt behaviors aligned with collaborative economy practices (Artese, 2020; Shin, 2020), impacting other generations' sustainable lifestyles and consumptions, particularly Gen-z (Djafarova and Foots, 2022). This collective consciousness indeed led to shaping societal norms and influenced other generations particularly, through social media interactions (Forbes, 2022; Forbes, 2021; Artese, 2020). Similarly, millennial generations are actively advocating the UN SDGs to facilitate sustainable consumption (Mohr et al., 2022). Collectively, their values including sustainable consumption patterns (Djafarova and Foots, 2022) sustainable fashion, (Williams and Hodges, 2022; Brun and Karaosman, 2020) often valuing economic benefits and using it to express their viewpoints (Shin, 2020; Mohr et al., 2022). Alongside their engagement in social media and with SMIs (Mohr et al., 2022). As a result, these characteristics create a ripple effect that extends beyond those generations impacting other members in the society particularly, Gen-z (Forbes, 2022; Sakdiyakorn et al., 2021). Particularly, normative influence that integrates Gen-z behavior into broader societal norms (Artese, 2020). The growing collectivist emphasis on environmental and sustainable consumerism in society has led to increased awareness and sometimes changes in behaviors among older generations, reinforcing these values within society (Sakdiyakorn et al., 2021).

The Conceptual Framework

The synthesis of prior studies served as a foundational framework for the current investigation to develop a new framework for analyzing and impacting complex behaviors, SFC, in social media contexts. It fills the literature gaps of three fields as mentioned before through two theoretical lenses: Nudge Theory from behavioral economy popularized by Thaler and Sunstein (2008) and Minority Influence Theory by (Moscovici and Lage,1976) from social psychology (see, Figure 5). The framework represents the interconnectivity between the two suggested theories to encourage a shift in behavior within social media platforms through SMIs. Influencers provide both visual and verbal cues that can significantly influence and stimulate specific behaviors, like repurposing, which could be reinforced by Minority Influence Theory. The framework indicates that minorities like SMIs generate information influence through four elements: behavioral style, thinking style, flexibility, and identification which reinforces nudging repurposing behavior. It serves as a foundation for the future development of effective behavioral intervention through SM platforms.

Figure 5. Conceptual framework: A bottom-up process of adopting SFC through edu-influencers (author own conceptual framework)

DISCUSSION AND IMPLICATIONS FOR FUTURE RESEARCH

Underpinned by a comprehensive critical literature review, this study explored existing research within three fields, behavioral change, social media, and sustainability literature, to identify gaps and propose a conceptual framework that fulfills the theoretical gaps and limitations. The current chapter emphasizes a theoretical gap in behavioral change, especially in social media/sustainable fashion contexts, and calls for academia to address this issue to enhance findings and develop interventions that positively impact sustainable fashion consumption. Particularly, the literature analysis revealed a predominant focus on traditional behavioral theories within SMIs' studies representing a major gap in theoretical contribution and hindering research findings. The behavioral theories that focus on internal/ individualistic factors and assume rational decision-making were the predominant way of the previous works demonstrated herein. Existing studies predominantly utilized behavioral theories that overlook the process of translating behavioral intentions into actual behavioral, hindering theory-driven behavior change interventions, which is like the discussion raised by Sun et al. (2021) and Zhang et al. (2021). Thus, it limits the breadth and depth of understanding, hinders the development of robust and generalizable knowledge, and limits the ability to address complex behavioral shifts effectively. The review also concluded that embracing a variety of theories in the behavioral field can enhance understanding, develop robust knowledge, and effectively address complex human behaviors. It also allows for a more nuanced exploration, contributing to a richer and more dynamic field of study.

Emphasizing the importance of identifying these gaps, this review argues that the suggested framework challenges the current drawbacks of behavioral change theories. It addresses the lack of a comprehensive framework for addressing complex and online behavior, proposing a comprehensive approach for developing effective behavioral interventions in the digital era. Additionally, the objective of the current work is to delineate future research directions through a comprehensive framework utilizing two distinctive lenses: behavioral Nudge and Minority Influence Theory envisioning a transformative impact on SFC and achieving multiple SDGs. The critical literature review encourages future studies within the realm of behavioral change, sustainable fashion, and SMIs' to empirically utilize the framework to diversify the findings yet contribute to multiple SDGs. The offered framework targets both System-1 (automatic thinking) and System-2 (reflective thinking) to impact behaviors.

This study highlights a significant gap in research on the impact of visual and verbal nudges on influencers' content, emphasizing the absence of a theory-based approach to selecting influencers' content. Alternatively, all studies examining influencer content in consumer behavior utilized theory to analyze the content exclusively neglecting the theory-based selection of visual and verbal cues in SM (e.g., Al-Emadi and Yahia, 2020; Ali et al. 2020; Argyris et al., 2020; Karimova, 2020). As a result, the negative impact of a lack of well-defined theoretical foundations on a subject leads to a less structured understanding and affects research design, methodology, analysis, and interpretation of findings as discussed by Filho, et al. (2022) and Vrontis et al. (2021). The discussion in the current chapter emphasizes the importance of using theory-based for selecting and analyzing influencers' visual and verbal content incorporating Nudge Theory. This is because theories provide a systematic method for researchers to understand, interpret, and predict behavioral patterns, aiding in discerning relevant content and its potential impact on audience behavior, thereby enhancing the analysis of SMIs' influence (Filho, et al., 2022).

This study distinguishes itself by adopting a novel approach in its selection process of SMI image and comment, assigning a distinct theory to guide the selection criteria. This approach sets it apart from other SM studies that do not use a theoretical lens. Furthermore, the study addresses the limitations of behavioral economics particularly, the Nudge Theory, by considering both system-1 thinking through nudge (heuristics, mental shortcuts, and biases) and system-2 thinking through Minority Influence Theory (reflective thinking) and its impact on behavior in a unified framework. Thus, it argues that both types of thinking System-1, heuristic and fast, and System-2, rational, can yield more effective results in providing a holistic approach to understanding and influencing human behavior. This is because the current literature revealed that minority influence is indeed acting as an external stimulus leading to behavioral changes (Henningsen and Henningsen, 2021). Furthermore, Minority Influence Theory posits that external stimuli from a minority group can catalyze behavioral change within a larger population (Moscovici and Lage 1976). This occurs due to the persistent communication of a specific viewpoint or behavior by a dedicated minority group, gradually leading the majority to adopt or conform to those perspectives (Moscovici, 1976).

The current review highlights that Dousay et al.'s 2018 study is the first official study on Edu-influencers within social media platforms. In addition, recent studies carried out in 2020 have initiated the categorization and documentation of the Edu-influencer phenomenon (Fiallos, and Figueroa, 2023; Carpenter et al., 2022; Marcelo and Marcelo, 2021). On the other hand, in 2018, this phenomenon had limited documentation under various diversified names such as Teacher-Influencers (e.g., Dousay et al., 2018). Primarily, in 2020, there was a formal categorization that unified what is known as "Educational influencers" under one comprehensive classification within influencers' marketing literature which has led to a surge in studies conducted under this unified classification, consolidating all research conducted from 2020 onward under this unified name (e.g., Fiallos, and Figueroa, 2023; Shelton et al., 2020). The formal classification of Edu-influencers has sparked in-depth research and scholarly inquiries into their unique characteristics, strategies, content, and effects, making them a new focus for future studies (Arantes and Buchanan, 2022; Gil-Quintana and Vida de León, 2021). As a result, it prompted researchers to explore various dimensions of the phenomenon such as pedagogical methods, learning behaviors, engagement strategies, knowledge dissemination, and their role in reshaping educational paradigms in different platforms. The review of the literature revealed major gaps related to Edu-influencers' studies. First, previous studies of Edu-influencers focused on schoolteachers, leaving a gap to explore higher education influencers like university lecturers, in various dimensions including their impact on behaviors. Secondly, there have been few theoretical and empirical implications of Edu-Influencers (Carpenter et al, 2022). Moreover, Shelton et al. (2020) study suggests future research on Edu-influencers' role in behavioral change. Carpenter et al. (2022) call for empirical analysis of Edu-influencer audiences to explore their content and expand the literature. Hudders et al. (2021) highlight the lack of research on SMIs' content strategies and their potential influence on behavior.

One of the key findings of the current review is that Instagram has significantly contributed to the socio-economic transformation of developing nations like Saudi Arabia, with Edu-influencers using visual and verbal nudges as a key strategy to engage with followers. This approach is particularly relevant to millennials and Gen-Z, who are influential demographics capable of exerting social pressure and promoting behavioral shifts through normative influence. In addition, both demographics are among the highest generations using social media platforms and among the highest demographics that interact and are influenced by SMIs. The current review also concluded that they possess a positive attitude towards sustainable consumption which has the potential to contribute to the SDGs. The study argues that initiating information influence, within Minority Influence Theory, to impact those generations could facilitate a greater behavioral shift toward repurposing behavior due to their unique characteristics that preserved SMIs as minorities impacting behavior. Also, these generations possess the ability to generate normative influence to spread repurposing behavior. Highlighting the importance of incorporating visual and verbal nudges in the content strategies of SMI is vital to appeal to those generations. This study classified Edu-influencers as minorities based on Moscovici's definition of minority influence, considering their distinctive characteristics and background, which align with this definition. Moscovici's concept refers to the capacity of a small group to wield influence over a larger population (Moscovici, 1976). Primarily, influencers' behavioral styles, thinking styles, flexibility, and identification contribute to their perception of minorities in the realm of online communication. Their distinctive attributes, strategic approach, adaptability, and ability to forge meaningful connections with audiences set them apart from the broader online population, positioning them as select individuals with significant influence and prominence within the digital landscape. Their influence on shaping the perspectives of educators and followers, especially among millennials and Gen-Z, is connected to their distinctive educational background, despite their limited numerical representation. This uniqueness positions them potentially as minorities impacting majorities. This study emphasizes how influencers, as minorities promote SFC through four constructs through the lens of Minority Influence Theory: consistency, behavioral and thinking styles, flexibility, and identification to impact repurposing behavior on social media. This is because the review revealed that when SMIs maintain a consistent presence across platforms, reinforcing the message that a repurposing fashion is compatible with normal life. Their argumentative style encourages systematic thinking among followers, challenging their existing beliefs and prompting them to reconsider their choices. By presenting relatable anecdotes and engaging followers in thoughtful discussions, influencers foster an environment conducive to attitude and behavior change. Also, adopting an approachable demeanor and addressing common concerns, facilitates identification with their audience, making their message more persuasive. Overall, Edu-influencers effectively leverage minority influence tactics to drive behavioral change among their followers.

On another note, the study highlights the lack of understanding in the emerging category of SMIs, Edu-Influencers, corresponding to Carpenter and Shelton group findings in 2022 & 2020 respectively. It calls for further research to analyze different types of content developed by different SMIs and contextualize Edu-influencers within behavioral change literature. Future studies should examine content from follower perspectives and fill previous gaps.

The chapter highlights the connection between minorities' information influence and normative influence, highlighting the dual social influences that reinforce behavioral change. It argues that informational social influence, used by SMIs, has a greater impact than normative influence, making it crucial to initiate information influence first by minorities. These findings align with Chwialkowska's (2019) and Lucas et al., (2019). The study concluded that Mutual Reinforcement, where informational and normative influences work together, can lead to a change in behavior. This is through Edu-influencers sharing information influence then millennials and Gen-z sharing normative influence. Also, the current study highlights the significant influence of millennials and Gen-Z on sustainable fashion consumption. Their advocacy not only influences their consumption patterns, but also influences their family and friends' behaviors (Forbes, 2022; Dabija et al., 2019). Initially, exposure to persuasive information presented by the minority group might change individuals' attitudes or behavior (informational influence), and over time, this change could lead to conformity with the group's norms or behaviors (normative influence) as explained by LaTour, and Manrai (1989). Both millennials and Gen-Z could play a vital role through normative influence on family and peers. Those highlights serve as a pivotal point of interest in the current study shedding light on the capacity of Millennials and Gen Z to disseminate normative influence instigated by minorities. Finally, the critical review reveals a previously unexplored gap in three synthesized fields that has not been previously addressed or mentioned by others which offers valuable insight for utilizing behavioral economy and social psychology in a theoretical framework to develop behavioral intervention in SM.

CONCLUSION

This paper introduces a comprehensive conceptual framework for social media behavioral change. Also, it synthesizes three distinct bodies of literature: consumer behavior, sustainable consumption, and social media while addressing limitations, gaps, and future research directions for developing a comprehensive framework. The framework consists of two distinct theories to address the limitations of those areas.

Although previous research in consumer behavior studied these variables in isolation (Pozharliev et al., 2022; Roozen et al., 2021; Chwialkowska, 2019), research integrating these notions in a unified nomological network is unknown. The critical literature review contributes to academic knowledge and practical applications by: First, the integration of diverse perspectives. The review combines three different literature bodies for a holistic understanding of the subject matter. Secondly, synthesized literature helps to identify connections, overlaps, and intersections among theories and fields. As a result, the review contributes by creating a novel conceptual framework that offers a more comprehensive explanation of impacting sustainable fashion consumption in the disposition stage within social media. This integrated framework provides a new lens through which to analyze and address complex online behaviors. Besides, it offers new insights and perspectives on interconnected fields. The review offers new insights and perspectives beyond individual theories, encouraging a more sophisticated understanding of the subject matter.

Additionally, it highlights practical implications for different stakeholders. Mailly, the framework offers practical insights into influencing sustainable fashion consumption behavior through social media, suggesting key messages, content types, and engagement techniques that resonate with the audience and drive positive behavioral changes. This study attempts to reduce the literature gaps mentioned before by exploring the narrative of how to impact SFC such as repurposing behavior through Edu-influencers' content, and providing insights to marketers, policymakers, and government entities to develop behavioral interventions through SM. Also, this insight can be utilized by brands and organizations to create influencer-led initiatives that resonate with the fashion-conscious demographic, potentially leading to significant changes in consumption behavior through Edu-influencers content. The study suggests that marketers and policymakers integrating sustainability messages into Edu-influencers' aesthetic and lifestyle content can enhance their audience's appeal and make sustainability more relatable.

Finally, it offers direction for future research: the review outlines gaps and inconsistencies in the three bodies of literature, urging further investigation into the combined effect of nudging and minority influence to overcome those gaps. It emphasizes the need to validate and expand existing theoretical foundations, adapting them to the unique features and complexities of digital platforms. These insights serve as a catalyst for future investigations, prompting researchers to delve deeper into the framework.

REFERENCES

A nudge in the right direction: Using social media to influence public health. (n.d.). Gies College of Business. https://giesbusiness.illinois.edu/news/2023/04/26/a-nudge-in-the-right-direction-using-social-media-to-influence-public-health.'

Abhyankar, A. (2019). *Behavioural Economics Towards Better Decision Making*. Academic Press.

Ajzen, I. (1991). The theory of planned behaviour. *Organizational Behavior and Human Decision Processes*, *50*(2), 179–211. doi:10.1016/0749-5978(91)90020-T

Akhtar, M. A., Khan, K. A., & Hoang, H. C. (2023). Role of Social Networking Sites in Financial Product Choice: An Investigation Through the Theory of Planned Behaviour. *Business Perspectives and Research, 11*(1), 44-62.

Al-Emadi, F., & Yahia, I. (2020). Ordinary celebrities related criteria to harvest fame and influence on social media. *Journal of Research in Interactive Marketing*, *14*(2), 195–213. doi:10.1108/JRIM-02-2018-0031

Ali, M., Baqir, A., Psaila, G., & Malik, S. (2020). Towards the Discovery of Influencers to Follow in Micro-Blogs (Twitter) by Detecting Topics in Posted Messages (Tweets). *Applied Sciences (Basel, Switzerland)*, *10*(16), 5715. doi:10.3390/app10165715

Apasrawirote, D., & Yawised, K. (2022). *Factors Influencing the Behavioral and Purchase Intention on Live-streaming Shopping*. Asian Journal of Business Research. doi:10.14707/ajbr.220119

Arantes, J., & Buchanan, R. (2022). Educational data advocates: Emerging forms of teacher agency in postdigital classrooms. *Learning, Media and Technology*, 1–21.

Argyris, Y., Wang, Z., Kim, Y., & Yin, Z. (2020). The effects of visual congruence on increasing consumers' brand engagement: An empirical investigation of influencer marketing on instagram using deep-learning algorithms for automatic image classification. *Computers in Human Behavior*, *112*, 106443. doi:10.1016/j.chb.2020.106443

Artese, F. (2020). In the digital world, all roads lead to Rome. But is Rome prepared? *Dental Press Journal of Orthodontics*, *24*(6), 7–8. doi:10.1590/2177-6709.24.6.007-008.edt PMID:31994650

Banerjee, S., & John, P. (2021). Nudge plus: Incorporating reflection into behavioral public policy. *Behavioural Public Policy*. Advance online publication. doi:10.1017/bpp.2021.9

Barbe, D., & Neuburger, L. (2021). *Generation Z and Digital Influencers in the Tourism Industry*. Generation Z Marketing and Management in Tourism and Hospitality. doi:10.1007/978-3-030-70695-1_7

Bazarova, N., Walther, J., & McLeod, P. (2012). Minority Influence in Virtual Groups. *Communication Research*, *39*(3), 295–316. doi:10.1177/0093650211399752

Bianchi, C., & Gonzalez, M. (2021). Exploring sustainable fashion consumption among eco-conscious women in Chile. *International Review of Retail, Distribution and Consumer Research*, *31*(4), 375–392. doi:10.1080/09593969.2021.1903529

Blackford, B. (2021). Nudging interventions on sustainable food consumption: a systematic review. *The Journal of Population and Sustainability*. . doi:10.3197/jps.2021.5.2.17

Borusiak, B., Szymkowiak, A., Horska, E., Raszka, N., & Żelichowska, E. (2020). Towards building sustainable consumption: A study of second-hand buying intentions. *Sustainability (Basel)*, *12*(3), 875. doi:10.3390/su12030875

Bouvier, L., & Cho, E. (2022, December). How Do Virtual Social Media Influencers Affect Millennial and Gen Z Female Consumers' Purchase Intentions? A Comparison of Fast Fashion Versus Luxury Fashion Brands. *International Textile and Apparel Association Annual Conference Proceedings, 79*(1). 10.31274/itaa.16012

Brandão, A., & da Costa, A. G. (2021). Extending the theory of planned behaviour to understand the effects of barriers towards sustainable fashion consumption. *European Business Review*, *33*(5), 742–774. doi:10.1108/EBR-11-2020-0306

Brijnath, B., Croy, S., Sabatés, J., Thodis, A., Ellis, S., Crespigny, F., Moxey, A., Day, R., Dobson, A., Elliott, C., Etherington, C., Geronimo, M., Hlis, D., Lampit, A., Low, L., Straiton, N., & Temple, J. (2022). Including ethnic minorities in dementia research: Recommendations from a scoping review. *Alzheimer's & Dementia: Translational Research & Clinical Interventions*, *8*(1), e12222. Advance online publication. doi:10.1002/trc2.12222 PMID:35505899

Brun, A., & Karaosman, H. (2020). Sustainability in the Luxury Fashion Supply Chain: Millennials'. *Perception*, (37), 99–121. doi:10.3917/maorg.037.0099

Busalim, A., Fox, G., & Lynn, T. (2022). Consumer behavior in sustainable fashion: A systematic literature review and future research agenda. *International Journal of Consumer Studies, 46*(5), 1804-1828. https://onlinelibrary.wiley.com/doi/abs/10.1111/ijcs.12794?casa_token=Xy5riLZnn7kAAAAA:ajOjnJVLJOfs0blCneH69tqVmLfx7zxf75u1Oe-Y4bGxK5AK2p_YtnEo7MwT8QGX23TFelvgA9M0eis

Carpenter, J. P., Shelton, C. C., & Schroeder, S. E. (2022). The education influencer: Is a new player in the educator professional landscape. *Journal of Research on Technology in Education*, 1–16. https://www.tandfonline.com/doi/abs/10.1080/15391523.2022.2030267

Chopra, A., Avhad, V., & Jaju, A. S. (2021). Influencer marketing: An exploratory study to identify antecedents of consumer behaviour among millennials. *Business Perspectives and Research*, *9*(1), 77–79. doi:10.1177/2278533720923486

Chwialkowska, A. (2019). How sustainability influencers drive green lifestyle adoption on social media: The process of green lifestyle adoption explained through the lenses of the minority influence model and social learning theory. *Management of Sustainable Development*, *11*(1), 33–42. doi:10.2478/msd-2019-0019

Crano, W., & Seyranian, V. (2007). Majority and Minority Influence. *Social and Personality Psychology Compass*, *1*(1), 572–589. doi:10.1111/j.1751-9004.2007.00028.x

Cummings, R., Huff, E., Mack, N., Womack, K., Reid, A., Ghoram, B., Gilbert, J., & Gosha, K. (2019). Vlog Commentary YouTube Influencers as Effective Advisors in College and Career Readiness for Minorities in Computing: An Exploratory Study. *2019 Research on Equity and Sustained Participation in Engineering, Computing, and Technology (RESPECT)*, 1-8. . doi:10.1109/RESPECT46404.2019.8985961

Curtis, B., Ashford, R., Magnuson, K., & Ryan-Pettes, S. (2019). Comparison of Smartphone Ownership, Social Media Use, and Willingness to Use Digital Interventions Between Generation Z and Millennials in the Treatment of Substance Use: Cross-Sectional Questionnaire Study. *Journal of Medical Internet Research*, *21*(4), e13050. Advance online publication. doi:10.2196/13050 PMID:30994464

Dabija, D. C., Bejan, B. M., & Dinu, V. (2019). How sustainability oriented is Generation Z in retail? A literature review. *Transformations in Business & Economics*, *18*(2). Advance online publication. doi:10.3390/jrfm13070152

Dahlquist, S., & Garver, M. (2022). Effects of Product and Product Company Information on Generation Zs' Purchasing Preferences. *American Business Review*, *25*(1), 209–220. Advance online publication. doi:10.37625/abr.25.1.209-220

Davis, S., & Yi, J. (2022). Double tap, double trouble: Instagram, teachers, and profit. *E-Learning and Digital Media*, *19*(3), 320–339. doi:10.1177/20427530211064706

Desa, I. S., Noviana, P., Yuniarsih, R. E., Farhana, Y., & Hasanah, N. (2023, May). Circular Economy: The Challenges and Opportunity in Fashion Recycling. In *Proceedings of the Business Innovation and Engineering Conference (BIEC 2022)* (*Vol. 236*, p. 204). Springer Nature. 10.2991/978-94-6463-144-9_20

Djafarova, E., & Foots, S. (2022). Exploring ethical consumption of generation Z: Theory of planned behaviour. *Young Consumers*, *23*(3), 413–431. doi:10.1108/YC-10-2021-1405

Dombrowski, S. U., Sniehotta, F. F., Avenell, A., Johnston, M., MacLennan, G., & Araújo-Soares, V. (2012). Identifying active ingredients in complex behavioural interventions for obese adults with obesity-related co-morbidities or additional risk factors for co-morbidities: A systematic review. *Health Psychology Review*, *6*(1), 7–32. doi:10.1080/17437199.2010.513298

Domínguez, M. F. O., & Bhatti, Y. A. (2022). From Waste to Luxury Fashion at Elvis & Kresse: A Business Model for Sustainable and Social Innovation in the Circular Economy. *Sustainability (Basel)*, *14*(19), 11805. doi:10.3390/su141911805

Dousay, T. A., Wolf, L. G., Green, L. S., & Asino, T. (2018, March). Rise of the "Teacher Influencers": Examining the benefits and conundrums. In *Society for Information Technology & Teacher Education International Conference* (pp. 1031-1033). Association for the Advancement of Computing in Education (AACE).

Duckworth, A. L., & Gross, J. J. (2020). Behavior change. *Organizational Behavior and Human Decision Processes*, *161*, 39–49. doi:10.1016/j.obhdp.2020.09.002 PMID:33716396

Eike, R., Irick, E., McKinney, E., Zhang, L., & Sanders, E. (2020). Repurposing design process. In Sustainability in the Textile and Apparel Industries: Sustainable Textiles, Clothing Design, and Repurposing (pp. 189-239). doi:10.1007/978-3-030-37929-2_9

Ensaff, H. (2021). A nudge in the right direction: The role of food choice architecture in changing populations' diets. *The Proceedings of the Nutrition Society, 80*(2), 195–206. doi:10.1017/S0029665120007983 PMID:33446288

Fiallos, A., & Figueroa, S. (2023, April). Detection of Educational Influencers and Communities on TikTok. In *2023 Ninth International Conference on eDemocracy & eGovernment (ICEDEG)* (pp. 1-6). IEEE. 10.1109/ICEDEG58167.2023.10122011

Filho, B., Tritany, É., & Struchiner, C. (2022). Theoretical report: Reflections and considerations for authors, reviewers, and editors. *Revista de Saude Publica, 56.* Advance online publication. doi:10.11606/s1518-8787.2022056003766 PMID:35476108

Filieri, R., Lin, Z., Pino, G., Alguezaui, S., & Inversini, A. (2021). The role of visual cues in eWOM on consumers' behavioral intentions and decisions. *Journal of Business Research, 135*, 663–675. doi:10.1016/j.jbusres.2021.06.055

Fischer, E., & Guzel, G. T. (2023). The case for qualitative research. *Journal of Consumer Psychology, 33*(1), 259–272. doi:10.1002/jcpy.1300

Forbes. (2021). *Gen Z is emerging as the sustainability generation.* https://www.forbes.com/

Forbes. (2022). *Gen Z and Sustainability: The Disruption Has Only Just Begun.* https://www.forbes.com/

Gao, X. (2023). *Wearing pineapple leaves?: Consumer responses to fashion products made from repurposed materials* (Doctoral dissertation, Wageningen University).

Garcés, P. (2022). Pragmatic Behaviour: Pragmatism as a philosophy for behavioural economics. *Journal of Philosophical Economics, 15*(Articles). doi:10.46298/jpe.8741

Garcia-Torres, S., Rey-Garcia, M., Sáenz, J., & Seuring, S. (2022). Traceability and transparency for sustainable fashion-apparel supply chains. *Journal of Fashion Marketing and Management, 26*(2), 344–364. doi:10.1108/JFMM-07-2020-0125

Geegamage, T., Ranaweera, A., & Halwatura, R. (2021). *Second-Hand Fashion Consumption: A Literature Review.* In The ERU Symposium 2021. 10.31705/ERU.2021.6

Gil-Quintana, J., & Vida de León, E. (2021). Educational influencers on Instagram: Analysis of educational channels, audiences, and economic performance. *Publications / MDPI, 9*(4), 43. doi:10.3390/publications9040043

Gillespie, E. (2019). The Instagram influencers hired to rehabilitate Saudi Arabia's image. *The Guardian.* https://www.theguardian.com/

Girgis, I. (2022). *Nudging sustainable fashion: how behavioural economics influence consumers pro-environmental clothing shopping online* (Bachelor's thesis, University of Malta). OAR@UM.

Gonçalves, A., & Silva, C. (2021). Looking for sustainability scoring in apparel: A review on environmental footprint, social impacts and transparency. *Energies, 14*(11), 3032. doi:10.3390/en14113032

Hallsworth, M., & Kirkman, E. (2020). *Behavioral insights.* MIT Press.

Hardecker, S., Vreden, C., & Alcan, E. (2023). Is the majority always right? Young children's normative interpretations of majority and dissenting peer behavior. *Social Development*, *32*(4), 1168–1191. Advance online publication. doi:10.1111/sode.12682

Hasbullah, N. N., Sulaiman, Z., Mas'od, A., & Ahmad Sugiran, H. S. (1945). Drivers of sustainable apparel purchase intention: An empirical study of Malaysian millennial consumers. *Sustainability (Basel)*, *14*(4), 1945. Advance online publication. doi:10.3390/su14041945

Hassan, S. H., Yeap, J. A., & Al-Kumaim, N. H. (2022). Sustainable fashion consumption: Advocating philanthropic and economic motives in clothing disposal behaviour. *Sustainability (Basel)*, *14*(3), 1875. doi:10.3390/su14031875

Henningsen, D., & Henningsen, M. (2021). *Persuasion and Social Influence in Groups*. The Emerald Handbook of Group and Team Communication Research. doi:10.1108/978-1-80043-500-120211018

Hickman, A. (2019). *Saudi Arabia turns to influencers to give nation's image a makeover*. Campaign US. https://www.campaignlive.com/

Hollebeek, L., & Rather, R. A. (2019). Service innovativeness and tourism customer outcomes. *International Journal of Contemporary Hospitality Management*, *31*(11), 4227–4246. doi:10.1108/IJCHM-03-2018-0256

Hoo, T. J. K. W. C., Chee, L. S. Q. D. T., & Foong, L. Y. P. C. Y. (2022). Consumers' Perceptions of Social Media Influencers and Its Influence on Purchase Intention in Malaysia. *Resmilitaris, 12*(3), 3012-3020.

Hudders, L., Jans, S., & Veirman, M. (2020). The commercialization of social media stars: A literature review and conceptual framework on the strategic use of social media influencers. *International Journal of Advertising*, *40*(3), 327–375. doi:10.1080/02650487.2020.1836925

Hulland, J. (2020). Conceptual review papers: Revisiting existing research to develop and refine theory. *AMS Review*, *10*(1-2), 27–35. doi:10.1007/s13162-020-00168-7

Iran, S. (2018). Sustainable fashion: from production to alternative consumption. In *Sustainable Fashion* (pp. 139–159). Governance and New Management Approaches. doi:10.1007/978-3-319-74367-7_13

Jaakkola, E. (2020). Designing conceptual articles: Four approaches. *AMS Review*, *10*(1-2), 18–26. doi:10.1007/s13162-020-00161-0

Jackson, T. (2004). Negotiating Sustainable Consumption: A review of the consumption debate and its policy Implications. *Energy & Environment*, *15*(6), 1027–1051. doi:10.1260/0958305043026573

Jacobson, J., & Harrison, B. (2022). Sustainable fashion social media influencers and content creation calibration. *International Journal of Advertising*, *41*(1), 150–177. doi:10.1080/02650487.2021.2000125

Jang, M. A., Lee, J. M., Bae, S., Jang, M. A., Lee, J. M., & Bae, S. (2022). A Study of Consumer Choice Behaviour Determination Applying the Theory of Planned Behaviour (TPB) of Functional Cosmetics. *Asian Journal of Beauty and Cosmetology*, *20*(1), 95–110. doi:10.20402/ajbc.2022.0003 PMID:31621194

Jia, C., & Mustafa, H. (2022). A Bibliometric analysis and review of nudge research using VOSviewer. *Behavioral Sciences (Basel, Switzerland)*, *13*(1), 19. doi:10.3390/bs13010019 PMID:36661591

Kardosh, R., Sklar, A., Goldstein, A., Pertzov, Y., & Hassin, R. (2022). Minority salience and the overestimation of individuals from minority groups in perception and memory. *Proceedings of the National Academy of Sciences of the United States of America,* 119. 10.1073/pnas.2116884119

Karimova, G. (2020). Exploring Visual Framing Strategies, Sentiment, and Product Presentation Modality in Instagram Posts of Fashion Influencers. *Exploring Visual Framing Strategies, Sentiment, and Product Presentation Modality in Instagram Posts of Fashion Influencers., 7*(1). Advance online publication. doi:10.29107/rr2020.1.6

Kende, J., Reiter, J., Coşkan, C., Doosje, B., & Green, E. G. (2023). The role of minority discrimination and political participation in shaping majority perceptions of discrimination: Two cross-national studies. *Group Processes & Intergroup Relations, 26*(3), 607–628. doi:10.1177/13684302221075711

Kidd, E., Ritch, E., & Carey, L. D. (2020, October). The Fashion Detox Challenge: An Experiment in Reduced Clothing Consumption. In *The Legacy of Fashion: Past, Present, and Future Global Fashion Conference. Université de la Mode* (pp. 21-23). https://researchonline.gcu.ac.uk/en/publications/the-fashion-detox-challenge-supporting-scotlands-transition-to-a-

Kim, D., & Park, S. (2020). Rethinking millennials: How are they shaping the tourism industry? *Asia Pacific Journal of Tourism Research, 25*(1), 1–2. doi:10.1080/10941665.2019.1667607

Kim, J., Yang, K., Min, J., & White, B. (2022). Hope, fear, and consumer behavioural change amid COVID-19: Application of protection motivation theory. *International Journal of Consumer Studies, 46*(2), 558–574. doi:10.1111/ijcs.12700 PMID:34220343

Kim, S., Jang, S., Choi, W., Youn, C., & Lee, Y. (2022). Contactless service encounters among Millennials and Generation Z: The effects of Millennials and Gen Z characteristics on technology self-efficacy and preference for contactless service. *Journal of Research in Interactive Marketing, 16*(1), 82–100. doi:10.1108/JRIM-01-2021-0020

Koch, K., & Domina, T. (1999). Consumer textile recycling as a means of solid waste reduction. *Family and Consumer Sciences Research Journal, 28*(1), 3–17. doi:10.1177/1077727X99281001

Konstantinou, I., & Jones, K. (2022). Investigating Gen Z attitudes to charitable giving and donation behaviour: Social media, peers and authenticity. *Journal of Philanthropy and Marketing, 27*(3), e1764. Advance online publication. doi:10.1002/nvsm.1764

Kovanci, E., & Karakoç, D. (2022). The effect of social media use on environmental awareness rating of university students. *Adıyaman Üniversitesi Sosyal Bilimler Enstitüsü Dergisi.* . doi:10.14520/adyusbd.1111999

Krismawan, D. A., Widagdo, S., & Puspitawati, D. (2021). Free Trade Area Agreement: Impact To The Fashion Industry And Environmental Protection In Indonesia. *International Journal of Global Community, 4*(2), 153-162. https://journal.riksawan.com/index.php/IJGC-RI/article/view/88

Kukulska-Hulme, A., Bossu, C., Charitonos, K., Coughlan, T., Ferguson, R., FitzGerald, E., Gaved, M., Guitert, M., Herodotou, C., Maina, M., & Prieto-Blázquez, J. (2022). *Innovating pedagogy 2022: exploring new forms of teaching, learning and assessment, to guide educators and policy makers.* open.ac.uk

Lamartora, V. (2021). *Z Houses. Nuovi servizi dedicati ai giovani nel Dipartimento Dipendenze della ASL Napoli2Nord*. MISSION, doi:10.3280/mis55-2020oa12159

LaTour, S., & Manrai, A. (1989). Interactive Impact of Informational and Normative Influence on Donations. *JMR, Journal of Marketing Research*, *26*(3), 327–335. doi:10.1177/002224378902600306

Leclercq-Machado, L., Alvarez-Risco, A., Gómez-Prado, R., Cuya-Velásquez, B. B., Esquerre-Botton, S., Morales-Ríos, F., Almanza-Cruz, C., Castillo-Benancio, S., Anderson-Seminario, M. M., Del-Aguila-Arcentales, S., & Yáñez, J. A. (2022). Sustainable fashion and consumption patterns in Peru: An environmental-attitude-intention-behavior analysis. *Sustainability (Basel)*, *14*(16), 9965. doi:10.3390/su14169965

Lee, E. J., Choi, H., Han, J., Kim, D. H., Ko, E., & Kim, K. H. (2020). How to 'Nudge' your consumers toward sustainable fashion consumption: An fMRI investigation. *Journal of Business Research*, *117*, 642–651. doi:10.1016/j.jbusres.2019.09.050

Lee, S., Chung, I., & Cho, Y. (2022). *Effect of the Ethical Consumption Tendency of Millennials and Members of Generation Z on the Purchase Intention of Social Enterprise Fashion Products*. Family and Environment Research. doi:10.6115/fer.2022.029

Lepesant, V. (2022). Redressing Sustainable Fashion Practices: Upcycling as a Defense to Trademark Infringement. Tex. A&M L. *Rev.*, *10*(2), 335–358. doi:10.37419/LR.V10.I2.5

Lewis, T. L., Park, H., Netravali, A. N., & Trejo, H. X. (2017). Closing the loop: A scalable zero-waste model for apparel reuse and recycling. *International Journal of Fashion Design, Technology and Education*, *10*(3), 353–362. doi:10.1080/17543266.2016.1263364

Li, L. (2023). Refashioning repair culture through the circle of value creation: A case study of the Japanese brand KUON. *International Journal of Sustainable Fashion & Textiles*, *2*(1), 53–62. doi:10.1386/sft_00020_1

Lidgren, J., & Major, M. (2021). *Social media influencers' impact on consumers' sustainable fashion consumption: A qualitative study on post-millennial consumers*. https://gupea.ub.gu.se/bitstream/handle/2077/69053/gupea_2077_69053_1.pdf?sequence=1&isAllowed=y

Lindstrom, K. N., Tucker, J. A., & McVay, M. (2023). Nudges and choice architecture to promote healthy food purchases in adults: A systematized review. *Psychology of Addictive Behaviors*, *37*(1), 87–103. doi:10.1037/adb0000892 PMID:36395010

Lotti, L., Barile, L., & Manfredi, G. (2023). Improving recycling sorting behaviour with human eye nudges. *Scientific Reports*, *13*(1), 10127. doi:10.1038/s41598-023-37019-x PMID:37349386

Madani, R. (2022). The new image of Saudi cultural shift; MDL Beast music festival; Saudi Vision 2030. *Cogent Arts & Humanities*, *9*(1), 2105511. doi:10.1080/23311983.2022.2105511

Marcella-Hood, M. (2023). Augmenting Sustainable Fashion on Instagram. *Sustainability (Basel)*, *15*(4), 3609. doi:10.3390/su15043609

Marcelo, C., & Marcelo, P. (2021). Educational influencers on Twitter. Analysis of hashtags and relationship structure. *Comunicar*, *29*(68), 73–83. doi:10.3916/C68-2021-06

Marchiori, D. R., Adriaanse, M. A., & De Ridder, D. T. (2017). Unresolved questions in nudging research: Putting the psychology back in nudging. *Social and Personality Psychology Compass, 11*(1), e12297. doi:10.1111/spc3.12297

Martín, A., Swaab, R., Sinaceur, M., & Vasiljevic, D. (2015). The double-edged impact of future expectations in groups: Minority influence depends on minorities' and majorities' expectations to interact again. *Organizational Behavior and Human Decision Processes, 128*, 49–60. doi:10.1016/j.obhdp.2015.03.002

Martin, G. L. (2021). *Nudges for all? The effect of power on the efficiency of nudges* (Doctoral dissertation). http://hdl.handle.net/10400.14/35406

Martin, N., & Morich, K. (2011). Unconscious mental processes in consumer choice: Toward a new model of consumer behavior. *Journal of Brand Management, 18*(7), 483–505. https://link.springer.com/article/10.1057/bm.2011.10. doi:10.1057/bm.2011.10

Mason, M. C., Pauluzzo, R., & Umar, R. M. (2022). Recycling habits and environmental responses to fast-fashion consumption: Enhancing the theory of planned behaviour to predict Generation Y consumers' purchase decisions. *Waste Management (New York, N.Y.), 139*, 146–157. doi:10.1016/j.wasman.2021.12.012 PMID:34971902

Mengyue, Z. (2021). *Based on Kahneman's two-system theory: presentation and application of the three-system theory*. Academic Journal of Humanities & Social Sciences. doi:10.25236/AJHSS.2021.040917

Mohr, I., Fuxman, L., & Mahmoud, A. B. (2022). A triple-trickle theory for sustainable fashion adoption: The rise of a luxury trend. *Journal of Fashion Marketing and Management, 26*(4), 640–660. doi:10.1108/JFMM-03-2021-0060

Montanaro, E. A., Kershaw, T. S., & Bryan, A. D. (2018). Dismantling the theory of planned behavior: Evaluating the relative effectiveness of attempts to uniquely change attitudes, norms, and perceived behavioral control. *Journal of Behavioral Medicine, 41*(6), 757–770. doi:10.1007/s10865-018-9923-x PMID:29671166

Moscovici, S. (1980). Toward a theory of conversion behavior. In Advances in experimental social psychology (Vol. 13, pp. 209–239). Academic Press. doi:10.1016/S0065-2601(08)60133-1

Moscovici, S. (2012). Minority influence. In Social Psychology: Revisiting the Classic Studies (pp. 91-106). Academic Press.

Moscovici, S., & Faucheux, C. (1972). Social Influence, Conformity Bias, and the Study of Active Minorities. *Advances in Experimental Social Psychology, 6*, 149–202. doi:10.1016/S0065-2601(08)60027-1

Moscovici, S., & Lage, E. (1976). Studies in social influence III: Majority versus minority influence in a group. *European Journal of Social Psychology, 6*(2), 149–174. doi:10.1002/ejsp.2420060202

Mukendi, A., Davies, I., McDonagh, P., & Glozer, S. (2020). Sustainable fashion: Current and future research directions. *European Journal of Marketing, 54*(11), 2873–2909. doi:10.1108/EJM-02-2019-0132

Nogueira, E., Gomes, S., & Lopes, J. M. (2023). Triple Bottom Line, Sustainability, and Economic Development: What Binds Them Together? A bibliometric approach. *Sustainability (Basel), 15*(8), 6706. doi:10.3390/su15086706

Özdil, N., Dalbaşı, E., Özgüney, A., & Atiker, L. (2023). *Multifunctional Modification with TiO2, SiO2, and Flame Retardant Agent on Upholstery Fabrics Produced From Recycled Cotton Fibers.* AATCC Journal of Research. doi:10.1177/24723444221147976

Palomo-Domínguez, I., Elías-Zambrano, R., & Álvarez-Rodríguez, V. (2023). Gen Z's Motivations towards Sustainable Fashion and Eco-Friendly Brand Attributes: The Case of Vinted. *Sustainability (Basel), 15*(11), 8753. doi:10.3390/su15118753

Paul, L. A., & Gray, M. J. (2011). Sexual assault programming on college campuses: Using social psychological belief and behavior change principles to improve outcomes. *Trauma, Violence & Abuse, 12*(2), 99–109. doi:10.1177/1524838010390710 PMID:21196434

Pérez, A. (2022). Behavioral Economics: Theoretical Conception to Understand Economic Behavior. *ESPOCH Congresses: The Ecuadorian Journal of S.T.E.A.M.* . doi:10.18502/espoch.v2i2.11403

Politi, E., Gale, J., & Staerklé, C. (2017). Flexible Solidarity with Refugees. *Integrating Minority Influence and Intergroup Communication., 30*(1), 172. doi:10.5334/irsp.24

Pozharliev, R., Rossi, D., & De Angelis, M. (2022). A picture says more than a thousand words: Using consumer neuroscience to study Instagram users' responses to influencer advertising. *Psychology and Marketing, 39*(7), 1336–1349. doi:10.1002/mar.21659

Prentice, D. A. (2022). Targeting ignorance to change behavior. In Routledge international handbook of ignorance studies (pp. 305-312). Routledge. doi:10.4324/9781003100607-34

Prestwich, A., Sniehotta, F. F., Whittington, C., Dombrowski, S. U., Rogers, L., & Michie, S. (2014). Does theory influence the effectiveness of health behavior interventions? Meta-analysis. *Health Psychology, 33*(5), 465–474. doi:10.1037/a0032853 PMID:23730717

Prislin, R. (2022). Minority Influence: An Agenda for Study of Social Change. *Frontiers in Psychology, 13*, 13. doi:10.3389/fpsyg.2022.911654 PMID:35814107

Roozen, I., Raedts, M., & Meijburg, L. (2021). Do verbal and visual nudges influence consumers' choice for sustainable fashion? *Journal of Global Fashion Marketing, 12*(4), 327–342. doi:10.1080/20932685.2021.1930096

Rotimi, E., Topple, C., & Hopkins, J. (2021). Towards A Conceptual Framework of Sustainable Practices of Post-consumer Textile Waste at Garment End of Lifecycle: A Systematic Literature Review Approach. *Sustainability (Basel), 13*(5), 2965. doi:10.3390/su13052965

Sah, Y. J., & Peng, W. (2023). Context-dependent Online Social Influence: Effect of Majority and Minority Comments on Posters and Lurkers. *Social Science Computer Review, 41*(4), 1316–1335. doi:10.1177/08944393211070527

Sakdiyakorn, M., Golubovskaya, M., & Solnet, D. (2021). Understanding Generation Z through collective consciousness: Impacts for hospitality work and employment. *International Journal of Hospitality Management, 94*, 102822. doi:10.1016/j.ijhm.2020.102822

Saksena, R. A. (2020). *Sustainable Fashion. [online] Circular Economy and Re-Commerce in the Fashion Industry.* Available at: https://www.semanticscholar.org/paper/Sustainable-Fashion-Saksena/e181956c3d183642cb2bda7cbceb410416f38e93

Sambargi & Tripathi. (2023). A Study on Awareness and Perceptions towards Sustainable Fashion. *International Scientific Journal of Engineering and Management, 2*(4), 1–10. Available at: https://isjem.com/download/a-study-on-the-awareness-and-perception-towards-sustainable-fashion/

Schlüter, M., Caniglia, G., Orach, K., Bodin, Ö., Magliocca, N., Meyfroidt, P., & Reyers, B. (2022). Why care about theories? Innovative ways of theorizing in sustainability science. *Current Opinion in Environmental Sustainability, 54,* 101154. doi:10.1016/j.cosust.2022.101154

Shelton, C., Schroeder, S., & Curcio, R. (2020). Instagramming their hearts out: What do edu-influencers share on Instagram? *Contemporary Issues in Technology & Teacher Education, 20*(3), 529–554. https://www.learntechlib.org/primary/p/215623/

Shin, H. K. (2020). A case study on value creation of fashion brands using content collaboration targeting MZ generation. *The Research Journal of Costume Culture, 28*(6), 830–844. doi:10.29049/rjcc.2020.28.6.830

Shirvanimoghaddam, K., Motamed, B., Ramakrishn, S., & Naebe, M. (2020). Death by Waste: A Fashion and Textile Circular Economy Case. *The Science of the Total Environment, 718,* 137317. doi:10.1016/j.scitotenv.2020.137317 PMID:32088483

Sniehotta, F. F., Presseau, J., & Araújo-Soares, V. (2014). Time to retire the theory of planned behaviour. *Health Psychology Review, 8*(1), 1–7. doi:10.1080/17437199.2013.869710 PMID:25053004

Stål, H. I., & Jansson, J. (2017). Sustainable consumption and value propositions: Exploring product–service system practices among Swedish fashion firms. *Sustainable Development (Bradford), 25*(6), 546–558. doi:10.1002/sd.1677

Statista. (2023a). *Fashion - Worldwide. Statista Market Forecast.* Retrieved from https://www.statista.com/outlook/90000000/100/fashion/worldwide

Statista. (2023b). *Global apparel market - statistics & facts.* Retrieved from https://www.statista.com/topics/4592/global-apparel-market/

Stroebe, W., Martin, R., & Hewstone, M. (2010). *Majority and minority influence and information processing: A theoretical and methodological analysis. Minority influence and innovation: Antecedents, processes and consequences, 201-225.* Processes and Consequences - Google Books.

Sugden, R. (2009). *On nudging: A review of nudge: Improving decisions about health, wealth and happiness by Richard H.* Thaler and Cass R. Sunstein., doi:10.1080/13571510903227064

Sun, J., Leung, X. Y., & Bai, B. (2021). How social media influencer's event endorsement changes attitudes of followers: The moderating effect of followers' gender. *International Journal of Contemporary Hospitality Management, 33*(7), 2337–2351. doi:10.1108/IJCHM-09-2020-0959

Tam, F. Y., & Lung, J. W. (2023). Impact of COVID-19 and innovative ideas for a sustainable fashion supply chain in the future. *Foresight, 25*(2), 225–248. doi:10.1108/FS-12-2021-0257

Testa, D. S., Bakhshian, S., & Eike, R. (2021). Engaging consumers with sustainable fashion on Instagram. *Journal of Fashion Marketing and Management, 25*(4), 569–584. doi:10.1108/JFMM-11-2019-0266

Thaler, R., & Sunstein, C. (2008). Human frailty caused this crisis. *Financial Times*, 11.

Thaler, R. H., & Sunstein, C. R. (2009). *Nudge: Improving decisions about health, wealth, and happiness*. Penguin.

Theunissen. (2023). *Why Fashion Is Betting Big on Saudi Arabia*. Business of Fashion. Retrieved from https://www.businessoffashion.com/articles/fashion-week/why-fashion-is-betting-big-on-saudi-arabia

Tzikas, A., & Koulierakis, G. (2023). A Systematic Review of Nudges on Hand Hygiene Against the Spread of COVID-19. *Journal of Behavioral and Experimental Economics, 102046*, 102046. Advance online publication. doi:10.1016/j.socec.2023.102046 PMID:37274754

UK Research & Innovation. (2023). *What is social science?* Retrieved from https://www.ukri.org/innovation/excellent-research/social-science/

UN. (2023). *Sustainable Lifestyles*. UNSSC | United Nations System Staff College. Retrieved from https://www.unssc.org/learn/sustainable-lifestyles/

UNFashionalliance. (2023). *The UN Alliance for Sustainable Fashion*. Retrieved from https://www.unfashionalliance.org/

Unilever, P. L. C. (2023). *Unilever reveals influencers can switch people on to sustainable living*. Unilever. Available at: https://www.unilever.com/news/press-and-media/press-releases/2023/unilever-reveals-influencers-can-switch-people-on-to-sustainable-living/#:~:text=The%20results%20revealed%20that%20both

United Nations. (2022). *The Sustainable Lifestyle Action Academy*. UNEP (UN Environment Programme). Retrieved from https://www.unep.org/resources/publication/sustainable-lifestyles-action-academy

United Nations. (2023). *Why Sustainable lifestyles matter. Retrieved from Why Sustainable lifestyles matter*. UNEP - UN Environment Programme.

Vesterinen, E., & Syrjälä, H. (2022). Sustainable anti-consumption of clothing: A systematic literature review. *Cleaner and Responsible Consumption, 100061*. Advance online publication. doi:10.1016/j.clrc.2022.100061

Vrontis, D., Makrides, A., Christofi, M., & Thrassou, A. (2021). Social media influencer marketing: A systematic review, integrative framework and future research agenda. *International Journal of Consumer Studies, 45*(4), 617–644. doi:10.1111/ijcs.12647

Williams, A., & Hodges, N. (2022). Adolescent Generation Z and sustainable and responsible fashion consumption: Exploring the value-action gap. *Young Consumers, 23*(4), 651–666. Advance online publication. doi:10.1108/YC-11-2021-1419

Wu, Y., Kim, K. J., & Mou, Y. (2022). Minority social influence and moral decision-making in human–AI interaction: The effects of identity and specialization cues. *New Media & Society*. Advance online publication. doi:10.1177/14614448221138072

Yıldırım, S. (2021). Do green women influencers spur sustainable consumption patterns? Descriptive evidences from social media influencers. *Ecofeminism and Climate Change, 2*(4), 198-210. https://www.emerald.com/insight/content/doi/10.1108/EFCC-02-2021-0003/full/html

Yilmaz, G., & Youngreen, R. (2016). The application of Minority Influence Theory in computer-mediated communication groups. *Small Group Research, 47*(6), 692–719. doi:10.1177/1046496416661033

Zhang, C., Lakens, D., & IJsselsteijn, W. A. (2021). Theory integration for lifestyle behavior change in the digital age: An adaptive decision-making framework. *Journal of Medical Internet Research, 23*(4), e17127. doi:10.2196/17127 PMID:33835036

Zhang, L., & Hale, J. (2022). Extending the lifetime of clothing through repair and repurpose: An investigation of barriers and enablers in UK citizens. *Sustainability (Basel), 14*(17), 10821. doi:10.3390/su141710821

KEY TERMS AND DEFINITIONS

Educational Influencers: Edu-influencers are individuals who offer free video and content beyond formal education programs, often working outside educational institutions.

Information Influence: It is based on minorities' behavioural style, thinking style, flexibility, and identification.

Minority Influence Theory: Minority Influence Theory posits that consistent minority positions, such as Edu-Influencers, can influence the majority's behaviors through information influence, highlighting the role of environmental and external factors in shaping behavior.

Nudge: Nudge Theory suggests that subtle changes in choice or information presentation can influence behavior without forbidding or mandating certain actions, highlighting the influence of environmental, external, and individual internal factors.

Repurposing: It is reusing old items into new products from a consumption standpoint.

Sustainable Fashion Consumption: It is supporting current and future generations' material and other needs without causing irreversible environmental damage or loss of function in natural systems.

Sustainable Fashion Consumption in the Disposition Stage: It is the responsible discarding of unwanted fashion items.

Verbal Nudge: Verbal nudges are messages that encourage sustainable fashion consumption through written language.

Visual Nudge: Visual nudges are images, graphics, or videos that encourage sustainable fashion consumption through visual cues.

APPENDIX (A)

Table 3. The recent studies exploring behavioural nudge to towards sustainability

Reference	Research aim	Findings	Method
(Torma et al. (2018)	This research explores the concept of 'self-nudging' in the experiences and understandings of customers in an organic food subscription scheme.	A change in behaviour within the context of sustainable food based on self-nudging.	Qualitative (interviews)
Andersson (2019)	The study aimed to explore the use of digital nudging to promote sustainable decisions on a travel company website, its design, and consumer perception of digital nudges.	The study found that digital nudges that offers design improvements can influence consumers to make sustainable decisions on a travel company's website, with a majority showing a positive attitude towards digital nudges.	Mix method (survey and interviews)
Huitink et al. (2020.)	It investigated the effect of a combination of two nudging strategies in shopping trolleys to increase the likelihood of healthy food purchase.	The results indicated positive change toward buying healthy food due to nudge interventions	Quantitative (experiment)
Isensee et al. (2022)	This study explores the use of mobile apps for fostering sustainability oriented corporate culture aiming to promote pro-environmental behaviour.	The study suggests the effectiveness of online behavioral change particularly through Apps to promote sustainability	Qualitative Analysis
Chu et al. (2022)	The study examined consumer perception of food packaging, focusing on portion control features, and gathered nudging ideas for improved healthy eating and downsizing packaging.	The study highlights the role of packaging as visual nudges in trust building, appetite stimulation, and self-identity, while portion control emphasizes structural reminders, healthy prompts, and portion awareness.	Qualitative- (Photo-Elicitations interviews)
Barker (2021)	What nudge techniques work for food waste behaviour change at the consumer level?	The study suggests that incorporating social norms, reminders, or disclosure as nudges into food waste recycling can effectively raise consumer awareness, potentially leading to positive waste reduction and household policy implications.	Systematic literature review
Morren et al. (2021)	It aim to create and evaluate four information nudges aimed at influencing dietary choices among a diverse group of Dutch consumers.	Pre-intervention knowledge about sustainable diets positively impacts participants' dietary choices, with procedural knowledge on healthier meal preparation influencing behavior, especially for those without prior dietary restrictions.	Mix-method (Survey followed by interviews)
Lotti et al. (2023)	Aim to tests whether visual nudges help direct attention towards existing instructions designed to increase waste sorting accuracy.	It concluded that combining both information with visual nudges significantly improves sustainable consumption behaviour within the disposition stage, recycling clothes. (Offline).	Quasi-experimental setting
Tening and Harder (2023)	Aim to use prior Nudging, with the aim of increasing the environmentallythemed transformedbehaviours.	It revealed most reported transformative behaviours were environmental, such as waste sorting, water and electricity conservation	Qualitative- (Photo-Elicitations Interviews)

Section 4
Influencers and Engagement

Chapter 11
Investigating the Impact of Influencer Wishful Identification and Parasocial Relationships on Purchasing Behavior:
Insights From Influencer Fan Data

Trinidee Mercado
Stetson University, USA

Ruonan Zhang
https://orcid.org/0000-0002-5872-7347
Rollins College, USA

ABSTRACT

Influencers are a powerful tool in the worlds of communication and marketing. The relationships that influencers build with audiences can affect consumer behaviors as can the brand that they create. Both the audience's perception of a relationship with the influencer as well as the audience's desire to be like the influencer can impact consumer purchasing behaviors. The purpose of this study is to explore how wishful identification and parasocial relationships serve as mediating factors in influencer impact on audience consumer behavior outcomes. This purpose is addressed via a quantitative survey (n = 948) in collaboration with a YouTube influencer disseminated to her audience. Results show that viewers' reported income, interactions with influencers, and parasocial relationships all have a positive impact on predicting participants' purchase behavior of influencer-recommended products. The findings contribute to an in-depth understanding of how wishful identification serves as a mediating variable between parasocial relationships and consumer purchasing behaviors in audiences.

DOI: 10.4018/979-8-3693-0912-4.ch011

INTRODUCTION

Influencers have the unique role of cultivating an individual brand that they sell to a viewing audience. Public figures have been used in advertising for hundreds of years to endorse products. The widely recognized first celebrity endorsement dates back to the 1760s when British royals endorsed pottery and chinaware products (Nair, Rajesh, & Singh, 2019). Endorsements have evolved and become more prevalent in society over time. Celebrity endorsements have become increasingly common throughout the 21st century as methods for advertising have boomed through the increased prevalence of digital media (Erdogan, 1999). Endorsements are now a common practice within marketing used to increase sales and overall brand awareness. As of 2009 an estimated 20 to 25% of all advertisements feature a celebrity or famous person (Sliburyte, 2009). While celebrity endorsements have historically been common in offline media, the rise of social media has created a vast digital landscape for advertisements (Segrave, 2015). Celebrity endorsements have become increasingly prevalent on social media applications including but not limited to Instagram, Facebook, X, and YouTube as they are easy platforms to disseminate mass communications (Burke, 2017; Burns, 2021; Segrave, 2017). Social media has also brought rise to the social media influencer (Burke, 2017; Burns, 2021). An influencer is a person who constantly shares their experiences and emotions with a given audience via content shared on a social media platform (2015; Burke, 2017; Burns, 2021; Enke & Borschers, 2021). A traditional influencer is someone who gained their fame via their content creation on social media platforms (2015; Burke, 2017; Burns, 2021; Enke & Borschers, 2021). Influencers offer a new way for brands to advertise products through both direct endorsements and indirect product placements (Campbell & Farrell, 2020; Leung et al, 2022). The ability for influencers to naturally and organically advertise and endorse products opens up a new realm for marketing (Campbell & Farrell, 2020). One study looking at K-Pop fans in Singapore found that participant parasocial interactions with social media have a positive impact on celebrity endorsement, improving perceived celebrity trustworthiness and brand credibility (Chung & Cho, 2017).

Influencers are unique in their impact on consumer behavior and often are more impactful than celebrities. Research has shown that influencers can successfully influence the purchase intentions of their audience (De Veirman et al., 2017), and have been perceived as being seen as more credible than traditional celebrities (Shareef et al., 2019). Using influencers instead of celebrities can improve brand credibility and trustworthiness by creating a more natural form of endorsement and product placement. Domingues Aguiar and van Reijmersdal (2018) found that users perceive a greater likeness to micro-influencers than meso- or macro-influencers with more followers. Organic and subtle influencer endorsements in social media are more greatly effective than celebrity endorsements (Gräve & Bartsch, 2022).

As influencers create their overarching brand, they also create the primary viewpoint from which their audience will perceive and interact with them. While viewers create their own perceptions of their relationship with a content creator, the creation and release of content by an influencer largely shapes how they will be perceived by their viewing audience. The branding an influencer creates for themselves largely shapes audiences' perception of the influencer. This impacts viewer perception of their relationship with the influencer as well as their desire to imitate the influencer. These behaviors are reflected through the concepts of parasocial relationships and wishful identification respectively. In this chapter, we will explore how wishful identification affects the relationship between parasocial relationships and consumer behaviors based on a real influencer's fan data.

LITERATURE REVIEW

Influencer Impact on Consumer Behaviors

As social media becomes increasingly prevalent throughout society, the frequency of user's parasocial interactions is increasing. Parasocial interactions account for the encounters a person has with a celebrity, influencer, or performer via a mass media platform (Horton & Wohl, 1956). By combining parasocial interactions with branded media, overall consumer engagement with product advertisements increases (Labrecque, 2014).In one study of 129 Russian social media users, participant engagement with social media influencer- and celebrity-created content found that purchase intention effect was dictated by user self-esteem (Piehler, 2022). Users with higher self-reported self-esteem were more positively affected by influencers and had higher purchase intention after viewing influencer content that promoted products as opposed to celebrity endorsement content. Consumer feelings of loyalty intentions towards a brand can also increase when paired with parasocial interactions. Influencers are a valuable asset to product advertisement (Chekima, Chekima, & Adis, 2020). Audience perception of factors including influencer authenticity, credibility, attractiveness, trustworthiness, and expertise impact advertising effectiveness and consumer product purchase intention. (Chekima, Chekima, & Adis, 2020; Wellman, Stoldt, Tully, & Ekdale, 2020). A study done by Hwang and Zhang (2018) found that parasocial relationships moderate the path between follower persuasion knowledge and purchase intention. Persuasion knowledge is a consumer's understanding of an advertiser's attempts to persuade, as well as their underlying motivation and tactics. This supports the idea that parasocial relationships can be a predictor of consumer purchasing behaviors. An influencer's overarching authenticity may be the most important factor in an influencer's rapport with their audience (Wellman et al., 2020). Influencers need to balance their sponsored content with their personal brand and image in order to remain authentic to their audience (Wellman et al., 2020). By remaining authentic to their personal brand and image through brand deals, sponsorships, and general recommendations this can strengthen their audience's trust (Giles, 2002).

Different types of content can elicit different audience behaviors and interactions with influencers. In 2021, researchers Le and Hancer discovered that audiences that viewed travel vlogs on YouTube were more inclined to visit locations featured within travel vlogs based on their perception of vloggers as credible and or attractive. The audience's desire to imitate the travel vloggers acted as a mediating factor in the relationship between the audience's intention to behave in ways that imitated these travel vloggers (Le and Hancer, 2021). While this impacted audience consumer behaviors, it also showed audiences imitating the traveling actions of the vloggers as well (Le and Hancer, 2021). Audiences who watched beauty vloggers on the other hand showed increased parasocial interactions with bloggers based on perceived similarities to and trustworthiness of vloggers (Nan & Park, 2018). These perceived factors then influenced consumer attitudes towards both the vlogs watched as well as the products shown. Another form of behavior content can elicit from the audience is the sharing of videos which increases the overall viewing audience. Viewers of product review videos tend to share YouTube testimonials of positive experiences due to their presumed influence on others and share negative videos due to their perceived self-effect (Bi & Zhang 2022). By framing review based content in a way that targets the audience's perception, consumer behavior can be shaped by influencers.

Influencer following size is also a predictor of consumer behavior impact. Micro-influencers are more impactfully persuasive than mega influencers when endorsing hedonic purchases due to higher audience perception of the authenticity of the endorsed brand which subsequently transfers from the perceptions of influencer authenticity (Park et al., 2021; Hernández-Méndez & Baute-Díaz, 2023). Micro-influencers who promoted the beauty product Focallure had a positive significant influence on respondent purchase intention (Isyanto, P., Sapitri, R. G., & Sinaga, 2020).

Different factors may serve as mediators between vlog watching and consumer purchasing behavior. Multiple factors have both been found to affect a viewing audience's percieved social norms (Bond, 2020; Bond & Drogos, 2014; Cohen et al., 2020). Cohen et al. (2020), found that wishful identification mediated the relative effects celebrities had on audience vaping norm perceptions (2020). One 2020 study found that audience parasocial relationships with television characters in an outgroup were predictive of viewer prejudice reduction (Bond). These examples showcase how audience parasocial relationships and wishful identification can largely impact viewers' social norms and actions. Using a mediation analysis, Lim et al. found that wishful identification and emotional engagement indirectly affected behavioral loyalty through PSR (Lim et al., 2020). Another found that factors relating to an influencer's attractiveness and perceived fairness increased viewer parasocial relationships which in turn increased following interest in products being advertised by the influencer (Yuan & Lou, 2020). While these studies explored audience parasocial relationships and wishful identification with social media influencers, rates of wishful identification and parasocial relationships were not explored across an audience for a singular influencer. By exploring a singular influencer's audiences, we can better determine the effect that wishful identification and parasocial relationships have on viewer behaviors, and what factors can increase or decrease wishful identification and parasocial relationships.

Wishful Identification

Influencers often display a desirable lifestyle or carefully cultivated personal branding that can be appealing to viewers. A person viewing an influencer can want to be like the influencer. Wishful identification is a person's desire to emulate a famous person (Feilitzen and Linne, 1975). This can include wanting to look like the person, act like them, or buy the same products as them. One study showed that it can even change a person's behavioral attitudes. Bond and Drogos (2013) found a positive relationship between young adults watching the television show—Jersey show and permissive sexual attitudes that were mediated by the participants' wishful identification and parasocial relationships with the show's cast members. Audiences may experience wishful identification towards influencers more often than towards traditional celebrities due to feeling more similar to influencers (Schouten, Janssen, & Verspaget, 2021). Previous research highlighted that viewers were more likely to experience wishful identification towards fictional characters whom they perceived to have similar characteristics and viewpoints (Hoffner & Buchanan, 2005). Viewers who had parasocial relationships with YouTubers were also likely to experience wishful identification towards the influencers (Tolbert & Drogos, 2019). Viewers who experience wishful identification have an indirect effect on behavioral loyalty or the likeliness of viewers to continue viewing an influencer's video content (Lim et al, 2020).

A study of wishful identification of fictional characters found that viewers who experienced wishful identification towards a particular character were more likely to be impacted by advertisements and product placements involving the character, which then influenced purchasing behavior (Schoenberger & Kim, 2019). When comparing celebrities and influencers a study found that audiences identified more with influencers and wishful identification served as a mediator between the type of endorser and the effectiveness of the advertising (Schouten, 2018). Wishful identification of influencers may also affect purchasing behavior. Viewer purchasing intention is affected by viewer attitudes towards influencers and environmental stimuli presented through livestreams (Zhang, Chao, Chiong, Hasan, Aljaroodi, & Tian, 2023). Viewers' positive attitudes toward the influencer positively mediated the effect between viewing the store an influencer was in and audience purchase behavior. A study also found when surveying users of Vietnamese social networking sites, wishful identification was positively associated with user parasocial relationships, which related to higher user purchase intentions (Bui et al., 2020).

Parasocial Relationships

While wishful identification is a person's desire to act like a certain public figure they do not know, oftentimes viewers feel like they do know the influencers they are watching. Parasocial relationships are one-sided relationships in which only one person exerts time, energy, and effort into a relationship with another person, typically a public figure, while the other person remains unaware of the other person's existence and perceived relationship (Dibble, Hartmann, & Rosaen, 2016). This creation of a relationship is essential in an influencer's creation of a strong loyal audience (Yesiloglu, 2020). Parasocial relationships with influencers are dependent on factors including influencer attractiveness, similarity with the viewer, and perceived fairness of their viewer interactions (Yuan & Lou, 2020). By creating content that highlights these factors influences may be able to create stronger parasocial relationships with viewers, which can then impact viewer purchasing behaviors. Parasocial interactions have been shown as positively related to viewer purchase intentions, as has the perceived credibility of the influencer (Sokolova & Perez, 2021). Factors including perceived credibility and informational influence created a strong relationship between parasocial relationships and audience purchase intentions (Su, Wu, Chang, & Hong, 2021). In addition, younger viewers are more inclined to be persuaded by an influencer, particularly vloggers, who have additional content posted about similar information as opposed to a content producer who may be objectively more credible (Sokolova & Kefi, 2020). The perceived credibility of the influencer as well as parasocial interactions were positively related to purchase intention. By understanding the factors that increase parasocial interactions viewer purchase intention can be increased.

Cultural Differences

The ways in which audiences perceive influencers, interact with their content, and alter their purchasing behaviors vary throughout different cultures. In this study, we will primarily be looking at Chinese and American influencer viewing audiences. Chinese and American consumer brand engagement varies (Men & Tsai, 2012). Both cultures as consumer markets vary in terms of legally required advertisement and brand deal disclosures as well as general perceptions on interacting directly with brands (Men & Tsai, 2012). Chinese study participants were shown to have a preference for two-way communication directly interacting with brands and gathering information from their official social media pages with very little negative feedback related to interactions with said brands. American participants were shown to have more negative interactions with brands on social media showing overall consumer attitude differences towards direct advertisement from brands. In addition, behaviors on social media platforms have been shown to be different, with Chinese TikTok users spending more time on average on the app and experiencing greater purchasing intention based on TikToks they have watched than their American counterparts (Yang, 2022).

In this study, we will be exploring how wishful identification and parasocial relationships impact consumer behavior. While prior research has looked at wishful identification and or parasocial relationships across content production platforms, we will be exploring the effects of wishful identification across one influencer's viewing audience on her main content creation platform YouTube. Working with a Chinese micro-influencer beauty vlogger living in the United States, we will recruit a sample from her viewing audience to determine the effects of wishful identification and parasocial relationships on audience consumer behavior. The behavior this study will look at consumer purchase intention. By exploring predictors of video preference and viewer interactions with the influencer we are also seeking to determine how these factors may predict wishful identification and parasocial relationships. Based on previous research in wishful identification, parasocial relationships, and consumer behavior, the following hypotheses are proposed. In this chapter, we will explore how viewer video preference and interactions with videos can predict wishful identification and parasocial relationships. We will explore how wishful identification and parasocial relationships serve as predictors for consumer purchasing behavior as the mediating variable in the relationship between parasocial relationships and consumer behaviors. We hypothesize as follows:

H1: Viewers' video preferences and social media interactions with the influencer are significantly associated with their parasocial relationships with the influencer.

H2: Viewers' video preference and social media interactions with the influencer are significantly associated with their wishful identification with the influencer.

H3: Viewers' social media interactions, parasocial relationships, and wishful identification with the influencer content are significantly associated with their purchasing behaviors of products recommended by the influencers.

METHOD

Sampling Techniques

With IRB approval, the sample of this study is recruited in collaboration with a real-time YouTube influencer CeciCchen, a Chinese beauty influencer with more than 70k followers (micro-influencer) and currently living in the United States. In her video posted on Jan. 15, 2023, she invited her viewers to participate in a survey that collaborated with the researchers of the study. In return, participants have a chance of winning one of the 20 gift cards of 50 US dollars. A total of 1,213 participants took the survey. After taking out cases with significant missing variables, the final sample size of the study is N=948.

Demographics

Out of the 948 participants, 443 (46.7%) held bachelor's degrees as their highest educational degree, 339 (35.8%) possessed Master's degrees as their highest educational degree, 40 (4.2%) held Doctoral degrees as their highest educational degree, and 34 (3.6%) held high school diplomas as their highest educational degree. In terms of gender distribution, female participants constituted 91.9% of the sample, males made up 0.4%, and 7.7% opted not to disclose their gender. Regarding age demographics, 9.9% of the participants were aged 22 or younger, 56.6% fell within the age bracket of 23 to 30, 29.2% were between 31 and 40, and 4.3% were aged above 40.

Measures

Video Preference. To assess the participants' preference for different types of videos created by the influencer, participants were asked: "How do you like the following categories of videos?" The categories include: "Get Ready With Me Makeup (GRWM)", "Shopping Hauls", "Vlogs Featuring Life Updates", "Favorites", "Festival Shopping Lists such as Sephora 20% off Recommendations", "Skin Care Thematic Series Covering Topics like Beauty Tools Recommendations, Medical Beauty, Brightening, and Hair Care", as well as "Empty Bottle Reviews."

Interactions with the Influencer. For assessing participants' interactions with the YouTuber, a 7-point scale ranging from "1 = never" to "7 = always" was employed across nine items, including "How often do you interact with me using the following method?" - "watch my videos", "rewatch my videos", "comment under my videos", "send live comments", "like my videos", "share my videos on social media", "share my videos through direct messages", "send me direct messages", and "join and communicate with me in my group message" (M = 2.91, SD = 1.02, Cronbach alpha $\alpha = .82$).

Parasocial Relationships. To assess participants' parasocial relationships with the YouTuber, a 7-point scale from "1 = strongly disagree" to "7 = strongly agree" was used on 10 items. The scale is adjusted from the scale developed by Rubin, Perse, and Powell (1985) and Rosaen and Dibble (2016). The items include: "You think I'm dependable when you need me", "Our relationship is like good friends", and "If I were your friend, you would share honestly with me the things about yourself" (M = 5.82, SD = .84, Cronbach alpha $\alpha = .93$).

Wishful Identification. To assess participants' wishful identification with the YouTuber, a 7-point scale from "1 = strongly disagree" to "7 = strongly agree" was used on 5 items, including: "I think Ceci is the kind of guy I want to be." "In some ways, I would like to be more like Ceci." "I wish I could be like Ceci at work." "I wish I could be like Ceci in life." and "In some ways, Ceci is someone I want to emulate." (M = 5.32, SD = 1.19, Cronbach alpha $\alpha = .94$). The scale is adapted from Hoffner and Buchanan (2005).

Purchase Behaviors. To assess participants' purchase behaviors of products recommended by the YouTuber, a 7-point scale was used on 5 items. Participants were asked: "Have you bought anything I recommend in the past year?" and the points include: "1 = Never bought it, never thought about buying it", "2 = I thought about buying it but haven't", "3 = bought one", "4 = Bought 2-3 pieces", "5 = Bought 4-6 pieces", "6 = Bought 7-10 pieces", and "7 = Bought more than 10 pieces". The items include: "clothing", "skincare products", "makeup products", "accessories", and "snacks" (M = 3.14, SD = 1.10, Cronbach alpha $\alpha = .84$).

Control variables. Control variables were employed to enhance comprehension of the association between the endogenous and exogenous variables. The demographic variables of age, gender, education, and income were measured for this purpose.

RESULTS

To test the hypotheses, three multiple linear regression analyses were performed. First, a multiple regression analysis was performed to predict participants' parasocial relationships with the influencer from video preference and interactions with the influencer (see Table 1).

Table 1. Multiple regression analysis predicting parasocial relationship

Predictor		Standardized Coefficients	Std. Error	t-value	p-value
Video Preference	GRWM	.106***	.022	3.748	.000
	Shopping Haul	.116***	.023	4.083	.000
	Vlogs	.229***	.019	8.170	.000
	Favorites	.091**	.032	3.133	.002
	Deals	.019	.021	.698	.485
	Skincare	-.019	.020	-.657	.511
	Makeup Empties	.119***	.023	4.056	.000
Interactions with the Influencer	Watch videos	.068	.011	2.555	.011
	Watch videos repeatedly	.168***	.016	5.607	.000
	Comment	.091**	.019	2.642	.008
	Send bullet screen	.007	.018	.227	.820
	Like videos	.144***	.012	5.025	.000
	Forward my videos to social media	-.049	.022	-1.332	.183
	Forward my videos directly to a friend(s)	.095**	.018	2.708	.007
	Private message	-.044	.032	-1.087	.277
	Communicate in WeChat group	-.059	.032	-1.556	.120

R-squared = 0.46, adjusted R-squared = 0.45.

$F(16, 933) = 50.33$, $p < 0.001$.

Second, a multiple regression analysis was performed to predict participants' wishful identification with the influencer from video preference and interactions with the influencer (see Table 2).

Third, a multiple regression analysis was performed to predict participants' purchase behavior of products recommended by the influencer from interactions with the influencer, parasocial relationships, wishful identification, and control variables, including age, gender, income, and education (see Table 3).

DISCUSSION

Influencers are increasingly becoming a prevalent part of society. The use of influencers as a resource for shaping consumer behaviors is already present throughout advertising and marketing as a whole. In order to efficiently use influencers in shaping consumer behaviors, we must first understand what factors impact the power influencers have over consumers. This study is designed to investigate the impact of YouTube video types on viewer-influencer parasocial relationships and wishful identification. Using data collected in collaboration with a YouTuber from her audience, we have explored how video preference and audience interactions with the influencer serve as predictors for wishful identification and parasocial relationships. Subsequently, we have also determined that income, interactions with the influencer, and parasocial relationships are all significant positive predictors of purchase behaviors.

Table 2. Multiple regression analysis predicting wishful identification

Predictor		Standardized Coefficients	Std. Error	t-value	p-value
Video Preference	GRWM	.030	.036	.929	.353
	Shopping Haul	.068*	.037	2.073	.038
	Vlogs	.203***	.030	6.266	.000
	Favorites	.092**	.053	2.746	.006
	Deals	.069*	.034	2.178	.030
	Skincare	.012	.032	.357	.721
	Makeup Empties	.041	.037	1.207	.228
Interactions with the Influencer	Watch videos	-.024	.017	-.775	.438
	Watch videos repeatedly	.154***	.025	4.477	.000
	Comment	.137**	.031	3.436	.001
	Send bullet screen	.020	.029	.543	.587
	Like videos	.048	.019	1.455	.146
	Forward my videos to social media	-.027	.035	-.645	.519
	Forward my videos directly to a friend(s)	.099*	.030	2.453	.014
	Private message	-.028	.052	-.594	.553
	Communicate in WeChat group	-.016	.052	-.372	.710

Table 2. (Continued)

Note. R-squared = 0.287, adjusted R-squared = 0.275.
F(16, 933) = 23.46, p < 0.001.

Table 3. Multiple regression analysis predicting purchase behaviors

Predictor	Standardized Coefficients	Std. Error	t-Value	p-Value
Gender	-.009	.282	-.309	.757
Education	-.028	.054	-.945	.345
Income	.304***	.019	10.234	.000
Interactions with the Influencer	.362***	.044	11.244	.000
Parasocial Relationship	.146***	.066	3.785	.000
Wishful Identification	.056	.045	1.481	.139

Note. R-squared = 0.31, adjusted R-squared = 0.30.
F(6, 865) = 63.64, p < 0.001.

To begin with, results showed that viewer interaction with content was a predictor of parasocial relationships and wishful identification. Interactions that were a positive predictor of parasocial relationships included commenting, watching videos repeatedly, and liking videos. Watching videos repeatedly, commenting, and forwarding videos were positive predictors for wishful identification. For influencers, this information can be a powerful tool in increasing overall engagement and viewer retention. By noting which content receives an increased frequency of these forms of viewer engagement, influencers can possibly track which forms of content best foster parasocial relationships and thus improve audience perceived trust and credibility in the influencer (Le & Hancer, 2021).

Being able to shape audience perception influencers can be a stronger tool for shaping audience purchasing behaviors. Using this information can also benefit advertisers, who can research possible influencers' comments and likes on videos prior to creating a partnership. By viewing these forms of engagement advertisers can create partnerships in which the influencer is more likely to have created a parasocial relationship with their audience and thus have created trust, a predictor for consumer brand loyalty (Labrecque, 2014). Our study also found that viewer parasocial relationships with the influencer had no significant effect on watching videos, sending bullet screens, or forwarding videos. This could mean that these forms of engagement analytics should not be solely relied upon by advertisers when choosing what influencers to partner with for branded content interactions.

Next, our results found that the types of videos that viewers watched were a positive predictor of viewer parasocial relationships with the influencer. Participants who reported watching vlogs had a moderate positive correlation with parasocial relationships and wishful identification. Watching shopping hauls, makeup empties, and favorite videos all were weak positive predictors of parasocial relationships. In addition, watching shopping hauls, favorites, and deals videos also had a weak positive correlation with wishful identification. These results support that different forms of video content created by influencers can foster the creation of parasocial relationships (Bi & Zhang, 2022). Content that supports the viewer's perception of influencer trustworthiness, such as vlogs, as opposed to product advertisements is also likely to be more effective at building a parasocial relationship (Chekima, Chekima, & Adis, 2020). Advertisers should use this information when deciding which influencers to partner with for ad content or paid product placements in videos, as influencers who create certain content such as vlogs, may have more influence on consumer purchasing behaviors. As similarity with viewers can strengthen the creation of parasocial relationships with the influencer, this supports prior findings that viewers who watch vlogs want to be more like the influencers they are viewing (Yuan & Lou, 2020). As vlogs are content that shows the influencer living their daily life, this may allow the viewer to perceive the influencer as more relatable and therefore more of a person that the viewer wishes to imitate.

Finally, our results show that viewer income, interactions with the influencer, and parasocial relationships with the influencer all were positive predictors of viewer purchasing behaviors. These results are supported by prior research by Hwang and Zhang (2018) which found that parasocial relationships moderated the relationship between viewer understanding of influencer persuasion and purchasing behavior. As these results showed that parasocial relationships are predictive of audience purchasing behaviors, this should be a factor that brands look at prior to partnering with an influencer. It may be more beneficial for a brand to partner with a smaller influencer who has cultivated an audience with a stronger parasocial relationship and high frequency of viewer interactions with the influencer, as opposed to a larger influencer with more viewers but less viewer interactions and a weaker relationship with the influencer. Income was also a predictor of audience purchase behaviors. Advertisers should take care to match the price point of the product they are pairing with an influencer in order to ensure that the audience income demographic has a higher likelihood of purchasing the product.

THEORETICAL AND MANAGERIAL IMPLICATIONS

This research is among the first empirical studies completed exploring the effects of wishful identification and parasocial relationships on purchase intention in influencer viewing audiences. The study is unique in that it has a large sample size gathered from a singular individual audience. By recruiting participants directly from an influencer's viewing audience, we are able to see how a single influencer's content creation affects their audience and what markers in audience interactions are predictive of consumer behaviors. This large sample from one influencer helps contribute to the literature on social media influencers as a whole as well as the use of beauty micro-influencers specifically. The findings in this research offer relevant theoretical contributions to influencer marketing.

This research highlights different forms of influencer content from a beauty influencer that have different impacts on viewer parasocial relationships and wishful identification as well as purchase intention. This can be used by markets to target which time of content from influencers is most likely to impact viewer purchase intention. The study also highlights that beauty vloggers in particular can be used as a marketing tool and they do effectively impact viewer purchase intention. This cross-cultural study also allows for the application across a wider viewing audience.

LIMITATIONS AND SUGGESTIONS FOR FUTURE RESEARCH

This study is limited in scope due to the data having been collected through convenience sampling via a self-report online questionnaire. This could have resulted in a sampling error or external validity issues. Secondly, this study was done in collaboration with an influencer whose content is largely beauty and fashion-related YouTube videos. Future research could be conducted looking at influencers who showcase content on a variety of other platforms including but not limited to Instagram, TikTok, or Facebook. In addition, future researchers are encouraged to conduct studies expanding the relationship between influencer video content and consumer behaviors in other markets such as travel or technology. Future researchers are also encouraged to complete longitudinal studies surveying the same viewers across time to see how their long-term viewing habits affect their consumer purchasing behaviors.

CONCLUSION

Influencers wield the power to affect consumer behavior. Factors of wishful identification and parasocial relationships can have a positive effect on audiences of micro-influencers. The unique ability to interact with influencer content and viewer preferences of videos impact these factors. Their position in modern communication strategies cannot be understated or left unknown. By being able to understand the factors that allow influencers to affect consumer behavior, and how to strengthen those factors influencers can more effectively be used in brand strategies. By improving and strengthening audience wishful identification and parasocial relationships with an influencer, brands can more effectively shape trust in brands and overall consumer behaviors.

REFERENCES

Bi, N. C., Zhang, R., & Ha, L. (2019). Does valence of product review matter? The mediating role of self-effect and third-person effect in sharing YouTube word-of-mouth (vWOM). *Journal of Research in Interactive Marketing*, *13*(1), 79–95. doi:10.1108/JRIM-04-2018-0049

Bond, B. J. (2021). The development and influence of parasocial relationships with television characters: A longitudinal experimental test of prejudice reduction through parasocial contact. *Communication Research*, *48*(4), 573–593. doi:10.1177/0093650219900632

Bond, B. J., & Drogos, K. L. (2014). Sex on the shore: Wishful identification and parasocial relationships as mediators in the relationship between Jersey Shore exposure and emerging adults' sexual attitudes and behaviors. *Media Psychology*, *17*(1), 102–126. doi:10.1080/15213269.2013.872039

Bui, M. T., Tran, T. T. H., Phi, H. M., Nguyen, N. D., Nguyen, T. T. M., & Pham, T. L. (2021). Impact of digital celebrities on their followers' purchase intention: Roles of wishful identification, parasocial relationship, and behavioral loyalty. In *2nd International Conference on Human-Centered Artificial Intelligence, Computing4Human* (pp. 191-198). Academic Press.

Burke, K. E. (2017). *Social butterflies: How social media influencers are the new celebrity endorsement* (Doctoral dissertation, Virginia Tech).

Burns, K. S. (2021). The history of social media influencers. *Research perspectives on social media influencers and brand communication*, 1-22.

Campbell, C., & Farrell, J. R. (2020). More than meets the eye: The functional components underlying influencer marketing. *Business Horizons*, *63*(4), 469–479. doi:10.1016/j.bushor.2020.03.003

Chekima, B., Chekima, F. Z., & Adis, A. A. A. (2020). Social media influencer in advertising: The role of attractiveness, expertise and trustworthiness. *Journal of Economics and Business*, *3*(4). Advance online publication. doi:10.31014/aior.1992.03.04.298

De Veirman, M., Cauberghe, V., & Hudders, L. (2017). Marketing through instagram influencers: The impact of number of followers and product divergence on brand attitude. *International Journal of Advertising*, *36*(5), 798–828. doi:10.1080/02650487.2017.1348035

Dibble, J. L., Hartmann, T., & Rosaen, S. F. (2016). Parasocial interaction and parasocial relationship: Conceptual clarification and a critical assessment of measures. *Human Communication Research*, *42*(1), 21–44. doi:10.1111/hcre.12063

Domingues Aguiar, T., & van Reijmersdal, E. (2018). *Influencer marketing. Amsterdam Stichting Wetenschappelijk Onderzoek Commerciële Communicatie*. SWOCC.

Enke, N., & Borchers, N. S. (2021). Social media influencers in strategic communication: A conceptual framework for strategic social media influencer communication. In *Social media influencers in strategic communication* (pp. 7-23). Routledge. https://www.cmgt.uni-leipzig.de/projekte/influencer/, May 20, 2019.

Erdogan, B. Z. (1999). Celebrity endorsement: A literature review. *Journal of Marketing Management*, *15*(4), 291–314. doi:10.1362/026725799784870379

Feilitzen, C., & Linne, O. (1975). Identifying with television characters. *Journal of Communication, 24*(4), 51–55. doi:10.1111/j.1460-2466.1975.tb00638.x PMID:1176636

Giles, D. C. (2002). Parasocial interaction: A review of the literature and a model for future research. *Media Psychology, 4*(3), 279–305. doi:10.1207/S1532785XMEP0403_04

Gräve, J. F., & Bartsch, F. (2022). # Instafame: Exploring the endorsement effectiveness of influencers compared to celebrities. *International Journal of Advertising, 41*(4), 591–622. doi:10.1080/02650487.2021.1987041

Hernández-Méndez, J., & Baute-Díaz, N. (2023). Influencer marketing in the promotion of tourist destinations: Mega, macro and micro-influencers. *Current Issues in Tourism*, 1–11. doi:10.1080/13683500.2023.2214354

Hoffner, C., & Buchanan, M. (2005). Young adults' wishful identification with television characters: The role of perceived similarity and character attributes. *Media Psychology, 7*(4), 325–351. doi:10.1207/S1532785XMEP0704_2

Isyanto, P., Sapitri, R. G., & Sinaga, O. (2020). Micro influencers marketing and brand image to purchase intention of cosmetic products focallure. *Systematic Reviews in Pharmacy, 11*(1), 601–605.

Khan, M. L., & Malik, A. (2022). Researching YouTube: Methods, tools, and analytics. The Sage Handbook of Social Media Research Methods, 651-663.

Leung, F. F., Gu, F. F., & Palmatier, R. W. (2022). Online influencer marketing. *Journal of the Academy of Marketing Science, 50*(2), 226–251. doi:10.1007/s11747-021-00829-4

Lim, J. S., Choe, M. J., Zhang, J., & Noh, G. Y. (2020). The role of wishful identification, emotional engagement, and parasocial relationships in repeated viewing of live-streaming games: A social cognitive theory perspective. *Computers in Human Behavior, 108*, 106327. doi:10.1016/j.chb.2020.106327

Men, L. R., & Tsai, W. H. S. (2012). How companies cultivate relationships with publics on social network sites: Evidence from China and the United States. *Public Relations Review, 38*(5), 723–730. doi:10.1016/j.pubrev.2011.10.006

Nair, P., Rajesh, G., & Singh, A. K. Multiple facets of celebrity brand endorsement. (2019) *Sustainable Resource Management through Innovative Management Practices*, 65.

Nan, M., & Park, J. S. (2018). Effects of beauty vloggers' parasocial interaction on Chinese consumers' attitudes toward vlogs and the products. *The Research Journal of the Costume Culture, 26*(5), 649–664. doi:10.29049/rjcc.2018.26.5.649

Piehler, R., Schade, M., Sinnig, J., & Burmann, C. (2022). Traditional or 'instafamous' celebrity? Role of origin of fame in social media influencer marketing. *Journal of Strategic Marketing, 30*(4), 408–420. doi:10.1080/0965254X.2021.1909107

Schouten, A. P., Janssen, L., & Verspaget, M. (2021). Celebrity vs. Influencer endorsements in advertising: the role of identification, credibility, and Product-Endorser fit. Leveraged Marketing Communications, 208-231.

Segrave, K. (2015). *Endorsements in advertising: A social history*. McFarland.

Shareef, M. A., Mukerji, B., Dwivedi, Y. K., Rana, N. P., & Islam, R. (2019). Social media marketing: Comparative effect of advertisement sources. *Journal of Retailing and Consumer Services*, *46*, 58–69. doi:10.1016/j.jretconser.2017.11.001

Shoenberger, H., & Kim, E. (2019). Product placement as leveraged marketing communications: The role of wishful identification, brand trust, and brand buying behaviours. *International Journal of Advertising*, *38*(1), 50–66. doi:10.1080/02650487.2017.1391678

Sliburyte, L. (2009). How celebrities can be used in advertising to the best advantage? *World Academy of Science, Engineering and Technology*, *58*, 934–939.

Sokolova, K., & Perez, C. (2021). You follow fitness influencers on YouTube. But do you actually exercise? How parasocial relationships, and watching fitness influencers, relate to intentions to exercise. *Journal of Retailing and Consumer Services*, *58*, 102276. doi:10.1016/j.jretconser.2020.102276

Su, B. C., Wu, L. W., Chang, Y. Y. C., & Hong, R. H. (2021). Influencers on social media as References: Understanding the Importance of Parasocial Relationships. *Sustainability (Basel)*, *13*(19), 10919. doi:10.3390/su131910919

Tolbert, A. N., & Drogos, K. L. (2019). Tweens' wishful identification and parasocial relationships with YouTubers. *Frontiers in Psychology*, *10*, 2781. doi:10.3389/fpsyg.2019.02781 PMID:31920829

Wellman, M. L., Stoldt, R., Tully, M., & Ekdale, B. (2020). Ethics of authenticity: Social media influencers and the production of sponsored content. *Journal of Medical Ethics*, *35*(2), 68–82. doi:10.1080/23736992.2020.1736078

Yang, Y. (2022). TikTok/Douyin use and its influencer video use: A cross-cultural comparison between Chinese and US users. *Online Media and Global Communication*, *1*(2), 339–368. doi:10.1515/omgc-2022-0016

Yesiloglu, S., & Costello, J. (Eds.). (2020). *Influencer marketing: building brand communities and engagement*. Routledge. doi:10.4324/9780429322501

Yuan, S., & Lou, C. (2020). How social media influencers foster relationships with followers: The roles of source credibility and fairness in parasocial relationship and product interest. *Journal of Interactive Advertising*, *20*(2), 133–147. doi:10.1080/15252019.2020.1769514

KEY TERMS AND DEFINITIONS

Digital Media: Any form of communication media spread via technical interface.

Influencers: A person who is able to influence an audience via social media.

Parasocial Relationships: A one-sided relationship in which one person exerts time, interest, and emotional energy onto a public figure that they do not know nor have a mutual relationship with.

Purchase Intentions: The likelihood that a person will purchase a good or service.

Social Media: A mode of interactive technology that allows users to create and share content across a social network.

Vlogs: Regularly posted video content posted on a public social media platform that is non-scripted and traditionally in video blog/log formatting.

Wishful Identification: A person's aspiration to behave as or become a character or public figure.

Chapter 12
Beyond the Borders:
Fashion Influencers Shaping Global Trends

Poornima Nair
https://orcid.org/0000-0001-9259-291X
Christ University, India

Sunita Kumar
https://orcid.org/0000-0002-0628-1873
Christ University, India

ABSTRACT

Social media has emerged as a powerful platform that revolutionized the way the fashion industry operates. Fashion influencers have significantly impacted global consumer trends and brand perceptions with their large followings and engaging content. This chapter investigated the ways in which fashion influencers leverage social media platforms to shape consumer behavior, promote sustainable fashion practices, and bridge cultural boundaries to create a more inclusive fashion community across borders. This chapter has contributed to a better understanding of fashion beyond borders, social media influencers' role in transforming the fashion landscape, and their potential to influence positive change in the industry by conducting a comprehensive literature review. This chapter explores social media influencers' multifaceted roles in redefining fashion globally.

INTRODUCTION

Very few sectors in global commerce can bring together the creativity, innovation, and culture of various countries and, of course, trade the way the fashion industry can in a very effortless manner. The fashion industry is one of the oldest and biggest export sectors (Gereffi, 1999). The industry is not just an amalgamation of fabrics, designs, and trends but also a perfect blend of culture, consumer societal aspirations, and a powerful means of self-expression. Fashion as a sector operates beyond boundaries, brings together people from various cultural backgrounds and constantly evolves to cater to customers' ever-changing requirements. Fashion drives a considerable portion of the global economy, one of the

DOI: 10.4018/979-8-3693-0912-4.ch012

most crucial sectors in the international economy. When considered in conjunction with the GDP of individual nations, the global fashion industry stands as the seventh largest economy globally (Amed et al., 2017). According to reports, the global apparel market generated 1.53 trillion dollars in revenue in 2022—a marginal decline from the year before. Nonetheless, revenue was predicted to rise to more than 1.7 trillion dollars in 2023 (Smith, 2023). In 2024, the fashion industry is anticipated to generate US$760.00 billion. It is projected that by 2028, there will be 2.9 billion users in the fashion market. The percentage of users will be 35.9% in 2024 and rise to 40.5% by 2028 (Statista,2023). The global fashion business has reached an evolutionary phase as an outcome of the digital age: rewriting the norms of engagement between companies and customers. Social media sites have evolved into virtual platforms where a global network of fashion aficionados not only follow the latest trends but also co-create them in addition to leading designers showcasing them. Pinterest, Instagram, etc., have developed into powerful catalysts that have brought fashion from the exclusive world of elite runways to the hands of the global population. Authentic, accessible content is becoming increasingly popular as fashion influencers, with their capacity to shape trends and influence purchase decisions, take center stage in the style world. The traditional retail industry is going through a digital transformation. "Fashion knowledge" is knowledge of a specific geography, which may or may not coincide with industrial production and retail locational geography (Weller, 2007). User-generated content (UGC), which is distinguished by relatability and authenticity, was made possible by the emergence of social media. It should come as no surprise that user-generated content (UGC) is more engaging and popular than platform-generated content (PGC), generating twice as much activity. User-generated content (UGC) will remain the most popular form of content consumption as more individuals use various social media platforms (Kumar, 2023). Since everyone has a different opinion about desirable or fashionable fashion items, the fashion market is primarily driven by material objects like shirts and skirts. However, fashion is also a very volatile and subjective field of study, and trends often come and go quickly due to wear and tear and shifting consumer preferences (Poorthuis et al., 2019).

The ease of purchasing from home for customers and the global platform that e-commerce companies offer manufacturers to display their products have made them into thriving marketplaces. Technology integration has transformed shopping experiences completely dependent on the traditional brick-and-mortar retail experience into a more engaging shopping space. Augmented reality, virtual fitting rooms, and customized shopping encounters are revolutionizing how customers engage with and perceive fashion.

The emergence of influencers as trendsetters is a transformational force altering the landscape of style and personal expression in the dynamic center of global fashion brands. In a time when digital platforms have replaced physical runways worldwide, influencers have a significant impact and can affect the rise and fall of fashion trends globally. This chapter provides insight into influencers' key role in the global fashion sector as vanguards of style. In the chapter, we will traverse digital spaces where fashion stories are being created in real-time as we delve into this examination of influencers as trendsetters. The global fashion industry and influencers are co-creating to redefine the fundamental principles of fashion conception, communication, and consumption globally and influence consumer preferences. There exists a confluence of fashion and influence, where the ability to create trends lies not only in the hands, or rather, on the screens, of well-known designers but also in the influencers who fascinate audiences and shape the ever-changing language of style.

The primary goal of this study is to examine how social media influencers affect consumer preferences and fashion trends across the globe. It will examine influencers' techniques to connect with audiences from different cultural backgrounds. The study assesses how social media has changed the global fashion community's efforts to promote inclusivity. This entails examining how influencers support a wider range of body shapes and fashion preferences while considering the potential and problems that social media pose for fostering a welcoming and culturally aware fashion industry. The study hopes to thoroughly understand influencers' complex role in constructing global fashion narratives by achieving these goals.

SOCIAL MEDIA AND THE FASHION INDUSTRY

Social media has become a trendsetter in the modern digital age as individuals spend more time online (Chu & Seock, 2020). With over half of everyone on the planet using social media, social media use is growing in popularity worldwide (Lakhan et al., 2023). Social media is an effective instrument for disseminating messages (Mason et al., 2021). Customers are product information providers and advocates in social commerce (Lamberton & Stephen, 2016). During the new normal, the number of social media users increased by up to 40% (Sinelnikov, 2022). Online purchasing has made Comparing products easier, allowing customers to quickly select the ones that best suit their needs (Mason et al., 2021). Consumers use social media to search for relevant information to help them make purchase decisions (Lu et al., 2016) and disseminate information based on their experiences and personal choices through social media (Kim & Kim, 2021). Because they are more inclined to shop through social media, young customers have primarily migrated to online shopping, which impacts how firms must function (Shopify,2021). Because social media participation is not confined to actual meetings, users have access to more chances for online participation (Lin & Kant, 2021). Fashion is one of the most important objects people use to convey their values and develop their self-image (Weismueller et al., 2020). Today's consumers get their information mostly from social media platforms, which are also one of the most effective marketing tools for the fashion industry (Chu & Seock, 2020). Social media influencers significantly influence their followers' choices (Hudders et al., 2020).

One of the major industries in the world, fashion drives a sizeable portion of the world economy. It is a vital industry that adds value to the global economy (Karl,2017). The apparel market includes all categories of clothing, spanning business and sportswear, as well as affordable and luxurious items. Fashion is multifaceted and difficult to understand. It can have a materialistic quality, particularly in relation to what covers the human body, but it can also have a symbolic quality, such as influencing how someone defines themselves (Orminski et al., 2020). The Internet is available almost everywhere thanks to the growing adoption and dissemination of technology, including smartphones and laptops, which has elevated how fashion is marketed to and purchased by customers (Barnes & Lea-Greenwood, 2006).

Due to the fierce competition and quick expansion of the fashion business, influencer marketing is becoming more popular on social media sites like Instagram (Tiwari et al., 2023; Handrimurtjahjo et al.). Influencers greatly impact how people dress, especially younger shoppers (Han et al.,2023). Consumers ' sentiments toward influencers positively impact purchase intentions and brand perceptions (Kondort et al., 2023). Consumer perceptions toward fashion influencers are influenced by various factors, including subjective norms, perceived behavioral control, and perceived trust (Saleem, 2023). Brand attachment, consumer happiness, and purchase intention are significantly impacted by the attributes of fashion influencers, including knowledge, attractiveness, and dependability. On the other hand, word-of-mouth and purchase intentions are not influenced directly by competence. Businesses must comprehend how consumers view Instagram fashion influencers to create successful digital strategies and cultivate enduring customer relationships.

INFLUENCERS AND THE FASHION INDUSTRY

Influencer marketing is the process by which well-known social media users work with brands to promote the brands' goods and services. Brands use influencer marketing because it benefits influencers, consumers, and brands themselves. (Mckinsey, 2023). Influencers on social media have grown in importance, especially for younger audiences, since they educate people on various subjects and even take stances on issues related to politics and society (Peter & Muth, 2023). Through their self-generated content and online interactions, these influencers significantly affect consumers' purchasing decisions and establish emotional connections with their followers (Zhang & Mac, 2023). Ads or content from social media influencers have been regarded as more reliable than those from celebrities or production companies (Ki et al., 2020). As a result, influencer advertisements receive more likes and comments (Lou & Yuan, 2019).

Additionally, they include product recommendations in their daily lives, which may impact their followers' future purchases (Zheng et al., 2023). Influencers on social media are significant in determining how customers interact with brands and how satisfied and favorable they perceive them to be (Nuji et al., 2023). Companies have discovered the benefits of social media influencers for cultivating direct connections with customers, boosting recognition of their brands, and fostering brand loyalty (P. Kumar et al., 2023). In terms of information distribution and consumer behavior, social media influencers have a significant overall impact on social media users. Influencers are outside parties engaged by the brands because they have the power to influence or impact the consumers' purchase decisions (Brown & Hayes, 2008). Influencers give their audience access to sources of information and creativity (Belanche et al., 2021). They indirectly create a chain reaction of influence through their followers and significantly impact a huge number of customers through their actions (De Veirman et al., 2017). Social media influencers (SMIs) are used by marketers on both a global and a local level (Ghosh & Islam, 2023). However, (Boerman 2020) classified social media users under three different categories of social media influencers based on the number of followers they have, from fewest to most: micro-influencers are those influencers that have less than 10,000 followers, Influencers who have between 10,000–1,000,000 followers are classified as meso-influencers, and macro-influencers are those influencers who have more than 1,000,000 followers. This classification helps brands find the best partners to meet their needs. An influencer's generated content includes sponsored and organic posts (Yalcin et al., 2021). Using social media influencers to promote items and boost a brand's online presence is known as sponsored content (Wibisono & Ruldeviyani, 2021). Although it may seem like corporations only want to collaborate with mega influencers, doing so isn't always the best course of action. Compared to their macro counterparts, who use a variety of advisers, including stylists, makeup artists, and professional photographers, to put together a post, micro-influencers may provide more relatable content. Conversely, micro-influencers can represent accessibility to their followers, whereas macro-influencers might promote a lifestyle many find unachievable. Working with macro influencers has clear advantages: their large followings enable marketers to reach hundreds of thousands or even millions of people (Mckinsey,2023).

Influencers, in contrast to traditional marketers, use electronic word-of-mouth, or E-WOM, to communicate with customers in an omnidirectional manner using social media (Yalcin et al., 2021). As a result of their expertise, the information they share will be useful to other people (Kim et al., 2020). Influencers typically form a partnership with their followers where their reputation is completely based on the content they publish and the engagement they have with them (Hu et al., 2020). Influencers concentrate on a more specifically defined audience that shares common interests and where they act as their online buddy (Belanche et al., 2021). After more than tripling in value from 2019 to 2023, the worldwide influencer marketing market was valued at 21.1 billion US dollars. Collaborations between brands and creators are now more profitable than ever because of the maturity of the influencer endorsement industry and the scale and worth of influencer marketing platforms, which are growing yearly (Statista,2023). Numerous brands depend extensively on social media influencers to endorse products, provide links to online stores, and use their corporate SNS pages to showcase new products and announce special promotions (Evans et al., 2017). Social media fashion influencers are people whose followers highly trust and connect with them because of their high credibility (Jin & Ryu, 2019; Lou & Yuan, 2018). SMIs are people who consistently express their opinions on their choice of social media channels and actively create material (such as texts, photos, and videos). Large social media audiences quickly absorb and follow these communications (Sun et al., 2021).

GLOBAL FASHION INDUSTRY AND INFLUENCER MARKETING

The apparel market includes every type of clothing, including business and sportswear, and affordable and luxurious items. With their significantly greater revenue generation rates, China and the United States make up the majority of this apparel demand (Smith, 2022). Influencer marketing is one of the most well-liked and successful online marketing strategies. It is hardly surprising that marketers are utilizing the influence of social media's most famous faces for advertising, given the millions of people who use social media platforms every day for inspiration, amusement, and product suggestions. As of 2023, the value of the worldwide influencer marketing market has more than tripled from 2019 to 21.1 billion US dollars (Dencheva,2023). The market for digital advertising expanded further, but more significantly, influencer marketing became the primary component of digital marketing. The days of marketing strategies focused on brands are long gone. The time has come for a more customer-centric strategy, especially as consumers are now more astute and favor companies that market their goods and/ or services by solving problems for them (Dadia,2022).

Today's consumers find information about products on social media, particularly by looking for posts from influencers recommending particular products. The necessity for brands to promote their products through viral and non-disruptive social media advertisements became apparent as the media landscape became more fragmented (De Veirman et al., 2017). A relevant example of the successful use of influencers, even by well-established brands, is to promote the debut of their new fragrance line, Gucci Bloom, the Italian fashion label Gucci, used influencer marketing in 2019. To produce incredibly imaginative content that reflects the artistic interpretation of the flowery universe surrounding the scent, Gucci teamed up with 23 artists on Instagram. 135 pieces of content were produced for the campaign, reaching around 750,000 followers and generating a great deal of awareness. Even their website and Facebook channel featured part of the content that was produced (Haenlein et al., 2020). But before engaging in any form of marketing by using influencers to promote their brands, managers need to understand and recognize that each Platform has a different user culture and language. Initially, businesses must choose the social media channels they wish to use with careful consideration. Additionally, before establishing their own presence, businesses must comprehend the user, and this comprehension takes time to build. Furthermore, companies must provide customers with an incentive to interact with them. Having a well-known brand alone might not always be sufficient (Haenlein et al., 2020). The influencer marketing campaign's goal should guide the decision-making process. Big influencers are the best choice for national or international brands looking to raise awareness of a new product. These accounts not only guarantee enough reach but also enable the company to be associated with a face that is immediately recognizable. On the other hand, smaller influencers might be a better option if a client's primary concerns are reaching an audience in a certain geographic area (e.g., national brands, local chains only available in some areas) or intending to create extremely relatable material (Haenlein et al., 2020).

GLOBAL FASHION TRENDS

At the center of rapidly evolving consumer products lies the dynamic fashion industry. The fashion industry encompasses more than just the design and style of apparel, accessories, and shoes. It also involves the production, supply, distribution, and sales of these products, all backed by a global network of manufacturers and workers in the retail and manufacturing sectors of the business. Unquestionably, the fashion industry has influenced people's lives worldwide. Since retail e-commerce sales have reached trillions of dollars globally, it is not surprising that the fashion e-commerce market is expanding annually (Staista, 2023). Fashion trends may spread quickly around the world thanks to influencers and the reach and immediacy of internet platforms. A browse through an influencer's Instagram feed provides a curated look into the newest trends in fashion, transforming it into a virtual tour of style. By bridging the gap between high-end clothing brands and the general public, these tastemakers democratize trends and make them approachable to a wider range of people. The fashion industry is the largest B2C eCommerce sector, with a projected worldwide market value of US$768.7 billion in 2023. By the end of 2027, it is anticipated that the market is expected to grow by 9.4% yearly to a total value of US$1,103.1 billion. In 2024, the fashion industry is expected to generate $746.80 billion in revenue. It is estimated that there will be 2.7 billion users in the fashion market by 2028, and the user penetration is predicted to reach 37.8%, up from 34.8% in the year 2024 (Statista,2023).

FASHION TREND ADOPTION PROCESS

Essentially, a fashion trend emerges from the creative ideas of designers who present fresh looks and the influencers who spread the latest fashion via various channels, including social media. These highly influential trailblazers serve as the initial sparks that ignite the adoption cascade. Various Communication channels and social media are crucial in enhancing these trends. Trends are quickly brought to the public's attention by disseminating information and images through fashion publications, websites, and social media platforms. Particularly, social media has become a democratizing force, enabling people to share their findings and styles, and so adding to the viral character of trend adoption.

The process by which a new style becomes popular among consumers once it is introduced to the market is known as fashion adoption (Forsythe et al., 1991). Adopting a fashion essentially refers to its gradual acceptance through several phases (Goldsmith & Flynn, 1992). Consumer behavior, technological breakthroughs, and social causes are some variables that impact the adoption of fashion trends.

Research indicates that when buyers relate to the social reason connected to a fashion product, they are more inclined to follow a trend (Mohr et al., 2021). Additionally, customers' intention to readily embrace new clothes fashion is influenced by aspects such as status, opinion leadership, and fashion involvement (Rahman et al., 2014). Social communication is the most effective means of spreading fashion (Goldsmith & Clark, 2008).

Furthermore, the adoption curve is heavily influenced by economic variables. Consumer preferences may shift toward classic and timeless styles during economic downturns, while they may embrace experimentation during economic upturns. Adoption is accelerated even more by rapid fashion and savvy retail techniques. Consumers may easily interact with the newest trends because of affordable prices and short manufacturing cycles, which promote a culture of continuous renewal. The diverse array of fashion trends is further enriched by seasonal variations, cultural influences, etc., rendering trend adoption a manifestation of personal expression and societal dynamics. Adopting fashion trends is an intriguing combination of communication, creativity, and cultural resonance that defines the constantly changing field of personal style.

CUSTOMER ENGAGEMENT

Customer engagement involves continuous interaction with the customers through dialogue and enabling and enhancing experiences that support the customers in a way that guides them to make optimal purchase decisions (Brodie et al., 2011). Beyond transactions, customer engagement behavior can be more accurately described as a consumer's behavioral expressions that are driven by a brand or organization and go beyond actual purchases (Van Doorn et al., 2010). Customer engagement is known as positive consumer motivation to engage with a brand through various channels, including social media interaction, brand referrals, and promotional activity participation (Eigenraa, 2023). A consumer-based taxonomy of digital engagement strategies has been developed as a result of the considerable attention it has received from academics and marketers alike (Kaur et al., 2023). Authentic brand interaction initiatives typically receive a more favorable response from consumers (Karunakaran & Raveendran, 2018). The notion of customer interaction has changed from classic marketing ideas and now takes several different forms. One way to define it is how deeply a person connects and participates in the services and events offered by an organization. Customers' participation and involvement are the antecedents of customer engagement; value, trust, and loyalty are a few of the outcomes. In an increasingly networked culture, client involvement is seen as a significant advancement in customer management. Providing customer ratings, blogging, WOM, and other activities are examples of various behaviors that make up customer engagement (Verhoef et al., 2010). Customer engagement is a behavior that extends beyond the purely transactional process and enables customers to contribute to a company's brand voluntarily (Jaakkola & Alexander, 2014). Engaging customers is one of the ways by which they contribute value to the business, either directly or indirectly (Pansari & Kumar, 2017).

BRAND ENGAGEMENT THROUGH CO-CREATION

Establishing a link between brands and their audiences through co-creation is a dynamic and cooperative approach to brand engagement. Co-creation takes place when customers, stakeholders, or communities actively participate in creating and developing new products, services, or brands. This strategy develops a sense of shared value, ownership, and cooperation as a supplement to traditional marketing. Co-creation fosters and promotes collective creativity. Brands may use a wide variety of viewpoints by asking customers to provide ideas, thoughts, and comments. Including customers in the creation process gives them a sense of empowerment and ownership over the finished good or experience. Brands may provide customized interactions tailored to their audience's interests through co-creation. Through collaborative efforts, brands can get insight into the distinct demands of consumers and customize their offerings, thereby improving customer satisfaction and loyalty. Customers have a better overall brand experience when they participate in co-creation. This engagement creates an ongoing conversation that extends beyond the moment of purchase. Brands can actively engage their audience in designing the complete customer journey through various channels such as focus groups, internet platforms, and collaborative events. Because brands engage in genuine partnerships with their audience, co-creation fosters authenticity. Co-creation connects customers with similar interests and beliefs to create a sense of community. This community, which is often made possible by social media and internet platforms, develops into an invaluable partner for the company and promotes it through word-of-mouth advertising and natural expansion. Engaging consumers in the co-creation process helps brands become more flexible and agile. Their ability to promptly adapt to dynamic market conditions, developing patterns, and evolving customer inclinations guarantees that their products and services are relevant and desirable.

Therefore, fashion brands can reach specifically targeted audiences who regularly follow fashion influencers and view their words and opinions as more trustworthy than fashion brands' promotion of their products, even though fashion brands typically have more Instagram followers than fashion influencers (Jin et al., 2019). By asking influencers to market their products to customers who already support their image or point of view, brands may take advantage of these strong connections (Rakuten, 2019).

However, engaging social media fashion influencers is pivotal in brands' social media marketing strategy in today's scenario (De Veirman et al., 2016). Social media platforms influence fashion trends and consumer behavior (Cao et al., 2021). The use of social media influencers to endorse companies and impact consumers' intention to buy has steadily risen in popularity (Delbaere et al., 2020). Consumers regard social media influencers' product reviews as trustworthy and relatable because they frequently integrate them into their personal lives (Schouten et al., 2020). A thorough review of the literature of previous researchers listed four popular categories of social media influencers: 1) social media influencers who act as advertisers for luxury brands, 2) opinion leaders and their followers, who seem to have a significant impact on customers' behavior, 3) friends and peers, and 4) celebrity endorsers (Sun et al., 2021). During the Covid period, there was another category of influencers identified as "Homefluencers", who are SMI's who stay home adhering to social distancing and creating content at home to connect with their followers (Ghosh, 2021) irrespective of the type of influencer during and post covid influencers have gained a larger platform and expanded base of audience across the globe.

RELATIONAL DIMENSIONS

Building and sustaining deep relationships between influencers, brands, and customers is referred to as the relational dimension in the context of fashion influencers. This relationship-building component is essential for obtaining feedback, marketing on social media, fostering co-creation with customers, boosting customer engagement, and helping to spread international fashion trends.

Figure 1. Relational dimension

"Beyond the Borders: Fashion Influencers Shaping Global Trends" is a concept that highlights the transformative impact of fashion influencers transcending geographical boundaries, shaping global trends through various means, particularly focusing on customer engagement, fashion trend adoption, feedback mechanisms, co-creation with consumers, and the pivotal role of social media.

Customer Engagement: This refers to the interaction and involvement of customers with a brand or influencer. In the context of fashion influencers, it involves creating content, fostering dialogues, and forming relationships with followers to understand their preferences and needs. Fashion influencers foster a sense of relatability and trust by frequently forming a personal connection with those who follow them. Through active engagement, marketers may use this pre-existing relationship with influencers, enhancing their marketing initiatives' authenticity and consumer appeal. By utilizing the influencer's familiarity with their audience, the relational component contributes to an increase in customer engagement.

Fashion Trend Adoption: Influencers play a significant role in setting and popularizing fashion trends. They introduce new styles, designs, and concepts to their audience, influencing their followers' preferences and consumption patterns. Influencers have the ability to establish and disseminate international fashion trends among their followers through their interpersonal relationships. The mutual trust these partnerships foster encourages followers to be more receptive to trends that influencers support, which helps fashion trends spread worldwide.

Feedback Mechanisms: Fashion influencers often rely on feedback from their audience to understand their tastes and preferences. They may use polls, comments, or surveys to gather insights, which in turn help them tailor content and endorse products that resonate with their followers. The relational dimension makes a constant feedback loop between influencers, brands, and customers possible. Influencers in fashion serve as go-betweens, communicating consumer preferences and feedback to brands. This open channel of contact helps the brand respond more quickly to its customers and improves its services and products overall.

Co-Creation with Consumers: Collaborating and involving consumers in the creation process. Fashion influencers engage their audience in designing collections, suggesting ideas, or creating content, fostering a sense of ownership and loyalty among followers. A platform for co-creation is provided by the interpersonal relationships that exist between influencers and their followers. Influencers in the fashion industry frequently involve their followers in creating content, including product evaluations, styling advice, and even joint venture designs. Customers are given the opportunity to actively shape the brand narrative through co-creation, which promotes inclusivity and a sense of community.

Social media: This is the primary platform for fashion influencers to engage with their audience. Channels like Instagram, YouTube, TikTok, and others allow influencers to showcase styles, share insights, and communicate directly with their followers, amplifying their influence and reach. Social media influencers are essential for the promotion of fashion brands. Since the influencer's genuine relationship with their followers lends credibility to promotional content, the relational factor is vital in this situation. The efficiency of social media promotions can be greatly enhanced by adding a personal touch, which can result in increased engagement and conversion rates.

In their role as global trendsetters, fashion influencers transcend borders by leveraging customer engagement, facilitating fashion trend adoption, actively seeking feedback, embracing co-creation with consumers, and harnessing the power of social media. Their engagement strategies involve fostering connections with followers, understanding their preferences, and initiating dialogues to shape trends. Feedback mechanisms aid in tailoring content and product endorsements to align with audience tastes, while co-creation initiatives foster a sense of inclusivity and ownership among consumers. Social media acts as the primary vehicle for these influencers, enabling them to showcase styles, share insights, and directly interact with their audience, amplifying their influence across international boundaries. Fashion influencers play a pivotal role in shaping and driving global fashion trends beyond geographical constraints through these multifaceted approaches.

IMPLICATIONS

Social media influencers play a big and diverse role in the fashion business, influencing customer behavior, sustainable fashion methods, and cultural inclusion. Through their curated content, they impact the information available to the consumers, which helps them make easier purchase decisions. Influencers and their followers form strong emotional bonds when their relationships are genuine. Marketing managers can take advantage of these relationships to increase consumer engagement because relatable and genuine content tends to be more engaging for users. Fashion brands can strategically partner with influencers who share their beliefs by understanding how these individuals alter consumer impressions of the company. This helps to build consumer trust and loyalty. Social media influencers can effectively promote fashion practices and sustainable fashion practices because of their vast reach and influence. Influencers are an excellent source of information and feedback from customers. These connections give marketing managers a better grasp of consumer trends, attitudes, and preferences, which helps them make better decisions and establish strategies. They can be crucial in promoting cultural interaction and appreciation, making the industry more inclusive and diverse. The current study suggests that influencers play a part in bridging cultural barriers within the fashion community. Influencers are very aware of the cultural background of their audience, which enables marketers to localize their messaging and campaigns for maximum impact. The present study emphasizes the significance of recognizing the worldwide influence of influencers, which enables firms to customize their approaches to cater to a wide range of consumers from different parts of the world. Businesses may reach a wider audience worldwide by creating themes and visuals that speak to various cultures and communities. The study's findings can be utilized by brands to ensure cultural sensitivity in their advertising campaigns, preventing cultural appropriation and promoting a more respectful portrayal of other identities by collaborating with influencers from various parts of the world to penetrate local markets. This study indicates that social media influencers substantially impact the fashion industry, transcend trends and geographic boundaries, and can lead to a more environmentally responsible and culturally inclusive fashion industry.

DISCUSSION AND CONCLUSION

Fashion influencers, distinguished by their vast virtual base of supporters and captivating material, have emerged as crucial agents in transforming consumer behavior and perceptions of brands. The emergence of influencers in the digital age and their capacity to serve as a point of contact between companies and customers have been the subject of previous research. Because of their significant audience reach, these influencers are important resources for organizations wanting to establish a more genuine and personal connection with their customers. A more interconnected world due to globalization and improved connections has made the fashion industry realize the importance of cultural inclusion. As cultural mediators, social media influencers are in a good position to blur cultural divides and help build a more varied and inclusive fashion community. Influencers in the fashion industry have become powerful forces that are changing how consumers behave and perceive brands. Influencers greatly influence consumers' purchase decisions and fashion choices due to their large followings on social media platforms, which make their posts highly coveted by their followers. Acknowledging influencers' critical role, the fashion industry strategically uses their reach to promote cultural inclusivity and establish connections with various audiences. Influencers are cultural bridge builders who can help create a more diverse and international fashion community by serving as ambassadors of trends and styles. Beyond just advertising items, they have a greater impact on a cultural movement that sees fashion as a unifying force that accepts variety and promotes individuality, which in turn changes the nature of the industry and what consumers expect. In conclusion, social media and fashion influencers have revolutionized the fashion world, playing a crucial part in influencing customer behavior, brand perceptions, and positive change. The fashion industry has seen a shift in its traditional mechanisms owing to the powerful platform social media provides. This chapter's thorough examination of the literature discusses the various ways that fashion influencers across the globe use social media platforms. Their substantial fan bases and captivating content have demonstrated their capacity to influence consumer trends, promote sustainability within the fashion industry, and cultivate a more diverse and inclusive fashion community. An important conclusion is that fashion influencers significantly impact how consumers behave. Their capacity to establish a personal connection with audiences has greatly influenced buying decisions, making them effective change agents in the business. In addition to improving their market presence, brands who recognize and proactively use this impact can help create a consumer base that is more aware of and thoughtful about products. The chapter also emphasizes how fashion influencers help navigate cultural divides and build a more welcoming fashion community. They can break down barriers and promote cultural interchange and appreciation because of their capacity to connect with a variety of audiences. In addition to being an advantage for society, this inclusion gives firms that want to appeal to a wide range of consumers worldwide a competitive edge. This book chapter, in its entirety, advances the understanding of the complex roles that social media influencers play in global fashion culture. It highlights their capacity to act as catalysts for improvement, guiding the fashion industry toward inclusivity, sustainability, and more thoughtful fashion consumption. The future of the fashion business is expected to be significantly shaped by the impact of fashion influencers, particularly as social media continues to develop.

REFERENCES

Amed, I., Berg, A., Brantberg, L., Hedrich, S., Leon, J., & Young, R. (2017). *The State of Fashion 2017.* The Business of Fashion. https://www.mckinsey.com/~/media/McKinsey/Industries/Retail/Our%20Insights/The%20state%20of%20fashion/The-state-of-fashion-2017-McK-BoF-report.pdf

Barnes, L., & Lea-Greenwood, G. (2006). Fast fashioning the supply chain: Shaping the research agenda. *Journal of Fashion Marketing and Management, 10*(3), 259–271. doi:10.1108/13612020610679259

Belanche, D., Casaló, L. V., Flavián, M., & Ibáñez-Sánchez, S. (2021). Understanding influencer marketing: The role of congruence between influencers, products and consumers. *Journal of Business Research, 132*, 186–195. doi:10.1016/j.jbusres.2021.03.067

Boerman, S. C. (2020). The effects of the standardized Instagram disclosure for Micro- and Meso-influencers. *Computers in Human Behavior, 103*, 199–207. doi:10.1016/j.chb.2019.09.015

Brodie, R. J., Hollebeek, L. D., Jurić, B., & Ilić, A. (2011). Customer engagement. *Journal of Service Research, 14*(3), 252–271. doi:10.1177/1094670511411703

Brown, D., & Hayes, N. (2008). *Influencer marketing*. Routledge. doi:10.4324/9780080557700

Cao, D., Meadows, M., Wong, D., & Xia, S. (2021). Understanding consumers' social media engagement behaviour: An examination of the moderation effect of social media context. *Journal of Business Research, 122*, 835–846. doi:10.1016/j.jbusres.2020.06.025

Chu, S.-C., & Seock, Y.-K. (2020). The power of social media in Fashion Advertising. *Journal of Interactive Advertising, 20*(2), 93–94. doi:10.1080/15252019.2020.1802955

Dadia, H. (2022, October 15). *The evolution of influencer marketing industry in post-Covid Digital Era!* Times of India Blog. https://timesofindia.indiatimes.com/blogs/voices/the-evolution-of-influencer-marketing-industry-in-post-covid-digital-era/

De Veirman, M., Cauberghe, V., & Hudders, L. (2017). Marketing through Instagram influencers: The impact of number of followers and product divergence on brand attitude. *International Journal of Advertising, 36*(5), 798–828. doi:10.1080/02650487.2017.1348035

Delbaere, M., Michael, B., & Phillips, B. J. (2020). Social Media influencers: A route to brand engagement for their followers. Psychology &amp. *Psychology and Marketing, 38*(1), 101–112. doi:10.1002/mar.21419

Dencheva, V. (2023a, December). *Topic: Influencer marketing worldwide*. Statista. https://www.statista.com/topics/2496/influence-marketing/

Dencheva, V. (2023b, December 18). *Influencer marketing worldwide - statistics & facts*. Statista. https://www.statista.com/topics/2496/influence-marketing/#topicOverview

Eigenraam, A. W. (2023). *Customer Engagement: Studies on Building Authentic Engagement Experiences in Online Evironments* [PhD-Thesis - Research and graduation internal, Vrije Universiteit Amsterdam]. doi:10.5463/thesis.79

Evans, N., Phua, J., Lim, J. I., & Jun, H. (2017). Disclosing Instagram Influencer advertising: The effects of disclosure language on advertising recognition, attitudes, and behavioral intent. *Journal of Interactive Advertising*, *17*(2), 138–149. doi:10.1080/15252019.2017.1366885

Fashion e-commerce worldwide - statistics & facts. (2023, December) https://www.statista.com/topics/9288/fashion-e-commerce-worldwide

Fashion eCommerce: market data & analysis. (2023, August) https://www.statista.com/study/38340/ecommerce-report-fashion

Forsythe, S., Butler, S. M., & Kim, M. S. (1991). Fashion Adoption: Theory and Pragmatics. *Clothing & Textiles Research Journal*, *9*(4), 8–15. doi:10.1177/0887302X9100900402

Gereffi, G. (1999). International Trade and industrial upgrading in the apparel commodity chain. *Journal of International Economics*, *48*(1), 37–70. doi:10.1016/S0022-1996(98)00075-0

Ghosh, M. (2021). Product placement by social media homefluencers during new normal. *South Asian Journal of Marketing*, *3*(1), 21–37. doi:10.1108/SAJM-05-2021-0069

Ghosh, M., & Islam, A. S. (2023). Homefluencers' endorsement of millennial consumers' purchase intention in new normal. *International Marketing Review*, *40*(5), 1188–1212. doi:10.1108/IMR-10-2021-0308

Goldsmith, R. E., & Clark, R. A. (2008). An analysis of factors affecting fashion opinion leadership and fashion opinion seeking. *Journal of Fashion Marketing and Management*, *12*(3), 308–322. doi:10.1108/13612020810889272

Goldsmith, R. E., & Flynn, L. R. (1992). Identifying innovators in consumer product markets. *European Journal of Marketing*, *26*(12), 42–55. doi:10.1108/03090569210022498

Haenlein, M., Anadol, E., Farnsworth, T., Hugo, H., Hunichen, J., & Welte, D. (2020). Navigating the new era of influencer marketing: How to be successful on Instagram, Tiktok, & Co. *California Management Review*, *63*(1), 5–25. doi:10.1177/0008125620958166

Han, M. S., Song, K. S., & Park, J. W. (2023). A Study on the Effect of Fashion Influencer on Consumer Purchase Intention and Word of Mouth Intention. *Journal of Service Management*, *24*(1), 1–25. Advance online publication. doi:10.15706/jksms.2023.24.1.001

Handrimurtjahjo, A. D., Handranata, Y. W., Permatasari, A., & Dewi, C. D. (n.d.). *Examining the Relationship Between Social Media Influencer Impact on Purchase Intention Towards Fashion Industry*. https://ieomsociety.org/proceedings/2022malaysia/414.pdf

Hu, L., Qi, M., Han, S., & Li, Y. (2020). Understanding followers' stickiness to digital influencers: The effect of psychological responses. *International Journal of Information Management, 54*, 102169. doi:10.1016/j.ijinfomgt.2020.102169

Hudders, L., De Jans, S., & De Veirman, M. (2020). The commercialization of social media stars: A literature review and conceptual framework on the strategic use of social media influencers. *International Journal of Advertising, 40*(3), 327–375. doi:10.1080/02650487.2020.1836925

Jaakkola, E., & Alexander, M. (2014). The role of customer engagement Behavior in Value Co-Creation. *Journal of Service Research, 17*(3), 247–261. doi:10.1177/1094670514529187

Jin, S. A., Muqaddam, A., & Ryu, E. (2019). Instafamous and social media influencer marketing. *Marketing Intelligence & Planning, 37*(5), 567–579. doi:10.1108/MIP-09-2018-0375

Jin, S. V., & Ryu, E. (2019). Celebrity fashion brand endorsement in Facebook viral marketing and social commerce: Interactive effects of social identification, materialism, fashion involvement, and opinion leadership. *Journal of Fashion Marketing and Management, 23*(1), 104–123. doi:10.1108/JFMM-01-2018-0001

Karl, C. (2017). *The State of Fashion 2017*. McKinsey Global Institute. https://www.mckinsey.com/~/media/McKinsey/Industries/Retail/Our%20Insights/The%20state%20of%20fashion/The-state-of-fashion-2017-McK-BoF-report.pdf

Karunakaran, M. S., & Raveendran, P. T. (2018). Customer Engagement - the Co Creation of value in the marketing process. *ICTACT Journal on Management Studies, 4*(1), 683–690. doi:10.21917/ijms.2018.0093

Kaur, G., Deshwal, P., & Dangi, H. K. (2023). Customer engagement: A systematic review and future research agenda. *International Journal of Internet Marketing and Advertising, 18*(2/3), 148. doi:10.1504/IJIMA.2023.129659

Ki, C., Cuevas, L., Chong, S. M., & Lim, H. (2020). Influencer marketing: Social media influencers as human brands attaching to followers and yielding positive marketing results by fulfilling needs. *Journal of Retailing and Consumer Services, 55*, 102133. doi:10.1016/j.jretconser.2020.102133

Kim, D. Y., & Kim, H.-Y. (2021). Influencer advertising on social media: The multiple inference model on Influencer-product congruence and sponsorship disclosure. *Journal of Business Research, 130*, 405–415. doi:10.1016/j.jbusres.2020.02.020

Kim, J., Kang, S., & Lee, K. H. (2020). How social capital impacts the purchase intention of sustainable fashion products. *Journal of Business Research, 117*, 596–603. doi:10.1016/j.jbusres.2018.10.010

Kondort, G., Pelău, C., Gáti, M., & Ciofu, I. (2023). The Role of Fashion Influencers in Shaping Consumers' Buying Decisions and Trends. *Proceedings of the International Conference on Business Excellence, 17*(1), 1009–1018. 10.2478/picbe-2023-0092

Kumar, M. (2023, January 3). *Influencer marketing*. Redseer Strategy Consultants. https://redseer.com/newsletters/influencer-marketing-a-solution-to-optimize-digital-ad-spends/

Kumar, P., Oberoi, S., & Jaitly, R. C. (2023). Impact of social media influencers on consumer engagement and its consequences in the emerging environment of metaverse. In Advances in marketing, customer relationship management, and e-services book series (pp. 225–240). doi:10.4018/978-1-6684-8898-0.ch014

Lakhan, R., Sharma, B., & Sharma, M. (2023). Social media: utility versus addiction. In *Effective Use of Social Media in Public Health* (pp. 65–97). Academic Press. doi:10.1016/B978-0-323-95630-7.00002-0

Lamberton, C., & Stephen, A. T. (2016). A thematic exploration of digital, social media, and Mobile Marketing: Research Evolution from 2000 to 2015 and an agenda for future inquiry. *Journal of Marketing*, *80*(6), 146–172. doi:10.1509/jm.15.0415

Lin, Y., & Kant, S. (2021). Using social media for citizen participation: Contexts, empowerment, and inclusion. *Sustainability (Basel)*, *13*(12), 6635. doi:10.3390/su13126635

Lou, C., & Yuan, S. (2019). Influencer Marketing: How message value and credibility affect consumer trust of branded content on social media. *Journal of Interactive Advertising*, *19*(1), 58–73. doi:10.1080/15252019.2018.1533501

Lu, B., Fan, W., & Zhou, M. (2016). Social Presence, trust, and Social Commerce Purchase Intention: An empirical research. *Computers in Human Behavior*, *56*, 225–237. doi:10.1016/j.chb.2015.11.057

Mason, A. N., Narcum, J., & Mason, K. (2021). Social media marketing gains importance after Covid-19. *Cogent Business & Management*, *8*(1), 1870797. Advance online publication. doi:10.1080/23311975.2020.1870797

Mohr, I., Fuxman, L., & Mahmoud, A. B. (2021). A triple-trickle theory for sustainable fashion adoption: The rise of a luxury trend. *Journal of Fashion Marketing and Management*, *26*(4), 640–660. doi:10.1108/JFMM-03-2021-0060

Nuji, M. N. N., Ali, A., Noordin, W. N. W., Thaheer, B. A. N. M., & Mathiew, V. (2023). Of Trust and Influence: A Look At Social Media Influencers and Brand Promotion. *International Journal of Academic Research in Business & Social Sciences*, *13*(6), 2152–2170. doi:10.6007/IJARBSS/v13-i6/15444

Orminski, J., Tandoc, E. C. Jr, & Detenber, B. H. (2020). #sustainablefashion – A Conceptual Framework for Sustainable Fashion Discourse on Twitter. *Environmental Communication*, *15*(1), 115–132. doi:10.1080/17524032.2020.1802321

Pansari, A., & Kumar, V. (2017). Customer engagement: The construct, antecedents, and consequences. *Journal of the Academy of Marketing Science*, *45*(3), 294–311. doi:10.1007/s11747-016-0485-6

Peter, C., & Muth, L. (2023). Social media influencers' role in shaping political opinions and actions of young audiences. *Media and Communication*, *11*(3). Advance online publication. doi:10.17645/mac.v11i3.6750

Poorthuis, A., Power, D., & Zook, M. (2019). Attentional social media: Mapping the spaces and networks of the Fashion Industry. *Annals of the American Association of Geographers*, *110*(4), 941–966. doi:10.1080/24694452.2019.1664887

Rahman, S. U., Saleem, S., Akhtar, S., Ali, T., & Khan, M. A. (2014). Consumers' adoption of apparel fashion: The role of innovativeness, involvement, and social values. *International Journal of Marketing Studies*, *6*(3). Advance online publication. doi:10.5539/ijms.v6n3p49

Saleem, Z. (2023). Impact of Instagram fashion influencers on consumer buying behavior. *MAIRAJ*, *1*(2), 24–32. doi:10.58760/mairaj.v1i2.9

Schouten, A., Janssen, L., & Verspaget, M. (2021). Celebrity vs. Influencer endorsements in advertising: The role of identification, credibility, and Product-Endorser fit. *International Journal of Advertising*, *39*(2), 258–281. doi:10.1080/02650487.2019.1634898

Shopify. (2021). *Future of Commerce.* https://cdn.shopify.com/static/future-of-commerce/Shopify%20Future%20of%20Commerce%202021.pdf

Sinelnikov, D. (2022). *The rise of influencer marketing: take your business international in 2022.* https://www.forbes.com/sites/forbesagencycouncil/2022/03/18/the-rise-of-influencer-marketing-take-your-business-international-in-2022/?sh=1bbc3bf36d9c

Smith, K. (2022, December 12). *How covid-19 increased influencer marketing.* Hurrdat Marketing. https://hurrdatmarketing.com/digital-marketing-news/how-covid-19-increased-influencer-marketing/

Smith, P. (2024). *Global apparel market - statistics & facts.* Statista https://www.statista.com/topics/5091/apparel-market-worldwide/#topicOverview

Statista. (2023). *Fashion eCommerce: Market data & analysis, August 2023.* Statista. https://www.statista.com/study/38340/ecommerce-report-fashion/

Sun, Y., Wang, R., Cao, D., & Lee, R. (2021). Who are social media influencers for luxury fashion consumption of the Chinese Gen Z? Categorisation and empirical examination. *Journal of Fashion Marketing and Management*, *26*(4), 603–621. doi:10.1108/JFMM-07-2020-0132

Tiwari, A., Kumar, A., Kant, R., & Jaiswal, D. (2023). Impact of fashion influencers on consumers' purchase intentions: Theory of planned behaviour and mediation of attitude. *Journal of Fashion Marketing and Management.* Advance online publication. doi:10.1108/JFMM-11-2022-0253

Van Doorn, J., Lemon, K. N., Mittal, V., Nass, S., Pick, D., Pirner, P., & Verhoef, P. C. (2010). Customer Engagement Behavior: Theoretical foundations and research directions. *Journal of Service Research*, *13*(3), 253–266. doi:10.1177/1094670510375599

Verhoef, P. C., Reinartz, W., & Krafft, M. (2010). Customer engagement as a new perspective in customer management. *Journal of Service Research*, *13*(3), 247–252. doi:10.1177/1094670510375461

Weismueller, J., Harrigan, P., Wang, S., & Soutar, G. N. (2020). Influencer endorsements: How advertising disclosure and source credibility affect consumer purchase intention on social media. *Australasian Marketing Journal*, *28*(4), 160–170. doi:10.1016/j.ausmj.2020.03.002

Weller, S. (2007). Fashion as viscous knowledge: Fashion's role in Shaping Trans-National Garment Production. *Journal of Economic Geography*, *7*(1), 39–66. doi:10.1093/jeg/lbl015

What is influencer marketing? (2023). https://www.mckinsey.com/featured-insights/mckinsey-explainers/what-is-influencer-marketing

Wibisono, A. I., & Ruldeviyani, Y. (2021, April). Detecting social media influencers of airline services through social network analysis on twitter: A case study of the Indonesian airline industry. In *2021 3rd East Indonesia Conference on Computer and Information Technology (EIConCIT)* (pp. 314-319). IEEE. 10.1109/EIConCIT50028.2021.9431876

Yalcin, T., Nistor, C., & Pehlivan, E. (2021). Sustainability Influencers: Between marketers and educators. *Social Science Research Network*. https://papers.ssrn.com/sol3/papers.cfm?abstract_id=3800316

Zhang, Y., & Mac, L. (2023). Social media influencers: The formation and effects of affective factors during online interactions. *International Journal of Consumer Studies*, *47*(5), 1824–1837. doi:10.1111/ijcs.12957

Zheng, L., Huang, B., Qiu, H., & Bai, H. (2023). The role of social media followers' agency in influencer marketing: A study based on the heuristic–systematic model of information processing. *International Journal of Advertising*, 1–26. doi:10.1080/02650487.2023.2229148

Chapter 13
The Role of Influencer Trust, Gender Congruency, and Expertise Congruency:
A Cross-national Comparison between Douyin and TikTok Users in China and the USA

Yang Yang
University of Southern Indiana, USA

ABSTRACT

This chapter explores the mediation role of influencer trust in gender and expertise congruency effects on consumers' attitudes and purchase intentions, focusing on a cross-national comparison between Douyin users in China and TikTok users in the U.S. It investigates how short video platforms, primarily TikTok and Douyin, have become integral in shaping consumer behavior and trust in influencers. The chapter explores the concepts of gender and expertise congruency in influencer marketing, examining how these factors impact the effectiveness of endorsements and consumer trust. The chapter presents a comprehensive analysis of endorsement effectiveness, contributing to the broader understanding of marketing strategies in the dynamic social media landscape. Through its findings, it provides theoretical and practical implications for marketers and advertisers aiming to enhance the efficiency and credibility of influencer collaborations in different cultural contexts.

INTRODUCTION

Short video platforms are gaining popularity in both the U.S. and China. Interestingly, TikTok, known as Douyin in China, serves as a comparable social media platform for China-U.S. comparison due to its widespread adoption in both regions. TikTok and Douyin share similar algorithms and formats, making them ideal for cross-cultural analysis. TikTok boasts over 1.7 billion users globally, with Douyin enjoy-

DOI: 10.4018/979-8-3693-0912-4.ch013

ing 750 million daily active users in China (Business of Apps, 2023). Despite bans in India and Iraq in 2021, TikTok remains the fastest-growing app worldwide (Iqbal, 2022). In 2022, there were 80 million active monthly TikTok users in the U.S. (Wallaroo Media, 2022), and as of January 2022, TikTok had 1 billion active monthly users globally (Geyser, 2022).

TikTok's success in advertising earned it the title of Marketer of the Year in 2020 in the U.S. (Ad Age, 2020), generating an estimated $500 million in revenue from the U.S. market alone in 2020 (Zhang & Dotan, 2020). Additionally, it was the most popular iPhone app in the U.S. in 2021 (Geyser, 2022), with continued growth projected in the U.S., reaching 89.7 million users by 2023 (Statista, 2022). Advertisers have capitalized on TikTok's global reach, with a reported 22.9% reach of global adults outside of China each month (Kemp, 2022). Notably, TikTok generated over $39.4 million in the U.S. from iOS alone in the second quarter of 2022 (Statista, 2022).

In the realm of social media, authenticity was once considered the paramount attribute for influencers. However, recent market research involving 700 marketers and creators indicates a shift. Relatability, or genuine connection with the audience, has overtaken authenticity as the primary factor in the influencer industry in 2024 (Aspire, 2024). Furthermore, the same research report reveals that 79% of brands and 89% of creators are now prioritizing TikTok.

The aim of this study is to investigate the influence of gender and expertise congruence between influencers and products on consumers' product attitudes and purchase intentions on short video platforms, specifically TikTok and Douyin. Additionally, the study aims to explore the role of influencer trust in these relationships.

This research is significant for several reasons. Firstly, it addresses a gap in the literature by examining the impact of gender and expertise congruence on consumer behavior across different cultural contexts, specifically comparing users of TikTok in the U.S. and Douyin in China. Although many researchers have paid attention to the cross-cultural comparison by applying Hofstede's cultural dimensions, less effort has been devoted to cross-country research in social media advertising and influencer marketing. Also, few studies have compared the cultural differences in online advertising between China and the USA. Secondly, by investigating the mediating effect of influencer trust, this study contributes to a deeper understanding of the mechanisms underlying influencer marketing effectiveness on short video platforms. Lastly, the findings of this study have practical implications for brands and influencers seeking to optimize their marketing strategies on these platforms, ultimately enhancing their effectiveness in reaching and persuading target consumers. Furthermore, these findings contribute to the development of a comprehensive model that elucidates the common relationships among Chinese and US users across various product types.

The research is organized into five chapters: Introduction, Literature Review, Method, Results, Discussion, and Conclusion.

LITERATURE REVIEW

Product-Gender Congruity on Endorser Effectiveness

Traditionally, women and men have been divided to accomplish different labor activities and play different social roles, for example, men take higher status or agentic role, while women concentrate on domestic work and caring roles (Meulenaer et al., 2019; Eagly & Wood, 2012). This perceived difference in terms of gender is not caused by biological differences but rather results from gender stereotypes inherent in the cultural environment (Diekman & Goodfriend, 2006). Typically, people observe certain roles women and men play in society and subsequently assume the appropriate characteristics each gender must possess to qualify for those roles (Clow et al., 2014). When one gender becomes associated with a range of social roles due to the societal labor division they are categorized into, people of the other gender are considered incongruent with those roles and are more likely to be viewed as less favorable candidates for them (Eagly, 2004). Men are associated with high agentic and low communal traits, such as independence, assertiveness, and competitiveness, while women are considered to have high communal and low agentic traits, such as kindness, sensitivity, caring, and dependence (Diekman & Goodfriend, 2006; Kaur et al., 2023).

Role congruity theory posits that the attitude toward a group is more positive if the characteristics of the group members align with the requirements and expectations of the group's distinctive social roles (Diekman & Goodfriend, 2006). Moreover, individuals who violate the boundaries of their assigned gender roles are punished; for example, women in typically male-dominated positions are viewed less favorably and likably (Heilman et al., 2004). People tend to believe that women and men should exhibit distinct differences from each other, especially when behaviors are associated with sex differences (Eagly & Karau, 2002). Men are also devalued when they attempt to enter women-dominated careers, such as nursing (Clow et al., 2014). Furthermore, gender values are integrated into individuals' social and cognitive schemata, and prior research has suggested that the congruence between gender norms and gender role stereotyping in advertising enhances advertising effects (Orth & Holancova, 2003).

Match-up Hypothesis and Congruency Theory

As an extension of social role theory, role congruity theory examines the perceived alignment between an individual's gender roles and other social roles they may occupy, and it identifies factors influencing congruity perceptions and their consequences for prejudice and discriminatory behaviors (Eagly & Karau, 2002). When inconsistencies arise between an individual's behavior and the expected norms of their social role, perceivers may interpret this as incongruent, leading to negative evaluations and potential prejudice (Eagly & Karau, 2005; Wood & Eagly, 2012). For example, people perceive nurses are women's jobs rather than man jobs.

The concept of congruence in marketing has been studied and examined for decades. For example, the theory of brand congruence argues that consumers feel more comfortable or satisfied with a brand when they find a congruence between the brand and their desired self-concept (Grubb & Grathwohl, 1967; Abosag, 2020). In their study, Misra and Beatty (1990) described congruence as "the highly relevant characteristics of the spokesperson are consistent with the highly relevant attributes of the brand" (p. 61). Within the field of congruence research, researchers have investigated the fit between the endorser and the product (Till & Busler, 1998; Kamins & Gupta, 1994; Lee & Thorson, 2008; McCormick, 2016; Schouten et al., 2021). Early research on the "match-up hypothesis" focused on an endorser's physical attractiveness and products related to appearance and physical attractiveness; in particular, a physically attractive endorser was found to be more persuasive and credible than an unattractive endorser for attractiveness-relevant products such as beauty products or cosmetics (Choi & Rifon, 2012). It is observed that with a high degree of congruence, a more favorable evaluation or effect will be produced (Misra & Beatty, 1990; Choi & Rifon, 2012). The congruence can be related to different aspects of meaning that are transferred from celebrities to products, such as gender fit and expertise fit (Eislend & Langner,

2010). Endorsers' expertise is also perceived as an important factor for endorsement effectiveness. A celebrity endorser with highly relevant expertise is more persuasive than a celebrity endorser with low relevant expertise (Ohanian, 1991).

In the era of social media, advertisers' focus on celebrity endorsement has been transferred to social media influencer endorsement. In 2015, 84% of marketing and advertising professionals expressed the expectation to launch at least one social media campaign involving one social media influencer in a year (eMarketer, 2015). However, compared to other forms of media, research focusing on advertising in social media is limited (Ha, 2017). It is known that influencer endorsements result in effective brand promotion and audience engagement. According to the Aspire 2024 market report, TikTok exhibits an average engagement rate of 2.06%, while nano-influencers consistently attain the highest engagement rates across all platforms, averaging 4.4%.

Prior studies suggest that endorser expertise positively impacts product attitude and purchase intention (Eisend & Langner, 2010;Schouten et al., 2019). Influencers are perceived as experts in their communities, and the congruency between the influencer and the product can build a high level of audiences' trust in the influencer (Chung & Cho, 2017). Moreover, influencers' self-claimed expertise makes them more knowledgeable and trustworthy than traditional celebrities in the domain of their interests (Schouten et al., 2019). Consumers value influencer endorsers as more trustworthy, authentic, and credible than traditional celebrities and advertisers; and expect to receive genuine advice about specific brands and products (Folkvord et al., 2020). Recent research emphasizes the importance of the match-up between the endorser's expertise and the endorsed product (Till & Busler, 2000; Fink et al., 2004; Schouten et al., 2021). Expertise refers to the extent to which a person is considered a valid source of information about a certain field/product (Choi & Rifon, 2012). It also refers to "the knowledge, experience, or skills possessed by an endorser (Erdogan, 1999, p. 298). McGuire (1969) understood expertise as an individual's perceived capacity to accurately understand and determine the correct stance on a matter. Siemens et al (2008) conducted an experimental study and found consumers could distinguish between endorser's expertise with products and endorser's expertise based on their profession. Siemens et al (2008) also defined product congruency as the fit between the product and an endorser's profession. Moreover, according to prior research, expertise is perceived to be more useful than an endorser's physical attractiveness when matching a brand with an appropriate endorser (Lynch & Schuler, 1994; Ohanian, 1991) as well as enhancing the positive effect on brand-level outcomes (Till & Busler, 2000; Fink et al., 2004; Schouten et al., 2021).

The Mediation Role of Trust

Social media influencers, as online opinion leaders, are perceived as knowledgeable and trusted sources (Ha & Yang, 2021; Yang & Ha, 2021). Gaining consumers' trust is vital to an influencer's endorsement effectiveness (Hu et al., 2019; Jin et al., 2021; Kim & Kim, 2021). Stubb and Colliander (2019) suggested that social media influencers should always disclose their sponsorship to improve consumer trust. Consumer trust is also a determinant of an endorser's credibility, referring to "the extent to which the source is perceived as possessing expertise relevant to the communication topic and can be trusted to give an objective opinion on the subject" (Goldsmith et al., 2000, p. 43). Martensen et al.'s (2018) focus group and interview study confirmed that trustworthiness was the primary contributor to citizen influencers' persuasive power. Hence, pairing a trustworthy influencer with the brand is key to the success of influencer marketing.

Trust is defined as “a willingness to rely on an exchange partner in whom one has confidence” (Moorman et al., 1992, p. 315). Brand trust is defined by Dwivedi and Johnson (2013) as “a consumer perception of a brand’s benevolence and integrity” (p. 37). It is a critical factor determining whether individuals purchase a product or not (Kauv & Blotnicky, 2020). Brand trust consists of two facets, functional and emotional brand trust (Kauv & Blotnicky, 2020). The former refers to a brand’s physical promises, such as product quality, and the latter to the value experienced by consumers, such as the brand’s social responsibility (Kauv & Blotnicky, 2020).

The relationship between endorser-product congruency and endorsement effectiveness is well-documented (Shan et al., 2019). Gender congruence, a specific type of congruency, when the gender of the endorser aligns with the product, has been shown to evoke positive attitudes towards the endorsement (Orth & Holancova, 2003). Based on these insights, the present research proposes that influencer trust mediates the relationship between endorser-product gender/expertise congruency and consumers’ attitudes towards products and their purchase intentions. This mediation is hypothesized because trust is fundamentally about the confidence consumers have in the endorser’s recommendations, which is likely to be stronger when there is a congruence between the endorser’s attributes (such as gender or expertise) and the product being endorsed. Trust, therefore, becomes the bridge that connects a consumer’s perception of congruency with their attitude towards the product and their intention to purchase.

Cultural Differences and Hofstede’s Cultural Dimensions

Hofstede introduced cultural dimensions in his seminal 1980 work “Culture’s Consequences,” with an updated edition in 2001, providing a foundation for thousands of studies in cross-cultural research and shaping the core concepts in the field (Venaik et al., 2013).

Hofstede (1980) describes individualism as a society where individuals prioritize themselves and their immediate families, while collectivism entails close-knit groups expecting loyalty and support. The individualism-collectivism dimension measures a country’s preference for individual or group actions (Hofstede, 1980). Power distance relates to the acceptance of unequal power distribution in society, and uncertainty avoidance is the extent to which structured and certain environments are preferred, avoiding ambiguity and uncertainty (Hofstede, 1980). Masculinity values assertiveness and material success, whereas femininity emphasizes compassion and relationships, affecting societal gender roles and their perceived flexibility in different cultures (Hofstede 1980; 2001). The fifth dimension is term orientation, whch refers to “long-term versus short-term orientation toward the future” (Yoo et al., 2011, p. 194). Contrary to the other four dimensions, which were developed based on Western cultures, Hofstede’s LTO dimension was formulated through a survey study in China, which aimed to examine Chinese cultural values (Venaik et al., 2013). Finally, the sixth dimension is Indulgence versus restraint (IVR), which refers to the extent to which society responds to the fulfillment of human desires, and this dimension is adopted from the World Values Survey (Hofstede et al., 2010). A high indulgence society embraces the individuals’ primitive needs of recreation and having fun with less control for individuals pursuing those gratifications, while in a low indulgence society, individuals’ gratification needs are constrained by social norms (Guo et al., 2018).

In advertising studies, masculinity-femininity and individualism-collectivism are widely examined cultural dimensions. Gender is a primary factor in developing strategic marketing plans and targeting favorable audiences (An & Kim, 2006). On the one hand, the cultural value in society influences the gender roles portrayed in advertising. On the other, the gender roles portrayed in advertising impact how people perceive gender value in real life (Odekerken-Schroder et al., 2002). Many studies suggest that gender role depiction in advertising varies by culture (Moon & Chen, 2002). However, previous research regarding gender role portrayals is limited to TV and print media, and few studies concern the most recent or other types of media (An & Kim, 2006). Additionally, most existing research on gender differences in TV advertising has focused on single-country studies; hence, there is a need for cross-country comparisons in the field (Matthes et al., 2016). In the feminine-value-dominant country, there are fewer differences in the roles played by male and female figures in advertising. In contrast, in the masculine-value-dominant country, there tends to be a significant difference between gender roles portrayed in advertising (Wiles et al., 1995).

Cross-country research has recognized China and the USA as representing two separate cultural clusters: the Confucian cluster for China and the Anglo cluster for the USA (Gupta et al., 2002).The two countries are similar to the Masculinity dimension and differ primarily on the Individualism (IDV), Uncertainty Avoidance (UA), and Power Distance (PD) dimensions (Shinnar et al., 2012). Masculinity, Power Distance, and Individualism dimensions are significantly linked with gender differences (Mathiyal-akan et al., 2018). Gender roles are more distinct in a masculine culture than feminine culture (Hofstede & McCrae, 2004). Individuals prefer socially acceptable jobs to their sex and avoid jobs appropriate for the opposite sex (Heilman, 1983).

A high masculine culture embraces that men should be successful outside their families, and women should care for the home and people (Hofstede & Hofstede, 2005). Parboteeah et al. (2008) found that power distance is negatively associated with gender equality, which means that a high power distance culture predicts a high gender inequality. Gender role ideology refers to the belief that men and women should behave appropriately based on social norms and cultural values (Kalin & Tilby, 1978). A traditional argument about gender ideology posits that men and women should behave differently and take different roles (Cota & Xinaris, 1993). Prior cultural studies suggested that a more traditional gender ideology was adopted in Chinese cultures than Western cultures (Marshall, 2008).

Therefore, based on the above arguments, five hypotheses are proposed regarding the effects of gender/expertise-product congruency on consumers' product attitudes and purchase intentions, along with the mediating effects of influencer trust and cross-country comparison.:

H1a: Influencer trust mediates the relationship between influencer's gender-product congruency and product attitude (Figure 1).

H1b: Influencer trust mediates the relationship between influencer's gender-product congruency and purchase intention (Figure 1).

H2a: Influencer trust mediates the relationship between influencer expertise-product congruency and product attitude (Figure 2).

Figure 1. The mediation effect of influencer trust on gender congruency and endorsement effectiveness (product attitude and purchase intention)

Figure 2. The mediation effect of influencer trust on expertise congruency and endorsement effectiveness (product attitude and purchase intention)

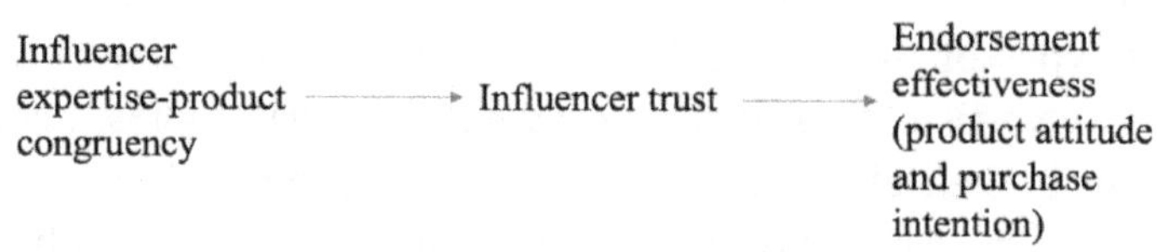

H2b: Influencer trust mediates the relationship between influencer expertise-product congruency and purchase intention (Figure 2).

H3: Chinese consumers have a higher level of expected influencer gender-product congruency than American consumers.

H4: The gender fit between an influencer and the product will have a greater impact on consumers' brand attitudes in China than in the USA.

H5: The gender fit between an influencer and the product will have a greater impact on consumers' purchase intentions in China than in the USA.

METHOD

Sampling

A self-administered online survey was employed as the data collection method for this study. The study population comprised US TikTok and China Douyin users. Eligible participants were regular TikTok/Douyin users over the age of 18 who had followed at least one TikTok/Douyin influencer who had endorsed or promoted commercial products. Two equivalent versions of the survey were utilized, one in Chinese and one in English, to cater to users in both countries. A quota sample was employed to ensure equal participation of men and women in the study, with approximately 110 male and 110 female participants recruited from each country. Participants from both countries were recruited through third-party recruiting companies, Survey Star (for the Chinese sample) and Amazon MTurk (for the US sample).

Questionnaire Design

The questionnaire was originally designed in English. Then it was translated into Chinese by the researcher who is native Chinese. There are two ways to secure the equivalence of items in both versions: 1) back translation (the researcher translated the English version into Chinese and asked another Chinese English speaker to translate it back to English, and check if they transmit the similar/same meaning); 2) pretest (asking Chinese friends of the researcher who studied/is studying in the USA to answer questions in both versions and pointing out the translation issues in the two questionnaires).

The respondent was asked to identify an influencer they follow. Then participants were presented with three scenarios of the products their identified influencer endorsed. The three product categories - beauty products (female product), food & drinks (gender-neutral product), and alcoholic products (male product) - were determined from Douyin's 30-Day Popular Goods List (CBNData, 2019). Participants answered questions measuring perceived influencer gender-product congruency, perceived expertise-product congruency, influencer trust, and endorsement effectiveness (product attitude and purchase intention) under each scenario. To prevent participants from being influenced by familiar brand names and to focus on influencers' importance for new brands, the researcher selected specific product categories but did not include brand names.

Measures

The items used in the questionnaire mostly consisted of a five-point Likert scales from strongly agree to strongly disagree, adopted from past research, to address the hypotheses of this study.

Perceived Influencer Gender-Product Congruency

The researcher created three items in the perceived influencer gender-product congruency scale to measure individuals' perception of the gender congruency between a specific TikTok influencer and the product he/she has ever endorsed/promoted. Items include: 1) The influencer gender fits the product category (For example, the female influencer endorses/promotes a beauty product; or a male influencer endorses/promotes an alcoholic product); 2) The influencer gender characteristic matches the product characteristic; 3) The influencer is fit to endorse/promote the product because of the gender fit between them.

Perceived Influencer Expertise-Product Congruency

Five items in the influencer expertise-product congruency scale were adapted from Ohanian (1990). Items include: 1) The influencer is an expert in the product relevant field; 2) The influencer is experienced in the product relevant field; 3) The influencer is knowledgeable in the product relevant field; 4) The influencer is qualified in the product relevant field; 5) The influencer is skilled in the product relevant field.

Social Media Influencer Trust

Four items in the social media influencer trust scale were adapted from the consumer trust measure of Chaudhuri and Holbrook (2001). Items are 1) I trust this influencer; 2) I rely on this influencer; 3) He/she is an honest influencer; 4) The brand/product endorsed by this influencer is safe.

Influencer Marketing (Endorsement) Effectiveness

The effectiveness of influencer marketing will be gauged by examining both the attitude toward the endorsed product and the purchase intentions for the influencer-endorsed product used in the study. Product attitude and purchase intention are recognized as two dimensions of the effectiveness of influencer endorsements. The former is an attitudinal response, while the latter concerns behavioral intentions. Although attitude change is associated with behavioral change, it does not directly predict consumer purchase intentions. For example, research on green purchase intentions has shown that despite the relationship between various factors and purchase intentions, consumers' attitudes toward green products do not necessarily predict their green purchasing behaviors (Xu et al., 2020). Additionally, purchase intention is contingent on the consumer's current product needs, whereas product attitude is consistent across all products, regardless of needs or purchasing conditions such as price. Therefore, both attitude toward the product and intentions to purchase the product were measured as dependent variables in this study.

Product Attitude. Six items in the brand attitude scale were adopted from Spears and Singh (2004). Participants indicate their attitudes toward the endorsed product by their favorite influencer by scoring on each item ranging from 1 to 7. Items include 1) "unappealing/appealing"; 2) "bad/good"; 3) "unpleasant/pleasant"; 4) "unfavorable/favorable"; 5) "boring/interesting"; 6) "unlikable/likable".

Purchase Intention. Five items in the purchase intention scale were adopted from Lu et al. (2014). Items include 1) "I would consider buying this product;" 2) "I have no intention to buy this product (Reverse scored);" 3) "It is possible that I would buy this product;" 4) "I will purchase (this brand) the next time I need a (product);" 5) "If I am in need, I would buy this (product)."

Hofstede's Cultural Dimensions at an Individual Level

Three out of six of Hofstede's cultural dimensions were chosen in this study measured at an individual level: masculinity, individualism, and power distance because they are most relevant to users' gender values. All the items are adopted from Yoo et al. (2011).

Individuals' Masculinity Value. Items include 1) It is vital for men to have a professional career than it is for women; 2) Men usually solve problems with logical analysis, and women usually solve problems with intuition; 3) Solving difficult problems usually requires an active, forcible approach, which is typical for men, and 4) There are some jobs that a man can always do better than a woman.

Individual's Individualism Value. Six items in the individualism scale were reversed scored. Items include: 1) Individuals should sacrifice self-interest for the group (*); 2) Individuals should stick with the group even through difficulties (*); 3) Group welfare is more important than individual rewards (*); 4) Group success is more important than individual success (*); 5) Individuals should only pursue their goals after considering the welfare of the group (*); 6) Group loyalty should be encouraged even if individual goals suffer (*).

Individual's Power Distance Value. Items include: 1) People in higher positions should make most decisions without consulting people in lower positions; 2) People in higher positions should not ask the opinions of people in lower positions too frequently; 3) People in higher positions should avoid social interaction with people in lower positions; 4) People in lower positions should not disagree with decisions by people in higher positions; 5) People in higher positions should not delegate important tasks to people in lower positions.

Respondent Profile

The survey included 221 Chinese respondents, comprising 111 males and 110 females, and 220 U.S. respondents, with 116 males and 104 females. The average age was 29.42 (SD = 5.87) for the Chinese respondents and 33.17 (SD = 6.93) for the U.S. respondents. Among the Chinese participants, the majority (74.9%) had over two years of experience using Douyin, and most (70.9%) spent between 11 to 59 minutes on Douyin daily. A significant proportion (91.5%) resided in urban areas, while 8.5% were from suburban and rural areas. In contrast, most U.S. respondents (68%) had less than two years of experience with TikTok, with the majority (78.9%) spending 11 minutes to 2 hours on TikTok each day. Approximately half of the U.S. respondents (54%) lived in urban locations, 32.5% in suburban areas, and 13.5% in rural areas.

RESULTS

Overall Mediation Effect on Influencer Gender-Product Congruency Effect: China

Hypotheses 1a and 1b posited a mediating effect of influencer trust on the relationship between the influencer's gender-product congruency and endorsement effectiveness, which includes product attitude and purchase intention. Regression analysis supported the mediating role of influencer trust in both countries. In the Chinese sample, influencer trust partially mediated the relationship between the influencer's gender-product congruency and product attitude. This was evidenced by a reduction in the strength of the relationship from $\beta = .37$, $p < .01$ to $\beta = .22$, $p < .01$ when influencer trust was included in the equation (Figure 3). Similarly, influencer trust partially mediated the relationship between the influencer's gender-product congruency and purchase intention, with the relationship weakening from $\beta = .47$, p

$< .01$ to $\beta = .22$, $p < .01$ upon the addition of influencer trust (Figure 4).

Figure 3. The standardized regression coefficient between gender congruency and product attitude for overall mediation model in China, controlling for influencer trust, is in the parentheses
$^{**}p < .01$.

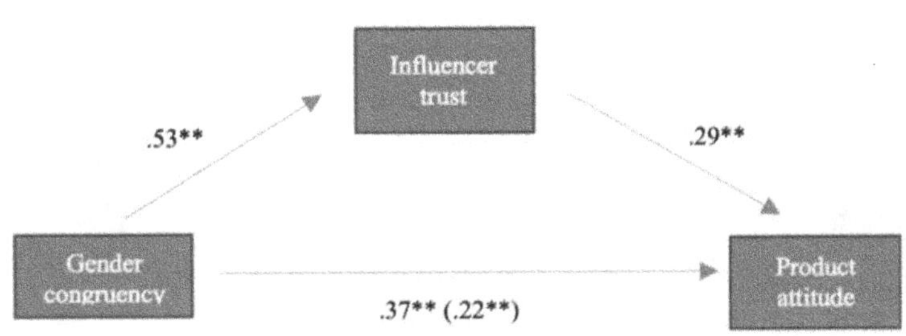

Figure 4. The standardized regression coefficient between gender congruency and purchase intention for the overall mediation model in China, controlling for influencer trust, is in the parentheses
$^{**}p < .01$.

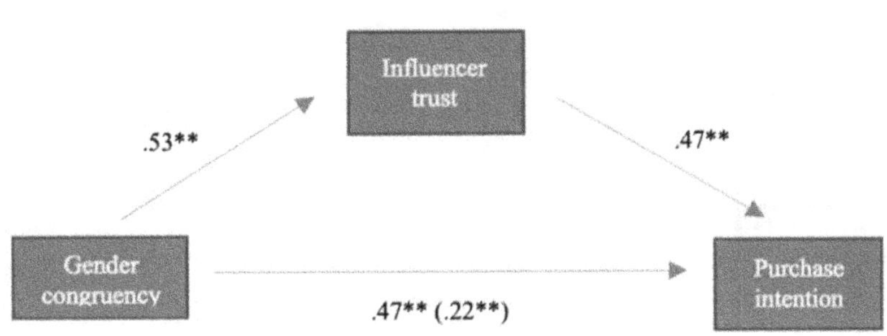

Overall Mediation Effect of Influencer Trust on Influencer Product-Expertise Effect: China

Hypotheses 2a and 2b investigated the mediating role of influencer trust in the relationship between influencer-product expertise congruency and endorsement effectiveness, encompassing both product attitude and purchase intention. In the Chinese sample, influencer trust was found to serve as a mediating variable. It partially mediated the relationship between influencer-product expertise congruency and product attitude, as well as purchase intention. This was evidenced by a decrease in the strength of the relationship for product attitude from β_attitude = .30, p < .01 to β_attitude = .19, p < .01, and for purchase intention from β_purchase = .40, p < .01 to β_purchase = .23, p < .01, once influencer trust was factored into the analysis. (Figures 5 and Figure 6).

Figure 5. The standardized regression coefficient between expertise congruency and product attitude for overall mediation model in China, controlling for influencer trust, is in the parentheses
***p < .01.*

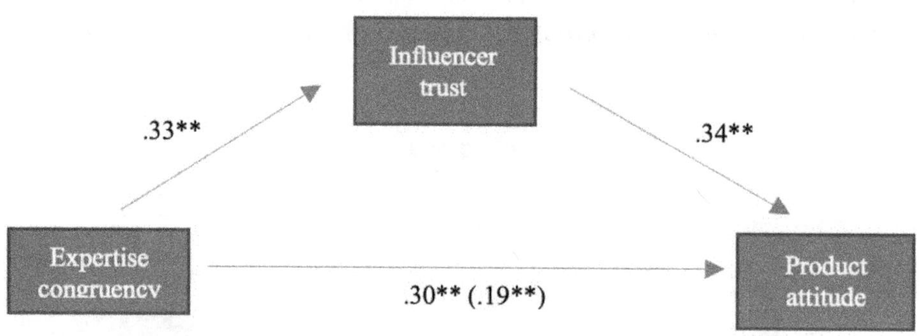

Figure 6. The standardized regression coefficient between expertise congruency and purchase intention for the overall mediation model in China, controlling for influencer trust, is in the parentheses
***p < .01.*

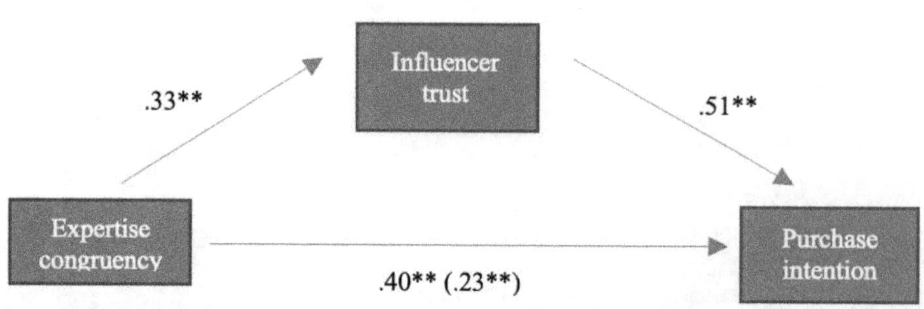

Overall Mediation Effect on Influencer Gender-Product Congruency Effect: The U.S.

In the U.S. sample, influencer trust served as a full mediator in the relationship between influencer gender-product congruency and product attitude, as well as between influencer gender-product congruency and purchase intention. Both relationships became non-significant when influencer trust was introduced into the model (Figure 7 and Figure 8).

Overall Mediation Effect of Influencer Trust on Influencer Product-Expertise Effect: The U.S.

In the U.S. sample, influencer trust was found to fully mediate the relationship between influencer-product congruency and both product attitude and purchase intention. This was evidenced by the positive relationships (β_attitude = .67, p < .01; β_purchase = .58, p < .01) becoming non-significant after the

Figure 7. The standardized regression coefficient between gender congruency and product attitude for the overall mediation model in the US, controlling for influencer trust, is in the parentheses
***p < .01.*

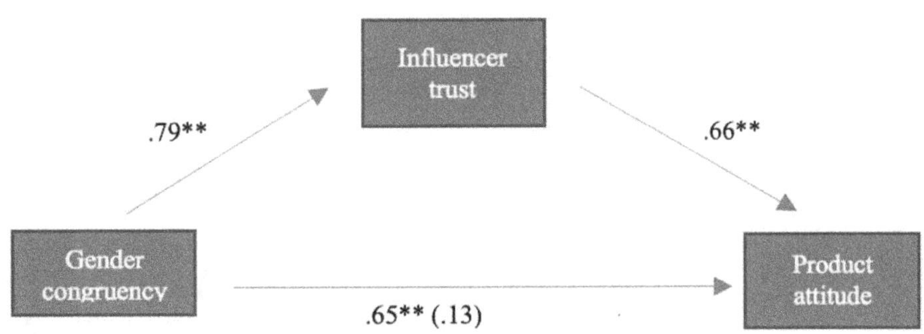

Figure 8. The standardized regression coefficient between gender congruency and purchase intention for the overall mediation model in the US, controlling for influencer trust, is in the parentheses
***p < .01.*

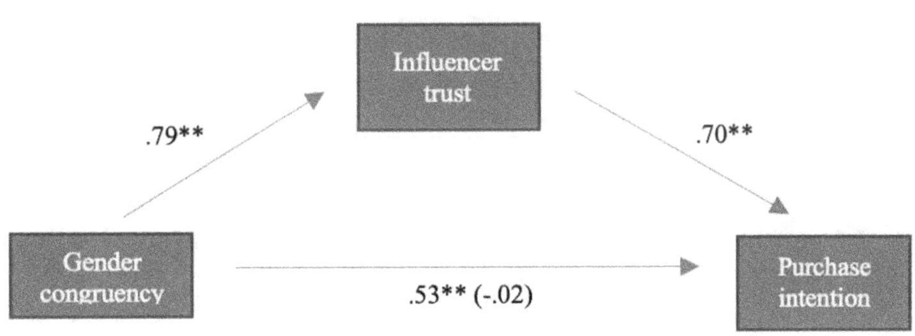

inclusion of influencer trust in both equations, as illustrated in Figures 9 and 10. Therefore, Hypotheses 3a and 3b, which proposed the mediation of influencer trust between influencer product expertise and endorsement effectiveness, are supported.

The research findings suggest a novel, common model elucidating the efficacy of influencer endorsements in both China and the U.S. This model posits that influencer gender-product congruency and influencer expertise-product congruency, each independently forecast product attitudes and purchase intentions. Furthermore, these two predictive relationships are mediated by consumers' trust in influencers (Diagram 1).

Cross-Country Comparison between China and the U.S.

Before proceeding with the analysis of Hypothesis 3, 4 and 5, descriptive statistics were examined concerning the individual users' scores for masculinity, individualism, and power distance. Table 1 presents the average scores for each value across the countries. Generally, Chinese Douyin users scored higher

Figure 9. The standardized regression coefficient between expertise congruency and product attitude for the overall mediation model in the US, controlling for influencer trust, is in the parentheses
***p < .01*

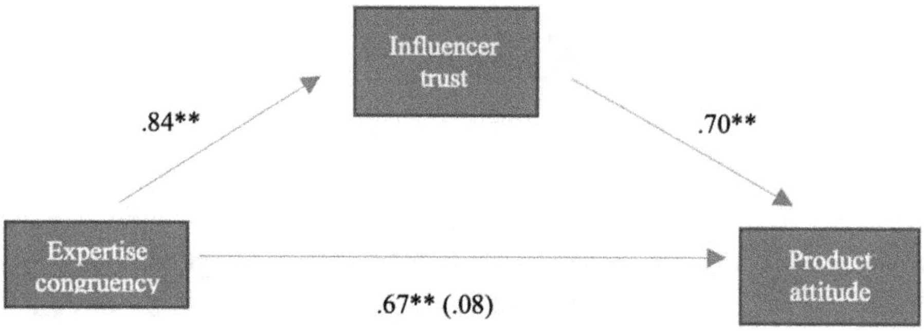

Figure 10. The standardized regression coefficient between expertise congruency and purchase intention for the overall mediation model in the US, controlling for influencer trust, is in the parentheses
***p < .01.*

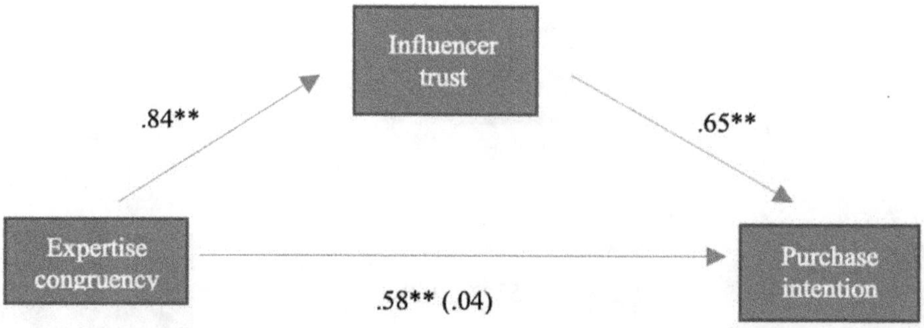

Figure 11. Common relationships among Chinese and US users across product types

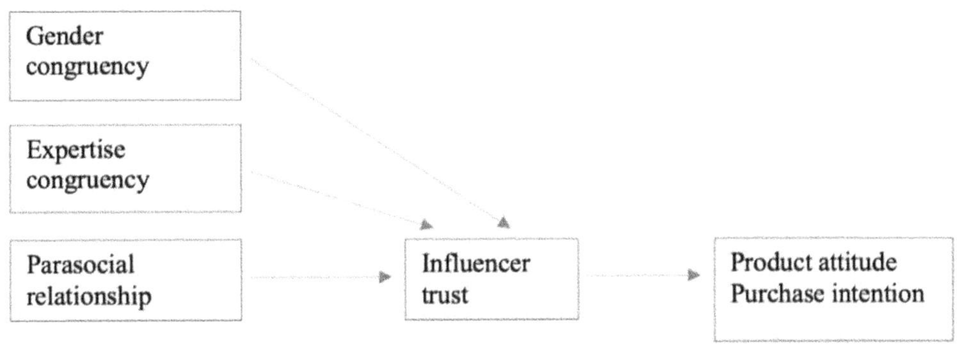

in masculinity (M_China = 3.50, SD = .85; M_US = 3.39, SD = 1.05) and individualism (M_China = 2.50, SD = .75; M_US = 2.43, SD = .90) compared to US TikTok users. Conversely, US TikTok users had higher power distance scores than their Chinese counterparts (M_China = 2.42, SD = .88; M_US = 3.12, SD = 1.16). Furthermore, within the US sample, male respondents scored higher in masculinity (M_male = 3.60, SD = .91; M_female = 3.15, SD = 1.14) and power distance (M_male = 3.32, SD = 1.08; M_female = 2.91, SD = 1.22) than female respondents. In contrast, female respondents outscored males in individualism (M_male = 2.30, SD = .80; M_female = 2.58, SD = .98), with all gender differences proving statistically significant. In the Chinese sample, male respondents also scored higher in masculinity (M_male = 3.69, SD = .74; M_female = 3.30, SD = .91) and power distance (M_male = 2.48, SD = .92; M_female = 2.36, SD = .85), but lower in individualism (M_male = 2.40, SD = .73; M_female = 2.60, SD = .77) compared to female respondents. However, gender differences were significant only for masculinity scores, $t(221) = 3.51$, $p < .01$, and not for power distance and individualism. When examining country differences after merging US and Chinese data, a t-test revealed that the only significant difference was for power distance in the combined dataset, $t(441) = 7.16$, $p < .01$, with no significant differences for masculinity, $t(441) = -1.21$, $p > .05$, or individualism, $t(441) = -.84$, $p > .05$.

To evaluate Hypothesis 3, descriptive analyses were conducted separately within US and Chinese samples, followed by a t-test on the combined US-China dataset to determine the significance of differences. The results indicated that Chinese users had higher expectations of influencer gender-product congruency than US users (M_China = 3.62, SD = .79; M_US = 3.51, SD = .95), but the country difference was not significant, $t(441) = -1.37$, $p > .05$. Thus, Hypothesis 5a was not supported. Additionally, in the combined dataset, male respondents expected higher influencer gender-product congruency than female respondents (Male = 3.72, SD = .80; M_female = 3.41, SD = .93), with a t-test confirming this gender difference as significant, $t(441) = 3.77$, $p < .01$.

Hierarchical regression analysis was applied to assess Hypotheses 4 and 5, with individual cultural values serving as control variables. Hypothesis 5b was not supported because the influence of gender-product congruency on product attitudes was stronger among US consumers ($\beta = .53$, $p < .01$) compared to Chinese consumers ($\beta = .38$, $p < .01$). Furthermore, the individualism value significantly influenced the regression models in both Chinese ($\beta = -.14$, $p < .05$) and US ($\beta = -.29$, $p < .01$) samples as a control variable. The negative coefficients indicate that higher individualism values correlate with a lower impact of influencer gender-product congruency on product attitudes.

Regression analysis also revealed support for Hypothesis 5c; the influence of influencer gender congruity with products on purchase intentions was stronger for Chinese users ($\beta = .49$, $p < .01$) than for US users ($\beta = .41$, $p < .01$). Additionally, in the Chinese sample, the power distance value acted as a significant negative control variable ($\beta = -.13$, $p < .05$), whereas in the US sample, individualism value was a significant negative control variable ($\beta = -.29$, $p < .01$).

(Tables 2 and 3)

DISCUSSION AND CONCLUSION

The Impact of Gender and Expertise Congruence on Users' Product Attitude/Purchase Intention

This study uncovers significant distinctions between Douyin users in China and TikTok users in the U.S. Drawing on a literature review, it was hypothesized that a gender match between an endorser and

Table 1. Individual cultural score grouped by country

	US			CH	
N = 220	Mean	SD	N = 221	Mean	SD
Individualism	2.43	0.9		2.50	0.75
Power distance	3.12	1.16		2.42	0.88
Masculinity	3.39	1.05		3.50	0.85

Table 2. Multiple regression analysis of gender congruency and product attitude with cultural value as control variables (China vs. the U.S.)

	China						US					
		Model 1			Model 2			Model 1			Model 2	
Variable	**B**	**SE.B**	**β**	**B**	**SE.B**	**β**	**B**	**SE.B**	**β**	**B**	**SE.B**	**β**
Masculinity	0.04	0.07	0.04	0.02	0.06	0.03	0.003	0.09	0.003	-0.06	0.08	-0.05
Powerdistance	0.04	0.06	0.04	0.04	0.06	0.04	0.12	0.08	0.13	0.07	0.07	0.07
Individualism	-0.17	0.07	-0.16	-0.15	0.06	0.14*	-0.58	0.09	-0.48	-0.35	0.08	0.29**
Gendercongruency				0.55	0.09	0.38**				0.90	0.10	.53**
R^2		.03			.18			.32			.52	
R^2 **change**					.15						.20	

Note: **$p < .01$.

Table 3. Multiple regression analysis of gender congruency and purchase intention with cultural value as control variables (China vs. the U.S.)

	China						US					
		Model 1			Model 2			Model 1			Model 2	
Variable	**B**	**SE.B**	***β***	**B**	**SE.B**	***β***	**B**	**SE.B**	***β***	**B**	**SE.B**	***β***
Masculinity	0.09	0.05	0.14	0.08	0.04	0.12	0.09	0.05	0.15	0.06	0.05	0.1
Powerdistance	-0.08	0.04	-0.14	-0.08	0.04	-.13*	-0.02	0.05	-0.03	-0.04	0.04	-0.08
Individualism	-0.04	0.05	-0.06	-0.03	0.04	-0.04	-0.3	0.05	-.43**	-0.2	0.05	-.29**
Gendercongruency				0.49	0.06	0.49**				0.4	0.1	.41**
R^2		.03			.26			.27			.39	
R^2 **change**					.23						.12	

Note: $^{**}p < .01$.

a product would positively influence the effectiveness of the endorsement. Gender compatibility is not the sole determinant of changes in attitude and purchase intentions towards a product endorsed by an influencer. The influencer's expertise regarding the product is equally critical. Many influencers were initially regular social media users who gained prominence due to their specialized knowledge in a particular area. They may have acquired this expertise through working in the field and possessing technical or professional knowledge, or they may have established their reputation by consistently using relevant products, thereby becoming grassroots experts. This latter path is particularly common among beauty and cosmetics enthusiasts who have become influencers on social media.

The regression analysis results from this study confirmed that influencer-product expertise congruency positively predicted participants' product attitudes and purchase intentions. Notably, influencer-product expertise congruency had a more substantial impact on participants in the U.S., suggesting that TikTok users in the U.S. were more readily influenced by an endorser's expertise on the topic. Conversely, Chinese Douyin users were less likely to be swayed by influencers based solely on expertise congruency with the product. Consequently, additional factors should be explored to understand the persuasive mechanisms of Douyin influencers on Chinese users.

Furthermore, when comparing the effects of influencer gender-product congruency and influencer expertise-product congruency on participants' product attitudes and purchase intentions, it was found that the former had a more substantial impact than the latter. Additionally, participants from both China and the U.S. were more significantly influenced by gender congruency than by expertise congruency. However, U.S. participants were comparatively more affected by both gender congruency and expertise congruency than Chinese participants. Moreover, gender and expertise congruency each independently influenced participants' product attitudes and purchase intentions.

The Role of Trust in Explaining Influencer's Effectiveness

Trust is a frequently examined factor that influences people's attitudes and behavioral changes when making decisions. Within influencer marketing, consumers' trust in influencers is indicative of the influencers' persuasive power over consumers' purchasing decisions. It is hypothesized that when the gender congruency between an influencer and a product aligns with consumers' gender or cultural values, it should positively influence consumers' trust in the influencer. Additionally, influencer gender-product congruency affected participants' trust in the influencer in both the U.S. and Chinese samples.

The subsequent mediation analysis confirmed the mediating role of influencer trust in the relationships between both influencer gender-product congruency and influencer expertise-product congruency, with product attitude and purchase intention. Across both samples and for all product categories, influencer trust accounted for part of the positive influence of gender congruency and expertise congruency on participants' product attitudes and purchase intentions. In essence, gender congruency and expertise congruency foster trust in the influencer, which in turn enhances participants' attitudes towards the product and their intentions to purchase. The mediation analysis also underscores trust as a pivotal element of an influencer's persuasive capacity on consumers. Therefore, to achieve influencer marketing objectives in terms of sales, brands and influencers should focus on fostering consumers' trust in the influencer. According to the results of this study, they should at least consider gender congruency and expertise congruency as key factors in building that trust.

Cultural Difference and Gender Congruence Effects between China and the U.S.

The individual cultural scores reported by participants in this study were the opposite of Hofstede's national scores. According to Hofstede's Insights (2021), China has a power distance score of 80, and the US has a score of 40, while the individualism scores for China and the US are 20 and 91, respectively, highlighting a significant difference in individualism levels between the two countries. Contrary to these findings, the present study revealed that participants from both countries reported low individualism scores, indicating a collectivistic orientation. Given that TikTok and Douyin are "twin" platforms under the Chinese parent company ByteDance, content transfer across the platforms is common (Su & Kaye, 2023). Content transfer is defined as the practice of 'borrowing, remixing, recreating, and reposting' trendy content either within the same platform or across different ones. Moreover, TikTok has a strategy of importing popular content from culturally influential markets to new markets, targeting specific regions for content deployment (Su & Kaye, 2023, p. 1539). This could explain why US TikTok users and Chinese Douyin users exhibit similar cultural values because they are influenced by some homogeneous content on both platforms.

The predominant demographic on TikTok/Douyin consists of younger generations. The majority of US TikTok users are young adults, aged 18 to 34, who make up 56% of US adults (Pew Research Center, 2024), with 47.4% of users being under 30 (Howarth, 2024). In China, as of November 2022, one-third of Douyin users are under 26 (Statista, 2023). Consequently, most TikTok users are from Generations Y and Z, with Generation Z (born after 1997) being the first to mature in a digital milieu and noted for being more receptive to change than Generation X or the baby boomers (Harari et al., 2023). This generational divide may help explain the differing cultural values between contemporary TikTok users and those from the year of 1980. With cultural globalization's advancement, the notions of a single world and global citizenship have emerged, which could explain why more US TikTok users favor community and group dynamics over individualism. Moreover, many Douyin users, having been raised during China's One-Child policy, received undivided attention and resources from their families, which may contribute to their higher individualism scores compared to their US counterparts and the older Chinese generation. Additionally, the increased educational attainment and rapid economic development in China may contribute to the younger generation's heightened awareness of gender equality's importance, potentially accounting for the lower power distance scores observed in this study.

Young TikTok users are more inclined than older generations to acknowledge other countries' strengths over the US (Hartig, 2021). Furthermore, 66% of American Gen Z individuals regard gender equality as a serious issue, compared to only 51% of those aged 65 and older (PRnewswire, 2022). Many participants, predominantly urban dwellers familiar with the Internet from a young age, are equipped to challenge traditional hierarchies and embrace new ideas. Over recent decades, China's rapid economic expansion and greater openness to the world have afforded Chinese people more opportunities to engage with global cultures and innovations. These factors — including the broad-mindedness of Chinese individuals and their age profile — may partially explain why findings related to cultural values do not align with Hofstede's original cultural dimension scores. Utilizing individual scores in this study suggests that country scores may not accurately reflect current consumer values in each country. Notably, the older average age of the US sample compared to the Chinese one could account for the higher power distance scores observed in the US sample.

In a later multiple regression analysis, the individual's power distance value was a negative control variable in the relationship between influencer gender-product congruency and purchase intention in the Chinese sample, opposite to the prior literature. However, the average power distance score of Chinese respondents was 2.42 on a 5-point Likert scale, which meant Chinese respondents disagreed with the statement of power distance. Therefore, the individual power distance and masculinity scores show that Chinese Douyin users did not accept power inequality in society and preferred gender and power justice. Moreover, the negative influence of power distance in people's purchase decisions also indicates that influencers are not higher up leaders to the general Douyin users. Instead, they are more influential because they are authentic, trustworthy, and building relationship with followers/consumers. Hence, it is understandable that power distance negatively correlated to consumers' purchase intentions in the Chinese sample because of their lower acceptance of societal inequality.

Theoretical Implications

As a successful global social media platform originating from China, TikTok/Douyin is garnering scholarly attention for its potential to significantly influence global trends. It is also a vital platform for cross-cultural studies, particularly for examining cultural differences between Western and non-Western countries. This research investigates the mechanisms behind social media influencers' persuasive power over their followers in product endorsements through the theoretical frameworks of gender congruity theory, the match-up hypothesis, and Hofstede's Cultural Dimensions. This pioneering study employs these theories to probe the influencer phenomenon across the U.S. and China on a leading social media and short video-sharing platform. The study underscores the significance of congruency between an endorser and a product in consumer decision-making, specifically concerning endorser-product gender and expertise congruency. The findings indicate that both gender and expertise congruency between the endorser and the product positively influence consumer product attitudes and purchase intentions.

It also elucidates that consumers' trust in influencers is pivotal in linking gender and expertise congruency, with positive product attitudes and purchase intentions. The derived model is applicable to TikTok users in both China and the U.S.

The present study also contributes to the literature in Hofstede's Cultural Dimensions by updating insights into this theory, demonstrating its applicability in modern digital contexts. In addition, the study also sheds light on the understanding of how generational differences impact cultural values. By utilizing individual scores instead of aggregating by country, the study emphasizes the importance of individual level analysis in cross-cultural studies.

Practical Implications

This research also enhances the practices of influencer marketing, particularly those on Douyin/TikTok targeting the U.S. and/or Chinese markets. It underscores the importance of gender congruity between the endorser and the product, especially as China and the U.S. exhibit masculine cultural dimensions where gender incongruity can lead to unfavorable influencer marketing outcomes. Therefore, marketing professionals planning influencer campaigns in these countries should carefully match the gender of the influencer with the product. For instance, skincare products or those with feminine traits should be endorsed by female influencers. Moreover, the importance of an influencer's expertise becomes more pronounced for products that are utilitarian rather than hedonic, influencing the effectiveness of the marketing strategy.

Furthermore, U.S. consumers place greater emphasis on the alignment of an influencer's expertise with the product compared to Chinese consumers. Therefore, marketers should give more consideration to the influence of expertise congruency on endorsement effectiveness in the U.S. Lastly, the trust in an influencer underpins the effectiveness of endorsements related to gender and expertise congruency. Thus, securing a trustworthy influencer is essential when aligning them with a product or marketing strategy.

Moreover, the cultural value has been changed in both countries; therefore, marketers and practitioners should consider the characteristics of current TikTok and Douyin users, and adapt their marketing efforts into different cultures.

CONCLUSION

This study evaluates the effectiveness of social media influencers' endorsements using the gender congruity theory, the match-up hypothesis, and the concept of cultural dimensions. It reaffirms the previous findings and indicate that gender and expertise congruency between an influencer and a product play a pivotal role in eliciting positive consumer attitudes towards products and intentions to purchase (Orth & Holancova, 2003;Schouten et al., 2019, Eisend & Langner, 2010). Moreover, these two factors are positively related to consumers' trust in influencers, which in turn predicts favorable product attitudes and purchase intentions. This trust accounts for the positive correlation between gender and expertise congruency, and endorsement effectiveness. Therefore, as previous study suggested, trust in influencers is a critical component of their endorsement efficacy (Hu et al., 2019; Jin et al., 2021; Kim & Kim, 2021). The insights from this research add to the body of knowledge regarding the theories explored and offer practical recommendations for successful influencer marketing strategies in both countries.

REFERENCES

Abosag, I., Romadan, Z. B., Baker, T., & Jin, Z. (2020). Customers' need for uniqueness theory versus brand congruence theory: The impact on satisfaction with social network sites. *Journal of Business Research, 117*, 862–872. doi:10.1016/j.jbusres.2019.03.016

Age, Ad. (2022). Ad Age names TikTok 'Marketer of the Year'. *PR Newswire*. https://www.prnewswire.com/news-releases/ad-age-names-tiktok-marketer-of-the-year-301187044.html

An, D., & Kim, S. (2006). Relating Hofstede's masculinity dimension to gender role portrayals in advertising. *International Marketing Review, 24*(2), 181–207. doi:10.1108/02651330710741811

Aspire. (2024) *The State of Influencer Marketing 2024*. Available at: https://www.aspire.io/ty-event/the-state-of-influencer-marketing-2024?utm_source=webinar&utm_medium=email-OD&utm_campaign=state-of-influencer marketing&mkt_tok=OTgyLURPTi0yNjYAAAGQvgcoNdhRhorW-3p1mW_2E3ct1sWuSbty-pmmZbIM282Xdn5zbq0M04WPm5zp2Oz35Nrz5QVP7Jl-iIDVnCd_vXXw7inTHDSZKCp6H6rpEA#watch

Bestvater, S. (2024, February 22). *How U.S. adults use TikTok*. Pew Research Center: Internet, Science & Tech. https://www.pewresearch.org/internet/2024/02/22/how-u-s-adults-use-tiktok/

Chaudhuri, A., & Holbrook, M. B. (2001). *Brand loyalty scale*. PsycTESTS Dataset. doi:10.1037/t11015-000

Choi, S., & Rifon, N. J. (2012). It is a match: The impact of congruence between celebrity image and consumer ideal self on endorsement effectiveness. *Psychology and Marketing, 29*(9), 639–650. doi:10.1002/mar.20550

Clow, K. A., Ricciardelli, R., & Bartfay, W. J. (2014). Are you man enough to be a nurse? The impact of ambivalent sexism and role congruity on perceptions of men and women in nursing advertisements. *Sex Roles, 72*(7-8), 363–376. doi:10.1007/s11199-014-0418-0

Cota, A. A., & Xinaris, S. (1993). Factor structure of the sex-role ideology scale: Introducing a short form. *Sex Roles, 29*(5-6), 345–358. doi:10.1007/BF00289428

De Meulenaer, S., Dens, N., De Pelsmacker, P., & Eisend, M. (2019). How consumers' values influence responses to male and female gender role stereotyping in advertising. *International Journal of Advertising, 37*(6), 893–913. doi:10.1080/02650487.2017.1354657

Delgado-Ballester, E., & Munuera-Alemén, J. L. (2001). Brand trust in the context of consumer loyalty. *European Journal of Marketing, 35*(11/12), 1238–1258. doi:10.1108/EUM0000000006475

Diekman, A. B., & Goodfriend, W. (2006). Rolling with the changes: A role congruity perspective on gender norms. *Psychology of Women Quarterly, 30*(4), 369–383. doi:10.1111/j.1471-6402.2006.00312.x

Dwivedi, A., & Johnson, L. (2013). Trust–Commitment as a mediator of the celebrity endorser–brand equity relationship in a service context. *Australasian Marketing Journal, 21*(1), 36–42. doi:10.1016/j.ausmj.2012.10.001

Eagly, A. H. (2004). Prejudice: Toward a more inclusive understanding. In A. H. Eagly, R. M. Baron, & V. L. Hamilton (Eds.), *The social psychology of group identity and social conflict: Theory, application, and practice* (pp. 45–64). doi:10.1037/10683-003

Eagly, A. H., & Karau, S. J. (2002). Role congruity theory of prejudice toward female leaders. *Psychological Review*, *109*(3), 573–598. doi:10.1037/0033-295X.109.3.573 PMID:12088246

Eagly, A. H., & Wood, W. (2012). Social role theory. Handbook of Theories of Social Psychology, 2, 458–476. doi:10.4135/9781446249222.n49

Erdogan, B. Z. (1999). Celebrity Endorsement: A Literature Review. *Journal of Marketing Management*, *41*(3), 291–314. doi:10.1362/026725799784870379

Geyser, W. (2022). *TikTok statistics – 63 TikTok stats you need to know* [2022 Update]. Influencer Marketing Hub. https://influencermarketinghub.com/tiktok-stats/

Goldsmith, R. E., Lafferty, B. A., & Newell, S. J. (2000). The impact of corporate credibility and celebrity credibility on consumer reaction to advertisements and brands. *Journal of Advertising*, *29*(3), 43–54. doi:10.1080/00913367.2000.10673616

Grubb, E., & Grathwohl, H. (1967). Consumer self-concept, symbolism and market behavior: A theoretical approach. *Journal of Marketing*, *31*(4), 22–27. doi:10.1177/002224296703100405

Guo, Q., Liu, Z., Li, X., & Qiao, X. (2018). Indulgence and long term orientation influence prosocial behavior at national level. *Frontiers in Psychology*, *9*, 9. doi:10.3389/fpsyg.2018.01798 PMID:30319499

Gupta, V., Hanges, P. J., & Dorfman, P. (2002). Cultural clusters: Methodology and findings. *Journal of World Business*, *37*(1), 11–15. doi:10.1016/S1090-9516(01)00070-0

Ha, L. (2017). Social media advertising and eWOM from 2011 to present. *Journal of Advertising*. http://explore.tandfonline.com/content/bes/ujoa-social-media-virtual-special-issue

Ha, L., & Yang, Y. (2021). Research about persuasive effects of social media influencers as online opinion leaders 1990-2020: A review. *International Journal of Internet Marketing and Advertising*.

Harari, T. T., Sela, Y., & Bareket-Bojmel, L. (2022). Gen Z during the COVID-19 Crisis: A Comparative Analysis of the Differences between Gen Z and Gen X in Resilience, Values and Attitudes. *Current Psychology (New Brunswick, N.J.)*, *42*(28), 24223–24232. doi:10.1007/s12144-022-03501-4 PMID:35967492

Hartig, H. (2022). *Younger Americans still more likely than older adults to say there are other countries better than the U.S.* Pew Research Center. Retrieved 8 September 2022, from https://www.pewresearch.org/fact-tank/2021/12/16/younger-americans-still-more-likely-than-older-adults-to-say-there-are-other-countries-better-than-the-u-s/

Heckler, S. E., & Childers, T. L. (1992). The role of expectancy and relevancy in memory for verbal and visual information: What is incongruency? *The Journal of Consumer Research*, *18*(4), 475–492. doi:10.1086/209275

Heilman, M. E. (1983). Sex bias in work settings: The lack of fit model. *Research in Organizational Behavior*, *5*, 269–298.

Hofstede, G., & Hofstede, G. J. (2005). *Cultures and organizations: Software of the mind*. McGraw-Hill.

Hofstede, G., Hofstede, G. J., & Minkov, M. (2010). *Cultures and organizations: Software of the mind* (3rd ed.). McGraw-Hill.

Hofstede, G., & McCrae, R. R. (2004). Personality and culture revisited: Linking traits and dimensions of culture. *Cross-Cultural Research, 38*(1), 52–88. doi:10.1177/1069397103259443

Hofstede, G. H. (1980). *Culture's consequences: International differences in work-related values*. Sage.

Hofstede, G. H. (2001). *Culture's consequences: Comparing values, behaviors, institutions, and organizations across nations*. Sage.

Hofstede Insights. (2021), *Country Comparison - Hofstede Insights*. Available at: https://www.hofstede-insights.com/country-comparison/china,the-usa/

Horton, D., & Wohl, R. (1956). Mass communication and para-social interaction. *Psychiatry, 19*(3), 215–229. doi:10.1080/00332747.1956.11023049 PMID:13359569

Howarth, J. (2024, January 12). *Tiktok user age, gender, & demographics (2024)*. Exploding Topics. https://explodingtopics.com/blog/tiktok-demographics

Hu, H., Zhang, D., & Wang, C. (2019). Impact of social media influencers' endorsement on application adoption: A trust transfer perspective'. *Social Behavior and Personality, 47*(11), 1–12. doi:10.2224/sbp.8518

Iqbal, M. (2022). *TikTok revenue and usage statistics 2022*. Business Of Apps. https://www.businessofapps.com/data/tik-tok-statistics/

Kalin, R., & Tilby, P. J. (1978). Development and validation of a sex-role ideology scale. *Psychological Reports, 42*(3), 731–738. doi:10.2466/pr0.1978.42.3.731 PMID:674496

Kaur, N., Ricciardelli, R., & Clow, K. (2023). Stereotypes of male nurses through the framework of social role theory and stereotype content model. *Journal of Men's Studies, 31*(1), 157–178. doi:10.1177/10608265221108209

Kauv, S., & Blotnicky, K. A. (2020). Brand loyalty, brand trust, peer influence and price sensitivity as influencer in student computer purchase. *Journal of Business and Behavioral Sciences, 31*(1), 131–150.

Kemp, S. (2022). *TikTok's ad audience hits 1.02 billion (And other mind-blowing stats)*. Social Media Marketing & Management Dashboard. https://blog.hootsuite.com/simon-kemp-social-media/

Kim, D. Y., & Kim, H.-Y. (2021). Trust me, Trust Me not: A nuanced view of influencer marketing on social media. *Journal of Business Research, 134*, 223–232. doi:10.1016/j.jbusres.2021.05.024

Lee, J. E., & Watkins, B. (2016). YouTube vloggers' influence on consumer luxury brand perceptions and intentions. *Journal of Business Research, 69*(12), 5753–5760. doi:10.1016/j.jbusres.2016.04.171

Lee, J.-G., & Thorson, E. (2008). The impact of celebrity–product incongruence on the effectiveness of product endorsement. *Journal of Advertising Research, 48*(3), 433–449. doi:10.2501/S0021849908080446

Lynch, J., & Schuler, D. (1994). The matchup effect of spokesperson and product congruency: A schema theory interpretation. *Psychology and Marketing*, *11*(5), 417–445. doi:10.1002/mar.4220110502

Marshall, T. (2008). Cultural differences in intimacy: The influence of gender-role ideology and individualism—collectivism. *Journal of Social and Personal Relationships*, *25*(1), 143–168. doi:10.1177/0265407507086810

Mathiyalakan, S., Heilman, G., Ho, K. K. W., & Law, W. (2018). An examination of the impact of gender and culture on Facebook privacy and trust in Guam. *Journal of International Technology and Information Management*, *27*(1), 29–56. doi:10.58729/1941-6679.1363

Matthes, J., Prieler, M., & Adam, K. (2016). Gender-role portrayals in television advertising across the globe. *Sex Roles*, *75*(7-8), 314–327. doi:10.1007/s11199-016-0617-y PMID:27688526

McCormick, K. (2016). Celebrity endorsements: Influence of a product-endorser match on millennials attitudes and purchase intentions'. *Journal of Retailing and Consumer Services*, *32*, 39–45. doi:10.1016/j.jretconser.2016.05.012

McGuire, W. J. (1969). The Nature of Attitudes and Attitude Change. The Handbook of Social Psychology, 3, 372–398.

Moon, Y. S., & Chen, K. (2002). Gender portrayals in Hong Kong and Korean children's TV commercials: A cross-cultural comparison. *Asian Journal of Communication*, *12*(2), 10–19. doi:10.1080/01292980209364825

Odekerken-Schroder, G. K., Wulf, D., & Hofstede, N. (2002). Is gender stereotyping in advertising more prevalent in masculine countries? A cross-national analysis. *International Marketing Review*, *19*(4), 408–419. doi:10.1108/02651330210435690

Orth, U. R., & Holancova, K. (2003). The influence of gender congruence on consumer attributions: A cross-cultural investigation. *Journal of International Consumer Marketing*, *15*(4), 79–107.

Parboteeah, K. P., Hoegl, M., & Cullen, J. B. (2008). Managers' gender role attitudes: A country institutional profile approach. *Journal of International Business Studies*, *39*(5), 795–813. doi:10.1057/palgrave.jibs.8400384

Research reveals Gen Z's priorities as Enterprise, Environment and Equality. (2022). Retrieved 8 September 2022, from https://www.prnewswire.com/news-releases/research-reveals-gen-zs-priorities-as-enterprise-environment-and-equality-301517764.html

Schouten, A. P., Janssen, L., & Verspaget, M. (2021). Celebrity vs. Influencer endorsements in advertising: The role of identification, credibility, and product-endorser fit. *International Journal of Advertising*, *39*(2), 258–281. doi:10.1080/02650487.2019.1634898

Shinnar, R., Giacomin, O., & Janssen, F. (2012). Entrepreneurial Perceptions and Intentions: The Role of Gender and Culture. *Entrepreneurship Theory and Practice*, *36*(3), 465–493. doi:10.1111/j.1540-6520.2012.00509.x

Siemens, J. C., Smith, S., Fisher, D., & Jensen, T. D. (2008). Product Expertise versus Professional Expertise: Congruency between an Endorser's Chosen Profession and the Endorsed Product. *Journal of Targeting. Measurement and Analysis for Marketing*, *16*(3), 159–168. doi:10.1057/jt.2008.8

Su, C., & Kaye, B. V. (2023). Borderline Practices on Douyin/TikTok: Content Transfer and Algorithmic Manipulation. *Media Culture & Society*, *45*(8), 1534–1549. doi:10.1177/01634437231168308

Thomala, L. L. (2023) *China: Douyin (TikTok)'s user age distribution 2022, Statista.* Available at: https://www.statista.com/statistics/1202727/china-douyin-user-age-distribution/

Till, B. D., & Busler, M. (1998). Matching products with endorsers: Attractiveness versus expertise. *Journal of Consumer Marketing*, *15*(6), 576–586. doi:10.1108/07363769810241445

Venaik, S., Zhu, Y., & Brewer, P. (2013). Looking into the future: Hofstede long term orientation versus GLOBE future orientation. *Cross Cultural Management*, *20*(3), 361–385. doi:10.1108/CCM-02-2012-0014

Wiles, J., Wiles, C., & Tjernlund, A. (1995). A comparison of gender role portrayals in magazine advertising. *European Journal of Marketing*, *29*(11), 35–49. doi:10.1108/03090569510100696

Wood, W., & Eagly, A. H. (2012). Biosocial construction of sex differences and similarities in behavior. In J. M. Olson & M. P. Zanna (Eds.), Advances in experimental social psychology. Academic Press. doi:10.1016/B978-0-12-394281-4.00002-7

Yang, Y., & Ha, L. (2021). Why people use TikTok (Douyin) and how their purchase decisions are affected by social media influencers in China: A uses & gratifications and para-social relationship perspective. *Journal of Interactive Advertising*, *21*(3), 297–305. doi:10.1080/15252019.2021.1995544

Yoo, B., Donthu, N., & Lenartowicz, T. (2011). Measuring Hofstede's five dimensions of cultural values at the individual level: Development and validation of CVSCALE. *Journal of International Consumer Marketing*, *23*, 193–210.

KEY TERMS AND DEFINITIONS

Celebrity: Individuals who have attained widespread recognition and fame through traditional media channels like film, music, or politics; they are often seen as aspirational figures or embodiments of ideal self-concepts, serving as role model to the public.

Endorsement Effectiveness: Product attitude and purchase intention are recognized as two dimensions of the effectiveness of influencer endorsements.

Hofstede's Cultural Dimensions: Five key differences in cultural values across societies: Power Distance, Individualism vs. Collectivism, Masculinity vs. Femininity, Uncertainty Avoidance, and Long-Term vs. Short-Term Orientation, explaining variations in workplace behavior.

Influencer Expertise-Product Congruency: The alignment of an influencer's specific domain with the category of the product they endorse.

Influencer Gender-Product Congruency: The alignment of an influencer's gender with the gendered attributes of the product they endorse.

Influencer Trust: The confidence consumer place in influencers, based on the influencers' perceived knowledge and authority in a specific domain of communication.

Opinion Leader: Individuals recognized for their early adoption of new technologies and innovative ideas. They possess the capability to influence and spread their views to those actively seeking guidance and insights.

Social Media Influencer: Individuals who have garnered a substantial following on digital platforms by consistently sharing content that resonates with a niche; they start as regular users and cultivate their expertise and reputation over time.

Chapter 14
Navigating Consumer Engagement:
Unveiling the Influence of Social Media Influencers

Rajni Bala
https://orcid.org/0000-0002-1225-939X
Chitkara Business School, Chitkara University, Punjab, India

Vinod Kumar
https://orcid.org/0000-0002-3578-8155
M.M. Institute of Management, Maharishi Markandeshwar University (deemed), Mullana-Ambala, India

Ritu Sharma
M.M. Institute of Management, Maharishi Markandeshwar University (deemed), Mullana-Ambala, India

ABSTRACT

Consumer engagement is paramount in the digital era, where people actively engage with brands. The importance of social media influencers in influencing customer behavior has grown in the current digital environment. The digital era has changed how consumers interact with brands and judge what to buy. Most information and engagement now occur on social media platforms, and customers frequently look to influencers to help them make decisions. Nowadays, influencer marketing is a multi-billion-dollar business. Brands are forming influencer partnerships with various industries to connect and interact with their target consumers. Given the significant investments in the field, evaluating influencer marketing's success and impact is essential. The study explores social media influencers' crucial role in influencing customer choice. This chapter's goals are to thoroughly examine consumer engagement dynamics and expose the power that social media influencers possess.

DOI: 10.4018/979-8-3693-0912-4.ch014

INTRODUCTION

Consumer engagement (CE) is a process that connects the consumer with a brand through the knot of trust, loyalty, and satisfaction. This two-way process involves communication from both ends as what the brand serves or sends is considered, analyzed, and responded to by the consumer. The success of a product largely depends upon the consumers' feedback as it is a way to attract new consumers. In other words, a consumer plays a crucial role in increasing the brand value in the market for a company, a brand, or a shopkeeper. The consumer is not a mere onlooker who watches and observes the brand's marketing activities but also becomes a part of the generation process (Sawhney et al., 2005, p.15). Based upon emotions, it is a practical activity in which a consumer is involved with a brand in multiple forms like cognitive, affective, behavioral, etc. "Cognitive engagement refers to the overall focused mental activity, involving attention and absorption; affective engagement involves enthusiasm and enjoyment about a focal object, while behavioral engagement denotes the active manifestations of the concept, including sharing, reviewing, learning, recommending, and endorsing behaviors (Dessart, 2017, p. 400). The involvement of the consumer with the brand is a process that takes time, consistent efforts, and innovative strategies to keep them intact and contribute. To achieve this objective, the method adopted by a firm is called consumer engagement marketing, in which the brand encourages and motivates them for their creative input in this process (Harmeling et al., 2017, p.331).

Adopting various marketing tools to convince consumers is not limited to traditional ways (face-to-face) but machine-to-human (telephonic communication) and machine-to-machine (Facebook, WhatsApp). In a world of digital advancement, online methods are gaining popularity in consumer engagement as they save time, money, and energy. Moreover, it works faster and reaches new people who were not associated with the brand earlier. Nowadays, business organizations invest more in online tools to engage consumers with their brands, and the reason behind this strategy is that people all over the world are more interested in online transactions and spend quality time shopping from online stores, booking transportation, using GPS for finding routes, pay bills of basic needs like water and electricity. During online activity, many people become a part of consumer engagement- active and passive. The active ones pay full attention to new products, attractive offers, and seasonal sales announced by the brand and share them with others. On the other hand, the passive group looks at the comments, shares, and reviews lightly given by others. As a result, active engagement is essential, and the passive side makes a significant contribution as a sole glance creates a lasting impression in the minds of the least interested consumers.

The rise of social media sites has made a tremendous change in consumer engagement marketing. Social media has become a mouthpiece of the brand, binding the company and the consumer together in a strong thread of mutual understanding that works slowly but steadily as it marks a significant impact on the inner state of the consumer. As a result, they start working as a source of brand representation and help increase the demand for their products. Social media sites like Facebook and WhatsApp for social networking, Twitter for micro blogging, YouTube for sharing videos, and Blogger for posting blogs make remarkable contributions to consumers and company interaction (Fischer & Reuber, 2011, p.12).

Facebook, the most used social networking site worldwide, has become a center of attraction for companies, spreading product awareness and giving cutthroat competition to their competitors. For this, they create a Facebook page, fill it with high-quality images and videos highlighting the remarkable features of their products, add reviews of happy and satisfied customers, and invite more people with similar interests to join the group. Many likes, comments, and shares for a post give tremendous rise in the demand for a product as people consider it worthwhile. Sometimes, there are some negative comments or complaints about the product, but these comments are a blessing in disguise for the companies. The reviews given by the users on social media allow the brand to analyze what the consumers want. If there is some gap between their expectations and reality, then it is a golden chance for them to make the desired changes to make it the consumer's first choice. Another popular social media platform for consumer engagement is WhatsApp. This is the most active and time-saving network, connecting people with the latest product and service updates and providing other valuable details. The brands create community groups and add customers immediately after they have done shopping from them. Now, people in the group find others with the same interests and feel free to express them, share their experiences, and learn from each other. The brand ties the community members in a relationship of mutual sharing, reviewing, and appreciating (Arora et al., 2019, p.479). While discussing and analyzing within a group, people come closer and feel a sense of belonging to the members and the brand. Gradually, they develop an emotional attachment to the company, which will have a significant impact on the company's sales in the future.

The contribution of other popular social media sites like YouTube and Twitter to influencing consumer behavior must be addressed. Using these platforms, companies put their best videos and images displaying their products at their best to create brand awareness. Conducting online demo sessions, workshops, and Q&A sessions are some helpful tools the brands use as a part of their marketing strategy. A professional, informative, and consumer-friendly approach undoubtedly leads to higher client commitment. To present valuable insight into the product, brands use blogs with internal links for detailed information. Interested people can click on them and get what they want. Here, the comment section is left open so that the users can write their views about the product and play an active role in consumer engagement. In this way, these internet-based applications have given a chance to involve consumers in determining brand value (Fournier & Avery, 2011, p.199).

CONSUMER ENGAGEMENT

Engaging with consumers has become increasingly important in business practices over time. In the past, marketing focused more on developing and distributing products with consumer interaction. It was one approach where companies pushed their products to the market. However, market research played a crucial role in understanding consumer behavior in the century. Businesses began to realize the significance of gathering insights and feedback from consumers. This led to a shift towards a consumer approach and the emergence of consumerism, which emphasized consumer rights and interests. Companies started prioritizing customer satisfaction. In the 20th century, relationship marketing gained prominence as businesses shifted from transactional marketing to building long-term customer connections (Grönroos, 1997, p.325). The focus was on fostering customer loyalty and retention. With the arrival of the internet and digital technologies, consumer engagement underwent further transformations. Platforms like media, email marketing, and e-commerce opened avenues for direct interaction between companies and consumers. Data analytics became instrumental in personalizing marketing efforts, while user-generated content on social media allowed consumer participation in brand discussions and product reviews (Han et al., 2018, p.609). As technology progressed, companies started embracing an omnichannel strategy to connect with customers through interaction points. The aim was to deliver a consistent experience, both online and offline.

The experience economy, where consumer participation goes beyond goods and services, characterizes the present (Pencarelli et al., 2016, p.208). Businesses aim to give customers unique and engaging experiences through events, narratives, and personalization. Today, data analytics and artificial intelligence significantly impact customer engagement. Businesses use data to understand consumer preferences and behavior to develop personalized marketing strategies. Customers now demand that companies take socially conscious actions and work towards sustainability. Nowadays, interacting with customers frequently entails committing to moral and environmental principles. In conclusion, consumer engagement has changed from a one-sided marketing strategy to a more interactive, data-driven, and customer-centric approach. It keeps altering in response to advancing technology and shifting consumer expectations.

These definitions demonstrate how different contexts can give customer engagement various meanings and applications, but that at its core, it always entails fostering connections, interactions, and relationships between individuals or groups and the entities they engage with, whether those entities are businesses, organizations, communities, or educational institutions.

Dimensions of Consumer Engagement

The literature stated the concept of engagement as one-dimensional, focusing instead on its emotional, cognitive, or behavioral components. Within the one-dimensional perspective, the behavioral component is particularly important. The one-dimensional techniques have the advantage of being straightforward, but they need to adequately capture the wide conceptual range of involvement.

The degree of involvement, interaction, and emotional connection that customers have with a brand, product, or organization is referred to by the complex concept of consumer engagement. It is essential for fostering consumer satisfaction, increasing revenue, and promoting brand loyalty (Holland et al., 2001, p.35). The definitions, concepts, and arguments used to describe the consumer engagement construct have changed significantly over time as it has evolved and been reinterpreted. However as of now, there is yet to be an overarching conceptualization in the literature. A number of frameworks have been developed to examine and comprehend consumer engagement. These models offer insightful information about the components, procedures, and results of consumer engagement.

Table 1. Definitions of consumer engagement

Orientation	Definition	Author's Name
Company and Brand oriented	Consumer engagement is the cognitive, emotional, and behavioral bond customers have with a company, brand, or product. Customers' loyalty, contentment, and advocacy are fostered through interactions, experiences, and connections.	Hollebeek et al., (2014) and Keller (2001)
Customer experience oriented	Consumer engagement is the process by which customers actively participate in experiences rather than just watching them.	McAlexander et al. (2002)
Brand and Customer relationship-oriented	Building a sustained, mutually beneficial relationship between a brand and its customers is called consumer engagement.	Rogers (2016)
Digital Marketing oriented	Consumer engagement in digital marketing space was defined as the act of establishing and upholding meaningful connections between brands and consumers across a various digital channels, including email, social media, mobile apps, and websites.	Labrecque et al. (2013)
Social Media oriented	Consumer engagement in the context of social media refers to the degree of interaction, participation, and connection that people or communities have with a brand's social media content. It involves comments, likes, shares, and other types of internet communication.	Wondwesen Tafesse (2016)

Table 2. Engagement dimensionality

One-Dimensional	
Emotional	**Roberts and Davenport (2002)**
	Catteeuw et al. (2007)
Cognitive	Blumenfeld and Meece (1988)
	Guthrie (2001)
	Guthrie and Cox (2001)
Behavioral	Peppers and Rogers (2005)
	Saczynski et al. (2006)
	Downer, Sara, and Robert (2007)
Multidimensional	
Emotional/Behavioral	Norris, Jean, and Garth (2003)
	Huo, Binning, and Molina (2009)
Cognitive/Emotional	Marks (2000)
	Passikoff (2006)
	London, Geraldine, and Shauna (2007)
Cognitive/Behavioral	Harvey (2005)
	Kane (2008)
	Matthews et al. (2010)
	Hu (2019)
Cognitive/Emotional/Behavioral	Appelbaum (2001)
	Macey and Schneider (2008)
	Van Doorn et al., (2010)
	Mollen, Anne and Hugh Wilson (2010),

Table 3. Summary of consumer engagement models

Author's Name	Engagement Model Name	Dimensions
Van Doorn et al. (2010)	Consumer Engagement Model	The cycle of customer engagement activates
Hollebeek (2011)	Engagement Decision Model	Customer interaction and Customer involvement
Vivek et al. (2012)	Engagement-Investment-Resource Model	Resources Allocation: Time, Money, Efforts
Pansari & Kumar (2017)	Engagement Marketing Model	Cognitive, Emotional, Behavioral and Social aspects and its effect on Brand Loyalty
Huang et al. (2017).	Motivation-Ability-Trigger (MAT) Model	Motivational and ability triggers for engagement in online communities
Vargo and Lusch (2004)	The Value Co-Creation Framework	Involvement and customer value
So et al. (2016)	3C Model of Brand Engagement	Content, Context and Customers

Consumer Engagement Model. The model describes a cycle of customer engagement that includes stages including brand or product awareness, the first interaction, engagement, and disengagement (Van Doorn et al., 2010, p. 260). It highlights the evolving character of engagement over time.

Four Dimensions of Consumer Engagement. The four elements of engagement identified by this mode were cognitive, emotional, behavioral, and social engagement (Brodie et al., 2011, p.259). It highlights how these qualities are interrelated and affect patron loyalty and advocacy. The conceptual framework of consumer involvement can be divided into subparts to comprehend it better. Cognitive engagement is defined as consumers' mental attachment to a brand or item. It entails being aware of, knowledgeable about, and understanding the brand's offerings (Vivek et al., 2012, p.131). Metrics, including brand memory, product awareness, and information retention, can be used to gauge cognitive engagement. Emotional engagement focuses on connecting with a brand or product (Pansari & Kumar, 2017, p.298). Strong emotional relationships require the presence of positive feelings like joy, trust, and love. Net Promoter Scores (NPS), Customer satisfaction surveys, and sentiment analysis can all be used to measure emotional engagement. Behavioral engagement is based on the acts consumers perform in response to a brand or product (De Vries et al., 2014, p.501). It includes making purchases, giving advice, using social media, and participating in loyalty programs. Measures of behavioral engagement include conversion rates, customer retention, and advocacy. The social interactions that customers experience with brands and their peers are highlighted by social engagement. Participating in user-generated content initiatives, sharing content on social media, and joining brand communities are all examples of social engagement. Likes, shares, comments, and community involvement are all examples of social engagement metrics.

The Engagement Decision Model. (Hollebeek, 2011, p. 152) proposed a paradigm emphasizing that customer interaction is vital in decision-making. It implies that involvement affects how information is processed, how brands are assessed, and ultimately, how consumers judge what to buy.

The Engagement-Investment-Resource Model. (Vivek et al., 2012, p.125) model addresses the notion that consumer engagement entails the allocation of resources (such as time, effort, and money) and looks at the elements that motivate customers to invest in their involvement with a brand or product.

The Engagement Marketing Model. (Pansari & Kumar, 2017, p. 303) created a model incorporating different engagement aspects, including cognitive, emotional, behavioral, and social. This model also described how engagement marketing techniques might affect brand loyalty and customer advocacy.

The Motivation-Ability-Trigger (MAT) Model. The MAT model focuses on the motivational, ability, and trigger aspects that drive consumer engagement in online brand communities. The importance of both intrinsic and external motives is emphasized.

The Social Identity Theory. The social identity theory proposes that consumers interact with brands or communities to identify with a specific group or brand. It highlights how crucial social identity is for promoting involvement.

The Value Co-Creation Framework. Vargo and Lusch (2004) developed this concept that goes beyond conventional marketing and emphasizes the co-creation of value between businesses and consumers. Consumer involvement is crucial to this co-creation.

The 3C Model of Brand Engagement. So et al. (2016) created a model stating that content, context, and customers are the three main factors influencing brand engagement. It implies that engaging material can increase customer engagement when used in the appropriate setting.

These models offer a range of methods for examining consumer interaction in various business settings. Researchers and marketers can use these models to increase their profits and create plans for boosting customer involvement and fortifying consumer-brand bonds.

SOCIAL MEDIA INFLUENCERS

People with a large following on social media who can alter the opinions of their followers are known as social media influencers. They use their expertise, credibility, or fame in a particular field to influence views, promote goods and services, and engage with their audience. These influencers can be prominent individuals, specialists, passionate fans, or regular people who have built large followings on social media sites like YouTube, Instagram, TikTok, Twitter, etc.

Social media influencers (SMIs) are innovative independent promoters who use tweets, blogs, and other social media platforms to shape audience impressions (Freberg, 2011, p.91). Social media platforms are becoming populated with social media influencers (SMIs). These content producers have built sizable audiences, frequently numbering in the thousands or even millions of followers on websites like YouTube, Facebook, or Instagram, enabling them to effectively communicate with and exert influence over a sizable audience with their messages (Uzunolu & Misci Kip, 2014, p.595). Brand marketers are drawn to these sizable followings because they can use them to their advantage when forming paid agreements with SMIs for advertising or product promotion (De Veirman et al., 2017, p.801). Brands, therefore, perceive social media influencers as persons with loyal and significant followings. They engage with these networks via various social media sites, allowing them to support products as unbiased third parties and fostering trust in the company. The loyalty of an influencer's audience gives them the capacity to drive customers to a company's website and increase its visibility on social media to influence the brand's image (Jaitly & Gautam, 2021, p.229). Influencers are adept content producers who create exciting and high-quality material. Their originality and capacity to create relatable content draw in viewers and promote likes, comments, and shares. Influencers frequently work with brands to promote goods and services. Their recommendations and reviews may impact customer choices, increasing interaction as followers enquire about the items they are being promoted, post queries, or share personal experiences. Influencers inspire followers to produce and distribute original content on a specific subject or problem. User-generated content campaigns increase engagement by directly involving customers and giving them a sense of belonging to the influencer's network. Social media influencers play a crucial role in fostering consumer engagement because of their reliability, authenticity, ability to create authentic content, and capacity for two-way communication.

Influencer marketing has two major obstacles: selecting the appropriate social media influencers for collaboration and evaluating the efficacy of the resulting campaigns. The manual assessment and evaluation of social media influencers is quite time-consuming. Furthermore, managers find it impractical to examine each sponsored post by SMIs as influencer marketing initiatives frequently involve multiple such posts. Brand marketers and agencies use a variety of measures as key performance indicators, known as KPIs, for both SMI selection and outcome measurement (Fay & Larkin (2017, p.139). For instance, they may utilize the number of followers or comments posted on each post to gauge the reach and impact of SMIs (Peters et al., 2013,p.291). These indicators are readily accessible to the general public, understandable, and comparative among the various social media platforms. Social media influencers can be further classified into macro, micro, nano, mega, and specialist or niche influencers.

CONSUMER ENGAGEMENT MODELS

A social media influencer is a person who engages the audience on social media sites. Influencers post content in a particular area on social media platforms, such as food, travel, fitness, or fashion (Haenlein et al., 2020, p.12). Academics and business experts are very interested in social media influencers because of their potential as a tool for brand promotion. Social media influencers significantly impact how consumers interact with brands in the current digital environment. Influencers have a devoted and active following. Higher engagement rates result from consumers being more likely to interact with material created by influencers they trust. Influencer marketing is a crucial component of many digital marketing strategies because brands understand the significance of influencers in reaching and interacting with their target audience. Consumer engagement models and social media influencers are closely related since influencers frequently function as essential elements of many engagement tactics.

The Consumer Engagement Continuum. Kabadayi & Price (2014) proposed a continuum model of consumer engagement, with low engagement (such as passive consumption) and high engagement (such as active participation and co-creation). This model takes into account the fact that consumer engagement levels can vary.

The Influencer Brand Collaboration Model. Schivinski & Dabrowski (2016) proposed that Brands are collaborating with social media influencers to engage their customers. Influencers who share a brand's values are partnered with by brands. They authentically advertise the brand's goods or services with the help of firm- generated content. The influencer's current following creates user-generated content and increases engagement. Brands monitor the engagement metrics (click-through rates, conversion rates, likes, shares, and comments) on which the influencer's activities have an impact.

The Influencer Funnel Model. This model states that how influencer created content links with marketing funnel and brand reputation (Colicev et al., 2019, p.111). This model provides crucial management insights into social media marketing based on the following stages. A) Awareness: Influencers introduce a brand or product to their audience. B) Interest: Users who follow the promoted content show interest. C) Desire: A desire for the product is sparked by the influencer's endorsement. D) Action: Followers take action by making a purchase or connecting with the brand.

The Brand Engagement Funnel Model. Rossolatos (2021) proposed this model for social media influencers and communities. This model states that Influencers propose brands or products to their audience. They engage their followers through likes, comments, and shares. The engaged followers take action, such as subscribing to emails or making purchases known as conversion. Influencers promote brand loyalty through maintaining interactions. Consistent clients become advocates by disclosing their favorable encounters.

Table 4. Summary of consumer engagement models of social media influencers

Author's Name	Engagement Model Name	Dimensions
Kabadayi & Price (2014)	Consumer Engagement Continuum	High and Low Engagement continuum
Schivinski & Dabrowski (2016)	Influencer Brand Collaboration Model	Brands and Social Media Influencers Collaboration
(Colicev et al., 2019).	Influencer Funnel Model	Social Media information processing stages: Awareness, Interest, Desire and Action
Rossolatos (2021)	Brand Engagement Funnel Model	Propose, Engage and Conversion.

Social media influencers are incorporated into several consumer engagement models to raise awareness, develop trust, encourage participation, and increase conversions. Brands and marketers strategically use Influencers to interact with their target demographic and improve the general user experience on social media platforms.

IMPACT OF SOCIAL MEDIA INFLUENCERS ON CONSUMER DECISION MAKING

Social media influencers considerably impact consumer decision-making in the Indian setting. They affect customer decision-making through product recommendations, demos, reviews, relatable material, social issues, partnerships, viral trends, and exciting video content. Because of their potential to influence customer tastes and habits, brands frequently collaborate with these influencers to reach a large and engaged audience. Social media influencers can affect consumer decisions in various instances such as Influencers often evaluate and provide recommendations for goods and services significantly impacting their following. For example, fashion influencers like @sherryshroff and culinary bloggers like @foodtalkindia routinely endorse dining establishments and clothes retailers (Umberia, 2022). They are trusted by their audience, who may decide to try or purchase what they advise. Many influencers show people how to use or apply things, giving them helpful advice and motivating them to make wise decisions. As an illustration, beauty influencers like @debasreee show followers how to apply cosmetics and maintain healthy skin by utilizing particular products, which can encourage followers to make purchases (Jaiswal, 2023). Influencers try to unwrap things, evaluate thoroughly, and share their personal experiences with their audience. Tech influencers like @geekyranjit, for instance, offer thorough assessments of smartphones, laptops, and other devices to assist customers in selecting the one that best meets their needs (Tech Influencers, 2023). Lifestyle influencers frequently present a luxurious lifestyle, including expensive products, exotic travel, and other things. An illustration of an Indian family travel influencer is @the.bucketlist.family. Followers might be motivated to buy things or book trips to imitate this ideal lifestyle. Influencers are relatable to their audience because they frequently share personal tales. This relatability has the potential to influence customer choices significantly. For instance, fitness influencers like @fitmuslimah and mother bloggers like @shinymathew stress their real-life experiences because they appeal to their target audiences (Li et. al., 2023). Influencers who utilize their platforms to promote social causes and activism are known as social activists. For instance, radio host and social influencer @rjraunac spread awareness of numerous social issues. Their fans could be more likely to back these causes or companies that share their ideals (Narasimha, 2023). Influencers frequently partner with brands to give their followers special discounts and deals. Customers are encouraged to buy because they feel exclusive. As an illustration, fashion bloggers often work with clothing companies to provide discount codes to their fans (Dhiman et al., 2018, p.191). Influencers can establish or participate in viral trends or challenges, encouraging their followers to follow suit. For instance, fitness influencers in India have publicized several fitness competitions, enticing their fans to take part, spend money on associated goods, and lead healthier lives. Influencers frequently promote events, limited-time deals, or products that make their followers feel pressed for time and FOMO. For instance, event and entertainment influencers may promote ticket sales for special events, encouraging ticket purchases. Thanks to the popularity of apps like TikTok and Instagram Reels, video influencers in India, like @riyaz.14, produce quick and exciting videos that highlight goods, ways of life, and entertainment, influencing customer decisions through visual storytelling. As a result, social media influencers significantly influence consumer behavior due to their authenticity, knowledge, active involvement, peer influence, skillful storytelling, usage of user-generated content, and creation of idealized lifestyles. Influencer marketing has become a well-known tactic in the digital era as brands recognize the importance of working with influencers to reach and persuade their target audiences.

ADVANTAGES OF INFLUENCER MARKETING

Advantages for Brands

Influencer marketing may provide Indian organizations with several vital advantages by utilizing the strength of social media and the reach of influencers to engage with their target customers effectively. There are a few possible advantages of influencer marketing for Indian brands. Influencers create more brand awareness. A company like Nykaa, an Indian retailer of cosmetics and beauty products, works with celebrities like Komal Pandey and Debasree Banerjee to promote and evaluate their goods. These influencers have sizable fan bases in the beauty and fashion industries, which help Nykaa reach a wider audience and build brand recognition. Influencers help a brand to reach its target audience. Like to sell its products, a fitness supplement firm like MuscleBlaze works with fitness influencers like Shilpa Shetty Kundra. They can adequately target people interested in health and well-being and exercise fanatics. Influencer marketing helps to create credibility and trust among customers. To advertise their line of Ayurvedic products, Dabur, a well-known Indian consumer goods firm, teamed up with actress and influencer Shilpa Shetty. Shilpa's affiliation with yoga and wellness complements Dabur's brand ideals, and her fans see her endorsement as trustworthy and credible. Zomato, a well-known Indian food delivery app, frequently works with food bloggers and reviews. These influencers provide exciting material about their culinary adventures that promote user-generated content and brand engagement. To generate material showcasing their jewelry lines, Tanishq, a well-known Indian jewelry brand, teamed up with influencers Sakshi Sindwani and Aashna Shroff. This saves the brand time and money spent on content creation and gives their products a new, relatable viewpoint. Influencers. Influencer marketing also helps to launch products in the market. To create hype and enthusiasm around new product introductions, smartphone manufacturer OnePlus frequently collaborates with tech influencers. Influencers receive early access to the products, produce unboxing videos, and write reviews, which aid OnePlus in generating interest and sales before the launch. An Indian regional clothing company like Fabindia can work with regional lifestyle influencers who are well-known locally. Thanks to this strategy, they may effectively engage a hyper-local audience. Campaigns encouraging users to make content using a brand's merchandise include Calvin Klein's #MyCalvins. Other Indian apparel companies have used similar marketing strategies to feature genuine people wearing their products, fostering a sense of belonging and authenticity. Influencer marketing is very cost-effective marketing. Despite a tight marketing budget, startups and small companies in India can work with micro-influencers. Despite smaller audiences, these influencers can offer highly focused exposure without the expenses associated with macro influencers. Through influencers, a brand can quickly boost its sales. Amazon India frequently works with influencers, including lifestyle, tech, and beauty, to promote their

Prime Day sales events. These influencers produce material that promotes the top offers and goods in the marketplace, increasing traffic and revenue (Jaitly, 2016, p.232).

Advantages for Indian Consumers

For Indian consumers, influencer marketing potentially offers several advantages. Indian customers frequently heed the advice of influencers in their sector of interest. For instance, if a famous food blogger recommends a restaurant, their followers are likelier to go there because they believe in the influencer's taste and judgment. Indian customers frequently find new brands and products through influencers' content. For instance, beauty influencers often introduce their followers to skincare and makeup products they might have yet to encounter. Influencers frequently offer actual product demonstrations and reviews. For instance, tech influencers in India routinely unbox and analyze new technology, assisting consumers in making purchase selections.

Many Indian influencers in their respective sectors produce instructional content. For instance, fitness influencers frequently provide training plans and nutritional guidance, which helps customers advance their understanding of health and fitness. Indian customers who follow influencers may be given access to special offers and discount vouchers. It benefits customers and brands when influencers work with them to offer unique bargains to their following. A few Indian influencers cater their suggestions to particular target demographics. For instance, a parenting influencer may suggest products pertinent to parents, ensuring their followers receive individualized information. Indian influencers frequently provide amusing and motivational content that connects with their audience. For instance, influencers in the travel industry share their experiences to encourage fans to visit new places and try new things. Many influencers support groups centered on common interests. For Indian consumers, this sense of belonging can be beneficial because it enables them to interact with others who share their interests and participate in conversations and events that cater to those passions. Indian customers frequently seek the advice and insights of influencers. For instance, a financial influencer may advise on spending, investing, and money management to assist followers in making wise financial choices. Indian shoppers frequently look for product reviews and influencer comments before making decisions. The sincere ideas and experiences of influencers might influence consumer decisions. A few Indian influencers use their platforms to advocate for causes and spread awareness of social concerns. This could serve as motivation and inspiration for shoppers.

EMERGING TOOLS IN MEASURING CONSUMER ENGAGEMENT

To assist businesses in learning more about consumer behavior and preferences, new trends and techniques for measuring and assessing consumer interaction are developing. A. Artificial intelligence (AI) and machine learning: Zendesk's Answer Bot, an AI-powered chatbot, uses natural language processing to shift through customer inquiries and give instantaneous solutions. These AI-powered products connect with clients while gathering helpful information about those encounters (Korman, 2023).B. Predictive Analytics: Based on past data, predictive analytics technologies like Salesforce Einstein Analytics assist companies in predicting customer behavior and engagement trends. Using this, data-driven decisions on marketing tactics may be made. C. Voice and Voice Analytics: Voice assistants like Google Assistant and Amazon Alexa are utilized to interact with customers via voice-activated products. To identify customer preferences and sentiment, voice analytics platforms such as Vayyoo analyze voice interactions (Jaybhaye et al., 2023, p.1898). D. Video Analytics: YouTube Analytics offers information on video engagement, such as watch time, click-through rates, and viewer demographics. It aids companies in assessing the value of video footage. E. Chatbots and Conversational AI: Drift's conversational marketing platform uses AI-driven chatbots to interact in real time with website visitors. During chats, these chatbots record information about user preferences and behavior. F. Social Media Listening and Monitoring: Brandwatch is a social listening platform that goes beyond simple analytics to assess sentiment, follow trends, and pinpoint influential individuals. It aids companies in comprehending consumer opinion and interaction on social media sites. G. Customer Journey Mapping: Solutions like Custify's customer journey mapping software let firms see and analyze the customer journey, finding key touchpoints and potential development areas. H. User-Generated Content (UGC) Analysis: TINT is a platform for collecting and curating UGC from social media. It enables companies to assess how UGC affects consumer engagement and brand impression. I. Augmented reality (AR) and virtual reality (VR): Oculus Insight, a feature of Oculus VR headsets, monitors user motions and interactions in VR settings. It offers information on user interaction with VR experiences. J. Blockchain for Data Verification: Blockchain-based platforms like Factom are examining data verification and transparency in consumer engagement data to guarantee data security and correctness. K. Personalization and Customer Segmentation: Dynamic Yield, a platform for personalization that employs machine learning to tailor content and recommendations based on unique user behavior and preferences, increasing engagement. L. Emotion identification: The emotion identification software Affective analyzes facial expressions and voice to identify clients' feelings in real-time video conversations. It assists companies in adjusting their responses to emotional stimuli. M. Cross-Channel Analytics: Google Analytics 4 (GA4) provides cross-channel tracking, allowing companies to assess consumer engagement across websites, mobile apps, and other digital touchpoints more comprehensively (Sharma, 2023). By empowering businesses to analyze and evaluate consumer involvement, these trends and tools help them make better decisions, enhance customer experiences, and forge stronger bonds with their target markets.

CONCLUSION

Consumer engagement has changed substantially in the current digital era, with social media influencers playing a crucial part in determining the dynamics of connections between brands and consumers. It is beyond dispute that these influencers significantly impact consumer engagement. The chapter has examined how social media influencers change marketing tactics and affect customer behavior. These influencers have become a potent force in digital marketing thanks to their ability to establish sincere relationships with their followers and to advertise goods and services interestingly and sympathetically. They are valuable resources for businesses looking to interact with their target consumers because of their capacity to reach a large and specific audience and their perceived genuineness. Understanding social media influencers' effects on consumer engagement is crucial for firms hoping to succeed in the ever-evolving world of online marketing. This is a dynamic and developing field.

REFERENCES

Abidin, C. (2016). Visibility labour: Engaging with Influencers' fashion brands and #OOTD advertorial campaigns on Instagram. *Media International Australia, Incorporating Culture & Policy*, *161*(1), 86–100. doi:10.1177/1329878X16665177

Appelbaum, A. (2001). *The constant consumer, The Gallup Group*. Retrieved from https://gmj.gallup.com/content/745/Constant-Customer.aspx

Arora, A. S., & Sanni, S. A. (2018). Ten Years of 'Social Media Marketing' Research in the Journal of Promotion Management: Research Synthesis, Emerging Themes, and New Directions. *Journal of Promotion Management*, *25*(4), 476–499. doi:10.1080/10496491.2018.1448322

Binning, K. R., Unzueta, M. M., Huo, Y. J., & Molina, L. E. (2009). The interpretation of multiracial status and its relation to social engagement and psychological well-being. *The Journal of Social Issues*, *65*(1), 35–49. doi:10.1111/j.1540-4560.2008.01586.x

Bratu, S. (2019). Can social media influencers shape corporate brand reputation? Online followers' trust, value creation, and purchase intentions. *Review of Contemporary Philosophy*, *18*, 157–163.

Brodie, R. J., Hollebeek, L. D., Jurić, B., & Ilić, A. (2011). Customer engagement: Conceptual domain, fundamental propositions, and implications for research. *Journal of Service Research*, *14*(3), 252–271. doi:10.1177/1094670511411703

Catteeuw, F., Flynn, E., & Vonderhorst, J. (2007). Employee engagement: Boosting productivity in turbulent times. *Organization Development Journal*, *25*(2).

Chen, Y., Fay, S., & Wang, Q. (2011). The role of marketing in social media: How online consumer reviews evolve. *Journal of Interactive Marketing*, *25*(2), 85–94. doi:10.1016/j.intmar.2011.01.003

Cho, J., & Park, D. (2013). Online celebrity endorsements and its potential impact on online purchase intention: The role of product type and celebrity fashion style. *Journal of Retailing and Consumer Services*, *20*(4), 322–332.

Colicev, A., Kumar, A., & O'Connor, P. (2019). Modeling the relationship between firm and user-generated content and the stages of the marketing funnel. *International Journal of Research in Marketing*, *36*(1), 100–116. doi:10.1016/j.ijresmar.2018.09.005

De Veirman, M., Cauberghe, V., & Hudders, L. (2017). Marketing through Instagram influencers: The impact of number of followers and product divergence on brand attitude. *International Journal of Advertising*, *36*(5), 798–828. doi:10.1080/02650487.2017.1348035

De Vries, N. J., & Carlson, J. (2014). Examining the drivers and brand performance implications of customer engagement with brands in the social media environment. *Journal of Brand Management*, *21*(6), 495–515. doi:10.1057/bm.2014.18

Dessart, L., Veloutsou, C., & Morgan-Thomas, A. (2016). Capturing consumer engagement: Duality, dimensionality, and measurement. *Journal of Marketing Management*, *32*(5-6), 399–426. doi:10.1080/0267257X.2015.1130738

Dhiman, R., Chand, P. K., & Gupta, S. (2018). Behavioural aspects influencing decision to purchase apparels amongst young Indian consumers. *FIIB Business Review*, *7*(3), 188–200. doi:10.1177/2319714518790308

Downer, J. T., Rimm-Kaufman, S. E., & Pianta, R. C. (2007). How do classroom conditions and children's risk for school problems contribute to children's behavioral engagement in learning? *School Psychology Review*, *36*(3), 413–432. doi:10.1080/02796015.2007.12087938

Engati. (2020). *What is engagement rate?* Retrieved from https://www.engati.com/glossary/engagement-rate

Fay, B., & Larkin, R. (2017). Why online word-of-mouth measures cannot predict brand outcomes offline: Volume, sentiment, sharing, and influence metrics yield scant online–offline WOM correlations. *Journal of Advertising Research*, *57*(2), 132–143. doi:10.2501/JAR-2017-021

Fischer, E., & Reuber, A. R. (2011). Social interaction via new social media: How can interactions on Twitter affect effectual thinking and behavior? *Journal of Business Venturing*, *26*(1), 1–18. doi:10.1016/j.jbusvent.2010.09.002

Fournier, S., & Avery, J. (2011). The uninvited brand. *Business Horizons*, *54*(3), 193–207. doi:10.1016/j.bushor.2011.01.001

Freberg, K., Graham, K., McGaughey, K., & Freberg, L. A. (2011). Who are the social media influencers? A study of public perceptions of personality. *Public Relations Review*, *37*(1), 90–92. doi:10.1016/j.pubrev.2010.11.001

Grönroos, C. (1997). Keynote paper From marketing mix to relationship marketing-towards a paradigm shift in marketing. *Management Decision*, *35*(4), 322–339. doi:10.1108/00251749710169729

Guthrie, J. P. (2001). High-involvement work practices, turnover, and productivity: Evidence from New Zealand. *Academy of Management Journal*, *44*(1), 180–190. doi:10.2307/3069345

Guthrie, J. T., & Cox, K. E. (2001). Classroom conditions for motivation and engagement in reading. *Educational Psychology Review*, *13*(3), 283–302. doi:10.1023/A:1016627907001

Hackworth, N. J., Matthews, J., Westrupp, E. M., Nguyen, C., Phan, T., Scicluna, A., Cann, W., Bethelsen, D., Bennetts, S. K., & Nicholson, J. M. (2018). What influences parental engagement in early intervention? Parent, program, and community predictors of enrollment, retention, and involvement. *Prevention Science*, *19*(7), 880–893. doi:10.1007/s11121-018-0897-2 PMID:29629506

Haenlein, M., Anadol, E., Farnsworth, T., Hugo, H., Hunichen, J., & Welte, D. (2020). Navigating the new era of influencer marketing: How to be successful on Instagram, TikTok, & Co. *California Management Review*, *63*(1), 5–25. doi:10.1177/0008125620958166

Han, W., McCabe, S., Wang, Y., & Chong, A. Y. L. (2018). Evaluating user-generated content in social media: An effective approach to encourage greater pro-environmental behavior in tourism? *Journal of Sustainable Tourism*, *26*(4), 600–614. doi:10.1080/09669582.2017.1372442

Harmeling, C. M., Moffett, J. W., Arnold, M. J., & Carlson, B. D. (2017). Toward a theory of customer engagement marketing. *Journal of the Academy of Marketing Science*, *45*(3), 312–335. doi:10.1007/s11747-016-0509-2

Holland, J., & Baker, S. M. (2001). Customer participation in creating site brand loyalty. *Journal of Interactive Marketing*, *15*(4), 34–45. doi:10.1002/dir.1021

Hollebeek, L. D., Glynn, M. S., & Brodie, R. J. (2014). Consumer brand engagement in social media: Conceptualization, scale development, and validation. *Journal of Interactive Marketing*, *28*(2), 149–165. doi:10.1016/j.intmar.2013.12.002

Jaiswal, S. (2023). *How India's 'brown beauty' makeup influencers are going global*. Retrieved from https://www.aljazeera.com/gallery/2023/4/6/how-indias-brown-beauty-makeup-influencers-are-going-global

Jaitly, R. C., & Gautam, O. (2021). Impact of social media influencers on customer engagement and brand perception. *International Journal of Internet Marketing and Advertising*, *15*(2), 220–242. doi:10.1504/IJIMA.2021.114336

Jaitly, V., Chowriappa, P., & Dua, S. (2016). A framework to identify influencers in signed social networks. In *International Conference on Advances in Computing, Communications and Informatics (ICACCI)* (pp. 2335-2340). 10.1109/ICACCI.2016.7732403

Jaybhaye, S., Manchekar, A., Dixit, A., Ingle, A., & Khatib, F. (2023). Comparative analysis of voice-powered assistants. *International Journal for Research*, *11*(4), 1892–1898.

Jin, S. A. A. (2020). The rise of influencer marketing: A conceptual framework for understanding its impact on message processing. *Journal of Interactive Advertising*, *20*(2), 58–74.

Kabadayi, S., & Price, K. (2014). Consumer–brand engagement on Facebook: Liking and commenting behaviors. *Journal of Research in Interactive Marketing*, *8*(3), 203–223. doi:10.1108/JRIM-12-2013-0081

Kane, T. J., & Staiger, D. O. (2008). *Estimating teacher impacts on student achievement: An experimental evaluation. (No. w14607)*. National Bureau of Economic Research. doi:10.3386/w14607

Keller, K. L. (2001). *Building customer-based brand equity: A blueprint for creating strong brands*. Retrieved from https://api.semanticscholar.org/CorpusID:10882841

Kim, A. J., & Ko, E. (2012). Do social media marketing activities enhance customer equity? An empirical study of luxury fashion brand. *Journal of Business Research*, *65*(10), 1480–1486. doi:10.1016/j.jbusres.2011.10.014

Korman, J. (2023). *Understanding how Answer Bot works with your content*. Retrieved from https://support.zendesk.com/hc/en-us/articles/4408830824474-Understanding-how-Answer-Bot-works-with-your-content/20/11/2023

Kumar, V., & Pansari, A. (2016). Competitive advantage through engagement. *JMR, Journal of Marketing Research*, *53*(4), 497–514. doi:10.1509/jmr.15.0044

Kuss, D. J., & Griffiths, M. D. (2017). Social networking sites and addiction: Ten lessons learned. *International Journal of Environmental Research and Public Health*, *14*(3), 311–321. doi:10.3390/ijerph14030311 PMID:28304359

Labrecque, L. I., Vor Dem Esche, J., Mathwick, C., Novak, T. P., & Hofacker, C. F. (2013). Consumer power: Evolution in the digital age. *Journal of Interactive Marketing*, *27*(4), 57–269. doi:10.1016/j.intmar.2013.09.002

Lee, J., Kim, H. J., & Hur, W. M. (2018). How does celebrity involvement affect brand attitude in social media? The mediating role of consumers' perceptions of celebrity credibility and product-brand relationship. *Journal of Global Fashion Marketing*, *9*(1), 52–66.

Li, W., Ding, H., Xu, G., & Yang, J. (2023). The impact of fitness influencers on a social media platform on exercise intention during the COVID-19 pandemic: The role of parasocial relationships. *International Journal of Environmental Research and Public Health*, *20*(2), 1113. doi:10.3390/ijerph20021113 PMID:36673868

Lipps, G., Norris, C., & Pignal, J. (2003). Measuring school engagement. *Education Quarterly Review*, *9*(2).

London, B., Downey, G., & Mace, S. (2007). Psychological theories of educational engagement: A multi-method approach to studying individual engagement and institutional change. *Vand. L. Rev.*, *60*, 455.

Luedicke, M. K., Thompson, C. J., & Giesler, M. (2010). Consumer identity work as moral protagonism: How myth and ideology animate a brand-mediated moral conflict. *The Journal of Consumer Research*, *36*(6), 1016–1032. doi:10.1086/644761

Macey, W. H., & Schneider, B. (2008). The meaning of employee engagement. *Industrial and Organizational Psychology: Perspectives on Science and Practice*, *1*(1), 3–30. doi:10.1111/j.1754-9434.2007.0002.x

Marks, H. M. (2000). Student engagement in instructional activity: Patterns in the elementary, middle, and high school years. *American Educational Research Journal*, *37*(1), 153–184. doi:10.3102/00028312037001153

McAlexander, J. H., Schouten, J. W., & Koenig, H. F. (2002). Building brand community. *Journal of Marketing*, *66*(1), 38–54. doi:10.1509/jmkg.66.1.38.18451

Meece, J. L., Blumenfeld, P. C., & Hoyle, R. H. (1988). Students' goal orientations and cognitive engagement in classroom activities. *Journal of Educational Psychology*, *80*(4), 514–523. doi:10.1037/0022-0663.80.4.514

Mollen, A., & Wilson, H. (2010). Engagement, telepresence and interactivity in online consumer experience: Reconciling scholastic and managerial perspectives. *Journal of Business Research*, *63*(9-10), 919–925. doi:10.1016/j.jbusres.2009.05.014

Narasimha, R. (2023). *The role of influencers in shaping social issues: A look at influencer activism.* Retrieved from https://www.cxotoday.com/press-release/the-role-of-influencers-in-shaping-social-issues-a-look-at-influencer-activism/05/12/2023

Pansari, A., & Kumar, V. (2017). Customer engagement: The construct, antecedents, and consequences. *Journal of the Academy of Marketing Science*, *45*(3), 294–311. doi:10.1007/s11747-016-0485-6

Passikoff, R. (2006). *Predicting market success: New ways to measure customer loyalty and engage consumers with your brand.* John Wiley & Sons.

Pencarelli, T., & Forlani, F. (2016). Marketing of touristic districts-viable systems in the experience economy. *Sinergie Italian Journal of Management, 34*(1), 199–238.

Peters, K., Chen, Y., Kaplan, A. M., Ognibeni, B., & Pauwels, K. (2013). Social media metrics—A framework and guidelines for managing social media. *Journal of Interactive Marketing, 27*(4), 281–298. doi:10.1016/j.intmar.2013.09.007

Prentice, C., Han, X. Y., Hua, L.-L., & Hu, L. (2019). The influence of identity-driven customer engagement on purchase intention. *Journal of Retailing and Consumer Services, 47*, 339–347. doi:10.1016/j.jretconser.2018.12.014

Roberts, D. R., & Davenport, T. O. (2002). Job engagement: Why it's important and how to improve it. *Employment Relations Today, 29*(3), 21–29. doi:10.1002/ert.10048

Rogers, D. L. (2016). *The digital transformation playbook: Rethink your business for the digital age.* Columbia University Press. doi:10.7312/roge17544

Rossolatos, G. (2021). The depth of brand engagement funnel: Dimensionalizing interaction in social media brand communities. *Qualitative Market Research, 24*(2), 200–220. doi:10.1108/QMR-03-2019-0041

Saczynski, J. S., Pfeifer, L. A., Masaki, K., Korf, E. S. C., Laurin, D., White, L., & Launer, L. J. (2006). The effect of social engagement on incident dementia: The Honolulu-Asia Aging Study. *American Journal of Epidemiology, 163*(5), 433–440. doi:10.1093/aje/kwj061 PMID:16410348

Sawhney, M., Verona, G., & Prandelli, E. (2005). Collaborating to create: The Internet as a platform for customer engagement in product innovation. *Journal of Interactive Marketing, 19*(4), 4–17. doi:10.1002/dir.20046

Schivinski, B., & Dabrowski, D. (2016). The effect of social media communication on consumer perceptions of brands. *Journal of Marketing Communications, 22*(2), 189–214. doi:10.1080/13527266.2013.871323

Sharma, A. (2023). *Google Analytics 4 and how it is changing the way we measure digital success.* Retrieved from https://www.addwebsolution.com/blog/google-analytics-4

So, K. K. F., King, C., Sparks, B. A., & Wang, Y. (2016). The role of customer engagement in building consumer loyalty to tourism brands. *Journal of Travel Research, 55*(1), 64–78. doi:10.1177/0047287514541008

Tafesse, W. (2016). An experiential model of consumer engagement in social media. *Journal of Product and Brand Management, 25*(5), 424–434. doi:10.1108/JPBM-05-2015-0879

Tech Influencers. (2023). *Stay up-to-date with these 10 must-follow tech influencers.* Retrieved from https://www.whosthat360.com/technology/stay-up-to-date-with-these-10-must-follow-tech-influencers-3997958 on 14/12/2023

Umberia. (2022). *Top bloggers in the fashion game.* Retrieved from https://isdi.in/blog/top-bloggers-in-the-fashion-game

Uzunoğlu, E., & Misci Kip, S. (2014). Brand communication through digital influencers: Leveraging blogger engagement. *International Journal of Information Management*, *34*(5), 592–602. doi:10.1016/j.ijinfomgt.2014.04.007

Van Doorn, J., Lemon, K. N., Mittal, V., Nass, S., Pick, D., Pirner, P., & Verhoef, P. C. (2010). Customer engagement behavior: Theoretical foundations and research directions. *Journal of Service Research*, *13*(3), 253–266. doi:10.1177/1094670510375599

Vargo, S. L., & Lusch, R. F. (2004). Evolving to a new dominant logic for marketing. *Journal of Marketing*, *68*(1), 1–17. doi:10.1509/jmkg.68.1.1.24036

Vivek, S. D., Beatty, S. E., & Morgan, R. M. (2012). Customer engagement: Exploring customer relationships beyond purchase. *Journal of Marketing Theory and Practice*, *20*(2), 122–146. doi:10.2753/MTP1069-6679200201

Wu, M. (2017). *Brandwatch- Social listening and analytics.* Retrieved from https://d3.harvard.edu/platform-digit/submission/brandwatch-social-listening-and-analytics/

Section 5

Influencers and Ethics

Chapter 15
Systematic Literature Review: Bibliometrics on Ethics Practised by Influencers

Albérico Travassos Rosário
https://orcid.org/0000-0003-4793-4110
GOVCOPP, IADE, Universidade Europeia, Portugal

Anna Carolina Boechat
https://orcid.org/0000-0002-9252-6602
UNIDCOM, IADE, Universidade Europeia, Portugal

ABSTRACT

The importance of ethics practiced by influencers must be considered. Influencers significantly impact their audience and can shape public opinion, attitudes, and behaviors. Ethical behavior helps influencers establish and maintain trust with their audience. Influencers are transparent, honest, and authentic in their content, which fosters trust and credibility. Ethical influencers are transparent about their partnerships, collaborations, and sponsored content. Ethical influencers have the potential to inspire and empower their audience to make a difference. They can influence their audience to adopt positive behaviors and attitudes, promoting social norms conducive to a more ethical and compassionate society. Influencers prioritizing ethical behavior contribute to a healthier online community and set a positive example for others in their field. Based on the above, it is intended to systematically review the bibliometric literature on ethics practiced by influencers using the Scopus database with the analysis of 134 academic and/or scientific documents.

INTRODUCTION

As social media platforms grow and evolve, brands have had to adjust their advertising strategy to reach and connect with their customers. With people spending more time on social media, businesses have embraced social media marketing as a tool to achieve their marketing goals. Dixon (2023) indicates that approximately 59% of the global population (4.59 billion people) use social media and spend about

DOI: 10.4018/979-8-3693-0912-4.ch015

151 minutes online daily. Global social media usage has significantly accelerated in recent years due to the increased eCommerce growth, access to cheap smartphones, and infrastructure development in less developed markets. This has given rise to the concept of social media influencers, individuals who have built a reputation on the internet with their knowledge and expertise. Influencers create and distribute high-quality content on social media, which attracts audiences interested in the topics they cover (Siddiqi & Bodolica, 2023). Due to their significant power and influence, working with influencers has become crucial in business marketing and communications. This has resulted in growth in influencer marketing, which was valued at US$101 billion in 2020 (Campbell & Farrell, 2020). Businesses leverage influencers' power and reach to connect with potential clients, thus creating numerous opportunities for these internet celebrities to monetize their skills and knowledge.

Unlike mainstream celebrities, influencers prioritize connecting with their audience through relatable content. This helps build trust and credibility, which grants them significant power to influence their followers' decisions and overall online behaviors. For instance, De Veirman et al. (2019) indicate that influencers share insights on brands they love and use daily and advise their followers on products they should or should not use. Due to their credibility and massive reach, these recommendations influence consumer purchasing decisions, thus increasing a company's sales and reputation. A study conducted by Twitter (X) and analytics firm Annalect found that 49% of surveyed internet users prefer recommendations from influencers (Woods, 2016). However, followers require influencers to adhere to certain ethical practices for this influencer-follower relationship to thrive. For instance, followers trust influencers to share unbiased information regarding brands and products they recommend (Kadekova & Holienčinova, 2018). In this case, some internet users consider the lack of transparency and disclosure in paid promotions as an unfair marketing practice that violates their trust. In addition, the lack of authenticity in sponsored content can undermine influencer credibility (Wellman et al., 2020). These issues indicate the need to address ethical practices influencers should maintain. Therefore, this systematic bibliometric literature review (LRSB) synthesizes findings from 134 sources on ethics practiced by influencers and highlights their potential impacts on marketing.

METHODOLOGICAL APPROACH

The global rise of influencers has established a rapidly growing industry backed by the increased adoption of technology and digital advertising practices. However, numerous ethical concerns have risen, such as the blurred lines between organic and sponsored content and the impacts on followers. As a result, researchers have published large volumes of data investigating and analyzing ethical standards guiding the influencer industry.

The systematic bibliometric literature review (LRSB) methodology provides a structured and rigorous method of analyzing large volumes of data. It helps illustrate how a specific field has evolved and sheds light on emerging areas (Donthu et al., 2022). In this case, the LRSB method was used to explore the evolution of the influencer industry, with a key focus on its related ethical practices.

The data collected and analyzed in this research was gathered from diverse sources. These included journal articles, proceedings and meeting papers, and books.

In contrast to conventional literature reviews, the LRSB adopts a comprehensive approach when examining the published literature pertaining to the research topic (Rosário & Dias, 2023; Raimundo & Rosário, 2202).

This method is designed to condense the volume of articles, concentrating on the most relevant ones. Additionally, the researcher provides a transparent audit trail, enabling readers to evaluate the research's methodologies, findings, and the quality of the aggregated studies. Thus, the LRSB encompasses a rigorous process of screening and selecting information sources to ensure the accuracy and validity of the presented data, involving a three-phase and six-step procedure (Rosário & Dias, 2023; Rosário et al., 2023; Raimundo & Rosário, 2022), as depicted in Table 1.

The Scopus database was used to identify and select relevant sources related to the research topic. This database was chosen since it allows researchers access to high-quality sources indexed through a rigorous selection and re-evaluation procedure conducted by an independent Content Selection and Advisory Board (Baas et al., 2020). In addition, Scopus continuously monitors and improves its data to maintain high-quality assurance.

It is crucial to underscore that this study had constraints as it solely concentrated on the Scopus database while overlooking other scholarly and scientific databases. When conducting literature searches up to October 2023, it is imperative to take into account peer-reviewed scientific and academic publications.

The search was performed to generate the largest number of documents in the database. During the initial search, the researcher used the keyword "ethics", generating 396,958 articles. With the addition of the keyword "influencers" the search was reduced to 134 documents (Table 2).

We employed content and thematic analysis methods to identify, examine, and present a range of documents, as specified by Rosário and Dias (2023), Rosário et al. (2023), and Raimundo and Rosario (2022).

Subsequently, the 134 scientific and academic documents, indexed in Scopus, were subject to both narrative and bibliometric analyses to delve into their content and potentially reveal recurring themes that directly addressed the research questions, in accordance with the guidelines provided by Rosário and Dias (2023), Rosário et al. (2023), and Raimundo and Rosario (2022).

Table 1. Process of systematic LRSB

Fase	Step	Description
Exploration	Step 1	formulating the research problem
	Step 2	searching for appropriate literature
	Step 3	critical appraisal of the selected studies
	Step 4	data synthesis from individual sources
Interpretation	Step 5	reporting findings and recommendations
Communication	Step 6	Presentation of the LRSB report

Source: adapted Rosário and Dias (2023), Rosário et al. (2023), Raimundo and Rosário (2022).

Table 2. Screening methodology

Database Scopus	Screening	Publications
Meta-search	Keyword: ethics	396,958
First Inclusion Criterion	Keyword: ethics, influencers	134
Screening	Keyword: ethics, influencers Published until October 2023	

Source: own elaboration

Of the 134 selected documents, 105 are articles; 11 books; 10 are Conference papers; and 8 are book series.

Publication Distribution

Peer-reviewed articles on how ethics are practiced by Influencers until October 2023. The year 2023 had the highest number of peer-reviewed publications on the subject, reaching 31. Figure 1 summarizes the peer-reviewed literature published until October 2023.

Figure 2 displays the countries exhibiting the highest levels of scientific output in specific research areas, with particular emphasis on the USA, UK, and AUSTRALIA, which boast the greatest number of publications.

Table 3, along with Figure 2, illustrates the top 10 nations with the most significant scientific contributions in the studied fields. This analysis seeks to discern which countries prioritize harnessing innovative marketing intelligence for business advantage over emphasizing their productivity.

The publications were sorted out as follows: International Journal Of Advertising (4); Public Relations Review (3); Journal Of Media Ethics Exploring Questions Of Media Morality (3); Journal Of Business Ethics (3); and with 2 publications (Sustainability Switzerland; Societies; Smart Innovation Systems And Technologies; Nursing Ethics; Journal Of Medical Internet Research; Developments In Marketing Science Proceedings Of The Academy Of Marketing Science); and the remaining publications with 1 document.

In Table 3 we analyze the Scimago Journal & Country Rank (SJR), the best quartile and the H index by Developments In Marketing Science Proceedings Of The Academy Of Marketing Science is the most quoted publication with 6,250 (SJR), Q1 and H index 194. There is a total of 49 publications in Q1, 17 publications in Q2, 16 publications Q3 and 10 publications in Q4.

Publications from best quartile Q1 represent 41% of the 119 publications titles; best quartile Q2 represents 14%, best Q3 represents 13% and best Q4 represents 8% of each of the titles of 119 publica-

Figure 1. Documents by year

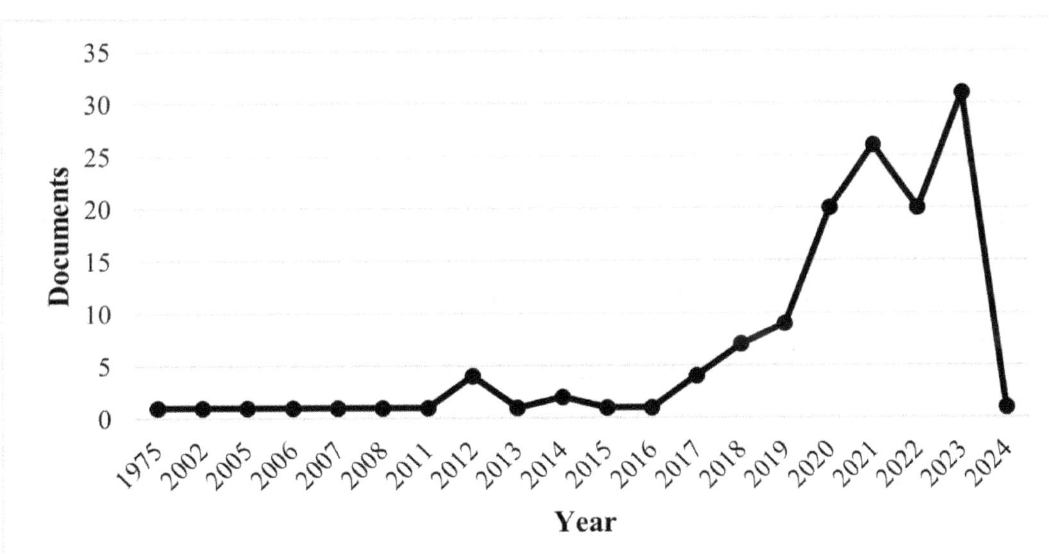

Figure 2. Scientific production by country

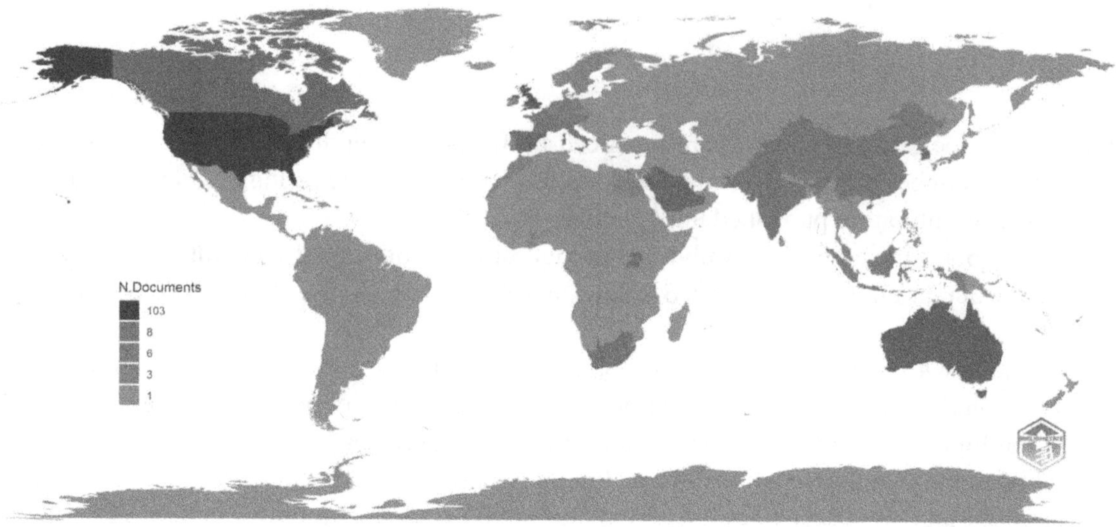

Table 3. Top 10 countries by number of publications

Country	Number of Publications
USA	103
UK	35
AUSTRÁLIA	24
SAUDI ARÁBIA	16
SPAIN	16
CANADA	15
SOUTH KOREA	13
SOUTH ÁFRICA	10
ÍNDIA	8
PAKISTAN	8

Source: own elaboration

tions. Finally, 27 publications without indexing data represent 23% of publications. As shown in Table 3, most publications do not have SJR.

The subject areas covered by the 134 scientific and/or academic documents were: Social Sciences (64); Business, Management and Accounting (37); Medicine (35); Computer Science (26); Arts and Humanities (22); Economics, Econometrics and Finance (13); Psychology (11); Nursing (10); Engineering (10); Decision Sciences (6); Environmental Science (5); Energy (4); Neuroscience (3); Health Professions (3); Mathematics (2); Biochemistry, Genetics and Molecular Biology (2); Materials Science (1); Dentistry (1); Chemical Engineering (1); Agricultural and Biological Sciences (1).

The most quoted article was "Insights in adolescents' advertising literacy, perceptions and responses regarding sponsored influencer videos and disclosures" by Binsardi and Ekwulugo Van Dam and Van

Table 4. Scimago journal and country rank impact factor

Title	SJR	Best Quartile	H index
Developments In Marketing Science Proceedings Of The Academy Of Marketing Science	6,250	Q1	194
IEEE Communications Magazine	5,290	Q1	227
Pediatrics	2,860	Q1	378
American Journal Of Transplantation	2,780	Q1	210
Journal Of Business Ethics	2,590	Q1	229
Big Data And Society	2,390	Q1	57
Environmental Research Letters	2,120	Q1	164
International Journal Of Advertising	2,080	Q1	74
Journal Of Medical Internet Research	1,990	Q1	178
Energy	1,990	Q1	232
Academy Of Management Learning And Education	1,940	Q1	90
Telematics And Informatics	1,880	Q1	93
Learning Media And Technology	1,880	Q1	56
Journal Of The American Academy Of Dermatology	1,620	Q1	229
Academic Medicine	1,580	Q1	173
Journal Of Psychiatric Research	1,550	Q1	155
Public Relations Review	1,410	Q1	96
Plastic And Reconstructive Surgery	1,350	Q1	198
Health Research Policy And Systems	1,350	Q1	61
BMC Public Health	1,310	Q1	178
Nursing Ethics	1,260	Q1	69
Industrial Management And Data Systems	1,220	Q1	117
Aesthetic Surgery Journal	1,200	Q1	71
Frontiers In Public Health	1,130	Q1	80
Journal Of Medical Ethics	1,110	Q1	81
Maternal And Child Nutrition	1,090	Q1	77
Convergence	1,060	Q1	49
BMJ Open	1,060	Q1	139
Nurse Education Today	0,950	Q1	92
Cyberpsychology	0,900	Q1	32
Profesional De La Informacion	0,870	Q1	40
Discourse Context And Media	0,840	Q1	28
Journal Of Eating Disorders	0,830	Q2	40
Social Responsibility Journal	0,820	Q1	45
Feminist Media Studies	0,820	Q1	49
International Journal Of Telemedicine And Applications	0,710	Q2	32
Journal Of Medicine And Philosophy United Kingdom	0,700	Q1	56
Revista Latina De Comunicacion Social	0,690	Q1	24

continued on following page

Table 4. Continued

Title	SJR	Best Quartile	H index
AI And Society	0,690	Q1	39
Big Data And Cognitive Computing	0,680	Q2	23
Ecancermedicalscience	0,670	Q3	42
Sustainability Switzerland	0,660	Q1	136
Journal Of Management Education	0,630	Q2	55
Education Sciences	0,610	Q2	40
Behavioral Sciences	0,600	Q2	39
American Journal Of Men S Health	0,600	Q2	46
Journal Of Academic Ethics	0,580	Q1	26
Frontiers In Communication	0,570	Q1	25
Journal Of Media Ethics Exploring Questions Of Media Morality	0,540	Q1	22
Journal Of The American Dental Association	0,520	Q2	128
Journal Of Human Trafficking	0,520	Q1	18
Ethics And Behavior	0,490	Q2	49
Kennedy Institute Of Ethics Journal	0,460	Q1	46
Fashion And Textiles	0,460	Q1	25
Tourism Analysis	0,440	Q3	43
Journal Of Information Communication And Ethics In Society	0,440	Q1	24
European Journal Of Women S Studies	0,440	Q2	50
Societies	0,420	Q2	33
Australasian Journal Of Information Systems	0,420	Q2	25
Education Policy Analysis Archives	0,410	Q2	53
Indian Journal Of Public Health	0,400	Q3	31
Revista Mediterranea De Comunicacion	0,370	Q1	6
IEEE Transactions On Professional Communication	0,370	Q2	50
Contemporary Family Therapy	0,360	Q1	38
Journal Of General Management	0,350	Q3	23
Religions	0,320	Q1	33
Journal Of Social Computing	0,320	Q2	6
BMJ Military Health	0,320	Q3	31
Cuadernos Info	0,310	Q2	12
Current Dermatology Reports	0,300	Q3	18
Studies In Health Technology And Informatics	0,290	Q3	64
Mind And Society	0,280	Q1	21
Ethics Medicine And Public Health	0,270	Q3	13
Proceedings Of The Association For Information Science And Technology	0,250	Q3	18
International Journal Of Internet Marketing And Advertising	0,250	Q3	23
Health SA Gesondheid	0,250	Q3	17

continued on following page

Table 4. Continued

Title	SJR	Best Quartile	H index
Canadian Public Administration	0,250	Q3	29
Studies In Computational Intelligence	0,210	Q4	81
Informing Science	0,210	Q3	26
Neuropsychiatrie De L Enfance Et De L Adolescence	0,190	Q3	19
Emerald Emerging Markets Case Studies	0,190	Q4	7
Jurnal Komunikasi Malaysian Journal Of Communication	0,180	Q3	12
Democracy And Security	0,180	Q3	15
Smart Innovation Systems And Technologies	0,170	Q4	31
Research In Ethical Issues In Organizations	0,160	Q2	9
Micro And Macro Marketing	0,13	Q4	3
Tijdschrift Voor Communicatiewetenschap	0,120	Q4	7
Revue De Chirurgie Orthopedique Et Traumatologique	0,120	Q4	47
Legal Ethics	0,110	Q4	13
Heart And Metabolism	0,110	Q4	10
Aesthetic Medicine	0,110	Q4	2
Medecine Et Droit	0,100	Q4	7
Proceedings Of The 2023 Communication Strategies In Digital Society Seminar 2023 Comsds 2023	0	-*	4
Proceedings New Security Paradigms Workshop	0	-*	5
Droit Deontologie Et Soin	0	-*	0
BMC Family Practice	0	-*	0
Atas Da Conferencia Da Associacao Portuguesa De Sistemas De Informacao	0	-*	5
Studia Ecologiae Et Bioethicae	-*	-*	-*
Springer Proceedings In Business And Economics	-*	-*	-*
Role Of Islamic Spirituality In The Management And Leadership Process	-*	-*	-*
Regulation Of Social Media Influencers	-*	-*	-*
Psycho Oncologie	-*	-*	*
Proceedings Of The 10th European Conference On Social Media Ecsm 2023	-*	-*	-*
Proceedings International Computer Software And Applications Conference	-*	-*	-*
Political Relevance Of Food Media And Journalism Beyond Reviews And Recipes	-*	-*	-*
Palgrave Handbook Of Interactive Marketing	-*	-*	-*
Lecture Notes In Computer Science Including Subseries Lecture Notes In Artificial Intelligence And Lecture Notes In Bioinformatics	-*	-*	-*
Idimt 2021 Pandemics Impacts Strategies And Responses 29th Interdisciplinary Information Management Talks	-*	-*	-*
Happiness Management And Social Marketing A Wave Of Sustainability And Creativity	-*	-*	-*
Global Media Ethics And The Digital Revolution	-*	-*	-*
Doing Performative Social Science Creativity In Doing Research And Reaching Communities	-*	-*	-*
Contemporary Issues In Marketing And Consumer Behaviour Third Edition	-*	-*	-*

continued on following page

Table 4. Continued

Title	SJR	Best Quartile	H index
Beyond The Dark Arts Advancing Marketing And Communication Theory And Practice	-*	-*	-*
BMJ	-*	-*	-*
Advertising Account Planning Planning And Managing Strategic Communication Campaigns	-*	-*	-*
Adam Smith And Modernity 1723 2023	-*	-*	-*
6th International Conference On Business And Industrial Research Icbir 202 Proceedings	-*	-*	-*
27th Annual Americas Conference On Information Systems Amcis 2021	-*	-*	-*
18th Annual International Symposium Of The International Council On Systems Engineering Incose 2008	-*	-*	-*

Note: *data not available. Source: own elaboration

Reijmersdal (2019), with 86 quotes published in Cyberpsychology 0,900 (SJR), the best quartile (Q1) and with H index (32), this article we investigate adolescents' awareness and understanding of the presence of persuasive content in influencer videos.

In Figure 3 we can analyze citation changes for documents published up to October 2023. The period 2013-2023 shows a positive net growth in citations with an R2 of 60%, reaching 419 citations in 2023.

The h-index is used to determine the productivity and impact of a published work based on the maximum number of included articles with at least the same number of citations. Of the documents considered for h-index, 19 were cited at least 19 times. Citations of all scientific and/or academic documents from the period 2013 to October 2023, with a total of 1278 citations, of the 134 documents 43 were not cited. The self-citation of documents in the period 2013 to September 2023 was self-cited.

The bibliometric analysis, conducted by employing the main keywords "ethics" and "influencers," unveiled key indicators of the changing landscape of scientific and academic information within documents, as illustrated in Figure 4. These insights were extracted using the VOSviewer scientific software, with a particular emphasis on identifying the primary search terms "ethics" and "influencers."

This study is grounded in scientific and academic literature investigating the role of ethics practiced by influencers Figure 5 allows us to closely examine the interrelated keywords, facilitating a focus on the connections between keywords within each academic article. This aids in identifying the topics addressed in these studies and offers valuable insights into potential directions for future research. Additionally, Figure 6 illustrates a significant number of co-citations and units, supporting the analysis of cited references.

THEORETICAL PERSPECTIVES

Social media influencers' large following and credibility give them significant power to influence consumer behaviors and brand perceptions. As a result, they have become crucial figures in contemporary marketing as businesses leverage influencer marketing to reach their target customers (Aengst et al., 2017). Influencers use their content creation skills to create niche communities, which they leverage to endorse products, services, and ideas. As a result, the rise of influencers has altered the advertising and communications field (Borchers & Enke, 2022; Jatho et al., 2020). However, influencers' popularity has evoked various ethical concerns.

Figure 3. Evolution of citations between 2013 and 2023

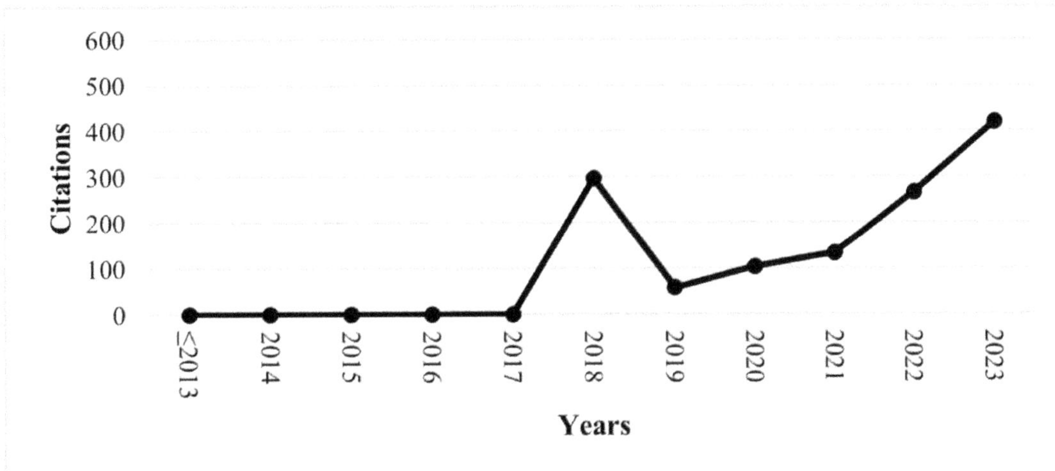

Figure 4. Network of all keywords

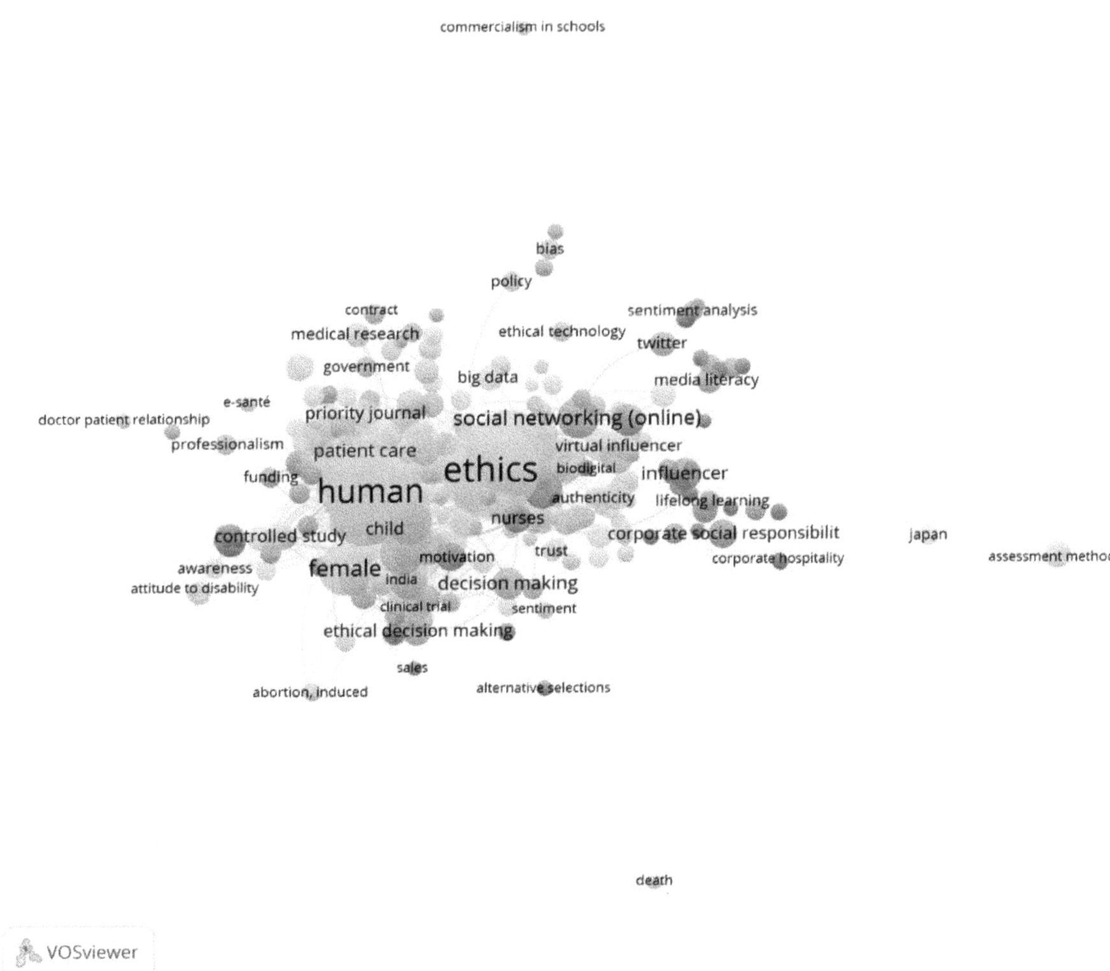

Figure 5. Network of linked keywords

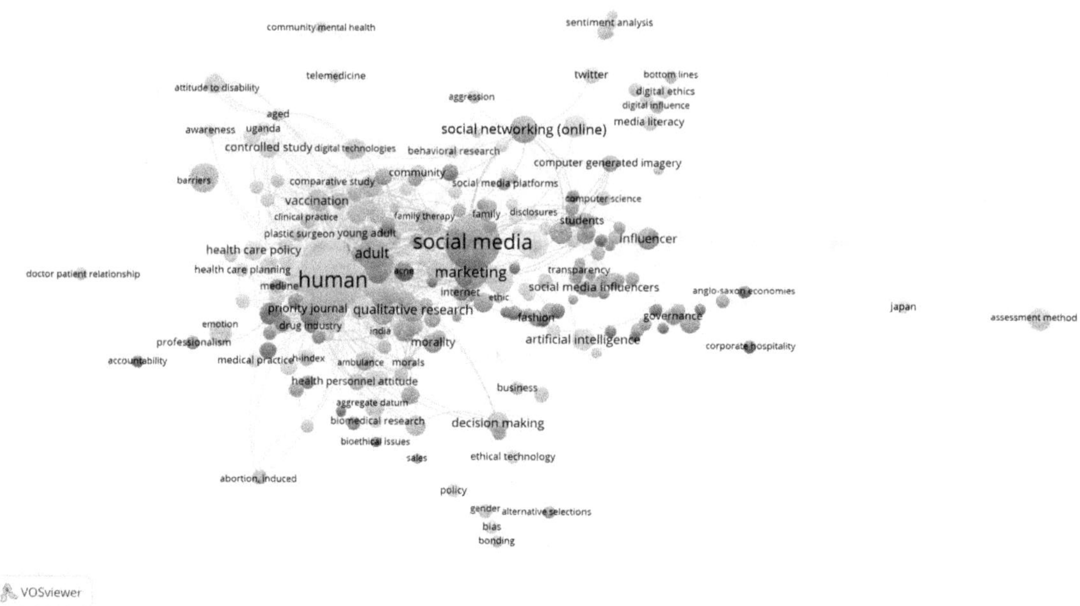

Figure 6. Network of co-citation

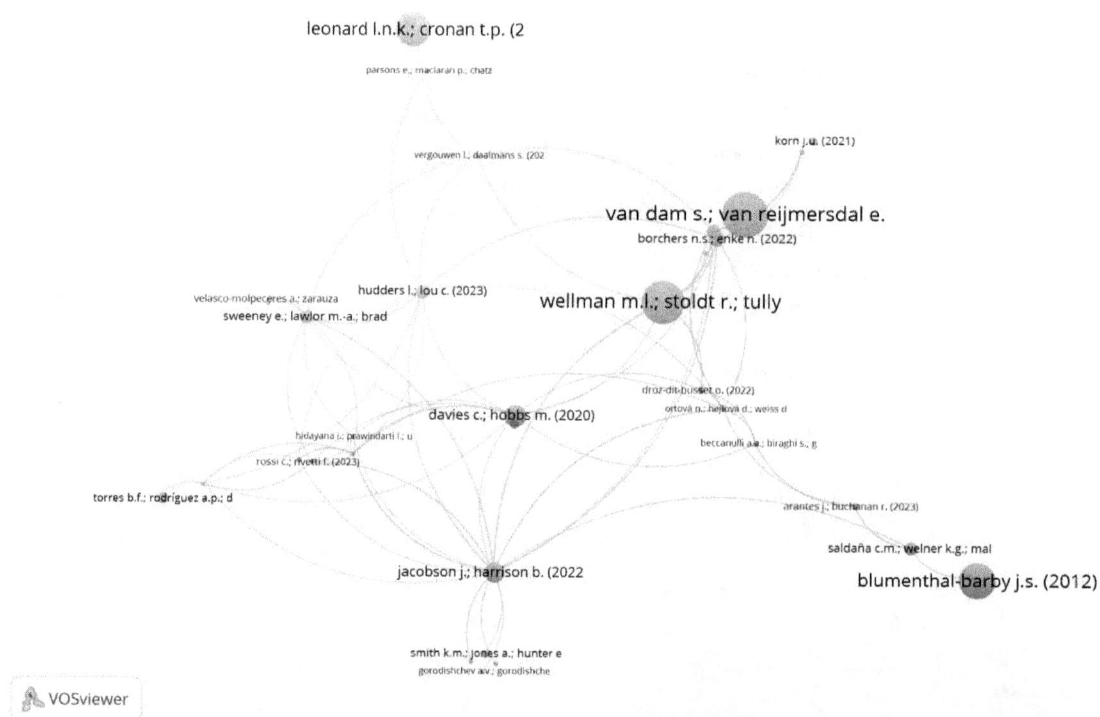

For instance, the relationship between influencers and their followers is characterized by trust, authenticity, and credibility, all built through relatable content and authentic interactions (Wellman et al., 2020; Silva & de Brito, 2020). However, increased focus on sponsored content can negatively affect this relationship, especially when the influencer provides misleading messages or engages in deceptive marketing practices. These issues indicate the need to thoroughly evaluate how influencers balance upholding ethical practices and monetizing their skills and knowledge online.

INFLUENCERS AND INFLUENCER MARKETING

Influencers are individuals who have built a substantial and engaged following on social media and online platforms within a specific niche or industry. Gómez (2019) defines social media influencers as digital content creators who have received recognition and created a community of followers beyond family and friends. Campbell and Farrell (2020, p.1) describe them as "specialists at generating content consumers interact with, which helps it spread more widely on social media." Influencers are digital opinion leaders and trendsetters with loyal audiences that trust their recommendations, opinions, and expertise (Van Dam & Van Reijmersdal, 2019; Gupta et al., 2020).

Influencers come in various forms, such as social media personalities, bloggers, vloggers, YouTubers, and celebrities. The ability to authentically connect with followers through personal stories, experiences, and insights differentiates influencers from other mainstream celebrities (Allen & Reese, 2016; Gorodishchev et al., 2023).

This personal connection gives them considerable influence over their audience's attitudes, behaviors, and purchasing decisions. Consequently, they monetize this influence by collaborating with brands to endorse products or services, leveraging their reach and credibility to create compelling, relatable, and persuasive content.

Campbell and Farrell (2020) identify five major categories of influencers: celebrity influencers, mega influencers, macro influencers, micro-influencers, and nano influencers. Celebrity influencers have a large follower base and are recognized beyond social media. While mega influencers have a celebrity status online, with more than 1 million followers, they are relatively unknown outside social media. They lacked celebrity status before social media. Macro influencers have an audience ranging from 100000 to 1 million followers and have strong engagement rates. Micro-influencers have an audience ranging between 10000 to 100000 followers, making them relatively smaller in scale and scope. Although these influencers have brand partnerships, they mainly earn through affiliate links and programs. Nano influencers have less than 10000 and are just beginning their careers (Figure 7).

However, these newcomers have the highest engagement rates due to their personal accessibility and high perceived authenticity. Bannigan & Shane (2019, p.249) explain the rise of nano influencers in the influencer marketing industry, noting that their "word seems as genuine as advice from a friend." Collaborating with each category of influencers yields varying outcomes due to factors like exposure and reach and followers' perceptions of an influencer's authenticity.

Influencer marketing is a strategic approach to advertising and promotion that capitalizes on the influencers' influence and credibility. Etheredge et al. (2021) describe this marketing technique as a collaboration between influencers and brands to create and disseminate content that promotes a brand's products or services to the influencer's audience. Influencer marketing leverages the trust and authenticity that influencers have built with their followers, making it an effective way to reach target demograph-

Figure 7. Types of influencers
Source: adapted from Campbell and Farrell (2020)

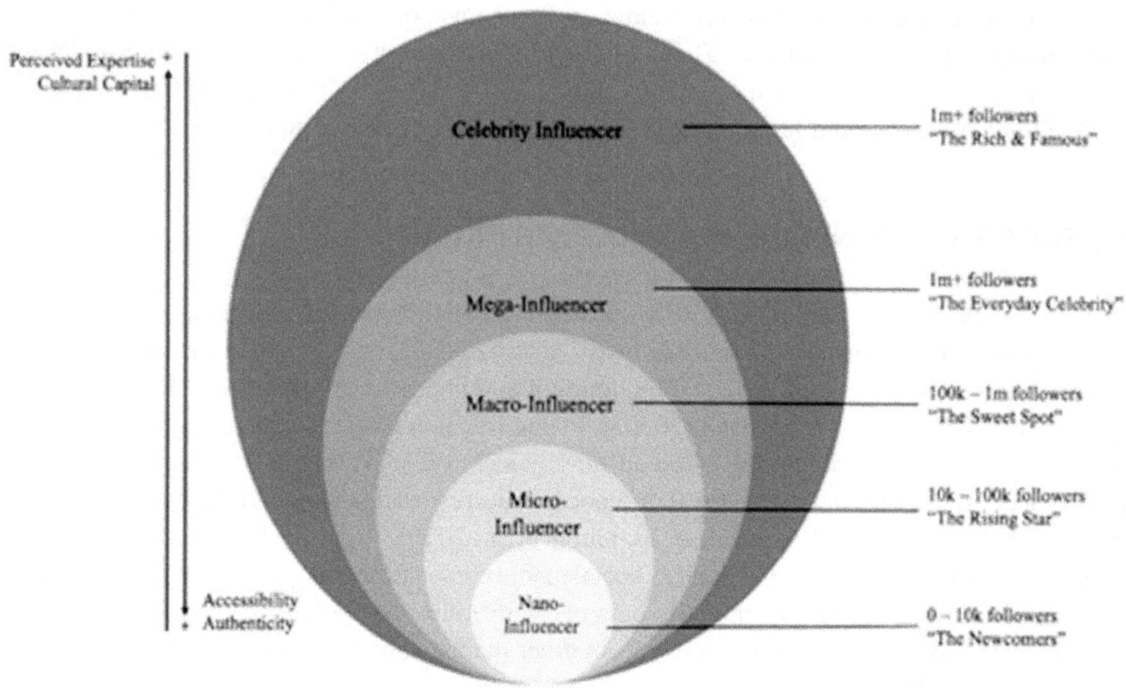

ics in a more personalized and engaging manner (Ebert & Sindermann, 2020; Fedeli & Cheng, 2023). According to El-Deeb (2022), consumers are more likely to purchase products recommended by influencers since they perceive them to be more credible than in-house marketing communications. Three factors contribute to consumers' perception of credibility, expertise, trustworthiness, and attractiveness (Hudders & Lou, 2023; Smith et al., 2023). These factors influence consumer purchasing decisions. For example, consumers are more likely to purchase a product recommended by an influencer perceived to be credible. El-Deeb (2022) found that the return on investment in influencer marketing is 11 times more times than in traditional marketing. Influencers promote brands through sponsored posts, product reviews, tutorials, and testimonials. They are typically compensated through money or free products, services, or experiences (Ortová et al., 2023; Bush et al., 2017). However, the value paid to each influencer depends on their following, engagement rates, skill set, branding and focus, and monetary requirements for collaboration. Besides, the success of influencer marketing lies in its ability to offer a less intrusive and more organic way of reaching potential customers.

ETHICS PRACTICED BY INFLUENCERS

Influencers can shape public opinions, behaviors, and attitudes. Their large following and strong relationships with their followers provide them with massive power and influence (Ebert & Sindermann, 2020). For instance, influencers' followers are more likely to trust their opinions and recommendations, consequently shaping behaviors and actions. Therefore, influencers should uphold ethical standards to ensure they have positive impacts on society and the people who admire them (Droz-dit-Busset, 2022; Ha & Yang, 2023). The various ethical practices influencers observe include promoting social responsibility and raising awareness, empowering and educating their followers, maintaining authenticity and credibility, transparency and disclosure, data privacy and security, content integrity, promoting ethical brands, and fact-checking and accuracy.

Social Responsibility and Raising Awareness

Social responsibility is a vital ethical practice among influencers. It reflects their commitment to the well-being of society, their followers, and the environment. Ethical influencers recognize their influence and use their platforms to promote positive values, social causes, and responsible behaviors (Hall et al., 2023). In addition, socially accountable influencers often leverage their reach to raise awareness about critical issues such as sustainability, mental health, social justice, or charitable causes (Campbell, 2012; Choi et al., 2021). They engage in partnerships and collaborations with organizations or nonprofits that align with their values and contribute to the betterment of society (Maheshwari & Fielding, 2019). They use their influence to advocate for positive change, educate their followers on important topics, and encourage socially responsible actions (Wang, 2023; Turnbull et al., 2023). Furthermore, these influencers maintain a high level of integrity in their personal and professional lives (Velasco-Molpeceres et al., 2023). For example, they avoid engaging in behaviors that can harm their audience, such as promoting unhealthy lifestyles, endorsing harmful products, or engaging in unethical practices (Davis et al., 2012). These practices enhance their credibility and contribute to a more ethical, compassionate, and informed digital environment.

Influencers can leverage their platforms to bring attention to lesser-known issues or critical topics not getting adequate mainstream coverage. For instance, they can share personal stories, relatable experiences, and empathetic messages that increase their audience's awareness of a certain topic or issue (Castillo-Abdul & Romero-Rodriguez, 2021). Due to their communication and storytelling skills, influencers use relatable ways to explain complex problems, making them accessible to a broad audience (Torres et al., 2021; Ssanyu et al., 2022). Moreover, their relatability and empathetic communication style foster a sense of community and drive a collective commitment to building a better world. As a result, influencers inspire change and foster a culture of social responsibility and collective action.

Empowering and Educating

Influencers leverage their digital platforms to share knowledge, foster personal growth, and inspire action among their audiences. They carefully blend curated personal experiences, expertise, and relatable storytelling to facilitate a dynamic form of engagement that transcends traditional educational paradigms (Stanberry et al., 2021; Saldaña et al., 2021). Influencers employ content strategies that prioritize accessibility and relatability, ensuring that their audience can readily absorb and apply the information imparted (Subramani et al., 2023; Thomas, 2019). Moreover, influencers often share narratives of resilience, personal growth, and triumph over adversity. These stories, often deeply personal and authentic, serve as powerful sources of inspiration, motivating their followers to persevere through life's challenges (Beccanulli et al., 2020; Clark et al., 2021). Consequently, influencers empower their audience by instilling self-belief, resilience, and the confidence to pursue their aspirations (De Pelsmacker et al.,

2023). Influencers also frequently address taboo subjects, dismantling societal stigmas and fostering open conversations on topics that might otherwise remain unaddressed (Collado-Alonso et al., 2023). In this way, they empower their audience to confront and understand their vulnerabilities, fostering a sense of solidarity and emotional growth.

Influencers act as informal educators, providing valuable insights, knowledge, and practical advice on a wide range of subjects. They deliver content that simplifies complex concepts, rendering them comprehensible and relevant to diverse audiences (Davies & Hobbs, 2020). Their instructional content is often presented in engaging and easily digestible formats to equip their followers with skills, information, and the capacity to make informed choices (Arantes & Buchanan, 2023; Hanson & Moore, 2014). Therefore, influencers bridge the gap between formal education and the everyday lived experiences of their audience by offering practical solutions and life hacks that enhance daily life (Degen, 2023). Influencers also serve as advocates for social and environmental causes, leveraging their reach to raise awareness, educate their followers on pressing issues, and encourage informed action and advocacy (Jatho et al., 2020; Gassas & Salem, 2022; Maloni et al., 2022). This multifaceted approach to education empowers individuals to expand their knowledge, refine their decision-making processes, and become more actively engaged in their communities.

Authenticity and Credibility

The trust between influencers and their audiences is significantly dependent on their authenticity and credibility. Authenticity embodies the influencers' commitment to sincerity and genuineness in their interactions with their followers (Rass, 2021). Wellman et al. (2020) explain that influencers maintain authenticity in two main ways: i) being true to themselves and their brands and ii) being true to their audience by creating and sharing the content they need. In this case, ethics of authenticity shape an influencer's decision-making in critical areas such as the type of content to produce, brands to work with, or the information to disclose or conceal (Robinson, 2020). Therefore, authenticity entails the disclosure of personal experiences, values, and opinions that reflect influencers' true selves, thereby fostering a connection built on transparency (Villamil & Wolbring, 2019; Amare et al., 2018). Ethical influencers avoid contrived personas or inauthentic narratives, ensuring that their content resonates with their audience's expectations and aligns with their brand identity (Antunes & Sebastiao, 2020). For instance, an authentic influencer's content is more relatable and relays a sense of vulnerability that humanizes their online presence. This adherence to authenticity safeguards their followers' trust, thus bolstering influencer credibility.

Credibility is the influencer's capacity to deliver accurate and trustworthy information, fostering a perception of expertise and reliability within their domain. Wellman et al. (2020) describe credibility as the believability of an influencer brand's ability to deliver as promised (based on the influencer's expertise) and trustworthiness. In this case, influencers establish credibility through consistent and factually accurate content that reflects a deep understanding of their niche (Dahill et al., 2022; Favre et al., 2020). They avoid disseminating false or misleading information, recognizing the potential harm it may cause to their audience and their reputation. Ethical influencers often provide evidence, sources, or endorsements from reputable experts or organizations to substantiate their claims (Dugdale & Braswell, 2021; El Kheir et al., 2022). Maintaining a high level of credibility enables influencers to earn their followers' respect and confidence since they are increasingly viewed as reliable sources of information (Rodenburg & Macdonald, 2021). Consequently, the ethical commitment to authenticity and credibility fosters enduring relationships with their audience and safeguards the long-term sustainability of their influencer careers.

Transparency and Disclosures

Transparency and clear disclosures are foundational ethical principles for successful influencer careers. Transparency entails openly communicating the nature of relationships between influencers and brands, especially when compensation or partnerships are involved (Hagelstein et al., 2021). Influencers should explicitly disclose when a piece of content, such as a social media post, blog article, or video, is sponsored or contains affiliate links. This disclosure ensures that the audience is aware that the content may have a promotional intent and allows them to distinguish between organic recommendations and paid endorsements (Josse-Eklund et al., 2014; Kim & Wang, 2023). Transparency is critical because it upholds the trust between influencers and their followers by being forthright about the commercial aspects of their content (Yao et al., 2017). It also complies with regulations and guidelines set by advertising standards authorities and social media platforms, ensuring ethical and honest marketing practices.

Sponsored content is designed to mirror non-paid content on social media and can deceive consumers if published without appropriate disclosures. Therefore, disclosures should be unambiguous and prominently placed to make it easy for the audience to notice (Korn, 2021; Vadíková, 2022). Influencers use various strategies to indicate that the content is sponsored or an ad. For example, they may include hashtags like #ad, #sponsored, or #paidpartnership, or captions explicitly stating the relationship with the brand. Ethical influencers understand that these disclosures are not merely legal obligations but ethical responsibilities to their audience (Triplett et al., 2022; Steele et al., 2020). Their followers can interpret failure to make proper disclosures as deception, causing trust issues (Kaler, 2002). Ultimately, practicing transparency and disclosures enables influencers to adhere to ethical standards and contribute to the overall integrity and transparency of influencer marketing (Rosas-Moreno, 2023; Ryu & Park, 2018). This transparency ensures that consumers can make informed decisions about the products or services they encounter in their online feeds, fostering an environment of trust and accountability.

Content Integrity

Maintaining content integrity is crucial for influencers looking to succeed in the competitive global influencer market. Integrity encompasses several critical elements that contribute to the honesty and reliability of the content they create and share with their audience (Alqahtani et al., 2021). For instance, influencers should prioritize accurate and truthful content. This includes verifying the information they present in aspects such as product claims, statistics, or health advice (Gisondi et al., 2022; Kim et al., 2013). This ethical practice is based on the understanding that misleading or false information can harm the trust that influencers have built with their followers and cause a backlash that can undermine an influencer's career (Lillywhite & Wolbring, 2020; Rossanty et al., 2021). Therefore, influencers who adhere to content integrity provide recommendations based on reliable and factual information and credible sources.

In addition, content integrity extends to the responsible use of editing and filters. Ethical influencers recognize that the use of excessive photo editing or filters can present unrealistic and unattainable beauty standards or lifestyle ideals (Yao et al., 2017). Therefore, these influencers balance using editing tools to enhance the visual appeal of their content while ensuring that it remains authentic and representative of reality (Pierce, 2018; Co Sy Su, 2018). They disclose when filters or significant alterations are used, enabling their audience to distinguish between genuine and modified content. This transparency reflects a commitment to content integrity, promoting more authentic and relatable interactions with their followers.

Data Privacy and Security

Influencers' interactions with followers and collaborations with brands require compliance with data privacy and security ethical standards. These practices revolve around the responsible handling of personal information and the protection of sensitive data (Morton & Sasse, 2012). Ethical influencers prioritize the safety of their followers' personal information, ensuring that it is collected, stored, and used in compliance with data protection regulations (Leonard & Cronan, 2005; Khan et al., 2020). They clearly communicate their data collection practices, obtain consent when necessary, and provide followers with the option to control their data preferences (Hancock & Ralph, 2021). This commitment to data privacy safeguards their audience's sensitive information, such as email addresses or personal messages, from misuse or unauthorized access. Moreover, influencers take measures to secure their digital presence (Rashi & Schleifer, 2023; Hockin-Boyers & Clifford-Astbury, 2021). They implement robust security practices to prevent unauthorized access to their accounts, ensuring that their content and personal data are not compromised (Rossi & Rivetti, 2023). These practices may include maintaining strong password protection, enabling two-factor authentication, and staying vigilant against phishing attempts. They help influencers reduce the risk of data breaches and hacking.

Ethical influencers are also cautious when sharing personal or sensitive information about themselves or others. They refrain from oversharing or exposing confidential details that could compromise their privacy or that of their followers or business partners (Hidayana et al., 2023). Additionally, they respect the privacy of individuals they encounter in their content, such as family members or friends, by obtaining consent before sharing personal stories or images (Fan et al., 2019; Fakazis & Fürsich, 2023). These strategies help protect digital rights and personal data and contribute to a safe and secure online environment characterized by trust (Jones, 2022). Robust data privacy and safety also ensure that individuals can engage with content creators without fear of privacy violations or data breaches.

Promoting Ethical Brands

Promoting ethical brands reflects an influencer's commitment to supporting companies with responsible and sustainable business practices. Ethical influencers understand the importance of aligning their endorsements with their values and principles (Jauffret & Aubrun, 2022). This may include endorsing brands that prioritize ethical, social, and environmental considerations. Influencers who promote ethical brands typically conduct thorough research and due diligence to ensure that the companies they collaborate with adhere to high ethical standards (Jansen van Vuuren & Jansen van Vuuren, 2022; Blumenthal-Barby, 2012). They evaluate factors such as fair labor practices, sustainable sourcing, environmental responsibility, and corporate social responsibility initiatives. Endorsing such brands helps promote businesses that are positively impacting society and the planet.

Additionally, influencers may use their platforms to educate their audience about the ethical choices they can make as consumers. For example, they can advocate for responsible shopping practices, such as supporting companies with fair trade policies, eco-friendly packaging, or charitable contributions to social causes (Boadi & Kolog, 2021). This educational role extends the ethical dimension of influencer marketing beyond the promotion of products and services by fostering a more conscious and ethical consumer culture. For instance, Jalali and Khalid (2021) found that social media influencers can leverage their platforms to promote green initiatives such as zero food waste. They can share content that improves the audience's attitudes toward sustainable consumption and purchasing decisions (Khan et al., 2018; Santoro & Bennett, 2018). Ultimately, promoting sustainability and endorsing ethical brands enhances influencers' credibility and integrity while also contributing to the growth of socially responsible and environmentally sustainable business practices.

Ensuring Accuracy and Fact-Checking

Influencers have an ethical responsibility to ensure the accuracy of the information they share with their audience. This ethical practice involves a commitment to providing reliable, evidence-based, and truthful content to their followers (Balas et al., 2015). Providing misleading or false information can have severe negative consequences that can harm users and break down trust (Bolly, 2011; Clifton, 2021). For example, influencers in the wellness and fitness niches must provide accurate information regarding the products, services, and actions they recommend since they can impact users' health and wellness (Mohamad & Damanhuri, 2019). Misinformation or unfair marketing practices can lead to misleading consumer decisions, which can result in dissatisfaction and negative user experiences (Nxumalo & McHunu, 2020; Yazdani et al., 2021). Therefore, influencers should prioritize accuracy by verifying the claims they make, consulting credible sources, and ensuring that their content is grounded in factual information.

Fact-checking is a major strategy used to ensure information accuracy. It encourages ethical influencers to rigorously verify the information presented in their content, ensuring it doesn't have inaccuracies, exaggerations, or unsubstantiated claims (Wu et al., 2020; Willis & Delbaere, 2022). This approach helps them avoid making statements that could misinform or deceive their audience, particularly in sensitive areas such as health, safety, or financial advice (Kalisch, 2023). In addition, influencers should acknowledge when they make mistakes or encounter new information that contradicts their previous statements (Waqas et al., 2019). They show humility by correcting errors and updating their audience. This showcases their commitment to accuracy and reinforces transparency and trustworthiness.

IMPORTANCE OF ETHICS IN INFLUENCER MARKETING

Ethics in influencer marketing help preserve consumer trust and brand reputation. Modern-day consumers are increasingly discerning and skeptical of marketing communications and other promotional initiatives. Unethical marketing practices, such as false advertising, deceptive messaging, or the manipulation of information, can lead to a breach of trust. For instance, Sweeney et al. (2022) found that consumers are less likely to engage with a brand in the future if they feel deceived or manipulated. These instances may occur when an influencer features a sponsored product in their content without appropriate disclosure, thus deceiving the audience into thinking that it is an unbiased recommendation (Núñez-Cansado et al., 2021; Money & Schepers, 2007). While such practices may have short-term positive outcomes, such as increased sales, they may have negative long-term consequences. This may happen when the followers discover it was an advertisement or if the products or services fail to deliver as promised (Militello et al., 2021). Therefore, maintaining a strong ethical stance in influencer marketing is crucial for fostering and building trust. Besides, ethical behavior reassures consumers that the brand's intentions are genuine and that its products or services are reliable (Miladi, 2021). The trust established translates into customer loyalty, positive word-of-mouth recommendations, and a solid brand reputation, which contribute to sustainable business growth.

Ethical marketing practices are intrinsically linked to legal compliance and risk mitigation. Adherence to ethical guidelines and industry standards preserves a company's reputation and safeguards it from legal entanglements (Kaler, 2006). Influencer-brand collaborations should prioritize consumer protection and ensure fair competition. In addition, they should be aligned with appropriate industry guidelines to reduce risks associated with non-compliance, such as fines, legal proceedings, and damage to a brand's credibility (Jacobson & Harrison, 2022; Ijabadeniyi & Govender, 2023). For example, the Federal Trade Commission (FTC) Act requires clear disclosure of an endorsement when an influencer has a material relationship with a brand that followers might not reasonably expect (Bladow, 2017). Although this Act is inadequately implemented and reinforced, failing to comply with laws and regulations increases the risk of costly lawsuits and reputational damage. Therefore, adopting a proactive approach to legal compliance ensures that marketing activities remain within the bounds of the law while creating a culture of responsibility within the organization.

Ethics in influencer marketing have a significant impact on a brand's long-term sustainability and customer retention. Ethical influencer marketing practices focus on building relationships with customers based on honesty, transparency, and respect (Mooz & Forsberg, 2008). Such relationships are more likely to be enduring, as they are built on trust and mutual benefit. When companies collaborate with influencers who prioritize ethical practices, they show a commitment to meeting customer needs and delivering on promises (Nichols & Pappas, 2022; Parsons et al., 2023). This commitment contributes to higher customer satisfaction and retention rates. Loyal customers are more likely to make repeat purchases, advocate for the brand, and refer others, thereby reducing customer acquisition costs and enhancing a company's overall sustainability (Perry et al., 2020). Therefore, ethics in influencer marketing supports the creation of a customer-centric culture that benefits the influencer, consumers, and the business.

ETHICAL ISSUES IN INFLUENCER MARKETING

Influencer marketing improves a brand's organic reach and helps connect with potential customers in a more personalized way. However, these collaborations are associated with multiple ethical issues that undermine their success. For instance, De Veirman et al. (2019) indicate that there has been a significant increase in influential children's vloggers partnering with brands to promote various products despite these minor influencers' limited advertising literacy knowledge. Children are a vulnerable group when it comes to marketing persuasion, indicating the need to assess the potential ethical issues associated with such collaboration practices (Choi, 2023). Other dominant ethical issues identified in the research are influencers' loss of creative control, which affects their authenticity, and increased deceptive marketing practices.

Loss of Creative Control

The loss of creative control when brands collaborate with influencers is a major ethical problem. Brands often partner with influencers to tap into the influencer's unique style, voice, and creativity, leveraging their authenticity and connection with their audience. However, this practice can sometimes lead to a loss of creative control for influencers or brands. For example, influencers may interpret brand guidelines differently or infuse their brand into the content, potentially deviating from the brand's intended message or values. On the other hand, brands can prioritize their marketing goals over influencers' authenticity and creative expression. This can result in influencers feeling pressured to create content that does not align with their usual style or values, potentially compromising their credibility with their audience. Additionally, when brands exert too much control, it can diminish the authenticity that influencer marketing is founded on. This tension between maintaining creative freedom for influencers and achieving brand objectives can lead to ethical dilemmas.

Advertising to Vulnerable Groups

Exploitative marketing to vulnerable consumer groups is an ethical issue in influencer marketing. It occurs when influencers and brands take advantage of individuals who may lack the capacity to evaluate advertising messages critically. These vulnerable groups include children, individuals with disabilities, or those suffering from serious diseases. They often face unique challenges, making them more susceptible to manipulation and exploitation through influencer marketing practices (Cosseron, 2018; Núñez-Cansado et al., 2019). For example, influencers may promote products or services that appeal to children through content that lacks age-appropriate guidelines or that encourages excessive consumption (De Veirman et al., 2019). Such practices exploit the vulnerability of children's limited comprehension of advertising intent and the consequences of their purchasing choices. Similarly, influencers may endorse products related to disabilities or diseases without adequately understanding the emotional or physical struggles of the affected individuals (Bouchalta et al., 2020; Collier et al., 2022). They may include content that potentially conveys a message that their condition can be entirely alleviated through a product or service, which may be misleading. These exploitative practices can lead to unethical profiteering at the expense of the well-being of vulnerable consumers and can damage the influencer's trust and credibility.

Brands that collaborate with influencers to target vulnerable consumer groups have an ethical responsibility to ensure that the marketing practices prioritize these individuals' best interests. They should encourage influencers to create content that has empathy and accurately represents product benefits to avoid capitalizing on the vulnerabilities of these groups (Clover-Brown et al., 2023). These ethical brands acknowledge their moral duty of prioritizing the protection and well-being of vulnerable consumer groups. Therefore, they should collaborate with influencers who share this commitment (Conti et al., 2022). Given the inadequate laws and regulations guiding influencer marketing practices, brands should ensure that their partnership agreements align with their brand values. This approach can contribute to an ethical influencer marketing industry that respects the unique needs of all consumers, including vulnerable consumer groups.

Deceptive Marketing

Deceptive marketing in influencer marketing represents a multifaceted ethical concern that encompasses various practices aimed at misleading, manipulating, or concealing essential information from the audience. For instance, some influencers may endorse products or services without genuine belief or personal experience (Davies & Li, 2020). This presents a facade of authenticity that erodes their credibility and the trust of their audience. Pursuing profit over integrity may prompt influencers and brands to exaggerate product benefits or omit crucial drawbacks, leading followers to make uninformed decisions (Py, 2023; Ramanayake et al., 2023). Other influencers may engage in undisclosed sponsorships or fail to transparently communicate their financial ties to brands, blurring the lines between genuine recommendations and paid endorsements (Pétursdóttir, 2017). For instance, Bannigan and Shane (2019) found that only 25% of Instagram influencers provided sponsorship disclosures that were compliant with the Federal Trade Commission (FTC) guidelines. These deceptive practices violate the principles of honesty and transparency and diminish the authenticity that influencer marketing relies upon. Ethical influencers should recognize that their audience is the primary focus, thereby prioritizing truthfulness and transparency to maintain trust.

Brands that prioritize short-term financial gains over ethical considerations may engage in deceptive marketing. For instance, Bannigan and Shane (2019) found that brands intentionally concealed their collaboration with influencers to preserve organic advertising and manipulate their products' market. Companies can encourage influencers to overhype their products, exaggerate claims, or omit negative aspects to boost sales (Deloria & Wolbring, 2019; Hewitt et al., 2023). This approach can lead to immediate gains but risks long-term damage to their reputation and legal consequences if exposed. However, ethical brands recognize the importance of responsible marketing and focus on building authentic and lasting relationships with their consumers (Mseer, 2021; Procházka, 2021). They collaborate with influencers who align with their values and advocate for transparency, honesty, and ethical practices in influencer marketing (Ranpariya et al., 2020; Sharma & Francis, 2020). As a result, they ensure that their marketing campaigns drive sales while also contributing to a sustainable and ethically sound business strategy.

CONCLUSION

The increased use of social media worldwide has led to the rise of social media influencers with the power to shape opinions, behaviors, and attitudes. These internet celebrities specialize in creating content in a specific niche that helps build online communities of loyal followers. As a result, these influencers leverage these communities to monetize their skills, leading to the massive growth of influencer marketing. However, the level of influence varies depending on one's follower base, reach, and engagement rates. The five main categories of influencers are nano influencers, micro-influencers, macro influencers, mega influencers, and celebrity influencers. However, an influencer's success, regardless of their celebrity status, depends on their ability to create authentic content, maintain credibility, and comply with ethical standards. However, the lack of adequate ethical guidelines and frameworks governing influencer marketing has evoked concerns about influencers' practices. For instance, there has been an increase in concerns regarding deceptive marketing practices where influencers partner with unethical brands or prioritize profit-making over followers' well-being.

However, ethical influencers engage in multiple practices that help build trust and strengthen relationships with their followers. These include embracing their social responsibility and raising awareness about issues affecting society, empowering and educating their followers, and maintaining authenticity, credibility, transparency and disclosures, and content integrity. These influencers also ensure data privacy and security, promote ethical promotes, and fact-check information before sharing to ensure the accuracy and reliability of their recommendations and opinions. However, ethical practices remain a huge challenge in influencer marketing. For example, the blurred line between authentic content and sponsored content poses a huge threat to consumer protection since most influencers do not provide proper disclosures. As a result, they often publish promotional content that mirrors organic content, thus potentially misleading their followers. In addition, marketing to vulnerable consumer groups such as children and patients remains a significant challenge. Some brands perceive these consumer groups as lucrative markets for their products and services, ignoring their vulnerabilities and prioritizing marketing goals. This results in unethical marketing practices. Therefore, more stringent solutions are needed to address these challenges and support ethical influencer practices.

In the realm of influencers, ethics play a crucial role in shaping their impact on society. Theoretical implications involve the broader understanding and discussions surrounding the ethical responsibilities of influencers, while practical implications are the tangible effects on their audience and the influencer industry. Influencers often operate within a framework of ethics that may vary. Understanding and analyzing these frameworks contribute to the ongoing discourse on ethical practices in the digital age.

The ethical considerations in influencer marketing raise questions about the audience's media literacy. How well can people critically assess the content they consume, especially when it's presented by influencers who may not always disclose their partnerships or may blur the lines between personal opinion and sponsored content? The power dynamics between influencers and their followers are important to explore. Influencers may have a significant impact on their audience, and ethical considerations arise when considering the potential manipulation or exploitation of this influence.

Ethical behavior enhances an influencer's trust and credibility. Followers are more likely to engage with and believe in influencers who are transparent, honest, and uphold ethical standards. Ethical practices influence the relationships between influencers and the brands they promote. Brands may choose influencers aligned with their values, and influencers need to navigate partnerships that align with their ethical stance.

Ethical behavior extends beyond individual transactions to the broader societal impact of influencer culture. Influencers can use their platforms for positive social change or contribute to societal issues. Ethical decisions can influence the social and cultural conversations they participate in. The theoretical implications involve the broader philosophical discussions around influencers and ethics, while the practical implications relate to the day-to-day impact on the relationships between influencers, brands, and their audience, as well as the broader societal consequences of their actions.

There are some fascinating directions that research on the ethics of influencer practices could take in the future. One area of exploration could focus on the impact of sponsored content and its potential to blur the lines between genuine recommendations and promotional material. It would be interesting to investigate how audiences perceive authenticity in influencer marketing and the ethical considerations surrounding disclosure.

Another avenue might involve delving into the social responsibility of influencers, especially in terms of the content they promote and the potential effects on their followers. This could extend to examining the ethical implications of endorsing certain products or ideologies, considering the significant influence influencers wield. Research could also explore the effectiveness and ethics of influencer self-regulation. Are influencers and the platforms they operate on doing enough to ensure transparency and ethical practices, or is there a need for external oversight and regulations?

Overall, as the landscape of influencer marketing evolves, so too will the ethical questions surrounding it. Exploring the dynamic nature of these ethical considerations and their implications for both influencers and their audiences could provide valuable insights for the future.

REFERENCES

Aengst, J. C., Harrington, E. K., Bahulekar, P., Shivkumar, P., Jensen, J. T., & Garg, B. S. (2017). Perceptions of nonsurgical permanent contraception among potential users, providers, and influencers in Wardha district and New Delhi, India: Exploratory research. *Indian Journal of Public Health, 61*(1), 3–8. doi:10.4103/0019-557X.200261 PMID:28218155

Allen, M. B., & Reese, P. P. (2016). The ethics of promoting living kidney donation using nonargumentative influence: Applications, concerns, and future directions. *American Journal of Transplantation, 16*(12), 3378–3384. doi:10.1111/ajt.13972 PMID:27438695

Alqahtani, M. M. J., Alkhamees, H. A., Alkhalaf, A. M., Alarjan, S. S., Alzahrani, H. S., AlSaad, G. F., Alhrbi, F. H., Wahass, S. H., Khayat, A. H., & Alqahtani, K. M. M. (2021). Toward establishing telepsychology guideline. Turning the challenges of COVID-19 into opportunity. *Ethics, Medicine, and Public Health, 16*, C7–C100612. doi:10.1016/j.jemep.2020.100612 PMID:33283033

Amare, Y., Scheelbeek, P., Schellenberg, J., Berhanu, D., & Hill, Z. (2018). Early postnatal home visits: A qualitative study of barriers and facilitators to achieving high coverage. *BMC Public Health, 18*(1 C7 - 1074). doi:10.1186/s12889-018-5922-7

Antunes, C., & Sebastiao, S. P. (2020). Ethical challenges in online social networks: The content production and the opinion of professionals. *Cuadernos.Info*, (46), 222–248. doi:10.7764/cdi.46.1473

Arantes, J., & Buchanan, R. (2023). Educational data advocates: Emerging forms of teacher agency in post digital classrooms. *Learning, Media and Technology, 48*(3), 493–513. doi:10.1080/17439884.2022.2087084

Baas, J., Schotten, M., Plume, A., Côté, G., & Karimi, R. (2020). Scopus as a curated, high-quality bibliometric data source for academic research in quantitative science studies. *Quantitative Science Studies, 1*(1), 377–386. doi:10.1162/qss_a_00019

Balas, E. A., Vernon, M., Magrabi, F., Gordon, L. T., & Sexton, J. (2015). Big Data Clinical Research: Validity, Ethics, and Regulation. *Studies in Health Technology and Informatics*. PMID:26262090

Bannigan, M. K., & Shane, B. (2019). Towards truth in influencing: Risks and rewards of disclosing influencer marketing in the fashion industry. *New York School Law Review, 64*(3), 247-263. https://digitalcommons.nyls.edu/cgi/viewcontent.cgi?article=1701&context=nyls_law_review

Beccanulli, A. A., Biraghi, S., & Gambetti, R. (2020). Migrant consumers, celebrity culture and technosociality. *Micro and Macro Marketing, 29*(2), 295–324. doi:10.1431/97320

Bladow, L. E. (2017). Worth the click: Why greater FTC enforcement is needed to curtail deceptive practices in influencer marketing. *William and Mary Law Review, 8*(3), 1123–1164. https://scholarship.law.wm.edu/cgi/viewcontent.cgi?article=3739&context=wmlr

Blumenthal-Barby, J. S. (2012). Between reason and coercion: Ethically permissible influence in health care and health policy contexts. *Kennedy Institute of Ethics Journal, 22*(4), 345–366. doi:10.1353/ken.2012.a495158 PMID:23420941

Boadi, C., & Kolog, E. A. (2021). Social media aggression: An assessment based on the contemporary deterrence theory. *27th Annual Americas Conference on Information Systems, AMCIS 2021.*

Bolly, C. (2011). Can the implementation of ethical processes have an influence on medical persons' suffering? *Psycho-oncologie, 5*(2), 98–108. doi:10.1007/s11839-011-0314-6

Borchers, N. S., & Enke, N. (2022). "I've never seen a client say: 'Tell the influencer not to label this as sponsored'": An exploration into influencer industry ethics. *Public Relations Review,48*(5 C7 - 102235). doi:10.1016/j.pubrev.2022.102235

Bouchalta, M., Belhouss, A., & Benyaich, H. (2020). The medical liability of the psychiatrist in Moroccan law. *Droit. Deontologie et Soin, 20*(3), 305–312. doi:10.1016/j.ddes.2020.07.011

Bush, V., Bush, A. J., Oakley, J., & Cicala, J. E. (2017). The Sales Profession as a Subculture: Implications for Ethical Decision Making. *Journal of Business Ethics, 142*(3), 549–565. doi:10.1007/s10551-015-2753-7

Campbell, A. T. (2012). Bioethics in the public square: Reflections on the how. *Journal of Medical Ethics, 38*(7), 439–441. doi:10.1136/medethics-2011-100057 PMID:22345555

Campbell, C., & Farrell, J. R. (2020). More than meets the eye: The functional components underlying influencer marketing. *Business Horizons, 63*(4), 1–11. doi:10.1016/j.bushor.2020.03.003

Castillo-Abdul, B., & Romero-Rodriguez, L. M. (2021). YouTubers as influencers in the responsible promotion and Happiness management of fashion brands. In *Happiness Management and Social Marketing: A Wave of Sustainability and Creativity* (pp. 189–206). Peter Lang AG.

Choi, E. (2023). Brand integration, disclosure, and ethics in child-targeted YouTube videos: A content analysis. *Journal of Media Ethics: Exploring Questions of Media Morality, 38*(1), 34–47. doi:10.1080/23736992.2022.2158829

Choi, Y. H., Yoon, S., Xuan, B., Lee, S. Y. T., & Lee, K. H. (2021). Fashion informatics of the Big 4Fashion Weeks using topic modeling and sentiment analysis. *Fashion and Textiles, 8*(1 C7 -33). doi:10.1186/s40691-021-00265-6

Clark, T., Moorhead, R., Vaughan, S., & Brener, A. (2021). Agency over technocracy: how lawyer archetypes infect regulatory approaches: the FCA example. *Legal Ethics (Oxford, England), 24*(2), 91–110. doi:10.1080/1460728x.2022.2059742

Clifton, S. (2021). Disability and the complexity of choice in the ethics of abortion and voluntary euthanasia. *The Journal of Medicine and Philosophy, 46*(4), 431–450. doi:10.1093/jmp/jhab008 PMID:34219161

Clover-Brown, I., Moore, B., Andrews, C. G., & Matheny Antommaria, A. H. (2023). Ethical Issues with Patient–Provider Interactions in an Evolving Social Media Landscape. *Pediatrics, 151*(6C7 - e2022060066). doi:10.1542/peds.2022-060066

Co Sy Su, C. (2018). The crossroads of plastination and pilgrimage. *Religions, 9*(3 C7 - 87). doi:10.3390/rel9030087

Collado-Alonso, R., Picazo-Sánchez, L., López-Pastor, A. T., & García-Matilla, A. (2023). What do social media teach? Influencers and followers in informal education in social media. *Revista Mediterrânea de Comunicacion, 14*(2), 259–270. doi:10.14198/MEDCOM.23658

Collier, B., Flynn, G., Stewart, J., & Thomas, D. (2022). Influence government: Exploring practices, ethics, and power in the use of targeted advertising by the UK state. *Big Data & Society, 9*(1). Advance online publication. doi:10.1177/20539517221078756

Conti, M., Gathani, J., & Tricomi, P. P. (2022). Virtual influencers in online social media. *IEEE Communications Magazine, 60*(8), 86–91. doi:10.1109/MCOM.001.2100786

Cosseron, F. (2018). The consent at the child between judicial constraint and support in the current care liberal. *Neuropsychiatrie de l'Enfance et de l'Adolescence, 66*(7-8), 438–442. doi:10.1016/j.neurenf.2018.04.006

Dahill, L. M., Morrison, N. M. V., Mannan, H., Mitchison, D., Touyz, S., Bussey, K., . . . Hay, P. (2022). Exploring associations between positive and negative valanced parental comments about adolescents' bodies and eating and eating problems: a community study. *Journal of Eating Disorders, 10*(1 C7 - 43). doi:10.1186/s40337-022-00561-6

Davies, C., & Hobbs, M. (2020). Irresistible possibilities: Examining the uses and consequences of social media influencers for contemporary public relations. *Public Relations Review, 46*(5C7 - 101983). doi:10.1016/j.pubrev.2020.101983

Davies, H., & Li, Z. (2020). Travel Frog: Traversing cultural borders with mobile games. *Convergence (London), 26*(5-6), 1194–1210. doi:10.1177/1354856519856619

Davis, S., Schrader, V., & Belcheir, M. J. (2012). Influencers of ethical beliefs and the impact on moral distress and conscientious objection. *Nursing Ethics, 19*(6), 738–749. doi:10.1177/0969733011423409 PMID:22736753

De Pelsmacker, P., Diehl, S., Neijens, P., & Terlutter, R. (2023). Editorial: Perspectives on advancing the advertising field for academics and practitioners. Celebrating 40 years of the International Journal of Advertising. *International Journal of Advertising, 42*(1), 1–12. doi:10.1080/02650487.2022.2131279

De Veirman, M., Hudders, L., & Nelson, M. R. (2019). What is influencer marketing and how does it target children? A review and direction for future research. *Frontiers in Psychology, 10*, 2685. doi:10.3389/fpsyg.2019.02685 PMID:31849783

Degen, J. L. (2023). Rationalizing fiction cues: Psychological effects of disclosing ads and the inaccuracy of the human mind when being in parasocial relationships. *Informing Science, 26*, 85–101. doi:10.28945/5108

Deloria, R., & Wolbring, G. (2019). Neuro-advancements and the role of nurses as stated in academic literature and Canadian newspapers. *Societies, 9*(3 C7 - 61). doi:10.3390/soc9030061

Dixon, S. J. (2023, Aug 29). Number of social media users worldwide from 2017 to 2027. *Statista*. https://www.statista.com/statistics/278414/number-of-worldwide-social-network-users/

Donthu, N., Kumar, S., Mukherjee, D., Pandey, N., & Lim, W. M. (2021). How to conduct a bibliometric analysis: An overview and guidelines. *Journal of Business Research, 133*, 285–296. doi:10.1016/j.jbusres.2021.04.070

Droz-dit-Busset, O. (2022). "So-called influencers": Stance taking and (de)legitimation in mediatized discourse about social media influencers. *Discourse, Context & Media, 49*, C7–C100629. doi:10.1016/j.dcm.2022.100629

Dugdale, L. S., & Braswell, H. (2021). Instacash: The ethics of leveraging medical student status on social media. *Academic Medicine, 96*(4), 507–511. doi:10.1097/ACM.0000000000003885 PMID:33298692

Ebert, I., & Sindermann, D. (2020). An ethical view on influencer marketing - dynamic interaction between individual and economy or a simple data-driven advertising model? In *The Regulation of Social Media Influencers* (pp. 74–97). Edward Elgar Publishing Ltd. doi:10.4337/9781788978286.00012

El-Deeb, S. (2022, December). Computer-generated imagery influencer marketing—which ends of the continuum will prevail? humans or avatars? In *International Conference on Marketing and Technologies* (pp. 3-15). Singapore: Springer Nature Singapore.

El Kheir, D. Y. M., Alnufaili, S. S., Alsaffar, R. M., Assad, M. A., & Alkhalifah, Z. Z. (2022). Physicians' Perspective of Telemedicine Regulating Guidelines and Ethical Aspects: A Saudi Experience. *International Journal of Telemedicine and Applications, 2022*, C7–C5068998. doi:10.1155/2022/5068998 PMID:36278028

Etheredge, H. R., Early, J., Norval, D., & Fabian, J. (2021). Influencer marketing by healthcare providers-Ethics and the law. *Aesthetic Medicine, 7*(4), 45–51.

Fakazis, E., & Fürsich, E. (2023). Introduction: from the racist sandwich to civil eats: how food journalism and media are engaging with politics. *The Political Relevance of Food Media and Journalism: Beyond Reviews and Recipes*, 1-16. doi:10.4324/9781003283942-1

Fan, K. L., Economides, J. M., & Song, D. H. (2019). To bot or not? Challenging the top social media influencers in #plasticsurgery. *Plastic and Reconstructive Surgery, 143*(1), 337–343. doi:10.1097/PRS.0000000000005103 PMID:30589813

Favre, J., Germond, T., Clavert, P., Collin, P., Michelet, A., & Lädermann, A. (2020). Want a betterh-index? – All you need to know about copyright and open access. *Revue de Chirurgie Orthopédique et Traumatologique, 106*(8), 930–936. doi:10.1016/j.rcot.2020.10.008

Fedeli, G., & Cheng, M. (2023). Influencer marketing and tourism: Another threat tointegrity for the industry? *Tourism Analysis, 28*(2), 323–328. doi:10.3727/108354222X16510114086370

Gassas, R., & Salem, O. (2022). Factors affecting nurses' professional values: A comprehensive integrative review. *Nurse Education Today, 118*, C7–C105515. doi:10.1016/j.nedt.2022.105515 PMID:36030580

Gisondi, M. A., Barber, R., Faust, J. S., Raja, A., Strehlow, M. C., Westafer, L. M., & Gottlieb, M. (2022). A Deadly Infodemic: Social Media and the Power of COVID-19 Misinformation. Journal *of Medical Internet Research, 24*(2 C7 - e35552). doi:10.2196/35552

Gómez, A. R. (2019). Digital fame and fortune in the age of social media: A Classification of social media influencers. *aDResearch. Revista Internacional de Investigación en Comunicación, 19*(19), 8–29. doi:10.7263/adresic-019-01

Gorodishchev, A. V., Gorodishcheva, A. N., & Kovalev, G. P. (2023). Digital influencer factory: the price of word authority. *Proceedings of the 2023 Communication Strategies in Digital Society Seminar 2023, ComSDS 2023.* 10.1109/ComSDS58064.2023.10130358

Gupta, N., Dorfman, R., Saadat, S., & Roostaeian, J. (2020). The plastic surgery social media influencer: Ethical considerations and a literature review. *Aesthetic Surgery Journal, 40*(6), 691–699. doi:10.1093/asj/sjz329 PMID:31738821

Ha, L., & Yang, Y. (2023). Research about persuasive effects of social media influencers as online opinion leaders 1990–2020: A review. *International Journal of Internet Marketing and Advertising, 18*(2-3), 220–241. doi:10.1504/IJIMA.2023.129661

Hagelstein, J., Einwiller, S., & Zerfass, A. (2021). The ethical dimension of public relations in Europe: Digital channels, moral challenges, resources, and training. *Public Relations Review, 47*(4 C7 - 102063). doi:10.1016/j.pubrev.2021.102063

Hall, P. F., Falconer Hall, T., Bailey, Z., & Horne, S. T. (2023). Medics as influencers: a historical analysis of British Army military medical exercises in Kenya over two decades. *BMJ Military Health.* doi:10.1136/military-2023-002442

Hancock, L., & Ralph, N. (2021). A framework for assessing fossil fuel 'retrofit' hydrogen exports: Security-justice implications of Australia's coal-generated hydrogen exports to Japan. *Energy, 223*, C7–C119938. doi:10.1016/j.energy.2021.119938

Hanson, W. R., & Moore, J. R. (2014). Business student moral influencers: Unseen opportunities for development? *Academy of Management Learning & Education, 13*(4), 525–546. doi:10.5465/amle.2012.0325

Hewitt, J., Parker, L., McQuilten, G., & Khan, R. (2023). Sustainability chic and the future of fashion marketing. In Beyond the Dark Arts: Advancing Marketing and Communication Theory and Practice (pp. 125-147). World Scientific Publishing Co. doi:10.1142/9789811276064_0007

Hidayana, I., Prawindarti, L., Umar, N., Ambarwati, K., & Rosatriani, F. (2023). Marketing of commercial milk formula during COVID-19 in Indonesia. *Maternal and Child Nutrition, 19*(3C7 - e13491). doi:10.1111/mcn.13491

Hockin-Boyers, H., & Clifford-Astbury, C. (2021). The politics of #diversifyyourfeed in the context of Black Lives Matter. *Feminist Media Studies, 21*(3), 504–509. doi:10.1080/14680777.2021.1925727

Hudders, L., & Lou, C. (2023). The rosy world of influencer marketing? Its bright and dark sides, and future research recommendations. *International Journal of Advertising, 42*(1), 151–161. doi:10.1080/02650487.2022.2137318

Ijabadeniyi, A., & Govender, J. P. (2023). Intrinsic drivers of the reputation for CSR: A cognitive analysis of consumer expectations. *Social Responsibility Journal.* Advance online publication. doi:10.1108/SRJ-10-2022-0451

Jacobson, J., & Harrison, B. (2022). Sustainable fashion social media influencers and content creation calibration. *International Journal of Advertising*, *41*(1), 150–177. doi:10.1080/02650487.2021.2000125

Jalali, S. S., & Khalid, H. B. (2021). The influence of Instagram influencers' activity on green consumption behavior. *Business Management and Strategy*, *12*(1), 78–90. doi:10.5296/bms.v12i1.18265

Jansen van Vuuren, C. J., & Jansen van Vuuren, J. M. (2022). Perspectives of healthcare workers in South Africa on COVID-19 vaccination passports. *Health SA*, *27*, C7–a1823. doi:10.4102/hsag.v27i0.1823 PMID:35548060

Jatho, A., Bikaitwoha, M. E., & Mugisha, N. M. (2020). Socio-culturally mediated factors and lower level of education are the main influencers of functional cervical cancer literacy among women in Mayuge, Eastern Uganda. *ecancermedicalscience, 14 C7 - 1004*. doi:10.3332/ecancer.2020.1004

Jauffret, M. N., & Aubrun, F. (2022). The biodigital rises: a new digital brand challenge. Lecture Notes in Computer Science (including subseries Lecture Notes in Artificial Intelligence and Lecture Notes in Bioinformatics).

Jones, K. (2022). Some conclusions, intrusions, and shock endings. In Doing Performative Social Science: Creativity in Doing Research and Reaching Communities (pp.237-247). Taylor and Francis. https://doi.org/ doi:10.4324/9781003187745-25

Josse-Eklund, A., Jossebo, M., Sandin-Bojö, A. K., Wilde-Larsson, B., & Petzäll, K. (2014). Swedish nurses' perceptions of influencers on patient advocacy: A phenomenographic study. *Nursing Ethics*, *21*(6), 673–683. doi:10.1177/0969733013515488 PMID:24477259

Kadekova, Z., & Holienčinova, M. (2018). Influencer marketing as a modern phenomenon creating a new frontier of virtual opportunities. *Communication Today, 9*(2), 90-104. https://www.communicationtoday.sk/download/22018/06.-KADEKOVA-HOLIENCINOVA-%E2%80%93-CT-2-2018.pdf

Kaler, J. (2002). Morality and strategy in stakeholder identification. *Journal of Business Ethics*, *39*(1/2), 91–100. doi:10.1023/A:1016336118528

Kaler, J. (2006). Evaluating stakeholder theory. *Journal of Business Ethics*, *69*(3), 249–268. doi:10.1007/s10551-006-9089-2

Kalisch, E. (2023). The ego-alter-tertius paradigm: Adam Smith's interaction model. In *Adam Smith and Modernity: 1723-2023* (pp. 161–174). Taylor and Francis. doi:10.4324/9781003301448-13

Khan, H. R., Onye, U. U., & Du, Y. (2018). Data-activism as civic engagement: Forming a narrative to foster social change on gun control in the United States. *Proceedings of the Association for Information Science and Technology*, *55*(1), 841–842. doi:10.1002/pra2.2018.14505501140

Khan, N., Rudoler, D., McDiarmid, M., & Peckham, S. (2020). A pay for performance scheme in primary care: Meta-synthesis of qualitative studies on the provider experiences of the quality and outcomes framework in the UK. *BMC Family Practice, 21*(1 C7 - 142). doi:10.1186/s12875-020-01208-8

Kim, D., & Wang, Z. (2023). The ethics of virtuality: Navigating the complexities of human-like virtual influencers in the social media marketing realm. *Frontiers in Communication*, *8*, C7–C1205610. doi:10.3389/fcomm.2023.1205610

Kim, H. S., Nam, S., Lee, W., Nam, K., & Kwon, D. (2013). Effects of moral judgement, emotional control and problem solving on information ethics of gifted students in computer science. *Proceedings - International Computer Software and Applications Conference C7 - 6605863*. doi:10.23919/JSC.2021.0026

Leonard, L. N. K., & Cronan, T. P. (2005). Attitude toward ethical behavior in computer use: A shifting model. *Industrial Management & Data Systems, 105*(9), 1150–1171. doi:10.1108/02635570510633239

Lillywhite, A., & Wolbring, G. (2020). Coverage of artificial intelligence and machine learning within academic literature, Canadian newspapers, and twitter tweets: The case of disabled people. *Societies, 10*(1 C7 - 23). doi:10.3390/soc10010023

Maheshwari, V., & Fielding, J. (2019). Importance of Ethics and Sustainability in the Fashion Industry: An Abstract. In *Developments in Marketing Science: Proceedings of the Academy of Marketing Science* (pp. 139-140). Springer Nature. 10.1007/978-3-030-02568-7_39

Maloni, M. J., Gligor, D. M., Blumentritt, T., & Gligor, N. (2022). Fear or Competition? Antecedents to U.S. Business Student Immigration Attitudes. *Journal of Management Education, 46*(4), 715–750. doi:10.1177/10525629211065623

Miladi, N. (2021). *Global Media Ethics and the Digital Revolution*. Taylor and Francis., doi:10.4324/9781003203551

Militello, M., Yang, R. A., Anderson, J. B., Szeto, M. D., Presley, C. L., & Laughter, M. R. (2021). Social Media and Ethical Challenges for the Dermatologist. *Current Dermatology Reports, 10*(4), 120–127. doi:10.1007/s13671-021-00340-7 PMID:34540357

Mohamad, E., & Damanhuri, N. H. A. (2019). Female health opinion leaders and ethics on Instagram. *Jurnal Komunikasi: Malaysian Journal of Communication, 35*(4), 193–210. doi:10.17576/JKMJC-2019-3504-12

Money, K., & Schepers, H. (2007). Are CSR and corporate governance converging? *Journal of General Management, 33*(2), 1–11. doi:10.1177/030630700703300201

Mooz, H. H., & Forsberg, K. (2008). *Making decisions that have global impact*. 18th Annual International Symposium of the International Council on Systems Engineering, INCOSE2008. 10.1007/978-3-030-62796-6_19

Nichols, K., & Pappas, R. (2022). The #ethics behind social media influencers in dentistry. *The Journal of the American Dental Association, 153*(10), 1010–1011. doi:10.1016/j.adaj.2022.07.008 PMID:36041963

Núñez-Cansado, M., López-López, A., & Somarriba-Arechavala, N. (2021). Covert advertising by kidsfluencers: A methodological proposal applied to the case study of the ten youngest youtubers with most followers in Spain. *Profesional de la Informacion, 30*(2 C7 - e300219). doi:10.3145/epi.2021.mar.19

Nxumalo, C. T., & McHunu, G. G. (2020). Zulu men's conceptions, understanding, and experiences of voluntary medical male circumcision in KwaZulu-Natal, South Africa. *American Journal of Men's Health, 14*(2). Advance online publication. doi:10.1177/1557988319892437 PMID:32131678

Ortová, N., Hejlová, D., & Weiss, D. (2023). Creation of a code of ethics for influencer marketing: The case of the Czech Republic. *Journal of Media Ethics: Exploring Questions of Media Morality, 38*(2), 65–79. doi:10.1080/23736992.2023.2193958

Parsons, E., Maclaran, P., Chatzidakis, A., & Ashman, R. (2023). *Contemporary Issues in Marketing and Consumer Behavior* (3rd ed.). Taylor and Francis., doi:10.4324/9781003201151

Perry, P., Ashman, R., & Stalker, I. D. (2020). Special session: corporate social responsibility and ai: the case of fashion: an abstract. In *Developments in Marketing Science: Proceedings of the Academy of Marketing Science* (pp. 143-144). Springer Nature. 10.1007/978-3-030-42545-6_36

Pétursdóttir, G. M. (2017). Fire-raising feminists: Embodied experience and activism in academia. *European Journal of Women's Studies*, *24*(1), 85–99. doi:10.1177/1350506815622513

Pierce, J. (2018). Storytelling through photos: A photovoice lens on ethical visual research. In *Research in Ethical Issues in Organizations* (Vol. 19, pp. 67–90). Emerald Group Publishing Ltd. doi:10.1108/S1529-209620180000019005

Potts, L., Small, R., & Trice, M. (2019). Boycotting the Knowledge Makers: How Reddit Demonstrates the Rise of Media Blacklists and Source Rejection in Online Communities. *IEEE Transactions on Professional Communication, 62*(4 C7 - 8894031), 351-363. doi:10.1109/TPC.2019.2946942

Procházka, D. A. (2021). Attitude of Czech influencers towards disinformation. *IDIMT 2021 -Pandemics: Impacts, Strategies and Responses, 29th Interdisciplinary Information Management Talks.*

Py, B. (2023). Les médecins, la communication et l'influence en santé après la loi du 9 juin 2023. *Médecine & Droit*, *2023*(183), 121–125. Advance online publication. doi:10.1016/j.meddro.2023.08.001

Raimundo, R., & Rosário, A. T. (2022). Cybersecurity in the Internet of Things in Industrial Management. *Applied Sciences (Basel, Switzerland)*, *12*(3), 1598. doi:10.3390/app12031598

Ramanayake, R., Wicke, P., & Nallur, V. (2023). Immune moral models? Pro-social rule breaking as a moral enhancement approach for ethical AI. *AI & Society*, *38*(2), 801–813. doi:10.1007/s00146-022-01478-z PMID:35645466

Ranpariya, V., Chu, B., Fathy, R., & Lipoff, J. B. (2020). Dermatology without dermatologists? Analyzing Instagram influencers with dermatology-related hashtags. *Journal of the American Academy of Dermatology*, *83*(6), 1840–1842. doi:10.1016/j.jaad.2020.05.039 PMID:32416205

Rashi, T., & Schleifer, R. (2023). The Ethics of Psychological Warfare–Lessons from Israel. *Democracy and Security*, *19*(2), 199–210. doi:10.1080/17419166.2023.2210472

Rass, S. (2021). Judging the quality of (fake) news on the internet. *Mind & Society*, *20*(1), 129–133. doi:10.1007/s11299-020-00249-x

Robinson, B. (2020). Towards an ontology and ethics of virtual influencers. *AJIS. Australasian Journal of Information Systems*, *24*, C7–C2807. doi:10.3127/ajis.v24i0.2807

Rodenburg, K., & Macdonald, K. (2021). Enhancing business schools' pedagogy on sustainable business practices and ethical decision-making. *Sustainability (Switzerland), 13*(10 C7 -5527). doi:10.3390/su13105527

Rosário, A. T., & Dias, J. C. (2023). How Industry 4.0 and Sensors Can Leverage Product Design: Opportunities and Challenges. *Sensors (Basel)*, *23*(3), 1165. doi:10.3390/s23031165 PMID:36772206

Rosário, A. T., Lopes, P. R., & Rosário, F. S. (2023). Metaverse in Marketing: Challenges and Opportunities. In A. Khang, V. Shah, & S. Rani (Eds.), *Handbook of Research on AI-Based Technologies and Applications in the Era of the Metaverse* (pp. 204–227). IGI Global. doi:10.4018/978-1-6684-8851-5.ch010

Rosas-Moreno, T. C. (2023). How Gendered Mediation Affects Local News Framing of Trafficking Victims: A Call for Ethics-Of-Care Journalism. *Journal of Human Trafficking*, 1–19. Advance online publication. doi:10.1080/23322705.2023.2225390

Rossanty, Y., Sari, P. B., Amlus, M. H., & Nasution, T. A. M. (2021). Islam, opinion leaders, and social media influencer. In *The Role of Islamic Spirituality in the Management and Leadership Process* (pp. 66–84). IGI Global. doi:10.4018/978-1-7998-6892-7.ch004

Rossi, C., & Rivetti, F. (2023). Virtual influencer marketing: is it effective in engaging younger generations? *Proceedings of the 10th European Conference on Social Media, ECSM 2023.* 10.34190/ecsm.10.1.1061

Ryu, S., & Park, B. (2018). Do I want to pay to download movies: Factors affecting acceptance of legal movie download services. *Journal of Information. Communication and Ethics in Society*, *16*(1), 45–60. doi:10.1108/JICES-03-2017-0019

Saldaña, C. M., Welner, K. G., Malcolm, S., & Tisch, E. (2021). Teachers as Market Influencers: Towards a Policy Framework for Teacher Brand Ambassador Programs in K-12 Schools. *Education Policy Analysis Archives*, *29*(August - December), C7–C109. doi:10.14507/epaa.29.5654

Santoro, J. D., & Bennett, M. (2018). Ethics of end of life decisions in pediatrics: A narrative review of the roles of caregivers, shared decision-making, and patient centered values. Behavioral *Sciences, 8*(5 C7 - 42). doi:10.3390/bs8050042

Sharma, P., & Francis, D. P. (2020). Social media influencers in cardiology/metabolism-a force for good or evil? *Heart and Metabolism*, (82), 36–40.

Siddiqi, A., & Bodolica, V. (2023). Bon voyage: A vacation from food wastage. *Emerald Emerging Markets Case Studies*, *13*(2), 1–31. doi:10.1108/EEMCS-05-2023-0148

Silva, S., & de Brito, P. Q. (2020). The Characteristics of Digital Influencers and Their Ethically Questionable Attitudes. *Smart Innovation, Systems and Technologies*. doi:10.1080/10508422.2021.1977935

Ssanyu, J. N., Kiguba, R., Olum, R., Kiguli, J., & Kitutu, F. E. (2022). Using community influencer groups to address COVID-19 misinformation and vaccine hesitancy in Uganda: a protocol for a prospective quasi-experimental study. *BMJ Open, 12*(8 C7 - 057994). doi:10.1136/bmjopen-2021-057994

Stanberry, K., Stanberry, C., & Reeves, T. (2021). A persistent academic ethical dilemma: Too few female students in STEM five decades after Title IX. *Journal of Academic Ethics*, *19*(1), 25–34. doi:10.1007/s10805-020-09370-5

Steele, L., Orefuwa, E., Bino, S., Singer, S. R., Lutwama, J., & Dickmann, P. (2020). Earlier Outbreak Detection—A Generic Model and Novel Methodology to Guide Earlier Detection Supported by Data From Low- and Mid-Income Countries. *Frontiers in Public Health*, *8*, C7–C452. doi:10.3389/fpubh.2020.00452 PMID:33014967

Subramani, N., Easwaramoorthy, S. V., Mohan, P., Subramanian, M., & Sambath, V. (2023). A Gradient Boosted Decision Tree-Based Influencer Prediction in Social Network Analysis. *Big Data and Cognitive Computing, 7*(1 C7 - 6). doi:10.3390/bdcc7010006

Sweeney, E., Lawlor, M. A., & Brady, M. (2022). Teenagers' moral advertising literacy in an influencer marketing context. *International Journal of Advertising*, *41*(1), 54–77. doi:10.1080/02650487.2021.1964227

Thomas, K. (2019). Key opinion leaders supercharged by the internet: Paid doctor and patient influencers on social media. *BMJ (Clinical Research Ed.)*, *365*, C7–l2336. doi:10.1136/bmj.l2336 PMID:31152003

Torres, B. F., Rodríguez, A. P., & Díaz, R. C. (2021). The credibility of social media and ethical implications for young people. *Revista Latina de Comunicacion Social*, *2021*(79), 51–68. doi:10.4185/RLCS-2021-1512

Triplett, N. T., Kingzette, A., Slivinski, L., & Niu, T. (2022). Ethics for Mental Health Influencers: MFTs as Public Social Media Personalities. *Contemporary Family Therapy*, *44*(2), 125–135. doi:10.1007/s10591-021-09632-3

Turnbull, S., Kelley, L., & Jugenheimer, D. (2023). *Advertising account planning: planning and managing strategic communication campaigns*. Taylor and Francis. doi:10.4324/9781003250449

Vadíková, K. M. (2022). On the Transformation of Thinking on Personal Responsibility Towards Requirements of Environmental Ethics in Slovakia. *Studia Ecologiae et Bioethicae*, *20*(2), 15–25. doi:10.21697/seb.2022.11

Van Dam, S., & Van Reijmersdal, E. A. (2019). Insights in adolescents' advertising literacy, perceptions and responses regarding sponsored influencer videos and disclosures. Cyberpsychology, *13*(2 C7 - 2). doi:10.5817/CP2019-2-2

Velasco-Molpeceres, A., Zarauza-Castro, J., Pérez-Curiel, C., & Mateos-González, S. (2023). Slow Fashion as a Communication Strategy of Fashion Brands on Instagram. *Sustainability(Switzerland), 15*(1 C7 - 423). doi:10.3390/su15010423

Villamil, V., & Wolbring, G. (2019). Role and scope coverage of speech-related professionals linked to neuro-advancements within the academic literature and Canadian newspapers. Education *Sciences, 9*(2 C7 - 98). doi:10.3390/educsci9020098

Wang, C. L. (2023). *The Palgrave Handbook of Interactive Marketing*. Springer International Publishing., doi:10.1007/978-3-031-14961-0

Waqas, A., Baig, A. A., Khalid, M. A., Aedma, K. K., & Naveed, S. (2019). Conflicts of interest and outcomes of clinical trials of antidepressants: An 18-year retrospective study. *Journal of Psychiatric Research, 116*, 83–87. doi:10.1016/j.jpsychires.2019.05.029 PMID:31212249

Wellman, M. L., Stoldt, R., Tully, M., & Ekdale, B. (2020). Ethics of authenticity: Social media influencers and the production of sponsored content. *Journal of Medical Ethics*, *35*(2), 68–82. doi:10.1080/23736992.2020.1736078

Wellman, M. L., Stoldt, R., Tully, M., & Ekdale, B. (2020). Ethics of Authenticity: Social Media Influencers and the Production of Sponsored Content. *Journal of Media Ethics: Exploring Questions of Media Morality, 35*(2), 68–82. doi:10.1080/23736992.2020.1736078

Willis, E., & Delbaere, M. (2022). Patient influencers: the next frontier in direct-to-consumer pharmaceutical marketing. *Journal of Medical Internet Research, 24*(3 C7 - e29422). doi:10.2196/29422

Woods, S. (2016). # Sponsored: The emergence of influencer marketing. *TRACE: Tennessee Research and Creative Exchange.* https://trace.tennessee.edu/cgi/viewcontent.cgi?article=3010&context=utk_chanhonoproj

Wu, Y., Xie, L., Yuan, Z., Jiang, S., Liu, W., & Sheng, H. (2020). Investigating public biodiversity conservation awareness based on the propagation of wildlife-related incidents on the Sina Weibo social media platform. *Environmental Research Letters, 15*(9 C7 - 094082). doi:10.1088/1748-9326/ab9ed1

Yao, Q., Perlmutter, D. D., & Liu, J. (2017). What are shaping the ethical bottom line?: Identifying factors influencing young readers' acceptance of digital news photo alteration. *Telematics and Informatics, 34*(1), 124–132. doi:10.1016/j.tele.2016.04.010

Yazdani, A. T., Muhammad, A., Nisar, M. I., Khan, U., & Shafiq, Y. (2021). Unveiling and addressing implementation barriers to routine immunization in the peri-urban slums of Karachi, Pakistan: A mixed-methods study. *Health Research Policy and Systems, 19*(S2), C7–C55. doi:10.1186/s12961-021-00691-4 PMID:34380526

ADDITIONAL READING

Barrientos-Baez, A., Cuesta, U., & Zito, M. (2023). Neurocommunication, Neuromarketing and Advertising: consumer behavior. *Revista latina de comunicacion social, 81*, 4-5.

Birchall, S. J., & Kehler, S. (2023). Denial and discretion as a governance process: How actor perceptions of risk and responsibility hinder adaptation to climate change. *Environmental Science & Policy, 147*, 1-10. doi:10.1016/j.envsci.2023.05.017

Cusnir, C. (2019). Mapping Romanian Influencers' Presence in the Online Environment. *Communication: strategic perspectives*, 121-129.

Dekavalla, M. (2020). Gaining trust: The articulation of transparency by You Tube fashion and beauty content creators. *Media Culture & Society, 42*(1), 75–92. doi:10.1177/0163443719846613

Johnstone, L., & Lindh, C. (2018). The sustainability-age dilemma: A theory of (un)planned behaviour via influencers. *Journal of Consumer Behaviour, 17*(1), E127–E139. doi:10.1002/cb.1693

Leavey, S. T. (2023). We're Not Just Telling Stories, We're Changing Lives": Dhar Mann's Progressive Neoliberalism. *International Journal of Communication, 17*, 1759–1776.

Marcella-Hood, M. (2021). Instagram versus reality: The design and use of self-curated photo elicitation in a study exploring the construction of Scottish identity amongst personal style influencers on Instagram. *Qualitative Research, 21*(6), 865–889. doi:10.1177/1468794120934404

Vilajoana-Alejandre, S., Rom-Rodríguez, J., & Miotto, G. (2019). Advertising self-regulation challenges in the light of legal and ethical risks of influencers' marketing. *Revista mediterranea comunicacion-journal of communication, 10*(2), 115-129.

KEY TERMS AND DEFINITIONS

Brand: It's a title, expression, design, symbol, or any distinguishing element that sets apart the goods or services of one seller from those of others.

Environmental responsibility: It's the moral responsibility that companies bear to safeguard natural resources, prevent pollution, and minimize other types of environmental damage.

Ethical: It refers to the ethical principles and values held by either an individual or a group.

Influencer: It's a marketing strategy that involves targeting individuals with influence or leadership among potential customers of a brand through specific actions.

Social Responsibility: It's a moral theory that emphasizes individual accountability in fulfilling civic duties, asserting that an individual's actions should contribute to the overall benefit of society.

Strategic: Involving the recognition of sustained or overarching objectives and interests, as well as the methods for accomplishing them.

Sustainable: It's a quality or state of a process or system that permits it to stay at a particular level over a specific duration.

Chapter 16
The Ethics of Collaborating With Social Media Influencers:
Influencers and Psychological Well-Being

Ranjit Singha
https://orcid.org/0000-0002-3541-8752
Christ University, India

Surjit Singha
https://orcid.org/0000-0002-5730-8677
Kristu Jayanti College, India

V. Muthu Ruben
https://orcid.org/0009-0006-7723-8596
Christ University, India

Melita Stephen Natal
https://orcid.org/0009-0004-1240-7817
Amity University, India

Amenla Longkumer
District Mental Health Program, India

Alphonsa Diana Haokip
https://orcid.org/0000-0003-2578-0114
Christ King High School, India

ABSTRACT

This study highlights the importance of placing influencers' psychological well-being as a top priority in influencer marketing. In light of the growing influencers' impact on brand perceptions and consumer behavior, addressing their obstacles is crucial to promoting an ethical and sustainable ecosystem. The demands of upholding genuineness and regulating personal limits can profoundly affect the psychological well-being of influencers. Acknowledging and giving precedence to the welfare of others is an ethical obligation and a critical factor in ensuring sustained success in collaborative endeavors. Suggested ideas for a genuine brand-influencer partnership encompass advocating for mental well-being and fostering open and honest communication. These suggestions can cultivate a more accountable, enduring, and genuine influencer marketing ecosystem.

INTRODUCTION

The marketing domain has experienced a significant paradigm shift in recent times due to the emergence and prominence of social media influencers. These individuals, who frequently amass substantial follow-

DOI: 10.4018/979-8-3693-0912-4.ch016

ings on social media platforms, including Instagram, YouTube, and TikTok, have emerged as influential figures in consumer trend formation and purchasing decision impact (Joshi et al., 2023; Kim & Kim, 2022). Undoubtedly, the proliferation of influencer marketing has created novel opportunities for strategic business communication, granting organizations exclusive and immediate entry into their intended demographics. Nevertheless, this phenomenon also raises numerous ethical concerns that necessitate meticulous scrutiny. The rise of influencer marketing signifies a divergence from conventional advertising approaches. As more and more companies rely on influencers to promote their products or services, ethical considerations arise (Joshi et al., 2023). A fundamental ethical consideration pertains to matters concerning authenticity and transparency. It is incumbent upon influencers, who serve as intermediaries between brands and consumers, to divulge any affiliations they may have with the products they promote. Refraining from failing to do so gives rise to apprehensions regarding the genuineness of suggestions and obscures the distinction between authentic content and sponsored advertisements (Kim & Wang, 2023).

As a bonus, exploitation and manipulation are possible when influencers place monetary profit at the expense of their followers' welfare. Influencers' endorsement of products in pursuit of sponsorships and partnerships may need more sincerity and comprehensive evaluation, thereby potentially undermining the trust of their audience. On the other hand, brands must ensure that their partnerships with influencers align with the welfare and principles of influencers and followers. In addition to the ethical implications linked to marketing strategies, there is an increasing need to address the psychological welfare of social media influencers. The pressure to maintain a curated online presence, constant engagement, and the scrutiny of a vast audience significantly impact the mental health of influencers. Influencers may experience fatigue, anxiety, and a sense of identity distortion as they confront the complexities of online celebrity (Hosszu et al., 2022; Kim & Kim, 2022).

Comprehending and attending to the psychological welfare of influencers is not merely a matter of ethics but also a critical business decision for organizations involved in influencer marketing. An influencer who maintains sound mental health is more adept at producing genuine and captivating content and cultivating a sincere rapport with their audience. Fostering enduring and mutually advantageous partnerships, brands that place a high value on the welfare of influencers positively impact the sustainability of the influencer marketing ecosystem. This chapter explores the complex network of ethical considerations that encircle business-social media influencer collaboration. Our study investigates the intricate facets of the psychological well-being of influencers and examines the potential ramifications for strategic business communication within the dynamic digital marketing environment.

Many theoretical frameworks offer significant perspectives on the ethical aspects of partnerships involving social media influencers. The Social Contract Theory, for example, illuminates the implicit agreements among brands, influencers, and their audience, emphasizing the criticality of honesty and transparency in preserving a harmonious rapport. When formulating ethical decisions regarding marketing practices, the utilitarian perspective urges businesses and influencers to prioritize the most significant benefit for the largest possible population (Kim & Wang, 2023). In recent years, the proliferation of digital platforms and the widespread accessibility of content generation have given rise to influencer marketing. The emergence of individuals who exploit their online presence to exert influence has resulted in the development of a vibrant environment conducive to brand collaborations. Nevertheless, as this domain progresses, ethical dilemmas also arise, demanding a comprehensive examination of the intricate relationship among influencers, brands, and their respective audiences.

The study's conceptual framework is based on a tripartite model that integrates strategic business communication, psychological well-being, and ethical considerations. This framework fundamentally asserts that ethical decision-making in influencer marketing is intricately intertwined with the psychological welfare of influencers and their audience. The model investigates how ethical practices contribute to the cultivation of a favorable influencer environment, thereby establishing a climate that is favorable for the generation of genuine content and the establishment of trust among audiences. The significance of strategic business communication is critical within this framework. To maintain ethical integrity, organizations must harmonize their objectives with the consequences of their partnerships with influencers and their respective audiences. The framework provides a comprehensive understanding of the dynamics within the influencer marketing sector by clarifying the interconnected relationship between influencers' psychological well-being, ethical decision-making, and effective strategic communication.

This chapter's principal objective is to critically analyze the ethical ramifications that arise from partnerships with social media influencers, with a particular emphasis on the psychological welfare of said influencers. This research aims to evaluate the moral aspects of influencer marketing, specifically focusing on the values of transparency, authenticity, and the conscientious application of influence. This study aims to comprehensively understand influencers' psychological challenges in influencer marketing, including intense online scrutiny, the responsibility to maintain a flawless image, and the potential impact on mental well-being. This inquiry examines the interdependent connection between ethical decision-making and the psychological well-being of influencers to clarify how ethical conduct can aid in developing a positive and sustainable influencer ecosystem. The chapter examines the strategic ramifications for companies involved in influencer marketing. Emphasizing the significance of harmonizing business objectives with ethical principles and fostering long-lasting, genuine connections with influencers, the chapter emphasizes the necessity of doing so. The chapter's contents provide valuable insights that transcend its academic focus, benefiting businesses, influencers, scholars, and practitioners equally as they navigate the ever-changing and dynamic realm of digital communication and brand endorsement.

The chapter extensively analyzes the ethical implications associated with collaborations involving social media influencers, particularly emphasizing the psychological welfare of said influencers. This study examines the moral aspects of influencer marketing, focusing on responsible influence, authenticity, and transparency. The study investigates the psychological obstacles that influencers encounter within the marketing domain, encompassing pressures to maintain an image on the internet, potential repercussions on their mental well-being, etc.

The chapter examines the complex correlation between ethical decision-making and the psychological welfare of influencers, placing particular emphasis on the potential of moral conduct to cultivate a positive and sustainable influencer ecosystem. The report analyzes the strategic implications that organizations engaged in influencer marketing may face. The importance of establishing genuine relationships with influencers and aligning business objectives with ethical principles is one of the central tenets emphasized. The chapter offers significant perspectives for academics, professionals, organizations, and influencers who encounter the intricate complexities of digital communication and brand endorsement in a constantly evolving setting.

The chapter utilizes a research methodology encompassing various dimensions to examine the subject matter comprehensively. The study begins with a comprehensive literature review on influencer marketing, ethics, and psychological well-being. This stage thoroughly examines scholarly articles, books, industry reports, and other relevant resources to comprehend the topic thoroughly. The methodology examines empirical case studies that exemplify ethical quandaries or psychological barriers that social media influencers confront while collaborating with brands. The practical insights these case studies provide regarding the complex dynamics of influencer marketing are invaluable.

INFLUENCERS AND PSYCHOLOGICAL WELL-BEING: RISKS AND CHALLENGES

Influencers bear a substantial psychological burden in their quest for authenticity, a fundamental aspect of effective influencer marketing. The constant pressure to present an authentic and relatable persona frequently causes influencers to contend with the obligation to divulge confidential information, authentic experiences, and content that is accessible to all. Although crucial for establishing rapport with the audience, this pressure can negatively impact the self-esteem of influencers. Felicity of inadequacy and the gradual erosion of an authentic sense of self may result from the perceived necessity to adhere to societal standards and satisfy the demands of one's audience (Zniva et al., 2023; Ao et al., 2023). Influencer marketing requires influencers to consistently present an idealized version of themselves, merging their personal and professional lives: the continuous self-presentation and performance-oriented nature of generating captivating content impact the mental health of influencers. The combination of the pressure to uphold an engaging online persona and the apprehension of negative feedback from one's audience can result in increased levels of stress, anxiety, and emotional fatigue. The increasing indistinctness between the curated online persona and the genuine self presents difficulties for the mental well-being of influencers (Kim & Kim, 2022). In their study, Bi et al. (2019) provided evidence that the perceived third-person effect significantly influences the dissemination of positive video-based electronic word-of-mouth (vWOM) on YouTube.

On the other hand, we found a stronger correlation between the perceived self-effect and the tendency to spread negative vWOM. The research, which was undertaken via a survey comprising 282 individuals attending a public university in the Midwest region of the United States of America, suggests that the sharing of vWOM is not directly influenced by the consumption of general electronic word-of-mouth (eWOM). The consistent dissemination of material on YouTube plays a substantial role in the proliferation of virtual word-of-mouth (vWOM), irrespective of its inherent quality (positive or negative). The research provides practical implications for marketers who aim to increase the visibility of promotional brand messages through social media platforms such as YouTube. As a result, the findings have become increasingly valuable. The study suggests that the perceived third-person effect, which underscores the assumed influence of others, increases the likelihood of sharing positive vWOM.

On the contrary, disseminating negative virtual word-of-mouth (vWOM) is linked to self-effect perception, suggesting that individuals are more likely to share unfavorable experiences. The results emphasize the criticality for marketers to expeditiously confront and control adverse evaluations, thereby thwarting their dissemination among users. It is critical, as it could influence viewers to believe that they, too, could undergo negative experiences, aiding in disseminating such content. The research makes a substantial theoretical contribution by further elucidating the literature on the third-person effect and presumed influence, focusing on product-related content on YouTube. Examining the mediating function of vWOM valence in its dissemination also fills a void in the current body of research regarding the consequences of electronic word-of-mouth (Bi et al., 2019).

The obligations of upholding an online persona transcend content generation and encompass the ceaseless struggle to remain pertinent and interactive. The perpetual need for ingenuity, regularity, and engagement from the audience all contribute to the potential for fatigue to affect influencers. Emotional fatigue, diminished enthusiasm, and disillusionment are all symptoms of burnout. The burdensome tasks of managing multiple social media platforms, responding to comments, and consistently producing content can compromise influencers' mental and emotional resilience. It underscores the necessity for an influencer marketing strategy that is more sustainable (Kim & Wang, 2023; Zniva et al., 2023; Kim & Kim, 2022). As the digital era progresses, influencers frequently confront the erosion of personal boundaries caused by the growing visibility of their private lives. The constant exposure of personal relationships, daily rituals, and intimate moments raises privacy concerns.

To sustain audience interest while also protecting personal details, influencers may need to strike a nuanced equilibrium between disclosure (Baker-Eveleth et al., 2021; Roth, 1999). Felicity, anxiety, and, in severe cases, a loss of agency over one's storyline may result from the ambiguity that exists between the public and private domains. Singha (2024) suggests that effective social media marketing strategies should emphasize authenticity, transparency, and community engagement, utilizing both quantitative metrics and qualitative analysis to gauge ROI. We envision the future of social media to revolve around personalized AI-driven interactions, immersive content experiences, and a shift towards audio-centric platforms. Despite hurdles such as algorithm changes and privacy concerns, opportunities exist for leveraging video dominance and integrating social commerce. To excel in this evolving sphere, businesses must exhibit adaptability, innovation, and a commitment to ethical standards. Singha (2023) suggests incorporating social media into economics education initiates a transformative journey characterized by innovation, overcoming challenges, and unveiling new opportunities. It emphasizes social media's efficacy in engaging students, simplifying economic concepts, and nurturing critical thinking abilities. It also underscores ethical concerns such as digital literacy, responsible usage, and the potential to foster cross-cultural connections.

Integrating emerging technologies like virtual reality, artificial intelligence, and blockchain holds promise for further revolutionizing economics education. Ultimately, the interconnectedness of technology, education, and economics presents substantial potential for equipping well-informed global citizens to address intricate economic issues. Both Singha (2024) and Singha (2023) underscore the transformative potential of incorporating social media in their respective fields: marketing and education. Singha (2024) highlights the importance of authenticity, transparency, and community engagement in social media marketing while discussing future trends such as AI-driven interactions and immersive content experiences. Similarly, Singha (2023) discusses the transformative journey of integrating social media into economics education, emphasizing its ability to engage students, simplify complex concepts, and promote critical thinking. Both articles address ethical considerations in their domains, whether regarding digital literacy and responsible usage in social media marketing (Singha, 2024) or ethical concerns surrounding digital education (Singha, 2023).

Additionally, both articles recognize the potential for cross-cultural connections facilitated by social media and the integration of emerging technologies like AI and blockchain. In essence, both Singha (2024) and Singha (2023) highlight the significant impact of social media on their respective fields, emphasizing innovation, overcoming challenges, and uncovering new opportunities. They collectively suggest that embracing social media and emerging technologies is essential for achieving success and preparing well-informed individuals to navigate the complexities of their industries.

Integrating AIoT (Artificial Intelligence of Things) technologies into businesses offers numerous benefits, including increased productivity, cost savings, data-driven insights, and enhanced consumer interactions. Challenges such as data privacy, ethical considerations, regulatory compliance, and technical complexities accompany these advantages. To address these challenges, recommendations include adopting transparent practices, ensuring accountability, mitigating biases, minimizing data collection, obtaining informed consent, and designing AIoT systems with ethics in mind. We urge policymakers to create flexible regulations that prioritize privacy and security, involving stakeholders. Additionally, a user-centric approach and data ethics training are essential components. The significant potential of AIoT for businesses highlights the importance of striking a delicate balance between innovation and responsibility. Prioritizing ethics, privacy, and policy compliance is crucial for ensuring the ethical and responsible integration of AIoT technologies into business operations (Singha & Singha, 2024). All three sources, Singha & Singha (2024), Singha (2024), and Singha (2023), underscore the significance of adopting technological advancements like social media and AIoT. While recognizing their potential benefits, they acknowledge the accompanying challenges and complexities. These sources emphasize maintaining a balanced approach that prioritizes innovation while addressing ethical considerations, privacy concerns, and compliance with relevant policies.

Hudders et al. (2020) conducted an extensive literature review about the strategic utilization of social media influencers in marketing, specifically focusing on their application in commercial settings. The review uncovered many empirical studies employing diverse methodologies, such as experiments, interviews, content analysis, and surveys. The research categorized the studies into three main strands using Stern's Revised Communication Model for Advertising as the conceptual framework: the perspectives of communication professionals and influencers, the execution of content strategies in sponsored posts, and the effectiveness of endorsements sponsored by influencers. While a few research studies investigated the potential of influencers to modify public sentiment or stimulate changes in behavior, the overwhelming majority of studies concentrated on the business aspects of influencer marketing. Notable is the growing concern regarding the transparency of influencer marketing strategies, specifically sponsored endorsements. It underscores the increasing acknowledgment of the importance of ethical and transparent conduct in influencer-brand partnerships. The review provides a comprehensive analysis of the scholarly literature about influencer marketing, clarifying its complex characteristics and implications for public policy and marketing tactics. Building upon Hudders et al. (2020) extensive literature review, which highlighted the ethical implications and commercial importance of influencer marketing, Booth & Matic (2011) developed a pragmatic approach to identify and engage with influential individuals within the influencer community. To identify "new somebodies" or influential members of the burgeoning influencer community, Booth & Matic (2011) developed a customizable valuation algorithm. The algorithm assesses various factors to quantify how much these users contribute to expanding brand awareness on social media platforms. Employing this influencer index, professionals in the field of communications can acquire significant insights into how these influencers mould traditional perceptions of their intended audience, thereby enabling them to devise effective outreach strategies. Integrating influencer index data into a comprehensive social media strategy facilitates a systematic approach to augmenting brand equity. The primary emphasis of the paper is on the significance of identifying and engaging with influential individuals within the realm of social media. It offers a highly beneficial instrument for streamlining brand communication tactics and augmenting brand exposure in the era of digitalization. Hudders et al. (2020) conducted research that illuminates the complex characteristics of influencer marketing, focusing on its commercial implications and the criticality of adhering to ethical standards. Expanding upon this groundwork, Booth & Matic (2011) algorithm presents a pragmatic resolution for discerning and interacting with influential constituents of the influencer community. Capitalizing on this influencer index, professionals in the field of communication can formulate influential outreach strategies and augment the prominence of their brands in the digital domain. The results of this study emphasize the significant impact that influencers have on influencing consumer opinions and the importance of establishing strategic partnerships with influential individuals to enhance brand communication tactics in the era of digitalization.

The metaverse offers significant opportunities for retail, especially amidst evolving consumer expectations and digital transformation. To thrive in metaverse-driven retail, businesses must develop a comprehensive strategy involving understanding metaverse dynamics, acquiring essential capabilities, assessing staff competencies, and implementing training initiatives. Crucial elements of metaverse-driven retail entail utilizing metaverse technology, creating immersive shopping experiences, implementing data-driven personalization, and ensuring robust cybersecurity measures. The chapter emphasizes the importance of workforce competencies such as digital literacy, collaboration, design proficiency, and cybersecurity awareness. Ultimately, it underscores the transformative potential of the metaverse in retail and the necessity of preparing for this emerging digital landscape (Singha & Singha, 2024a). Singha & Mukthar (2024) explore the intersection of the metaverse and the retail industry, emphasizing a fundamental shift towards digital goods and immersive purchasing experiences. They explore the foundational concepts, historical evolution, and current impact of the metaverse on retail. The chapter highlights digital products like non-fungible tokens (NFTs), virtual goods, and augmented reality items as critical elements with the potential to revolutionize shopping experiences. Despite facing technological complexities, security concerns, and customer adoption challenges during this transition, the chapter discusses future trends. It offers practical strategies for seamless integration, enhanced customer engagement, and effective marketing within the metaverse. Ultimately, Singha and Mukthar underscore that the metaverse presents a revolutionary era for retail, offering limitless opportunities for businesses that embrace it. They urge retailers to embark on this journey to meet evolving consumer expectations and maintain competitiveness in the future retail landscape.

Although influencers possess considerable sway and capability in moulding consumer conduct and brand image, it is critical to recognize the potential hazards and difficulties they encounter concerning their mental health. Mental health issues may result from the demands of sustaining a curated online presence, constant scrutiny, and the competitive nature of the industry. By acknowledging these obstacles and executing approaches to bolster the psychological welfare of influencers, interested parties can cultivate a more robust and enduring influencer ecosystem. Advocating for mental health awareness and offering self-care resources can enhance the equilibrium and positivity of influencers as they navigate the digital landscape.

ETHICAL RESPONSIBILITIES IN INFLUENCER COLLABORATIONS

In influencer collaborations, ethical considerations require adherence to the principles of equitable remuneration and precise contractual arrangements. It is imperative for brands that collaborate with influencers to acknowledge the significance of their innovative contributions and the magnitude of their following, guaranteeing that compensation corresponds to benchmarks set by the industry. Explicit agreements regarding deliverables, expectations, and compensation structures foster a just and courteous collaboration. The transparency above fosters trust between brands and influencers by maintaining ethical standards (Joshi et al., 2023; Hugh et al., 2022). Brands should treat influencers' autonomy and creative control with the utmost regard in ethical collaborations. Brands ought to exercise restraint in exerting excessive influence on influencers, who possess distinctive writing styles and voices, not to compromise authenticity. Moral responsibility entails the preservation of influencers' genuine self-expression and guaranteeing that brand communications are consistent with their convictions and legitimately connect with their followers (Botes, 2022; Hugh et al., 2022). In their study, Bi & Zhang (2022) elucidated the intricate dynamics at play within influencer marketing, emphasizing the moderating effect of self-esteem and the mediating function of influencer credibility (IC) in determining how individuals react to YouTube influencers. Bi and Zhang (2022) revealed a sequential mediation model where individuals' parasocial relationships (PSR) with YouTube influencers and their purchase intentions (PIs) are mediated by product attitudes and influencer credibility. The study findings indicate that individuals with diminished self-esteem are likelier to purchase an endorsed product when they perceive the influencer's credibility as low.

On the contrary, individuals exhibit a reduced propensity to purchase endorsed products when their self-esteem is elevated, notwithstanding robust parasocial connections with the influencers. It highlights the moderating effect of self-esteem on purchase intentions, affecting influencer credibility and parasocial relationships. The study's originality and value come from exploring new dimensions of influencer credibility and discovering the complex effects of personal differences, especially self-esteem, on the persuasive power of relationships between influencers and users. The significant ramifications for brands highlight the criticality of considering customers' personalities, motivations, and preferences when developing influencer marketing strategies on social media platforms such as YouTube.

A fundamental ethical obligation in influencer collaborations is to give precedence to the influencers' mental health and overall well-being. It is imperative for brands to be conscious of the pressures and difficulties that influencers face and to endeavor to establish a sustainable and nurturing professional atmosphere. It may entail setting reasonable expectations for workload and deadlines, being flexible concerning deadlines, and having compassion for the psychological toll of maintaining a constant online presence. Ethical brands proactively cultivate an atmosphere that advances mental health and holistic well-being, positively contributing to the influencer ecosystem (Lajnef, 2023; Triplett et al., 2022). Establishing transparent protocols for ethical brand-influencer collaborations is an aspect of moral responsibility. Brands must develop and communicate ethical principles consistent with prevailing industry standards and legal obligations. These encompass policies regarding the authenticity of content, disclosure of sponsored content, and compliance with advertising regulations (Jhawar et al., 2023). By establishing these ethical standards, brands guarantee adherence to the law and bolster the trustworthiness and legitimacy of influencer marketing as a strategic means of communication. Moral obligations within influencer collaborations comprise equitable remuneration, openness, regard for independence of thought, protection of psychological well-being, and establishing protocols for conscientious alliances. Adhering to these principles is critical to establishing confidence, nurturing enduring connections, and making a constructive contribution to the advancement of influencer marketing.

CASE STUDIES

Case Study 1 examines an analysis of a highly successful collaboration that exemplifies socially and ethically responsible influencer marketing. In 2023, a partnership emerged between Influencer X, a reputable advocate for mental health awareness and personal hygiene, and a skincare brand with a similar commitment to holistic wellness. Using a symbiotic partnership, Influencer X and the skincare brand generated content promoting mental health consciousness while underscoring the importance of incorporating self-care practices. The content skillfully integrated the positive impacts of the cosmetics brand's products on overall well-being, thus constructing a storyline beyond product promotion. The ethical value of the collaboration is derived from its adherence to the influencer's genuine principles and its support for a socially responsible discourse surrounding mental health. Audience members who were conscious of and grateful for the influencer's commitment to mental health initiatives responded positively to the collaboration. The audience reacted positively to the conversation that Influencer X sparked concerning mental health, which led to the forming of a more informed and engaged community.

Besides providing product endorsements, the content facilitated a constructive dialogue about mental health, establishing a favorable precedent for the influencer marketing sector. This case study illustrates how partnerships between brands and influencers can have a constructive effect on society, uphold ethical standards, and make substantial contributions to discourse. Carefully choosing partnerships based on influential individuals' principles and convictions, brands can enhance their reputation and engage in meaningful discussions regarding important issues. Case Study 1 aptly illustrates the positive outcomes that can result from the ethical and transparent implementation of influencer marketing, coupled with a steadfast commitment to social responsibility. The collaboration between the skincare brand and Influencer X was founded upon their mutual appreciation for personal hygiene and mental health awareness. This alignment exemplifies a commitment to integrity and moral accountability, guaranteeing that the partnership is established upon sincere principles instead of solely profit-driven objectives. The partnership extended its reach beyond conventional product endorsements by promoting awareness regarding mental health. The collaboration's inclusion of mental health discussions in the promotional materials enhanced public consciousness. It diminished the social stigma associated with mental health concerns, thus effecting a beneficial change in society. The favorable response from Influencer X's audience serves as additional evidence of the beneficial outcomes that resulted from the collaboration. The positive feedback from the audience suggests that the material struck a chord with them and stimulated substantial discourse regarding mental health subjects, ultimately resulting in a more informed and involved community.

Regarding the collaboration, Influencer X has published content on various platforms, including but not limited to Instagram, YouTube, Twitter, and TikTok. Electronic word-of-mouth (e-WOM) can be defined as audience members expressing their gratitude and approval of the collaboration with others through online platforms. This activity contributes to a broader discourse concerning self-care practices and promoting mental health awareness. As X previously stated, "Concerning the recent partnership with a cosmetics brand, I would like to express my initial enthusiasm for collaborating with an organization that espouses my principles. However, I have been significantly burdened by the expectations and pressures associated with this collaboration. The complexities involved have induced feelings of tension and anxiety within me, which the public's scrutiny has further exacerbated. X pursued professional counseling to manage the difficulties that arose due to the collaboration. The collaboration depicted in Case Study 1 illustrates how ethical and responsible practices can be upheld while influencer-brand collaborations accomplish marketing objectives. The partnership establishes a favorable precedent for influencer marketing by emphasizing social responsibility and facilitating significant dialogues. In its entirety, Case Study 1 presents persuasive proof that partnerships between brands and influencers can effectuate positive societal change, promote ethical conduct, and stimulate substantive discourse regarding significant matters. Demonstrating authentic solidarity with the values of influencers and a dedication to social responsibility, these partnerships can foster constructive transformation and enhance the realm of responsible and influential influencer marketing.

Case Study 2 highlights the negative ramifications of partnerships with influencers who compromise ethical standards. A prominent influencer and follower, Y, partnered with a well-known fast-fashion brand notorious for its exploitative labor practices. Throughout 2023, the collaboration endorsed products duly acknowledged for their adverse environmental effects. A critical factor was the influencer's failure to reveal any financial investment or affiliation with the fast-fashion brand. The immediate and adverse repercussions of this collaboration were evident. The audience of Y, who had previously admired and followed her, reacted unfavorably to her endorsing of products associated with unethical practices and the obscure nature of her financial connections with the brand. This case study aptly demonstrates the profound consequences that influencers may face when they engage in partnerships that contradict their principles and compromise ethical standards. The implications of the partnership had a profound effect on Y. The collaboration had a substantial negative impact on the influencer's mental health and public image. Following increased public scrutiny and ethical criticism, adherents decreased significantly. The erosion of credibility and trust resulted from the influencer's opaqueness concerning a financial interest and the audience's disillusionment with their ethical conduct. "The backlash from the collaboration with the fast-fashion brand has been overwhelming," Y once stated. I am overcome with remorse and sorrow for endorsing products that contradict my beliefs.

The public scrutiny has negatively impacted my mental health, and I am finding it difficult to cope with the criticism. Before the collaboration, Y was recognized for producing engaging and positive content. However, since the partnership, their posts' frequency and calibre have declined significantly. The videos depicted Y in a withdrawn state, and their captions conveyed sentiments indicative of anxiety and tension. According to Y, she has been grappling with elevated levels of anxiety and depression ever since the collaboration controversy surfaced. The adverse remarks and decline in followers have significantly impacted my self-esteem, making it progressively more challenging to sustain a constructive perspective on social media. The family and acquaintances of Y have observed a substantial transformation in their personality and general state of health.

Additionally, Y conveyed a desire to seek assistance from a mental health professional. A decline in mental health is indicated by the fact that Y appears more withdrawn, irritable, and preoccupied with negative feedback from the collaboration, as reported. The insights these statements and observations offer concern the collaboration's potential ramifications on Y's mental health and overall well-being. Although speculative, they mirror the circumstances's potential impact on the influencer's cognitive processes and conduct. Case Study 2 underscores the importance of influencers establishing brand partnerships and participating in alliances that align with their ethical tenets. This observation highlights the adverse consequences that ethical concessions in collaborations can impose on the mental well-being, standing, and involvement of influencers' audiences. This case is an instructive example of influencer marketing partnerships, emphasizing the importance of transparency, ethical consideration, and value congruence for brands and influencers. This collaborative effort occurred in influencer marketing on widely utilized social media platforms such as Instagram, YouTube, and TikTok. The audience members' online dissemination of their disapproval of the collaboration was e-WOM; this was how Y's audience expressed discontent. In Case Study 2, the partnership significantly impacted Y's mental health.

The case studies mentioned illustrate the ethical dimensions inherent in influencer marketing. The case studies above emphasize value alignment, transparency maintenance, and societal impact assessment when evaluating influencer-brand collaborations. Both brands and influencers can derive advantages from the insights gained in these situations as they navigate the complex landscape of influencer marketing responsibly and ethically.

MENTAL HEALTH OF SOCIAL MEDIA INFLUENCERS

In recent years, the rise of social media platforms has led to the emergence of new celebrities known as social media influencers. These individuals leverage their online presence to cultivate large followings, often partnering with brands for sponsored content and collaborations. However, behind the glamorous facade of curated posts and sponsored partnerships lies a complex landscape of psychological well-being challenges that many influencers face. Mental health among social media influencers has become a pressing concern as they navigate the pressures of maintaining a polished online image while dealing with the demands of their digital careers. The constant scrutiny of their appearance, lifestyle, and personal choices can take a toll on their mental well-being, leading to issues such as anxiety, depression, and low self-esteem (Lajnef, 2023; Sadagheyani & Tatari, 2020).

One notable example is that of Essena O'Neill, an Australian social media influencer who gained fame on platforms like Instagram and YouTube. In 2015, O'Neill made headlines when she publicly announced her decision to quit social media, citing the negative impact it had on her mental health. Despite having hundreds of thousands of followers and lucrative brand partnerships, O'Neill revealed that she struggled with feelings of inadequacy and loneliness behind the scenes. Similarly, many other influencers have spoken out about the challenges they face in maintaining authenticity while meeting the expectations of their audience and brand partners. The pressure to constantly curate aspirational content can create a disconnect between their online persona and authentic selves, leading to emptiness and disillusionment.

The competitive nature of the influencer industry exacerbates mental health issues among content creators. Pursuing likes, comments, and followers can become all-consuming, fueling a never-ending cycle of comparison and self-doubt. Influencers may feel pressured to constantly outdo themselves and their peers, leading to burnout and emotional exhaustion (O'Connor et al., 2018). Despite these challenges, there is growing awareness within the influencer community and among brands about the importance of prioritizing mental health. Some influencers have taken proactive steps to promote self-care and authenticity, sharing their struggles openly with their followers and advocating for greater transparency in the industry. The mental health of social media influencers necessitates thoughtful deliberation from both the influencers and the brands with which they partner. Cultivating an environment that promotes empathy, authenticity, and self-care, brands and influencers can collaborate harmoniously to establish a digital ecosystem that is both more sustainable and beneficial for all participants. Singha (2024a) explores the pivotal juncture within digital capitalism, where promise and complexity converge. The necessity of understanding the challenges and opportunities presented by emerging media technologies during the transition into the digital era is emphasized. The insights derived from this study serve as a foundation for envisioning policies, strategies, and collaborative efforts to foster significant social transformation within digital capitalism.

The research sheds light on the transformative potential of the digital landscape in addressing deeply ingrained gender biases and promoting inclusivity, thus propelling progress towards gender equality. It foresees a future where technology is a powerful tool for dismantling existing gender biases and fostering a digital environment where equality flourishes. Ultimately, the core finding underscores the profound impact of technology in advocating for gender equality and unlocking limitless opportunities for individuals from diverse backgrounds. Singha (2024a) explores the pivotal moments within digital capitalism, highlighting the convergence of promise and complexity and the necessity of understanding the challenges and opportunities presented by emerging media technologies. This exploration serves as a foundation for envisioning policies, strategies, and collaborative efforts aimed at fostering significant social transformation in the digital realm. This connection can be drawn from the observation of O'Connor et al. (2018) regarding the mental health challenges social media influencers face. The competitive nature of the influencer industry, driven by metrics such as likes, comments, and followers, can lead to mental health issues such as comparison, self-doubt, burnout, and emotional exhaustion. Despite these challenges, there is a growing awareness within the influencer community and among brands about the importance of prioritizing mental health. Some influencers have taken proactive steps to promote self-care and authenticity, advocating for greater transparency in the industry. Acknowledging and addressing these mental health challenges, influencers and brands can work together to cultivate an environment that promotes empathy, authenticity, and self-care, as advocated in Singha's exploration of digital capitalism. This collaborative effort contributes to establishing a more sustainable and beneficial digital ecosystem for all participants. The connection between Singha (2024a) and O'Connor et al. (2018) lies in their shared emphasis on understanding and addressing the challenges faced within the digital landscape, whether regarding social transformation or mental health awareness among influencers.

An influencer's mental health can substantially affect their capacity to consistently produce content and interact with their audience. For example, an influencer who is grappling with anxiety or depression might discover it challenging to maintain a regular publishing schedule or provide timely responses to audience engagements. Prioritize brands searching for dependable partnerships with influencers who exhibit sound mental health practices and maintain a consistent online persona. Mental health challenges can impact the authenticity and transparency of an influencer's content. For instance, an influencer grappling with exhaustion or emotional distress might need help upholding the authenticity standard their audience anticipates. In pursuit of authentic collaborations, brands might be drawn to influencers who candidly address mental health difficulties and demonstrate a steadfast dedication to candidness in their material. Collaborating with influencers who highly value mental health can benefit a brand's reputation and value congruence. For example, when an influencer endorses self-care practices and advocates for mental health awareness, a collaboration with them may convey to viewers that the brand places a high value on the welfare of its audience. By achieving this alignment, the brand can enhance its reputation and cultivate a more profound bond with its intended demographic.

Allocating resources towards influencers who adhere to sound mental health practices may enhance the long-term viability of collaborations. Prioritizing mental health, influencers can effectively manage their professional and personal lives, prevent exhaustion, and thus guarantee the longevity and prosperity of brand collaborations. Brands prioritize influencers who exhibit a proactive stance towards mental health management in search of long-lasting partnerships. It is imperative for brands seeking to forge enduring, dependable, and genuine collaborations to address the mental well-being of influencers. Emphasizing influencers prioritizing their mental well-being, brands can bolster their reputation, foster significant connections with their target audience, and align with their core values.

DISCUSSION

Influencer marketing is replete with ethical difficulties and complexities that necessitate meticulous contemplation. Maintaining an intricate equilibrium between commercial interests and authenticity poses a significant obstacle. Influencers encounter the moral quandary of reconciling the need to enhance brand collaborations with the authenticity of their persona. Engaging in a curated and marketable persona may undermine the confidence of one's audience, thereby giving rise to ethical considerations about authenticity and transparency. An additional noteworthy ethical dilemma pertains to corporations' possible exploitation of influencers. In the early phases of their professional journeys, influencers may encounter power imbalances during negotiations that raise concerns regarding equitable remuneration and contractual transparency. The allure of compromising ethical principles in pursuit of financial benefit could jeopardize the influencer's reputation and undermine the credibility of influencer marketing as a strategic communication instrument.

The perpetually changing and dynamic characteristics of digital marketing present difficulties in the observance of legal and ethical standards. Influencers face moral dilemmas when disclosing brand partnerships due to the need for standardized guidelines and the ambiguity surrounding disclosure requirements. Bi and Zhang (2022a) emphasize the substantial impact that electronic word-of-mouth (eWOM) and user-generated content (UGC) have on social media platforms such as YouTube, Facebook, and Instagram. This impact goes beyond simply influencing consumers' information acquisition strategies; it also directs their actions when obtaining product evaluations and, ultimately, their purchasing choices. Electronic word-of-mouth (eWOM) comprises evaluations and firsthand experiences of products or services disseminated via online platforms and significantly influences the complex mechanisms by which consumers make decisions. The extent to which social media impacts information access and decision-making underscores the critical significance of eWOM in this dynamic. The definition of eWOM that has been provided serves as the basis for understanding its importance in consumer behavior.

Additionally, the text recognizes the vast array of subjects addressed by electronic word-of-mouth (eWOM) on social media platforms. These topics span from assessments of healthcare providers and vacation experiences to conversations regarding restaurants and technological products. The text emphasizes the pervasive impact of electronic word-of-mouth (eWOM) on individuals' daily lives, highlighting the proactive involvement of social media users who disseminate a wide range of evaluations and experiences. This proactive involvement contributes to the diffusion of eWOM's pervasive influence.

Various approaches can be adopted to mitigate the intrinsic ethical complexities of influencer marketing and promote ethical and responsible conduct. To navigate ethical concerns, brands and influencers must adhere to standardized, unambiguous industry guidelines. The guidelines must encompass suggestions about equitable compensation practices, transparent disclosure, and responsible content creation. Understanding ethical considerations in influencer marketing is advantageous for both brands and influencers. By providing resources and training programs, brands can assist influencers in comprehending their obligation to cultivate a favorable influencer ecosystem and enable them to make well-informed, ethical decisions. Promoting the value of authenticity above commercial interests among influencers is a cornerstone of ethical conduct. Brands should identify influencers whose principles are congruent with their own to cultivate partnerships that harmonize with the influencer's authentic expression and the audience's anticipated standards.

The discourse on the psychological well-being of social media influencers underscores the significant ramifications of online celebrity status on individuals' health. It highlights the significance of recognizing influencers' difficulties and demands when balancing a curated online persona with their personal lives. The fierce competition within the industry and the quest for validation via quantifiable indicators such as followers and likes contribute to a detrimental cycle of self-criticism and comparison. Conversely, this situation has a positive aspect, as many brands and influencers acknowledge the importance of placing mental health first and promoting authenticity and self-care. This continuous discourse is essential to cultivating a more salubrious digital environment for influencers and their audiences.

In light of the mental strain that influencers endure, it is imperative that brands proactively integrate mental health support services into their collaborations. It may involve addressing concerns regarding fatigue, fostering a healthy work-life balance, and establishing reasonable expectations. Advocates for more precise industry regulations and standards may include brands and influencers. Engaging in dialogues and undertakings to develop ethical standards can bolster the influencer marketing sector's integrity and credibility. By implementing these strategies, brands and influencers can establish a collaborative, ethical framework that emphasizes the welfare of all participants, authenticity, and transparency. This methodology not only enhances the efficacy of individual partnerships but also positively impacts the progression of influencer marketing.

CONCLUSION

This investigation into influencer marketing highlights the importance of placing influencers' mental health first. Given the growing influence on consumer behavior and brand perceptions, it is crucial to recognize and confront the obstacles they face to cultivate a sustainable and ethical influencer ecosystem. The consistent maintenance of authenticity, perpetual self-presentation, and the progressive erosion of personal boundaries are all factors that can significantly affect the mental well-being of influencers. To guarantee the enduring success of influencer collaborations, it is both a moral obligation and a strategic imperative to acknowledge and prioritize the welfare of influencers. Expanding upon these observations, we suggest direct ethical partnerships between brands and influencers, including advocating for industry standards, promoting transparent communication, aligning values, providing mental health support programs, and offering education on ethical practices. Adhering to these suggestions, brands and influencers can cultivate honest partnerships that make a constructive contribution to the ever-changing realm of digital communication and brand endorsement. Ultimately, this will establish a more sustainable, genuine, and accountable influencer marketing ecosystem.

REFERENCES

Ao, L., Bansal, R., Pruthi, N., & Khaskheli, M. B. (2023). Impact of social media influencers on customer engagement and purchase Intention: A meta-analysis. *Sustainability (Basel), 15*(3), 2744. doi:10.3390/su15032744

Baker-Eveleth, L., Stone, R. W., & Eveleth, D. M. (2021). Understanding social media users' privacy-protection behaviours. *Information and Computer Security, 30*(3), 324–345. doi:10.1108/ICS-07-2021-0099

Bi, N. C., & Zhang, R. (2022). I will buy what my 'friend' recommends: The effects of parasocial relationships, influencer credibility and self-esteem on purchase intentions. *Journal of Research in Interactive Marketing, 17*(2), 157–175. doi:10.1108/JRIM-08-2021-0214

Bi, N. C., & Zhang, R. (2022a). Electronic word-of-mouth and social media. In Emerald Publishing Limited eBooks (pp. 37–50). doi:10.1108/978-1-80071-597-420221003

Bi, N. C., Zhang, R., & Ha, L. (2019). Does the valence of product review matter? *Journal of Research in Interactive Marketing, 13*(1), 79–95. doi:10.1108/JRIM-04-2018-0049

Booth, N., & Matic, J. A. (2011). Mapping and leveraging influencers in social media to shape corporate brand perceptions. *Corporate Communications, 16*(3), 184–191. doi:10.1108/13563281111156853

Botes, M. (2022). Autonomy and the social dilemma of online manipulative behaviour. *AI and Ethics, 3*(1), 315–323. doi:10.1007/s43681-022-00157-5

Hosszu, A., Rughiniş, C., Rughiniş, R., & Rosner, D. E. (2022). Webcams and social interaction during online classes: Identity work, presentation of self, and well-being. *Frontiers in Psychology, 12*, 761427. Advance online publication. doi:10.3389/fpsyg.2021.761427 PMID:35082716

Hudders, L., De Jans, S., & De Veirman, M. (2021). The commercialization of social media stars: A literature review and conceptual framework on the strategic use of social media influencers. *International Journal of Advertising, 40*(3), 327–375. doi:10.1080/02650487.2020.1836925

Hugh, D. C., Dolan, R., Harrigan, P., & Gray, H. (2022). Influencer marketing effectiveness: The mechanisms that matter. *European Journal of Marketing, 56*(12), 3485–3515. doi:10.1108/EJM-09-2020-0703

Joshi, Y., Lim, W. M., Jagani, K., & Kumar, S. (2023). Social media influencer marketing: Foundations, trends, and ways forward. *Electronic Commerce Research*. Advance online publication. doi:10.1007/s10660-023-09719-z

Kim, D., & Wang, Z. (2023). The ethics of virtuality: Navigating the complexities of human-like virtual influencers in the social media marketing. *Frontiers in Communication, 8*, 1205610. Advance online publication. doi:10.3389/fcomm.2023.1205610

Kim, J., & Kim, M. (2022). Rise of social media influencers as a new marketing channel: Focusing on the roles of psychological well-being and perceived social responsibility among consumers. *International Journal of Environmental Research and Public Health, 19*(4), 2362. doi:10.3390/ijerph19042362 PMID:35206553

Lajnef, K. (2023). The effect of social media influencers on teenagers behavior: An empirical study using cognitive map technique. *Current Psychology (New Brunswick, N.J.), 42*(22), 19364–19377. doi:10.1007/s12144-023-04273-1 PMID:36742063

O'Connor, K., Muller Neff, D., & Pitman, S. (2018). Burnout in mental health professionals: A systematic review and meta-analysis of prevalence and determinants. *European Psychiatry, 53*, 74–99. doi:10.1016/j.eurpsy.2018.06.003 PMID:29957371

Roth, L. M. (1999). The right to privacy is political: Power, the boundary between public and private, and sexual harassment. *Law & Social Inquiry, 24*(01), 45–71. doi:10.1111/j.1747-4469.1999.tb00792.x

Sadagheyani, H. E., & Tatari, F. (2020). Investigating the role of social media on mental health. *Mental Health and Social Inclusion, 25*(1), 41–51. doi:10.1108/MHSI-06-2020-0039

Singha, R., & Singha, S. (2024). Transitioning to digital merchandise: Integrating metaverse into retail offerings. In S. Rezaei & A. Ansary (Eds.), *Artificial Intelligence of Things (AIoT) for Productivity and Organizational Transition* (Vol. 1, pp. 26–51). IGI Global. doi:10.4018/979-8-3693-0993-3.ch002

Singha, R., & Singha, S. (2024a). Building capabilities and workforce for metaverse-driven retail formats. In B. E. Singla, K. Shalender, & N. Singh (Eds.), *Creator's Economy in Metaverse Platforms: Empowering Stakeholders Through Omnichannel Approach* (Vol. 1, pp. 111–131). IGI Global. doi:10.4018/979-8-3693-3358-7.ch007

Singha, S. (2023). Exploring the role of social media in enhancing K-12 Economics education. In B. Scott & M. E. Fox (Eds.), *Cases on Economics Education and Tools for Educators* (Vol. 1, pp. 160–182). IGI Global. doi:10.4018/978-1-6684-7583-6.ch007

Singha, S. (2024). Social media's influence on consumer decision-making: A roadmap for success. In F. Sahin & C. E. Soylemez (Eds.), *Globalized Consumer Insights in the Digital Era* (Vol. 1, pp. 85–109). IGI Global. doi:10.4018/979-8-3693-3811-7.ch004

Singha, S. (2024a). Unveiling gender dynamics in digital capitalism: Navigating the path to social gender equality. In C. Topçu (Ed.), *Digital Capitalism in the New Media Era* (Vol. 1, pp. 161–186). IGI Global. doi:10.4018/979-8-3693-1182-0.ch009

Singha, S., & Mukthar, J. (2024). Transitioning to digital merchandise: Integrating metaverse into retail offerings. In B. E. Singla, K. Shalender, & N. Singh (Eds.), *Creator's Economy in Metaverse Platforms: Empowering Stakeholders Through Omnichannel Approach* (Vol. 1, pp. 71–96). IGI Global. doi:10.4018/979-8-3693-3358-7.ch005

Triplett, N. T., Kingzette, A., Slivinski, L., & Niu, T. (2022). Ethics for mental health influencers: MFTs as public social media personalities. *Contemporary Family Therapy*, *44*(2), 125–135. doi:10.1007/s10591-021-09632-3

Zniva, R., Weitzl, W., & Lindmoser, C. (2023). Be constantly different! How to manage influencer authenticity. *Electronic Commerce Research*, *23*(3), 1485–1514. doi:10.1007/s10660-022-09653-6

ADDITIONAL READING

Booth, N., & Matic, J. A. (2011). Mapping and leveraging influencers in social media to shape corporate brand perceptions. *Corporate Communications*, *16*(3), 184–191. doi:10.1108/13563281111156853

Brown, D., & Fiorella, S. (2013). *Influence marketing: How to create, manage, and measure brand influencers in social media marketing*. Que Publishing.

Hudders, L., De Jans, S., & De Veirman, M. (2021). The commercialization of social media stars: A literature review and conceptual framework on the strategic use of social media influencers. *International Journal of Advertising*, *40*(3), 327–375. doi:10.1080/02650487.2020.1836925

KEY TERMS AND DEFINITIONS

Burnout: A state of emotional, physical, and mental exhaustion resulting from prolonged stress or overwork, often experienced by influencers due to high content demands.

Ethics: Influencer behaviour's moral principles encompass transparency, honesty, and responsibility in content creation and brand collaborations.

Influencer Marketing: Strategic collaboration between brands and influencers to promote products or services, utilizing the influencer's credibility and reach.

Mental Health: The state of one's mental and emotional well-being, encompassing emotional resilience, coping mechanisms, and psychological balance.

Privacy: The right of individuals to control their personal information is a crucial consideration in influencer marketing, where the boundary between public and private life can blur.

Psychological Well-Being: Relationships, stress management, and overall life satisfaction influence an individual's mental and emotional health.

Social Media Influencers: Individuals who leverage their online presence to impact and persuade their followers, often through content creation and endorsements.

Chapter 17
Leveraging Artificial Intelligence for Ethical Social Media Influencer Communication

Isuru Udayangani Hewapathirana
https://orcid.org/0000-0003-4843-0993
Faculty of Science, University of Kelaniya, Sri Lanka

ABSTRACT

This chapter explores the connections between artificial intelligence (AI) and the ethical dimensions of influencer communication on social media. The ethical aspects are evaluated according to the criteria outlined in the Professional Code of Ethics of the Public Relations Society of America (PRSA). The study reviews the multiple aspects of influencer communication, including emerging challenges and legal implications resulting from the continued development of AI in social media. Furthermore, a dataset was collected from the social media platform Reddit, and a case study analysis was performed using the NodeXL software. This empirical investigation aims to investigate social media users' perspectives on specific ethical concerns associated with integrating artificial intelligence (AI). The findings presented in this chapter provide scholars with an advanced understanding of AI capabilities, offer industry professionals valuable guidance for ethical decision-making, and offer lawmakers guidance for developing regulatory frameworks.

INTRODUCTION

In the era of digital interconnectivity, social media has seamlessly integrated into the essence of our everyday existence, fundamentally altering how we communicate, establish connections, and navigate through extensive volumes of information. Artificial intelligence (AI) is the main driving force behind the development of social media platforms in this revolutionary environment. The growing need for efficient content management and improved user experiences has driven the development of artificial intelligence (AI) solutions. Content recommendation systems and other AI algorithms integrated into social media platforms are crucial for this change. These systems thoroughly examine user preferences,

DOI: 10.4018/979-8-3693-0912-4.ch017

patterns of engagement, and contextual information in order to provide customized feeds and suggest pertinent material. Their flexibility improves user engagement by customizing material to meet individual needs. Moreover, AI explores user sentiments and engagement data, offering vital insights to enhance platforms and tackle problems such as malware or offensive content.

Notwithstanding the significant influence of AI, enduring obstacles and ethical considerations persist. Ongoing challenges arise from issues such as bias in AI tools, the spread of misinformation, and the possibility of unforeseen outcomes. Existing literature on the ethical implications of social media fails to address the ethical integration of AI into social media platforms within a theoretical framework. For example, Davies & Hobbs (2020), Hagelstein et al. (2021), and Hudders et al. (2021) examine the ethical implications of social media influencing within theoretical frameworks, but do not discuss the ethical dimensions of using AI tools in social media influencing. This book chapter seeks to fill this gap by examining the ethical aspects of incorporating artificial intelligence (AI) into social media, with a specific emphasis on the theoretical framework outlined in the Professional Code of Ethics of the Public Relations Society of America (PRSA).

The Public Relations Society of America (PRSA) has a crucial role in establishing ethical standards and advocating for responsible practices in public relations. PRSA, founded in 1947, is a professional association that advocates for the concerns and interests of communication and public relations experts in several sectors. PRSA is dedicated to promoting the profession and maintaining ethical standards. The PRSA Code of Ethics (Hunt & Tirpok, 1993) serves as a reliable instrument for professionals seeking to address ethical dilemmas with diligence and responsibility effectively. The PRSA Code of Ethics outlines key values and principles essential for maintaining ethical standards within public relations. As a comprehensive guide, it emphasizes the importance of accountability, truthfulness, and openness in communication practices. Furthermore, it underscores the professional obligation to conduct oneself with integrity, transparency, and a steadfast dedication to the welfare of the public. This code serves as more than a set of rules; it acts as a framework for practitioners to ensure ethical conduct in their interactions with various stakeholders. In an era where ethical communication is critical to the success of organizations, the PRSA Code functions as a benchmark to ensure that public relations practitioners uphold the ethical standard of society through the promotion of trust, transparency, and responsible communication methodologies.

The ethical implications of incorporating AI into social media influence are conceptualized within this book chapter using the PRSA Code of Ethics framework. By adhering to the ethical principles delineated in The PRSA Code of Ethics, the following research questions (RQs) seek to investigate the specific ethical aspects of AI integration by social media influencers:

RQ1: How do social media influencers maintain honesty and integrity in their communication practices when integrating AI tools into their content creation, and what impact does this have on audience trust and perception?

RQ2: To what extent do social media influencers openly disclose the use of AI technologies in their content, and how does this transparency influence audience perceptions of authenticity and trustworthiness?

RQ3: How do social media influencers ensure fairness in their AI-influenced content creation, particularly in terms of representing diverse perspectives and avoiding biases that may compromise the public interest?

RQ4: In what ways do social media influencers navigate the balance between advocating for brands or organizations and demonstrating loyalty to the public interest when incorporating AI tools into their content strategies?

RQ5: How are social media influencers engaging in continuous professional development to stay informed about AI technologies, and how does this commitment contribute to the ethical integration of AI in their communication practices?

RQ6: How do individuals on social media platforms articulate their perspectives on the integration of AI tools by social media influencers?

In order to answer the research questions RQ1-RQ5, this book chapter first provides a comprehensive discussion pertaining to the integration of artificial intelligence in social media supported by published academic research articles. Next, to address RQ6, a case study is conducted by gathering data from a social network consisting of posts about integrating artificial intelligence in social media. The analysis employs social network analysis and text analysis techniques to get insights into public attitudes regarding this issue, thus enhancing the understanding of AI in the context of social media influencer communication.

The importance of this book chapter is emphasized by its pertinence to scholars, practitioners, and policymakers negotiating the continually evolving environment of digital communication. The complete literature evaluation offers academics a cohesive comprehension of the existing knowledge environment, while the empirical analysis contributes a practical viewpoint. Professionals in the industry can get vital knowledge about the groundbreaking capabilities of artificial intelligence, which can be used to make ethical and strategic decisions in influencer marketing initiatives. Policymakers gain crucial insights to balance innovation and ethical responsibilities appropriately. This chapter facilitates an informed discussion on the ethical use of AI and the evolving dynamics of digital influence, specifically within the context of AI, ethics, and communication by social media influencers.

LEVERAGING AI FOR PRESERVING HONESTY AND INTEGRITY

To uphold the highest standards of integrity in communication, public relations practitioners need to provide the public with accurate and reliable information. The implication is clear: honesty is not simply a praiseworthy characteristic but a fundamental requirement that ensures the credibility of organizational communications and inspires trust among stakeholders. Influencers collect enormous followings on social media platforms such as Instagram, YouTube, and TikTok and have a distinctive capacity to engage and connect with audiences worldwide. In addition to crafting personal narratives, they carefully curate images, videos, and communications that mirror their distinct brand identity and establish a connection with their audience. The review paper by Chintalapati & Pandey (2022) classifies this type of influencing as integrated digital marketing. According to them, social media influencers are increasingly implementing AI tools to optimize content creation procedures to ensure continued audience engagement and relevance. By utilizing technologies such as content recommendation algorithms (Tatiya, 2014), AI-powered photo retouching (Shanmukhaprasanthi et al., 2023), and video enhancements (Bouaafia et al., 2022), influencers optimize their output and captivate their audience. Although these improvements may help create a more refined and visually appealing feed, they also provoke inquiries regarding how influencers manage the delicate balance between enhancement and distortion. To maintain credibility amidst the integration of artificial intelligence, influencers must effectively manage the interplay between harnessing technological advancements and keeping an authentic rapport with their followers. For instance, an influencer might use AI-powered filters to enhance the lighting in a photo while consciously avoiding excessive retouching to preserve natural features. It will ensure that AI contributes to visual appeal without erasing the human touch. Such a procedure will require an influencer to determine when and how to implement AI enhancements judiciously. Hermann (2021) emphasizes the need for AI literacy to empower individuals in such situations. According to them, when influencers have a basic understanding of AI inputs, functioning, agency, and outcomes, they will utilize AI tools to preserve authenticity.

The ethical framework in the domain of social media advertising is significantly impacted by occurrences of influencer fraud. Influencers place a high priority on authenticity in their content; however, the integrity of this authenticity may be compromised using deceitful techniques such as acquiring fake followers and engagement (Wellman et al., 2020). Fake followers are purchased by influencers to present themselves as highly influential. A variety of AI techniques have been employed to detect influencer fraud and ensure authenticity. Anklesaria et al. (2021) conducted research with the main objective of identifying fraudulent accounts on the Instagram platform. Machine learning algorithms such as Random Forest, Artificial Neural Network, and AdaBoost were implemented on a dataset acquired from Instagram, and performance was compared using receiver operating characteristics. The random forest algorithm depicted superior performance in detecting fraudsters compared to the others. The spreading of rumors or misinformation is another harmful phenomenon in social networks. AbdulAmeer et al., (2022) concentrated on identifying influencers who spread negative information on Twitter. Their findings present a scoring technique to identify influencers spreading misinformation.

The production of virtual models and characters entails the construction of realistic personas that appeal to the intended audience. Virtual influencers, which are frequently driven by cutting-edge technologies like computer graphics and artificial intelligence, are made to fit in well with the digital world. They provide a fresh and engrossing method of promoting brands that surpass conventional marketing techniques (Belova, 2021). By utilizing these entities, brands can convey captivating narratives, exhibit their products in digital settings, and craft indelible consumer experiences. Customer engagement is significantly improved by the interactive and immersive qualities of virtual endorsements, which fosters a sense of connection and loyalty (Zhong, 2022). Although there are ongoing apprehensions regarding the authenticity and trustworthiness of virtual influencers, they have proven their effectiveness by cultivating consumer loyalty, influencing purchase intentions, and fostering trust (Sánchez et al., 2022).

ENSURING TRANSPARENCY IN AI INTEGRATION

Integrity in public relations is predicated on transparency. It entails candid communication and the explicit disclosure of facts and motivations to establish and preserve public confidence. In all communication efforts, transparency is a commitment to lucidity, guaranteeing that stakeholders have a complete and unobstructed view of organizational motivations, procedures, and decisions. Ethical communication is built on transparency. Influencers need to make sure that their audience is aware that AI tools are used in content development. Openness and honesty are promoted when the use of AI-driven improvements or filters is made transparent. Influencers can inform their audience about the tools used and how they affect the content by adding disclaimers to captions or video descriptions. Transparency was highlighted as a driving factor in the design of ethical content by Woodroof et al. (2020). According to the study, influencers who were transparent about their creative processes, including the usage of AI, built closer bonds with their followers. The work of Woodroof et al., (2020) examined the landscape of AI disclosure practices and the various tactics adopted by influencers. Influencers who were subtle and those who freely talked about using AI tools were both featured in the study. Researchers were able to obtain important insights into the complex ways influencers handle AI disclosure by comprehending these techniques. Steils et al., (2022) investigated audience perceptions of authenticity in influencer material through a case study. According to the research, the extent to which disclosure messages impact authenticity and participation varies with community size. The study also emphasizes the link between positive audience impressions of authenticity and transparency in AI deployment. The facet of trust-building underscores the significance of transparency in influencer-audience connections. Trust is developed among followers when the usage of AI tools is discussed openly. Influencers who openly share details about their content creation process, including the involvement of AI, show a dedication to honesty. For example, in travel and tourism, followers are better able to discern between genuine situations and augmented graphics thanks to this transparency. To give followers a true picture of the content creation process, a travel influencer may write a narrative or highlight specifically addressing the use of AI editing tools for vacation photos.

THE CHALLENGE OF PRESERVING FAIRNESS AND MITIGATING BIAS

In public relations, fairness entails treating all parties involved equitably and refraining from taking any actions that could undermine the public interest. This principle requires public relations professionals to guarantee that their communication endeavors are impartial, just, and cognizant of a wide range of viewpoints. Fairness promotes constructive and morally upright connections between organizations and their stakeholders; it is not merely an ideal but a pragmatic obligation. AI systems employed for content filtering may unintentionally manifest biases or discriminatory conduct. This can happen if the training data used to construct the AI models includes prejudiced information or if the algorithms themselves are not designed to be impartial and inclusive. It is imperative to confront these biases to guarantee equitable treatment of all users and avoid exacerbating current disparities. Belenguer (2022) examined the problem of algorithmic bias in AI-powered content production. The study showed that AI algorithms may unintentionally reinforce preexisting biases in training data if they are not carefully created. Influencers on social media must handle this difficulty by being aware of how biased algorithms affect how different viewpoints are represented. Influencers need to take measures to counteract algorithmic bias since they understand the importance of objective material. According to Belenguer's research, influencers can actively select a variety of datasets, use moral AI systems, and monitor ongoing biases to detect and correct them. These proactive approaches facilitate the fair and equal depiction of content.

Influencers are crucial in forming the narratives that shape society. Li and Feng (2022) emphasize the significance of influencers as cultural bridges that can dispel prejudices and advance inclusivity. Influencers must actively promote diversity in their material to assure fairness, and they should use AI techniques to facilitate diversity rather than reinforce prejudice. Gerlich (2023) investigated the use of virtual influencers for inclusive storytelling. The findings made clear that virtual influencers may help break down stereotypes, elevate marginalized perspectives, and create a more welcoming online space by utilizing AI ethically. Thus, influencers on social media can rewrite stories and magnify different viewpoints by carefully integrating AI. However, it is important that influencers put fairness first in the creation of AI-influenced content to preserve public confidence, given their position as opinion leaders.

THE ROLE OF AI IN ADVOCACY AND LOYALTY

Maintaining an equilibrium between advocating for clients or organizations and upholding the public interest is an intricate yet vital component of practicing ethical public relations. This equilibrium is acknowledged by the PRSA Code, which defines loyalty and advocacy as a dedication to serving the client and the public interest. Public relations professionals must effectively manage the occasionally divergent expectations of clients and ethical standards, guaranteeing that the objectives of the organization are in line with the collective welfare. The ethical dimension of social media influencers is intricate and diverse. According to Goanta and Ranchordás (2020), the activities of influencers are predominantly unregulated, presenting obstacles to safeguarding consumer interests. Influencers frequently function within a paradigm of genuineness, carefully managing their brand image and connection with their audience while fulfilling the requirement of creating sponsored content (Wellman et al., 2020). However, the capacity of influencers to mislead their followers and the necessity for regulation in this domain are emphasized by Nafi & Ahmed (2019). Public relations professionals who collaborate with influencers might tend to employ covert operations and persuasive tactics (Davies & Hobbs, 2020). These considerations are further complicated by the absence of official standards forcreating and disseminating content on social media (Lama & Shrook, 2020). Notwithstanding these obstacles, the level of professionalism in influencers' communication is on the rise, and under specific circumstances, their followers are inclined to embrace advertising (Kolo & Haumer, 2018). On another note, social workers who interact with clients on social media encounter distinct ethical dilemmas, such as maintaining confidentiality and avoiding boundary violations (Boddy & Dominelli, 2016).

Sophisticated machine learning algorithms can process and analyze large volumes of data and enhance the security of influencer marketing platforms (Raimundo & Rosário, 2021). However, the use of personal data for influencer marketing also raises concerns about data privacy and security. A range of methods have been proposed to protect user information in AI-driven social media influencer campaigns. Beigi et al., (2018) and Xue et al., (2020) highlight the importance of anonymization and de-anonymization algorithms in protecting user privacy. Lewis & Moorkens (2020) emphasize the need for governance and regulation, with a focus on collective rights and shared data ownership. Weth et al., (2020) propose the use of machine learning and computational intelligence for real-time user nudging and security techniques, respectively. AI and blockchain technology can provide innovative data models and improve data authenticity (B et al., 2022).

THE NEED FOR CONTINUOUS PROFESSIONAL DEVELOPMENT

A crucial aspect of ethical conduct in public relations involves a resolute commitment to ongoing professional development and making meaningful contributions that promote the advancement of the profession. Public relations (PR) professionals are motivated to consistently improve their abilities, remain updated on developments in the field, and make contributions that advance the profession. In a domain characterized by swift advancements in methodologies and technologies, continuous education is not merely a discretionary choice but an ethical obligation. Ho (2021) studies the shortcomings in the existing curriculum planning of PR educators in China due to the rapidly changing social environment and technological intelligence. The need to include topics on deep learning AI techniques is emphasized in their discussion.

As highlighted in previous sections, there is widespread anticipation that artificial intelligence (AI) should adhere to ethical principles. However, the public's understanding, assumptions, and expectations regarding the ethical use of AI can be diverse. Although private organizations and research establishments have recognized the current and potential ethical dilemmas linked to artificial intelligence, there remains a lack of research on the public's perception of what constitutes ethical use of AI by social media influencers. The next section presents a case study analysis of a real-world social network to investigate individuals' perspectives on the use of AI tools in social media.

EXPLORING PUBLIC DISCOURSE ON AI INTEGRATION IN SOCIAL MEDIA: A REDDIT NETWORK ANALYSIS

Collecting data from a social media platform can be an acceptable alternative to traditional surveys for understanding public sentiments on specific topics (Fownes et al., 2018). While it may not offer the same structured approach as a survey, harnessing the information readily available on social media platforms has been shown to provide valuable insights into real- time, unfiltered opinions and discussions (Brett et al., 2019; Eskandari et al., 2022; Hudaefi et al., 2023; Ocal, 2023). Reddit is an online platform where registered users share content by submitting links or text posts. Users, referred to as "Redditors", can comment on posts and engage in a threaded conversation through comments and replies to the comments. Content entries, known as posts, are categorized according to specific topics or sub-communities referred to as "subreddits", such as politics, programming, or science. Users on Reddit can cast their votes in favor or against each post, which affects its ranking and determines its position or visibility on the site's pages. Highly favored content ascends to the highest position, while content that receives downvotes (e.g. less favored) becomes less prominent. Each subreddit commences with the URL reddit.com/r, for example, reddit.com/r/marketing. According to the information provided by the official Reddit home page, by October 2023, the number of daily active users on Reddit exceeded 70 million. There were over 100,000 active communities and more than 16 billion posts and comments. Given the unique characteristics of Reddit, this case study aims to investigate the way discussions revolve around the utilization of AI technology in social media.

Data Collection

The NodeXL Pro Reddit Search Network Importer was utilized to gather posts, comments, and related metadata from multiple subreddits. The search queries were 'AI', 'AI Tools', and 'Artificial Intelligence'. Based on the restrictions imposed by Reddit API as of October 2023, the NodeXL importer collected the most recent Reddit posts related to a specific search term within a maximum limit of 250. This also includes all comments and replies associated with the posts. The subreddits systematically examined and analyzed were as follows:

r/socialmedia
r/socialmedia_marketing
r/SocialMediaMarketing
r/SocialMediaManagers
r/socialmediaresearch

r/socialmedianews
r/SocialMediaPromotion
r/DigitalMarketing
r/ContentMarketing

All of these subreddits contain publicly accessible content. To compile a comprehensive list of subreddits, Reddit's built-in subreddit search feature (https://www.reddit.com/reddits) was used to search for subreddits related to "social media". A preliminary filtering process was conducted on the search results to narrow the focus exclusively to relevant subreddits discussing concerns and issues related to social media communication.

Data Preprocessing and Social Network Analysis

The dataset collected consisted of 740 Reddit posts, 2025 comments, and 1220 replies by 1723 Reddit users across the selected subreddits. Using this data, a social network graph was created using NodeXL Pro (Figure 1). Here, a vertex represents a user, and an edge between two vertices represents a post, a comment in a post, or a reply to a comment. The graph is directed. The vertices of the graph are clustered using the Clauset-Newman-Moore algorithm (Clauset et al., 2004). This algorithm efficiently grouped vertices according to their connectivity patterns, assuming the network is generated using a Stochastic Block Model (Zhang & Zhou, 2016). The edge opacities in the graph are based on edge weight values, and the vertex size is proportional to the number of edges directed to each vertex. Text analysis is performed on the content of the posts, comments, and replies. This is done to identify sentiment-related words (positive or negative words), top words, and top word pairs. Accordingly, each cluster in the graph in Figure 1 is labeled based on the top 10 most frequently used words in that cluster.

Table 1 provides a detailed description of the top words and top word pairs identified in the text pertaining to Cluster 1 (G1), Cluster 2 (G2), …, and Cluster 10 (G10).

The discussions in G1 explore various facets of social media marketing. Participants discuss the effectiveness of Google Ads and TikTok Ads, strategies for optimizing content to reach a wider audience, and the impact of recent updates from major platforms like Twitter and Meta. Topics include hashtags, such as #youtube and #meta, to boost visibility and engagement. The discussions in G2 explore social media marketing, content creation, and data analysis. It discusses the benefits and challenges of AI integration in small businesses, its creative potential, and its impact on search engine optimization (SEO). Participants discuss successful AI-powered campaigns, ethical considerations, and AI's role in digital content quality. G3 cluster explores marketing strategies and community engagement on platforms like Discord and social media subreddits. This includes AI bot actions, automation, and interactions between moderators and users. Other topics include AI implementation, communication channels, and content creation. The discussions in G4 explore the effectiveness of the collaborative writing tool Cowriter, its impact on creative processes, and the experiences of its users. The discussions in G5 revolve around the integration of AI in social media marketing, with a specific focus on the recent launch of Feature X. The positive impact of integrating AI into content creation is explored in G6. Experiences and insights on the effective utilization of AI tools, such as ChatGPT, for enhancing content marketing strategies are shared. Benefits, challenges and the preservation of human connection are also discussed. G7 further discuss the proper functioning of AI-powered tools like ChatGPT, their role in media management, and the effectiveness of integrating AI for enhanced content strategies. The use of AI in direct messaging

Figure 1. NodeXL social network graph of Reddit posts

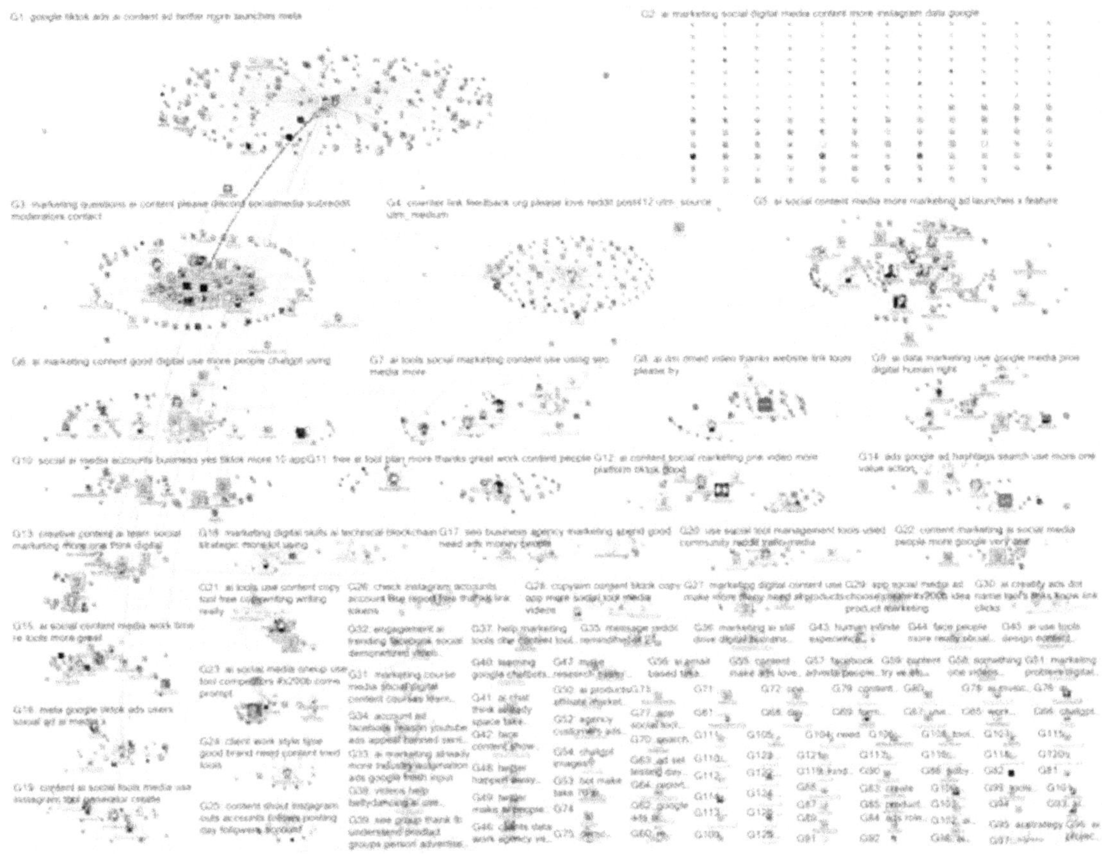

(DM) and video repurposing is discussed in G8. The conversations cover various aspects, such as linking in DMs, expressing gratitude for DMs received, and exploring tools like Opus Clip for video repurposing. Participants share experiences and insights on content formats and website links. G9 discusses the use of AI in digital marketing and its impact on data usage, and its role in social media platforms like TikTok and Twitch. The advantages and drawbacks such as ensuring ethical considerations and respect for human rights are highlighted. The use of AI in managing social media accounts for businesses, specifically on platforms like TikTok, and its automatic lead generation is pointed out in G10. Participants share their experiences of managing multiple accounts and discuss the benefits of AI in handling cold leads and engaging a larger number of users.

Sentiment analysis performed on the entire network identified 8310 positive words and 3289 negative words. Table 2 depicts a selected list of positive and negative single words with their relevant frequencies.

Table 2 reveals a positive outlook towards AI integration in social media, with words like "work," "free," "better," and "great" dominating the discourse. Users appreciate AI's utility, creativity, and overall positive impact, emphasizing its worth, support, and personalized benefits. However, concerns emerge with terms such as "discord," "issues," and "negative," highlighting potential challenges and drawbacks. The negative sentiments suggest that users grapple with problems, limitations, and difficulties associated with AI implementation, reflecting the need for addressing

Table 1. Top words and word pairs pertaining to discussions in 10 major groups

Group	Top Words	Top Word Pairs
G1	google tiktok ads ai content ad twitter more launches meta	social,media link,bio updates,week google,ads #youtube,youtube #meta,meta #top,updates #google,google social,juice #tiktok,tiktok
G2	ai marketing social digital media content more instagram data google	social,media digital,marketing artificial,intelligence digital,leaders ai,generated small,businesses high,quality ai,powered search,engine using,ai
G3	marketing questions ai content please discord socialmedia subreddit moderators contact	bot,action action,performed subreddit,message moderators,subreddit automatically,please performed,automatically questions,concerns contact,moderators please,contact message,compose
G4	cowriter link feedback org please love reddit post412 utm_source utm_medium	cowriter,org utm_source,reddit utm_medium,post412 reddit,utm_medium org,utm_source link,cowriter here's,link canny,io cowriter,canny io,feedback
G5	ai social content media more marketing ad launches x feature	social,media social,juice artificial,intelligence juice,newsletter media,manager media,management credits,social ai,generated ad,revenue content,creation
G6	ai marketing content good digital use more people chatgpt using	digital,marketing chat,gpt much,time use,ai using,ai generation,tools started,using human,connection tell,ai content,marketing
G7	ai tools social marketing content use using seo media more	social,media ai,tools app,social boost,app digital,marketing content,creation media,management chat,gpt ai,powered properly,work
G8	ai dm dmed video thanks website link tools please try	dm,link dmed,thanks opus,clip social,media link,please love,try hey,everyone video,repurposing formats,content media,marketing
G9	ai data marketing use google media pros digital human right	very,simple pros,free simple,use social,media digital,marketing website,traffic tiktok,twitch ig,tiktok smart,data cons,basic
G10	social ai media accounts business yes tiktok more 10 app	social,media amazely,co media,accounts ig,tiktok leads,automatically accounts,10 10,social cold,leads users,200 end,result

negative aspects. Striking a balance between positive attributes and addressing concerns is crucial for successful AI integration in social media. Emphasizing solutions to potential problems and highlighting positive aspects such as personalization and support can enhance user confidence in embracing AI technologies in the social media landscape. Table 3 provides a summary of the top word-pairs that appeared in the graph.

The analysis of word-pairs regarding AI integration in social media in Table 2 reveals overwhelmingly positive sentiments. Phrases like "good luck," "pretty good," and "super helpful" dominate, indicating users' positive experiences and perceived advantages. The word-pair "best free" suggests users appreciate AI offerings that are both high-quality and cost-free. On the negative side, concerns are primarily centered around the platform Discord, with pairs like "discord discord" and "adversarial threat" pointing to potential issues. Users express concern about crises, warned against fake content, and highlight cons, including expense and restrictions. The pairs "catastrophic risk" and "fundamentalism worse" underline apprehensions about severe consequences and the potential deterioration of circumstances. Addressing concerns surrounding specific platforms and emphasizing transparency and security is crucial for fostering a positive reception of AI integration in social media.

Overall, the social network of 740 Reddit posts, 2025 comments, and 1220 replies across 1723 users reveals diverse discussions in ten identified clusters on the use of AI in social media. Positive sentiments dominate, with users expressing appreciation for AI's utility, creativity, and impact on social media marketing and content creation. Moreover, discussions about community engagement, AI bot actions, and strategies for content creation underscore an effort to enhance the

Table 2. Word analysis results on the entire graph Reddit network

Top Positive Word Count	Top Negative Word Count
work 395	discord 236
free 378	concerns 185
better 319	bad 84
good 291	problem 64
great 269	issues 56
best 250	hard 56
well 191	hate 37
thank 169	flair 37
love 162	limit 33
available 162	wrong 32
right 149	limited 28
creative 142	difficult 26
pretty 114	sorry 26
top 106	fake 25
works 105	expensive 24
important 102	mistake 24
useful 100	rival 22
helpful 99	negative 21
easier 81	pain 21
Intelligence 73	complex 21
Support 69	limits 21
Interesting 62	lost 20
Worth 60	cold 20
Boost 51	risk 15
personalized 44	violation 6

profession ethically. Conversations addressing the impact of updates from major platforms, ethical considerations in AI-powered campaigns, and experiences with collaborative writing tools reflect accountability and a commitment to truthfulness and accuracy. However, concerns highlight potential challenges and drawbacks, emphasizing the need to address specific issues and maintain a balance. Leveraging AI for ethical social media communication involves addressing concerns related to privacy, transparency, and potential negative consequences. Emphasizing positive aspects such as personalized benefits and support can enhance user confidence in adopting AI technologies in social media. Striking this balance is essential for a successful and widely accepted integration of AI in social media platforms.

Table 3. Word-pair analysis results on the entire graph Reddit network

Top Positive	Top Negative
Word 1 Word 2 Count	**Word 1 Word 2 Count**
good luck 13	discord discord 88
pretty good 12	adversarial threat 6
best free 8	discord slack 6
super helpful 8	crisis bad 4
good enough 7	warned fake 3
amazing thank 7	cons expensive 3
pretty well 6	restrictive limits 2
pros free 6	slow burn 2
works well 6	expensive clunky 2
helpful better 5	leak discord 2
helpful thank 5	denies allegations 2
great work 5	hype dying 2
great free 4	catastrophic risk 2
good good 4	creepy confusing 2
faster easy 4	harmful misleading 2
best luck 4	fundamentalism worse 2
super useful 3	
nice work 3	
generous free 3	
great thank 3	
love thank 3	
works pretty 3	
work complementary 3	
competitive advantage 3	
pretty helpful 3	
pretty effective 3	

GENERAL DISCUSSION AND CONCLUSION

This book chapter provides an in-depth investigation of utilizing artificial intelligence for ethical communication with social media influencers. The findings uncover perspectives on technological progress, ethical concerns, and the ever-changing field of influencer marketing. First and foremost, there are opportunities and difficulties with using AI in influencer marketing. The benefits include better campaign performance metrics, more effective audience targeting, and optimized content. AI-powered solutions help minimize problems like audience analysis, influencer fraud, and salary negotiations. These developments have the potential to significantly alter influencer tactics and improve the general efficacy of influencer marketing initiatives.

Nevertheless, ethical considerations play a significant role in this context. The possibility of AI being used inappropriately, concerns about privacy, and the necessity for transparency in the influencer communication process highlight the significance of establishing strong ethical guidelines. These guidelines should prioritize fairness, accountability, and user privacy. These guidelines serve as a guide, offering influencers and marketers a structure to navigate the ethical considerations linked to AI technologies. Transparency is also a fundamental element that requires influencers and brands to disclose the utilization of AI in their communication strategies ethically. Effective communication establishes trust with the audience, enabling them to make well-informed decisions regarding the content they interact with. Safeguarding user privacy is of utmost importance when integrating ethical AI. It is essential to prioritize the acquisition of explicit consent from social media users before implementing AI for personalized content, targeted advertising, or data analysis in order to adhere to best practices. Regular evaluations of AI algorithms and influencer communication strategies help ensure continuous ethical compliance. Algorithmic accountability mechanisms must be implemented to evaluate the influence of AI on content generation, guaranteeing its adherence to ethical norms.

The integration of AI has implications that extend beyond individual influencers and brands to encompass broader societal impacts. The discourse revolves around the crucial aspects of data privacy, security concerns, and the necessity for regulatory frameworks. Ensuring the sustainable growth of AI-driven influencer marketing requires a careful equilibrium between technological innovation and protecting user interests.

In conclusion, this book chapter highlights AI's significant impact in redefining how social media influencers communicate. In order to fully harness the potential of AI, it is essential to adopt a conscientious and ethical approach despite the numerous opportunities offered by technological advancements. As the use of artificial intelligence in social media influencer communication continues to evolve, collaboration, education, and adherence to ethical guidelines are crucial for influencers, brands, and regulators to ensure responsible and impactful integration. The insights garnered from this exploration serve as a foundation for continued research, industry practices, and the ethical evolution of influencer marketing in the age of artificial intelligence.

Funding. This research received funding through the University Research Grant (RP/03/02/09/01/2022) awarded by the Research Council of the University of Kelaniya, Sri Lanka.

REFERENCES

AbdulAmeer, A. A., Salman, M. A., & Mahdi, M. A. (2022, May). Influencers Detection Algorithm to Combat Rumors in Social Networks. *2022 5th International Conference on Engineering Technology and Its Applications (IICETA).*

Anaya-Sánchez, Aurora, Ruiz, Molinillo, & Japutra. (2022). *Virtual influencers: generation of trust, loyalty and purchase intentions.* Academic Press.

Anklesaria, K., Desai, Z., Kulkarni, V., & Balasubramaniam, H. (2021, December). A Survey on Machine Learning Algorithms for Detecting Fake Instagram Accounts. *2021 3rd International Conference on Advances in Computing, Communication Control and Networking (ICAC3N).*

B, V. K., Kubsad, S. S., & G, S. A. (2022, December). Survey on Data Security with Intersection of AI and Blockchain. *2022 Fourth International Conference on Cognitive Computing and Information Processing (CCIP).*

Beigi, G., Shu, K., Zhang, Y., & Liu, H. (2018, July). Securing Social Media User Data. *Proceedings of the 29th on Hypertext and Social Media.* 10.1145/3209542.3209552

Belenguer, L. (2022). AI bias: Exploring discriminatory algorithmic decision-making models and the application of possible machine-centric solutions adapted from the pharmaceutical industry. *AI and Ethics, 2*(4), 771–787. doi:10.1007/s43681-022-00138-8 PMID:35194591

Belova, A. (2021). *Virtual influencers in multimodal advertising*. Academic Press.

Boddy, J., & Dominelli, L. (2016). Social Media and Social Work: The Challenges of a New Ethical Space. *Australian Social Work, 70*(2), 172–184. doi:10.1080/0312407X.2016.1224907

Bouaafia, S., Khemiri, R., Messaoud, S., Ben Ahmed, O., & Sayadi, F. E. (2022). Deep learning-based video quality enhancement for the new versatile video coding. *Neural Computing & Applications, 34*(17), 14135–14149. doi:10.1007/s00521-021-06491-9 PMID:34511732

Brett, E. I., Stevens, E. M., Wagener, T. L., Leavens, E. L. S., Morgan, T. L., Cotton, W. D., & Hébert, E. T. (2019). A content analysis of JUUL discussions on social media: Using Reddit to understand patterns and perceptions of JUUL use. *Drug and Alcohol Dependence, 194*, 358–362. doi:10.1016/j.drugalcdep.2018.10.014 PMID:30472576

Chintalapati, S., & Pandey, S. K. (2022). Artificial intelligence in marketing: A systematic literature review. *International Journal of Market Research, 64*(1), 38–68. doi:10.1177/14707853211018428

Clauset, A., Newman, M. E. J., & Moore, C. (2004). Finding community structure in very large networks. *Physical Review. E, 70*(6), 066111. doi:10.1103/PhysRevE.70.066111 PMID:15697438

Davies, C., & Hobbs, M. (2020). Irresistible possibilities: Examining the uses and consequences of social media influencers for contemporary public relations. *Public Relations Review, 46*(5), 101983. Advance online publication. doi:10.1016/j.pubrev.2020.101983

Eskandari, F., Lake, A. A., & Butler, M. (2022). COVID-19 pandemic and food poverty conversations: Social network analysis of Twitter data. *Nutrition Bulletin, 47*(1), 93–105. doi:10.1111/nbu.12547 PMID:36045084

Fownes, J. R., Yu, C., & Margolin, D. B. (2018). Twitter and climate change. *Sociology Compass, 12*(6), e12587. Advance online publication. doi:10.1111/soc4.12587

Gerlich, M. (2023). The Power of Virtual Influencers: Impact on Consumer Behaviour and Attitudes in the Age of AI. *Administrative Sciences, 13*(8), 178. doi:10.3390/admsci13080178

Goanta, C., & Ranchordás, S. (2020). The regulation of social media influencers: an introduction. In *The Regulation of Social Media Influencers*. Edward Elgar Publishing. doi:10.4337/9781788978286.00008

Hagelstein, J., Einwiller, S., & Zerfass, A. (2021). The ethical dimension of public relations in Europe: Digital channels, moral challenges, resources, and training. *Public Relations Review*, *47*(4), 102063. Advance online publication. doi:10.1016/j.pubrev.2021.102063

Hermann, E. (2021). Artificial intelligence and mass personalization of communication content—An ethical and literacy perspective. *New Media &amp. Society*, *24*(5), 1258–1277.

Ho, C. H. (2021). A Preliminary Study of Artificial Intelligence Deep Learning Amid Teaching of Public Relations Course. *2021 2nd International Conference on Education, Knowledge and Information Management (ICEKIM)*, 539–542. 10.1109/ICEKIM52309.2021.00124

Hudaefi, F. A., Hassan, M. K., Abduh, M., & Beik, I. S. (2023). Knowledge discovery of zakat administration worldwide from YouTube and Zoom via text mining. *Journal of Islamic Accounting and Business Research*, *14*(1), 159–180. doi:10.1108/JIABR-03-2022-0067

Hudders, L., De Jans, S., & De Veirman, M. (2021). The commercialization of social media stars: A literature review and conceptual framework on the strategic use of social media influencers. *International Journal of Advertising*, *40*(3), 327–375. doi:10.1080/02650487.2020.1836925

Hunt, T., & Tirpok, A. (1993). Universal ethics code: An idea whose time has come. *Public Relations Review*, *19*(1), 1–11. doi:10.1016/0363-8111(93)90025-8

Kolo & Haumer. (2018). *Social media celebrities as influencers in brand communication: An empirical study on influencer content, its advertising relevance and audience expectations*. Academic Press.

Lama, A. B., & Shrook, A. F. (2020). Ethical Considerations for Using Social Media: "Is it Okay to Share?" *The Arab Journal of Media and Communication Research*, *2020*(31), 172–187.

Lewis, D., & Moorkens, J. (2020). A Rights-Based Approach to Trustworthy AI in Social Media. *Social Media + Society*, *6*(3), 205630512095467. doi:10.1177/2056305120954672

Li, X., & Feng, J. (2022). Influenced or to be influenced: Engaging social media influencers in nation branding through the lens of authenticity. *Global Media and China*, *7*(2), 219–240. doi:10.1177/20594364221094668

Nafi & Ahmed. (2019). *The Ethical Standpoint of Social Influencers on Hotel EServicescape: A Theoretical Perspective on the Existing Literature*. Academic Press.

Ocal, A. (2023). Perceptions of AI Ethics on Social Media. *2023 IEEE International Symposium on Ethics in Engineering, Science, and Technology (ETHICS)*. 10.1109/ETHICS57328.2023.10155069

Raimundo, R., & Rosário, A. (2021). The Impact of Artificial Intelligence on Data System Security: A Literature Review. *Sensors (Basel)*, *21*(21), 7029. doi:10.3390/s21217029 PMID:34770336

Shanmukhaprasanthi, T., Rayavarapu, S. M., Lavanya, Y. L., & Rao, G. S. (2023). A Comprehensive Study of Image Inpainting Techniques with Algorithmic approach. *2023 6th International Conference on Information Systems and Computer Networks (ISCON)*, 1–5. 10.1109/ISCON57294.2023.10112205

Steils, N., Martin, A., & Toti, J.-F. (2022). Managing the Transparency Paradox Of Social-Media Influencer Disclosures. *Journal of Advertising Research*, *62*(2), 148–166. doi:10.2501/JAR-2022-008

Tatiya, R. V. (2014). A Survey of Recommendation Algorithms. *IOSR Journal of Computer Engineering, 16*(6), 16–19. doi:10.9790/0661-16651619

von der Weth, C., Abdul, A., Fan, S., & Kankanhalli, M. (2020, October). Helping Users Tackle Algorithmic Threats on Social Media: A Multimedia Research Agenda. *Proceedings of the 28th ACM International Conference on Multimedia.* 10.1145/3394171.3414692

Wellman, M. L., Stoldt, R., Tully, M., & Ekdale, B. (2020). Ethics of Authenticity: Social Media Influencers and the Production of Sponsored Content. *Journal of Medical Ethics, 35*(2), 68–82. doi:10.1080/23736992.2020.1736078

Woodroof, P. J., Howie, K. M., Syrdal, H. A., & VanMeter, R. (2020). Whats done in the dark will be brought to the light: Effects of influencer transparency on product efficacy and purchase intentions. *Journal of Product &amp. Brand Management, 29*(5), 675–688.

Xue, H., Liu, B., Din, M., Song, L., & Zhu, T. (2020, December). Hiding Private Information in Images From AI. *ICC 2020 - 2020 IEEE International Conference on Communications (ICC).*

Zhang, A. Y., & Zhou, H. H. (2016). Minimax rates of community detection in stochastic block models. *Annals of Statistics, 44*(5). Advance online publication. doi:10.1214/15-AOS1428

Zhong, L. (2022). Analyses of the Relationship between Virtual Influencers Endorsements and Customer Brand Engagement in Social Media. *Proceedings of the 2022 International Conference on Creative Industry and Knowledge Economy (CIKE 2022).* 10.2991/aebmr.k.220404.007

KEY TERMS AND DEFINITIONS

Artificial Intelligence (AI): Denotes the replication of human intelligence within machines, empowering them to execute duties that conventionally demand human intelligence, including but not limited to decision-making, learning, and problem-solving.

Empirical Analysis: The use of real-world data and observations to draw conclusions and insights.

Ethical Considerations: The examination and evaluation of moral principles and values related to influencer communication, with a focus on ensuring responsible and just practices.

Influencer Communication: A procedure by which influencers interact with their followers via social media platforms; includes the creation of content, interaction, and influence on their audience.

NodeXL Pro: A social network analysis application that offers valuable insights into the dynamics and structure of user interactions.

Professional Code of Ethics: A collection of principles and guidelines, demonstrated by the code established by the Public Relations Society of America (PRSA), which prescribes ethical standards for the behavior of professionals within a particular domain.

Regulatory Frameworks: Legislative entities or governing bodies establish rules and guidelines with the objective of overseeing and controlling the ethical utilization of artificial intelligence and influencer communication practices.

Social Network Analysis: The investigation of social structures via networks and graph theory constitutes social network analysis. Networked structures are defined by the connections between nodes (representing individual actors, people, or objects within the network) and ties, edges, or links (representing relationships or interactions).

Text Analysis: Text analysis, also known as text mining or natural language processing, is extracting meaningful information and insights from written or spoken language. It involves the use of computational methods and algorithms to analyze and interpret large volumes of text data.

Compilation of References

@allygroom. (2019, April 11). "Our boy" lol i love it. like give him a commercial at this point... maybe one where its just him being surrounded by nuggets. Twitter. https://twitter.com/allygroom/status/851805748719964160

@astitchtowear. (2019). *Instagram photos and videos*. Retrieved May 17, 2019, from https://www.instagram.com/astitchtowear/

@BenBriggs34. (2017). @Wendys I bet @McDonalds would give him the nuggets for the effort. Quit slacking. Twitter. https://twitter.com/BenBriggs34/status/850091859808595968?s=19

@calekiekhaefer2. (2017, Apr. 6). @Wendys lower this for this man. Twitter. https://twitter.com/calekiekhaefer2/status/850024284487548928?s=19

@cwilso… (2017, Apri. 6). Records were made to be broken,haha! Twitter.

@ocean_bythesea. (2019). *Instagram photos and videos*. Retrieved May 17, 2019, from https://www.instagram.com/ocean_bythesea/

@Seth_Kaplan. (2017, Apr. 6). Wendy's is playing this perfectly. Twitter. https://twitter.com/Seth_Kaplan/status/850149089928990721?s=19

@su.krita. (2019). *Instagram photos and videos*. Retrieved May 17, 2019, from https://www.instagram.com/su.krita/

@thecolormustard. (2019). *Instagram photos and videos*. Retrieved May 17, 2019 from https://www.instagram.com/thecolormustard/

@tina.say.knits. (2019). *Instagram photos and videos*. Retrieved May 17, 2019, from https://www.instagram.com/tina.say.knit/

@transitory. (2019). *Instagram photos and videos*. Retrieved May 17, 2019, from https://www.instagram.com/transitory/

@Wendys. (2017a, Apr. 8). Attempt? It's still climbing. He's going to crush that record. Twitter. https://twitter.com/Wendys/status/850821313920991234?s=19

@Wendys. (2017b), Apr. 6). He's doing well. Don't doubt the hustle. Twitter. https://twitter.com/Wendys/status/850024538305961984?s=19

@wendys. (2017c, Apr. 7). It can definitely happen. Twitter. https://twitter.com/Wendys/status/850443001428144129?s=19

@Wendys. (2017d, Apr. 9). It's over 2 million. Twitter. https://twitter.com/Wendys/status/851195851972202498?s=19

@Wendys. (2017e, Apr. 6). Just be patient, have faith, and let a beautiful thing happen. Twitter. https://twitter.com/Wendys/status/850092618881130496?s=19

@Wendys. (2017f, Apr. 7). That's the spirit right there. Twitter. https://twitter.com/Wendys/status/850418239729545216?s=19

A nudge in the right direction: Using social media to influence public health. (n.d.). Gies College of Business. https://giesbusiness.illinois.edu/news/2023/04/26/a-nudge-in-the-right-direction-using-social-media-to-influence-public-health.'

AbdulAmeer, A. A., Salman, M. A., & Mahdi, M. A. (2022, May). Influencers Detection Algorithm to Combat Rumors in Social Networks. *2022 5th International Conference on Engineering Technology and Its Applications (IICETA).*

Abhyankar, A. (2019). *Behavioural Economics Towards Better Decision Making*. Academic Press.

Abidin, C. (2016). Visibility labour: Engaging with Influencers' fashion brands and #OOTD advertorial campaigns on Instagram. *Media International Australia, Incorporating Culture & Policy*, *161*(1), 86–100. doi:10.1177/1329878X16665177

Abosag, I., Romadan, Z. B., Baker, T., & Jin, Z. (2020). Customers' need for uniqueness theory versus brand congruence theory: The impact on satisfaction with social network sites. *Journal of Business Research*, *117*, 862–872. doi:10.1016/j.jbusres.2019.03.016

Absolom, S., & Roberts, A. (2011). Connecting with others: The meaning of social eating as an everyday occupation for young people. *Journal of Occupational Science*, *18*(4), 339–346. doi:10.1080/14427591.2011.586324

Adebonojo, R. (2023). *Remi Bader*. Forbes. https://www.forbes.com/profile/remi-bader/?sh=17ab80cf7de2

Aengst, J. C., Harrington, E. K., Bahulekar, P., Shivkumar, P., Jensen, J. T., & Garg, B. S. (2017). Perceptions of nonsurgical permanent contraception among potential users, providers, and influencers in Wardha district and New Delhi, India: Exploratory research. *Indian Journal of Public Health*, *61*(1), 3–8. doi:10.4103/0019-557X.200261 PMID:28218155

Age, Ad. (2022). Ad Age names TikTok 'Marketer of the Year'. *PR Newswire*. https://www.prnewswire.com/news-releases/ad-age-names-tiktok-marketer-of-the-year-301187044.html

Agostino, D. (2013). Using social media to engage citizens: A study of Italian municipalities. *Public Relations Review*, *39*(3), 232–234. doi:10.1016/j.pubrev.2013.02.009

Ahmed, S. (2010). *The Promise of Happiness*. Duke University Press.

Ahmed, S. (2021). *Complaint!* Duke University Press.

Ajzen, I. (1991). The theory of planned behaviour. *Organizational Behavior and Human Decision Processes*, *50*(2), 179–211. doi:10.1016/0749-5978(91)90020-T

Akhtar, M. A., Khan, K. A., & Hoang, H. C. (2023). Role of Social Networking Sites in Financial Product Choice: An Investigation Through the Theory of Planned Behaviour. *Business Perspectives and Research*, *11*(1), 44-62.

Al-Emadi, F., & Yahia, I. (2020). Ordinary celebrities related criteria to harvest fame and influence on social media. *Journal of Research in Interactive Marketing*, *14*(2), 195–213. doi:10.1108/JRIM-02-2018-0031

AlFarraj, O., Alalwan, A. A., Obeidat, Z. M., Baabdullah, A., Aldmour, R., & Al-Haddad, S. (2021). Examining the impact of influencers' credibility dimensions: Attractiveness, trustworthiness and expertise on the purchase intention in the aesthetic dermatology industry. *Review of International Business and Strategy*, *31*(3), 355–374. doi:10.1108/RIBS-07-2020-0089

Alhothali, G. T., & Aljefree, N. M. (2023). Young adults' sought gratifications from, and perceptions of food advertising by, social media influencers: A qualitative approach. *Journal of Health, Population and Nutrition*, *42*(1), 1–12. doi:10.1186/s41043-023-00449-4 PMID:37752524

Ali, M., Baqir, A., Psaila, G., & Malik, S. (2020). Towards the Discovery of Influencers to Follow in Micro-Blogs (Twitter) by Detecting Topics in Posted Messages (Tweets). *Applied Sciences (Basel, Switzerland), 10*(16), 5715. doi:10.3390/app10165715

Allen, M. B., & Reese, P. P. (2016). The ethics of promoting living kidney donation using nonargumentative influence: Applications, concerns, and future directions. *American Journal of Transplantation, 16*(12), 3378–3384. doi:10.1111/ajt.13972 PMID:27438695

Alqahtani, M. M. J., Alkhamees, H. A., Alkhalaf, A. M., Alarjan, S. S., Alzahrani, H. S., AlSaad, G. F., Alhrbi, F. H., Wahass, S. H., Khayat, A. H., & Alqahtani, K. M. M. (2021). Toward establishing telepsychology guideline. Turning the challenges of COVID-19 into opportunity. *Ethics, Medicine, and Public Health, 16*, C7–C100612. doi:10.1016/j.jemep.2020.100612 PMID:33283033

Alrwashdeh, M., Ali, H., Helalat, A., & Alkhodar, D. (2022). The mediating role of brand credibility between social media influencers and patronage intentions. *International Journal of Data and Network Science, 6*(2), 305–314. doi:10.5267/j.ijdns.2022.1.007

Alvaro, E. M., Crano, W. D., Siegel, J. T., Hohman, Z., Johnson, I., & Nakawaki, B. (2013). Adolescents' attitudes toward antimarijuana ads, usage intentions, and actual marijuana usage. *Psychology of Addictive Behaviors, 27*(4), 1027–1035. doi:10.1037/a0031960 PMID:23528197

Amare, Y., Scheelbeek, P., Schellenberg, J., Berhanu, D., & Hill, Z. (2018). Early postnatal home visits: A qualitative study of barriers and facilitators to achieving high coverage. *BMC Public Health, 18*(1 C7 - 1074). doi:10.1186/s12889-018-5922-7

Amed, I., Berg, A., Brantberg, L., Hedrich, S., Leon, J., & Young, R. (2017). *The State of Fashion 2017.* The Business of Fashion. https://www.mckinsey.com/~/media/McKinsey/Industries/Retail/Our%20Insights/The%20state%20of%20fashion/The-state-of-fashion-2017-McK-BoF-report.pdf

Anaya-Sánchez, Aurora, Ruiz, Molinillo, & Japutra. (2022). *Virtual influencers: generation of trust, loyalty and purchase intentions.* Academic Press.

An, D., & Kim, S. (2006). Relating Hofstede's masculinity dimension to gender role portrayals in advertising. *International Marketing Review, 24*(2), 181–207. doi:10.1108/02651330710741811

Anderson, M. (2023, September 13). *How brands are embracing the "realness movement."* Forbes. https://www.forbes.com/sites/forbescommunicationscouncil/2023/09/13/how-brands-are-embracing-the-realness-movement/

Andrii. (2023). *How many influencers are there in 2023.* trendHERO. Available at: https://trendhero.io/blog/how-many-influencers-are-there/

Angraini, N. (2023). Social media marketing influencer: Literature review on promotional strategies using the influence of social media celebrities. *International Journal of Economic Research and Financial Accounting, 1*(4). Advance online publication. doi:10.55227/ijerfa.v1i4.42

Anklesaria, K., Desai, Z., Kulkarni, V., & Balasubramaniam, H. (2021, December). A Survey on Machine Learning Algorithms for Detecting Fake Instagram Accounts. *2021 3rd International Conference on Advances in Computing, Communication Control and Networking (ICAC3N).*

Antunes, C., & Sebastiao, S. P. (2020). Ethical challenges in online social networks: The content production and the opinion of professionals. *Cuadernos.Info*, (46), 222–248. doi:10.7764/cdi.46.1473

Ao, L., Bansal, R., Pruthi, N., & Khaskheli, M. B. (2023). Impact of social media influencers on customer engagement and purchase Intention: A Meta-Analysis. *Sustainability (Basel), 15*(3), 2744. doi:10.3390/su15032744

Apasrawirote, D., & Yawised, K. (2022). *Factors Influencing the Behavioral and Purchase Intention on Live-streaming Shopping*. Asian Journal of Business Research. doi:10.14707/ajbr.220119

Appelbaum, A. (2001). *The constant consumer, The Gallup Group*. Retrieved from https://gmj.gallup.com/content/745/Constant-Customer.aspx

Appel, G., Grewal, L., Hadi, R., & Stephen, A. T. (2020). The future of social media in marketing. *Journal of the Academy of Marketing Science, 48*(1), 79–95. doi:10.1007/s11747-019-00695-1 PMID:32431463

Arantes, J., & Buchanan, R. (2022). Educational data advocates: Emerging forms of teacher agency in postdigital classrooms. *Learning, Media and Technology*, 1–21.

Arantes, J., & Buchanan, R. (2023). Educational data advocates: Emerging forms of teacher agency in post digital classrooms. *Learning, Media and Technology, 48*(3), 493–513. doi:10.1080/17439884.2022.2087084

Argyris, Y., Wang, Z., Kim, Y., & Yin, Z. (2020). The effects of visual congruence on increasing consumers' brand engagement: An empirical investigation of influencer marketing on instagram using deep-learning algorithms for automatic image classification. *Computers in Human Behavior, 112*, 106443. doi:10.1016/j.chb.2020.106443

Arora, A. S., & Sanni, S. A. (2018). Ten Years of 'Social Media Marketing' Research in the Journal of Promotion Management: Research Synthesis, Emerging Themes, and New Directions. *Journal of Promotion Management, 25*(4), 476–499. doi:10.1080/10496491.2018.1448322

Arrington, M. (2005, November 14). Yahoo Shoposphere just launched. *TechCrunch*. https://techcrunch.com/2005/11/14/yahoo-shoposphere-launches-tonight/

Artese, F. (2020). In the digital world, all roads lead to Rome. But is Rome prepared? *Dental Press Journal of Orthodontics, 24*(6), 7–8. doi:10.1590/2177-6709.24.6.007-008.edt PMID:31994650

Arula, K. (2021, December 1). *The evolution of social commerce: What, when, how and why?* Insights for Professionals. https://www.insightsforprofessionals.com/marketing/ecommerce/evolution-of-social-commerce

Aspire. (2024) *The State of Influencer Marketing 2024*. Available at: https://www.aspire.io/ty-event/the-state-of-influencer-marketing-2024?utm_source=webinar&utm_medium=email-OD&utm_campaign=state-of-influencermarketing&mkt_tok=OTgyLURPTi0yNjYAAAGQvgcoNdhRhorW-3p1mW_2E3ct1sWuSbty-pmmZbIM282Xdn5zbq0M04WPm5z-p2Oz35Nrz5QVP7Jl-iIDVnCd_vXXw7inTHDSZKCp6H6rpEA#watch

Atika, A., Kusumawati, A., & Iqbal, M. (2018). The effect of electronic word of mouth, message source credibility, information quality on brand image and purchase intention. *Jurnal Ekonomi dan Keuangan, 20*, 94-108. doi:10.24034/j25485024.y2016.v20.i1.94

Audrezet, A., de Kerviler, G., & Guidry Moulard, J. (2020). Authenticity under threat: When social media influencers need to go beyond self-presentation. *Journal of Business Research, 117*, 557–569. doi:10.1016/j.jbusres.2018.07.008

Avalos, L., Tylka, T. L., & Wood-Barcalow, N. (2005). The Body Appreciation Scale: Development and psychometric evaluation. *Body Image, 2*(3), 285–297. doi:10.1016/j.bodyim.2005.06.002 PMID:18089195

B, V. K., Kubsad, S. S., & G, S. A. (2022, December). Survey on Data Security with Intersection of AI and Blockchain. *2022 Fourth International Conference on Cognitive Computing and Information Processing (CCIP)*.

Baas, J., Schotten, M., Plume, A., Côté, G., & Karimi, R. (2020). Scopus as a curated, high-quality bibliometric data source for academic research in quantitative science studies. *Quantitative Science Studies, 1*(1), 377–386. doi:10.1162/qss_a_00019

Baker-Eveleth, L., Stone, R. W., & Eveleth, D. M. (2021). Understanding social media users' privacy-protection behaviours. *Information and Computer Security, 30*(3), 324–345. doi:10.1108/ICS-07-2021-0099

Balabanis, G., & Chatzopoulou, E. (2019). Under the influence of a blogger: The role of information-seeking goals and issue involvement. *Psychology and Marketing, 36*(4), 342–353. doi:10.1002/mar.21182

Balas, E. A., Vernon, M., Magrabi, F., Gordon, L. T., & Sexton, J. (2015). Big Data Clinical Research: Validity, Ethics, and Regulation. *Studies in Health Technology and Informatics*. PMID:26262090

Balestra, D. (2022, December 19). *WhatNot app: Pros & cons of auction apps like WhatNot*. Vendoo. https://blog.vendoo.co/live-selling-the-pros-cons-of-selling-on-whatnot-app

Ballantine, P., & Martin, B. (2005). Forming parasocial relationships in online communities. *Advances in Consumer Research. Association for Consumer Research (U. S.), 32*, 197–201.

Bandura, A. (2001). Social cognitive theory: An agentic perspective. *Annual Review of Psychology, 52*(1), 1–26. doi:10.1146/annurev.psych.52.1.1 PMID:11148297

Banerjee, S., & John, P. (2021). Nudge plus: Incorporating reflection into behavioral public policy. *Behavioural Public Policy*. Advance online publication. doi:10.1017/bpp.2021.9

Bannigan, M. K., & Shane, B. (2019). Towards truth in influencing: Risks and rewards of disclosing influencer marketing in the fashion industry. *New York School Law Review, 64*(3), 247-263. https://digitalcommons.nyls.edu/cgi/viewcontent.cgi?article=1701&context=nyls_law_review

Barbe, D., & Neuburger, L. (2021). *Generation Z and Digital Influencers in the Tourism Industry*. Generation Z Marketing and Management in Tourism and Hospitality. doi:10.1007/978-3-030-70695-1_7

Barnes, L., & Lea-Greenwood, G. (2006). Fast fashioning the supply chain: Shaping the research agenda. *Journal of Fashion Marketing and Management, 10*(3), 259–271. doi:10.1108/13612020610679259

Bastos, M. T., Mercea, D., & Charpentier, A. (2015). Tents, tweets, and events: The interplay between ongoing protests and social media. *Journal of Communication, 65*(2), 320–350. doi:10.1111/jcom.12145

Baxter, P., & Jack, S. (2015). Qualitative case study methodology: Study design and implementation for novice researchers. *The Qualitative Report*. Advance online publication. doi:10.46743/2160-3715/2008.1573

Bazarova, N., Walther, J., & McLeod, P. (2012). Minority Influence in Virtual Groups. *Communication Research, 39*(3), 295–316. doi:10.1177/0093650211399752

Beccanulli, A. A., Biraghi, S., & Gambetti, R. (2020). Migrant consumers, celebrity culture and technosociality. *Micro and Macro Marketing, 29*(2), 295–324. doi:10.1431/97320

Beigi, G., Shu, K., Zhang, Y., & Liu, H. (2018, July). Securing Social Media User Data. *Proceedings of the 29th on Hypertext and Social Media*. 10.1145/3209542.3209552

Belanche, D., Casalo, L. V., Flavian, M., & Ibanez-Sanchez, S. (2021). Understanding influencer marketing: The role of congruence between influencers, products and consumers. *Journal of Business Research, 132*, 186–195. doi:10.1016/j.jbusres.2021.03.067

Belch, G. E., & Belch, M. A. (2013). A content analysis of the use of celebrity endorsers in magazine advertising. *International Journal of Advertising, 32*, 369–389. doi:10.2501/IJA-32-3-369-389

Belenguer, L. (2022). AI bias: Exploring discriminatory algorithmic decision-making models and the application of possible machine-centric solutions adapted from the pharmaceutical industry. *AI and Ethics, 2*(4), 771–787. doi:10.1007/s43681-022-00138-8 PMID:35194591

Belk, R. W. (2013). Extended self in a digital world: Table 1. *The Journal of Consumer Research, 40*(3), 477–500. doi:10.1086/671052

Bellissimo, N., Pencharz, P. B., Thomas, S. G., & Anderson, G. H. (2007). Effect of television viewing at mealtime on food intake after a glucose preload in boys. *Pediatric Research, 61*(6), 745–749. doi:10.1203/pdr.0b013e3180536591 PMID:17426650

Belova, A. (2021). *Virtual influencers in multimodal advertising.* Academic Press.

Bennett, W. L., & Segerberg, A. (2012). The logic of connective action: Digital media and the personalization of contentious politics. *Information Communication and Society, 15*(5), 739–768. doi:10.1080/1369118X.2012.670661

Berlant, L. (2012). *Cruel Optimism.* Duke University Press.

Bernard, P., Hanoteau, F., Gervais, S., Servais, L., Bertolone, I., Deltenre, P., & Colin, C. (2019). Revealing clothing does not make the object: ERP evidences that cognitive objectification is driven by posture suggestiveness, not by revealing clothing. *Personality and Social Psychology Bulletin, 45*(1), 16–36. doi:10.1177/0146167218775690 PMID:29877123

Berné-Manero, C., & Marzo-Navarro, M. (2020). Exploring how influencer and relationship marketing serve corporate sustainability. *Sustainability (Basel), 12*(11), 4392. doi:10.3390/su12114392

Berzleja, Z., & Kertész, F. (2019). *The furry side of Instagram: A study about dog influencers on Instagram.* Unpublished thesis. Malmö Universitet.

Bestvater, S. (2024, February 22). *How U.S. adults use TikTok.* Pew Research Center: Internet, Science & Tech. https://www.pewresearch.org/internet/2024/02/22/how-u-s-adults-use-tiktok/

Beverland, M. B., & Farrelly, F. J. (2010). The quest for authenticity in consumption: Consumers' purposive choice of authentic cues to shape experienced outcomes. *The Journal of Consumer Research, 36*(5), 838–856. doi:10.1086/615047

Bi, N. C., & Zhang, R. (2022a). Electronic word-of-mouth and social media. In Emerald Publishing Limited eBooks (pp. 37–50). doi:10.1108/978-1-80071-597-420221003

Bianchi, C., & Gonzalez, M. (2021). Exploring sustainable fashion consumption among eco-conscious women in Chile. *International Review of Retail, Distribution and Consumer Research, 31*(4), 375–392. doi:10.1080/09593969.2021.1903529

Biefeld, S. D., & Brown, C. S. (2022). Fat, sexy, and human? Perceptions of plus-size sexualized women and dehumanization. *Body Image, 42*, 84–97. doi:10.1016/j.bodyim.2022.05.002 PMID:35671637

Bi, N. C., & Zhang, R. (2022). I will buy what my 'friend' recommends: The effects of parasocial relationships, influencer credibility and self-esteem on purchase intentions. *Journal of Research in Interactive Marketing, 17*(2), 157–175. doi:10.1108/JRIM-08-2021-0214

Bi, N. C., Zhang, R., & Ha, L. (2019). Does valence of product review matter? The mediating role of self-effect and third-person effect in sharing YouTube word-of-mouth (vWOM). *Journal of Research in Interactive Marketing, 13*(1), 79–95. doi:10.1108/JRIM-04-2018-0049

Binning, K. R., Unzueta, M. M., Huo, Y. J., & Molina, L. E. (2009). The interpretation of multiracial status and its relation to social engagement and psychological well-being. *The Journal of Social Issues*, *65*(1), 35–49. doi:10.1111/j.1540-4560.2008.01586.x

Blackford, B. (2021). Nudging interventions on sustainable food consumption: a systematic review. *The Journal of Population and Sustainability*. . doi:10.3197/jps.2021.5.2.17

Black, S. (2017). Knit + Resist: Placing the Pussyhat project in the context of craft activism. *Gender, Place and Culture*, *24*(5), 696–710. doi:10.1080/0966369X.2017.1335292

Bladow, L. E. (2017). Worth the click: Why greater FTC enforcement is needed to curtail deceptive practices in influencer marketing. *William and Mary Law Review*, *8*(3), 1123–1164. https://scholarship.law.wm.edu/cgi/viewcontent.cgi?article=3739&context=wmlr

Blowers, H. (2012). Measuring social media and the greater digital landscape. *Computers in Libraries*, *32*, 27–29.

Blumenthal-Barby, J. S. (2012). Between reason and coercion: Ethically permissible influence in health care and health policy contexts. *Kennedy Institute of Ethics Journal*, *22*(4), 345–366. doi:10.1353/ken.2012.a495158 PMID:23420941

Boadi, C., & Kolog, E. A. (2021). Social media aggression: An assessment based on the contemporary deterrence theory. *27th Annual Americas Conference on Information Systems, AMCIS 2021*.

Boddy, J., & Dominelli, L. (2016). Social Media and Social Work: The Challenges of a New Ethical Space. *Australian Social Work*, *70*(2), 172–184. doi:10.1080/0312407X.2016.1224907

Boerman, S. C. (2020). The effects of the standardized Instagram disclosure for micro-and meso-influencers. *Computers in Human Behavior*, *103*, 199–207. doi:10.1016/j.chb.2019.09.015

Boerman, S. C., Kruikemeier, S., & Zuiderveen Borgesius, F. J. (2017). Online behavioral advertising: A literature review and research agenda. *Journal of Advertising*, *46*(3), 363–376. doi:10.1080/00913367.2017.1339368

Bolly, C. (2011). Can the implementation of ethical processes have an influence on medical persons' suffering? *Psycho-oncologie*, *5*(2), 98–108. doi:10.1007/s11839-011-0314-6

Bond, B. J. (2021). The development and influence of parasocial relationships with television characters: A longitudinal experimental test of prejudice reduction through parasocial contact. *Communication Research*, *48*(4), 573–593. doi:10.1177/0093650219900632

Bond, B. J., & Drogos, K. L. (2014). Sex on the shore: Wishful identification and parasocial relationships as mediators in the relationship between Jersey Shore exposure and emerging adults' sexual attitudes and behaviors. *Media Psychology*, *17*(1), 102–126. doi:10.1080/15213269.2013.872039

Booth, N., & Matic, J. A. (2011). Mapping and leveraging influencers in social media to shape corporate brand perceptions. *Corporate Communications*, *16*(3), 184–191. doi:10.1108/13563281111156853

Borchers, N. S., & Enke, N. (2022). "I've never seen a client say: 'Tell the influencer not to label this as sponsored'": An exploration into influencer industry ethics. *Public Relations Review*,*48*(5 C7 - 102235). doi:10.1016/j.pubrev.2022.102235

Borchers, N. S. (2019). Social media influencers in strategic communication. *International Journal of Strategic Communication*, *13*(4), 255–260. doi:10.1080/1553118X.2019.1634075

Borusiak, B., Szymkowiak, A., Horska, E., Raszka, N., & Żelichowska, E. (2020). Towards building sustainable consumption: A study of second-hand buying intentions. *Sustainability (Basel)*, *12*(3), 875. doi:10.3390/su12030875

Bosch, T. (2017). Twitter activism and youth in South Africa. The case of #RhoeesMustFall. *Information Communication and Society*, *20*(2), 221–232. doi:10.1080/1369118X.2016.1162829

Bosch, T., & Mutsvairo, B. (2017). Pictures, Protests and politics: Mapping Twitter images during South Africa's fees must fall campaign. *African Journalism Studies*, *38*(2), 71–89. doi:10.1080/23743670.2017.1368869

Botes, M. (2022). Autonomy and the social dilemma of online manipulative behaviour. *AI and Ethics*, *3*(1), 315–323. doi:10.1007/s43681-022-00157-5

Bouaafia, S., Khemiri, R., Messaoud, S., Ben Ahmed, O., & Sayadi, F. E. (2022). Deep learning-based video quality enhancement for the new versatile video coding. *Neural Computing & Applications*, *34*(17), 14135–14149. doi:10.1007/s00521-021-06491-9 PMID:34511732

Bouchalta, M., Belhouss, A., & Benyaich, H. (2020). The medical liability of the psychiatrist in Moroccan law. *Droit. Deontologie et Soin*, *20*(3), 305–312. doi:10.1016/j.ddes.2020.07.011

Bourdieu, P. (1986). The forms of capital. In J. G. Richardson (Ed.), *Handbook of theory and research for the sociology of education* (pp. 241–258). Greenwood.

Bouvier, L., & Cho, E. (2022, December). How Do Virtual Social Media Influencers Affect Millennial and Gen Z Female Consumers' Purchase Intentions? A Comparison of Fast Fashion Versus Luxury Fashion Brands. *International Textile and Apparel Association Annual Conference Proceedings, 79*(1). 10.31274/itaa.16012

Brandão, A., & da Costa, A. G. (2021). Extending the theory of planned behaviour to understand the effects of barriers towards sustainable fashion consumption. *European Business Review*, *33*(5), 742–774. doi:10.1108/EBR-11-2020-0306

Brathwaite, K. N., & DeAndrea, D. C. (2022). BoPopriation: How self-promotion and corporate commodification can undermine the body positivity (BoPo) movement on Instagram. *Communication Monographs*, *89*(1), 25–46. doi:10.1080/03637751.2021.1925939

Bratu, S. (2019). Can social media influencers shape corporate brand reputation? Online followers' trust, value creation, and purchase intentions. *Review of Contemporary Philosophy*, *18*, 157–163.

Brems, C., Temmerman, M., Graham, T., & Broersma, M. (2016). Personal branding on Twitter. *Digital Journalism (Abingdon, England)*, *5*(4), 443–459. doi:10.1080/21670811.2016.1176534

Brett, E. I., Stevens, E. M., Wagener, T. L., Leavens, E. L. S., Morgan, T. L., Cotton, W. D., & Hébert, E. T. (2019). A content analysis of JUUL discussions on social media: Using Reddit to understand patterns and perceptions of JUUL use. *Drug and Alcohol Dependence*, *194*, 358–362. doi:10.1016/j.drugalcdep.2018.10.014 PMID:30472576

Brijnath, B., Croy, S., Sabatés, J., Thodis, A., Ellis, S., Crespigny, F., Moxey, A., Day, R., Dobson, A., Elliott, C., Etherington, C., Geronimo, M., Hlis, D., Lampit, A., Low, L., Straiton, N., & Temple, J. (2022). Including ethnic minorities in dementia research: Recommendations from a scoping review. *Alzheimer's & Dementia: Translational Research & Clinical Interventions*, *8*(1), e12222. Advance online publication. doi:10.1002/trc2.12222 PMID:35505899

Britt, R. K., Hayes, J. L., Britt, B. C., & Park, H. (2020). Too big to sell? A computational analysis of network and content characteristics among mega and micro beauty and fashion social media influencers. *Journal of Interactive Advertising*, *20*(2), 111–118. doi:10.1080/15252019.2020.1763873

Brodie, R. J., Hollebeek, L. D., Jurić, B., & Ilić, A. (2011). Customer engagement. *Journal of Service Research*, *14*(3), 252–271. doi:10.1177/1094670511411703

Brooks, G., Drenten, J., & Piskorski, M. J. (2021). Influencer celebrification: How social media influencers acquire celebrity capital. *Journal of Advertising*, *50*(5), 528–547. doi:10.1080/00913367.2021.1977737

Brown, D., & Hayes, N. (2008). *Influencer marketing*. Routledge. doi:10.4324/9780080557700

Browne, M. W., & Cudeck, R. (1992). Alternative ways of assessing model fit. *Sociological Methods & Research, 21*(2), 230–258. doi:10.1177/0049124192021002005

Brown, Z., & Tiggemann, M. (2020). A picture is worth a thousand words: The effect of viewing celebrity Instagram images with disclaimer and body positive captions on women's body image. *Body Image, 33*, 190–198. doi:10.1016/j.bodyim.2020.03.003 PMID:32289571

Brumbaugh, A. M. (1993). Physical attractiveness and personality in advertising: More than just a pretty face? In L. McAlister & M. L. Rothschild (Eds.), *Advances in consumer research* (Vol. 20, pp. 159–164). Association for Consumer Research.

Brun, A., & Karaosman, H. (2020). Sustainability in the Luxury Fashion Supply Chain: Millennials'. *Perception*, (37), 99–121. doi:10.3917/maorg.037.0099

Bueno, C. C. (2017). *The attention economy: Labour, time and power in cognitive capitalism.* Rowman & Littlefield International.

Bui, M. T., Tran, T. T. H., Phi, H. M., Nguyen, N. D., Nguyen, T. T. M., & Pham, T. L. (2021). Impact of digital celebrities on their followers' purchase intention: Roles of wishful identification, parasocial relationship, and behavioral loyalty. In *2nd International Conference on Human-Centered Artificial Intelligence, Computing4Human* (pp. 191-198). Academic Press.

Bullock, O. M., & Hubner, A. Y. (2020). Candidates' use of informal communication on social media reduces credibility and support: Examining the consequences of expectancy violations. *Communication Research Reports, 37*(3), 87–98. doi:10.1080/08824096.2020.1767047

Burchill, A. (2024, January). *Influencer marketing statistics to know in 2024.* Dash. Retrieved from: https://www.dash.app/blog/influencer-marketing-statistics#:~:text=65%25%20of%20influencers%20on%20Instagram,to%20work%20with%20content%20creators

Burgoon, J. K. (1978). A communication model of personal space violations: Explication and an initial test. *Human Communication Research, 4*(2), 129–142. doi:10.1111/j.1468-2958.1978.tb00603.x

Burgoon, J. K. (2015). Expectancy Violations Theory. In C. R. Berger, M. E. Roloff, S. R. Wilson, J. P. Dillard, J. Caughlin, & D. Solomon (Eds.), *The International Encyclopedia of Interpersonal Communication* (Vol. 26, pp. 1–9). John Wiley & Sons, Inc.

Burke, K. E. (2017). *Social butterflies: How social media influencers are the new celebrity endorsement* (Doctoral dissertation, Virginia Tech).

Burns, K. S. (2021). The history of social media influencers. *Research perspectives on social media influencers and brand communication*, 1-22.

Burton, J. L., Gollins, J., McNeely, L. E., & Walls, D. M. (2019). Revisiting the relationship between ad frequency and purchase intentions: How affect and cognition mediate outcomes at different levels of advertising frequency. *Journal of Advertising Research, 59*(1), 27–39. doi:10.2501/JAR-2018-031

Busalim, A., Fox, G., & Lynn, T. (2022). Consumer behavior in sustainable fashion: A systematic literature review and future research agenda. *International Journal of Consumer Studies, 46*(5), 1804-1828. https://onlinelibrary.wiley.com/doi/abs/10.1111/ijcs.12794?casa_token=Xy5riLZnn7kAAAAA:ajOjnJVLJOfs0blCneH69tqVmLfx7zxf75u1Oe-Y4bGxK5AK2p_YtnEo7MwT8QGX23TFelvgA9M0eis

Bush, V., Bush, A. J., Oakley, J., & Cicala, J. E. (2017). The Sales Profession as a Subculture: Implications for Ethical Decision Making. *Journal of Business Ethics, 142*(3), 549–565. doi:10.1007/s10551-015-2753-7

Caballero, M. J. (1989). Using physical attractiveness as an advertising tool: An empirical test of the attraction phenomenon. *Journal of Advertising Research, 29*(4), 16.

Caldeira, S. P., & De Ridder, S. (2017). Representing diverse femininities on Instagram: A case study of the body-positive@ effyourbeautystandards Instagram account. *Catalan Journal of Communication & Cultural Studies, 9*(2), 321–337. doi:10.1386/cjcs.9.2.321_1

Camiciottoli, C. B. (2015). All those Elvis-Meets-Golf-Player looks: A corpus-assisted analysis of creative compounds in fashion blogging. *Discourse, Context & Media, 12*, 77–86. doi:10.1016/j.dcm.2015.10.002

Campagna, C. L., Donthu, N., & Yoo, B. (2023). Brand authenticity: Literature review, comprehensive definition, and an amalgamated scale. *Journal of Marketing Theory and Practice, 31*(2), 129–145. doi:10.1080/10696679.2021.2018937

Campbell, A. T. (2012). Bioethics in the public square: Reflections on the how. *Journal of Medical Ethics, 38*(7), 439–441. doi:10.1136/medethics-2011-100057 PMID:22345555

Campbell, C., & Farrell, J. R. (2020). More than meets the eye: The functional components underlying influencer marketing. *Business Horizons, 63*(4), 469–479. doi:10.1016/j.bushor.2020.03.003

Campopiano, J. (2014). Memory, temporality, & manifestations of our tech-nostalgia. *Preservation. Digital Technology & Culture, 43*(3), 75–85. doi:10.1515/pdtc-2014-0004

Cao, D., Meadows, M., Wong, D., & Xia, S. (2021). Understanding consumers' social media engagement behaviour: An examination of the moderation effect of social media context. *Journal of Business Research, 122*, 835–846. doi:10.1016/j.jbusres.2020.06.025

Carpenter, J. P., Shelton, C. C., & Schroeder, S. E. (2022). The education influencer: Is a new player in the educator professional landscape. *Journal of Research on Technology in Education*, 1–16. https://www.tandfonline.com/doi/abs/10.1080/15391523.2022.2030267

Carrillat, F. A., & Ilicic, J. (2019). The celebrity capital life cycle: A framework for future research directions on celebrity endorsement. *Journal of Advertising, 48*(1), 61–71. doi:10.1080/00913367.2019.1579689

Carroll, B. A., & Ahuvia, A. C. (2006). Some antecedents and outcomes of brand love. *Marketing Letters, 17*(2), 79–89. doi:10.1007/s11002-006-4219-2

Castillo-Abdul, B., & Romero-Rodriguez, L. M. (2021). YouTubers as influencers in the responsible promotion and Happiness management of fashion brands. In *Happiness Management and Social Marketing: A Wave of Sustainability and Creativity* (pp. 189–206). Peter Lang AG.

Catteeuw, F., Flynn, E., & Vonderhorst, J. (2007). Employee engagement: Boosting productivity in turbulent times. *Organization Development Journal, 25*(2).

Chae, J. (2018). Explaining females' envy toward social media influencers. *Media Psychology, 21*(2), 246–262. doi:10.1080/15213269.2017.1328312

Chang, S., & Wu, J. (2023). A content-based metric for social media influencer marketing. *Industrial Management & Data Systems, 124*(1), 344–360. doi:10.1108/IMDS-05-2022-0303

Charon, J. (1992). *Sociology: A conceptual approach.* Allyn & Bacon.

Chaudhuri, A., & Holbrook, M. B. (2001). *Brand loyalty scale.* PsycTESTS Dataset. doi:10.1037/t11015-000

Chekima, B., Chekima, F. Z., & Adis, A. A. A. (2020). Social media influencer in advertising: The role of attractiveness, expertise and trustworthiness. *Journal of Economics and Business, 3*(4). Advance online publication. doi:10.31014/aior.1992.03.04.298

Cheng, Y. (2018). Looking back, moving forward: A review and reflection of the organization–public relationship (OPR) research. *Public Relations Review, 44*(1), 120–130. doi:10.1016/j.pubrev.2017.10.003

Cheng, Y., Wei, W., & Zhang, L. (2020). Seeing destinations through vlogs: Implications for leveraging customer engagement behavior to increase travel intention. *International Journal of Contemporary Hospitality Management, 32*(10), 3227–3248. doi:10.1108/IJCHM-04-2020-0319

Chen, H. (2018). College-aged young consumers' perceptions of social media marketing: The story of Instagram. *Journal of Current Issues and Research in Advertising, 39*(1), 22–36. doi:10.1080/10641734.2017.1372321

Chen, Y., Fay, S., & Wang, Q. (2011). The role of marketing in social media: How online consumer reviews evolve. *Journal of Interactive Marketing, 25*(2), 85–94. doi:10.1016/j.intmar.2011.01.003

Chen, Y.-L., Chang, C.-L., & Sung, A.-Q. (2021). Predicting eWOM's influence on purchase intention based on helpfulness, credibility, information quality and professionalism. *Sustainability (Basel), 13*(13), 7486. doi:10.3390/su13137486

Cheung, C. M. K., Lee, M. K. O., & Rabjohn, N. (2008). The impact of electronic word-of-mouth: The adoption of online opinions in online customer communities. *Internet Research, 18*(3), 229–247. doi:10.1108/10662240810883290

Childs, K. M. (2022). "the shade of it all": How Black women use Instagram and YouTube to contest colorism in the beauty industry. *Social Media + Society, 8*(2). doi:10.1177/20563051221107634

Chintalapati, S., & Pandey, S. K. (2022). Artificial intelligence in marketing: A systematic literature review. *International Journal of Market Research, 64*(1), 38–68. doi:10.1177/14707853211018428

Choi, Y. H., Yoon, S., Xuan, B., Lee, S. Y. T., & Lee, K. H. (2021). Fashion informatics of the Big 4Fashion Weeks using topic modeling and sentiment analysis. *Fashion and Textiles, 8*(1 C7 -33). doi:10.1186/s40691-021-00265-6

Choi, E. (2023). Brand integration, disclosure, and ethics in child-targeted YouTube videos: A content analysis. *Journal of Media Ethics: Exploring Questions of Media Morality, 38*(1), 34–47. doi:10.1080/23736992.2022.2158829

Choi, S., & Rifon, N. J. (2012). It is a match: The impact of congruence between celebrity image and consumer ideal self on endorsement effectiveness. *Psychology and Marketing, 29*(9), 639–650. doi:10.1002/mar.20550

Choi, W., & Lee, Y. (2019). Effects of fashion vlogger attributes on product attitude and content sharing. *Fashion and Textiles, 6*(1), 1–18. doi:10.1186/s40691-018-0161-1

Cho, J., & Park, D. (2013). Online celebrity endorsements and its potential impact on online purchase intention: The role of product type and celebrity fashion style. *Journal of Retailing and Consumer Services, 20*(4), 322–332.

Chopra, A., Avhad, V., & Jaju, A. S. (2021). Influencer marketing: An exploratory study to identify antecedents of consumer behaviour among millennials. *Business Perspectives and Research, 9*(1), 77–79. doi:10.1177/2278533720923486

Christel, D. A., & Dunn, S. C. (2017). Average American women's clothing size: Comparing national health and nutritional examination surveys (1988–2010) to ASTM international misses & women's plus size clothing. *International Journal of Fashion Design, Technology and Education, 10*(2), 129–136. doi:10.1080/17543266.2016.1214291

Chung, J., Ding, Y., & Kalra, A. (2023). I really know you: How influencers can increase audience engagement by referencing their close social ties. *The Journal of Consumer Research, 50*(4), 683–703. doi:10.1093/jcr/ucad019

Chung, S., & Cho, H. (2017). Fostering parasocial relationships with celebrities on social media: Implications for celebrity endorsement. *Psychology and Marketing*, *34*(4), 481–495. doi:10.1002/mar.21001

Chu, S.-C., & Kamal, S. (2008). The effect of perceived blogger credibility and argument quality on message elaboration and brand attitudes: An exploratory study. *Journal of Interactive Advertising*, *8*(2), 26–37. doi:10.1080/15252019.2008.10722140

Chu, S.-C., & Seock, Y.-K. (2020). The power of social media in fashion advertising. *Journal of Interactive Advertising*, *20*(2), 93–94. doi:10.1080/15252019.2020.1802955

Chwialkowska, A. (2019). How sustainability influencers drive green lifestyle adoption on social media: The process of green lifestyle adoption explained through the lenses of the minority influence model and social learning theory. *Management of Sustainable Development*, *11*(1), 33–42. doi:10.2478/msd-2019-0019

Cirucci, A. (2020). Facebook and Unintentional Celebrification. In C. Abidin & M. L. Brown (Eds.), *Microcelebrity Around the Globe: Approaches to cultures of internet fame* (pp. 33–47). Emerald Publishing Group.

Clark, T., Moorhead, R., Vaughan, S., & Brener, A. (2021). Agency over technocracy: how lawyer archetypes infect regulatory approaches: the FCA example. *Legal Ethics (Oxford, England)*, *24*(2), 91–110. doi:10.1080/1460728x.2022.2059742

Clauset, A., Newman, M. E. J., & Moore, C. (2004). Finding community structure in very large networks. *Physical Review. E*, *70*(6), 066111. doi:10.1103/PhysRevE.70.066111 PMID:15697438

Clayton, R. B., Ridgway, J. L., & Hendrickse, J. (2017). Is plus size equal? The positive impact of average and plus-sized media fashion models on women's cognitive resource allocation, social comparisons, and body satisfaction. *Communication Monographs*, *84*(3), 406–422. doi:10.1080/03637751.2017.1332770

Clendenen, V. I., Herman, C. P., & Policy, J. (1994). Social facilitation of eating among friends and strangers. *Appetite*, *23*(1), 1–13. doi:10.1006/appe.1994.1030 PMID:7826053

Clifton, S. (2021). Disability and the complexity of choice in the ethics of abortion and voluntary euthanasia. *The Journal of Medicine and Philosophy*, *46*(4), 431–450. doi:10.1093/jmp/jhab008 PMID:34219161

CloudFlare. (n.d.). *What is live streaming? How live streaming works.* https://www.cloudflare.com/learning/video/what-is-live-streaming/

Clover-Brown, I., Moore, B., Andrews, C. G., & Matheny Antommaria, A. H. (2023). Ethical Issues with Patient–Provider Interactions in an Evolving Social Media Landscape. *Pediatrics*, *151*(6C7 - e2022060066). doi:10.1542/peds.2022-060066

Clow, K. A., Ricciardelli, R., & Bartfay, W. J. (2014). Are you man enough to be a nurse? The impact of ambivalent sexism and role congruity on perceptions of men and women in nursing advertisements. *Sex Roles*, *72*(7-8), 363–376. doi:10.1007/s11199-014-0418-0

Clow, K., James, K., Kranenburg, K., & Berry, C. (2006). The relationship of the visual element of an advertisement to service quality expectations and source credibility. *Journal of Services Marketing*, *20*(6), 404–411. doi:10.1108/08876040610691293

Co Sy Su, C. (2018). The crossroads of plastination and pilgrimage. *Religions*, *9*(3 C7 - 87). doi:10.3390/rel9030087

Coates, A. E., Hardman, C. A., Halford, J. C. G., Christiansen, P., & Boyland, E. J. (2019). Food and beverage cues featured in youtube videos of social media influencers popular with children: An exploratory study. *Frontiers in Psychology*, *10*, 21–42. doi:10.3389/fpsyg.2019.02142 PMID:31616344

Cohen, R., Fardouly, J., Newton-John, T., & Slater, A. (2019). #BoPo on Instagram: An experimental investigation of the effects of viewing body positive content on young women's mood and body image. *New Media & Society*, *21*(7), 1546–1564. doi:10.1177/1461444819826530

Cohen, R., Irwin, L., Newton-John, T., & Slater, A. (2019). #bodypositivity: A content analysis of body positive accounts on Instagram. *Body Image*, *29*, 47–57. doi:10.1016/j.bodyim.2019.02.007 PMID:30831334

Colicev, A., Kumar, A., & O'Connor, P. (2019). Modeling the relationship between firm and user-generated content and the stages of the marketing funnel. *International Journal of Research in Marketing*, *36*(1), 100–116. doi:10.1016/j.ijresmar.2018.09.005

Collado-Alonso, R., Picazo-Sánchez, L., López-Pastor, A. T., & García-Matilla, A. (2023). What do social media teach? Influencers and followers in informal education in social media. *Revista Mediterrânea de Comunicacion*, *14*(2), 259–270. doi:10.14198/MEDCOM.23658

Collier, B., Flynn, G., Stewart, J., & Thomas, D. (2022). Influence government: Exploring practices, ethics, and power in the use of targeted advertising by the UK state. *Big Data & Society*, *9*(1). Advance online publication. doi:10.1177/20539517221078756

Conti, M., Gathani, J., & Tricomi, P. P. (2022). Virtual influencers in online social media. *IEEE Communications Magazine*, *60*(8), 86–91. doi:10.1109/MCOM.001.2100786

Convertino, A. D., Rodgers, R. F., Franko, D. L., & Jodoin, A. (2019). An evaluation of the *Aerie Real* campaign: Potential for promoting positive body image? *Journal of Health Psychology*, *24*(6), 726–737. doi:10.1177/1359105316680022 PMID:27888254

Cosseron, F. (2018). The consent at the child between judicial constraint and support in the current care liberal. *Neuropsychiatrie de l'Enfance et de l'Adolescence*, *66*(7-8), 438–442. doi:10.1016/j.neurenf.2018.04.006

Cota, A. A., & Xinaris, S. (1993). Factor structure of the sex-role ideology scale: Introducing a short form. *Sex Roles*, *29*(5-6), 345–358. doi:10.1007/BF00289428

Cramer, E. M., Song, H., & Drent, A. M. (2016). Social comparison on Facebook: Motivation, affective consequences, self-esteem, and Facebook fatigue. *Computers in Human Behavior*, *64*, 739–746. doi:10.1016/j.chb.2016.07.049

Crano, W., & Seyranian, V. (2007). Majority and Minority Influence. *Social and Personality Psychology Compass*, *1*(1), 572–589. doi:10.1111/j.1751-9004.2007.00028.x

Crnjak-Karanović, B., Milaković, I. K., & Elez, J. (2023). Which decision-making stages matter more? Influencer's perceived credibility, sponsorship and moderating role of trust. *Young Consumers*, *24*(6), 649–668. doi:10.1108/YC-08-2022-1590

Crunchbase. (2023). *Whatnot financials.* https://www.crunchbase.com/organization/Whatnot

Cummings, R., Huff, E., Mack, N., Womack, K., Reid, A., Ghoram, B., Gilbert, J., & Gosha, K. (2019). Vlog Commentary YouTube Influencers as Effective Advisors in College and Career Readiness for Minorities in Computing: An Exploratory Study. *2019 Research on Equity and Sustained Participation in Engineering, Computing, and Technology (RESPECT)*, 1-8. . doi:10.1109/RESPECT46404.2019.8985961

Curtis, B., Ashford, R., Magnuson, K., & Ryan-Pettes, S. (2019). Comparison of Smartphone Ownership, Social Media Use, and Willingness to Use Digital Interventions Between Generation Z and Millennials in the Treatment of Substance Use: Cross-Sectional Questionnaire Study. *Journal of Medical Internet Research*, *21*(4), e13050. Advance online publication. doi:10.2196/13050 PMID:30994464

Cwynar-Horta, J. (2016). The commodification of the body positive movement on Instagram. *Stream: Culture/Politics/Technology, 8*(2), 36-56.

Dabija, D. C., Bejan, B. M., & Dinu, V. (2019). How sustainability oriented is Generation Z in retail? A literature review. *Transformations in Business & Economics, 18*(2). Advance online publication. doi:10.3390/jrfm13070152

Dadia, H. (2022, October 15). *The evolution of influencer marketing industry in post-Covid Digital Era!* Times of India Blog. https://timesofindia.indiatimes.com/blogs/voices/the-evolution-of-influencer-marketing-industry-in-post-covid-digital-era/

Dahill, L. M., Morrison, N. M. V., Mannan, H., Mitchison, D., Touyz, S., Bussey, K., . . . Hay, P. (2022). Exploring associations between positive and negative valanced parental comments about adolescents' bodies and eating and eating problems: a community study. *Journal of Eating Disorders, 10*(1 C7 - 43). doi:10.1186/s40337-022-00561-6

Dahlquist, S., & Garver, M. (2022). Effects of Product and Product Company Information on Generation Zs' Purchasing Preferences. *American Business Review, 25*(1), 209–220. Advance online publication. doi:10.37625/abr.25.1.209-220

Dam, L., Basaran, A., & Burroughs, B. (2024). (Over)Eating with our eyes: An examination of Mukbang influencer marketing and consumer engagement with food brands. *Journal of Promotion Management, 30*(2), 227–251. doi:10.1080/10496491.2023.2253244

Dao, W. (2014). Social media advertising value: The case of transitional economies in Southeast Asia. *International Journal of Advertising, 33*(2), 271–294. doi:10.2501/IJA-33-2-271-294

Davies, C., & Hobbs, M. (2020). Irresistible possibilities: Examining the uses and consequences of social media influencers for contemporary public relations. *Public Relations Review, 46*(5C7 - 101983). doi:10.1016/j.pubrev.2020.101983

Davies, H., & Li, Z. (2020). Travel Frog: Traversing cultural borders with mobile games. *Convergence (London), 26*(5-6), 1194–1210. doi:10.1177/1354856519856619

Davis, S., Schrader, V., & Belcheir, M. J. (2012). Influencers of ethical beliefs and the impact on moral distress and conscientious objection. *Nursing Ethics, 19*(6), 738–749. doi:10.1177/0969733011423409 PMID:22736753

Davis, S., & Yi, J. (2022). Double tap, double trouble: Instagram, teachers, and profit. *E-Learning and Digital Media, 19*(3), 320–339. doi:10.1177/20427530211064706

Dawkins, N. (2011). Do-it-yourself: The precarious work and postfeminist politics of handmaking (in) Detroit. *Utopian Studies, 22*(2), 261–284. doi:10.5325/utopianstudies.22.2.0261

De Cicco, R., Silva, S. C., & Alparone, F. R. (2020). Millennials' attitude toward chatbots: an experimental study in a social relationship perspective. *International Journal of Retail & Distribution Management, 48*(11), 1213–1233. doi:10.1108/IJRDM-12-2019-0406

De Meulenaer, S., Dens, N., De Pelsmacker, P., & Eisend, M. (2019). How consumers' values influence responses to male and female gender role stereotyping in advertising. *International Journal of Advertising, 37*(6), 893–913. doi:10.1080/02650487.2017.1354657

De Pelsmacker, P., Diehl, S., Neijens, P., & Terlutter, R. (2023). Editorial: Perspectives on advancing the advertising field for academics and practitioners. Celebrating 40 years of the International Journal of Advertising. *International Journal of Advertising, 42*(1), 1–12. doi:10.1080/02650487.2022.2131279

De Veirman, M., Cauberghe, V., & Hudders, L. (2017). Marketing through Instagram influencers: The impact of number of followers and product divergence on brand attitude. *International Journal of Advertising, 36*(5), 798–828. doi:10.1080/02650487.2017.1348035

De Veirman, M., & Hudders, L. (2020). Disclosing sponsored Instagram posts: The role of material connection with the brand and message-sidedness when disclosing covert advertising. *International Journal of Advertising*, *39*(1), 94–130. doi:10.1080/02650487.2019.1575108

De Veirman, M., Hudders, L., & Nelson, M. R. (2019). What is influencer marketing and how does it target children? A review and direction for future research. *Frontiers in Psychology*, *10*, 2685. doi:10.3389/fpsyg.2019.02685 PMID:31849783

De Vries, N. J., & Carlson, J. (2014). Examining the drivers and brand performance implications of customer engagement with brands in the social media environment. *Journal of Brand Management*, *21*(6), 495–515. doi:10.1057/bm.2014.18

Deci, E. L., & Ryan, R. M. (2000). The "what" and "why" of goal pursuits: Human needs and the self-determination of behavior. *Psychological Inquiry*, *11*(4), 227–268. doi:10.1207/S15327965PLI1104_01

Degen, J. L. (2023). Rationalizing fiction cues: Psychological effects of disclosing ads and the inaccuracy of the human mind when being in parasocial relationships. *Informing Science*, *26*, 85–101. doi:10.28945/5108

Delbaere, M., Michael, B., & Phillips, B. J. (2021). Social media influencers: A route to brand engagement for their followers. *Psychology and Marketing*, *38*(1), 101–112. doi:10.1002/mar.21419

Delgado-Ballester, E., & Munuera-Alemén, J. L. (2001). Brand trust in the context of consumer loyalty. *European Journal of Marketing*, *35*(11/12), 1238–1258. doi:10.1108/EUM0000000006475

Deloitte Analysis. (2023, February). *The rise of social commerce: A growth opportunity for brands.* https://www2.deloitte.com/content/dam/Deloitte/nl/Documents/deloitte-nl-consumer-the-rise-of-social-commerce.pdf

Deloria, R., & Wolbring, G. (2019). Neuro-advancements and the role of nurses as stated in academic literature and Canadian newspapers. *Societies, 9*(3 C7 - 61). doi:10.3390/soc9030061

Dencheva, V. (2023). *Influencer marketing –worldwide—statistics & facts*. Statista. Available at: https://www.statista.com/topics/2496/influence-marketing/#topicOverview

Dencheva, V. (2023a, December). *Topic: Influencer marketing worldwide*. Statista. https://www.statista.com/topics/2496/influence-marketing/

Dencheva, V. (2023b, December 18). *Influencer marketing worldwide - statistics & facts*. Statista. https://www.statista.com/topics/2496/influence-marketing/#topicOverview

Desa, I. S., Noviana, P., Yuniarsih, R. E., Farhana, Y., & Hasanah, N. (2023, May). Circular Economy: The Challenges and Opportunity in Fashion Recycling. In *Proceedings of the Business Innovation and Engineering Conference (BIEC 2022)* (*Vol. 236*, p. 204). Springer Nature. 10.2991/978-94-6463-144-9_20

Deshpandé, R., & Stayman, D. (1994). A tale of two cities: Distinctiveness theory and advertising effectiveness. *JMR, Journal of Marketing Research*, *31*(1), 57–64. doi:10.1177/002224379403100105

Dessart, L., Veloutsou, C., & Morgan-Thomas, A. (2016). Capturing consumer engagement: Duality, dimensionality, and measurement. *Journal of Marketing Management*, *32*(5-6), 399–426. doi:10.1080/0267257X.2015.1130738

Devos, S., Eggermont, S., & Vandenbosch, L. (2022). Instagram influencers as superwomen: Influencers' lifestyle presentations observed through framing analysis. *Media and Communication*, *10*(1), 173–184. doi:10.17645/mac.v10i1.4717

Dhanesh, G. S. (2017). Putting engagement in its PRoper place: State of the field, definition and model of engagement in public relations. *Public Relations Review*, *43*(5), 925–933. doi:10.1016/j.pubrev.2017.04.001

Dhanesh, G. S., & Duthler, G. (2019). Relationship management through social media influencers: Effects of followers' awareness of paid endorsement. *Public Relations Review*, *45*(3), 101765. doi:10.1016/j.pubrev.2019.03.002

Dhanesh, G., Duthler, G., & Li, K. (2022). Social media engagement with organization-generated content: Role of visuals in enhancing public engagement with organizations on Facebook and Instagram. *Public Relations Review*, *48*(2), 102174. Advance online publication. doi:10.1016/j.pubrev.2022.102174

Dhiman, R., Chand, P. K., & Gupta, S. (2018). Behavioural aspects influencing decision to purchase apparels amongst young Indian consumers. *FIIB Business Review*, *7*(3), 188–200. doi:10.1177/2319714518790308

Dibble, J. L., Hartmann, T., & Rosaen, S. F. (2016). Parasocial interaction and parasocial relationship: Conceptual clarification and a critical assessment of measures. *Human Communication Research*, *42*(1), 21–44. doi:10.1111/hcre.12063

Diekman, A. B., & Goodfriend, W. (2006). Rolling with the changes: A role congruity perspective on gender norms. *Psychology of Women Quarterly*, *30*(4), 369–383. doi:10.1111/j.1471-6402.2006.00312.x

Dimofte, C. V., Forehand, M. R., & Deshpande, R. (2003). Ad schema incongruity as elicitor of ethnic self-awareness and differential advertising response. *Journal of Advertising*, *32*(4), 7–17. doi:10.1080/00913367.2003.10639142

Dittmar, H., & Howard, S. (2004). Professional hazards? The impact of models' body size on advertising effectiveness and women's body-focused anxiety in professions that do and do not emphasize the cultural ideal of thinness. *British Journal of Social Psychology*, *43*(4), 477–497. doi:10.1348/0144666042565407 PMID:15601505

Dixon, S. J. (2023, Aug 29). Number of social media users worldwide from 2017 to 2027. *Statista*. https://www.statista.com/statistics/278414/number-of-worldwide-social-network-users/

Dixon, S. J. (2023, August 25). *Instagram: distribution of global audiences 2023, by age group*. Statista. https://www.statista.com/statistics/325587/instagram-global-age-group/

Djafarova, E., & Foots, S. (2022). Exploring ethical consumption of generation Z: Theory of planned behaviour. *Young Consumers*, *23*(3), 413–431. doi:10.1108/YC-10-2021-1405

Djafarova, E., & Rushworth, C. (2017). Exploring the credibility of online celebrities' Instagram profiles in influencing the purchase decisions of young female users. *Computers in Human Behavior*, *68*, 1–7. doi:10.1016/j.chb.2016.11.009

Dodd, M. D. (2016). Intangible resource management: Social capital theory development for public relations. *Journal of Communication Management (London)*, *20*(4), 289–311. doi:10.1108/JCOM-12-2015-0095

Dombrowski, S. U., Sniehotta, F. F., Avenell, A., Johnston, M., MacLennan, G., & Araújo-Soares, V. (2012). Identifying active ingredients in complex behavioural interventions for obese adults with obesity-related co-morbidities or additional risk factors for co-morbidities: A systematic review. *Health Psychology Review*, *6*(1), 7–32. doi:10.1080/17437199.2010.513298

Domingues Aguiar, T., & van Reijmersdal, E. (2018). *Influencer marketing. Amsterdam Stichting Wetenschappelijk Onderzoek Commerciële Communicatie*. SWOCC.

Domínguez, M. F. O., & Bhatti, Y. A. (2022). From Waste to Luxury Fashion at Elvis & Kresse: A Business Model for Sustainable and Social Innovation in the Circular Economy. *Sustainability (Basel)*, *14*(19), 11805. doi:10.3390/su141911805

Donthu, N., Kumar, S., Mukherjee, D., Pandey, N., & Lim, W. M. (2021). How to conduct a bibliometric analysis: An overview and guidelines. *Journal of Business Research*, *133*, 285–296. doi:10.1016/j.jbusres.2021.04.070

Dousay, T. A., Wolf, L. G., Green, L. S., & Asino, T. (2018, March). Rise of the "Teacher Influencers": Examining the benefits and conundrums. In *Society for Information Technology & Teacher Education International Conference* (pp. 1031-1033). Association for the Advancement of Computing in Education (AACE).

Downer, J. T., Rimm-Kaufman, S. E., & Pianta, R. C. (2007). How do classroom conditions and children's risk for school problems contribute to children's behavioral engagement in learning? *School Psychology Review, 36*(3), 413–432. doi:10.1080/02796015.2007.12087938

Driver, R. (2018). *Instagram reigns supreme for fashion and beauty influencers*. Fashionnetwork.com. https://us.fashionnetwork.com/news/instagram-reigns-supreme-for-fashion-and-beauty-influencers,942744.html

Droz-dit-Busset, O. (2022). "So-called influencers": Stance taking and (de)legitimation in mediatized discourse about social media influencers. *Discourse, Context & Media, 49*, C7–C100629. doi:10.1016/j.dcm.2022.100629

Druckman, J. N. (2001). The Implications of Framing Effects for Citizen Competence. *Political Behavior, 23*(3), 225–256. doi:10.1023/A:1015006907312

Dubrofsky, R. E., & Ryalls, E. D. (2014). The Hunger Games: Performing not-performing to authenticate femininity and whiteness. *Critical Studies in Media Communication, 31*(5), 395–409. doi:10.1080/15295036.2013.874038

Duckworth, A. L., & Gross, J. J. (2020). Behavior change. *Organizational Behavior and Human Decision Processes, 161*, 39–49. doi:10.1016/j.obhdp.2020.09.002 PMID:33716396

Ducoffe, R. H. (1996). Advertising value and advertising on the web. *Journal of Advertising Research, 36*(5), 21–35. https://link.gale.com/apps/doc/A76914157/AONE?u=anon~4e336c6a&sid=googleScholar&xid=c32e5dbb

Duffy, B. (2015). The Romance of work: Gender and aspirational labour in the digital culture industries. *International Journal of Cultural Studies, 19*(4), 441–457. doi:10.1177/1367877915572186

Duffy, B. E. (2013). *Remake, remodel: Women's magazines in the digital age*. University of Illinois Press. doi:10.5406/illinois/9780252037962.001.0001

Duffy, B. E. (2017). *Not Getting Paid to Do What You Love: Gender, Social Media, and Aspirational Work*. Yale University Press. doi:10.12987/yale/9780300218176.001.0001

Duffy, B. E., & Wissinger, E. (2017). Mythologies of Creative Work in the Social Media Age: Fun, Free, and "Just Being Me.". *International Journal of Communication*, 11.

Dugdale, L. S., & Braswell, H. (2021). Instacash: The ethics of leveraging medical student status on social media. *Academic Medicine, 96*(4), 507–511. doi:10.1097/ACM.0000000000003885 PMID:33298692

Dumont, G., & Ots, M. (2020). Social dynamics and stakeholder relationships in personal branding. *Journal of Business Research, 106*, 118–128. doi:10.1016/j.jbusres.2019.09.013

Dwivedi, A., & Johnson, L. (2013). Trust–Commitment as a mediator of the celebrity endorser–brand equity relationship in a service context. *Australasian Marketing Journal, 21*(1), 36–42. doi:10.1016/j.ausmj.2012.10.001

Eagly, A. H., & Wood, W. (2012). Social role theory. Handbook of Theories of Social Psychology, 2, 458–476. doi:10.4135/9781446249222.n49

Eagly, A. H. (2004). Prejudice: Toward a more inclusive understanding. In A. H. Eagly, R. M. Baron, & V. L. Hamilton (Eds.), *The social psychology of group identity and social conflict: Theory, application, and practice* (pp. 45–64). doi:10.1037/10683-003

Eagly, A. H., Ashmore, R. D., Makhijani, M. G., & Longo, L. C. (1991). What is beautiful is good, but…: A meta-analytic review of research on the physical attractiveness stereotype. *Psychological Bulletin, 110*(1), 109–128. doi:10.1037/0033-2909.110.1.109

Eagly, A. H., & Karau, S. J. (2002). Role congruity theory of prejudice toward female leaders. *Psychological Review, 109*(3), 573–598. doi:10.1037/0033-295X.109.3.573 PMID:12088246

Ebert, I., & Sindermann, D. (2020). An ethical view on influencer marketing - dynamic interaction between individual and economy or a simple data-driven advertising model? In *The Regulation of Social Media Influencers* (pp. 74–97). Edward Elgar Publishing Ltd. doi:10.4337/9781788978286.00012

Ehlers, K. (2021, June 2). *Micro-influencers: When smaller is better*. Forbes. https://www.forbes.com/sites/forbesagencycouncil/2021/06/02/micro-influencers-when-smaller-is-better/?sh=2795a40b539b

Eigenraam, A. W. (2023). *Customer Engagement: Studies on Building Authentic Engagement Experiences in Online Evironments* [PhD-Thesis - Research and graduation internal, Vrije Universiteit Amsterdam]. doi:10.5463/thesis.79

Eike, R., Irick, E., McKinney, E., Zhang, L., & Sanders, E. (2020). Repurposing design process. In Sustainability in the Textile and Apparel Industries: Sustainable Textiles, Clothing Design, and Repurposing (pp. 189-239). doi:10.1007/978-3-030-37929-2_9

Eisend, M., & Langner, T. (2010). Immediate and delayed advertising effects of celebrity endorsers' attractiveness and expertise. *International Journal of Advertising, 29*(4), 527–546. doi:10.2501/S0265048710201336

El Kheir, D. Y. M., Alnufaili, S. S., Alsaffar, R. M., Assad, M. A., & Alkhalifah, Z. Z. (2022). Physicians' Perspective of Telemedicine Regulating Guidelines and Ethical Aspects: A Saudi Experience. *International Journal of Telemedicine and Applications, 2022*, C7–C5068998. doi:10.1155/2022/5068998 PMID:36278028

El-Deeb, S. (2022, December). Computer-generated imagery influencer marketing—which ends of the continuum will prevail? humans or avatars? In *International Conference on Marketing and Technologies* (pp. 3-15). Singapore: Springer Nature Singapore.

Ellison, N. B., Steinfield, C., & Lampe, C. (2007). The benefits of Facebook "friends:" Social capital and college students' use of online social network sites. *Journal of Computer-Mediated Communication, 12*(4), 1143–1168. doi:10.1111/j.1083-6101.2007.00367.x

Engati. (2020). *What is engagement rate?* Retrieved from https://www.engati.com/glossary/engagement-rate

Enke, N., & Borchers, N. S. (2021). Social media influencers in strategic communication: A conceptual framework for strategic social media influencer communication. In *Social media influencers in strategic communication* (pp. 7-23). Routledge. https://www.cmgt.uni-leipzig.de/projekte/influencer/, May 20, 2019.

Ensaff, H. (2021). A nudge in the right direction: The role of food choice architecture in changing populations' diets. *The Proceedings of the Nutrition Society, 80*(2), 195–206. doi:10.1017/S0029665120007983 PMID:33446288

Entrupy. (2023). *Luxury retailers.* https://www.entrupy.com/luxury-reinfluencers/

Erdogan, B. Z. (1999). Celebrity endorsement: A literature review. *Journal of Marketing Management, 15*(4), 291–314. doi:10.1362/026725799784870379

Erz, A., & Heeris Christensen, A.-B. (2018). Transforming consumers into brands: Tracing transformation processes of the practice of blogging. *Journal of Interactive Marketing, 43*, 69–82. doi:10.1016/j.intmar.2017.12.002

Eskandari, F., Lake, A. A., & Butler, M. (2022). COVID-19 pandemic and food poverty conversations: Social network analysis of Twitter data. *Nutrition Bulletin, 47*(1), 93–105. doi:10.1111/nbu.12547 PMID:36045084

Etheredge, H. R., Early, J., Norval, D., & Fabian, J. (2021). Influencer marketing by healthcare providers-Ethics and the law. *Aesthetic Medicine, 7*(4), 45–51.

Evans, M. (1989). Consumer behaviour towards fashion. *European Journal of Marketing*, *23*(7), 7–16. doi:10.1108/EUM0000000000575

Evans, N., Phua, J., Lim, J. I., & Jun, H. (2017). Disclosing Instagram Influencer advertising: The effects of disclosure language on advertising recognition, attitudes, and behavioral intent. *Journal of Interactive Advertising*, *17*(2), 138–149. doi:10.1080/15252019.2017.1366885

Everett, Y., Martin, C. G., & Zalewski, M. (2021). A Systematic Review Focusing on Psychotherapeutic Interventions that Impact Parental Psychopathology, Child Psychopathology and Parenting Behavior. *Clinical Child and Family Psychology Review*, *24*(3), 579–598. doi:10.1007/s10567-021-00355-3 PMID:34254219

Fakazis, E., & Fürsich, E. (2023). Introduction: from the racist sandwich to civil eats: how food journalism and media are engaging with politics. *The Political Relevance of Food Media and Journalism: Beyond Reviews and Recipes*, 1-16. doi:10.4324/9781003283942-1

Faliagka, E., Ramantas, K., Rigou, M., & Sirmakessis, S. (2018). Measuring personal branding in social media: Towards an influence indication score. In I. Garrigós & M. Wimmer (Eds.), *Current trends in web engineering*. Springer. doi:10.1007/978-3-319-74433-9_23

Fan, K. L., Economides, J. M., & Song, D. H. (2019). To bot or not? Challenging the top social media influencers in #plasticsurgery. *Plastic and Reconstructive Surgery*, *143*(1), 337–343. doi:10.1097/PRS.0000000000005103 PMID:30589813

Fardouly, J., & Vartanian, L. R. (2015). Negative comparisons about one's appearance mediate the relationship between Facebook usage and body image concerns. *Body Image*, *12*, 82–88. doi:10.1016/j.bodyim.2014.10.004 PMID:25462886

Fashion e-commerce worldwide - statistics & facts . (2023, December) https://www.statista.com/topics/9288/fashion-e-commerce-worldwide

Fashion eCommerce: market data & analysis. (2023, August) https://www.statista.com/study/38340/ecommerce-report-fashion

Favre, J., Germond, T., Clavert, P., Collin, P., Michelet, A., & Lädermann, A. (2020). Want a betterh-index? – All you need to know about copyright and open access. *Revue de Chirurgie Orthopédique et Traumatologique*, *106*(8), 930–936. doi:10.1016/j.rcot.2020.10.008

Fay, B., & Larkin, R. (2017). Why online word-of-mouth measures cannot predict brand outcomes offline: Volume, sentiment, sharing, and influence metrics yield scant online–offline WOM correlations. *Journal of Advertising Research*, *57*(2), 132–143. doi:10.2501/JAR-2017-021

Fedeli, G., & Cheng, M. (2023). Influencer marketing and tourism: Another threat tointegrity for the industry? *Tourism Analysis*, *28*(2), 323–328. doi:10.3727/108354222X16510114086370

Feedspot. (2023). *Top 100 pet influencers*. Available at: https://influencers.feedspot.com/pet_instagram_influencers/

Feilitzen, C., & Linne, O. (1975). Identifying with television characters. *Journal of Communication*, *24*(4), 51–55. doi:10.1111/j.1460-2466.1975.tb00638.x PMID:1176636

Ferraro, C., Sands, S., Zubcevic-Basic, N., & Campbell, C. (2024). Diversity in the digital age: How consumers respond to diverse virtual influencers. *International Journal of Advertising*, 1–23. Advance online publication. doi:10.1080/02650487.2023.2300927

Fiallos, A., & Figueroa, S. (2023, April). Detection of Educational Influencers and Communities on TikTok. In *2023 Ninth International Conference on eDemocracy & eGovernment (ICEDEG)* (pp. 1-6). IEEE. 10.1109/ICEDEG58167.2023.10122011

Filho, B., Tritany, É., & Struchiner, C. (2022). Theoretical report: Reflections and considerations for authors, reviewers, and editors. *Revista de Saude Publica, 56*. Advance online publication. doi:10.11606/s1518-8787.2022056003766 PMID:35476108

Filieri, R., Lin, Z., Pino, G., Alguezaui, S., & Inversini, A. (2021). The role of visual cues in eWOM on consumers' behavioral intentions and decisions. *Journal of Business Research, 135*, 663–675. doi:10.1016/j.jbusres.2021.06.055

Fioravanti, G., Bocci Benucci, S., Ceragioli, G., & Casale, S. (2022). How the exposure to beauty ideals on social networking sites influences body image: A systematic review of experimental studies. *Adolescent Research Review, 7*(3), 419–458. doi:10.1007/s40894-022-00179-4

Fischer, E., & Guzel, G. T. (2023). The case for qualitative research. *Journal of Consumer Psychology, 33*(1), 259–272. doi:10.1002/jcpy.1300

Fischer, E., & Reuber, A. R. (2011). Social interaction via new social media: How can interactions on Twitter affect effectual thinking and behavior? *Journal of Business Venturing, 26*(1), 1–18. doi:10.1016/j.jbusvent.2010.09.002

Forbes. (2019, April 2). *Taking a stand on authenticity in influencer marketing*. Forbes Media LLC. Retrieved from https://www.forbes.com/sites/forbesagencycouncil/2019/03/29/taking-a-stand-on-authenticity-in-influencer-marketing/#3abc5a6c7270

Forbes. (2021). *Gen Z is emerging as the sustainability generation*. https://www.forbes.com/

Forbes. (2021, March 25). 16 Inspiring ways to build a community on social media. *Forbes*. https://www.forbes.com/sites/forbescommunicationscouncil/2021/03/25/16-inspiring-ways-to-build-a-community-on-social-media/?sh=46770f7f30b9

Forbes. (2022). *Gen Z and Sustainability: The Disruption Has Only Just Begun*. https://www.forbes.com/

Forsythe, S., Butler, S. M., & Kim, M. S. (1991). Fashion Adoption: Theory and Pragmatics. *Clothing & Textiles Research Journal, 9*(4), 8–15. doi:10.1177/0887302X9100900402

Fournier, S. (1998). Consumers and their brands: Developing relationship theory in consumer research. *The Journal of Consumer Research, 24*(4), 343–373. doi:10.1086/209515

Fournier, S., & Avery, J. (2011). The uninvited brand. *Business Horizons, 54*(3), 193–207. doi:10.1016/j.bushor.2011.01.001

Fownes, J. R., Yu, C., & Margolin, D. B. (2018). Twitter and climate change. *Sociology Compass, 12*(6), e12587. Advance online publication. doi:10.1111/soc4.12587

Foxwell, B. (2020). A Guide to Social Media Influencers: Mega, Macro, Micro, and Nano. *Iconosquare*. https://blog.iconosquare.com/guide-to-social-media-influencers/

Freberg, K. (2022). *Social media for strategic communication: Creative strategies and research-based applications*. Sage Publications.

Freberg, K., Graham, K., McGaughey, K., & Freberg, L. A. (2011). Who are the social media influencers? A study of public perceptions of personality. *Public Relations Review, 37*(1), 90–92. doi:10.1016/j.pubrev.2010.11.001

Frederick, D. A., Daniels, E. A., Bates, M. E., & Tylka, T. L. (2017). Exposure to thin-ideal media affect most, but not all, women: Results from the Perceived Effects of Media Exposure Scale and open-ended responses. *Body Image, 23*, 188–205. doi:10.1016/j.bodyim.2017.10.006 PMID:29132044

Freelon, D., McIlwain, C., & Clark, M. (2018). Quantifying the power and consequences of social media protest. *New Media & Society, 20*(3), 990–1011. doi:10.1177/1461444816676646

Fryar, C. D., Kruszon-Moran, D., Gu, Q., & Ogden, C. L. (2018, December 20). *Mean body weight, waist circumference, and body mass index among adults: United States, 1999-2000 through 2015-2016*. Centers for Disease Control and Prevention. https://www.cdc.gov/nchs/data/nhsr/nhsr122-508.pdf

Fuchs, C. (2014). Social Media and the Public Sphere. *tripleC: Communication, Capitalism & Critique. Open Access Journal for a Global Sustainable Information Society*, *12*(1), 57–101. https://doi.org/https://triple-c.at/index.php/tripleC/article/view/552

Fuchs, C. (2013). Digital prosumption labour on social media in the context of the capitalist regime of time. *Time & Society*, *23*(1), 97–123. doi:10.1177/0961463X13502117

Gagne, N., & Maini, S. (2022, October 29). *Whatnot*. Contrary Research. https://research.contrary.com/reports/Whatnot

Gannon, V., & Prothero, A. (2016). Beauty blogger selfies as authenticating practices. *European Journal of Marketing*, *50*(9/10), 1858–1878. doi:10.1108/EJM-07-2015-0510

Gao, X. (2023). *Wearing pineapple leaves?: Consumer responses to fashion products made from repurposed materials* (Doctoral dissertation, Wageningen University).

Garcés, P. (2022). Pragmatic Behaviour: Pragmatism as a philosophy for behavioural economics. *Journal of Philosophical Economics*, *15*(Articles). doi:10.46298/jpe.8741

García-Rapp, F. (2017). 'Come join and let's BOND': Authenticity and legitimacy building on YouTube's beauty community. *Journal of Media Practice*, *18*(2–3), 120–137. doi:10.1080/14682753.2017.1374693

Garcia-Torres, S., Rey-Garcia, M., Sáenz, J., & Seuring, S. (2022). Traceability and transparency for sustainable fashion-apparel supply chains. *Journal of Fashion Marketing and Management*, *26*(2), 344–364. doi:10.1108/JFMM-07-2020-0125

Gassas, R., & Salem, O. (2022). Factors affecting nurses' professional values: A comprehensive integrative review. *Nurse Education Today*, *118*, C7–C105515. doi:10.1016/j.nedt.2022.105515 PMID:36030580

Geegamage, T., Ranaweera, A., & Halwatura, R. (2021). *Second-Hand Fashion Consumption: A Literature Review*. In The ERU Symposium 2021. 10.31705/ERU.2021.6

Gereffi, G. (1999). International Trade and industrial upgrading in the apparel commodity chain. *Journal of International Economics*, *48*(1), 37–70. doi:10.1016/S0022-1996(98)00075-0

Gerlich, M. (2023). The Power of Virtual Influencers: Impact on Consumer Behaviour and Attitudes in the Age of AI. *Administrative Sciences*, *13*(8), 178. doi:10.3390/admsci13080178

Getting closer: Influencers help brands build more personal consumer connections. (May 2022). Nielsen. https://www.nielsen.com/insights/2022/getting-closer-influencers-help-brands-build-more-personal-consumer-connections/

Geyser, W. (2021). *The state of influencer marketing 2021*. Benchmark report. Influencer Marketing (Influencer Marketing Hub). https://influencermarketinghub.com/influ encer-marketing-benchmark-report-2021/

Geyser, W. (2022). *TikTok statistics – 63 TikTok stats you need to know* [2022 Update]. Influencer Marketing Hub. https://influencermarketinghub.com/tiktok-stats/

Ghosh, M. (2021). Product placement by social media homefluencers during new normal. *South Asian Journal of Marketing*, *3*(1), 21–37. doi:10.1108/SAJM-05-2021-0069

Ghosh, M., & Islam, A. S. (2023). Homefluencers' endorsement of millennial consumers' purchase intention in new normal. *International Marketing Review*, *40*(5), 1188–1212. doi:10.1108/IMR-10-2021-0308

Giles, D. C. (2002). Parasocial interaction: A review of the literature and a model for future research. *Media Psychology, 4*(3), 279–305. doi:10.1207/S1532785XMEP0403_04

Giles, D. C. (2017). How do fan and celebrity identities become established on Twitter? A study of 'social media natives' and their followers. *Celebrity Studies, 8*(3), 445–460. doi:10.1080/19392397.2017.1305911

Gillespie, E. (2019). The Instagram influencers hired to rehabilitate Saudi Arabia's image. *The Guardian*. https://www.theguardian.com/

Gill, J. D., Grossbart, S., & Laczniak, R. N. (1988). Influence of involvement, commitment and familiarity on brand beliefs and attitudes of viewers exposed to alternative claim strategies. *Journal of Advertising, 17*(2), 33–43. doi:10.1080/00913367.1988.10673111

Gill, R. (2023). *Perfect: Feeling judged on social media*. Polity Press.

Gill, R., & Pratt, A. (2008). In The Social Factory?: Immaterial Labour, Precariousness and Cultural Work. *Theory, Culture & Society, 25*(7-8), 1–30. doi:10.1177/0263276408097794

Gil-Quintana, J., & Vida de León, E. (2021). Educational influencers on Instagram: Analysis of educational channels, audiences, and economic performance. *Publications / MDPI, 9*(4), 43. doi:10.3390/publications9040043

Girgis, I. (2022). *Nudging sustainable fashion: how behavioural economics influence consumers pro-environmental clothing shopping online* (Bachelor's thesis, University of Malta). OAR@UM.

Gisondi, M. A., Barber, R., Faust, J. S., Raja, A., Strehlow, M. C., Westafer, L. M., & Gottlieb, M. (2022). A Deadly Infodemic: Social Media and the Power of COVID-19 Misinformation. Journal *of Medical Internet Research, 24*(2 C7 - e35552). doi:10.2196/35552

Goanta, C., & Ranchordás, S. (2020). The regulation of social media influencers: an introduction. In *The Regulation of Social Media Influencers*. Edward Elgar Publishing. doi:10.4337/9781788978286.00008

Goldsmith, R. E., & Clark, R. A. (2008). An analysis of factors affecting fashion opinion leadership and fashion opinion seeking. *Journal of Fashion Marketing and Management, 12*(3), 308–322. doi:10.1108/13612020810889272

Goldsmith, R. E., & Flynn, L. R. (1992). Identifying innovators in consumer product markets. *European Journal of Marketing, 26*(12), 42–55. doi:10.1108/03090569210022498

Goldsmith, R. E., Lafferty, B. A., & Newell, S. J. (2000). The impact of corporate credibility and celebrity credibility on consumer reaction to advertisements and brands. *Journal of Advertising, 29*(3), 43–54. doi:10.1080/00913367.2000.10673616

Gómez, A. R. (2019). Digital fame and fortune in the age of social media: A Classification of social media influencers. *aDResearch. Revista Internacional de Investigación en Comunicación, 19*(19), 8–29. doi:10.7263/adresic-019-01

Gonçalves, A., & Silva, C. (2021). Looking for sustainability scoring in apparel: A review on environmental footprint, social impacts and transparency. *Energies, 14*(11), 3032. doi:10.3390/en14113032

Gong, W., & Li, X. (2017). Engaging fans on microblog: The synthetic influence of parasocial interaction and source characteristics on celebrity endorsement. *Psychology and Marketing, 34*(7), 720–732. doi:10.1002/mar.21018

Gorodishchev, A. V., Gorodishcheva, A. N., & Kovalev, G. P. (2023). Digital influencer factory: the price of word authority. *Proceedings of the 2023 Communication Strategies in Digital Society Seminar 2023, ComSDS 2023*. 10.1109/ComSDS58064.2023.10130358

Grabe, S., Ward, L. M., & Hyde, J. S. (2008). The role of the media in body image concerns among women: A meta-analysis of experimental and correlational studies. *Psychological Bulletin, 134*(3), 460–476. doi:10.1037/0033-2909.134.3.460 PMID:18444705

Gräve, J.-F. (2017). Exploring the perception of influencers vs. Traditional celebrities: Are social media stars a new type of endorser? *Proceedings of the 8th International Conference on Social Media & Society - #SMSociety17.*

Gräve, J. F., & Bartsch, F. (2022). # Instafame: Exploring the endorsement effectiveness of influencers compared to celebrities. *International Journal of Advertising, 41*(4), 591–622. doi:10.1080/02650487.2021.1987041

Griffin, R. J., Neuwirth, K., Giese, J., & Dunwoody, S. (2002). Linking the heuristic-systematic model and depth of processing. *Communication Research, 29*(6), 705–732. doi:10.1177/009365002237833

Grönroos, C. (1997). Keynote paper From marketing mix to relationship marketing-towards a paradigm shift in marketing. *Management Decision, 35*(4), 322–339. doi:10.1108/00251749710169729

Grubb, E., & Grathwohl, H. (1967). Consumer self-concept, symbolism and market behavior: A theoretical approach. *Journal of Marketing, 31*(4), 22–27. doi:10.1177/002224296703100405

Grunig, J. E. (2006). Furnishing the edifice: Ongoing research on public relations as a strategic management function. *Journal of Public Relations Research, 18*(2), 151–176. doi:10.1207/s1532754xjprr1802_5

Guo, Q., Liu, Z., Li, X., & Qiao, X. (2018). Indulgence and long term orientation influence prosocial behavior at national level. *Frontiers in Psychology, 9*, 9. doi:10.3389/fpsyg.2018.01798 PMID:30319499

Gupta, N., Dorfman, R., Saadat, S., & Roostaeian, J. (2020). The plastic surgery social media influencer: Ethical considerations and a literature review. *Aesthetic Surgery Journal, 40*(6), 691–699. doi:10.1093/asj/sjz329 PMID:31738821

Gupta, V., Hanges, P. J., & Dorfman, P. (2002). Cultural clusters: Methodology and findings. *Journal of World Business, 37*(1), 11–15. doi:10.1016/S1090-9516(01)00070-0

Guthrie, J. P. (2001). High-involvement work practices, turnover, and productivity: Evidence from New Zealand. *Academy of Management Journal, 44*(1), 180–190. doi:10.2307/3069345

Guthrie, J. T., & Cox, K. E. (2001). Classroom conditions for motivation and engagement in reading. *Educational Psychology Review, 13*(3), 283–302. doi:10.1023/A:1016627907001

Ha, L. (2017). Social media advertising and eWOM from 2011 to present. *Journal of Advertising*. http://explore.tandfonline.com/content/bes/ujoa-social-media-virtual-special-issue

Ha, L., & Yang, Y. (2021). Research about persuasive effects of social media influencers as online opinion leaders 1990-2020: A review. *International Journal of Internet Marketing and Advertising.*

Ha, T. (2020). *Báo cáo về thị trường KOLs, influencer Việt Nam* [Report on Vietnam KOLs and influencer market]. https://issuu.com/tuanha/docs/state_of_influencer_marketing_in_vietnam_2020_7sat

Hackney, F. (2013). Quiet Activism and the New Amateur. *Design and Culture, 5*(2), 169–193. doi:10.2752/175470813X13638640370733

Hackworth, N. J., Matthews, J., Westrupp, E. M., Nguyen, C., Phan, T., Scicluna, A., Cann, W., Bethelsen, D., Bennetts, S. K., & Nicholson, J. M. (2018). What influences parental engagement in early intervention? Parent, program, and community predictors of enrollment, retention, and involvement. *Prevention Science, 19*(7), 880–893. doi:10.1007/s11121-018-0897-2 PMID:29629506

Haenlein, M., Anadol, E., Farnsworth, T., Hugo, H., Hunichen, J., & Welte, D. (2020). Navigating the new era of influencer marketing: How to be successful on Instagram, Tiktok, & Co. *California Management Review, 63*(1), 5–25. doi:10.1177/0008125620958166

Hagelstein, J., Einwiller, S., & Zerfass, A. (2021). The ethical dimension of public relations in Europe: Digital channels, moral challenges, resources, and training. *Public Relations Review, 47*(4 C7 - 102063). doi:10.1016/j.pubrev.2021.102063

Haigh, M. M., & Wigley, S. (2015). Butter, Facebook, and Paula Deen: Examining fans' use of social media in crisis. In A. Slade, A. Narro, & D. Given-Carroll (Eds.), *Television, Social Media, and Fan Culture* (pp. 261–275). Lexington Books.

Haimson, O. L., Liu, T., Zhang, B. Z., & Corvite, S. (2021). The online authenticity paradox: What being" authentic" on social media means, and barriers to achieving it. *Proceedings of the ACM on Human-Computer Interaction, 5*(2), 1–18. doi:10.1145/3479567

Ha, L., & Yang, Y. (2023). Research about persuasive effects of social media influencers as online opinion leaders 1990–2020: A review. *International Journal of Internet Marketing and Advertising, 18*(2-3), 220–241. doi:10.1504/IJIMA.2023.129661

Hall, P. F., Falconer Hall, T., Bailey, Z., & Horne, S. T. (2023). Medics as influencers: a historical analysis of British Army military medical exercises in Kenya over two decades. *BMJ Military Health.* doi:10.1136/military-2023-002442

Hallahan, K. (1999). Seven Models of Framing: Implications for Public Relations. *Journal of Public Relations Research, 11*(3), 205–242. doi:10.1207/s1532754xjprr1103_02

Hallahan, K., Holtzhausen, D., Van Ruler, B., Vercic, D., & Sriramesh, K. (2007). Defining strategic communication. *International Journal of Strategic Communication, 1*(1), 3–35. doi:10.1080/15531180701285244

Halliwell, E. (2013). The impact of thin idealized media images on body satisfaction: Does body appreciation protect women from negative effects? *Body Image, 10*(4), 509–514. doi:10.1016/j.bodyim.2013.07.004 PMID:23972728

Hallsworth, M., & Kirkman, E. (2020). *Behavioral insights.* MIT Press.

Hancock, L., & Ralph, N. (2021). A framework for assessing fossil fuel 'retrofit' hydrogen exports: Security-justice implications of Australia's coal-generated hydrogen exports to Japan. *Energy, 223*, C7–C119938. doi:10.1016/j.energy.2021.119938

Handrimurtjahjo, A. D., Handranata, Y. W., Permatasari, A., & Dewi, C. D. (n.d.). *Examining the Relationship Between Social Media Influencer Impact on Purchase Intention Towards Fashion Industry.* https://ieomsociety.org/proceedings/2022malaysia/414.pdf

Han, M. S., Song, K. S., & Park, J. W. (2023). A Study on the Effect of Fashion Influencer on Consumer Purchase Intention and Word of Mouth Intention. *Journal of Service Management, 24*(1), 1–25. Advance online publication. doi:10.15706/jksms.2023.24.1.001

Hanson, W. R., & Moore, J. R. (2014). Business student moral influencers: Unseen opportunities for development? *Academy of Management Learning & Education, 13*(4), 525–546. doi:10.5465/amle.2012.0325

Han, W., McCabe, S., Wang, Y., & Chong, A. Y. L. (2018). Evaluating user-generated content in social media: An effective approach to encourage greater pro-environmental behavior in tourism? *Journal of Sustainable Tourism, 26*(4), 600–614. doi:10.1080/09669582.2017.1372442

Harari, T. T., Sela, Y., & Bareket-Bojmel, L. (2022). Gen Z during the COVID-19 Crisis: A Comparative Analysis of the Differences between Gen Z and Gen X in Resilience, Values and Attitudes. *Current Psychology (New Brunswick, N.J.), 42*(28), 24223–24232. doi:10.1007/s12144-022-03501-4 PMID:35967492

Hardecker, S., Vreden, C., & Alcan, E. (2023). Is the majority always right? Young children's normative interpretations of majority and dissenting peer behavior. *Social Development, 32*(4), 1168–1191. Advance online publication. doi:10.1111/sode.12682

Hardt, M. (1999). Affective Labor. *Boundary, 26*(2), 89-100.

Harmeling, C. M., Moffett, J. W., Arnold, M. J., & Carlson, B. D. (2017). Toward a theory of customer engagement marketing. *Journal of the Academy of Marketing Science, 45*(3), 312–335. doi:10.1007/s11747-016-0509-2

Harnish, R. J., & Bridges, K. R. (2016). Mall haul videos: Self-presentational motives and the role of self-monitoring. *Psychology and Marketing, 33*(2), 113–124. doi:10.1002/mar.20858

Hart, B. (2017, October 30). *Why 2018 Will Be the Year of the Micro-Influencer, According to a Millennial Expert.* Retrieved May 23, 2019, from Inc.com website: https://www.inc.com/brian-hart/this-game-changing-strategy-will-help-your-business-reach-millennials-heres-how-to-use-it.html

Hartama, E. (2021). *Possibilities of influencer marketing through pet Instagram accounts: A fast lane to a pet owner's pocket?* Lut University. https://lutpub.lut.fi/handle/10024/163069

Hartig, H. (2022). *Younger Americans still more likely than older adults to say there are other countries better than the U.S.* Pew Research Center. Retrieved 8 September 2022, from https://www.pewresearch.org/fact-tank/2021/12/16/younger-americans-still-more-likely-than-older-adults-to-say-there-are-other-countries-better-than-the-u-s/

Hasbullah, N. N., Sulaiman, Z., Mas'od, A., & Ahmad Sugiran, H. S. (1945). Drivers of sustainable apparel purchase intention: An empirical study of Malaysian millennial consumers. *Sustainability (Basel), 14*(4), 1945. Advance online publication. doi:10.3390/su14041945

Hassan, S. H., Yeap, J. A., & Al-Kumaim, N. H. (2022). Sustainable fashion consumption: Advocating philanthropic and economic motives in clothing disposal behaviour. *Sustainability (Basel), 14*(3), 1875. doi:10.3390/su14031875

Hayes, A. F. (2022). *Introduction to mediation, moderation, and conditional process analysis: A regression-based approach* (3rd ed.). The Guilford Press.

Hayes, R. A., & Carr, C. T. (2015). Does being social matter? Effects of enabled commenting on credibility and brand attitudes in Social Media. *Journal of Promotion Management, 21*(3), 371–390. doi:10.1080/10496491.2015.1039178

Heckler, S. E., & Childers, T. L. (1992). The role of expectancy and relevancy in memory for verbal and visual information: What is incongruency? *The Journal of Consumer Research, 18*(4), 475–492. doi:10.1086/209275

Heide, M., von Platen, S., Simonsson, C., & Falkheimer, J. (2018). Expanding the scope of strategic communication: Towards a holistic understanding of organizational complexity. *International Journal of Strategic Communication, 12*(4), 452–468. doi:10.1080/1553118X.2018.1456434

Heilman, M. E. (1983). Sex bias in work settings: The lack of fit model. *Research in Organizational Behavior, 5*, 269–298.

Henningsen, D., & Henningsen, M. (2021). *Persuasion and Social Influence in Groups.* The Emerald Handbook of Group and Team Communication Research. doi:10.1108/978-1-80043-500-120211018

Hermann, E. (2021). Artificial intelligence and mass personalization of communication content—An ethical and literacy perspective. *New Media &amp. Society, 24*(5), 1258–1277.

Hernández-Méndez, J., & Baute-Díaz, N. (2023). Influencer marketing in the promotion of tourist destinations: Mega, macro and micro-influencers. *Current Issues in Tourism*, 1–11. doi:10.1080/13683500.2023.2214354

Hewitt, J., Parker, L., McQuilten, G., & Khan, R. (2023). Sustainability chic and the future of fashion marketing. In Beyond the Dark Arts: Advancing Marketing and Communication Theory and Practice (pp. 125-147). World Scientific Publishing Co. doi:10.1142/9789811276064_0007

Hickman, A. (2019). *Saudi Arabia turns to influencers to give nation's image a makeover.* Campaign US. https://www.campaignlive.com/

Hidayana, I., Prawindarti, L., Umar, N., Ambarwati, K., & Rosatriani, F. (2023). Marketing of commercial milk formula during COVID-19 in Indonesia. *Maternal and Child Nutrition, 19*(3C7 - e13491). doi:10.1111/mcn.13491

Ho, C. H. (2021). A Preliminary Study of Artificial Intelligence Deep Learning Amid Teaching of Public Relations Course. *2021 2nd International Conference on Education, Knowledge and Information Management (ICEKIM)*, 539–542. 10.1109/ICEKIM52309.2021.00124

Hockin-Boyers, H., & Clifford-Astbury, C. (2021). The politics of #diversifyyourfeed in the context of Black Lives Matter. *Feminist Media Studies, 21*(3), 504–509. doi:10.1080/14680777.2021.1925727

Hoffner, C., & Buchanan, M. (2005). Young adults' wishful identification with television characters: The role of perceived similarity and character attributes. *Media Psychology, 7*(4), 325–351. doi:10.1207/S1532785XMEP0704_2

Hofstede Insights. (2021), *Country Comparison - Hofstede Insights.* Available at: https://www.hofstede-insights.com/country-comparison/china,the-usa/

Hofstede, G. H. (1980). *Culture's consequences: International differences in work-related values.* Sage.

Hofstede, G. H. (2001). *Culture's consequences: Comparing values, behaviors, institutions, and organizations across nations.* Sage.

Hofstede, G., & Hofstede, G. J. (2005). *Cultures and organizations: Software of the mind.* McGraw-Hill.

Hofstede, G., & McCrae, R. R. (2004). Personality and culture revisited: Linking traits and dimensions of culture. *Cross-Cultural Research, 38*(1), 52–88. doi:10.1177/1069397103259443

Ho, J. Y. C., & Dempsey, M. (2010). Viral marketing: Motivations to forward online content. *Journal of Business Research, 63*(9-10), 1000–1006. doi:10.1016/j.jbusres.2008.08.010

Holland, E., & Haslam, N. (2013). Worth the weight: The objectification of overweight versus thin targets. *Psychology of Women Quarterly, 37*(4), 462–468. doi:10.1177/0361684312474800

Holland, J., & Baker, S. M. (2001). Customer participation in creating site brand loyalty. *Journal of Interactive Marketing, 15*(4), 34–45. doi:10.1002/dir.1021

Hollebeek, L. D., Glynn, M. S., & Brodie, R. J. (2014). Consumer brand engagement in social media: Conceptualization, scale development, and validation. *Journal of Interactive Marketing, 28*(2), 149–165. doi:10.1016/j.intmar.2013.12.002

Hollebeek, L., & Rather, R. A. (2019). Service innovativeness and tourism customer outcomes. *International Journal of Contemporary Hospitality Management, 31*(11), 4227–4246. doi:10.1108/IJCHM-03-2018-0256

Hoo, T. J. K. W. C., Chee, L. S. Q. D. T., & Foong, L. Y. P. C. Y. (2022). Consumers' Perceptions of Social Media Influencers and Its Influence on Purchase Intention in Malaysia. *Resmilitaris, 12*(3), 3012-3020.

Horton, D., & Wohl, R. (1956). Mass communication and para-social interaction: Observations on intimacy at a distance. *Psychiatry, 19*(3), 215–229. doi:10.1080/00332747.1956.11023049 PMID:13359569

Hosie, R. (2019, April 9). Why brands are turning away from big Instagram influencers to work with people who have small followings instead. *Business Insider*. https://www.businessinsider.com/brands-turning-to-micro-influencers-instead-of-instagram-stars-2019-4

Hosszu, A., Rughiniş, C., Rughiniş, R., & Rosner, D. E. (2022). Webcams and social interaction during online classes: Identity work, presentation of self, and well-being. *Frontiers in Psychology*, *12*, 761427. Advance online publication. doi:10.3389/fpsyg.2021.761427 PMID:35082716

Hou, F., Guan, Z., Li, B., & Chong, A. Y. L. (2020). Factors influencing people's continuous watching intention and consumption intention in live streaming: Evidence from China. *Internet Research*, *30*(1), 141–163. doi:10.1108/INTR-04-2018-0177

Hovland, C. I., & Weiss, W. (1951). The influence of source credibility on communication effectiveness. *Public Opinion Quarterly*, *15*(4), 635–650. doi:10.1086/266350

Howarth, J. (2024, January 12). *Tiktok user age, gender, & demographics (2024)*. Exploding Topics. https://explodingtopics.com/blog/tiktok-demographics

Huang, Q., Peng, W., & Ahn, S. (2021). When media become the mirror: A meta-analysis on media and body image. *Media Psychology*, *24*(4), 437–489. doi:10.1080/15213269.2020.1737545

Hudaefi, F. A., Hassan, M. K., Abduh, M., & Beik, I. S. (2023). Knowledge discovery of zakat administration worldwide from YouTube and Zoom via text mining. *Journal of Islamic Accounting and Business Research*, *14*(1), 159–180. doi:10.1108/JIABR-03-2022-0067

Hudders, L., De Jans, S., & De Veirman, M. (2020). The commercialization of social media stars: A literature review and conceptual framework on the strategic use of social media influencers. *International Journal of Advertising*, *40*(3), 327–375. doi:10.1080/02650487.2020.1836925

Hudders, L., & Lou, C. (2023). The rosy world of influencer marketing? Its bright and dark sides, and future research recommendations. *International Journal of Advertising*, *42*(1), 151–161. doi:10.1080/02650487.2022.2137318

Hugh, D. C., Dolan, R., Harrigan, P., & Gray, H. (2022). Influencer marketing effectiveness: The mechanisms that matter. *European Journal of Marketing*, *56*(12), 3485–3515. doi:10.1108/EJM-09-2020-0703

Hughes, C., Swaminathan, V., & Brooks, G. (2019). Driving brand engagement through online social media influencers: An empirical investigation of sponsored blogging campaigns. *Journal of Marketing*, *83*(5), 78–96. doi:10.1177/0022242919854374

Hu, H., Zhang, D., & Wang, C. (2019). Impact of social media influencers' endorsement on application adoption: A trust transfer perspective'. *Social Behavior and Personality*, *47*(11), 1–12. doi:10.2224/sbp.8518

Hu, L., Qi, M., Han, S., & Li, Y. (2020). Understanding followers' stickiness to digital influencers: The effect of psychological responses. *International Journal of Information Management*, *54*, 102169. doi:10.1016/j.ijinfomgt.2020.102169

Hulland, J. (2020). Conceptual review papers: Revisiting existing research to develop and refine theory. *AMS Review*, *10*(1-2), 27–35. doi:10.1007/s13162-020-00168-7

Hund, E., & McGuigan, L. (2019). A shoppable life: Performance, selfhood, and influence in the social media storefront. *Communication, Culture & Critique*, *12*(1), 18–35. doi:10.1093/ccc/tcz004

Hunt, T., & Tirpok, A. (1993). Universal ethics code: An idea whose time has come. *Public Relations Review*, *19*(1), 1–11. doi:10.1016/0363-8111(93)90025-8

Ijabadeniyi, A., & Govender, J. P. (2023). Intrinsic drivers of the reputation for CSR: A cognitive analysis of consumer expectations. *Social Responsibility Journal*. Advance online publication. doi:10.1108/SRJ-10-2022-0451

Infanger, M., & Sczesny, S. (2015). Communion-over-agency effects on advertising effectiveness. *International Journal of Advertising*, *34*(2), 285–306. doi:10.1080/02650487.2014.993794

Influencity. (2023). *The largest influencer study in the U.S. in 2023. The state of influencer marketing in the United States in 2023*. Available at: https://influencity.com/resources/studies/the-largest-influencer-study-of-the-united-states-2023/

Iqbal, M. (2022). *TikTok revenue and usage statistics 2022*. Business Of Apps. https://www.businessofapps.com/data/tik-tok-statistics/

Iran, S. (2018). Sustainable fashion: from production to alternative consumption. In *Sustainable Fashion* (pp. 139–159). Governance and New Management Approaches. doi:10.1007/978-3-319-74367-7_13

Isyanto, P., Sapitri, R. G., & Sinaga, O. (2020). Micro influencers marketing and brand image to purchase intention of cosmetic products focallure. *Systematic Reviews in Pharmacy*, *11*(1), 601–605.

Jaakkola, E. (2020). Designing conceptual articles: Four approaches. *AMS Review*, *10*(1-2), 18–26. doi:10.1007/s13162-020-00161-0

Jaakkola, E., & Alexander, M. (2014). The role of customer engagement Behavior in Value Co-Creation. *Journal of Service Research*, *17*(3), 247–261. doi:10.1177/1094670514529187

Jackson, T. (2004). Negotiating Sustainable Consumption: A review of the consumption debate and its policy Implications. *Energy & Environment*, *15*(6), 1027–1051. doi:10.1260/0958305043026573

Jacobson, J. (2020). You are a brand: Social media managers' personal branding and "the future audience". *Journal of Product and Brand Management*, *29*(6), 715–727. doi:10.1108/JPBM-03-2019-2299

Jacobson, J., & Harrison, B. (2022). Sustainable fashion social media influencers and content creation calibration. *International Journal of Advertising*, *41*(1), 150–177. doi:10.1080/02650487.2021.2000125

Jain, V., & Roy, S. (2016). Understanding meaning transfer in celebrity endorsements: A qualitative exploration. *Qualitative Market Research*, *19*(3), 266–286. doi:10.1108/QMR-03-2015-0020

Jaiswal, S. (2023). *How India's 'brown beauty' makeup influencers are going global*. Retrieved from https://www.aljazeera.com/gallery/2023/4/6/how-indias-brown-beauty-makeup-influencers-are-going-global

Jaitly, R. C., & Gautam, O. (2021). Impact of social media influencers on customer engagement and brand perception. *International Journal of Internet Marketing and Advertising*, *15*(2), 220–242. doi:10.1504/IJIMA.2021.114336

Jaitly, V., Chowriappa, P., & Dua, S. (2016). A framework to identify influencers in signed social networks. In *International Conference on Advances in Computing, Communications and Informatics (ICACCI)* (pp. 2335-2340). 10.1109/ICACCI.2016.7732403

Jalali, S. S., & Khalid, H. B. (2021). The influence of Instagram influencers' activity on green consumption behavior. *Business Management and Strategy*, *12*(1), 78–90. doi:10.5296/bms.v12i1.18265

Jamil, R., Qayyum, U., ul Hassan, S., & Khan, T. (2023). Impact of social media influencers on consumers' well-being and purchase intention: a TikTok perspective. *European Journal of Management and Business Economics*. doi:10.1108/EJMBE-08-2022-0270

Jang, M. A., Lee, J. M., Bae, S., Jang, M. A., Lee, J. M., & Bae, S. (2022). A Study of Consumer Choice Behaviour Determination Applying the Theory of Planned Behaviour (TPB) of Functional Cosmetics. *Asian Journal of Beauty and Cosmetology*, *20*(1), 95–110. doi:10.20402/ajbc.2022.0003 PMID:31621194

Janseen, L., Schouten, A. P., & Croes, E. A. J. (2022). Influencer fit and number of followers affect advertising outcomes and influencer evaluations via credibility and identification. *International Journal of Advertising*, *41*(1), 101–127. doi:10.1080/02650487.2021.1994205

Jansen van Vuuren, C. J., & Jansen van Vuuren, J. M. (2022). Perspectives of healthcare workers in South Africa on COVID-19 vaccination passports. *Health SA*, *27*, C7–a1823. doi:10.4102/hsag.v27i0.1823 PMID:35548060

Jarrett, K. (2017). *Feminism, Labour and Digital Media: The Digital Housewife*. Routledge, Taylor & Francis Group.

Jatho, A., Bikaitwoha, M. E., & Mugisha, N. M. (2020). Socio-culturally mediated factors and lower level of education are the main influencers of functional cervical cancer literacy among women in Mayuge, Eastern Uganda. *ecancermedicalscience, 14 C7 - 1004*. doi:10.3332/ecancer.2020.1004

Jauffret, M. N., & Aubrun, F. (2022). The biodigital rises: a new digital brand challenge. Lecture Notes in Computer Science (including subseries Lecture Notes in Artificial Intelligence and Lecture Notes in Bioinformatics).

Jaybhaye, S., Manchekar, A., Dixit, A., Ingle, A., & Khatib, F. (2023). Comparative analysis of voice-powered assistants. *International Journal for Research*, *11*(4), 1892–1898.

Jefferies, J. (2016). Crocheted Strategies: Women Crafting their Own Communities. *Textile (Oxford)*, *14*(1), 14–35. doi:10.1080/14759756.2016.1142788

Jenkins, H., Green, J., & Ford, S. (2018). *Spreadable media: Creating value and meaning in a networked culture*. New York University Press.

Jia, C., & Mustafa, H. (2022). A Bibliometric analysis and review of nudge research using VOSviewer. *Behavioral Sciences (Basel, Switzerland)*, *13*(1), 19. doi:10.3390/bs13010019 PMID:36661591

Jiménez-Castillo, D., & Sánchez-Fernández, R. (2019). The role of digital influencers in brand recommendation: Examining their impact on engagement, expected value and purchase intention. *International Journal of Information Management*, *49*, 366–376. doi:10.1016/j.ijinfomgt.2019.07.009

Jin, S. A. A. (2020). The rise of influencer marketing: A conceptual framework for understanding its impact on message processing. *Journal of Interactive Advertising*, *20*(2), 58–74.

Jin, S. V., Muqaddam, A., & Ryu, E. (2019). Instafamous and social media influencer marketing. *Marketing Intelligence & Planning*, *37*(5), 567–579. doi:10.1108/MIP-09-2018-0375

Jin, S. V., & Ryu, E. (2019). Celebrity fashion brand endorsement in Facebook viral marketing and social commerce: Interactive effects of social identification, materialism, fashion involvement, and opinion leadership. *Journal of Fashion Marketing and Management*, *23*(1), 104–123. doi:10.1108/JFMM-01-2018-0001

Jin, S. V., Ryu, E., & Muqaddam, A. (2021). I trust what she's #endorsing on Instagram: Moderating effects of parasocial interaction and social presence in fashion influencer marketing. *Journal of Fashion Marketing and Management*, *25*(4), 665–681. doi:10.1108/JFMM-04-2020-0059

Jin, S.-A. A., & Phua, J. (2014). Following celebrities' tweets about brands: The impact of twitter-based electronic word-of-mouth on consumers' source credibility perception, buying intention, and social identification with celebrities. *Journal of Advertising*, *43*(2), 181–195. doi:10.1080/00913367.2013.827606

Johnston, J., & Taylor, J. (2008). Feminist consumerism and fat activists: A comparative study of grassroots activism and the Dove Real Beauty campaign. *Signs (Chicago, Ill.)*, *33*(4), 941–966. doi:10.1086/528849

Jones, K. (2022). Some conclusions, intrusions, and shock endings. In Doing Performative Social Science: Creativity in Doing Research and Reaching Communities (pp.237-247). Taylor and Francis. https://doi.org/ doi:10.4324/9781003187745-25

Joshi, Y., Lim, W. M., Jagani, K., & Kumar, S. (2023). Social media influencer marketing: Foundations, trends, and ways forward. *Electronic Commerce Research.* Advance online publication. doi:10.1007/s10660-023-09719-z

Josse-Eklund, A., Jossebo, M., Sandin-Bojö, A. K., Wilde-Larsson, B., & Petzäll, K. (2014). Swedish nurses' perceptions of influencers on patient advocacy: A phenomenographic study. *Nursing Ethics*, *21*(6), 673–683. doi:10.1177/0969733013515488 PMID:24477259

Jun, S., & Yi, J. (2020). What makes followers loyal? The role of influencer interactivity in building influencer brand equity. *Journal of Product and Brand Management*, *29*(6), 803–814. doi:10.1108/JPBM-02-2019-2280

Kabadayi, S., & Price, K. (2014). Consumer–brand engagement on Facebook: Liking and commenting behaviors. *Journal of Research in Interactive Marketing*, *8*(3), 203–223. doi:10.1108/JRIM-12-2013-0081

Kadekova, Z., & Holienčinova, M. (2018). Influencer marketing as a modern phenomenon creating a new frontier of virtual opportunities. *Communication Today, 9*(2), 90-104. https://www.communicationtoday.sk/download/22018/06.-KADEKOVA-HOLIENCINOVA-%E2%80%93-CT-2-2018.pdf

Kaler, J. (2002). Morality and strategy in stakeholder identification. *Journal of Business Ethics*, *39*(1/2), 91–100. doi:10.1023/A:1016336118528

Kaler, J. (2006). Evaluating stakeholder theory. *Journal of Business Ethics*, *69*(3), 249–268. doi:10.1007/s10551-006-9089-2

Kalin, R., & Tilby, P. J. (1978). Development and validation of a sex-role ideology scale. *Psychological Reports*, *42*(3), 731–738. doi:10.2466/pr0.1978.42.3.731 PMID:674496

Kalisch, E. (2023). The ego-alter-tertius paradigm: Adam Smith's interaction model. In *Adam Smith and Modernity: 1723-2023* (pp. 161–174). Taylor and Francis. doi:10.4324/9781003301448-13

Kamins, M. A. (1990). An investigation into the "match-up" hypothesis in celebrity advertising: When beauty may be only skin deep. *Journal of Advertising*, *19*(1), 4–13. doi:10.1080/00913367.1990.10673175

Kanai, A., & Gill, R. (2020). Woke? affect, neoliberalism, marginalised identities and consumer culture. *New Formations*, *102*(102), 10–27. doi:10.3898/NewF:102.01.2020

Kane, T. J., & Staiger, D. O. (2008). *Estimating teacher impacts on student achievement: An experimental evaluation. (No. w14607).* National Bureau of Economic Research. doi:10.3386/w14607

Kaplan, A. M., & Haenlein, M. (2011). Two hearts in three-quarter time: How to waltz the Social Media/viral marketing dance. *Business Horizons*, *54*(3), 253–263. doi:10.1016/j.bushor.2011.01.006

Kardosh, R., Sklar, A., Goldstein, A., Pertzov, Y., & Hassin, R. (2022). Minority salience and the overestimation of individuals from minority groups in perception and memory. *Proceedings of the National Academy of Sciences of the United States of America,* 119. 10.1073/pnas.2116884119

Karimova, G. (2020). Exploring Visual Framing Strategies, Sentiment, and Product Presentation Modality in Instagram Posts of Fashion Influencers. *Exploring Visual Framing Strategies, Sentiment, and Product Presentation Modality in Instagram Posts of Fashion Influencers.*, *7*(1). Advance online publication. doi:10.29107/rr2020.1.6

Karl, C. (2017). *The State of Fashion 2017*. McKinsey Global Institute. https://www.mckinsey.com/~/media/McKinsey/Industries/Retail/Our%20Insights/The%20state%20of%20fashion/The-state-of-fashion-2017-McK-BoF-report.pdf

Karlovitz, T. J. (2020). The democratization of technology – and its limitation. In *Managing Customer Experiences in an Omnichannel World: Melody of Online and Offline Environments in the Customer Journey* (pp. 13–25). Emerald Publishing Limited. doi:10.1108/978-1-80043-388-520201004

Karunakaran, M. S., & Raveendran, P. T. (2018). Customer Engagement - the Co Creation of value in the marketing process. *ICTACT Journal on Management Studies*, *4*(1), 683–690. doi:10.21917/ijms.2018.0093

Kaur, G., Deshwal, P., & Dangi, H. K. (2023). Customer engagement: A systematic review and future research agenda. *International Journal of Internet Marketing and Advertising*, *18*(2/3), 148. doi:10.1504/IJIMA.2023.129659

Kaur, N., Ricciardelli, R., & Clow, K. (2023). Stereotypes of male nurses through the framework of social role theory and stereotype content model. *Journal of Men's Studies*, *31*(1), 157–178. doi:10.1177/10608265221108209

Kauv, S., & Blotnicky, K. A. (2020). Brand loyalty, brand trust, peer influence and price sensitivity as influencer in student computer purchase. *Journal of Business and Behavioral Sciences*, *31*(1), 131–150.

Kay, S., Mulcahy, R., & Parkinson, J. (2020). When less is more: The impact of macro and micro social media influencers' disclosure. *Journal of Marketing Management*, *36*(3–4), 248–278. doi:10.1080/0267257X.2020.1718740

Keel, A., & Nataraajan, R. (2012). Celebrity endorsements and beyond: New avenues for celebrity branding. *Psychology and Marketing*, *29*(9), 690–703. doi:10.1002/mar.20555

Keller, K. L. (2001). *Building customer-based brand equity: A blueprint for creating strong brands*. Retrieved from https://api.semanticscholar.org/CorpusID:10882841

Kelman, H. C. (1958). Compliance, identification, and internalization three processes of attitude change. *The Journal of Conflict Resolution*, *2*(1), 51–60. doi:10.1177/002200275800200106

Kelman, H. C. (1961). Processes of Opinion Change. *Public Opinion Quarterly*, *25*(1), 57. doi:10.1086/266996

Kemp, S. (2022). *TikTok's ad audience hits 1.02 billion (And other mind-blowing stats)*. Social Media Marketing & Management Dashboard. https://blog.hootsuite.com/simon-kemp-social-media/

Kemp, S. (2023, February 13). *Digital 2023: Vietnam*. DataReportal. https://datareportal.com/reports/digital-2023-vietnam

Kende, J., Reiter, J., Coşkan, C., Doosje, B., & Green, E. G. (2023). The role of minority discrimination and political participation in shaping majority perceptions of discrimination: Two cross-national studies. *Group Processes & Intergroup Relations*, *26*(3), 607–628. doi:10.1177/13684302221075711

Kennan, W. R., & Hazelton, V. (2006). Internal public relations, social capital, and the role of effective organizational communication. In C. H. Botan & V. Hazelton (Eds.), *Public relations theory II* (pp. 311–341). Lawrence Erlbaum.

Kenny, D. A. (1979). *Correlation and causality*. Wiley-Interscience.

Kenrick, D. T., Montello, D. R., Gutierres, S. E., & Trost, M. R. (1993). Effects of physical attractiveness on affect and perceptual judgments: When social comparison overrides social reinforcement. *Personality and Social Psychology Bulletin*, *19*(2), 195–199. doi:10.1177/0146167293192008

Kent, M. L., & Taylor, M. (2021). Fostering dialogic engagement: Toward an architecture of social media for social change. *Social Media + Society*, *7*(1), 205630512098446. Advance online publication. doi:10.1177/2056305120984462

Kerpen, D., Greenbaum, M., & Berk, R. (2019). *Likeable social media*. McGraw Hill.

Khamis, S., & Munt, A. (2010). The three Cs of fashion media today: convergence, creativity and control. *SCAN Journal of Media Arts Culture, 7*(3).

Khamis, S., Ang, L., & Welling, R. (2017). Self-branding, 'micro-celebrity' and the rise of Social Media Influencers. *Celebrity Studies, 8*(2), 191–208. doi:10.1080/19392397.2016.1218292

Khan, M. L., & Malik, A. (2022). Researching YouTube: Methods, tools, and analytics. The Sage Handbook of Social Media Research Methods, 651-663.

Khan, N., Rudoler, D., McDiarmid, M., & Peckham, S. (2020). A pay for performance scheme in primary care: Meta-synthesis of qualitative studies on the provider experiences of the quality and outcomes framework in the UK. *BMC Family Practice, 21*(1 C7 - 142). doi:10.1186/s12875-020-01208-8

Khan, H. R., Onye, U. U., & Du, Y. (2018). Data-activism as civic engagement: Forming a narrative to foster social change on gun control in the United States. *Proceedings of the Association for Information Science and Technology, 55*(1), 841–842. doi:10.1002/pra2.2018.14505501140

Khan, S., & Khan, M. A. (2021). Effect of social media influencer marketing on consumers' purchase intention and the mediating role of credibility. *Journal of Promotion Management, 27*(4), 503–523. doi:10.1080/10496491.2020.1851847

Ki, C.-W., Cuevas, L. M., Chong, S. M., & Lim, H. (2020). Influencer marketing: Social media influencers as human brands attaching to followers and yielding positive marketing results by fulfilling needs. *Journal of Retailing and Consumer Services, 55*(102133), 102133. doi:10.1016/j.jretconser.2020.102133

Ki, C.-W., & Kim, Y.-K. (2019). The mechanism by which social media influencers persuade consumers: The role of consumers' desire to mimic. *Psychology and Marketing, 36*(10), 905–922. doi:10.1002/mar.21244

Kidd, E., Ritch, E., & Carey, L. D. (2020, October). The Fashion Detox Challenge: An Experiment in Reduced Clothing Consumption. In *The Legacy of Fashion: Past, Present, and Future Global Fashion Conference. Université de la Mode* (pp. 21-23). https://researchonline.gcu.ac.uk/en/publications/the-fashion-detox-challenge-supporting-scotlands-transition-to-a-

Kim, A. J., & Ko, E. (2012). Do social media marketing activities enhance customer equity? An empirical study of luxury fashion brand. *Journal of Business Research, 65*(10), 1480–1486. doi:10.1016/j.jbusres.2011.10.014

Kim, D. (2023). Racialized beauty, visibility, and empowerment: Asian American women influencers on YouTube. *Information Communication and Society, 26*(6), 1159–1176. doi:10.1080/1369118X.2021.1994626

Kim, D. Y., & Kim, H. (2022). Social media influencers as human brands: An interactive marketing perspective. *Journal of Research in Interactive Marketing, 17*(1), 94–109. doi:10.1108/JRIM-08-2021-0200

Kim, D. Y., & Kim, H.-Y. (2021). Influencer advertising on social media: The multiple inference model on Influencer-product congruence and sponsorship disclosure. *Journal of Business Research, 130*, 405–415. doi:10.1016/j.jbusres.2020.02.020

Kim, D. Y., & Kim, H.-Y. (2021). Trust me, trust me not: A nuanced view of influencer marketing on social media. *Journal of Business Research, 134*, 223–232. doi:10.1016/j.jbusres.2021.05.024

Kim, D., & Park, S. (2020). Rethinking millennials: How are they shaping the tourism industry? *Asia Pacific Journal of Tourism Research, 25*(1), 1–2. doi:10.1080/10941665.2019.1667607

Kim, D., & Wang, Z. (2023). The ethics of virtuality: Navigating the complexities of human-like virtual influencers in the social media marketing realm. *Frontiers in Communication, 8*, C7–C1205610. doi:10.3389/fcomm.2023.1205610

Kim, H. S., Nam, S., Lee, W., Nam, K., & Kwon, D. (2013). Effects of moral judgement, emotional control and problem solving on information ethics of gifted students in computer science. *Proceedings - International Computer Software and Applications Conference C7 - 6605863*. doi:10.23919/JSC.2021.0026

Kim, J. H., Song, H., & Youn, H. (2020). The chain of effects from authenticity cues to purchase intention: The role of emotions and restaurant image. *International Journal of Hospitality Management, 85*, 102354. doi:10.1016/j.ijhm.2019.102354

Kim, J.-H., & Lennon, S. J. (2007). Mass media and self-esteem, body image, and eating disorder tendencies. *Clothing & Textiles Research Journal, 25*(1), 3–23. doi:10.1177/0887302X06296873

Kim, J., Kang, S., & Lee, K. H. (2020). How social capital impacts the purchase intention of sustainable fashion products. *Journal of Business Research, 117*, 596–603. doi:10.1016/j.jbusres.2018.10.010

Kim, J., & Kim, M. (2022). Rise of social media influencers as a new marketing channel: Focusing on the roles of psychological well-being and perceived social responsibility among consumers. *International Journal of Environmental Research and Public Health, 19*(4), 2362. doi:10.3390/ijerph19042362 PMID:35206553

Kim, J., Yang, K., Min, J., & White, B. (2022). Hope, fear, and consumer behavioural change amid COVID-19: Application of protection motivation theory. *International Journal of Consumer Studies, 46*(2), 558–574. doi:10.1111/ijcs.12700 PMID:34220343

Kim, S., Jang, S., Choi, W., Youn, C., & Lee, Y. (2022). Contactless service encounters among Millennials and Generation Z: The effects of Millennials and Gen Z characteristics on technology self-efficacy and preference for contactless service. *Journal of Research in Interactive Marketing, 16*(1), 82–100. doi:10.1108/JRIM-01-2021-0020

Kingfisher, C. (2013). Happiness: Notes on History, Culture and Governance. *Health, Culture and Society (Pittsburgh, Pa.), 5*(1), 67–82. doi:10.5195/HCS.2013.145

Kirmani, A. (1997). Advertising repetition as a signal of quality: If it's advertised so much, something must be wrong. *Journal of Advertising, 26*(3), 77–86. doi:10.1080/00913367.1997.10673530

Kitchen, P. J., & Moss, D. (1995). Marketing and public relations: The relationship revisited. *Journal of Marketing Communications, 1*(2), 105–106. doi:10.1080/13527269500000012

Kleemans, M., Daalmans, S., Carbaat, I., & Anschütz, D. (2018). Picture perfect: The direct effect of manipulated Instagram photos on body image in adolescent girls. *Media Psychology, 21*(1), 93–110. doi:10.1080/15213269.2016.1257392

Kline, R. B. (2005). *Principles and practice of structural equation modeling*. Guilford publications.

Koch, K., & Domina, T. (1999). Consumer textile recycling as a means of solid waste reduction. *Family and Consumer Sciences Research Journal, 28*(1), 3–17. doi:10.1177/1077727X99281001

Kohan, S. E. (2020, June 28). *AEO's Aerie brand, built on body positivity and inclusion, is slowly edging out sexy supermodel juggernaut Victoria's Secret*. Forbes. https://www.forbes.com/sites/shelleykohan/2020/06/28/aeos-aerie-brand-built-on-body-positivity-and-inclusion-is-slowly-edging-out-sexy-supermodel-juggernaut-victorias-secret/?sh=2d3d4d3d42ba

Kolo & Haumer. (2018). *Social media celebrities as influencers in brand communication: An empirical study on influencer content, its advertising relevance and audience expectations*. Academic Press.

Kondort, G., Pelău, C., Gáti, M., & Ciofu, I. (2023). The Role of Fashion Influencers in Shaping Consumers' Buying Decisions and Trends. *Proceedings of the International Conference on Business Excellence, 17*(1), 1009–1018. 10.2478/picbe-2023-0092

Konstantinou, I., & Jones, K. (2022). Investigating Gen Z attitudes to charitable giving and donation behaviour: Social media, peers and authenticity. *Journal of Philanthropy and Marketing*, *27*(3), e1764. Advance online publication. doi:10.1002/nvsm.1764

Korman, J. (2023). *Understanding how Answer Bot works with your content.* Retrieved from https://support.zendesk.com/hc/en-us/articles/4408830824474-Understanding-how-Answer-Bot-works-with-your-content/20/11/2023

Kovanci, E., & Karakoç, D. (2022). The effect of social media use on environmental awareness rating of university students. *Adıyaman Üniversitesi Sosyal Bilimler Enstitüsü Dergisi.* . doi:10.14520/adyusbd.1111999

Kowalczyk, C. M., & Pounders, K. R. (2016). Transforming celebrities through social media: The role of authenticity and emotional attachment. *Journal of Product and Brand Management*, *25*(4), 345–356. doi:10.1108/JPBM-09-2015-0969

Kozar, J. M., & Lynn Damhorst, M. (2008). Older women's responses to current fashion models. *Journal of Fashion Marketing and Management*, *12*(3), 338–350. doi:10.1108/13612020810889290

Krismawan, D. A., Widagdo, S., & Puspitawati, D. (2021). Free Trade Area Agreement: Impact To The Fashion Industry And Environmental Protection In Indonesia. *International Journal of Global Community, 4*(2), 153-162. https://journal.riksawan.com/index.php/IJGC-RI/article/view/88

Kukulska-Hulme, A., Bossu, C., Charitonos, K., Coughlan, T., Ferguson, R., FitzGerald, E., Gaved, M., Guitert, M., Herodotou, C., Maina, M., & Prieto-Blázquez, J. (2022). *Innovating pedagogy 2022: exploring new forms of teaching, learning and assessment, to guide educators and policy makers.* open.ac.uk

Kumar, M. (2023, January 3). *Influencer marketing.* Redseer Strategy Consultants. https://redseer.com/newsletters/influencer-marketing-a-solution-to-optimize-digital-ad-spends/

Kumar, P., Oberoi, S., & Jaitly, R. C. (2023). Impact of social media influencers on consumer engagement and its consequences in the emerging environment of metaverse. In Advances in marketing, customer relationship management, and e-services book series (pp. 225–240). doi:10.4018/978-1-6684-8898-0.ch014

Kumar, V., & Pansari, A. (2016). Competitive advantage through engagement. *JMR, Journal of Marketing Research*, *53*(4), 497–514. doi:10.1509/jmr.15.0044

Kurtin, K. S., O'Brien, N., Roy, D., & Dam, L. (2018). The development of parasocial relationship on YouTube. *The Journal of Social Media in Society*, *7*, 233–252.

Kuss, D. J., & Griffiths, M. D. (2017). Social networking sites and addiction: Ten lessons learned. *International Journal of Environmental Research and Public Health*, *14*(3), 311–321. doi:10.3390/ijerph14030311 PMID:28304359

Labrecque, I. I. (2014). Fostering consumer-brand relationships in social media environments: The role of parasocial interaction. *Journal of Interactive Marketing*, *28*(2), 134–148. doi:10.1016/j.intmar.2013.12.003

Labrecque, L. I., Vor Dem Esche, J., Mathwick, C., Novak, T. P., & Hofacker, C. F. (2013). Consumer power: Evolution in the digital age. *Journal of Interactive Marketing*, *27*(4), 57–269. doi:10.1016/j.intmar.2013.09.002

Lajnef, K. (2023). The effect of social media influencers on teenagers Behavior: An empirical study using cognitive map technique. *Current Psychology (New Brunswick, N.J.)*, *42*(22), 19364–19377. doi:10.1007/s12144-023-04273-1 PMID:36742063

Lakhan, R., Sharma, B., & Sharma, M. (2023). Social media: utility versus addiction. In *Effective Use of Social Media in Public Health* (pp. 65–97). Academic Press. doi:10.1016/B978-0-323-95630-7.00002-0

Lama, A. B., & Shrook, A. F. (2020). Ethical Considerations for Using Social Media: "Is it Okay to Share?" *The Arab Journal of Media and Communication Research*, *2020*(31), 172–187.

Lamartora, V. (2021). *Z Houses. Nuovi servizi dedicati ai giovani nel Dipartimento Dipendenze della ASL Napoli2Nord.* MISSION, doi:10.3280/mis55-2020oa12159

Lamberton, C., & Stephen, A. T. (2016). A thematic exploration of digital, social media, and Mobile Marketing: Research Evolution from 2000 to 2015 and an agenda for future inquiry. *Journal of Marketing*, *80*(6), 146–172. doi:10.1509/jm.15.0415

LaTour, S., & Manrai, A. (1989). Interactive Impact of Informational and Normative Influence on Donations. *JMR, Journal of Marketing Research*, *26*(3), 327–335. doi:10.1177/002224378902600306

Lawson, C. E. (2020). Skin deep: Callout strategies, influencers, and racism in the online beauty community. *New Media & Society*, *23*(3), 596–612. Advance online publication. doi:10.1177/1461444820904697

Lazuka, R. F., Wick, M. R., Keel, P. K., & Harriger, J. A. (2020). Are we there yet? Progress in depicting diverse images of beauty in Instagram's body positivity movement. *Body Image*, *34*, 85–93. doi:10.1016/j.bodyim.2020.05.001 PMID:32534269

Leclercq-Machado, L., Alvarez-Risco, A., Gómez-Prado, R., Cuya-Velásquez, B. B., Esquerre-Botton, S., Morales-Ríos, F., Almanza-Cruz, C., Castillo-Benancio, S., Anderson-Seminario, M. M., Del-Aguila-Arcentales, S., & Yáñez, J. A. (2022). Sustainable fashion and consumption patterns in Peru: An environmental-attitude-intention-behavior analysis. *Sustainability (Basel)*, *14*(16), 9965. doi:10.3390/su14169965

Lee, D., & Wan, C. (2023). The impact of Mukbang live streaming commerce on consumers' overconsumption behavior. *Journal of Interactive Marketing*, *58*(2-3), 198–221. doi:10.1177/10949968231156104

Lee, E. J., Choi, H., Han, J., Kim, D. H., Ko, E., & Kim, K. H. (2020). How to 'Nudge' your consumers toward sustainable fashion consumption: An fMRI investigation. *Journal of Business Research*, *117*, 642–651. doi:10.1016/j.jbusres.2019.09.050

Lee, J. A., & Eastin, M. S. (2021). Perceived authenticity of social media influencers: Scale development and validation. *Journal of Research in Interactive Marketing*, *15*(4), 822–841. doi:10.1108/JRIM-12-2020-0253

Lee, J. E., & Watkins, B. (2016). YouTube vloggers' influence on consumer luxury brand perceptions and intentions. *Journal of Business Research*, *69*(12), 5753–5760. doi:10.1016/j.jbusres.2016.04.171

Lee, J.-G., & Thorson, E. (2008). The impact of celebrity–product incongruence on the effectiveness of product endorsement. *Journal of Advertising Research*, *48*(3), 433–449. doi:10.2501/S0021849908080446

Lee, J., & Hong, I. B. (2016). Predicting positive user responses to social media advertising: The roles of emotional appeal, informativeness, and creativity. *International Journal of Information Management*, *36*(3), 360–373. doi:10.1016/j.ijinfomgt.2016.01.001

Lee, J., Kim, H. J., & Hur, W. M. (2018). How does celebrity involvement affect brand attitude in social media? The mediating role of consumers' perceptions of celebrity credibility and product-brand relationship. *Journal of Global Fashion Marketing*, *9*(1), 52–66.

Lee, S., Chung, I., & Cho, Y. (2022). *Effect of the Ethical Consumption Tendency of Millennials and Members of Generation Z on the Purchase Intention of Social Enterprise Fashion Products.* Family and Environment Research. doi:10.6115/fer.2022.029

Leonard, L. N. K., & Cronan, T. P. (2005). Attitude toward ethical behavior in computer use: A shifting model. *Industrial Management & Data Systems*, *105*(9), 1150–1171. doi:10.1108/02635570510633239

Lepesant, V. (2022). Redressing Sustainable Fashion Practices: Upcycling as a Defense to Trademark Infringement. Tex. A&M L. *Rev.*, *10*(2), 335–358. doi:10.37419/LR.V10.I2.5

Leung, F. F., Gu, F. F., & Palmatier, R. W. (2022). Online influencer marketing. *Journal of the Academy of Marketing Science*, *50*(2), 226–251. doi:10.1007/s11747-021-00829-4

Lewis, D., & Moorkens, J. (2020). A Rights-Based Approach to Trustworthy AI in Social Media. *Social Media + Society*, *6*(3), 205630512095467. doi:10.1177/2056305120954672

Lewis, R. (2019). Modest body politics: The commercial and ideological intersect of fat, black, and Muslim in the modest fashion market and media. *Fashion Theory*, *23*(2), 243–273. doi:10.1080/1362704X.2019.1567063

Lewis, T. L., Park, H., Netravali, A. N., & Trejo, H. X. (2017). Closing the loop: A scalable zero-waste model for apparel reuse and recycling. *International Journal of Fashion Design, Technology and Education*, *10*(3), 353–362. doi:10.1080/17543266.2016.1263364

Lidgren, J., & Major, M. (2021). *Social media influencers' impact on consumers' sustainable fashion consumption: A qualitative study on post-millennial consumers*. https://gupea.ub.gu.se/bitstream/handle/2077/69053/gupea_2077_69053_1.pdf?sequence=1&isAllowed=y

Li, L. (2023). Refashioning repair culture through the circle of value creation: A case study of the Japanese brand KUON. *International Journal of Sustainable Fashion & Textiles*, *2*(1), 53–62. doi:10.1386/sft_00020_1

Lillywhite, A., & Wolbring, G. (2020). Coverage of artificial intelligence and machine learning within academic literature, Canadian newspapers, and twitter tweets: The case of disabled people. *Societies*, *10*(1 C7 - 23). doi:10.3390/soc10010023

Limatius, H. (2020). *Communities of empowerment: Exploring the discourse practices of plus-size fashion bloggers* [Tampere University]. https://urn.fi/URN:ISBN:978-952-03-1489-7

Lim, J. S., Choe, M. J., Zhang, J., & Noh, G. Y. (2020). The role of wishful identification, emotional engagement, and parasocial relationships in repeated viewing of live-streaming games: A social cognitive theory perspective. *Computers in Human Behavior*, *108*, 106327. doi:10.1016/j.chb.2020.106327

Lim, M. (2018). Roots, Routes, and Routers: Communications and Media of Contemporary Social Movements. *Journalism & Communication Monographs*, *20*(2), 92–136. doi:10.1177/1522637918770419

Lin, C. A., Crowe, J., Pierre, L., & Lee, Y. (2021). Effects of parasocial interaction with an *Instafamous* influence on brand attitudes and purchase intentions. *Journal of Social Media in Society*, *10*, 55–78.

Lindstrom, K. N., Tucker, J. A., & McVay, M. (2023). Nudges and choice architecture to promote healthy food purchases in adults: A systematized review. *Psychology of Addictive Behaviors*, *37*(1), 87–103. doi:10.1037/adb0000892 PMID:36395010

Lin, L., Hoegg, J., & Aquino, K. (2018). When beauty backfires: The effects of server attractiveness on consumer taste perceptions. *Journal of Retailing*, *94*(3), 296–311. doi:10.1016/j.jretai.2018.04.003

Linqia. (2019). *The State of Influencer Marketing 2019*. https://linqia.com/wp-content/uploads/2019/04/Linqia-State-of-Influencer-Marketing-2019-Report.pdf

Linquia. (2019). *2020 Influencer Marketing Playbook*. Retrieved November 27, 2019, from https://linqia.com/insights/the-2020-influencer-marketing-playbook/

Lin, Y., & Kant, S. (2021). Using social media for citizen participation: Contexts, empowerment, and inclusion. *Sustainability (Basel), 13*(12), 6635. doi:10.3390/su13126635

Lipps, G., Norris, C., & Pignal, J. (2003). Measuring school engagement. *Education Quarterly Review, 9*(2).

Lissavoy, N. W. (2013). Pedagogy of the Impossible: Neoliberalism and the Ideology of Accountability. *Policy Futures in Education, 11*(4), 423–435. doi:10.2304/pfie.2013.11.4.423

Littler, J. (2018). *Against Meritocracy: Culture, Power and Myths of Mobility.* Routledge.

Liu, B., Yan, J., Briones, R., & Kuch, B. (2012). Managing turbulence in the blogosphere: Evaluating the blog-mediated crisis communication model with the American Red Cross. *Journal of Public Relations Research, 24*(4), 353–370. doi:10.1080/1062726X.2012.689901

Liu, Z., Li, J., Wang, X., & Guo, Y. (2023). How search and evaluation cues influence consumers' continuous watching and purchase intentions: An investigation of live-stream shopping from an information foraging perspective. *Journal of Business Research, 168*, 114233. Advance online publication. doi:10.1016/j.jbusres.2023.114233

Li, W., Ding, H., Xu, G., & Yang, J. (2023). The impact of fitness influencers on a social media platform on exercise intention during the COVID-19 pandemic: The role of parasocial relationships. *International Journal of Environmental Research and Public Health, 20*(2), 1113. doi:10.3390/ijerph20021113 PMID:36673868

Li, X., & Feng, J. (2022). Influenced or to be influenced: Engaging social media influencers in nation branding through the lens of authenticity. *Global Media and China, 7*(2), 219–240. doi:10.1177/20594364221094668

Llopis, G. (2013, April 8). Personal branding is a leadership requirement, not a self-promotion campaign. *Forbes.* https://www.forbes.com/sites/glennllopis/2013/04/08/personal-branding-is-a-leadership-requirement-not-a-self-promotion-campaign/?sh=50b73bd8226f

London, B., Downey, G., & Mace, S. (2007). Psychological theories of educational engagement: A multi-method approach to studying individual engagement and institutional change. *Vand. L. Rev., 60*, 455.

Lotti, L., Barile, L., & Manfredi, G. (2023). Improving recycling sorting behaviour with human eye nudges. *Scientific Reports, 13*(1), 10127. doi:10.1038/s41598-023-37019-x PMID:37349386

Lou, C., & Kim, H. K. (2019). Fancying the new rich and famous? Explicating the roles of influencer content, credibility, and parental mediation in adolescents' parasocial relationship, materialism, and purchase intentions. *Frontiers in Psychology, 10*, 2567. doi:10.3389/fpsyg.2019.02567 PMID:31803110

Lou, C., & Yuan, S. (2019). Influencer marketing: How message value and credibility affect consumer trust of branded content on social media. *Journal of Interactive Advertising, 19*(1), 58–73. doi:10.1080/15252019.2018.1533501

Lu, B., Fan, W., & Zhou, M. (2016). Social Presence, trust, and Social Commerce Purchase Intention: An empirical research. *Computers in Human Behavior, 56*, 225–237. doi:10.1016/j.chb.2015.11.057

Lubitz, R. (2016, June 22). *Model Denise Bidot wants you to know that there is no wrong way to be a woman.* Yahoo News. https://news.yahoo.com/news/model-denise-bidot-wants-know-140226584.html?guccounter=1&guce_referrer=aHR0cHM6Ly93d3cuZ29vZ2xl

Luckman, S. (2013). The Aura of the Analogue in a Digital Age: Women's Crafts, Creative Markets and Home-Based Labour After Etsy. *Cultural Studies Review, 19*(1), 249–270. doi:10.5130/csr.v19i1.2585

Luedicke, M. K., Thompson, C. J., & Giesler, M. (2010). Consumer identity work as moral protagonism: How myth and ideology animate a brand-mediated moral conflict. *The Journal of Consumer Research, 36*(6), 1016–1032. doi:10.1086/644761

Lundblad, L., & Davies, I. A. (2016). The values and motivations behind sustainable fashion consumption. *Journal of Consumer Behaviour, 15*(2), 149–162. doi:10.1002/cb.1559

Luong, T.-B., & Ho, C.-H. (2023). The influence of food vloggers on social media users: A study from Vietnam. *Heliyon, 9*(7), e18259. doi:10.1016/j.heliyon.2023.e18259 PMID:37501978

Luo, X., Lim, W. M., Cheah, J. H., Lim, X. J., & Dwivedi, Y. K. (2023). Live streaming commerce: A review and research agenda. *Journal of Computer Information Systems*, 1–24. doi:10.1080/08874417.2023.2290574

Luvaas, B. (2017). What does a fashion influencer look like? Portraits of the Instafamous. *Fashion, Style & Popular Culture, 4*(3), 341–363. doi:10.1386/fspc.4.3.341_7

Lynch, J., & Schuler, D. (1994). The matchup effect of spokesperson and product congruency: A schema theory interpretation. *Psychology and Marketing, 11*(5), 417–445. doi:10.1002/mar.4220110502

Macey, W. H., & Schneider, B. (2008). The meaning of employee engagement. *Industrial and Organizational Psychology: Perspectives on Science and Practice, 1*(1), 3–30. doi:10.1111/j.1754-9434.2007.0002.x

MacKenzie, S. B., & Lutz, R. J. (1989). An empirical examination of the structural antecedents of attitude toward the ad in an advertising pretesting context. *Journal of Marketing, 53*(2), 48–65. doi:10.1177/002224298905300204

MacKenzie, S. B., Lutz, R. J., & Belch, G. E. (1986). The role attitude toward the ad as a mediator of advertising effectiveness: A test of competing explanations. *JMR, Journal of Marketing Research, 23*(2), 130–143. doi:10.1177/002224378602300205

Madani, R. (2022). The new image of Saudi cultural shift; MDL Beast music festival; Saudi Vision 2030. *Cogent Arts & Humanities, 9*(1), 2105511. doi:10.1080/23311983.2022.2105511

Maddox, J. (2020). The secret life of pet Instagram accounts: Joy, resistance, and commodification in the Internet's cute economy. *New Media & Society, 23*(11), 3332–3348. doi:10.1177/1461444820956345

Maheshwari, V., & Fielding, J. (2019). Importance of Ethics and Sustainability in the Fashion Industry: An Abstract. In *Developments in Marketing Science: Proceedings of the Academy of Marketing Science* (pp. 139-140). Springer Nature. 10.1007/978-3-030-02568-7_39

Malik, M. J., Ahmad, M., Kamran, M. R., Aliza, K., & Elahi, M. Z. (2020). Student use of social media, academic performance, and creativity: The mediating role of intrinsic motivation. *Interactive Technology and Smart Education, 17*(4), 403–415. doi:10.1108/ITSE-01-2020-0005

Maloni, M. J., Gligor, D. M., Blumentritt, T., & Gligor, N. (2022). Fear or Competition? Antecedents to U.S. Business Student Immigration Attitudes. *Journal of Management Education, 46*(4), 715–750. doi:10.1177/10525629211065623

Manzerolle, V. (2010). Mobilizing the audience commodity: Digital labour in a wireless world. *Ephemera, 10*(4), 455–469.

Marcella-Hood, M. (2023). Augmenting Sustainable Fashion on Instagram. *Sustainability (Basel), 15*(4), 3609. doi:10.3390/su15043609

Marcelo, C., & Marcelo, P. (2021). Educational influencers on Twitter. Analysis of hashtags and relationship structure. *Comunicar, 29*(68), 73–83. doi:10.3916/C68-2021-06

Marchiori, D. R., Adriaanse, M. A., & De Ridder, D. T. (2017). Unresolved questions in nudging research: Putting the psychology back in nudging. *Social and Personality Psychology Compass, 11*(1), e12297. doi:10.1111/spc3.12297

Marks, H. M. (2000). Student engagement in instructional activity: Patterns in the elementary, middle, and high school years. *American Educational Research Journal, 37*(1), 153–184. doi:10.3102/00028312037001153

Marshall, T. (2008). Cultural differences in intimacy: The influence of gender-role ideology and individualism—collectivism. *Journal of Social and Personal Relationships, 25*(1), 143–168. doi:10.1177/0265407507086810

Martensen, A., Brockenhuus-Schack, S., & Zahid, A. L. (2018). How citizen influencers persuade their followers. *Journal of Fashion Marketing and Management, 22*(3), 335–353. doi:10.1108/JFMM-09-2017-0095

Martin, G. L. (2021). *Nudges for all? The effect of power on the efficiency of nudges* (Doctoral dissertation). http://hdl.handle.net/10400.14/35406

Martín, A., Swaab, R., Sinaceur, M., & Vasiljevic, D. (2015). The double-edged impact of future expectations in groups: Minority influence depends on minorities' and majorities' expectations to interact again. *Organizational Behavior and Human Decision Processes, 128*, 49–60. doi:10.1016/j.obhdp.2015.03.002

Martínez-López, F. J., Anaya-Sánchez, R., Fernández Giordano, M., & Lopez-Lopez, D. (2020). Behind influencer marketing: Key marketing decisions and their effects on followers' responses. *Journal of Marketing Management, 36*(7–8), 579–607. doi:10.1080/0267257X.2020.1738525

Martin, M. C., & Gentry, J. W. (1997). Stuck in the model trap: The effects of beautiful models in ads on female preadolescents and adolescents. *Journal of Advertising, 26*(2), 19–34. doi:10.1080/00913367.1997.10673520

Martin, N., & Morich, K. (2011). Unconscious mental processes in consumer choice: Toward a new model of consumer behavior. *Journal of Brand Management, 18*(7), 483–505. https://link.springer.com/article/10.1057/bm.2011.10. doi:10.1057/bm.2011.10

Marwick, A. E. (2013). They're really profound women, they're entrepreneurs. Conceptions of Authenticity in Fashion Blogging.

Mason, A. N., Narcum, J., & Mason, K. (2021). Social media marketing gains importance after Covid-19. *Cogent Business & Management, 8*(1), 1870797. Advance online publication. doi:10.1080/23311975.2020.1870797

Mason, M. C., Pauluzzo, R., & Umar, R. M. (2022). Recycling habits and environmental responses to fast-fashion consumption: Enhancing the theory of planned behaviour to predict Generation Y consumers' purchase decisions. *Waste Management (New York, N.Y.), 139*, 146–157. doi:10.1016/j.wasman.2021.12.012 PMID:34971902

Mathiyalakan, S., Heilman, G., Ho, K. K. W., & Law, W. (2018). An examination of the impact of gender and culture on Facebook privacy and trust in Guam. *Journal of International Technology and Information Management, 27*(1), 29–56. doi:10.58729/1941-6679.1363

Matthes, J., Prieler, M., & Adam, K. (2016). Gender-role portrayals in television advertising across the globe. *Sex Roles, 75*(7-8), 314–327. doi:10.1007/s11199-016-0617-y PMID:27688526

McAlexander, J. H., Schouten, J. W., & Koenig, H. F. (2002). Building brand community. *Journal of Marketing, 66*(1), 38–54. doi:10.1509/jmkg.66.1.38.18451

McComb, S. E., Gobin, K. C., & Mills, J. S. (2021). The effects of self-disclaimer Instagram captions on young women's mood and body image: The moderating effect of participants' own photo manipulation practices. *Body Image, 38*, 251–261. doi:10.1016/j.bodyim.2021.04.011 PMID:33964566

McCormick, H., & Livett, C. (2012). Analysing the influence of the presentation of fashion garments on young consumers' online behaviour. *Journal of Fashion Marketing and Management, 16*(1), 21–41. doi:10.1108/13612021211203014

McCormick, K. (2016). Celebrity endorsements: Influence of a product-endorser match on millennials attitudes and purchase intentions'. *Journal of Retailing and Consumer Services*, *32*, 39–45. doi:10.1016/j.jretconser.2016.05.012

McCroskey, J. C. (1966). Scales for the measurement of ethos. *Speech Monographs*, *33*(1), 65–72. doi:10.1080/03637756609375482

McDermott, V., & Caslin, T. (in press). Day 206 of being a girl: How LGBTQ+ GenZ are communicatively performing and disrupting traditional expectations of gender on TikTok. In R. R. Reynolds (Ed.), *Mediating Sex, Gender, and Sexuality in the Gen Z Era*. New York University Press.

McGuire, W. J. (1969). The Nature of Attitudes and Attitude Change. The Handbook of Social Psychology, 3, 372–398.

McGuire, W. J. (1985). Attitudes and Attitude Change. In Handbook of Social Psychology (vol. 2, pp. 233–346). Random House.

McKee, A. (2003). *Textual Analysis: A Beginner's Guide*. Sage Publications. doi:10.4135/9780857020017

McPherson, M., Smith-Lovin, L., & Cook, J. M. (2001). Birds of a feather: Homophily in social networks. *Annual Review of Sociology*, *27*(1), 415–444. doi:10.1146/annurev.soc.27.1.415

Meece, J. L., Blumenfeld, P. C., & Hoyle, R. H. (1988). Students' goal orientations and cognitive engagement in classroom activities. *Journal of Educational Psychology*, *80*(4), 514–523. doi:10.1037/0022-0663.80.4.514

Mehta, A. (2000). Advertising attitudes and advertising effectiveness. *Journal of Advertising Research*, *40*(3), 67–72. doi:10.2501/JAR-40-3-67-72

Mengyue, Z. (2021). *Based on Kahneman's two-system theory: presentation and application of the three-system theory*. Academic Journal of Humanities & Social Sciences. doi:10.25236/AJHSS.2021.040917

Men, L. R., & Tsai, W. H. S. (2012). How companies cultivate relationships with publics on social network sites: Evidence from China and the United States. *Public Relations Review*, *38*(5), 723–730. doi:10.1016/j.pubrev.2011.10.006

Men, L. R., & Tsai, W. H. S. (2013). Beyond liking or following: Understanding public engagement on social networking sites in China. *Public Relations Review*, *39*(1), 13–22. doi:10.1016/j.pubrev.2012.09.013

Men, L. R., Tsai, W. S., Chen, Z. F., & Ji, Y. G. (2018). Social presence and digital dialogic communication: Engagement lessons from top social CEOs. *Journal of Public Relations Research*, *30*(3), 83–99. doi:10.1080/1062726X.2018.1498341

Miladi, N. (2021). *Global Media Ethics and the Digital Revolution*. Taylor and Francis., doi:10.4324/9781003203551

Militello, M., Yang, R. A., Anderson, J. B., Szeto, M. D., Presley, C. L., & Laughter, M. R. (2021). Social Media and Ethical Challenges for the Dermatologist. *Current Dermatology Reports*, *10*(4), 120–127. doi:10.1007/s13671-021-00340-7 PMID:34540357

Minocher, X. (2019). Online consumer activism: Challenging companies with Change. org. *New Media & Society*, *21*(3), 620–638. doi:10.1177/1461444818803373

Mohamad, E., & Damanhuri, N. H. A. (2019). Female health opinion leaders and ethics on Instagram. *Jurnal Komunikasi: Malaysian Journal of Communication*, *35*(4), 193–210. doi:10.17576/JKMJC-2019-3504-12

Mohr, I., Fuxman, L., & Mahmoud, A. B. (2022). A triple-trickle theory for sustainable fashion adoption: The rise of a luxury trend. *Journal of Fashion Marketing and Management*, *26*(4), 640–660. doi:10.1108/JFMM-03-2021-0060

Mollen, A., & Wilson, H. (2010). Engagement, telepresence and interactivity in online consumer experience: Reconciling scholastic and managerial perspectives. *Journal of Business Research*, *63*(9-10), 919–925. doi:10.1016/j.jbusres.2009.05.014

Money, K., & Schepers, H. (2007). Are CSR and corporate governance converging? *Journal of General Management, 33*(2), 1–11. doi:10.1177/030630700703300201

Monge-Benito, S., Elorriaga-Illera, A., & Olabarri-Fernandez, E. (2020). YouTube celebrity endorsement: Audience evaluation of source attributes and response to sponsored content. A case study of influencer Verdeliss. *Communicatio Socialis, 33*, 149–166.

Montanaro, E. A., Kershaw, T. S., & Bryan, A. D. (2018). Dismantling the theory of planned behavior: Evaluating the relative effectiveness of attempts to uniquely change attitudes, norms, and perceived behavioral control. *Journal of Behavioral Medicine, 41*(6), 757–770. doi:10.1007/s10865-018-9923-x PMID:29671166

Moon, Y. S., & Chen, K. (2002). Gender portrayals in Hong Kong and Korean children's TV commercials: A cross-cultural comparison. *Asian Journal of Communication, 12*(2), 10–19. doi:10.1080/01292980209364825

Mooz, H. H., & Forsberg, K. (2008). *Making decisions that have global impact.* 18th Annual International Symposium of the International Council on Systems Engineering, INCOSE2008. 10.1007/978-3-030-62796-6_19

Morgan, G., & Nelligan, P. (2018). *The creativity hoax: Precarious work in the Gig Economy.* Anthem Press. doi:10.2307/j.ctt1z27hwj

Morimoto, M., & La Ferle, C. (2008). Examining the influence of culture on perceived source credibility of Asian Americans and the mediating role of similarity. *Journal of Current Issues and Research in Advertising, 30*(1), 49–60. doi:10.1080/10641734.2008.10505237

Morrow, P. C. (1990). Physical attractiveness and selection decision making. *Journal of Management, 16*(1), 45–60. doi:10.1177/014920639001600104

Moscovici, S. (2012). Minority influence. In Social Psychology: Revisiting the Classic Studies (pp. 91-106). Academic Press.

Moscovici, S. (1980). Toward a theory of conversion behavior. In Advances in experimental social psychology (Vol. 13, pp. 209–239). Academic Press. doi:10.1016/S0065-2601(08)60133-1

Moscovici, S., & Faucheux, C. (1972). Social Influence, Conformity Bias, and the Study of Active Minorities. *Advances in Experimental Social Psychology, 6*, 149–202. doi:10.1016/S0065-2601(08)60027-1

Moscovici, S., & Lage, E. (1976). Studies in social influence III: Majority versus minority influence in a group. *European Journal of Social Psychology, 6*(2), 149–174. doi:10.1002/ejsp.2420060202

Mudambi & Schuff. (2010). Research note: What makes a helpful online review? A study of customer reviews on Amazon.com. *MIS Quarterly: Management Information Systems, 34*(1), 185. doi:10.2307/20721420

Mukendi, A., Davies, I., McDonagh, P., & Glozer, S. (2020). Sustainable fashion: Current and future research directions. *European Journal of Marketing, 54*(11), 2873–2909. doi:10.1108/EJM-02-2019-0132

Muniz, A. M. Jr, & O'guinn, T. C. (2001). Brand community. *The Journal of Consumer Research, 27*(4), 412–432. doi:10.1086/319618

Munnukka, J., Maity, D., Reinikainen, H., & Luoma-aho, V. (2019). "Thanks for watching." The effectiveness of YouTube vlogendorsements. *Computers in Human Behavior, 93*, 226–234. 10.1016/j.chb.2018.12.014

Munnukka, J., Maity, D., Reinikainen, H., & Luoma-aho, V. (2019). "Thanks for watching". The effectiveness of YouTube vloendorsements. *Computers in Human Behavior, 93*, 226–234. doi:10.1016/j.chb.2018.12.014

Munnukka, J., Uusitalo, O., & Toivonen, H. (2016). Credibility of a peer endorser and advertising effectiveness. *Journal of Consumer Marketing, 33*(3), 182–192. doi:10.1108/JCM-11-2014-1221

Myers, S. (2021). Instagram source effects: The impact of familiarity and likeability of influencer outcomes. *Journal of Marketing Development and Competitiveness, 15*, 50–55.

Myers, S., Sen, S., Syrdal, H., & Woodroof, P. (2022). The impact of persuasion knowledge cues on social media engagement: A look at pet influencer marketing. *Journal of Marketing Theory and Practice*, 1–18. doi:10.1080/10696679.2022.2093224

Nafi & Ahmed. (2019). *The Ethical Standpoint of Social Influencers on Hotel EServicescape: A Theoretical Perspective on the Existing Literature.* Academic Press.

Nair, P., Rajesh, G., & Singh, A. K. Multiple facets of celebrity brand endorsement. (2019) *Sustainable Resource Management through Innovative Management Practices*, 65.

Nan, M., & Park, J. S. (2018). Effects of beauty vloggers' parasocial interaction on Chinese consumers' attitudes toward vlogs and the products. *The Research Journal of the Costume Culture, 26*(5), 649–664. doi:10.29049/rjcc.2018.26.5.649

Narasimha, R. (2023). *The role of influencers in shaping social issues: A look at influencer activism.* Retrieved from https://www.cxotoday.com/press-release/the-role-of-influencers-in-shaping-social-issues-a-look-at-influencer-activism/05/12/2023

Neely, E., Walton, M., & Stephens, C. (2014). Young people's food practices and social relationships. A thematic synthesis. *Appetite, 82*, 50–60. doi:10.1016/j.appet.2014.07.005 PMID:25017130

Nelson, A. (2023, May 18). *Charlize Theron's net worth, "Monster" Bank Account—Charlize Theron's Net Worth Is Almost as Big as Her Acting Range!* Parade. https://parade.com/celebrities/charlize-theron-net-worth

Neuendorf, K. A. (2017). The content analysis guidebook. *Sage (Atlanta, Ga.).*

Nicholls, S. B., & Rice, R. E. (2017). A dual-identity model of responses to deviance in online groups: Integrating social identity theory and expectancy violations theory. *Communication Theory, 27*(3), 243–268. doi:10.1111/comt.12113

Nichols, K., & Pappas, R. (2022). The #ethics behind social media influencers in dentistry. *The Journal of the American Dental Association, 153*(10), 1010–1011. doi:10.1016/j.adaj.2022.07.008 PMID:36041963

Niemeyer, K., & Siebert, O. (2023). Nostalgia, media, and technologies of the future. *Current Opinion in Psychology, 50*, 101561. doi:10.1016/j.copsyc.2023.101561 PMID:36889050

Niemietz, B. (2020, January 5). They bark, we buy: Pet influencers having big impact on what humans spend. *New York Dailey News.* https://www.nydailynews.com/2020/01/05/they-bark-we-buy-pet-influencers-having-big-impact-on-what-humans-spend/

Nogueira, E., Gomes, S., & Lopes, J. M. (2023). Triple Bottom Line, Sustainability, and Economic Development: What Binds Them Together? A bibliometric approach. *Sustainability (Basel), 15*(8), 6706. doi:10.3390/su15086706

Nuji, M. N. N., Ali, A., Noordin, W. N. W., Thaheer, B. A. N. M., & Mathiew, V. (2023). Of Trust and Influence: A Look At Social Media Influencers and Brand Promotion. *International Journal of Academic Research in Business & Social Sciences, 13*(6), 2152–2170. doi:10.6007/IJARBSS/v13-i6/15444

Núñez-Cansado, M., López-López, A., & Somarriba-Arechavala, N. (2021). Covert advertising by kidsfluencers: A methodological proposal applied to the case study of the ten youngest youtubers with most followers in Spain. *Profesional de la Informacion, 30*(2 C7 - e300219). doi:10.3145/epi.2021.mar.19

Nxumalo, C. T., & McHunu, G. G. (2020). Zulu men's conceptions, understanding, and experiences of voluntary medical male circumcision in KwaZulu-Natal, South Africa. *American Journal of Men's Health*, *14*(2). Advance online publication. doi:10.1177/1557988319892437 PMID:32131678

O'Connor, K., Muller Neff, D., & Pitman, S. (2018). Burnout in mental health professionals: A systematic review and meta-analysis of prevalence and determinants. *European Psychiatry*, *53*, 74–99. doi:10.1016/j.eurpsy.2018.06.003 PMID:29957371

Ocal, A. (2023). Perceptions of AI Ethics on Social Media. *2023 IEEE International Symposium on Ethics in Engineering, Science, and Technology (ETHICS)*. 10.1109/ETHICS57328.2023.10155069

Odekerken-Schroder, G. K., Wulf, D., & Hofstede, N. (2002). Is gender stereotyping in advertising more prevalent in masculine countries? A cross-national analysis. *International Marketing Review*, *19*(4), 408–419. doi:10.1108/02651330210435690

Ogden, C., Fryar, C. D., Carroll, M. D., & Flegal, K. M. (2004, October 27). Mean body weight, height, and body mass index, United States 1960+2002. *Centers for Disease Control and Prevention*. https://www.cdc.gov/nchs/data/ad/ad347.pdf

Ogden, J., Coop, N., Cousins, C., Crump, R., Field, L., Hughes, S., & Woodger, N. (2013). Distraction, the desire to eat and food intake. Towards an expanded model of mindless eating. *Appetite*, *62*, 119–126. doi:10.1016/j.appet.2012.11.023 PMID:23219989

Ohanian, R. (1990). Construction and validation of a scale to measure celebrity endorsers' perceived expertise, trustworthiness, and attractiveness. *Journal of Advertising*, *19*(3), 39–52. doi:10.1080/00913367.1990.10673191

Ohanian, R. (1991). The impact of celebrity spokespersons' perceived image on consumers' intentions to purchase. *Journal of Advertising*, *31*, 46–54.

Olney, T. J., Holbrook, M. B., & Batra, R. (1991). Consumer responses to advertising: The effects of ad content, emotions, and attitude toward the ad on viewing time. *The Journal of Consumer Research*, *17*(4), 440–453. doi:10.1086/208569

Oprea, C. (2023). Influencer branding in brand management. In Innovatives Markenmanagement (pp. 51–60). doi:10.1007/978-3-658-41364-4_6

Orminski, J., Tandoc, E. C. Jr, & Detenber, B. H. (2020). #sustainablefashion – A Conceptual Framework for Sustainable Fashion Discourse on Twitter. *Environmental Communication*, *15*(1), 115–132. doi:10.1080/17524032.2020.1802321

Orth, U. R., & Holancova, K. (2003). The influence of gender congruence on consumer attributions: A cross-cultural investigation. *Journal of International Consumer Marketing*, *15*(4), 79–107.

Orton-Johnson, K. (2012). Knit, purl and upload: New technologies, digital mediations and the experience of leisure. *Leisure Studies*, *33*(3), 305–321. doi:10.1080/02614367.2012.723730

Ortová, N., Hejlová, D., & Weiss, D. (2023). Creation of a code of ethics for influencer marketing: The case of the Czech Republic. *Journal of Media Ethics: Exploring Questions of Media Morality*, *38*(2), 65–79. doi:10.1080/23736992.2023.2193958

Ott, H. K., Vafeiadis, M., Kumble, S., & Waddell, T. F. (2016). Effects of message interactivity on product attitudes and purchase intentions. *Journal of Promotion Management*, *22*(1), 89–106. doi:10.1080/10496491.2015.1107011

Özdil, N., Dalbaşı, E., Özgüney, A., & Atiker, L. (2023). *Multifunctional Modification with TiO2, SiO2, and Flame Retardant Agent on Upholstery Fabrics Produced From Recycled Cotton Fibers*. AATCC Journal of Research. doi:10.1177/24723444221147976

Palomo-Domínguez, I., Elías-Zambrano, R., & Álvarez-Rodríguez, V. (2023). Gen Z's Motivations towards Sustainable Fashion and Eco-Friendly Brand Attributes: The Case of Vinted. *Sustainability (Basel)*, *15*(11), 8753. doi:10.3390/su15118753

Pansari, A., & Kumar, V. (2017). Customer engagement: The construct, antecedents, and consequences. *Journal of the Academy of Marketing Science*, *45*(3), 294–311. doi:10.1007/s11747-016-0485-6

Parboteeah, K. P., Hoegl, M., & Cullen, J. B. (2008). Managers' gender role attitudes: A country institutional profile approach. *Journal of International Business Studies*, *39*(5), 795–813. doi:10.1057/palgrave.jibs.8400384

Park, S. Y., Cho, M., & Kim, S. (2021). The effect of CSR expectancy violation: Value from expectancy violation theory and confirmation bias. *Journal of Marketing Communications*, *27*(4), 365–388. doi:10.1080/13527266.2019.1671478

Parsons, E., Maclaran, P., Chatzidakis, A., & Ashman, R. (2023). *Contemporary Issues in Marketing and Consumer Behavior* (3rd ed.). Taylor and Francis., doi:10.4324/9781003201151

Passikoff, R. (2006). *Predicting market success: New ways to measure customer loyalty and engage consumers with your brand.* John Wiley & Sons.

Patton, M. Q. (2014). Qualitative research & evaluation methods: Integrating theory and practice. *Sage (Atlanta, Ga.).*

Paul, L. A., & Gray, M. J. (2011). Sexual assault programming on college campuses: Using social psychological belief and behavior change principles to improve outcomes. *Trauma, Violence & Abuse*, *12*(2), 99–109. doi:10.1177/1524838010390710 PMID:21196434

Pawar, A. (2016). The power of personal branding. *International Journal of Engineering and Management Research*, *6*(2), 840–847.

Pawar, A., Kusmiati, M., & Sundari, S. (2022). The building of online personal branding. *Journal of Business and Management Inaba*, *1*(1), 1–15. doi:10.56956/jbmi.v1i1.6

Peleg-Oren, N. (2002). Group intervention for children of drug-addicted parents—Using expressive techniques. *Clinical Social Work Journal*, *30*(4), 403–418. doi:10.1023/A:1020768011128

Pencarelli, T., & Forlani, F. (2016). Marketing of touristic districts-viable systems in the experience economy. *Sinergie Italian Journal of Management*, *34*(1), 199–238.

Pentney, B. A. (2018). Feminism, Activism, and Knitting: Are the Fibre Arts a Viable Mode for Feminist Political Action? *Thirdspace: A Journal of Feminist Theory & Culture*, *8*(1), 14.

Pérez, A. (2022). Behavioral Economics: Theoretical Conception to Understand Economic Behavior. *ESPOCH Congresses: The Ecuadorian Journal of S.T.E.A.M.* . doi:10.18502/espoch.v2i2.11403

Perry, P., Ashman, R., & Stalker, I. D. (2020). Special session: corporate social responsibility and ai: the case of fashion: an abstract. In *Developments in Marketing Science: Proceedings of the Academy of Marketing Science* (pp. 143-144). Springer Nature. 10.1007/978-3-030-42545-6_36

Peter, C., & Muth, L. (2023). Social media influencers' role in shaping political opinions and actions of young audiences. *Media and Communication*, *11*(3). Advance online publication. doi:10.17645/mac.v11i3.6750

Peters, K., Chen, Y., Kaplan, A. M., Ognibeni, B., & Pauwels, K. (2013). Social media metrics—A framework and guidelines for managing social media. *Journal of Interactive Marketing*, *27*(4), 281–298. doi:10.1016/j.intmar.2013.09.007

Pétursdóttir, G. M. (2017). Fire-raising feminists: Embodied experience and activism in academia. *European Journal of Women's Studies*, *24*(1), 85–99. doi:10.1177/1350506815622513

Pham, M.-H. T. (2011). Blog ambition: Fashion, feelings, and the political economy of the digital raced body. *Camera Obscura, 26*(1), 1–37. doi:10.1215/02705346-2010-013

Philbrick, J. L., & Cleveland, A. D. (2015). Personal branding: Building your pathway to professional success. *Medical Reference Services Quarterly, 34*(2), 181–189. doi:10.1080/02763869.2015.1019324 PMID:25927510

Phillips, K. W., Northcraft, G. B., & Neale, M. A. (2006). Surface-level diversity and decision-making in groups: When does deep-level similarity help? *Group Processes & Intergroup Relations, 9*(4), 467–482. doi:10.1177/1368430206067557

Piehler, R., Schade, M., Sinnig, J., & Burmann, C. (2022). Traditional or 'instafamous' celebrity? Role of origin of fame in social media influencer marketing. *Journal of Strategic Marketing, 30*(4), 408–420. doi:10.1080/0965254X.2021.1909107

Pierce, J. (2018). Storytelling through photos: A photovoice lens on ethical visual research. In *Research in Ethical Issues in Organizations* (Vol. 19, pp. 67–90). Emerald Group Publishing Ltd. doi:10.1108/S1529-209620180000019005

Pierucci, S. (2018, January 17). *Why MICRO-INFLUENCER Marketing is still 'The Game' in 2019.* Retrieved May 23, 2019, from Medium website: https://medium.com/swlh/why-micro-influencer-marketing-is-the-game-in-2018-fdeda0993c36

Politi, E., Gale, J., & Staerklé, C. (2017). Flexible Solidarity with Refugees. *Integrating Minority Influence and Intergroup Communication., 30*(1), 172. doi:10.5334/irsp.24

Poorthuis, A., Power, D., & Zook, M. (2019). Attentional social media: Mapping the spaces and networks of the Fashion Industry. *Annals of the American Association of Geographers, 110*(4), 941–966. doi:10.1080/24694452.2019.1664887

Pornpitakpan, C. (2004). The persuasive effect of circadian arousal, endorser expertise, and argument strength in advertising. *Journal of Global Marketing, 17*(2-3), 141–172. doi:10.1300/J042v17n02_07

Portal, S., Abratt, R., & Bendixen, M. (2019). The role of brand authenticity in developing brand trust. *Journal of Strategic Marketing, 27*(8), 714–729. doi:10.1080/0965254X.2018.1466828

Potts, L., Small, R., & Trice, M. (2019). Boycotting the Knowledge Makers: How Reddit Demonstrates the Rise of Media Blacklists and Source Rejection in Online Communities. *IEEE Transactions on Professional Communication, 62*(4 C7 - 8894031), 351-363. doi:10.1109/TPC.2019.2946942

Pöyry, E., Pelkonen, M., Naumanen, E., & Laaksonen, S.-M. (2019). A call for authenticity: Audience responses to social media influencer endorsements in strategic communication. *International Journal of Strategic Communication, 13*(4), 336–351. doi:10.1080/1553118X.2019.1609965

Pöyry, E., Pelkonen, M., Naumanen, E., & Laaksonen, S.-M. (2021). A Call for Authenticity: Audience Responses to Social Media Influencer Endorsements in Strategic Communication. In N. S. Borchers (Ed.), *Social Media Influencers in Strategic Communication.* Routledge. doi:10.4324/9781003181286-6

Pozharliev, R., Rossi, D., & De Angelis, M. (2022). A picture says more than a thousand words: Using consumer neuroscience to study Instagram users' responses to influencer advertising. *Psychology and Marketing, 39*(7), 1336–1349. doi:10.1002/mar.21659

Prentice, D. A. (2022). Targeting ignorance to change behavior. In Routledge international handbook of ignorance studies (pp. 305-312). Routledge. doi:10.4324/9781003100607-34

Prentice, C., Han, X. Y., Hua, L.-L., & Hu, L. (2019). The influence of identity-driven customer engagement on purchase intention. *Journal of Retailing and Consumer Services, 47*, 339–347. doi:10.1016/j.jretconser.2018.12.014

Prestwich, A., Sniehotta, F. F., Whittington, C., Dombrowski, S. U., Rogers, L., & Michie, S. (2014). Does theory influence the effectiveness of health behavior interventions? Meta-analysis. *Health Psychology, 33*(5), 465–474. doi:10.1037/a0032853 PMID:23730717

Prislin, R. (2022). Minority Influence: An Agenda for Study of Social Change. *Frontiers in Psychology, 13*, 13. doi:10.3389/fpsyg.2022.911654 PMID:35814107

Priya, A. (2021). Case study methodology of qualitative research: Key attributes and navigating the conundrums in its application. *Sociological Bulletin, 70*(1), 94–110. doi:10.1177/0038022920970318

Procházka, D. A. (2021). Attitude of Czech influencers towards disinformation. *IDIMT 2021 -Pandemics: Impacts, Strategies and Responses, 29th Interdisciplinary Information Management Talks.*

Py, B. (2023). Les médecins, la communication et l'influence en santé après la loi du 9 juin 2023. *Médecine & Droit, 2023*(183), 121–125. Advance online publication. doi:10.1016/j.meddro.2023.08.001

Rahman, S. U., Saleem, S., Akhtar, S., Ali, T., & Khan, M. A. (2014). Consumers' adoption of apparel fashion: The role of innovativeness, involvement, and social values. *International Journal of Marketing Studies, 6*(3). Advance online publication. doi:10.5539/ijms.v6n3p49

Raimundo, R., & Rosário, A. (2021). The Impact of Artificial Intelligence on Data System Security: A Literature Review. *Sensors (Basel), 21*(21), 7029. doi:10.3390/s21217029 PMID:34770336

Raimundo, R., & Rosário, A. T. (2022). Cybersecurity in the Internet of Things in Industrial Management. *Applied Sciences (Basel, Switzerland), 12*(3), 1598. doi:10.3390/app12031598

Ramanayake, R., Wicke, P., & Nallur, V. (2023). Immune moral models? Pro-social rule breaking as a moral enhancement approach for ethical AI. *AI & Society, 38*(2), 801–813. doi:10.1007/s00146-022-01478-z PMID:35645466

Ranpariya, V., Chu, B., Fathy, R., & Lipoff, J. B. (2020). Dermatology without dermatologists? Analyzing Instagram influencers with dermatology-related hashtags. *Journal of the American Academy of Dermatology, 83*(6), 1840–1842. doi:10.1016/j.jaad.2020.05.039 PMID:32416205

Rashi, T., & Schleifer, R. (2023). The Ethics of Psychological Warfare–Lessons from Israel. *Democracy and Security, 19*(2), 199–210. doi:10.1080/17419166.2023.2210472

Rass, S. (2021). Judging the quality of (fake) news on the internet. *Mind & Society, 20*(1), 129–133. doi:10.1007/s11299-020-00249-x

Research reveals Gen Z's priorities as Enterprise, Environment and Equality. (2022). Retrieved 8 September 2022, from https://www.prnewswire.com/news-releases/research-reveals-gen-zs-priorities-as-enterprise-environment-and-equality-301517764.html

Robert, Y. (2018, October 23). *How ASOs is making E-commerce all-inclusive.* Forbes. https://www.forbes.com/sites/yolarobert1/2018/10/23/now-trending-how-asos-is-making-e-commerce-all-inclusive/?sh=521a65b9297d

Roberts, R. (2021, March 10). *Pet industry trends, growth & statistics in 2021 and beyond: Unleashing your ecommerce pet marketing strategies.* Common Thread. https://commonthreadco.com/blogs/coachs-corner/pet-industry-trendsgrowth-ecommerce-marketing

Roberts, D. R., & Davenport, T. O. (2002). Job engagement: Why it's important and how to improve it. *Employment Relations Today, 29*(3), 21–29. doi:10.1002/ert.10048

Robinson, B. (2020). Towards an ontology and ethics of virtual influencers. *AJIS. Australasian Journal of Information Systems, 24*, C7–C2807. doi:10.3127/ajis.v24i0.2807

Rocamora, A. (2011). Personal fashion blogs: Screens and mirrors in digital self-portraits. *Fashion Theory, 15*(4), 407–424. doi:10.2752/175174111X13115179149794

Rocamora, A. (2012). Hypertextuality and remediation in the fashion media: The case of fashion blogs. *Journalism Practice, 6*(1), 92–106. doi:10.1080/17512786.2011.622914

Roccapriore, A. Y., & Pollock, T. G. (2023). I don't need a degree, I've got abs: Influencer warmth and competence, communication mode, and stakeholder engagement on social media. *Academy of Management Journal, 66*(3), 979–1006. doi:10.5465/amj.2020.1546

Rodenburg, K., & Macdonald, K. (2021). Enhancing business schools' pedagogy on sustainable business practices and ethical decision-making. *Sustainability (Switzerland), 13*(10 C7 -5527). doi:10.3390/su13105527

Rodgers, R. F., Kruger, L., Lowy, A. S., Long, S., & Richard, C. (2019). Getting Real about body image: A qualitative investigation of the usefulness of the Aerie Real campaign. *Body Image, 30*, 127–134. doi:10.1016/j.bodyim.2019.06.002 PMID:31260946

Rodgers, S. (2003). The effects of sponsor relevance on consumer reactions to internet sponsorships. *Journal of Advertising, 32*(4), 67–76. doi:10.1080/00913367.2003.10639141

Rogers, D. L. (2016). *The digital transformation playbook: Rethink your business for the digital age*. Columbia University Press. doi:10.7312/roge17544

Roozen, I., Raedts, M., & Meijburg, L. (2021). Do verbal and visual nudges influence consumers' choice for sustainable fashion? *Journal of Global Fashion Marketing, 12*(4), 327–342. doi:10.1080/20932685.2021.1930096

Rosário, A. T., & Dias, J. C. (2023). How Industry 4.0 and Sensors Can Leverage Product Design: Opportunities and Challenges. *Sensors (Basel), 23*(3), 1165. doi:10.3390/s23031165 PMID:36772206

Rosário, A. T., Lopes, P. R., & Rosário, F. S. (2023). Metaverse in Marketing: Challenges and Opportunities. In A. Khang, V. Shah, & S. Rani (Eds.), *Handbook of Research on AI-Based Technologies and Applications in the Era of the Metaverse* (pp. 204–227). IGI Global. doi:10.4018/978-1-6684-8851-5.ch010

Rosas-Moreno, T. C. (2023). How Gendered Mediation Affects Local News Framing of Trafficking Victims: A Call for Ethics-Of-Care Journalism. *Journal of Human Trafficking*, 1–19. Advance online publication. doi:10.1080/23322705.2023.2225390

Rossanty, Y., Sari, P. B., Amlus, M. H., & Nasution, T. A. M. (2021). Islam, opinion leaders, and social media influencer. In *The Role of Islamic Spirituality in the Management and Leadership Process* (pp. 66–84). IGI Global. doi:10.4018/978-1-7998-6892-7.ch004

Rossi, C., & Rivetti, F. (2023). Virtual influencer marketing: is it effective in engaging younger generations? *Proceedings of the 10th European Conference on Social Media, ECSM 2023*. 10.34190/ecsm.10.1.1061

Rossolatos, G. (2021). The depth of brand engagement funnel: Dimensionalizing interaction in social media brand communities. *Qualitative Market Research, 24*(2), 200–220. doi:10.1108/QMR-03-2019-0041

Roth, L. M. (1999). The right to privacy is political: Power, the boundary between public and private, and sexual harassment. *Law & Social Inquiry, 24*(01), 45–71. doi:10.1111/j.1747-4469.1999.tb00792.x

Rotimi, E., Topple, C., & Hopkins, J. (2021). Towards A Conceptual Framework of Sustainable Practices of Post-consumer Textile Waste at Garment End of Lifecycle: A Systematic Literature Review Approach. *Sustainability (Basel), 13*(5), 2965. doi:10.3390/su13052965

Ryan, R. M., & Deci, E. L. (2000). Self-determination theory and the facilitation of intrinsic motivation, social development, and well-being. *The American Psychologist, 55*(1), 68–78. doi:10.1037/0003-066X.55.1.68 PMID:11392867

Ryu, S., & Park, B. (2018). Do I want to pay to download movies: Factors affecting acceptance of legal movie download services. *Journal of Information. Communication and Ethics in Society, 16*(1), 45–60. doi:10.1108/JICES-03-2017-0019

Saczynski, J. S., Pfeifer, L. A., Masaki, K., Korf, E. S. C., Laurin, D., White, L., & Launer, L. J. (2006). The effect of social engagement on incident dementia: The Honolulu-Asia Aging Study. *American Journal of Epidemiology, 163*(5), 433–440. doi:10.1093/aje/kwj061 PMID:16410348

Sadagheyani, H. E., & Tatari, F. (2020). Investigating the role of social media on mental health. *Mental Health and Social Inclusion, 25*(1), 41–51. doi:10.1108/MHSI-06-2020-0039

Sah, Y. J., & Peng, W. (2023). Context-dependent Online Social Influence: Effect of Majority and Minority Comments on Posters and Lurkers. *Social Science Computer Review, 41*(4), 1316–1335. doi:10.1177/08944393211070527

Sakdiyakorn, M., Golubovskaya, M., & Solnet, D. (2021). Understanding Generation Z through collective consciousness: Impacts for hospitality work and employment. *International Journal of Hospitality Management, 94*, 102822. doi:10.1016/j.ijhm.2020.102822

Saksena, R. A. (2020). *Sustainable Fashion. [online] Circular Economy and Re-Commerce in the Fashion Industry.* Available at: https://www.semanticscholar.org/paper/Sustainable-Fashion-Saksena/e181956c3d183642cb2bda7cb-ceb410416f38e93

Saldaña, C. M., Welner, K. G., Malcolm, S., & Tisch, E. (2021). Teachers as Market Influencers: Towards a Policy Framework for Teacher Brand Ambassador Programs in K-12 Schools. *Education Policy Analysis Archives, 29*(August - December), C7–C109. doi:10.14507/epaa.29.5654

Saleem, Z. (2023). Impact of Instagram fashion influencers on consumer buying behavior. *MAIRAJ, 1*(2), 24–32. doi:10.58760/mairaj.v1i2.9

Sambargi & Tripathi. (2023). A Study on Awareness and Perceptions towards Sustainable Fashion. *International Scientific Journal of Engineering and Management, 2*(4), 1–10. Available at: https://isjem.com/download/a-study-on-the-awareness-and-perception-towards-sustainable-fashion/

Sanderon, J. (2009). "You are all loved so much" Exploring relational maintenance within the context of parasocial relationships. *Journal of Media Psychology, 21*(4), 171–182. doi:10.1027/1864-1105.21.4.171

Santoro, J. D., & Bennett, M. (2018). Ethics of end of life decisions in pediatrics: A narrative review of the roles of caregivers, shared decision-making, and patient centered values. Behavioral *Sciences, 8*(5 C7 - 42). doi:10.3390/bs8050042

Sastre, A. (2014). Towards a radical body positive: Reading the online "body positive movement". *Feminist Media Studies, 14*(6), 929–943. doi:10.1080/14680777.2014.883420

Sawhney, M., Verona, G., & Prandelli, E. (2005). Collaborating to create: The Internet as a platform for customer engagement in product innovation. *Journal of Interactive Marketing, 19*(4), 4–17. doi:10.1002/dir.20046

Saxena, J. (2019). *Racism in the knitting community is finally being talked about.* Retrieved Feb 27, 2019, from *Vox* website: https://www.vox.com/the-goods/2019/2/25/18234950/knitting-racism-instagram-stories

Scaraboto, D., & Fischer, E. (2013). Frustrated fashionistas: An institutional theory perspective on consumer quests for greater choice in mainstream markets. *The Journal of Consumer Research*, *39*(6), 1234–1257. doi:10.1086/668298

Schaefer, L. M., Burke, N. L., Thompson, J. K., Dedrick, R. F., Heinberg, L. J., Calogero, R. M., & Anderson, D. A. (2016). Development and validation of the sociocultural attitudes towards appearance questionnaire-4 (SATAQ-4). *Psychological Assessment*, *27*(1), 54–67. doi:10.1037/a0037917 PMID:25285718

Scharff, C. (2016). The Psychic Life of Neoliberalism: Mapping the Contours of Entrepreneurial Subjectivity. *Theory, Culture & Society*, *33*(6), 107–122. doi:10.1177/0263276415590164

Schivinski, B., & Dabrowski, D. (2016). The effect of social media communication on consumer perceptions of brands. *Journal of Marketing Communications*, *22*(2), 189–214. doi:10.1080/13527266.2013.871323

Schlüter, M., Caniglia, G., Orach, K., Bodin, Ö., Magliocca, N., Meyfroidt, P., & Reyers, B. (2022). Why care about theories? Innovative ways of theorizing in sustainability science. *Current Opinion in Environmental Sustainability*, *54*, 101154. doi:10.1016/j.cosust.2022.101154

Schmidt, J. (2007). Blogging practices: An analytical framework. *Journal of Computer-Mediated Communication*, *12*(4), 1409–1427. doi:10.1111/j.1083-6101.2007.00379.x

Schouten, A. P., Janssen, L., & Verspaget, M. (2021). Celebrity vs. Influencer endorsements in advertising: the role of identification, credibility, and Product-Endorser fit. Leveraged Marketing Communications, 208-231.

Schouten, A. P., Janssen, L., & Verspaget, M. (2019). Celebrity vs. Influencer endorsements in advertising: The role of identification, credibility, and Product-Endorser fit. *International Journal of Advertising*, *39*(2), 258–281. doi:10.1080/02650487.2019.1634898

Scott, D. M. (2015). *The new rules of marketing and PR: How to use social media, online video, mobile applications, blogs, news releases, and viral marketing to reach buyers directly* (D. M. Scott, Ed.; 5th ed.). John Wiley & Sons. doi:10.1002/9781119172499.ch02

Segrave, K. (2015). *Endorsements in advertising: A social history*. McFarland.

Senft, T. M. (2008). *Camgirls: Celebrity and community in the age of social networks*. Peter Lang Publishing.

Shah, S. (2021, September 17). *'A monstrous market': Whatnot co-founder Grant Lafontaine on what's next for the livestream shopping unicorn*. ModernRetail. https://www.modernretail.co/retailers/a-monstrous-market-Whatnot-co-founder-grant-lafontaine-on-whats-next-for-the-livestream-shopping-unicorn/

Shang, S. S. C., Wu, Y.-L., & Sie, Y.-J. (2017). Generating consumer resonance for purchase intention on social network sites. *Computers in Human Behavior*, *69*, 18–28. doi:10.1016/j.chb.2016.12.014

Shanmukhaprasanthi, T., Rayavarapu, S. M., Lavanya, Y. L., & Rao, G. S. (2023). A Comprehensive Study of Image Inpainting Techniques with Algorithmic approach. *2023 6th International Conference on Information Systems and Computer Networks (ISCON)*, 1–5. 10.1109/ISCON57294.2023.10112205

Shan, Y., Chen, K., & Lin, J. (2020). When social media influencers endorse brands: The effects of self-influencer congruence, parasocial identification, and perceived endorser motive. *International Journal of Advertising*, *39*(5), 590–610. doi:10.1080/02650487.2019.1678322

Shareef, M. A., Mukerji, B., Dwivedi, Y. K., Rana, N. P., & Islam, R. (2019). Social media marketing: Comparative effect of advertisement sources. *Journal of Retailing and Consumer Services*, *46*, 58–69. doi:10.1016/j.jretconser.2017.11.001

Sharma, A. (2023). *Google Analytics 4 and how it is changing the way we measure digital success.* Retrieved from https://www.addwebsolution.com/blog/google-analytics-4

Sharma, P., & Francis, D. P. (2020). Social media influencers in cardiology/metabolism-a force for good or evil? *Heart and Metabolism*, (82), 36–40.

Shelton, C., Schroeder, S., & Curcio, R. (2020). Instagramming their hearts out: What do edu-influencers share on Instagram? *Contemporary Issues in Technology & Teacher Education*, *20*(3), 529–554. https://www.learntechlib.org/primary/p/215623/

Shin, H. K. (2020). A case study on value creation of fashion brands using content collaboration targeting MZ generation. *The Research Journal of Costume Culture*, *28*(6), 830–844. doi:10.29049/rjcc.2020.28.6.830

Shinnar, R., Giacomin, O., & Janssen, F. (2012). Entrepreneurial Perceptions and Intentions: The Role of Gender and Culture. *Entrepreneurship Theory and Practice*, *36*(3), 465–493. doi:10.1111/j.1540-6520.2012.00509.x

Shirvanimoghaddam, K., Motamed, B., Ramakrishn, S., & Naebe, M. (2020). Death by Waste: A Fashion and Textile Circular Economy Case. *The Science of the Total Environment*, *718*, 137317. doi:10.1016/j.scitotenv.2020.137317 PMID:32088483

Shiv, B., Edell, J. A., & Payne, J. W. (1997). Factors affecting the impact of negatively and positively framed ad messages. *The Journal of Consumer Research*, *24*(3), 285–294. doi:10.1086/209510

Shodipe-Dosunmu, A. (2023, June 9). *The history and evolution of live streaming.* Make Use Of. https://www.makeuseof.com/history-of-live-streaming/

Shoenberger, H., & Kim, E. (2019). Product placement as leveraged marketing communications: The role of wishful identification, brand trust, and brand buying behaviours. *International Journal of Advertising*, *38*(1), 50–66. doi:10.1080/02650487.2017.1391678

Shoenberger, H., Kim, E. A., & Johnson, E. K. (2020). #BeingReal about Instagram ad models: the effects of perceived authenticity: How image modification of female body size alters advertising attitude and buying intention. *Journal of Advertising Research*, *60*(2), 197–207. doi:10.2501/JAR-2019-035

Shopify. (2021). *Future of Commerce.* https://cdn.shopify.com/static/future-of-commerce/Shopify%20Future%20of%20Commerce%202021.pdf

Siddiqi, A., & Bodolica, V. (2023). Bon voyage: A vacation from food wastage. *Emerald Emerging Markets Case Studies*, *13*(2), 1–31. doi:10.1108/EEMCS-05-2023-0148

Siemens, J. C., Smith, S., Fisher, D., & Jensen, T. D. (2008). Product Expertise versus Professional Expertise: Congruency between an Endorser's Chosen Profession and the Endorsed Product. *Journal of Targeting. Measurement and Analysis for Marketing*, *16*(3), 159–168. doi:10.1057/jt.2008.8

Silva, S., & de Brito, P. Q. (2020). The Characteristics of Digital Influencers and Their Ethically Questionable Attitudes. *Smart Innovation, Systems and Technologies.* doi:10.1080/10508422.2021.1977935

Sinelnikov, D. (2022). *The rise of influencer marketing: take your business international in 2022.* https://www.forbes.com/sites/forbesagencycouncil/2022/03/18/the-rise-of-influencer-marketing-take-your-business-international-in-2022/?sh=1bbc3bf36d9c

Singha, R., & Singha, S. (2024). Transitioning to digital merchandise: Integrating metaverse into retail offerings. In S. Rezaei & A. Ansary (Eds.), *Artificial Intelligence of Things (AIoT) for Productivity and Organizational Transition* (Vol. 1, pp. 26–51). IGI Global. doi:10.4018/979-8-3693-0993-3.ch002

Singha, R., & Singha, S. (2024a). Building capabilities and workforce for metaverse-driven retail formats. In B. E. Singla, K. Shalender, & N. Singh (Eds.), *Creator's Economy in Metaverse Platforms: Empowering Stakeholders Through Omnichannel Approach* (Vol. 1, pp. 111–131). IGI Global. doi:10.4018/979-8-3693-3358-7.ch007

Singha, S. (2023). Exploring the role of social media in enhancing K-12 Economics education. In B. Scott & M. E. Fox (Eds.), *Cases on Economics Education and Tools for Educators* (Vol. 1, pp. 160–182). IGI Global. doi:10.4018/978-1-6684-7583-6.ch007

Singha, S. (2024). Social media's influence on consumer decision-making: A roadmap for success. In F. Sahin & C. E. Soylemez (Eds.), *Globalized Consumer Insights in the Digital Era* (Vol. 1, pp. 85–109). IGI Global. doi:10.4018/979-8-3693-3811-7.ch004

Singha, S. (2024a). Unveiling gender dynamics in digital capitalism: Navigating the path to social gender equality. In C. Topçu (Ed.), *Digital Capitalism in the New Media Era* (Vol. 1, pp. 161–186). IGI Global. doi:10.4018/979-8-3693-1182-0.ch009

Singha, S., & Mukthar, J. (2024). Transitioning to digital merchandise: Integrating metaverse into retail offerings. In B. E. Singla, K. Shalender, & N. Singh (Eds.), *Creator's Economy in Metaverse Platforms: Empowering Stakeholders Through Omnichannel Approach* (Vol. 1, pp. 71–96). IGI Global. doi:10.4018/979-8-3693-3358-7.ch005

Sliburyte, L. (2009). How celebrities can be used in advertising to the best advantage? *World Academy of Science, Engineering and Technology*, *58*, 934–939.

Smith, K. (2022, December 12). *How covid-19 increased influencer marketing*. Hurrdat Marketing. https://hurrdatmarketing.com/digital-marketing-news/how-covid-19-increased-influencer-marketing/

Smith, P. (2024). *Global apparel market - statistics & facts*. Statista https://www.statista.com/topics/5091/apparel-market-worldwide/#topicOverview

Smith, B. G., Krishna, A., & Al-Sinan, R. (2019). Beyond Slactivism: Examining the entanglement between social media engagement, empowerment, and participation in activism. *International Journal of Strategic Communication*, *13*(3), 182–196. doi:10.1080/1553118X.2019.1621870

Sniehotta, F. F., Presseau, J., & Araújo-Soares, V. (2014). Time to retire the theory of planned behaviour. *Health Psychology Review*, *8*(1), 1–7. doi:10.1080/17437199.2013.869710 PMID:25053004

So, K. K. F., King, C., Sparks, B. A., & Wang, Y. (2016). The role of customer engagement in building consumer loyalty to tourism brands. *Journal of Travel Research*, *55*(1), 64–78. doi:10.1177/0047287514541008

Sokolova, K., & Kefi, H. (2020). Instagram and YouTube bloggers promote it, why should I buy? How credibility and parasocial interaction influence purchase intentions. *Journal of Retailing and Consumer Services*, *53*(101742), 101742. doi:10.1016/j.jretconser.2019.01.011

Sokolova, K., Kefi, H., & Dutot, V. (2022). Beyond the shallows of physical attractiveness: Perfection and objectifying gaze on Instagram. *International Journal of Information Management*, *67*, 102546. doi:10.1016/j.ijinfomgt.2022.102546

Sokolova, K., & Perez, C. (2021). You follow fitness influencers on YouTube. But do you actually exercise? How parasocial relationships, and watching fitness influencers, relate to intentions to exercise. *Journal of Retailing and Consumer Services*, *58*, 102276. doi:10.1016/j.jretconser.2020.102276

Sommer, V. (2020). Multimodal analysis in qualitative research: Extending grounded theory through the lens of social semiotics. *Qualitative Inquiry*, *27*(8-9), 1102–1113. Advance online publication. doi:10.1177/1077800420978746

Spears, N., & Singh, S. N. (2004). Measuring attitude toward the brand and purchase intentions. *Journal of Current Issues and Research in Advertising*, *26*(2), 53–66. doi:10.1080/10641734.2004.10505164

Sprecher, S., & Hatfield, E. (2022). Ratings of the physical attractiveness of an interaction partner after a getting-acquainted interaction. *Personal Relationships*, *29*(2), 366–385. doi:10.1111/pere.12422

Springgay, S. (2010). Knitting as an Aesthetic of Civic Engagement: Re-conceptualizing Feminist Pedagogy through Touch. *Feminist Teacher*, *20*(2), 111–123. doi:10.1353/ftr.2010.0009

Ssanyu, J. N., Kiguba, R., Olum, R., Kiguli, J., & Kitutu, F. E. (2022). Using community influencer groups to address COVID-19 misinformation and vaccine hesitancy in Uganda: a protocol for a prospective quasi-experimental study. *BMJ Open, 12*(8 C7 - 057994). doi:10.1136/bmjopen-2021-057994

Stål, H. I., & Jansson, J. (2017). Sustainable consumption and value propositions: Exploring product–service system practices among Swedish fashion firms. *Sustainable Development (Bradford)*, *25*(6), 546–558. doi:10.1002/sd.1677

Stanberry, K., Stanberry, C., & Reeves, T. (2021). A persistent academic ethical dilemma: Too few female students in STEM five decades after Title IX. *Journal of Academic Ethics*, *19*(1), 25–34. doi:10.1007/s10805-020-09370-5

Statista. (2023). *Fashion eCommerce: Market data & analysis, August 2023*. Statista. https://www.statista.com/study/38340/ecommerce-report-fashion/

Statista. (2023a). *Fashion - Worldwide. Statista Market Forecast*. Retrieved from https://www.statista.com/outlook/90000000/100/fashion/worldwide

Statista. (2023a). *Influencer marketing worldwide – statistics & facts.* Retrieved from: https://www.statista.com/topics/2496/influence-marketing/#topicOverview

Statista. (2023b). *Global apparel market - statistics & facts*. Retrieved from https://www.statista.com/topics/4592/global-apparel-market/

Statista. (2023b). *YouTube food & drink industry sponsored video views in the U.S. & Canada 2020.* Retrieved from: https://www.statista.com/statistics/1269589/youtube-food-drink-industry-sponsored-video-views/#statisticContainer

Steele, L., Orefuwa, E., Bino, S., Singer, S. R., Lutwama, J., & Dickmann, P. (2020). Earlier Outbreak Detection—A Generic Model and Novel Methodology to Guide Earlier Detection Supported by Data From Low- and Mid-Income Countries. *Frontiers in Public Health*, *8*, C7–C452. doi:10.3389/fpubh.2020.00452 PMID:33014967

Steils, N., Martin, A., & Toti, J.-F. (2022). Managing the Transparency Paradox Of Social-Media Influencer Disclosures. *Journal of Advertising Research*, *62*(2), 148–166. doi:10.2501/JAR-2022-008

Stein, J.-P., Krause, E., & Ohler, P. (2021). Every (Insta)gram counts? Applying cultivation theory to explore the effects of Instagram on young users' body image. *Psychology of Popular Media Culture*, *10*(1), 87–97. doi:10.1037/ppm0000268

Stevens, A., & Griffiths, S. (2020). Body Positivity (#BoPo) in everyday life: An ecological momentary assessment study showing potential benefits to individuals' body image and emotional wellbeing. *Body Image*, *35*, 181–191. doi:10.1016/j.bodyim.2020.09.003 PMID:33068893

Stojanovic, I., Andreu, L., & Curras-Perez, R. (2018). Effects of the intensity of use of social media on brand equity: An empirical study in a tourist destination. *European Journal of Management and Business Economics*, *27*(1), 83–100. doi:10.1108/EJMBE-11-2017-0049

Stroebe, W., Martin, R., & Hewstone, M. (2010). *Majority and minority influence and information processing: A theoretical and methodological analysis. Minority influence and innovation: Antecedents, processes and consequences, 201-225.* Processes and Consequences - Google Books.

Stubb, C., Nystrom, A. G., & Colliander, J. (2019). Influencer marketing: The impact of disclosing sponsorship compensation justification on sponsored content effectiveness. *Journal of Communication Management (London), 23*(2), 109–122. doi:10.1108/JCOM-11-2018-0119

Su, B., Wu, L., Chang, Y., & Hong, R. (2021). Influencers on social media as references: Understanding the importance of parasocial relationships. *Sustainability (Basel), 13*(19), 10919. doi:10.3390/su131910919

Subramani, N., Easwaramoorthy, S. V., Mohan, P., Subramanian, M., & Sambath, V. (2023). A Gradient Boosted Decision Tree-Based Influencer Prediction in Social Network Analysis. *Big Data and Cognitive Computing, 7*(1 C7 - 6). doi:10.3390/bdcc7010006

Su, C., & Kaye, B. V. (2023). Borderline Practices on Douyin/TikTok: Content Transfer and Algorithmic Manipulation. *Media Culture & Society, 45*(8), 1534–1549. doi:10.1177/01634437231168308

Sugden, R. (2009). *On nudging: A review of nudge: Improving decisions about health, wealth and happiness by Richard H.* Thaler and Cass R. Sunstein., doi:10.1080/13571510903227064

Suhr, H. C. (2014). *Online Evaluation of Creativity and the Arts*. Routledge. doi:10.4324/9781315795836

Suk, H. (2021). The characteristics of democratization of fashion and fashionocracy in the global fashion industry. *The Research Journal of the Costume Culture, 29*(4), 488–504. doi:10.29049/rjcc.2021.29.4.488

Sundermann, G., & Raabe, T. (2019). Strategic communication through social media influencers: Current state of research and desiderata. *International Journal of Strategic Communication, 13*(4), 278–300. doi:10.1080/1553118X.2019.1618306

Sun, J., Leung, X. Y., & Bai, B. (2021). How social media influencer's event endorsement changes attitudes of followers: The moderating effect of followers' gender. *International Journal of Contemporary Hospitality Management, 33*(7), 2337–2351. doi:10.1108/IJCHM-09-2020-0959

Sun, Y., Shao, X., Li, X., Guo, Y., & Nie, K. (2019). How live streaming influences purchase intentions in social commerce: An IT affordance perspective. *Electronic Commerce Research and Applications, 37*, 100886. Advance online publication. doi:10.1016/j.elerap.2019.100886

Sun, Y., Wang, R., Cao, D., & Lee, R. (2021). Who are social media influencers for luxury fashion consumption of the Chinese Gen Z? Categorisation and empirical examination. *Journal of Fashion Marketing and Management, 26*(4), 603–621. doi:10.1108/JFMM-07-2020-0132

Sweeney, E., Lawlor, M. A., & Brady, M. (2022). Teenagers' moral advertising literacy in an influencer marketing context. *International Journal of Advertising, 41*(1), 54–77. doi:10.1080/02650487.2021.1964227

Tafesse, W. (2016). An experiential model of consumer engagement in social media. *Journal of Product and Brand Management, 25*(5), 424–434. doi:10.1108/JPBM-05-2015-0879

Taillon, B. J., Mueller, S. M., Kowalczyk, C. M., & Jones, D. N. (2020). Understanding the relationships between social media influencers and their followers: The moderating role of closeness. *Journal of Product and Brand Management, 29*(6), 767–782. doi:10.1108/JPBM-03-2019-2292

Talavera, M. (2015, July 14). 10 reasons why influencer marketing is the next big thing. *Adweek*. https://www.adweek.com/digital/10-reasons-why-influencer-marketing-is-the-next-big-thing/

Talbot, K. (2019, June 2). *Diversity in influencer marketing: Why representation matters.* Forbes. https://www.forbes.com/sites/katetalbot/2019/06/02/diversity-in-influencer-marketing-why-representation-matters/?sh=9f5aad47a3e6

Tam, F. Y., & Lung, J. W. (2023). Impact of COVID-19 and innovative ideas for a sustainable fashion supply chain in the future. *Foresight, 25*(2), 225–248. doi:10.1108/FS-12-2021-0257

Tan, D. (2017). *The Commercial Appropriation of Fame.* Cambridge University Press. doi:10.1017/9781316488744

Tatiya, R. V. (2014). A Survey of Recommendation Algorithms. *IOSR Journal of Computer Engineering, 16*(6), 16–19. doi:10.9790/0661-16651619

Tech Influencers. (2023). *Stay up-to-date with these 10 must-follow tech influencers.* Retrieved from https://www.whosthat360.com/technology/stay-up-to-date-with-these-10-must-follow-tech-influencers-3997958 on 14/12/2023

Templer, K. (2019, January 12). *Words Matter.* Retrieved April 22, 2019, from Fringe Association: Knit and Let Knit website: fringeassociation.com/2019/01/12/words-matter.

Templer, K. (2019, January 7). *2019: My year of color.* Retrieved July 3, 2019, from Fringe Association website: https://fringeassociation.com/2019/01/07/2019-my-year-of-color/

Testa, D. S., Bakhshian, S., & Eike, R. (2021). Engaging consumers with sustainable fashion on Instagram. *Journal of Fashion Marketing and Management, 25*(4), 569–584. doi:10.1108/JFMM-11-2019-0266

Tewksbury, D., & Scheufele, D. A. (2009). News framing theory and research. In J. Bryant & M. B. Oliver (Eds.), Media Effects: Advances in theory and research (3rd ed., pp. 17–33). New York: Routledge.

Thaler, R. H., & Sunstein, C. R. (2009). *Nudge: Improving decisions about health, wealth, and happiness.* Penguin.

Thaler, R., & Sunstein, C. (2008). Human frailty caused this crisis. *Financial Times,* 11.

Theunissen. (2023). *Why Fashion Is Betting Big on Saudi Arabia.* Business of Fashion. Retrieved from https://www.businessoffashion.com/articles/fashion-week/why-fashion-is-betting-big-on-saudi-arabia

Thomala, L. L. (2023) *China: Douyin (TikTok)'s user age distribution 2022, Statista.* Available at: https://www.statista.com/statistics/1202727/china-douyin-user-age-distribution/

Thomas, K. (2019). Key opinion leaders supercharged by the internet: Paid doctor and patient influencers on social media. *BMJ (Clinical Research Ed.), 365,* C7–l2336. doi:10.1136/bmj.l2336 PMID:31152003

Thorson, K. S., & Rodgers, S. (2006). Relationships between blogs as eWOM and interactivity, perceived interactivity, and parasocial interactions. *Journal of Interactive Advertising, 6*(2), 34–44. doi:10.1080/15252019.2006.10722117

Tiggemann, M., & Anderberg, I. (2020). Social media is not real: The effect of 'Instagram vs reality' images on women's social comparison and body image. *New Media & Society, 22*(12), 2183–2199. doi:10.1177/1461444819888720

Tiggemann, M., Anderberg, I., & Brown, Z. (2020). #Loveyourbody: The effect of body positive Instagram captions on women's body image. *Body Image, 33,* 129–136. doi:10.1016/j.bodyim.2020.02.015 PMID:32151992

Tiggemann, M., Brown, Z., Zaccardo, M., & Thomas, N. (2017). "Warning: This image has been digitally altered": The effect of disclaimer labels added to fashion magazine shoots on women's body dissatisfaction. *Body Image, 21,* 107–113. doi:10.1016/j.bodyim.2017.04.001 PMID:28456058

Till, B. D., & Busler, M. (1998). Matching products with endorsers: Attractiveness versus expertise. *Journal of Consumer Marketing, 15*(6), 576–586. doi:10.1108/07363769810241445

Tiwari, A., Kumar, A., Kant, R., & Jaiswal, D. (2023). Impact of fashion influencers on consumers' purchase intentions: Theory of planned behaviour and mediation of attitude. *Journal of Fashion Marketing and Management*. Advance online publication. doi:10.1108/JFMM-11-2022-0253

Tolbert, A. N., & Drogos, K. L. (2019). Tweens' Wishful Identification and Parasocial Relationships With YouTubers. *Frontiers in Psychology*, *10*, 2781. Advance online publication. doi:10.3389/fpsyg.2019.02781 PMID:31920829

Torres, B. F., Rodríguez, A. P., & Díaz, R. C. (2021). The credibility of social media and ethical implications for young people. *Revista Latina de Comunicacion Social*, *2021*(79), 51–68. doi:10.4185/RLCS-2021-1512

Torres, P., Augusto, M., & Matos, M. (2019). Antecedents and outcomes of digital influencer endorsement: An exploratory study. *Psychology and Marketing*, *36*(12), 1267–1276. doi:10.1002/mar.21274

Tracy, S. J. (2019). *Qualitative research methods: Collecting evidence, crafting analysis, communicating impact*. John Wiley & Sons.

Trequattrini, R., Manfredi, S., Lardo, A., & Cuozzo, B. (2019). Social media as a new opportunity for female entrepreneurs: An analysis of the fashion industry. In *Advances in Gender and Cultural Research in Business and Economics* (pp. 287–298). Springer International Publishing. doi:10.1007/978-3-030-00335-7_19

Triplett, N. T., Kingzette, A., Slivinski, L., & Niu, T. (2022). Ethics for Mental Health Influencers: MFTs as Public Social Media Personalities. *Contemporary Family Therapy*, *44*(2), 125–135. doi:10.1007/s10591-021-09632-3

Trivedi, J., & Sama, R. (2019). The effect of influencer marketing on consumers' brand admiration and online purchase intentions: An emerging market perspective. *Journal of Internet Commerce*, *19*(1), 103–124. doi:10.1080/15332861.2019.1700741

Turnbull, S., Kelley, L., & Jugenheimer, D. (2023). *Advertising account planning: planning and managing strategic communication campaigns*. Taylor and Francis. doi:10.4324/9781003250449

Turner, P. G., & Lefevre, C. E. (2017). Instagram use is linked to increase symptoms of orthorexia nervosa. *Eating and Weight Disorders*, *22*(2), 227–284. doi:10.1007/s40519-017-0364-2 PMID:28251592

Tusken, M. (2019, January 23). *Knitting, Instagram, and some new bases for the shop!* YouTube [Video]. Retrieved May 17, 2019, from YouTube website: https://www.youtube.com/watch?v=Dv1TxdkwdIY

Tzikas, A., & Koulierakis, G. (2023). A Systematic Review of Nudges on Hand Hygiene Against the Spread of COVID-19. *Journal of Behavioral and Experimental Economics*, *102046*, 102046. Advance online publication. doi:10.1016/j.socec.2023.102046 PMID:37274754

UK Research & Innovation. (2023). *What is social science?* Retrieved from https://www.ukri.org/innovation/excellent-research/social-science/

Umberia. (2022). *Top bloggers in the fashion game*. Retrieved from https://isdi.in/blog/top-bloggers-in-the-fashion-game

UN. (2023). *Sustainable Lifestyles*. UNSSC | United Nations System Staff College. Retrieved from https://www.unssc.org/learn/sustainable-lifestyles/

UNFashionalliance. (2023). *The UN Alliance for Sustainable Fashion*. Retrieved from https://www.unfashionalliance.org/

Unilever, P. L. C. (2023). *Unilever reveals influencers can switch people on to sustainable living*. Unilever. Available at: https://www.unilever.com/news/press-and-media/press-releases/2023/unilever-reveals-influencers-can-switch-people-on-to-sustainable-living/#:~:text=The%20results%20revealed%20that%20both

United Nations. (2022). *The Sustainable Lifestyle Action Academy*. UNEP (UN Environment Programme). Retrieved from https://www.unep.org/resources/publication/sustainable-lifestyles-action-academy

United Nations. (2023). *Why Sustainable lifestyles matter. Retrieved from Why Sustainable lifestyles matter*. UNEP - UN Environment Programme.

Urbany, J. E., Bearden, W. O., Kaicker, A., & Borrero, M. S. (1997). Transaction utility effects when quality is uncertain. *Journal of the Academy of Marketing Science*, *25*(1), 45–55. doi:10.1007/BF02894508

Uribe, R., Buzeta, C., & Velasquez, M. (2016). Sidedness, commercial intent, and expertise in blog advertising. *Journal of Business Research*, *69*(10), 4403–4410. doi:10.1016/j.jbusres.2016.04.102

Uzunoğlu, E., & Misci Kip, S. (2014). Brand communication through digital influencers: Leveraging blogger engagement. *International Journal of Information Management*, *34*(5), 592–602. doi:10.1016/j.ijinfomgt.2014.04.007

Vadíková, K. M. (2022). On the Transformation of Thinking on Personal Responsibility Towards Requirements of Environmental Ethics in Slovakia. *Studia Ecologiae et Bioethicae*, *20*(2), 15–25. doi:10.21697/seb.2022.11

Vaidhyanathan, S. (2021, September 18). Leaks just exposed how toxic Facebook and Instagram are to teen girls and, well, everyone. *The Guardian*. https://www.theguardian.com/commentisfree/2021/sep/18/facebook-instagram-zuckerberg-teenagers

Van Dam, S., & Van Reijmersdal, E. A. (2019). Insights in adolescents' advertising literacy, perceptions and responses regarding sponsored influencer videos and disclosures. Cyberpsychology, *13*(2 C7 - 2). doi:10.5817/CP2019-2-2

Van Dijck, J., & Poell, T. (2013). Understanding social media logic. *Media and Communication*, *1*(1), 2–14. doi:10.17645/mac.v1i1.70

Van Doorn, J., Lemon, K. N., Mittal, V., Nass, S., Pick, D., Pirner, P., & Verhoef, P. C. (2010). Customer Engagement Behavior: Theoretical foundations and research directions. *Journal of Service Research*, *13*(3), 253–266. doi:10.1177/1094670510375599

van Esch, P., Arli, D., Castner, J., Talukdar, N., & Northey, G. (2018). Consumer attitudes towards bloggers and paid blog advertisements: What's new? *Marketing Intelligence & Planning*, *36*(7), 778–793. doi:10.1108/MIP-01-2018-0027

Vargo, S. L., & Lusch, R. F. (2004). Evolving to a new dominant logic for marketing. *Journal of Marketing*, *68*(1), 1–17. doi:10.1509/jmkg.68.1.1.24036

Velasco-Molpeceres, A., Zarauza-Castro, J., Pérez-Curiel, C., & Mateos-González, S. (2023). Slow Fashion as a Communication Strategy of Fashion Brands on Instagram. *Sustainability(Switzerland)*, *15*(1 C7 - 423). doi:10.3390/su15010423

Venaik, S., Zhu, Y., & Brewer, P. (2013). Looking into the future: Hofstede long term orientation versus GLOBE future orientation. *Cross Cultural Management*, *20*(3), 361–385. doi:10.1108/CCM-02-2012-0014

Vendemia, M. A., DeAndrea, D. C., & Brathwaite, K. N. (2021). Objectifying the body positive movement: The effects of sexualizing and digitally modifying body-positive images on Instagram. *Body Image*, *38*, 137–147. doi:10.1016/j.bodyim.2021.03.017 PMID:33887562

Vendemia, M. A., & Robinson, M. J. (2022). Promoting body positivity through stories: How protagonist body size and esteem influence readers' self-concepts. *Body Image*, *42*, 315–326. doi:10.1016/j.bodyim.2022.07.005 PMID:35908298

Ventre, I., Mollá-Descals, A., & Frasquet, M. (2021). Drivers of social commerce usage: A multi-group analysis comparing Facebook and Instagram. *Ekonomska Istrazivanja*, *34*(1), 570–589. doi:10.1080/1331677X.2020.1799233

Verhoef, P. C., Reinartz, W., & Krafft, M. (2010). Customer engagement as a new perspective in customer management. *Journal of Service Research, 13*(3), 247–252. doi:10.1177/1094670510375461

Vesterinen, E., & Syrjälä, H. (2022). Sustainable anti-consumption of clothing: A systematic literature review. *Cleaner and Responsible Consumption, 100061.* Advance online publication. doi:10.1016/j.clrc.2022.100061

Villamil, V., & Wolbring, G. (2019). Role and scope coverage of speech-related professionals linked to neuro-advancements within the academic literature and Canadian newspapers. Education *Sciences, 9*(2 C7 - 98). doi:10.3390/educsci9020098

Vitelar, A. (2019). Like me: Generation Z and the use of social media for personal branding. *Management Dynamics in the Knowledge Economy*, 7(2), 257–268. Advance online publication. doi:10.25019/mdke/7.2.07

Vivek, S. D., Beatty, S. E., & Morgan, R. M. (2012). Customer engagement: Exploring customer relationships beyond purchase. *Journal of Marketing Theory and Practice*, *20*(2), 122–146. doi:10.2753/MTP1069-6679200201

von der Weth, C., Abdul, A., Fan, S., & Kankanhalli, M. (2020, October). Helping Users Tackle Algorithmic Threats on Social Media: A Multimedia Research Agenda. *Proceedings of the 28th ACM International Conference on Multimedia.* 10.1145/3394171.3414692

Vrontis, D., Makrides, A., Christofi, M., & Thrassou, A. (2021). Social media influencer marketing: A systematic review, integrative framework and future research agenda. *International Journal of Consumer Studies*, *45*(4), 617–644. doi:10.1111/ijcs.12647

Wang, C. L. (2023). *The Palgrave Handbook of Interactive Marketing*. Springer International Publishing., doi:10.1007/978-3-031-14961-0

Wang, E. S. T., & Weng, Y. J. (2024). Influence of social media influencer authenticity on their followers' perceptions of credibility and their positive word-of-mouth. *Asia Pacific Journal of Marketing and Logistics*, *36*(2), 356–373. doi:10.1108/APJML-02-2023-0115

Wang, S. W., & Scheibaum, A. C. (2018). Enhancing brand credibility via celebrity endorsement: Trustworthiness trumps attractiveness and expertise. *Journal of Advertising Research*, *58*(1), 16–32. doi:10.2501/JAR-2017-042

Wang, Y., & Yang, Y. (2020). Dialogic communication on social media: How organizations use twitter to build dialogic relationships with their publics. *Computers in Human Behavior*, *104*, 106183. Advance online publication. doi:10.1016/j.chb.2019.106183

Waqas, A., Baig, A. A., Khalid, M. A., Aedma, K. K., & Naveed, S. (2019). Conflicts of interest and outcomes of clinical trials of antidepressants: An 18-year retrospective study. *Journal of Psychiatric Research*, *116*, 83–87. doi:10.1016/j.jpsychires.2019.05.029 PMID:31212249

Weil, J. (2017, August 28). Dior launches digital 'Love Chain' initiative. *The Los Angeles Times*. https://www.latimes.com/fashion/la-ig-wwd-dior-love-chain-20170828-story.html

Wei, P.-S., & Lu, H.-P. (2013). An examination of the celebrity endorsements and online customer reviews influence female consumers' shopping behavior. *Computers in Human Behavior*, *29*(1), 193–201. doi:10.1016/j.chb.2012.08.005

Weismueller, J., Harrigan, P., Wang, S., & Soutar, G. N. (2020). Influencer endorsements: How advertising disclosure and source credibility affect consumer purchase intention on social media. *Australasian Marketing Journal*, *28*(4), 160–170. doi:10.1016/j.ausmj.2020.03.002

Weller, S. (2007). Fashion as viscous knowledge: Fashion's role in Shaping Trans-National Garment Production. *Journal of Economic Geography*, *7*(1), 39–66. doi:10.1093/jeg/lbl015

Wellman, M. L., Stoldt, R., Tully, M., & Ekdale, B. (2020). Ethics of authenticity: Social media influencers and the production of sponsored content. *Journal of Medical Ethics*, *35*(2), 68–82. doi:10.1080/23736992.2020.1736078

West, C. (2023, October 26). *22 influencer marketing statistics to guide your brand's strategy in 2023.* Sprout Social. https://sproutsocial.com/insights/influencer-marketing-statistics/

What is influencer marketing? (2023). https://www.mckinsey.com/featured-insights/mckinsey-explainers/what-is-influencer-marketing

Whatnot. (2023a). https://www.Whatnot.com/

Whatnot. (2023b). *About us.* https://www.Whatnot.com/about-us

Whatnot. (2023c). *Browse by category.* https://www.Whatnot.com/explore

Whatnot. (2023d). *Bags & accessories.* https://www.Whatnot.com/category/bags_jewelry_accessories

Whatnot. (2023e). *Understanding how rankings work on Whatnot.* https://help.Whatnot.com/hc/en-us/articles/12190921464461-Understanding-how-ranking-works-on-Whatnot

Whatnot. (2023f, December 22). *Giveaways overview.* https://help.Whatnot.com/hc/en-us/articles/11329417780365-Giveaways-Overview

Whatnot. (2023g, December 22). *Whatnot return policy.* https://help.Whatnot.com/hc/en-us/articles/360061194552-Whatnot-Return-Policy

Wibisono, A. I., & Ruldeviyani, Y. (2021, April). Detecting social media influencers of airline services through social network analysis on twitter: A case study of the Indonesian airline industry. In *2021 3rd East Indonesia Conference on Computer and Information Technology (EIConCIT)* (pp. 314-319). IEEE. 10.1109/EIConCIT50028.2021.9431876

Wiedmann, K. P., & von Mettenheim, W. (2021). Attractiveness, trustworthiness, and expertise-social media influencers' winning formula? *Journal of Product and Brand Management*, *30*(5), 707–725. doi:10.1108/JPBM-06-2019-2442

Wiles, J., Wiles, C., & Tjernlund, A. (1995). A comparison of gender role portrayals in magazine advertising. *European Journal of Marketing*, *29*(11), 35–49. doi:10.1108/03090569510100696

Williams, A., & Hodges, N. (2022). Adolescent Generation Z and sustainable and responsible fashion consumption: Exploring the value-action gap. *Young Consumers*, *23*(4), 651–666. Advance online publication. doi:10.1108/YC-11-2021-1419

Willis, E., & Delbaere, M. (2022). Patient influencers: the next frontier in direct-to-consumer pharmaceutical marketing. *Journal of Medical Internet Research*, *24*(3 C7 - e29422). doi:10.2196/29422

Winslow, L. (2018). Frame Analysis. In The Sage Encyclopdia of Communication Research Methods (pp. 584-586). doi:10.4135/9781483381411

Wongkitrungrueng, A., Dehouche, N., & Assarut, N. (2020). Live streaming commerce from the sellers' perspective: Implications for online relationship marketing. *Journal of Marketing Management*, *36*(5-6), 488–518. doi:10.1080/0267257X.2020.1748895

Woodcock, J., & Johnson, M. R. (2018). Gamification: What it is, and how to fight it. *The Sociological Review*, *66*(3), 542–558. doi:10.1177/0038026117728620

Woodroof, P. J., Howie, K. M., Syrdal, H. A., & VanMeter, R. (2020). Whats done in the dark will be brought to the light: Effects of influencer transparency on product efficacy and purchase intentions. *Journal of Product &amp. Brand Management*, *29*(5), 675–688.

Woods, S. (2016). # Sponsored: The emergence of influencer marketing. *TRACE: Tennessee Research and Creative Exchange.* https://trace.tennessee.edu/cgi/viewcontent.cgi?article=3010&context=utk_chanhonoproj

Wood, W., & Eagly, A. H. (2012). Biosocial construction of sex differences and similarities in behavior. In J. M. Olson & M. P. Zanna (Eds.), Advances in experimental social psychology. Academic Press. doi:10.1016/B978-0-12-394281-4.00002-7

Wrenn, M. V., & Waller, W. (2017). Care and the Neoliberal Individual. *Journal of Economic Issues*, *51*(2), 495–502. doi:10.1080/00213624.2017.1321438

Wróblewski, Ł., & Grzesiak, M. (2020). The impact of social media on the brand capital of famous people. *Sustainability (Basel)*, *12*(16), 6414. doi:10.3390/su12166414

Wu, M. (2017). *Brandwatch- Social listening and analytics.* Retrieved from https://d3.harvard.edu/platform-digit/submission/brandwatch-social-listening-and-analytics/

Wu, Y., Xie, L., Yuan, Z., Jiang, S., Liu, W., & Sheng, H. (2020). Investigating public biodiversity conservation awareness based on the propagation of wildlife-related incidents on the Sina Weibo social media platform. *Environmental Research Letters, 15*(9 C7 - 094082). doi:10.1088/1748-9326/ab9ed1

Wu, Y., Kim, K. J., & Mou, Y. (2022). Minority social influence and moral decision-making in human–AI interaction: The effects of identity and specialization cues. *New Media & Society*. Advance online publication. doi:10.1177/14614448221138072

Xiao, M., Wang, R., & Chan-Olmstead, S. (2018). Factors affecting YouTube influencer marketing credibility: A heuristic-systematic model. *Journal of Media Business Studies*, *15*(3), 188–213. doi:10.1080/16522354.2018.1501146

Xue, H., Liu, B., Din, M., Song, L., & Zhu, T. (2020, December). Hiding Private Information in Images From AI. *ICC 2020 - 2020 IEEE International Conference on Communications (ICC).*

Yalcin, T., Nistor, C., & Pehlivan, E. (2021). Sustainability Influencers: Between marketers and educators. *Social Science Research Network.* https://papers.ssrn.com/sol3/papers.cfm?abstract_id=3800316

Yan, G., Pegoraro, A., & Watanabe, N. (2018). Student-athletes' organization of activism at the University of Missouri: Resource mobilization on Twitter. *Journal of Sport Management*, *32*(1), 24–37. doi:10.1123/jsm.2017-0031

Yang, J., Teran, C., Battocchio, A. F., Bertellotti, E., & Wrzesinski, S. (2021). Building brand authenticity on social media: The impact of Instagram ad model genuineness and trustworthiness on perceived brand authenticity and consumer responses. *Journal of Interactive Advertising*, *21*(1), 34–48. doi:10.1080/15252019.2020.1860168

Yang, Y. (2022). TikTok/Douyin use and its influencer video use: A cross-cultural comparison between Chinese and US users. *Online Media and Global Communication*, *1*(2), 339–368. doi:10.1515/omgc-2022-0016

Yang, Y., & Ha, L. (2021). Why people use TikTok (Douyin) and how their purchase decisions are affected by social media influencers in China: A uses & gratifications and para-social relationship perspective. *Journal of Interactive Advertising*, *21*(3), 297–305. doi:10.1080/15252019.2021.1995544

Yaniv, I., Choshen-Hillel, S., & Milyavsky, M. (2011). Receiving advice on matters of taste: Similarity, majority influence, and taste discrimination. *Organizational Behavior and Human Decision Processes*, *115*(1), 111–120. doi:10.1016/j.obhdp.2010.11.006

Yan, Y., & Bissell, K. (2014). The globalization of beauty: How is ideal beauty influenced by globally published fashion and beauty magazines? *Journal of Intercultural Communication Research*, *43*(3), 194–214. doi:10.1080/17475759.2014.917432

Yao, Q., Perlmutter, D. D., & Liu, J. (2017). What are shaping the ethical bottom line?: Identifying factors influencing young readers' acceptance of digital news photo alteration. *Telematics and Informatics*, *34*(1), 124–132. doi:10.1016/j.tele.2016.04.010

Yazdani, A. T., Muhammad, A., Nisar, M. I., Khan, U., & Shafiq, Y. (2021). Unveiling and addressing implementation barriers to routine immunization in the peri-urban slums of Karachi, Pakistan: A mixed-methods study. *Health Research Policy and Systems*, *19*(S2), C7–C55. doi:10.1186/s12961-021-00691-4 PMID:34380526

Yesiloglu, S., & Costello, J. (Eds.). (2020). *Influencer marketing: building brand communities and engagement*. Routledge. doi:10.4324/9780429322501

Yıldırım, S. (2021). Do green women influencers spur sustainable consumption patterns? Descriptive evidences from social media influencers. *Ecofeminism and Climate Change, 2*(4), 198-210. https://www.emerald.com/insight/content/doi/10.1108/EFCC-02-2021-0003/full/html

Yilmaz, C., Telci, E. E., Bodur, M., & Iscioglu, T. E. (2011). Source characteristics and advertising effectiveness: The roles of message processing motivation and product category knowledge. *International Journal of Advertising*, *30*(5), 889–915. doi:10.2501/IJA-30-5-889-914

Yilmaz, G., & Youngreen, R. (2016). The application of Minority Influence Theory in computer-mediated communication groups. *Small Group Research*, *47*(6), 692–719. doi:10.1177/1046496416661033

Yim, M. C. (2019). CEOs' political tweets and perceived authenticity: Can expectancy violation be a pleasant surprise? *Public Relations Review*, *45*(3), 101785. doi:10.1016/j.pubrev.2019.05.006

Yin, R. K. (2009). *Case study research: Design and methods*. SAGE Publications.

Yoo, B., Donthu, N., & Lenartowicz, T. (2011). Measuring Hofstede's five dimensions of cultural values at the individual level: Development and validation of CVSCALE. *Journal of International Consumer Marketing*, *23*, 193–210.

Yuan, S., & Lou, C. (2020). How social media influencers foster relationships with followers: The roles of source credibility and fairness in parasocial relationship and product interest. *Journal of Interactive Advertising*, *20*(2), 133–147. doi:10.1080/15252019.2020.1769514

Zerfass, A., Verčič, D., Nothhaft, H., & Werder, K. P. (2018). Strategic communication: Defining the field and its contribution to research and practice. *International Journal of Strategic Communication*, *12*(4), 487–505. doi:10.1080/1553118X.2018.1493485

Zhang, L., & Wei, W. (2021). Influencer Marketing: A comparison of traditional celebrity, social media influencer, and AI influencer. *Boston Hospitality Review*. https://www.bu.edu/bhr/2021/10/04/influencer-marketing-a-comparison-of-traditional-celebrity-social-media-influencer-and-ai-influencer

Zhang, A. Y., & Zhou, H. H. (2016). Minimax rates of community detection in stochastic block models. *Annals of Statistics*, *44*(5). Advance online publication. doi:10.1214/15-AOS1428

Zhang, C., Lakens, D., & IJsselsteijn, W. A. (2021). Theory integration for lifestyle behavior change in the digital age: An adaptive decision-making framework. *Journal of Medical Internet Research*, *23*(4), e17127. doi:10.2196/17127 PMID:33835036

Zhang, L., & Hale, J. (2022). Extending the lifetime of clothing through repair and repurpose: An investigation of barriers and enablers in UK citizens. *Sustainability (Basel)*, *14*(17), 10821. doi:10.3390/su141710821

Zhang, L., Wei, W., Rathjens, B., & Zheng, Y. (2023). Pet influencers on social media: The joint effect of message appeal and narrator. *International Journal of Hospitality Management*, *110*, 103453. doi:10.1016/j.ijhm.2023.103453

Zhang, X., & Choi, J. (2022). The importance of social influencer-generated content for user cognition and emotional attachment: An information relevance perspective. *Sustainability (Basel), 14*(11), 6676. doi:10.3390/su14116676

Zhang, Y., & Mac, L. (2023). Social media influencers: The formation and effects of affective factors during online interactions. *International Journal of Consumer Studies, 47*(5), 1824–1837. doi:10.1111/ijcs.12957

Zheng, L., Huang, B., Qiu, H., & Bai, H. (2023). The role of social media followers' agency in influencer marketing: A study based on the heuristic–systematic model of information processing. *International Journal of Advertising*, 1–26. doi:10.1080/02650487.2023.2229148

Zhong, L. (2022). Analyses of the Relationship between Virtual Influencers Endorsements and Customer Brand Engagement in Social Media. *Proceedings of the 2022 International Conference on Creative Industry and Knowledge Economy (CIKE 2022)*. 10.2991/aebmr.k.220404.007

Zitzmann, J., Rombold-George, L., Rosenbach, C., & Renneberg, B. (2024). Emotion regulation, parenting, and psychopathology: A systematic review. *Clinical Child and Family Psychology Review, 27*(1), 1–22. doi:10.1007/s10567-023-00452-5 PMID:37704867

Zniva, R., Weitzl, W., & Lindmoser, C. (2023). Be constantly different! How to manage influencer authenticity. *Electronic Commerce Research, 23*(3), 1485–1514. doi:10.1007/s10660-022-09653-6

Zweiman, J., & Suh, K. (n.d.). *Our Story*. Retrieved May 29, 2019, from PUSSYHAT PROJECT™ website: https://www.pussyhatproject.com/our-story

About the Contributors

Nicky Chang Bi, Ph.D., is an assistant professor of public relations and advertising of the School of Communication at the University of Nebraska, Omaha, U.S.A. Her research interests include prosocial strategic communication, brand activism, media psychology, and health communication. Her current research explores why and how people engage with social influencers and electronic word-of-mouth communication. She teaches both undergraduate and graduate students and courses including Capstone for Public Relations and Advertising, Strategic Communication, Journalism and Mass Communication Theories, Computer-Mediated Communication, Social Media, and Quantitative Research Methods.

Ruonan Zhang received her PhD in media and communication at Bowling Green State University. She is currently an assistant professor at Rollins College, FL, USA. Her research is centered around social media marketing and digital culture, with a specialization in exploring how digital technologies shape human communication, both in advancement and hindrance. Her research has been featured in the Journal of Computer Assisted Learning, the Journal of Research in Interactive Marketing, and Asian Communication Research.

* * *

Rajni Bala is presently working as an Assistant Professor in Chitkara Business School, Chitkara University, Punjab, India. She is having 15.5 years of teaching experience. She is having 30 research publications in her account indexed in Scopus and UGC care. She has presented a number of papers in various national and international conferences. She is having 4 patents and 3 copyrights in her account. She has delivered workshops on Writing Literature Review, Statistical Tools on Excel & Innovative technologies in education etc. She is having keen interest in updating students with upcoming technology to fill Industry-Academia gap.

Anna Boechat is a PhD in Strategic Communication with the highest grade at University NOVA of Lisbon, and has worked as an Assistant Professor at prestigious Portuguese institutions such as IADE, University NOVA of Lisbon, Lusíada University of Lisbon, and the Portuguese Catholic University. She is also Marketing & Communication Scientific and Pedagogical Coordinator at IADE, Academic Supervisor, and participates in national and international scientific events as a speaker/conferencist. She develops Business Consulting projects in the areas of Marketing and Strategic Communication and is specialized in the following topics: Marketing, Strategic Marketing, Sports Marketing, Advertising, Communication, Strategic Communication, Project Management, Consumer Psychology, Market Research,

Brand Management, and Corporate Social Responsibility. As an Integrated Researcher at UNIDCOM/IADE, Anna Carolina Boechat has been developing projects and publications in the areas of Strategic Communication, Marketing, Brands, Consumer Behavior, Corporate Social Responsibility, Sustainability, and Metaverse. Complementing the academic spectrum, she has over 10 years of exclusive professional experience in Marketing and Communication, having contributed to companies in different markets, assuming various roles over time.

Linda Dam is an Assistant Professor in the Hank Greenspun School of Journalism and Media Studies. Her primary research specialization is in strategic communication, working at the intersection of social and digital media, public relations, and health communication. Her work explores the persuasive impact of social and digital media with a focus on health behaviors and consumer brand relationships.

Tricia M. Farwell, Ph.D. joined the Middle Tennessee State University faculty in 2008 to teach in the advertising and public relations concentrations in the School of Journalism. Farwell holds a Ph.D., two Masters degrees (obtained concurrently), and a Bachelor of Arts from Arizona State University. Prior to her academic career, she had a successful career in small business communication in the industrial sector. Farwell's research has appeared in a variety of publication outlets including book chapters in editions published by Sage and journals such as MEIEA, the Journal of Public Relations Education, the American Journal of Qualitative Research, and Advertising & Society Quarterly. She is author of the book, Love and Death in Edith Wharton's Fiction. She is currently the associate editor of the Journal of Advertising Education.

Camilla Guimaraes (A.B., Rollins College) was an honor's student who earned a wide range of honors. Camilla's research interests focus on fashion marketing, public relations, and social media promotions.

Michel M. Haigh (Ph.D., University of Oklahoma) is a professor in the School of Journalism and Mass Communication at Texas State University. She teaches in the public relations area. Her research area is in the areas of persuasion, crisis communication, and news framing.

Alphonsa Haokip is currently the Headmistress of Christ King High School, Chingjaroi Khullen, Manipur. She has completed her doctorate entitled, "Attitude, Problem Solving Ability, and Achievement in Mathematics Learning among the Secondary School Students of Thadou Kuki Tribe in Manipur". Her areas of interest are Mathematics Learning of Secondary School Students, their problem-solving ability, their academic achievement, mathematics teachers and their concerns, paradigm shift in higher education, and gender issues. ORCID: 0000-0003-2578-0114.

Lujan Hassoubah is a current PhD student in Fashion Marketing at the University of Manchester, Science and Engineering, Department of Material. Parallel to this, Hassoubah is currently holding a lecturing position at the Business School, University of Jeddah, Saudi Arabia. A distinction Master of international Marketing, University of Sussex. Hassoubah is the first on the 2015 batch at the University of Business and Technology, Bachelor of Marketing. Hassoubah is interested in publication within the field of fashion marketing, sustainable consumption, social media influencers and destination-branding.

Isuru Udayangani Hewapathirana serves as a Senior Lecturer at the Faculty of Science, University of Kelaniya, Sri Lanka. Holding a prestigious B.Sc. degree with First Class honours from the University of Colombo, Sri Lanka, Dr. Hewapathirana furthered her academic journey by obtaining a Ph.D. in Statistics from the University of Canterbury, New Zealand. With a diverse research portfolio, Dr. Hewapathirana's research interests span across machine learning, computational social science, and operations research. With several research publications in indexed journals, she actively engages in scholarly discourse, pushing the boundaries of knowledge in her respective fields. Currently, as an editor of one of the most well-known internationally peer-reviewed journals in Sri Lanka, Sri Lanka Journal of Applied Statistics (SLJAS), she plays a pivotal role in shaping scholarly discourse and advancing research within the country. Dr. Hewapathirana's expertise extends to teaching statistics, data science, and management science subjects to students following the computing domain, enriching their educational experience with her depth of knowledge and practical insights. Additionally, her role as a Senior Academic Advisor and Academic Career Counselor at the Faculty of Science, University of Kelaniya, Sri Lanka, underscores her commitment to nurturing the academic and professional growth of her peers and students alike.

Truc Ngoc Hoang is a graduate of the Bachelor of Public Relations program at Van Lang University, Vietnam. With her research, she looks to contribute to the sustainable development of the public relations industry within the community.

Faren Karimkhan, Ph. D., is an assistant professor of advertising at the Newhouse School of Public Communications at Syracuse University. Her research focuses on social media influencer advertising and understanding audience-influencer relationships, especially within the realms of fashion and cosmetics. Her current research centers around understanding the concept of authenticity among social media influencers and its impact on the effectiveness of their advertising.

Sunita Kumar is a dedicated educator with over 19 years of experience, encompassing 5+ years in the industry and 14+ years in teaching. Her areas of expertise and research focus include advertising, branding, digital marketing, consumer behavior, and marketing analytics. Over the last 12 years, she has published over 20 papers in Scopus-indexed journals, book chapters, and conference proceedings. Dr. Kumar has also received commendable evaluations for her teaching in various marketing units, such as Brand Management, Consumer Behavior, Social Media and Digital Marketing, and Marketing Analytics. She is actively involved in supervising master's & PhD candidates at Christ University Bangalore, showcasing a strong interest in research and consultancy projects.

Vinod Kumar is an Associate Professor in Maharishi Markandeshwar (Deemed to be University), Mullana, Ambala. His research interest areas are branding and service marketing. He has 14 years of experience in management teaching. He has published more than 30 publications in reputed journals along with various patents and copyrights.

Amenla Longkumer, a licensed Clinical Psychologist under the Rehabilitation Council of India (RCI), currently practices in Nagaland. With a teaching background spanning over three years and four years of dedicated service to individuals with Intellectual disabilities, she brings a wealth of experience to her practice. Amenla is keenly interested in mental health promotion, mindfulness, and psychotherapy.

She has actively conducted numerous mental health awareness programs in Wokha, showcasing her commitment to fostering well-being in the community. ORCID: 0000-0001-6318-9654.

Tuong-Minh Ly-Le is dean of the School of Applied Arts and Media Production at the University of Management and Technology, Vietnam. She is also a professional communications consultant and managing director of EloQ Communications, a leading PR and marketing agency based in Ho Chi Minh, Vietnam. Dr. Ly-Le has been involved in many successful public relations and integrated marketing projects at both national and regional scales. She has put her professional knowledge and extensive connections with business media and influencers to serve clients from a diversified clientele, including hospitality, education, technology, finance, healthcare, etc. Along with her professional career, Dr. Ly-Le is also interested in academic research activities. Her research foci include public relations, crisis communication, and social media. She strongly believes in the complementary power between practical experience and academic knowledge. ORCID: 0000-0001-8203-7357

Amy May, PhD is an Associate Professor and Chair of the Department of Communication at the University of Alaska Troth Yeddha'. She remains committed to understanding how messages related to science and health are created, distributed, and received by target audiences. From developing a text messaging system for low income pregnant to understanding the impact of parental disclosure of HIV on children, Dr. May is committed to using communication as a tool to promote health and wellness. Additionally, Dr. May maintains an active research agenda related to challenging existing power structures across contexts. She has served as co-editor for three edited volumes, including *Women educators' experiences during COVID-19: On the front lines* (2023), *Women of the wild: Challenging gender disparities in field stations and marine laboratories* (2022), and *Supporting the Military-Affiliated Learner: Communication Approaches to Military Pedagogy & Education* (2020). Her research is available for review in *Patient Education and Counseling, Qualitative Research Reports in Communication, Journal of GLTB Family Studies,* and *the Journal of Communication Pedagogy.* ORCID: 0000-0003-2108-7013

Victoria McDermott (Ph.D., University of Maryland) is an assistant professor in the Department of Communication at the University of Alaska Fairbanks Troth Yeddha'. She serves as the Foundational Communication Course Director and the co-director of graduate studies. Victoria's research explores the communication of power in traditionally masculine environments, specifically within academia and the military. She is the first editor of three edited volumes *Women educators' experiences during COVID-19: On the front lines* (2023), *Women of the wild: Challenging gender disparities in field stations and marine laboratories* (2022), and *Supporting the Military-Affiliated Learner: Communication Approaches to Military Pedagogy & Education* (2020). Her research can be found in the *Journal of Communication Pedagogy*, *Public Relations Review*, *Communication Education*, and the *Bulletin of the Ecological Society of America*. ORCID: 0000-0001-9837-5545

Trinideé Mercado is a graduate student at Stetson University in the Clinical Mental Health Counseling master's program. She received her bachelor's from Rollins College, double majoring in Psychology and Communication Studies with a minor in Sexuality, Women, and Gender Studies. She was awarded Outstanding Senior Scholar in the Social Sciences Applied Division at Rollins College in 2023. She is interested in the utilization of social media in trauma-based mental health interventions.

Poornima Nair is an entrepreneur with an experience of more than 6 years in the fashion industry. She is also a qualified assistant professor, having taught marketing at post-graduation level. She is currently a research scholar at Christ University, School of Business and Management, Bangalore, pursuing her doctoral research in branding and co-creation. Her research is motivated by her passion to encourage fresh entrepreneurship. Her areas of interest include branding, advertising, social media marketing, Co-creation and Fashion.

Melita Stephen Natal is an Assistant Professor at Amity Business School, Amity University, Greater Noida, India. With a wealth of academic expertise, she brings dedication and passion to her role in shaping the minds of future business leaders. Her commitment to fostering a dynamic learning environment is reflected in her contributions to the academic realm. Melita's professional journey is characterized by a steadfast dedication to education and a firm commitment to the growth and development of her students. ORCID: 0009-0004-1240-7817.

David Lynn Painter (Ph.D., University of Florida) is an Associate Professor of Communication at Rollins College. David's research interests focus on social media and political communication, with particular expertise in quantitative methodologies. Since 2009, David has authored more than 25 publications and 40 papers that were competitively selected for presentation at national and international conferences.

Albérico Travassos Rosário is a Ph.D. Marketing and Strategy of the Universities of Aveiro (UA), Minho (UM) and Beira Interior (UBI). With affiliation to the GOVCOPP research center of the University of Aveiro. Master in Marketing and Degree in Marketing, Advertising and Public Relations, degree from ISLA Campus Lisbon-European University | Laureate International Universities. Has the title of Marketing Specialist and teaches with the category of Assistant Professor at IADE-Faculty of Design, Technology and Communication of the European University and as a visiting Associate Professor at the Santarém Higher School of Management and Technology (ESGTS) of the Polytechnic Institute of Santarém. He taught at IPAM-School of Marketing | Laureate International Universities, ISLA- Higher Institute of Management and Administration of Santarém (ISLA-Santarém), was Director of the Commercial Management Course, Director of the Professional Technical Course (TeSP) of Sales and Commercial Management, Chairman of the Pedagogical Council and Member of the Technical Council and ISLA-Santarém Scientific Researcher. He is also a marketing and strategy consultant for SMEs.

V. Muthu Ruben is a distinguished Associate Professor at the School of Law, Christ University, situated in Bengaluru, Karnataka, India. Driven by an extensive scholarly foundation and a steadfast dedication to legal education, Dr. Ruben makes substantial contributions to both the academic community and the domain of law. His proficiency transcends numerous spheres within the realm of law, and he significantly influences the educational journeys of students enrolled at Christ University. Motivated by an ardent interest in legal research, he actively participates in scholarly endeavors, thereby making significant contributions to the ongoing legal dialogue. In addition to his scholarly responsibilities, Dr. V. Muthu Ruben is renowned for his commitment to cultivating an atmosphere that encourages intellectual engagement. His mentorship and counsel motivate pupils to explore into the complexities of the law, fostering the development of critical thinking skills and a profound comprehension of legal principles. In his role as an Associate Professor, Dr. Ruben provides the School of Law with an abundance of expertise, experience, and a forward-thinking perspective, thereby enhancing the institution's dedication to providing superior legal education. ORCID: 0009-0006-7723-8596.

Daniella Ryding is a senior lecturer in Fashion Marketing, and faculty lead for the New Academics Programme (Academic Development) and Foundations of Teaching and Learning Programme (Post Doctoral Scholar Development) at The University of Manchester.

Ritu Sharma is presently working as Assistant professor of English in Maharishi Markandeshwar deemed to be University Mullana. Her area of research is gender studies. She has 20 publications in international journals.

Ranjit Singha is a Doctorate Research Fellow at Christ (Deemed to be University) and holds the prestigious American Psychological Association (APA) membership. With a strong background in Research and Development, he has significantly contributed to various fields such as Mindfulness, Addiction Psychology, Women Empowerment, UN Sustainable Development Goals, and Data Science. With over 15 years of experience in Administration, Teaching, and Research, both in Industry and Higher Education Institutions (HEI), Mr Ranjit has established himself as a seasoned professional. Mr Ranjit is dedicatedly involved in research and teaching endeavours, primarily focusing on mindfulness and compassion-based interventions. His work in these areas aims to promote well-being and foster positive change in individuals and communities. ORCID: 0000-0002-3541-8752.

Surjit Singha is an academician with a broad spectrum of interests, including UN Sustainable Development Goals, Organizational Climate, Workforce Diversity, Organizational Culture, HRM, Marketing, Finance, IB, Global Business, Business, AI, K12 & Higher Education, Gender and Cultural Studies. Currently a faculty member at Kristu Jayanti College, Dr. Surjit also serves as an Editor, reviewer, and author for prominent global publications and journals, including being on the Editorial review board of Information Resources Management Journal and contributor to various publications. With over 13 years of experience in Administration, Teaching, and Research, Dr. Surjit is dedicated to imparting knowledge and guiding students in their research pursuits. As a research mentor, Dr. Surjit has nurtured young minds and fostered academic growth. Dr. Surjit has an impressive track record of over 75 publications, including articles, book chapters, and textbooks, holds two US Copyrights, and has successfully completed and published two fully funded minor research projects from Kristu Jayanti College. ORCID: 0000-0002-5730-8677.

David Stephens is an Assistant Professor of the Media Studies in the Department of Communication and Film at the University of Memphis. His research spans multiple forms of media with an emphasis on critical cultural analysis of digital media phenomena.

Olivia Truban (M.A.) is a Ph.D. Candidate at the University of Maryland in the public relations and strategic communication track. She received her B.A. in Communication Studies from James Madison University and her M.A. in Communication with concentrations in health communication and public relations from Johns Hopkins University. Her current research explores internal communication, crisis communication, and ethics in public relations. She teaches communication courses at the University of Maryland, Northern Virginia Community College, and the University of Alaska Fairbanks.

Tanja Vierrether (Ph.D., Bowling Green State University) is currently a Visiting Assistant Professor in the Communication Department at Rollins College. Her research interests focus on narrative engagement, psychological reactance, and attitude change. Her work was selected for presentation at national and international conferences and published in journals such as Media Psychology and the International Journal of Communication among, others.

Gianpaolo Vignali is a Professor of Sustainable Fashion Business and co-lead of The SAFE Futures (Sustainable Approaches in Fashion Entrepreneurship) Research Group. Gianpaolo's notable contributions to academia encompass the publication of over 70 papers and books in the realm of Marketing and Management including Springer Nature and Palgrave texts and papers included in the Journal of Consumer Behaviour, The Social Enterprise Journal and The Journal of Fashion Marketing and Management. Additionally, he has established himself as a distinguished presenter at various international conferences.

Shelley Wigley is an associate professor in the Department of Communication at the University of Texas at Arlington where she teaches graduate courses in persuasion and crisis communication and undergraduate courses in public relations. She has more than a decade of professional public relations experience that includes media training, media relations, and crisis preparation, as well as experience as both a newspaper and broadcast journalist.

Yang Yang (PhD, Bowling Green State University) is assistant professor in the Department of Communication and Media, University of Southern Indiana, U.S.A. Her research interests are social media influencer, audience research, consumer behavior and psychology research, social media use, and advertising effect of brand collaboration.

Index

O

P

R

S

T

V

W

Y

www.ingramcontent.com/pod-product-compliance
Lightning Source LLC
LaVergne TN
LVHW062110300926
849161LV00010B/2420